It Was
Nevada

TONY LESPERANCE

It Was
Nevada

ARPress
ILLUMINATING IDEAS
EMPOWERING VOICES

ARPress
45 Dan Road Suite 5
Canton, MA 02021

Hotline: 1(888) 821-0229
Fax: 1(508) 545-7580

Ordering Information:
Quantity sales. Special discounts are available on quantity purchases by corporations, associations, and others. For details, contact the publisher at the address above.

Printed in the United States of America.

ISBN-13:	Softcover	979-8-89330-100-7
	eBook	979-8-89330-102-1
	Hardback	979-8-89330-101-4

Library of Congress Control Number: 2024900510

TABLE OF CONTENTS

DEDICATION

This book would never have materialized if it had not been for the support and constant encouragement of my wife. Nancy Ann. The story contained in this book occurred before our marriage, most of it long before. However, it did not take Nancy Ann long after our marriage for her to realize the terrible impacts certain actions taken by the University of Nevada had on Nevada Agriculture, rural Nevada, and much less myself. Her steadfast belief was that the story must be told and told in its entirety. That belief has never wavered to this day. It is rare for a man to be so blessed with a mate that not only totally loves him but has undying faith in him as well. Nancy Ann, you are indeed a treasure of treasures. I love you dearly. (The Lesperance's Nancy Ann and Tony, Christmas, 2015

FOREWORD

I*t was Nevada* is a post-World War II snapshot of the making of modern Nevada through the eyes of Anthony Lesperance, PhD. Tony's career and fate gave him a unique front-row seat to the political forces that would wrest Nevada from being populated by more cattle and sheep than people to the most urban state in America. He witnessed the making of some of Nevada's most prominent national politicians. He tangled with the military industrial complex in a high-stake land grab for the MX missile system. His work took him to ground zero at the Nevada Test Site during the nuclear testing program, for which he was fortunate to come out alive, to playing an instrument role in developing the premier university agriculture research station in the West.

Lesperance takes the reader on a very personal journey that is at the same time historical, rollicking fun, and gut-wrenching. He recounts hilarious escapades during his college years at Cal Poly, both San Dimas and San Luis Obispo, acts for which a student would be arrested today. For the first time in these pages, Lesperance is able to reveal a dreadful secret incident that occurred during the above-ground testing of nuclear bombs on the Nevada Test Site. From his accidental unveiling of some of the military's darkest secrets to political scandals and brothels, cattle drives, and Basque sheepherders, the accounts in this book are true. Some of the characters are not identified by their Christian names to protect the innocent.

Tony was born and raised in the height of the Depression, but his father made sure that he would learn how to deal with his world. As a teenager, Tony was shipped to Nevada by his father to work on a ranch to give him direction in life. His teenage diversion turned into a lifelong love for Nevada, particularly, Nevada ranching and farming.

Lesperance arrived in the state when the range livestock industry was in its heyday and cattle and sheep outnumbered people. Little could he then imagine that eventually his career as a professor at the third-ranked Fleischman College of Agriculture would place him in the middle of a political tug-of-war to destroy Nevada's range livestock industry and, ultimately, the rangelands themselves. Today, the cowboy is closer to being eligible for listing on the endangered species list than the spotted owl. Desert tortoise, or sage hen ever were.

Lesperance foresaw that a war would be waged on the western stockman and agriculture in general by the federal government through the Bureau of Land Management and U.S. Forest Service, with the backing of a new political phenomenon — environmentalists. While federal bureaucrats were intent on sending the cowboy into the sunset, Las Vegas and Reno began looking to Nevada's dessert valleys to water the growing cities. Ultimately, Lesperance found himself in a political blender as some of Nevada's power brokers became openly hostile to Nevada agriculture.

It Was Nevada documents a part of Nevada and national history that may ever be read anywhere else but on these pages. A gifted storyteller, Lesperance takes the reader on a journey they won't soon forget.

I am a second-generation friend of Dr. Lesperance. I had the great pleasure of serving with tony on the Board of Agriculture while he was director of the department. Before then, I often relied upon his expertise of the livestock industry in my work. In addition, he served as a critical expert witness in my father's constitutional Fifth Amendment takings case against the BLM and U.S. Forest Service involving our ranch. He appeared at the trial in true Lesperance style, with his arm in a sling after having a wreck with his haystack. Wayne Hage, my father, was one of Dr. Lesperance's students while he attended the Fleischman College of Agriculture at the University of Nevada, Reno, and considered Lesperance one of the best professors at Fleschman. They remained lifelong friends and, as the reader will see, part-time cohorts in the effort to see Nevada agriculture survive.

Ramona Hage Morrison

Sparks, Nevada

INTRODUCTION

It was a different sort of day, at least by anything that I had ever experienced. I had been to Disneyland when I was perhaps 10, but this was the first time that I had really spent time in Southern California. The morning had started under fog; fog thick enough to cut with a knife. The dew had made everything soaked, including my clothes, but by 1:00 in the afternoon the fog had lifted to display a brilliant blue sky against fluffy white clouds.

I stood by the grave contemplating life in general, and my grandfather in particular. So much had occurred in his life that I really never knew about until the very end; and I was sure there was much more that I could only speculate on. Under the beautiful oak and sycamore trees in the Bardsdale cemetery, looking at the blue sky and white clouds, and smelling the fragrance of orange blossoms seemed to make my mind go in circles. How did it all happen? What did his death bring to a close? There were so many questions left unanswered, yet he answered so many in the end.

I was brought back to reality by my Aunt Holly, along with my Mom, saying; "Come on Jon, let's go to Ventura for a dinner, all your aunts, uncles and cousins are hungry, and you know as well as I do, your Grandpa never missed a dinner". I really didn't want to leave, but I had to admit that I was hungry too. I took one last long look around the Cemetery, looked at Nancy's grave, and all of her family's graves, going clear back to the 1800's. I gazed across the Santa Clara Valley, still basically covered with citrus; however, it was obvious that the urban sprawl was winning. I looked across the Santa Clara Valley at the majestic San Cayetano Range, thought about my Grandpa as a boy riding his horse throughout those beautiful, but rugged mountains. Then I reflected on all the events of his life that followed. I got to admit, I shed a tear then, not so much for him, for he was a hard man to understand, much less love, but the tears were for his world that had changed so much, despite his efforts to the contrary.

My aunts had made reservations at the Pierpont Inn for dinner. It sat on a bluff on the edge of Ventura, overlooking the Pacific. The fog bank had rolled way out to sea: One could look at distant islands - it was a beautiful sight. Holly informed me that my Grandpa and Nancy, and her parents often came to dinner here. She also said that Grandpa had told her that his parents also frequented the Pierpont when he was a little boy. So many figures had gone through my head in recent days that my math was a bit fuzzy, but it didn't take long for me to realize that we were talking close to 100 years or so of time!

Throughout dinner, my aunts and Mom pestered me as to why I spent so much time with Grandpa during the last month. "I simply wanted to get to know him better, and besides he liked telling me about how things were long, long ago" I responded. But I had to think to myself that if I tried to relate some of the wild tales he had told me, it would definitely change the complexion of dinner!

After dinner, we drove back to Fillmore, some stayed at the family citrus ranch, however, I choose to stay in town at a motel. Once there and in bed, I began to review the events that had led up to today. Grandpa had gotten sick, likely in January. He really hadn't said a word to anybody, some of us grandkids noticed that he had lost weight and looked tired, but he was still distant. When asked, he would grouch back that likely at his worst he could out work any of us, which was true. He was still feeding about 50 cows all by himself on the family ranch in Paradise Valley.

Grandpa loved Nevada, and he loved Paradise Valley, but he long since had asked to be buried in the Bardsdale Cemetery. It's where he grew up, besides, more than anything he wanted to be by his wife, Nancy. They grew up together, but went there separate ways after graduating from Fillmore High School. But fate has strange ways, they both went to their 35th high school class reunion, her husband had passed away, he was separated and in the process of a divorce. As they liked to tell everybody, they danced once and it was love forever after. Nancy had preceded him in death by only a couple of years but it was a long two years for Grandpa. He probably had missed her something fierce, but in a way, it probably brought him and all of his grandchildren a bit closer. Our whole family missed Nancy; Mom always said she was the best thing that ever happened to us.

By February, Grampa was showing obvious signs of sickness, he finally agreed to go to Reno and see a doctor in March. By then the cancer had progressed to a point that no treatment including surgery could be helpful. Grandpa drove back to the ranch, made arrangements to sell all of the cattle, and by early April he had given away his favorite dogs to old friends in Paradise. He was admitted to Renown Medical on April 15th, and passed away on June 5th.

There was a service held in the community church at Paradise Valley, Nevada with burial five days later at Bardsdale, California. The Paradise service was well attended by many old time Nevadan's as well as all the locals and our family. Most of his old friends had long since passed away, but even at that I had to laugh, having learned some of the things that I had in the last few days. I could well visualize the reaction that some might have had at that service if they knew what I had learned. I speculated that a lot of people shedding tears were in fact greatly relieved that the old man had never talked of certain "events" until his death. The burial ceremony at Bardsdale was simply that, and attended by basically our family plus a few surviving friends from his high school days. Although it was a sad event, in a way it was a good time. Our family, both Nancy and Grandpa's, had grown and spread all over the West. We hadn't been totally together for years, so there was lots of tall tales to tell, mostly however, involving the known escapades of Grandpa.

One day after being admitted to Renown, Grandpa called me at work at the Gazette-Journal, and asked if I could come by and spend a little time, as there were some things he "wanted to get off his chest." I was there early the next morning, he was medicated for pain, but his mind was crystal clear as always. After a few minutes of not much of anything, he asked if I might like to write a book someday. I joked that after getting a journalism degree at the University and landing the job at the Reno Gazette-Journal, I hadn't really graduated to writing books yet. He laughed and said that he understood, but that in the next week or two before the pain became unbearable he might tell me a story, a story that if I were clever enough might just make a good book. I knew there were many dark sides to Grandpa, some that we just simply didn't ever talk about, but it dawned on me that what he was trying to impress on me was the fact that he might just let it all come out.

My journalistic appetite, especially for investigative reporting was such that it was worth a shot. I asked him how long it would take and his response, as always, was very blunt, "Boy, it may well take until I die, and if the good Lord lets me live long enough, I promise it will all come out, even everything I have known about Nevada politicians, Salt Wells, the MX issue, even the Test Site, but more than anything else, why and how the University of Nevada turned its back on agriculture. Not only that, but the long term political impacts that turning your back on agriculture has had, and will surely have, not only on Nevada, the West, but ultimately our great Nation. Things you, or hardly anybody else anymore, never knew existed or even understood, much less fully understand the ultimate consequences of some of those actions." That was good enough for me, for in the few years that I had worked for the Gazette-Journal, mostly doing research to support investigative reporting, I had long since learned that somehow his name always seemed to surface with just about every fiasco that had occurred in Nevada during the last 60-70 years.

I arranged for a full month leave from work that afternoon, purchased a new tape recorder, lap top computer, volumes of paper, pencils, high liters and everything else that I could think of, and the following morning, with the permission of the head nurse, Grandpa's doctor and a few other people, I set up office along side his bed. He talked, albeit with ever increasing difficulty, for the next 30 days, or so.

What follows is his story, verified with factual research wherever possible. It is his life up to and through his years at the University. There was much more after he left the University, perhaps even more intriguing, but to him, the University were the most important years of his life, and that's what he wanted to talk about the most. They were also the most frustrating years of his life, in that in his mind, his efforts of those years were pretty much failures. He had tried to do the impossible, slow down the inevitable growth that our Nation faces, protect agriculture, and the resources that make agriculture possible. Noble efforts, indeed, but efforts that the advance of civilization has always had a tendency to simply ignore. Some people, like my grandfather, could clearly see the ultimate consequences of replacing food production with industrial growth. Perhaps one day, the rest of us will finally realize the folly of that philosophy.

This is a story of old Nevada in a time where anything was possible, often as much bad as good. Like the nursery rhyme goes, when it was bad it was very, very bad, but when it was good, it was oh so very good. It was an era in this country that never occurred before, and could never occur again. It was, after all, Nevada!

THE EARLY YEARS

The year was 1943, and we had just moved to a house on the Sespe River, west of Fillmore. For a nine-year-old boy, it was a paradise! There was a small citrus grove, bordered by an irrigation drainage ditch loaded with wild berries. A trail led down to the river, where several acres belonged to my folks. Although many changes had occurred throughout California by that time, one change had not yet occurred, the annual running of the steelhead. I'll never forget the first time I witnessed these gigantic, to a nine year old, fish traverse the rocky ponds of the Sespe on their annual migration to spawn. I didn't understand all aspects of life at that tender age, but I can still recall the despair I felt when a few weeks later the dead, dying and tattered fish floated back down the river. It took a lot of explaining to make me accept their fate!

This residence was the closest I had ever lived to a town. My parents came from very wealthy stock in Southern California, but that was before The Depression. By 1932 all of my grandparents had essentially lost everything. My dad, Ed Hope, headed out to find work, which he did in the infant oil industry of the southern San Joaquin Valley. After making a small grubstake, he put a deposit on a small oil field on top of Sulfur Mountain, located midway between Santa Paula and Ojai. That was 1937, and it's just about my earliest memories. Dad pumped the lone well in the field, hauling a load of crude to the refinery in Ventura every week. It was 18 miles, one way, to the local school in Summit, or upper Ojai Valley, and that was only a one-room school with outhouses

1

for restrooms. Mom hauled both my older sister and myself to school, once I reached the first grade, every single day in a Model A.

I loved Sulfur Mountain, it was totally isolated, and it provided my first memory of cattle. I was fascinated by the cows, but to this day, I can't remember what breed they were, not that it was important. I can just remember sitting on the front porch watching them graze on the rolling hills, eating the lush green grass under the towering oak trees.

Life was peaceful on Sulfur Mountain, but the transition must have been hard for Mom. She came from a family in Santa Monica, where everything was provided, including a private boarding school, and ultimately USC. Now she found herself stuck on top of an isolated mountain, nearly 30 miles from the nearest grocery store, and we didn't have electricity and only hot water when the sun was out. And, on cold nights the only heat was the wood Dad cut and burned in the homemade stove, a stove he made out of a fifty-gallon metal drum. Much to her credit, I have no recollection of her ever complaining. Her life was nothing but work, seven days a week, from sun up to sun down. I remember the day we graduated from an icebox to a gas refrigerator, and she made ice cream with fresh cream she purchased with money she had scraped together somehow. What a treat, and one of those memories that lasted all the rest of my days. I also remember when she graduated from the tub and scrub board to a gasoline driven Maytag washer/ringer. That didn't leave as much a memory, but as the years have gone by, I began to realize the significance that this event must have been for her.

One of my strongest memories from Sulfur Mountain was the start of World War II and the threat of Japanese attack. Where we lived we could clearly see the ocean, in fact from Ventura, north towards Santa Barbara. The civil patrols, reinforced by the military started almost immediately thereafter. No place on the coast could have lights on at night for fear of attack. We were told that we couldn't have any lights at all because of our location, not that we had much in the way of light to begin with. Dad rigged up shutters on all the windows, and he allowed us two kerosene lanterns, barely lit. Dad also shortly joined the civil patrol, which required him to be out all over Sulfur Mountain at night. We didn't have any kind of a radio in the house that worked at night, we could get some Los Angeles' stations during the day. The nights were lonely when Dad was out. My sister Joy, Mom and I tried to play games under the kerosene lanterns, but that never worked very well. Dad always tried to be home Friday nights, because he loved to listen to the Friday night fights, as he was a great fight fan. His truck had a powerful radio, so he and I would sit in the truck every Friday night and listen to the fights on the car radio. After the war started, I can remember Friday nights as being the only night that I felt safe on Sulfur Mountain.

Although life on the mountain was a true adventure, there was danger. Danger existed in the occasional rattlesnake, although none of us ever came close to getting bit. The danger came from the cattle, or more correctly the cattle's owner. His name was Mr. Freeman, and he was a powerful district judge in Ventura. On several occasions he had approached Dad about buying the property; however, he never offered as much as my folks paid for it to begin with. Dad had developed water from a dry oil well hole. That was the water we used at the house, and for everything else that needed water. It was stored in a large tank, with the excess allowed to run down the mountain. I remember Dad offering to let Mr. Freeman use the surplus water for his cattle, providing he installed a water trough somewhere below the house. My memory is such that this was done, sometime around 1938 or '39. However, within a year, Mr. Freeman claimed that Dad let some oil get into the water, and ultimately the livestock trough. He further claimed that it killed a number of his purebred cows, and he brought suit against Mom and Dad for just about what he offered to buy the place for originally. Dad couldn't afford a lawyer, and he knew just how powerful Mr. Freeman was, being a District Judge for Ventura County.

I remember lying awake at night listening to Mom and Dad talk about their options, which probably weren't many. In early 1942, right after the war started, they made the decision to sign over the property to Mr. Freeman if he would drop all of the charges, which he agreed to do.

We left the mountain with Dad's truck, Mom's model A, and whatever we could carry. It was the first time that I realized that the world isn't always fair. But I also learned another lesson, and that is you have to fight back on your terms, terms that you can live with. In all Mr. Freeman's legal wisdom, he never described the water source in his eagerness to get his hands on that all-important commodity. So, Dad figured the water source was his, and seeing how he couldn't figure out how to move it, he simply dumped a half case of dynamite down the well casing as we were leaving.

We heard later that Judge Freeman was defeated in the next election. We also later heard the District Attorney was investigating him for wrongdoing while in office. Neither Dad nor Mom ever made any comment about his status, nor did they ever talk about that water well. But Sulfur Mountain had taught my family how to survive, and it was probably my first beginning education in the ways of the world.

In hindsight, leaving Sulfur Mountain was a godsend. My Dad had met a man from Long Beach by the name of Freeman Fairfield. Mr. Fairfield owned what was called the Oil Tool Corporation, located in Long Beach, as well as a large oil lease on South Mountain, immediately to the south of Santa Paula. Fairfield must have liked what he knew about Dad, because he gave him the chance of a lifetime. He asked him to head up the development of the South Mountain Lease that he owned to see if there was as much oil there as he had been led to believe.

Fairfield had two drilling rigs moved up from Long Beach, the initial sites were staked out, and Dad began hiring crews. In those days, a drilling crew consisted of a driller, a derrick man and two floor roustabouts, for a total of four men. It took four crews to run a rig, including a tool pusher, thus for each rig a total of 17 men were required. For both rigs, 34 men were hired, as well as a welder and two mechanics. Needless to say, for 1942, the hiring of 36-40 men in Santa Paula was big news! The war made it difficult, but Dad found the men and started drilling in late 1942. The first well was a gusher, and South Mountain became of age immediately.

When we left Sulfur Mountain, Mom and Dad rented an old house in Bardsdale, a citrus dominated community to the south of Fillmore. We lived there for about three years and I went to the Bardsdale Grammar School, which was a three-room schoolhouse. It was so much larger than the Summit School, that I almost got lost the first day there! Not much in my life was exciting living in Bardsdale. I did have friends, something that was rare on Sulfur Mountain. We lived about a quarter mile from the cemetery. The family that managed the cemetery had three kids, all older than I was. I use to peddle my tricycle over there in the evenings, and we would all play hide-n-seek in the cemetery.

Dad worked long hours so he was seldom home. Mom raised frying chickens for the war effort; I helped her a lot with that project. Every week a truck would arrive with new day old baby chicks, and every week another truck would arrive to take the fryers away. I don't remember how many chickens Mom was turning out every week, but it was a lot! By late 1943 I think Mom was getting tired of the chicken business, and I can remember not ever wanting to eat chicken again. Anyway, by early 1944, Dad had saved enough money to buy the place on the Sespe River, so the chicken business came to an end when we moved! Thank God!!

As I said earlier, living by the river was a paradise. I was in the fifth grade and had become overtaken by fishing. In addition to the annual migration of steelhead, in those days there were a lot of trout in the

Sespe. I remember Mom saying that she hoped we wouldn't get as tired of trout as we had become of chicken.

I kept pestering my folks that there was enough grass on our property around the citrus grove, as well as on the other side of the river to raise a steer or two so that we would have something to eat besides trout!

Maybe my pestering made the point, or maybe Dad just wanted to see me get involved in something besides school and fishing. At any rate around 1946, shortly after the end of the War, he asked if I would be interested in raising a few heifers. My response was in the affirmative, so we set out to build some corrals. He had enough old drill pipe and sucker rods left over from drilling oil wells to get the job done. In hindsight, it was one of the very few times my Dad and I did something together, every night we would dig holes, mix concrete, cut and weld pipe. It took about two months, but in the end we had a dandy corral, and in the process, I learned to weld. He bought two Hereford X Angus heifers, that I remember to be about 8 months old, and that was the beginning of my first cowherd!

It didn't take Mr. Fairfield long to hear of our project. One night when he came by for dinner, he wanted to know what in the world I was going to do with those heifers. My response was; "I am going to build a cow herd", not giving any thought as to how in the world this might be accomplished! He asked a lot of questions, not many for which I had an answer. He felt I needed some things to work the cattle with, such as a horse. And he wanted to know where I was going to find enough grass to support this herd.

Well, it didn't take long to answer the first question, for about a month after his visit, he showed up with the prettiest little Morgan gelded horse you ever wanted to see, and a bridle, saddle and all the gear necessary was there as well! His name was Chubby, and we became fast friends. I had never ridden a horse in my life at that point, but it didn't take me long! I took to it like a duck takes to water. He was an easy horse, certainly with no bad habits. I was soon riding far from our house, up into the Sespe backcountry, just about as far as I could venture in a day's time, and still return before dark. I worked him around the heifers, but they were so tame that didn't accomplish much.

About six months after Mr. Fairfield gave me Chubby, he asked if I might be looking to expand my herd beyond two heifers (open at that time). My answer was obvious, however, I was quick to point out that I didn't have the slightest idea where that might occur. He came back and said he thought I was old enough (I was maybe 12 at that time) to work a deal with him to graze some of his fee owned oil property. In particular, he had a 240-acre property in Santa Paula Canyon that surely was going to burn up if something didn't eat that grass up. He always referred to it as the "Fee Lease". He guessed if I were interested in fencing the property, he would let me graze cattle on it until I graduated from college. First of all, I didn't have the slightest idea of how big 240 acres was: I hadn't built any fence, except when I helped Dad fix some on our place, and I sure hadn't thought about college at that point in my life. However, it didn't take me long to fire an answer back, "you bet!"

If I had the slightest idea how far it is around 240 acres I might have been a bit more hesitant. Fortunately, two sides of Mr. Fairfield's property had natural barriers, and a third side, where Santa Paula Creek ran through the property was already fenced by a neighboring ranch, so I only had to fence about a mile on one side of the property. Furthermore, I hadn't given any thought to what it was going to cost to fence this place. Again, Mr. Fairfield sort of took pity, as he shortly informed me of what kind of a fence he wanted, 5 strand barb wire, corner braces and in line braces ever eighth of a mile, swinging metal gates, etc. He guessed because he was so particular, that it was only fair that he bought the material if I did the work. So the summer of 1947, I built a mile of the prettiest fence you ever saw. Dad helped me some on weekends, but I can honestly say I did most of it myself. There was a WW II jeep on the property that I could use, but Mom or Dad took me every day and brought me back every night to Fillmore. Although I could drive plenty well, I just looked to darn young to get home by myself, even using the back roads. Besides, the jeep wasn't licensed. By the end of summer, I had learned just about every trick there was to fence building, and a good deal of just plain old fashioned work in general. I had also learned some painful experiences about poison oak!

At any rate, by the fall of 1947, we moved the two heifers to the Fee Lease. Dad loaned me the money to buy a bull, four more bred heifers, and four yearling steers, so I was in the cattle business at last! Mr. Fairfield said he wanted to come by and see how my operation was going, so I had everything spruced up for his arrival. He liked the bull; I'll never forget his name "California Hero #16". He was a purebred Hereford that we had found north of Ventura on a ranch that raised registered Herefords. After reviewing everything, Mr. Fairfield took my hand and shook it, saying, "You kept up your part of the bargain. The fence looks great - now you can graze as many cattle as you want here. Just keep the place up, don't overgraze it, and as I said, you can stay here until you graduate from college." I'll never forget the handshake, and the look of sincerity in his eyes. I never had any reason to doubt, or mistrust anybody in my life, but between Dad and Mr. Fairfield, they reinforced my belief in the good of people and the trust that goes with it.

During the next year, I learned to rope, doctor, castrate, dehorn, brand and just about everything that goes with cattle. We even had to pull a calf or two (successfully)! It turned out that Chubby had never been used for roping before, so it was a learning experience for both of us. Mom and Dad, along with Mr. Fairfield were totally supportive.

I started raising day old dairy calves on two milk cows that I bought from a neighboring dairy. So, we just about always had some fresh milk

and cream, and even once in awhile butter. I was on top of the world:
- I had a business, the first cattle were taken to market in late spring of
1948: I made enough to pay off some of my debt to Dad. We had kept
all of the heifer's calves, so I was up to about eight cows and a bull, and
I hadn't put even a dent in the grass on the Fee Lease.

Although Mr. Fairfield made his money in the oil business, he always
loved the land. He had been raised in Meeker, Colorado, and came to
California in the height of The Depression, and it was said with only the
shirt on his back. He had made his first million in the junk business,
and then he went into oil. But he never forgot his roots - so, in about
1946 or 47, he bought a ranch straddling the Nevada/California border
along the east slope of the Sierra Nevada mountain range near Coleville,
California. Some of the ranch was in Nevada along the Walker River,
while the summer range was high in the Sierra's, in Slinkard Valley. I
had just finished the seventh grade, it was June of 1948, when he told
me that he thought I was old enough to go the "Ranch" and help put in
a pipeline. Summers were the slack time in "my" operation, and both
Mom and Dad felt it was all right for me to go to Nevada, since this
job would only last 2-3 weeks. I guess I didn't really understand until
years later, but all of these deals that Mr. Fairfield kept bringing to me
were worked out in detail between him and my parents long before I
was asked.

So, at any rate, in late July, I headed to Nevada with my Dad. Seeing
how Dad was Mr. Fairfield's overall headman, he had already been to the
ranch, and knew quite a bit about Nevada. The trip up U.S. 395 was an
experience I'll never forget. I had never seen country like Owens Valley
or Bishop. There was water everywhere! Once into the mountains, I
couldn't believe how high the passes were, close to 10,000'! That was
far higher then the highest point in Ventura County. Dad had much to
say along the way about Nevada. He explained how it was a wide-open
state, gambling, prostitution, etc. He asked if I knew what prostitution
was, and I reckoned I did. He was never long on the birds and the bee's

theory that parents are supposed to tell their children about. I guess he figured out that after watching California Hero #16 breed everything in sight that I had things figured anyway. As to prostitution, I didn't really have that figured out, and I didn't totally understand gambling, albeit, my parents did have a roulette table that they occasionally used at parties. Seeing how they let me run the table for the guests, that gave me a leg up on anybody my age as to gambling.

Dad also cautioned me that people in Nevada drink a lot, or so he thought. "There are lots of saloons", he said, and "probably the ones in the small towns would serve someone as young as you." Well, I only had $5 in my pocket, and I wouldn't get a paycheck for this job until I got back to Fillmore, so I speculated to Dad that I couldn't get in too much trouble. Anyway Dad was going to be there some of the time, at least so I thought. It turned out however, he had to go right back to Fillmore and didn't return to Nevada until the job was over. At the end of the job I hitched a ride back with some of the crew that I had worked with.

We stayed at Palmer's Resort, near Topaz Lake, and every day I went up into Slinkard Valley with two other men. One was a welder and one was a roustabout. I guess my title was helper. We laid a 16" pipeline about one and one half miles long: The pipe was all strung out before we got there. The joints were 16', with each joint having to be butt-welded. The pipe had to be bent around boulders and trees, although a road had been built good enough so that we could get the welder and an "A" frame hoist truck all the way. Nobody ever mentioned, but I figured up that there are 495 joints of 16' pipe in a mile and a half. It took about 20 minutes to make a butt weld, so that meant it would take 165 hours, or 21 days just to make the butt welds. That's when I learned what this was all about: - We weren't going to work 8 hour days, no, my welder was anxious to get back to Santa Paula where his family lived, so we were going to work 10 or 12 hour days! And, we did! Keeping in mind I was only 13 years old, probably stood only 5'2"

10

at the outside, and maybe weighed 115#, I didn't do too bad! I was chipping slag as fast as the welder could weld. On his final pass, I was helping the roustabout, Gene; line up the next joint for welding. And if we had a minute or two to spare, we shot his 22 rifle.

Gene was an excellent shot, he would have me pitch rocks in the air, and he would hit them nine times out of ten. He showed me the trick of just following the rock up to the peak, and just as it tops its arc, it holds for a bit of a second, and that's when you have to shoot, not going up, not going down. It took me twenty tries before I finally hit a rock, even though it was larger then the ones I threw for him. Buy the end of the job I could hit just about every other rock. However, we didn't spend that much time shooting - no if I wasn't chipping slag, or lining Gene up with the "A" frame truck with the next joint, I was fixing the torch to cut or bend pipe. Sometimes, we would cut a notch to facilitate the bend, sometimes we would just heat the pipe with a "rosebud", bend it enough to put a ripple in the pipe, and go on. All told we did lay about 500 joints, put in one large valve and two pressure relief valves, and we finished the whole project in 22 days. The stream where the intake was, had just about dried up by the time we finished, but it was clear to me how much water could be delivered on a meadow at the end of the pipe. Ditches had been flagged out, but not put in yet. Before I left, Mr. Fairfield had said that it was his plan to ultimately put in about 12-15 miles of pipe, bringing all of the tributary streams in Slinkard down to the main meadows. He felt that he could double the size of the meadows by doing this.

As we were building the pipeline, I thought a lot about his plans. I didn't know if he would want me to come back or not, but if he did, there was work every summer for me for a long time! And I had grown to like this Nevada. Its beauty was beyond belief. I loved the mountains of the Santa Clara Valley, especially the San Cayetano range, but these were real mountains - the head of Slinkard Valley topped out at over 10,000'. There were deer and we saw a bear on several occasions.

We saw mountain lion tracks nearly every day. In the evenings when we returned out of the mountains, there often were antelope along U.S. 395 before we got to Palmers. No, this Nevada could definitely grow on a fellar!

After about 5 days on the Job, our welder, Huck, said, "lets all go to Holbrook Junction tonight after dinner for a drink." By that time, I was so tired that I could hardly hold my eyes open, but if I were to be a "Nevadan", I was beginning to realize that you didn't say no! At any rate, after our boarding house supper, we all piled into a jeep and went up 395 about 10 miles until we came to a bar at the junction of the road to Smith Valley. I'll never forget the owners, Bill and Mary, they were a pair! Huck and Gene had been there before, I guessed quite a few times by how they knew everyone. Mary took a liking to me, as I was the only kid on the premise. She said, "we all have heard how hard Huck and Gene are working you on that pipeline. We took bets on if you would make it or not"! Now that was the first time that I realized that being the "boss's" kid had its bad sides as well as good. I guess there had been speculation that I was too young and small, and probably pampered, to cut the mustard! It was about right then that Nevada became a challenge, and I was secretly glad that I hadn't gone to sleep in the jeep ride!

Well anyway, Mary and I hit it off. She wanted to know all about how I liked working at the ranch, about my home in Ventura County, on and on. She said she had only been in Southern California once, and that was when she was a kid during the early days of The Depression.

Huck and Gene had a drink or two along with two other locals while we were talking. Bill came over to where I was sitting at the bar and talking to Mary and said in a voice loud enough for everybody to hear, "by God, if Terry is old enough to do a man's work, then he is old enough to drink at my bar"!

And so, there it was in front of me at a Nevada bar, a bourbon and water, a ditch, a highball, call it what you want - I was 13 years old and I was served a man's drink, and I drank it like a man - one long swallow. I reported to Bill, that, "I was mighty thirsty and that hit the spot!" Bill said that's fine, but he was only buying me the first one. Huck came to my rescue and bought the next round, but drinks were only fifty cents, so it didn't set him back too far. This one I took a lot slower!

After listening to all the stories that come out at a bar, and having a few drinks, I thought about learning more about Nevada, and started eying the antique slot machines lining the far wall. There was a quarter machine, and four nickel machines, all old, very old. I asked Bill, if he could break the $5.00 bill still in my pocket for ones, which he did. Then I screwed up my nerve, handed him back a dollar, and asked for 20 nickels. He laughed, and guessed he wouldn't be in any more trouble by letting me play the slots than he would be if he were caught letting me drink at the bar.

Well, it didn't take long for that 20 to be gone, but Gene came to my rescue and handed me a drink, "Here kid, that will ease the pain of loosing all that money", and it did. In fact, it eased the pain so much I promptly lost the other four dollars, nickel by nickel, but it did take some time, and it didn't all go into the slots, at least one dollar went for two more drinks. Wow, this Nevada was great!

Or so it seemed! When we got back into the jeep, the "boys" made me sit in the back. I tried, I tried very hard, but after about five miles I lost it all, in fact all over everybody, the jeep, and I suppose a goodly stretch of Highway 395. By the time we got back to Palmer's, Huck and Gene got back enough of their sense of humor, at least enough to laugh while I washed out the jeep with a nearby hose. We all went to our rooms a mess. I pulled off my clothes, got sick once more, at least this time in the toilet, climbed in bed, despites its attempt to twirl me right back out. I was strong, so I held on desperately with both hands to the singlewide cot and I succeeded in taming the beast. As I more or less drifted off to sleep, I thought about the five dollar bill that I had lost (spent). That was so unpleasant, I tried to think about something else. Prostitution maybe? I wasn't sure what all that entailed, so I concentrated on the German brown trout in Slinkard Creek. That seemed to work for a while until my head started hurting; at that point I just gave up.

Bang, bang, "Come on get up. Your breakfast is on the table"! What is this all about? Gradually, I realized that kindly Mrs. Palmer was telling me that it was far past time to get up. I was just thinking about trying to catch more of the fish in Slinkard, when she started yelling: I never got more sleep. I knew I was in trouble by the angle of the sunlight in the window. So I did my best, which wasn't much, but I did make it to breakfast. Huck and Gene were there, but they didn't look all that good either. At least, they were there on time. There was orange juice at my place along with a fresh hot cup of coffee. Orange juice in my entire life never tasted better, and the coffee went down good also. Mr. Palmer was serving us this morning, and it was eggs and bacon with homemade bread for toast. He brought over the bacon, which seemed greasier than usual, and then he slid two eggs, up, off onto my plate. The sight of those two eggs, kind of quivering in their juice, just about did it all over again. If their had been anything but juice in my stomach, it would have been all over. Huck looked my way and quietly said, "Boy, you best eat, we have a long day, and I am still mad about what you did to my back last night". Huck was a big man, probably stood 6'1" or 2", maybe weighed 225 pounds. He would have made twice of me normally, but this morning I felt like it was quadruple. I just sat there and stared at him, until it finally dawned on me that he was right, for more reasons than one, I had better eat. You know what, after I ate, especially the homemade bread, I did feel better.

We were just finishing our last cup of coffee, when Mrs. Palmer came into the room and asked where we went last night. She said, "I saw you leave about 7:00, but never heard you come home, must have been pretty quiet". Gene tried to explain, but then she laughed and said, "Don't tell me stories, I bet you all went to the Junction, and I'll bet that you tried to get Terry drunk - but it looks to me like you either failed or he drank you under the table. Now I know Terry's a good boy, I know his Dad and I have met his Mom, so I bet he just sat there and behaved himself while you guys made fools of yourselves"! With that I somewhat felt like the resurrection! The look on both Gene and Huck's faces was great. Maybe it was their turn to loose their cookies, or whatever. Huck had a habit of coughing every time he wanted to change the subject, and this time he must have wanted to change it real bad!

A Young Tony Lesperance, 14 years of Age, on his Prize Morgan Cow Pony, Chubby. At the time this picture was taken, 1948, young Lesperance had accumulated a cowherd of 25 mostly hereford cows and was will on his way to being a top "Cow Hand".

It was a long day, we didn't work a ten, maybe an eight if you don't count the breaks - but by five we were past ready to go home. Gene and Huck talked about having a beer on the drive to Palmers, I opted for a coke. Yup, this Nevada could grow on you!

After the trip to Nevada, returning to Fillmore seemed like an awful big let down, even seeing my cattle at the Fee Lease. Nevada had gotten into my blood in a big way! It wasn't long before eighth grade started, and I couldn't contain myself. Nobody really believed that I had sat at a bar drinking mixed shots and gambled, but if I told the story once, I probably told it a hundred times. Well, the word got around. Although Fillmore Junior and Senior High School was a small outfit, it, nevertheless, had a disciplinarian, the Vice Principal, Harry Bigger. I had already spent one year in this institution and had long since learned that you didn't let yourself get hauled into Mr. Bigger's office - under any circumstances! School hadn't been in session for two weeks, when in Ms. Weaver's eighth grade class, she suddenly announced, right in the middle of class, that Mr. Bigger wanted to see me - pronto! It seemed like a long walk from the Junior High Building to the main building. Once inside, it was even longer down the hall. Well, I gently opened the office door, and barely able to peer over the counter, I just stood there. The school secretary looked at me and inquired what my business was. I said, "My name is Terry Hope, and Ms. Weaver said that Mr. Bigger wanted to see me". "Oh yes, indeed, he does", was her rapid response in a tone that just about made me wet my pants.

Well, Mr. Bigger surely did want to see me, because as soon as I was escorted into his office, he greeted me like a long last friend. His first response was concerning the welfare of my parents, whom both he and his wife occasionally socialized with. Gosh I thought, maybe this is all he wants to talk about, my parents! No such luck! For the very next sentence had something to do with wild tales that I was spreading on campus concerning my adventures in Nevada last summer. His version made mine seem pretty simple. It didn't take me long to realize that even though I didn't think my school chums believed my story about Nevada; it had spread like wildfire throughout the campus. It seemed like I had gambled hundreds of dollars, and maybe even stayed drunk all summer.

I was stunned, I tried to look hurt, and most of all I was scared. Rumors of Mr. Bigger's treatment to wayward kids was legendary, and there was always Los Prietos, the reform school. I did some fast thinking, decided to be fairly honest, and told Mr. Bigger about me working as a welder's helper for three weeks on Mr. Fairfield's ranch in Nevada. I fessed up to the fact that the crew took me to a bar one night, and although, they had a drink or two, I just sat in the corner and drank seven-up while I watched them play the slot machines. Boy - I am glad I didn't learn about prostitution, because I don't believe that I could have explained that one!

I told Mr. Bigger that I loved the drive up Highway 395, especially in the June Lake area. Now, it didn't hurt to know that Mr. Bigger's pride and joy was his cabin at June Lake. His eyes lit up on that subject, especially when I told him how pretty the country was. Before the conversation ended, he even invited me to stop in next summer if I went back to Nevada, and he would take me fishing on June Lake. About then, I realized how important it was to have advance knowledge, especially, in trying times such as this.

Well, as I began to leave the office, he suddenly forgot about June Lake and fishing, because the real Mr. Bigger just came back to life, in fact bigger than life. He stood towering over me, glaring down, and in a snarling voice indicated just how disappointed my Dad, and of course, my Mom would be if they found out about my escapades. That was a thought that I didn't care to contemplate at that time, or any time for that matter. "Now of course you told me that you didn't drink or gamble, but I think you've told the exact opposite to everybody in the eighth grade, and just about every man that would listen to you in high school. Now that's not so bad, but some of the girls that you told this story to have become down right upset with your behavior. They told me that they just don't believe this school is the place for anyone bragging about this type of behavior!" "Now if this keeps up, I am going to invite both of your parents in and we will all sit down and talk about this, and some of the girls have even promised me that they will repeat the story exactly as you told it". I never really wet my pants since my earliest memory, but right there I started dribbling! The thought of Mr. Bigger, my folks, and of course myself sitting there and listening to some of the eighth grade girls, and probably some of the ninth grade girls, as well, repeat my stories in detail was just more than I could handle. As I backed out, I promised Mr. Bigger that I wouldn't fabricate such tales ever again, and all I really ever wanted to do was fish anyway. He grinned, and said, "I hope so. The offer is still open, if you can get to June Lake I'll take you fishing, and then you will have something to really brag about"! Well, I never got to June Lake to go fishing with Mr. Bigger, but I sure never bragged about any Nevada experience from that point on, no never again. I took a little heckling, especially from the high school boys, as I gently let out the rumor that everything that I had bragged about was so much hogwash! For the remainder of my days at Fillmore, I didn't talk about Nevada again - it was just plain safer, and besides no one would have believed me ever again anyway.

The remainder of the eighth grade wasn't too eventful, except along about winter I got pretty sick. Nobody knew what my problem was, except I had a real fever, close to 105 degrees. Mom said I smelled like I was putrid, and I remember feeling worse. In those days, doctors still came to the house. Fillmore had two doctors, Dr. Kerr being our doctor. He came to the house every day and gave me sulfa pills, but they got harder and harder to swallow. He finally determined that I had a throat infection, and that the sulfa wasn't doing any good. After about two weeks of being flat on my back and not remembering anything except how every joint hurt beyond belief, he finally brought some new medicine. He said it had been developed during the war and it was called penicillin, but that he had to inject it into my sit down. I guessed that was OK, as a needle couldn't make me hurt any worse than I already did. He gave me a shot every day for about four days, and it worked! The fever and pain finally went away.

I guessed in hindsight that I was a bit sicker than anybody realized. Doc had been taking urine and blood samples and sent them to the county hospital in Ventura. About six months later, somebody from the county came to the house with Dr. Kerr and said that I had rheumatic fever, whatever that was, along with a strep throat. They were concerned about how I got the fever and asked all kinds of questions, and that's when they found out that we all had been drinking the milk from my cows without boiling it first. I guessed that none of us knew anything about that, but somehow I imagined that boiled milk just wouldn't taste right. We probably were fortunate that nobody else got the fever, and we all thought that was the end of the situation. However, two things happened. First, I quit raising dairy calves, and we got rid of the dairy cows - that didn't bother me too much, as I was getting sick and tired of milking them, and I hadn't really made very much off of the calves. The second had a bit more lasting impact, I developed a heart mummer, and over the years I learned that I became a permanent carrier of the strep germ. This required periodic penicillin shots, some of which occurred under some mighty humorous situations. The fortunate thing about all of these events was by the time I finally got back to school, most everybody had forgotten about my fabrication of Nevada stories, and that was just as well!

For the remainder of my years at Fillmore, both through the eighth grade as well as high school were relatively uneventful. I worked hard in building my cowherd, went to Nevada every chance I had (which was about once a year), and was a mediocre student. Working and cows just took priority over studying. I took vocational agriculture, and did get very active in FFA. My folks restored an old house on the Fee Lease, so we stayed there on weekends and much of the summer. It made life much easier for me with the cows. Also I had learned to ride my horse from the Fee Lease to Fillmore, the back way. There was a good trail up Santa Paula Creek, in fact just about all the way to the top. It was a relatively short trip across the backside of the San Cayetano range, down a ridge, to an old oil well road, probably constructed in the 1920's. From there it was only an hour to our house on the Sespe River. Times were different in those days. I doubt if it is even possible to take that ride today, because of the Condor sanctuary and the heavy handedness of the Forest Service in general.

During my senior year in high school, I was president of our FFA chapter, and used my cowherd as my FFA project, resulting in becoming Fillmore's first recipient of the State Farmers Degree. I dated a little bit, but most of the girls that I really would like to have dated I just didn't have nerve to ask. One in particular was in the same grade that I was in; she was into everything, including getting straight A's in her schoolwork. Her name was Nancy, and she was senior class president. She still remembered my bragging about my Nevada escapades clear back in the eighth grade, but I gradually grew to believe that my apparent "clean act" ever since had somewhat softened her feelings toward me. However, whatever chance I had of dating her was likely ruined, again all by myself.

It seems that every year the FFA chapter sponsored a father-son banquet, featuring either chicken or beef for our bar-b-q. That year we had decided on chicken, we had been raising them all winter for the spring event. On the day of the dinner, about 11:00 a.m., we brought the live chickens into the Ag shop for processing. The Ag shop was located on one side of a service alley, while the high school cafeteria was located on the other side. Along about 11:30 in the morning, our instructor, Mr. Madsen told us it was time to start killing and dressing the chickens. We had about 75. We started by chopping heads, but that got old and messy after a few. One of the other senior students, Glen Canada, said he had learned how to simply snap a chicken's head off, it would happen so fast that they never knew what hit them. Glen picked up a chicken by its feet, held it upside down, gave it a hard snap, and sure enough the chicken's head came right off. Glen was careful to hold the chicken in such a fashion that when he snapped it, the head went straight to the floor.

I was fascinated by this technique, and said that I was going to try the next one. He cautioned me that the real trick was to give it a hard and fast snap, much like popping a towel. Well, that's exactly what I did; only I forgot to hold it so its head would go down. In fact, I held it just like I would hold a towel to snap someone's rump in gym class. The only other problem I had is I forgot about which direction the head might go. Well, sure enough, my luck couldn't have been any worse, even by design. I snapped the chicken's head all right, in fact if records of that nature were kept, it was probably an Olympic qualifying snap. The head came off with ease, in fact it came off in a great arc, rising across the service alley with all eyes following. Now it was about lunchtime, and across the alley, students were lining up for lunch at the cafeteria. Right in the middle of the line stood Nancy in a beautiful gleaming white dress. We all watched, as if in slow motion, the arc of the chicken's head, topping out at about the middle of the service alley, and slowly starting its decent towards the other side, the damn chicken was oblivious to what was about to happen. There was a loud "plop" as the head hit Nancy's butt, there was even a louder scream, and then there was general pandemonium! Sure enough that damn chicken's head hit her beautiful white dress squarely on her rump leaving a series of ever fading rings of bright red blood radiating out from the point of impact. There was, as I said, pandemonium on the student side of the alley, and there was total laughter on the vo-ag side of the alley, except for me of course - I couldn't believe what I had accomplished, I just stood there in disbelief.

Mr. Madsen, who had just walked out of his office couldn't believe it either. Nor for that matter could Mr. Bigger, who as luck would have it, was just walking down to the cafeteria as well. I guess if I had any luck at all it would be just plain bad. Bigger just growled at me, however, he put his efforts into calming the girls. Nancy probably took it better

21

than her friends; they all wanted me for a variety of reasons, none of which were good. I think Nancy might have even laughed about all of this, except I think right about then she was wondering how to get the blood out of her white skirt. Well, Mr. Bigger consoled her, and took her home, up Foothill, not far from school, so she could change. Mr. Madsen, who wasn't real good at discipline, didn't know whether to laugh or cry, but simply said all heads will be chopped off from this point on, with the shop door closed.

That night the father son banquet went off without a hitch. As President, I gave a short talk, and nobody said a word to my Dad about the day's events. A few days later we graduated, Nancy was class valedictorian, and gave a beautiful speech. As I sat there listening, somewhat mellowed by having passed a bottle around amongst us boys, I thought about what a beautiful person Nancy was, and how I had blown any chance of ever dating her by my actions. The events of many years to come would be one more lesson on how much about life I really didn't know.

The summer after graduation was spent primarily working and building my cowherd. The herd was up to about 25 cows, and I ran approximately half of the calves as yearlings. At any one time there could be over 50 head on the Fee Lease, which seemed to keep the grass grazed to a healthy level, and somewhat diminish the fire danger. Anyway, Mr. Fairfield was happy, and so was I. Much to my disappointment, I didn't make it to the Nevada ranch that summer. Besides taking care of the cows, I was also preparing for college. J. Cordner Gibson, Dean of the San Dimas Campus of Cal Poly, had recruited me, based on the fact that they wanted to recruit every FFA president of every chapter in southern California. So I enrolled at San Dimas starting the fall of 1953.

The San Dimas campus of Cal Poly was a very small school at that time, having only about 300 students. It was pretty much a party atmosphere, although the academics were not to be dismissed. I majored in animal science, but my knowledge of the livestock industry was such, that courses in my major were pretty easy. At Cal Poly, the hard courses, chemistry, biology, physics, etc., started in your junior year, so I faced a pretty easy academic time for the next two years, which of course, being only 18 years old could only lead to some other occupations.

I usually went back to Fillmore every weekend to check on the cattle, and, hopefully, convince Mom to do my laundry. Checking on the cattle proved more fruitful of the two objectives. However, one trip in particular back to Fillmore almost ruined my academic career before it hardly got started. It seems that my folks, and in particular my dad, must have entered a second childhood. During my senior year he bought an English MG Mark II, which is the racing model. Now this machine was off limits to me, except under the strictest of supervision. But it was a goer! In addition to having the gears to make it really perform, it also had a dual exhaust system, with porter mufflers, meaning, properly back shifted, the muffled rumble could be heard a mile away. After starting college, I had returned home on several occasions when my folks were out of state on business. Sometimes they used the MG, but during the winter months they preferred a big Buick sedan. So, what that meant was that both the MG and I were home alone - a bad combination!

I had taken it into town on more than one occasion, and just let the mufflers roar enough to catch the attention of the Fillmore Police Department, headed up by Earl Hume. They had turned on their lights twice, but it was no contest, once I was out of town there was no way they could catch me! And, I always went a different direction so that they would never connect the MG with Dad, as I was sure both he and Mom had driven it into town on more than one occasion. Fillmore is ideally situated for "dragging Main", Main or more correctly Central Avenue bisects the town in a north south fashion, heading toward the foothills. As Central hits the foothills, it becomes Foothill, and forms a large circle of about one half mile in length. On this part of Foothill, houses line both sides of the street, not ordinary houses, but houses of Fillmore's "rich and affluent", and of course, this is also where all the "girls" live. So, it has always been a natural for the "boys" to drag Central, including up and around Foothill, and back down Central. And Earl didn't have too much problem with this as long as it was done with a certain degree of respect and not too late at night.

I had returned to Fillmore during November, and my folks were in Las Vegas, and of course the MG was in the garage. A combination of things more tempting than I could handle! I slipped into town about 9:30, negotiated up a side street past the high school, and then headed up Central. It was a cool crisp clear night, and the porters sounded magnificent. I went up around Foothill, shifting at every possible occasion. The more RPM I was able to generate, the more the porters sounded off. It was fabulous! Well, I successfully negotiated the circle once, probably waking up a few old folks to say the least, and certainly letting every high school girl know that Terry had returned from college!

On many occasions throughout life I have learned that once your mission is accomplished, you should let it alone, and I must say that most of the times that I have learned that, it was a difficult lesson. Well, I guess that night I just hadn't learned it well enough yet. Anyway, at the bottom of Foothill I had a choice, either get down Central and the hell out of Fillmore, or tour Foothill one more time. I chose the latter - big mistake.

As I came down around Foothill, this time letting the porters go from a muffled roar to a full all out roar, I almost crashed into a road block, manned by none other than Chief Earl Hume himself. His car was parked sideways in the middle of the road, a deputy filled the gap on either side between the cruiser and the sidewalk, and Earl was standing directly between me and the MG and his cruiser. Now, Earl was not a big man, at least not in height. Probably 5' 6" or thereabouts, but he probably weighed a good two hundred pounds, so he made a formidable object. Besides that, he was standing there with his legs far apart, hands on his hips, and smoking a bigger than usual cigar. I slid to a stop, in fact, to avoid hitting him, I slid broadside to a stop, and unfortunately, my side, the drivers side, slid right up literally to his cigar. His only comment was, "I gotcha now, you little son-of-a-bitch"!

I didn't really have much to say at that point in time. Oh, several thoughts went through my mind, but I was beginning to realize that it was time to let well enough alone, so my only response was "Damn, it's sure a pretty evening Earl, how in the world have you been anyway?"

That didn't work really good, we all went to the Police Department, the deputies in his cruiser, and Earl driving the MG. He had some trouble shifting, but with my help he figured it out soon enough. By the time we finally got to the Department, which included three trips around the central part of Fillmore, he had mellowed a bit. The agreement was that I had to deposit a hundred-dollar check with the court, by hand delivering it to him, before I left Sunday afternoon for College, and that he would inform Dad of my activities on their return from Las Vegas. Fortunately, I had the hundred in my checking account, and my folks wouldn't be back until Wednesday. Well Earl got his check, and the following weekend when I got home, I got a pretty good chewing out. Before it went too far, however, Mom reminded Dad about the time he got a ticket driving his Dad's Lincoln in 1924 when he and Mom tried to outrun the San Fernando Police Department on Van Nuys Boulevard! That helped, to say the least, - and we all agreed that I couldn't afford to drive the MG anymore. You know - I never knew who wrote the script for the motion picture Smokey and the Bandit, but when I saw it, I was pretty sure whoever wrote that script had to base it on my encounters with Earl Hume!

Life at Cal Poly was fun to say the least. I lived in Smith Hall, which was immediately across the road from the campus swimming pool. Smith housed about 35 students, and it wasn't a bit uncommon for a mass exodus across the road to occur about midnight for an hour or so of skinny-dipping. As I said, life at the San Dimas branch of Cal Poly was indeed fun, one factor that lead to that was the fact that the campus, albeit all male in those days, was surrounded by four campuses of all women colleges and universities! So girls did play a major part of our daily lives.

On several occasions I almost cut my academic life short because of the copious quantity of women about the vicinity of the campus. Obviously, entertaining women on campus after hours, much less in your room, was strictly forbidden. Women and alcohol were, of course, the cardinal sin! Smith Hall also seemed to play home to a lot of the school's basketball team. Two in particular, Tom Peltzer and Ken Kelly, both from Antelope Valley High School located in Lancaster, seemed to be not only good at basketball, but were equally adept at scoring with the opposite sex. Tom and Ken always had girls coming and going, and they were not averse to sneaking them on campus late at night for extra curricular activities! This did, however, come with certain risks. In addition to students living on campus, there were several staff members as well, including Dean Gibson, and Professor Weeks, who taught English and music. Now Dean Gibson was normally one to go to bed early, and we had already learned that he must sleep pretty tight, as several late night events had failed to waken him. Professor Weeks was another story, he liked to roam the campus halls late at night, checking up on us to make sure we were studying and doing everything that young male college students were expected to do. I might add that these late night v–isits were unannounced.

One winter night, when I was actually studying, I noticed loud laughter coming from down the hall, and it had the distinct tones of female laughter mixed in as well. That sounded a lot more enticing then trying to remember the distinctive traits on approximately 15 different breeds of pigs, so I opted to go see what was cooking. Well, needless to say, the laughter was coming from Ken and Tom's room, and with the amount of noise, it didn't occur to me that the door was locked, so I just went in. Well, both Ken and Tom were there along with two other students, Bill Weinberger, and Jim "Hot Dog" Wiley, all drinking beer. Now that wasn't so bad, but the two high school girls that were there were also drinking beer, which obviously compounded the situation somewhat! However, what really made the situation bad was the fact that the two girls were giving a lingerie show, a real personal lingerie show! Well, I couldn't help but watch, Tom offered me a beer, which just seemed the natural thing to do, so I enjoyed the show!

At the end of Smith Hall, one room faced the vicinity of the campus chapel, which was also in the vicinity of where Professor Weeks and his wife lived. Probably the most studious kid living on campus occupied that room, John English. Now, John wasn't a prude, he simply was going to college to learn something, a type of conduct which hadn't really registered on some of us at that point in time, including myself. But John was also an all right kind of guy; in fact his conduct probably saved my academic life! John was studying at his desk throughout all of this activity, but fortunately, there was a big window that looked out on Campus Way, the street that ran by Smith Hall, and fortunately, Campus Way was well lit. Anyway, John happened to look up and see Professor Weeks just leaving the hall next door, Aunt Nell, and head for Smith. John made a dash to Tom and Ken's room, through open the door, and stood there looking in amazement for perhaps ten seconds, before he uttered words I remember to this day, "Prof. Weeks is coming, and I'll try to stop him before he comes in --"!

With that he ran out of the room, slamming the door. I figured we had somewhere between one to three minutes to hide the evidence, by now I was as guilty as anybody else. Our room had the biggest closet, and when I had gone away to college, Mom and Dad had bought a large hanging closet for my clothes. Now, for reasons I'll never understand, that hanging closet was exactly the same length as the distance from the hanging rod in the closet as it was to the floor. So the hanging closet's bottom rested perfectly on the floor.

Anyway, without a second thought, I shouted, "gather up their clothes, there's no time for them to dress, we'll put them in my hanging closet in my room, throw the beer cans out the back window, and turn your lights off, this room smells, and if Weeks comes in here we are dead." It probably didn't occur to me that the smell, cheap perfume, beer, etc., would follow right along with the girls, but there wasn't time to be concerned with details. Anyway, Tom and Ken helped me put the girls into the hanging closet, shoved their various garments in as well, and as it was being zipped shut, I told the girls in my sternest, adult voice, "If you make a peep, I'll personally see to it you spend the rest of your lives in reform school". Well, my message must have connected, for sure enough they didn't utter a peep for the duration of that evening, although none of us realized just how long that might be.

Once everything was accomplished, Tom and Ken left my room like nothing had ever happened. I could hear them walking down the hall joking, and as they got near the door, I could hear them greet Prof. Weeks, saying they were going to the dining hall to get a coke. He briefly inquired how their studies were going, and after a short discussion I could hear the front door close, and Prof. Weeks head down the hall. About then it suddenly dawned on me that they were home scot-free, in fact everyone was, with the lone exception of myself. I didn't know the girls, I didn't know there names, I hadn't bought the beer, I hadn't brought them on campus, however, I figured, if I ever survived this night, Ken and Tom would owe me, in fact they would owe me an incalculable amount! Finally, Prof. Weeks gently knocked on my door, which was slightly ajar. There were four beds in my room, but two of the students were away on a field trip, so there was just Whisky and myself. Whisky, as he was lovingly called, was a Korean War Veteran, by the name of Ken Weiss. He had acquired the name Whiskey, I guess, because he enjoyed whiskey, and he had survived some of the worst of the Korean conflict. He was also over 21 years of age. Now Whiskey had missed all the excitement, except that he came into the room just as we were zipping the girls up. He saw their state of their dress (undress), his eyes lit up, but it didn't take long to explain our predicament, of which I more or less implied that now that he was here he was also part of the problem. Whiskey had told me about some of the tight spots that he had been in Korea, so adversity was no stranger to him, and it was also obvious that he had already enjoyed his "whiskey" that evening at his favorite bar in San Dimas.

When Prof Weeks entered, Whiskey was getting ready to climb into his bunk, and I was sitting at my desk memorizing the characteristics of various hog breeds. Now Prof Weeks knew Whiskey drank, he had caught him at it several times, but Whiskey was clever enough to never get caught drinking on campus, besides he was over 21. Weeks had told him if he ever got caught giving alcohol to any of us students under age, or if he was ever drunk on campus, he, Weeks, would personally get him kicked out of school. Well, anyway, Weeks came in to the room, gave Whiskey a scrawl, and came over to my desk, pulled up a chair, and inquired about what I was studying. I explained how I was really interested in hog production, and was attempting to learn as much about hogs as I could possibly learn, and right now I was just reading and studying about different breeds of hogs. Keeping in mind that Prof. Weeks taught English and music, the furthermost thing that could have been from my mind was the fact that he had been raised on an Iowa hog farm! So, I sat and listened about Iowa hog farms for what seemed like an eternity. As he droned on, I began to notice an odor drifting about, an odor that I had run into earlier that evening, cheap perfume! Apparently, the sides of the hanging closet were not holding back the fragrant odors, whatever the damned stuff was.

Weeks droned on, Whiskey had climbed into bed and was snoring, and although I was sweating profusely, I started yawning. Finally, Weeks got the idea and as he stood up he said, "I fear I have bored you with all my memories about Iowa." I assured him that I had enjoyed every moment of the discussion, and that the knowledge that he imparted on me would surely help me in my class work. Well, as he started to leave, he stopped and looked at the closet, and my heart sank to an all time low level. "What is that obnoxious smell, god, it smells like cheap perfume!" he stated.

With that Whiskey sat bolt upright in bed, looked at the Prof, and said, "Don't you remember the lecture you gave me last week about body odor? You said I stank, so I bought a new after shave lotion, and that's what you are smelling. I hope tomorrow in your class that it will eliminate the problem my body odor must be causing."

Professor Weeks looked at Whiskey in disgust, and said, "It wasn't body odor, it was your breath, and the whiskey on it. It not only disturbs everybody, but it sets a horrible example for good, young students like Terry here. I hope you don't try to drink that horrible stuff that you claim is shaving lotion - on the other hand it might eliminate a big problem we seem to have on this campus"! With that he turned and looked at me saying, "Keep up the good work Terry, and I am sorry that our overcrowded facilities cause your having to bunk with the likes of Mr. Weiss"! With that, he turned, left the room, closed the door and was gone. I sat there for what seemed like an eternity, afraid to move, say a word, or do anything. Whiskey lay back down in bed, grinning, and gradually broke into a laugh. I was too nervous to do anything but just sweat!

After about five minutes, Tom and Ken came into the room, followed by several other Smith residents, even John English. Everybody was saying how I saved the day by having the presence of mind to put the girls into the closet. About that time it dawned on all of us to see how the girls were. Tom went to the closet saying, "It's all right now ladies, everybody is gone, we'll get you out and home". Well, it wasn't quite that simple - they both had been locked up in that hanging closet for well over an hour, they were probably drunk when they went in, and to their eternal credit they had been absolutely as quiet as church mice for the entire ordeal. But, after awhile, the heat generated by their bodies in the confinement of the closet, along with all of the beer that they had drank must have just got too much for them to handle. They both had gotten sick, not only all over each other, but on all of my hanging clothes as well. Also it went without saying that their clothes, which we had rather unceremoniously dumped into the closet along with them had all landed on the floor. Needless to say, they were in about two inches of plain old-fashioned beer puke!

It's pointless to say how long it took me to clean up my portion of the mess, but for sure that's one load of washing I didn't take home for Mom to do. I don't know how Tom and Ken got the girls home, or how the mess was explained, nor did I really care at that point. I do remember about six months later, on a field trip one day, with Tom, asking how he took care of that problem. He just grinned and said there wasn't enough time left in the day to explain that one! I didn't mess with girls on campus ever again, and I'll bet those two high school girls never let somebody talk them to going on campus again either!

Academically, life at San Dimas was easy for me. I hardly ever had to study at night and, I went home just about every weekend to take care of my cattle. I took a class in journalism during my freshman year, which required writing for the student newspaper. Near the end of my freshman year, the student newspaper advisor, Hugh LaBounty, suggested I should try to become the editor of the newspaper the following year, which was an elected position. I agreed, and ran for the office, and much to my amazement won! The following year, my sophomore year, as editor I had two distinct responsibilities, one, make sure the paper got out, and two, write the editorials. The editorials took a lot of imagination, and at first, I was really stuck on this point. But after the first week or two, I decided that being editor gave me some real power and authority, so I started writing editorials about anything that I heard a gripe about, or that bothered me or anybody else that I believed had a problem or was causing a problem. No one was beyond my reach, students, staff or administration. Some were in fun, some were deadly serious, but they must have worked because they produced results. We built a new amphitheater because of the paper's agenda: We cleaned up the campus; we even "reinvigorated" a professor or two. We challenged the student body to build a prize-winning float for the annual Rose Bowl parade, which they did! In general, the student paper not only added to student life and pride, we even won several awards for college newspapers throughout California!

During my freshman year I started working in the student cafeteria, mostly doing dishes and mopping floors. By the end of the year, I had advanced to working on the food line. Dean Gibson, who more or less oversaw the operation of the cafeteria, asked if I would like to be student manager during the following year. It meant that I had to work all three meals every day, as well as help with food projection and food buying. During my freshman year, in order to save funds, the cafeteria had served a lot of mutton. Now there are only so many ways you can fix mutton, probably the most palatable is to serve it with gravy on bread or toast. This was affectionately referred to by the Korean War veterans as "shit on a shingle", and they weren't too far off base. I thought about Dean Gibson's offer a bit, and thought if we serve "shit on a shingle" for another year, I might get tarred and feathered, if I were lucky. So I said I would be manager, but we weren't going to have mutton but twice a month. We would feature beef at least three days a week, and by beef, I didn't necessarily mean hamburger. We had the facilities on campus to process beef halves and to prepare both roasts and steaks. I agreed to poultry once a week, but nothing more.

Gibson said he didn't see how we could afford to do that, and not raise student meal rates to a prohibitive level. I inquired where the beef went that we raised in the beef unit (I full well knew the answer to that! They were sold.). Gibson said he wasn't sure, but maybe we could have some of them processed for the cafeteria. Well we did, and it proved to be a money making project for my sophomore year, and far beyond as far as I ever knew. I never got an award for my efforts at the cafeteria, but a whole lot of veterans didn't mind buying me a beer now and then!

I had one other notable adventure while at San Dimas, and that involved fireworks. Fireworks in those days were just beginning to be outlawed, although we could all remember from our youth, almost unrestricted fireworks being available. One of my best friends while at San Dimas was Raul Galvan, a Mexican student from the Imperial Valley. However, much of Raul's family lived south of the border. He had been telling us that anyone could buy as much fireworks in Tijuana as they wanted to. That sounded OK; until somebody asked how do you get them across the border. Raul seemed to have an answer to everything. "That's easy, we just have them wrapped like ordinary merchandise that tourists buy in TJ. They never inspect them when you cross." That may seem strange by today's standards, but you have to remember back in those days, the border crossing was pretty lax. Anyway, five of us chipped in $20 apiece and we headed south in my Chevrolet.

It was easy getting to Tijuana. Raul knew exactly where the stores were that sold fireworks. And he was right, did they ever have fireworks. We bought $100 worth of rockets and some change, wrapped them in some old burlap sacks and headed towards the boarder. Just like Raul said, the crossing was easy, they looked at the trunk, had me open it, and noted the burlap sacks. I responded, "these are saddles and things that we bought for a ranch where I work". With a friendly nod, we were on our way back to Smith Hall.

It took a better part of a week to figure out how to launch everything we purchased, but between the metal shop and the wood shop, it didn't take too long. We had decided that on an upcoming Saturday, at about midnight, we would liven up that part of Southern California. There was a football field on the south end of campus, and we figured that if we launched from the field, sort of to the east, the rockets should be readily seen from San Dimas and even further east. So we picked our Saturday, and after dark began constructing our launch structures. Now you have to realize that these weren't ordinary rockets, some were three feet long and up to six inches in diameter. There wasn't much in the way of directions, but they all had fuses, and we reasoned we didn't need much more. Raul seemed to know more about this than all of the rest of us put together, so he took charge. It took us about three hours to have everything ready, we had eight rockets all told. It was quite a sight, all of them lined up, pointing to the northeast. Good old Whiskey provided us with some beer, so we fortified our nerve!

As the hour approached, several "what ifs" surfaced, but Raul calmed us down, saying that he was experienced in this sort of thing and nothing could go wrong. There were only four of us at this point in time, so we had each agreed to light two rockets, then vaporize. Rumors had spread throughout the campus as to an event likely occurring at this hour. So unknown to us, we had lots of spectators. Well, we each had a punk type wick; we lit all of them at the same time, then progressed towards our assigned rockets. I was amazed at how fast the fuses took off when the punks were touched to them, almost instantaneously. It probably didn't take more than eight to ten seconds, but we had eight fuses lit. Lift off occurred at approximately 12:02 A. M. Nobody had sent anything to the moon in 1954, much less into orbit, but in hindsight, I am sure we were pioneers in that regard. The rockets performed beyond belief. Their fiery trails arched into the heavens for what seemed to be thousands of feet before exploding into arrays of color beyond description! The sounds of the exploding rockets came back with near deafening booms! We all were thunderstruck, just standing there in disbelief observing what we had brought to the otherwise peaceful Southern California night. Our first jolt to reality was the honking of horns everywhere on campus. I guess people were wondering what the rumors were all about and had been outside their dorms on that warm night. We were beginning to congratulate each other, especially Raul, as everything had gone just as he described. I was shaking his hand, when his smile seemed to descend to a deep frown underlain by sheer panic. "Christ, here comes Dean Gibson", was all he could manage to say.

Looking over my shoulder, I could see his brand new Ford sedan pull out of his garage and head towards the football field, kind of like he had to put a fire out. Well, the four of us didn't waste much time. There was nothing of value in the launchers that we had built. There was only one way out. The football stadium was small, stands only existed on the west side. On the east side of the field was the chain link fence, which surrounded the whole facility. About ten yards past the fence, the country fell off rapidly into a steep gorge that San Dimas Creek passed through. Without another word, we were at and over the fence, and down to San Dimas Creek. We soon lost track of each other, but the sounds were obvious, serious cussing and the crack of small branches. Probably none of us had ever been down the side of this gorge before. We knew if we hit the creek it would be a short walk to the main road, and we could sneak back to our rooms. What we didn't know, or contemplate, was the amount of underbrush under the oak trees, berry vines, scrub oak, schumack, and yes, poison oak. It took me the better part of an hour to get back to my room, and it took another hour to clean and doctor the bruises and scratches, but a quick check proved we all made it. It was reported that after about ten minutes Dean Gibson had gone home. We were a success! Or so it seemed.

Dean Gibson knew full well where we went after he showed up, and he probably knew full well what was in store for us. So all he had to do was wait his time, visit all of the students daily by going to the cafeteria, walking the halls or whatever. As each of us came down with poison oak, we were politely called into his office to explain how in the world we got into the poison oak. I was the last to get it, and I got it the worst, all over my face, in my ears, eyes, even my nose. Well, when my time came, I just went in and sat down for my lecture. Dean Gibson had recruited me here to begin with, so he knew me well. Besides, I was editor of the student newspaper, and he liked my editorials. The only lecture was about safety, and he was really concerned that we hadn't blown ourselves up. When he looked at my face we both agreed that I had paid a pretty good price. Dean Gibson asked if I was going to write an editorial about the event, I said "Naw, I'll think I'll write about something else this week". Then he proceeded to surprise me beyond my wildest expectations. He reminisced about visiting me at Fillmore High School, about how I had taken to journalism, about how the paper was so much better this year than before, and how he appreciated me livening up the campus.

He summarized it all by saying how much he, and the whole campus would miss me next year when I transferred to Cal Poly at San Luis Obispo. I started to say that I didn't really have to transfer next year, I could go to my junior year here, then go to San Luis for my senior year. San Dimas didn't have all of the classes necessary to graduate in animal science, so a student had to go to San Luis. That argument didn't go far - he calmly stated "You have two choices, even enforced by the Los Angeles County Sheriffs Department, you either go to San Luis, or you are expelled! Now they don't have the slightest idea, who masterminded the fireworks, nor do I for that matter, but you are the likely suspect. I don't want to turn you over to them under any circumstances, in fact I won't. So you will go to San Luis. Its best for you, the animal science curriculum here is a joke. Up there you will truly learn something. But as I said, we will miss you - most students just don't know how to liven up a campus"!

Well it was settled, I would go to San Luis Obispo for the last two years of college. I need to say in hindsight, my job being the student manager of the cafeteria, and being the editor of the student newspaper had taught me far more valuable lessons about life than anything I had learned academically at San Dimas.

The summer between San Dimas and San Luis Obispo was different in that I had to work in Santa Paula all summer, so I didn't get to go to Nevada. Well, I didn't really have to work, but Jack Gilbertson, who owned an extensive welding shop on the east end of Santa Paula asked if I would stay home this summer and work for him. He had several welding trucks on the go all over Ventura County, but he was having difficulty keeping welder's helpers on each truck. Jack was a very close friend of my Dad's, and he did lots of work for Dad and Mr. Fairfield, so I could hardly so no. Jack, who was also mayor of Santa Paula, and at that time, had about four welders working in the shop. Two normally stayed there all of the time, and two were out in the field with trucks.

My job was to gin up the acetylene generator for the shops source of acetylene first thing every morning. Nobody liked doing that because it was kind of dangerous. I kept hearing stories of how welding shops kept being blown up by their acetylene generators. Well, I never blew the shop up, but I also noticed there weren't a lot of people around when I ginned up the generator. My welder was an old guy, by the name of Gus. He just plain and simple talked too much. When we were out in the field he just talked more than he worked, which bothered me. So it wasn't long before I had him talked into letting me do the welding. Dad had taught me some about welding, but this gave me a real opportunity. Gus was a good teacher, and soon I was doing most of the welding.

I'll never forget one day - we had gone to do some welding above Val Verde, which was a black community across the county line in Los Angeles County. It was a blistering hot day: It was supposed to be over 110 degrees in Fillmore, and you can bet Val Verde would be at least five to ten degrees hotter. We were supposed to weld some pipe on an oil well head that was out of production. Gus wasn't talking about anything except the temperature, so it didn't require much for me to do the welding. I sweat so bad that my helmet was continually fogging

37

up. I had Gus hold a wet rag over my head while I was running vertical beads, but even that didn't help much. By eleven o'clock it was 121 degrees on our thermometer. Gus wasn't sure it was accurate, and I hoped it wasn't. We had one last weld to make, about a six-inch lateral on two heavy pieces of plate. I speculated that it would require two passes, probably each taking two to three minutes, but these welds were in a grassy area and about all I could imagine was starting a fire. We had a big CO_2 fire canister, so I wanted that close to where I was going to weld, along with what was left of our five gallons of water and a shovel. Gus was glad to comply, and sat in the truck. Our hoses weren't real long so we had backed the truck up close to the job, and I began. I made the first pass OK, and after cooling off a bit I began the second pass. I could see the end when a crashing boom exploded along side my head, followed by a long, harsh, hissing sound. I knew that I had either burned through an acetylene hose, or the acetylene tank had blown. In either case, I was probably already dead. My helmet was thrown off while I rolled backwards. However, after coming to a stop I heard the distinct sounds of laughter. As I got to my feet examining myself to make sure most of the vital parts were still attached I observed that Gus was bent over with laughter. That didn't impress me too much, but my composure was such that I couldn't do too much about it anyway. To make a long story short, the safety release on the CO_2 container had blown, releasing all of the CO_2. Likely the extra heat from my welding, along with the 120 degree temperature was all she wrote. Well, I didn't die, but I surely thought I was well on my way. It didn't help my sense of humor to realize that I had added to Gus's amusement to that extent. It didn't take more than a few minutes to finish the job. All the way home I listened to Gus's version about how big my eyes were as I was rolling over backwards. However, I did make him stop in Piru and buy me a six-pack of beer for medicinal purposes only.

When we would come in at the end of the day, the welders like to sit around and have a beer or two. They were a fun loving bunch, so the stories got pretty good. Their favorite was the day they blew up the red anthill. Red ant mounds were pretty frequent around places like Santa Paula, and I had noticed several behind the welding shop. Well, it seems their story went something like this: One day a year or two before they had gotten everything done about 4:30 in the afternoon, so it was beer time. Jack was out of town, so they were a bit more relaxed. The subject came up about doing something a bit different, and someone suggested running acetylene down a red aunt hill to see how much it would take. It wasn't long before a big tip on the end of a long hose was inserted in a red anthill, with a little mud over the top to insure a good fit. The boys got to drinking beer and kind of lost track of time. Directly, someone remembered the anthill and the acetylene hose. Wade, my favorite welder told the story best - as he remembered, they sort of panicked when they realized how long the hose had been on, but Wade said, "Oh, hell, boys you only live once, besides most of that acetylene surely has found a way out by now and it's long gone", as he threw a match in the direction of the mound. Hearing the story it's hard to imagine exactly what happened next, but it was a dandy at any rate. Wade claimed he was the only one left standing. Gus claimed his feet went right out from under him like everybody else. There was a large cement pad behind the shop, the remnant of a long lost, outer building. I had noticed how cracked up the cement was, but never questioned why. Well, that's why, most of the colony was right under the cement. I guess chunks flew every direction according to Wade's description. One went right through a shop window. When the dust settled and everybody decided they had had enough for the day, the shop was closed and that was that. Wade was still laughing when he brought out the torn copy of the Santa Paula Chronicle, dated July 15, 1954, describing the sharp earth quake reported throughout the Santa Paula area at 5:45 P.M. the day before. They all agreed that was one that would be hard to top.

Anyway that story relived, over another beer or two, led to a discussion of what could be done to top the red ant explosion. This crew was great friends with my Dad's crew over at his shop. Jack's shop was about two blocks due east from where my Dad's office and shop were. There was absolutely nothing in between except two vacant lots. So Wade, whom I had long suspected of being the ringleader of all such pranks, felt it was time to wake up my Dad's crew. He said, "You know, we could build a cannon and knock Ed's gang into the Pacific." I agreed, it was a clear shot, but I didn't like the idea of blowing them to the ocean. Wade calmed my nerves, "We'll just blow a sound shot at them. They'll think they are going to the ocean". Gus was getting nervous and so were the rest, but Wade said he had seen it done before. It won't hurt a thing, just wake everybody up. I should have left at this point, but as usual curiosity got the best of me. They got a length of drill collar pipe, which is about ten inches in diameter, with an internal hole of about six inches, and set it on some metal horses, generally aimed at Dad's shop. The length of drill collar pipe was about 16 or 20 feet long. Wade and Gus got out their torches, both put on rose buds, and heated the last five to seven feet of the pipe to a glowing red. After that was accomplished, a torch was placed in the other end, with the acetylene turned on full force. Wade had mixed up a five gallon bucket of mud which he packed into the drill stem around the torch tip, so the acetylene had only one way to go, up the pipe towards the red hot end. We all sat back with one more beer, speculating on how long it would take to get to the other end. I was good with math, and I knew about how many cubic feet per second of acetylene were going out of that size of the tips. So I sat there with a beer in one hand, and a pencil in the other doing some quick calculations. I was getting close to the answer when the damned thing went off - and it went off! I'll swear to this day that that drill stem, which weighed literally thousands of pounds rose up into the air about five feet and just stayed there. The mudpack blew out along with the torch, but not as hard as one would expect. The vast amount of the force went the other direction - straight at my Dad's shop. You could see the sound waves going, as if in slow motion. Dust was raised as the wave went along, to, and then right past the shop. I wasn't sure anybody was still there. Dad wasn't for sure, but I saw somebody come out that looked like Huck. He must have known what happened, because he jumped into a car and came straight over to our shop. I guess I had never really seen Huck mad before. Certainly not even years before when I threw up all over his back at Coleville, but he was mad. When he calmed down, he finally started laughing, because he had pulled the same stunt years before, but on a much smaller scale. Then he finally said what was really funny was how we were going to explain to Ed the next morning about his front window being knocked out! Well, right then and there, I knew I had a problem, even though I was only a welder's helper. We all went over to inspect the damage. Fortunately there was some old form plywood behind the shop. It didn't take long to cut a piece to fit the window: I had already cleaned up the glass inside. About then, the Santa Paula version of Earl Hume came by to see what blew up. Wade and Huck explained that there was no problem, just a gas can with only vapor in it somehow ignited and blew the window out, but we had everything under control.

The next night Dad and Jack cornered me about the whole incident. I said don't worry, even though it wasn't my idea, I'll pay for fixing the window. It turned out Dad and Jack didn't care as much about the window, as to learning what happened. I was awfully relieved to find out just how much of a prankster Jack Gilbertson, as well as my Dad really was. Their version of what happened, which was only hearsay, was much greater than the true facts. They both loved pranks: They just wanted to know how it was done. I suggested that Wade might have some idea, but it was time for me to go to San Luis Obispo and learn something of value.

Cal Poly at San Luis Obispo was a whole lot different than Cal Poly at San Dimas. First of all, it had about ten times the students. And it had real classes with real professors that gave real homework assignments. My first quarter in school was a dandy. It took me about two weeks to get through the academic shock and realize exactly what I had gotten myself into. Between my cattle operation and schoolwork, there wasn't time to work. I had saved up a bit of money. Besides in those days, if you were an elected campus leader, your tuition was waved. I never was so glad to have been the editor of the paper at San Dimas! I quickly outlined my school program, and realized with a little help that it might be possible to actually graduate a quarter early, in March, instead of June. Mr. Fairfield had mentioned once or twice that it just might be possible for me to work on his Nevada ranch full time when I graduated. So, it didn't take me long to get the word to him that I might just be able to graduate in March of 1957, rather than June! He seemed to think that might be OK!

Even though life at San Luis was hard, it wouldn't be right to say that we didn't periodically have fun. Every spring, the school puts on a real show called Poly Royal, where all students have projects on display, alumni return, and in general a real celebration occurs, including a formal dance on Saturday night in the campus gym. Girls weren't admitted to Cal Poly yet, so the availability of females at San Luis was very limited compared to San Dimas. Besides, I was going pretty steady with a girl I had met at San Dimas. When Poly Royal rolled around, several of us had participated in just about every event, except no one had a girl to take to the formal dance. One enterprising student, Julian Smith, felt that we ought to do something extraordinary for Poly Royal. So over a beer or two, we compared ideas. Julian had the best, by far! He had been working at the swine unit and knew of a barren sow, that he claimed to weigh over 600 pounds - he said she was kind of ornery, but she hadn't ever bitten anybody, yet. Anyway, his idea was to load her into his pickup, back the truck up to the rear door of the gym and release her onto the floor during the dance. Well, that all seemed simple enough, and I knew that there was a back door with a ramp at the gym. Tom Peltzer, who had come from San Dimas at the same time I did, knew where there were some panels that he could put at the back of the gym beforehand to facilitate our madness.

At about 6:00 P.M., the Saturday night of Poly Royal, we all went to the swine unit, gently backed Julian's pickup up to one of the loading ramps, and went to get the sow. Seeing how Julian nearly ran the swine unit, we didn't have too many problems. The old sow was even pretty cooperative. She grunted a lot, but once we had our panels in place, we moved her right along. She slid right into Julian's pickup with ease. His side racks kept her well confined. It didn't take more than 15 minutes to return to the back of the gym. The front was packed with cars, as there were several thousand people at the dance, but the alley behind the building was clear, except for some barricades, which we easily removed. When we got to the door, both Tom and Julian suggested, once the sow went in that we hide the pickup, run around to the front, go upstairs to the balcony bleachers and watch the fun. We put the panels in place, Julian got behind the sow, I dropped the tailgate, Tom opened the doors of the gym, and within a second or two she was gone and the doors were closed!

It took us a minute or two to hide Julian's pickup and run up stairs. I'll never forget the sight that unfolded before us. The gym floor was totally covered with dancing couples, men mostly in tuxedoes, all the girls in formals. The band was at the balcony at the end of the gym above one of the baskets. There was simply a mass of humanity everywhere, as well as a great deal of noise. As we looked down, it wasn't hard to spot our sow. Things were pretty peaceful throughout the gym except in the general vicinity of the sow, but right there it was bedlam! There were screams; parts of girl's formals were flying; once we saw the sow running with the better part of a formal in her mouth; there were men jumping over each other. I never knew if they were trying to get away or trying to protect their dates. After a few minutes of this bedlam, Julian said as one of the student managers of the sow unit, it was his honor bound duty to help get that sow off the dance floor. Julian McPhee, President of the San Luis Campus knew Julian, and was very relieved to see Julian and the rest of us show up. Julian immediately told McPhee that he had heard what happened, and that he rushed right over, along with some of his friends to get the sow out - McPhee said, "Don't stand around talking, do something"! It only took us about five minutes to convince the sow that she would be a lot better outside than in, even if she were still wearing about half of a formal. Well, we got her out, and generally headed towards the swine unit, but that took the better part of the night. A little beer didn't hurt that part of the project. After the dust all settled, President McPhee never did catch the culprits that put the sow in Poly Royal. That event was talked about for years to come!

At the start of my senior year I married Jan, the girl from San Dimas that I had been dating. She had just graduated from junior college, but there were no jobs in San Luis. We lived fairly cheaply in those days, and I had saved enough money to make it through, providing I graduated in March.

In the stretch of my senior year to graduate in March, things became a bit hectic. Mr. Fairfield promised me a job, but he also reminded me about our agreement about the Fee Lease. "I told you when you graduated, your cattle had to leave. Besides, I plan on selling that place next year anyway, and you can't take care of those cattle and work for me in Nevada at the same time". I agreed, so the cattle were all sold, including Chubby, who had grown old by that time. Anyway, Chubby went to a friend of my younger sister's in Fillmore, so that wasn't all bad.

Cal Poly had a requirement to graduate that was often hard for senior students, namely, a senior project. The project could be just about anything in your major, but a committee of professors had to approve it, and when completed, the project had to be presented in front of the senior students and staff, with approval of the staff a necessary requirement for graduation. For me the project was easy, I chose a management plan for Mr. Fairfield's Nevada ranch. The ranch brand chosen by Fairfield was fittingly enough, OIL. My project included maximizing production, using a number of innovative management techniques. I passed the senior class project with an A+, the highest

44

grade awarded in the class, and after review of my project by Fairfield, he promised to apply some of the techniques I had described.

However, to graduate in March wasn't as easy as it seemed. There were many requirements to obtain a degree in animal science, some which didn't make too much sense. I went along with most, but in that last quarter, there was a political science class that conflicted with biochemistry. Now I was interested in biochemistry, but the political science class was such that I couldn't have cared less. If I couldn't resolve the conflict, I wouldn't be able to move to Nevada in March and that was unacceptable. Now that was the year that Cal Poly allowed women to enroll. About a thousand had, so the campus population had swelled significantly. Generally, there were two types of women that enrolled at Poly that first year, ones that loved horses, and ones that love the social odds of a three to one male to female ratio. Consequently, there had been some real campus turmoil, clear up to and including the registrars office. Thank god there weren't computers then to keep track of which student was in what class - and that allowed me to arrive at the very solution to my scheduling problems.

It didn't take me long to contact my old friend Tom Peltzer, and further, I learned that his academic progress was such that he had no designs on graduating in March or June for that matter. He was simply having too much fun since the advent of girl students! I reminded him of our adventure in Smith Hall a few years back, and how my actions had saved his very being. He agreed by asking what I finally wanted in return. My answer was simply, "Register for Poly Sci 205, under my name; take the class, and if you pass with a C, we are even. If you get a D, or heaven forbid an F, then you owe me $500. If you get either a B or an A, I'll pay you $100." Tom laughed, he loved anything that would beat the system, so to speak, and this was his cup of tea, not to mention mine. There were a few discrepancies. Tom stood about 6'2", and probably weighed in at 225#, while I stood 5'7", and weighed about 140#. Tom's hair was coal black, and mine was very light, in fact beginning to turn grey. Other than that, we matched up fairly even! Fortunately, having only been there for our junior year, and one quarter of our senior year, we weren't well known on campus. Besides neither of us knew the prof. So we registered, with Tom taking Poly Sci 205 under my name. It made me appear to be taking 25 units that quarter, but fortunately no red flags were raised. Tom got a C, I passed all of my classes, and on March 15, 1957, I received official notice that I had earned a Bachelor of Science Degree in Animal Science from California State Polytechnic College at San Luis Obispo, California! Three days later, Jan and I headed for Nevada and we never looked back!

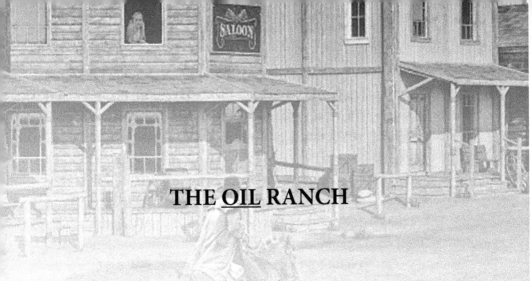

THE OIL RANCH

The OIL was a large ranch by any standard. The headquarters were at Holbrook Junction, in Nevada. However, all of the late spring, summer and early fall range was in California, lying entirely within Slinkard Valley, and Antelope Valley. Mr. Fairfield had purchased Antelope Valley a few years before I graduated, and it just about doubled the grazing capacity of the ranch. Antelope Valley lay to the east of the Coleville/Walker area, rose from an elevation of around 5,000' to over 10,000'. The upper end of the valley represented some of the highest grazing range anywhere in the Sierra. In fact from the top of the range, it was possible to look down on Pickle Meadows, the Marine cold weather and survival training facility located on Sonora Pass.

Basically, Fairfield owned the vast majority of both Slinkard and Antelope valleys, thus his operation had little to do with the United States Forest Service. A small Forest Service permit did exist in both valleys, however, his ownership pattern was such that the forest ranger paid little attention to it. Cattle wintered in Nevada, again exclusively on deeded property. Fairfield owned a great rectangular shape piece of property, stretching from Topaz Lake to Holbrook Junction, then easterly to Hoyt Canyon, where the Walker River flowed into Smith Valley, and then east to the Sweetwater Range. I never did know exactly how many acres were in the winter range, but by my guess it would be about 75,000 acres.

Mr. Fairfield had put a great deal of effort into developing the winter range. There were some old water wells there when he originally bought the property, but it didn't take him long to develop real water. He drilled about six water wells, all producing over 1,000 gallon per minute. After he realized how much water he had, he tried growing potatoes as an enterprise. The potato production was above expectations, however, marketing was such that the enterprise didn't work. The ranch did end up with a very large potato cellar that made an excellent equipment storage area. After potatoes, he went into alfalfa hay production, as a source of winter feed for his cattle. This gradually expanded, along with some grain production to the point that the ranch could support close to 2,000 mother cows; with enough feed left over to support a feedlot to fatten about 500 head of steers annually. Mr. Fairfield was a Hereford man through and through, so the commercial herd was Hereford, along with a small purebred herd for a source of breeding bulls.

When we arrived at the ranch, our living quarters were directly below the manager's house, adjacent to U.S Highway 395, and just a stone's throw from the bar at Holbrook Junction. Needless to say Bill and Mary were glad to see me in Nevada on a permanent basis, and they were happy to meet Jan.

The manager's name was Jim Kilduff, and he had been manager for about the last five years. Jim had grown up in Meeker, with Mr. Fairfield, so they were life long friends. Now don't think Jim got the job because he was Mr. Fairfield's friend, far from it. First of all, Mr. Fairfield was not that sort of person, and furthermore, Jim Kilduff was probably one of the most qualified ranch managers in the West. I had gotten to know Jim during my periodic summer visits to the ranch. He seemed to like the way I worked, and on several occasions he indicated that he would like to see me at the ranch when I graduated. Jim was a striking individual, about 6'4", skinny as a pole, probably didn't weigh over 175 pounds. He had long wavy grey hair, and strong features. We use to kid him that he looked like a cross between Jimmy Stewart and John Wayne. The "Duke" side of Jim emerged when we worked cattle, and the Jimmy Stewart side seemed to emerge when farming became a priority! Regardless of what mood Jim was in, he had become a highly respected member of the Nevada Cattlemen's Association in the few short years that he had lived in Nevada. He had headed up many committees and was some sort of an officer of that organization at our arrival date.

When we arrived, the ranch crew consisted in addition to Jim, the cow boss, Jack Davis, Arnold Stoudmeister, pretty much in charge of equipment, Slim Beck, who had worked for my Dad in the oil fields at Santa Paula, and in fact I had gone to school with Slim's kids. Slim was in charge of the farming operation. Also a local Indian by the name of Gene Ramboux, in addition to myself, rounded out the crew. We didn't put up hay, as it was done by a custom farmer in Smith Valley. However, Jim liked to top the stacks out with an elevator, which pretty much fell to myself and Gene. If we had to put up the hay, it would have taken several more hands, as the ranch was putting over 4,000 tons into the stack at that time.

Each member of the crew was not only unique in their appearance and manor, but they were also unique in how they approached work. Jack should have been called "Silent Jack", for he hardly ever said a word before 10:00 A.M., and then it wasn't much. If you were going to ride with Jack, it paid to get your instructions the evening before, because it was cold turkey the next morning. But Jack was a great cow man. He knew his cows, pretty much by sight, and he had a good handle on their production. Jack was a small man, probably 5'6" and 140 pounds dripping wet. He sat a horse real well, didn't mind bucking one out in the morning if necessary. He could sort cows as good as anybody, and he threw a mean loop. Jack was married: Her name was Bessie, and she was just about the exact opposite. Bessie was 4 inches taller, and likely 100 pounds heavier. And if "Silent Jack" was appropriate for him, then "Babbling Bessie" would have been appropriate for her! You couldn't be around Bessie for more than a few minutes without knowing just about everything that was of importance in Western Nevada and Eastern California.

All the crew lived down by the feedlot and general ranch headquarters, which was about 10 miles from where Jim and I lived. So, we only got to visit with Bessie infrequently, and that probably saved Jan's mentality!

Slim was about 6'2" tall and probably weighed around 225 pounds. And he was equally strong. Slim came directly from Oklahoma during the dust bowl days, so he knew hard times. Slim was always happy, always had a smile. Slim's specialty was serving bar-b-qued sage hen breasts. Sage hens were everywhere around the hay fields in those days. In the evening Slim would drive along the edge of the fields with his 22 rifle, shooting the birds in the head. About every two weeks Slim and his wife would put on a bar-b-que for the ranch, and just about every one would come. We always kept an eye out for the game warden, but in those days they were pretty rare.

Arnold and Gene were probably the two biggest characters on the ranch. Arnold was of direct German decent, and had grown up in Pennsylvania. Arnold wasn't very well educated. He said he made it through the fourth grade. He couldn't write very well, but he did read. In fact, he had read every western novel ever written! His house was filled with novels that he had already read, and he never went to town without purchasing several new books. Arnold didn't bother with a checking account, just cashed his checks, and always carried around his money in a roll in his front pocket. He wasn't much on clothes, as I don't think women interested him much. He always wore Levi's. In fact, he always wore new Levi's. When Arnold would go to town, he would come home with a new pair on. Now, Arnold didn't believe in washing very much, because he would wear that pair of "new" Levi's until he went to town again, regardless. Sometimes they would get pretty ripe, especially if we had been working cattle. It didn't make much difference if they stayed on until he went to town. I once inquired of him what became of the old pair when he bought a new one. He didn't really know, as he always changed in the dressing room, and simply left them there. I suppose in those days at the Gardnerville Mercantile you could do that sort of thing! Jim had tried to change his habits, and after coming to the conclusion that he couldn't, assigned him his own ranch vehicle, and forbade him to ride in any other company vehicle!

Gene, or Genie as we all called him, was a Paiute from the local band. Genie was small, probably 5'2" and I doubt if he weighed 120 pounds. But for what ever he lacked in size, he made up for quickness, in fact he was cat quick. And pound for pound, he probably was the strongest around. Genie loved to have fun. He was always pulling practical jokes, and you simply would never catch him without a smile on his face.

Gene had a problem common to many Paiutes, he couldn't handle alcohol. Now that didn't mean that he didn't drink, far from it, no he simply couldn't handle it! A few drinks and Gene would simply enter another world - around other Paiutes, that world often ended up in a brawl. After his days off, he would invariably come back with some new scars, he already had about half of his right ear bitten off in one such brawl, but he always smiled when he told that or any other similar story.

My job on the OIL was primarily putting in new alfalfa fields and irrigating, then helping Jack with cow work. Although my degree was in animal science, I loved farming just about as much. In fact, I had a minor in farm production. Anyway after arriving, Jim showed me a new field that had been broken out of sagebrush adjacent to a new water well that had just been drilled. He thought that the well would produce about 2,000 gallons per minute, so he reckoned that we ought to be able to irrigate at least 150 acres. The field was still rough, basically. Arnold had done nothing more than bunch up the sage brush with the ranch D-8 on about 200 acres of pretty flat land. So, the first thing I did was burn the sagebrush piles. It was a bitter cold March day, so that wasn't too bad. After it was all burned, I hooked up a large scraper to the D-8 dozer and tried to fill in the low spots.

After about two days of pushing dirt around and making little progress, Slim happened by. Slim must have had a surveying instrument for an eyeball, because he could look across a field and in short order have all the low spots and high spots staked out. After a couple of hours, he had me pretty well organized, so it didn't take more than a few days more until the Cat and I had about 175 acres pretty level. Fortunately, this whole area drained towards the Walker River in a very gentle, but constant slope of about 2%, so the field didn't have to be perfect.

I ripped it with a big ripper that we borrowed from the neighbors, disked it, then used a land plain to get it as uniform as possible. This all took about 3 weeks, but it passed merit as far as Jim was concerned. I seeded the field with a mixture of oats and vetch for the first year, corrugated it and was ready to irrigate. In the meantime, my old friends Huck and Gene had come up from Santa Paula to install the pipe necessary for irrigation. Fairfield had almost unlimited access to junk pipe and hardware of all kinds. The plan for this field was to install a stand pipe about 20 feet into the air coming off of the well outlet pipe that was 16' in diameter. After the standpipe, the 16' pipe "T'ed" with a lateral going to each end of the field. Fairfield had found a ton of 3/4" faucets somewhere, so every three feet a faucet with a 3/4" nipple about 4" long was tapped into the main line. It took Huck and Gene about two weeks to put all of this together, with a lot of grumbling about never wanting to see a faucet again! The field was about 1,900' deep, and 3,500' across the top. The well was just about in the middle, so each main line was about 1750' long. Putting a faucet every 3' resulted in almost 1,200 faucets being welded in place - no wonder Huck and Gene were grouchy. However, they never invited me to the Junction for a drink!

It was about May 1, when we turned the well on. The whole object was to turn on just enough faucets to keep the water from going over the top of the standpipe. I started with about 50 faucets on, and started the well. I hadn't really thought the whole process through, but neither had Arnold, Slim or Jim for that matter, as they all stood by and watched. This well at full throttle would produce about 2,000 gallons per minute. Under normal pressure you can shove about five gallons per minute through a 3/4 faucet. And it didn't take long for the extra 1,750 gallons per minute to go over the top of the standpipe, a beautiful sight to say the least! By the time Slim got to the clutch, we had rained several thousand gallons down on my new furrows, resulting in a bit more than moderate damage to the field! With a loader, dump truck, and a lot of shovel work I was ready to start over in about two days.

The next time I figured we would run the well at 80%, producing about 1,500 gallon per minute. I opened 300 faucets full, turned the well on, and everything worked, except it soon became apparent that five gallons per minute was more than the furrows could handle. So I started closing faucets to an estimated 3 gallons per minute, and opened an additional 200 faucets, and everything worked like a charm. It didn't take me long to figure that I could run one full lateral, with all of the faucets and get just about the right amount of flow for the furrows. It took about four days to get the water clear through, and wet clear across, so I completed a full set every eight days. When it was all over, we irrigated that field eight days on and about 16 days off. Later that year about 2.5 tons of oat/vetch hay/acre was harvested, for a total of 375 tons. The plan was to drill in alfalfa in September without disturbing the furrows. Jim hoped that the oats and vetch would reemerge enough to make a cover crop for the alfalfa. That plan ultimately worked perfect, the only problem was that I didn't get to do it - for reasons which I will discuss later on!

After the new field got in, I continued irrigating it and several hundred additional acres of alfalfa. Sometimes I got to go to either Antelope or Slinkard and help Slim or Arnold irrigate the native meadows. I probably enjoyed that kind of irrigation the most of all. Sometimes, when I was really lucky I got to ride with Jack in the high country.

Ridding that summer was a totally new experience for me. My old horse Chubby, had only offered to buck with me once, and in hindsight it wasn't much of a buck, but it sure scared me. We were riding in what is called North Canyon on the Fee Lease when we rode right over a rattlesnake. Chubby realized it about the same time I did, he went straight up, and all I can remember is hanging on, because I sure wasn't going to fall on that snake. It all calmed down about as fast as it happened, the snake disappeared in the brush, Chubby got his composure, and I relieved myself! Well on the OIL riding was a bit different. The ranch had about 10 broke horses, most of them were pretty good, but they weren't ridden enough. Besides, during the summer they were kept in pastures with an abundance of fresh green grass. As I said earlier, Jack didn't mind breaking a horse out early in the morning, but the first time I rode with him, I didn't understand the protocol! Jack had come by my place about 4:30 A.M. and we headed to Slinkard. The horses were in a small field at the lower end of the valley. It didn't take more than a few minutes to get them in the corral. Jack cut out his favorite old grey gelding. He suggested that I catch a little roan filly, which I didn't have much problem doing. As we were getting the gear ready, Jack mentioned that the filly hadn't been ridden in a week or two, and she might be a bit "touchy". I can't remember rather that advice went right over my head or I just didn't pay any attention. Anyway, once we were saddled, Jack climbed on his grey, and as usual he popped once or twice, but caused Jack no problem. Well, I climbed on the filly, and she never moved a muscle. I was sure that I was good enough a rider that even if she had popped, I could handle the situation. We were going to move some cattle out of a field adjacent to the corral, on up to the upper pastures in Slinkard. So, Jack opened the gate and we headed out. We were about twenty feet past the corral gate when the filly began to quiver - I braced for something, I wasn't quite sure what. Well she blew, arched her back, all four feet off the ground. I thought I might go to new heights! My legs were strong, but not that strong - I grabbed leather, and held on with every ounce of energy I had. Jack went by pretty fast, but at least he talked this time. "Spur her boy, ride her out, get it over with" Yeah, you bet, first of all I didn't have any spurs on. I offered a small prayer for at least that!

It was all over about as quick as it started, but we covered the better part of 50 acres. The filly got it out of her system. I guess, I was too scared to be scared, if that's possible. Jack paid both me and my alma mater a high compliment. "I guess they taught you something about ridding at that school you went to. You did good on her. She dumped both Arnold and Genie last time they tried", he kind of laughed as he uttered those early morning words. I didn't say anything, just acted like it was an every day occurrence, but I guessed by luck or something I had passed Jack's horsemanship test. I never really had the heart to tell Jack that they never had any horses like that at Poly, unless it was in the rodeo string!

We rode most all day, pushed several hundred cattle about five miles up Slinkard to new pasture, got back to the corral, unsaddled and got ready to go back to the ranch without saying a word. On the way back, I guessed that I had better unpack my spurs if most of the ranch horses were like this, and Jack agreed that would be a good thing. I probably rode with Jack 20 or more times that summer, and no horse ever bucked to any extent with me again. However, I did give Jack's little roan filly, or his test horse, as I liked to call her, a wide berth from that point on!

I guess the highlight of that year was riding with Jack. Didn't get to do it every day, but whenever we rode it was always higher in the mountains as the summer progressed, especially in Antelope Valley. As I said, the upper end of the range overlooked Sonora Pass and Pickle Meadows. Pickle Meadows was known as a cold weather-training center, and I had no doubt that was correct along about January 15, but it was also a survival training camp. Marines that trained there in the summer had to pass a survival class, which included among other things being on your own for 4-5 days in the high Sierra with nothing more than the clothes on your back, a knife and a few matches. The camp commander had long since warned the ranch that summer riders were not to help participants, rather give them a wide berth, don't offer them anything. He stressed their ultimate survival during times of war would be dependent on how they survived here. Jack had warned me that occasionally we would run into marines in survival training, and to just ignore them. I only ran into them once, and I was pretty much by myself. Jack was a draw or two away. I was pushing some cow towards another group of cows, which included two bulls. We were drifting through some big pines, when suddenly two marines confronted me; at least, I guessed they were marines. They were eying my saddlebags, and based on their appearance I could well understand why. By the growth of their beards, I guessed they had been out at least three days. Their clothes were in tatters, and their faces were scratched and blistered. They looked at me, I looked at them, then I said, "You poor guys, if I had a bite of anything I would give it to you". You could see the look of disappointment: They both sat down, and I climbed off and walked over to where they were. They hadn't had a bite of real food in three and a half days, just some plants which they knew to be edible. They were issued a plant guidebook on which ones to eat and not to eat. In talking to them I soon realized botany was not their long suit. They described how the day before they finally spotted a porcupine, and the chase that followed. They had the porcupine twice, but in the end all they got was a handful and a face full of quills. Finally, the porcupine went up a tall pine, and they followed. One got up 20 or so feet, and was nearly up to the animal when he fell. Describing his tumultuous fall from branch to branch made me laugh, but watching him try to laugh with some pretty sore ribs soon sobered me up. They were due back into camp the following day, so I guessed they made it. I had always wondered why I never saw porcupines in the upper reaches of Antelope Valley before; but now, I began to understand why. On the way home that night I told Jack of my experience. He laughed and described some he had run into over the years. He claimed they would get hungry enough to wrestle a bear down: He had watched them eat porcupine raw, including the fat. And snakes were considered the best delicacy of all, but they were scarce at that elevation. To Jack's knowledge, the only thing they hadn't eaten to that point was some of the ranch's beef! My respect for Marines in general, and specifically survivors of Pickle Meadows grew pretty much after that.

We worked six days on and Sundays off at the ranch. However, being in charge of irrigation of about 500 acres of alfalfa, 150 acres of vetch and oats, as well as helping with the meadows, I sometimes worked at least a half day Sunday. I had rearranged the alfalfa irrigation schedules considerably, attempting to maximizing the use of water, not that it was in short supply, but I had been taught that by maximizing water usage, it would challenge the crop to grow more rapidly. Comparing the first and second cuttings with previous years seemed to make my point, certainly Jim, Arnold and Slim were pleased.

Even though we worked hard long hours at the OIL, there was always time for fun. Slim's sage hen bar-b-ques were a great get together, with lots of story telling about the week's activities. And with Genie around, there was never a dull moment. We were always talking about the actions of the various neighbors to the ranch. Most of the ranches in the valley were long standing third and fourth generation operations. In that regard, we were all outsiders, the only local being Genie. Some of the old families used to look at us like we were from a foreign country, which to their minds, we pretty well were. Some of the families got to know the ranch and the crew, and we even got invited for some special events. The Parks family and the Chichester families finally had began to realize that some of the innovative techniques being developed on the OIL were well worth considering. Everybody always brags about their weaning percentages and their weaning weights on ranches like these. Jim never said very much about ours, but where we knew the facts, ours were far superior. But Jim was not the kind of person to rub it in. If somebody wanted to know the facts, he was only too glad to share them, but you had to ask first.

There were some real characters in the valley as well, some we liked, and some we just hoped we'd never see again! One in particular was an individual by the name of Billy Wilson. I don't think Billy owned the ranch he was on. I believe it was an absentee owner, but nevertheless, Billy acted like he owned it. Whatever you might say, Billy could always top it. He was just one of those kind of guys.

Billy's place was on the east side of the valley, and the only reason we had anything to do with it, was that our range on the east side of the Walker River could more readily be accessed by going through Billy's place. Also, Jim had rented some pasture for replacement heifers from Billy. Jack would go over there once or twice a week to check on the heifers, but none of us liked to go because we just didn't like Billy's constant BS. The last two or three times Jack had gone, after returning, he would tell us about the problems Billy was having with coyotes. Coyotes were always a problem anywhere, but it seems like the coyotes had just decided to set up camp at Billy's headquarters. They had decimated his chickens, and a flock of ducks and geese that he had on his pond. They had also ripped his prize flock of Suffolk ewes something fierce. According to Jack, Billy claimed it was all the fault of one old bitch coyote that he had wounded the previous year. She recovered, but had apparently decided to even up on Billy and put him out of business, if at all possible, at least that was Billy's reasoning. Knowing Billy, I could imagine the amount of bitching, ranting, raving and general cussing that was aimed at the poor coyote. Without knowing any more of the facts, my vote at this point generally went for the coyote, although in general they were far from my favorite animal!

One day, when everything seemed caught up by noon, Jack said he had to go check the heifers at Billy's, and asked if Genie and I would like to go. I probably should have said no, I just had that feeling for some reason that things were going too good that day, and we should let well enough alone. I didn't. Genie agreed as well, but suggested we take his pick-up, as Jacks had left him high and dry the last two days. So we all piled into Gene's truck headed to Coleville and across the valley. The heifers were fine; in fact, they were doing better than average on the pasture. Fortunately, the fences were in good shape, as none of Billy's crossbred bulls had gotten in yet. We were laughing over what Jim's response would be if that happened to his prize Herefords. Well, anyway, on the return we went through Billy's headquarters.

Just as we drove in, there was dust everywhere, two Indian boys went by on their ponies at an all out gallop, with Billy in hot pursuit in his brand new Ford pick-up. We slowed down and got out of the way, as we didn't quite know what was happening. Genie knew the two boys well. They were cousins of one kind or another. He speculated, because they were excellent ropers, that they were trying to rope a coyote. Sure enough, as the dust settled, the two Indian lads were heading back towards us with a coyote in unwilling tow, and Billy was closely following with his pick-up. You could hear Billy giving directions to the boys at 300 yards at least. They stopped out in a large clearing, so Genie drove over to see what Billy's plan was, although by that time, both Jack and I were kind of suggesting that maybe it would be a good time to leave. Anyway, Billy drove up and looked at Genie, exclaiming, "Genie, you got any dynamite in that rig of yours"? He knew Gene would have dynamite, he always did, as Genie's true love was being a powder monkey, at least when he was sober.

Gene answered, "Yup, I got a few sticks in the back. Why?"

Billy responded, "Let me have one, I'm going to tie it to that bitch then turn her loose. She's caused me too much misery, so we won't waste ammunition today"! One of the Indian boys threw another loop around the poor coyote, who was just about warn out. A couple of half hitches and she was well secured. Billy had already helped himself to Genie's dynamite and fuse stash. It didn't take him more than a few seconds to use some electrician's tape to tie the stick to the coyote's back. He instructed both boys to dismount and get ready to get their loops off, but to hold the animal down, which they did with their boots. He lit the fuse, and everyone ran like hell. We were mesmerized by the whole event. I knew neither Jack nor Genie liked to see animals hurt, nor certainly did I, but it all happened faster than we could think. Jack yelled at Genie to get the hell out of here, which Genie did by putting his truck in reverse. We all watched as the coyote stood up, shook something fierce and then lit out in a straight line for protection of some kind.

The only thing she could see was Billy's brand new shinny Ford pickup, and that's where she stopped. From our angle we really couldn't tell if that was where she was or not, but the ungodly cussing coming from Billy's mouth would lead one to believe that's where she landed. It only took about 15 seconds for the fuse to burn down, as Genie liked short fuses. It went with an awful bang, Billy's truck disappeared in a cloud of dust, I saw glass and metal, and I thought an aerial go by. When the dust settled, Billy's pick-up just didn't look the same. Three of the four tires were flat, the spare was still rolling about two hundred yards downhill. The windows were broken, and the hood had a new bow to it. But the thing that was going to be hard to fix was the bow to the main frame. The poor coyote had sat right under the middle of the pick-up, apparently right between the cab and the bed. She must have stood up just as it went off, because the front half of the pick up went up on about a 20-degree angle to the end of the cab, then down at a similar angle to the rear bumper.

We all just sat there, sort of in disbelief to what we had just witnessed. Jack finally broke the silence saying in an extra slow drawl, "You know, I don't think Billy's legs are long enough to get into his new pick-up anymore"!

Genie was kind of shaking, I couldn't tell if he was laughing, or it was because of fear, but he finally said, "You know, by the grace of God, that could of been us! Thank you Lord!" I didn't know Genie to be religious before, but I guessed at that point he kind of was. As to Billy, he had given up yelling at that point, he just sat down in the dirt, held his head in his hands, and I honestly believe he was crying. The two Indian boys were kneeling in front of their horses, contemplating their fate. I kind of thought their careers as buckaroos, at least for Billy, might be coming to an end, but I also knew once the story got out, they would have lots of opportunities. We didn't know what more to do, Billy didn't want to talk, and so we just drove back to the ranch kind of quiet and peaceful. Later, on the way home Genie thought it might be a good idea to bring him some of the ranch chickens to start his flock over now that the coyote was gone. Jack thought better, in fact, he said for the next week or two he would take the long way around over the Hoyt Canyon Bridge to check the heifers. I didn't say anything, just chucked the whole thing away as one more experience that probably some place, some time, would be worth something.

Working on the OIL taught you survival: You didn't have to go to Pickle Meadows for that. We all tried to know where everybody was every day, at least by the time they headed out. Jack was the hardest to figure, often he just headed out, but we didn't worry as he usually had a horse nearby if all else failed. It was kind of up to each of us to tell somebody where you were going, just in case something went wrong. One day I broke that cardinal rule, and I almost paid dearly for it.

Arnold had been doing some Cat work on the road at the upper end of Slinkard. Fairfield wanted a road good enough over the top and into Antelope, that he could drive it in a pick-up, and as it was, it was little more than a jeep road. The day before Arnold had some problem with the starting motor on the Cat, so I went up with him, took my tools, and we fixed it. Like an idiot, however, I left my toolbox on the tracks along side of the starting motor. The next morning, first thing when I woke up, I realized where I had left my tools. Arnold was on a few days off, and no one else was going to Slinkard that I knew of, and we had noticed some things disappearing, so I came to the conclusion that I had better go get the tools. I felt so dumb about it that I didn't want to tell anybody, so after I got all of my alfalfa irrigation set, I jumped in one of the ranch jeeps, and headed for Slinkard. It's about ten miles from Holbrook Junction to the Monitor Pass road to Markleville. About five miles up the Monitor Pass road, the road to Slinkard takes off to the left. It's about 18 miles to the head of Slinkard where the Cat was parked, so all told it took me about one hour to go from Holbrook to the head of Slinkard. I didn't get away until about two in the afternoon so it was about three when I got there.

After I got to the caterpillar, I noticed something move off to my left in a little grove of pines, so my curiosity got the best of me and away I went. There were fresh deer tracks, and there was also fresh cat tracks, so I nosed around for a while to see what I could see, which turned out to be nothing. After about an hour, I returned to the jeep, put the tools in the back and got ready to head for home, only thing, the damn jeep wouldn't start. The battery was completely dead. I checked all of the terminals and everything else, but to no avail - plain and simple the battery was dead. I had parked in a little swell, so pushing it was out of the question. I looked down the valley, and could see the monitor Pass highway in the distance, but 18 miles and it was already 4:30, I figured I could make it in four hours, but the likely hood of another car coming by on that highway after dark was somewhere between slim and none, so I figured to get to 395 would be at least a five hour jaunt - yuk! I thought about firing up the 8, but it really couldn't travel much faster than I could walk, and there was no way to take it down to 395 once I hit the Monitor road, so other than saving some shoe leather, that didn't offer much of an alternative. I didn't have a jacket; I didn't have any food; I didn't have a gun. In fact I didn't even have a match. I thought about just sitting down and crying, but that reminded me of

Billy Wilson, so that didn't sound like a good idea either. Well, like I said, working on the OIL taught you survival!

And feeling sorry for yourself only added to the desire to conquer the enemy. I looked at the Cat; I looked at the jeep; then it hit me, if I could get the Cat started, I could push the jeep to a little rise in the road about 20 yards away. Once there, it was a fairly clear shot for about 100 yards down a gentle slope. We had fixed the starting motor yesterday, so at least that was in my favor. And it started on the second pull, shortly I had the big diesel idling.

I put the jeep in neutral, positioned the Cat directly behind, with the blade about a foot off the ground, and started pushing. It took a bit of jockeying, but pretty soon I had the jeep to the top of the rise ready to go. I put her in second, turned the switch on, pulled the choke out a bit, climbed on the cat and started forward. Everything worked just about as good as if it were in the bible. The jeep coughed once and that little four-cylinder motor started purring, only a bit too fast. For some reason the throttle was sort of stuck on fast, so the jeep pulled right away from the cat. I got that 8 shut down as quick as I knew how, hit the ground running, but was already about 50 yards in second place. I prayed that she might start going in circles, no such luck, she went dead ahead, towards a pretty good size bunch of boulders about 200 yards off in the distance. I never was a very fast runner, but it must have been the elevation, because it seemed that I was going a mite bit faster than usual - I was probably picking up a yard for every yard the jeep went, I was too busy for my usual mental math calculations, but it was obvious that this was to be a close race. One thing I hadn't counted on was that if I got a hold on the rear of the jeep, that extra effort might make the difference, and it did. For as soon as my hand hit the ridge above the rear seat, I propelled myself along side the drivers seat, grabbed the steering wheel and pulled her to the left, just missing the first rock.

I was about done, but as the jeep turned left, it kind of helped me roll in, and just as quick as it happened, we were idling back towards the cat. About then, I realized that the elevation here was close to 8,500 feet - I was totally out of breath and my heart felt like it might break a motor mount. But time cures most problems and it cured that one. I got back to the house about 6 P.M., Jan asked how my day went - I didn't have a very good answer, because I really didn't want anyone to know that I had left my tools in Slinkard!

Jim's wife Barb, had left to go back east to visit her mother during most of June, so Jim was batching. One night we felt sorry for him, so we asked if he would like to come down and Bar-b-que some steaks. It didn't take him long to show up, and with a fifth of bourbon in hand! After dinner and a few drinks, Jim reminisced about his life in Colorado, and here in Nevada. Gradually the conversation turned to what Jim saw for the future of the livestock industry in the West. What followed was pretty much a one-way conversation, but its one of those conversations that didn't go away very easy. In hindsight, it undoubtedly was one of the most profound discussions of not only the future of the livestock industry, but also the future of the West, and for all practical purposes, the future of this country. I didn't have the knowledge at that point in my life to understand much of what he said, much less the ramifications, for I hadn't quite yet turned twenty two years of age.

Jim wanted to know what I had learned about range management at Cal Poly, and more specifically, what I had learned about the management of the federal lands. I responded by saying, "I didn't have a real strong professor in range management. I learned far more about pasture management. But I do remember spending a few lectures discussing the management of the federal lands. He went over the history of the grazing service, and how the Taylor Grazing Act eventually resulted in the formation of the Bureau of Land Management. And we also learned about the early history of the Forest Service. But most of our time was spent on plant communities, and the limited knowledge there was about grazing impacts and things of that nature". Jim wanted to know what I had learned about Political Science, but I didn't have the heart to tell him about that fiasco! So, I truthfully answered not much.

I don't know what prompted Jim to start in with his philosophy about federal lands, but whatever it was it took several hours until the wee hours of the morning. I can't remember every word, and as I said, I was too young to even understand much of what he was saying, but I never forgot. And as the years have gone, I have often reflected on that conversation, not only how true his words were, but also what a profound effect that conversation ultimately had on my life.

He discussed his fears about the continuation of livestock grazing on the federal lands, which of course was critical for the survival of the industry throughout the western states. He knew of attempts in the past, before the development of the BLM, to grant large tracts of this land to each ranch, so that they could manage their land. Every time discussion of this nature came up in Congress, the livestock producers united to fight to keep the system the same. They didn't want to own the land; their claim always was that it wasn't productive enough to pay the taxes. Jim went on to say, "They wanted free forage, or since the formation of the BLM and the Forest Service, forage cheaper than the county would charge in taxes for fee land, in short they want their cake and eat it too"! Even though Jim was an officer in the Nevada Cattlemen's Association, it was pretty obvious that he didn't hold them in high regard. "Sure, there's a few that understand, and have done everything in their power to get title to the land that they graze, but the vast majority of producers always shout them down", he went on to say.

He asked what I thought might become of these lands, and my answer was pretty simple, "I don't have any idea". Well it was pure speculation on his part, but he believed that as the years went on the general public would express ever more interest in the so-called federal lands, including every detail as well as management. He went on to theorize that as that happened, there would be more and more outcry to either get livestock, and for that matter timber and mining, off the federal lands, or make them pay dearly for the resource they used. It was obvious to me that Jim had become very frustrated with the inability of people to understand just how important the conversion of resources from the federal lands into usable products was to the overall economy of the nation. He felt that politicians were nearly useless in this regard. "They will always bend to the will of the majority, that's how you keep in public office. As this whole issue becomes more political, you mark my words, the politicians will sell us down the river, even the western politicians who know best of all". He made reference to the Eisenhower Report on federal lands, a report that Ike had called for, because no one in national government really knew what the government owned.

Jim inquired what I knew about the constitution, which again my answer was pretty simple, not much, as I hadn't really paid that much attention to it in college, and in high school, only one teacher, Mr. Mozley, tried to help us understand it, but he struck us as not understanding it well enough to teach about it. Anyway, Jim went on to say that the constitution pretty well sums up the government's position on federal lands, they were to be disposed of in an orderly fashion. The government was never to own any lands, except for forts, postal services, and things of that nature. He blamed Teddy Roosevelt for starting the whole issue of government ownership of vast tracts of land, but he also speculated that Teddy never envisioned the holding of one third of this nation as federal land.

Finally Jim switched the conversation to Nevada. "Did you know that there are more cattle than people in Nevada"? he asked. That I did know, and I said, I believe there is only about a quarter of a million people in Nevada. He laughed indicating that he was pleased that I knew something. But he went on to say, " In some ways that's the problem. We send two senators to Washington, that's two out of 96, which puts Nevada on an even footing with New York, which has millions of people in it. It's damn difficult to become a senator from New York, but it's far too easy to become a senator from Nevada. Only about half the people in this state are eligible to vote, and only about half of them vote, so to win you've got to get 50% plus one, which means that about 35,000 votes is about all you have to get to become a United States senator from Nevada. This makes it awfully easy for us to send somebody to Washington that would be better off in jail"! And that was Jim's fear, that we would send people to Washington that would sell out Nevada for personal gain - he went on to say how easy it would be to do both; send them to Washington, and for them to take advantage of Nevada. It was a genuine fear on his part, and it all went back to the federal lands. Jim recognized the value, something far in excess of what the tax dollars for grazing might represent.

The night wore on, the level of the bourbon went down, but I never forgot the conversation, no never. I didn't understand the full significance of his words on that warm June night in 1957, but it didn't take many years before I wished I had picked Jim's brain far more than I did that night. That was the only real time that we talked "politics" at least at that level. The next morning when I saw Jim, he had a kind of "Jimmy Stewart" sheepish grin on his face, and said that he hoped that I didn't take him too serious. To tell the truth, at that point in time, I really didn't know what to take of the conversation. Much of what he said was foreign to what I knew, what I had learned, even the way I was raised, but yet on the surface there was a certain truth to the whole spectrum of issues that we talked about that just wouldn't go away. It would take me a long time to digest it all, and in hindsight as I said, I never had been through a conversation with anyone, anywhere, that would so ultimately impact my life as the years went by.

We all planned to celebrate the Fourth of July with a special bar-b-que at Slims house. Jim said let everything go but what had to be done, and he would buy the beer. It sounded like a great time, but I was sad to hear Genie wasn't going to be there. He always went to the Reno Rodeo, which was held on the Fourth. Well anyway, we had a dandy time. About half way through the afternoon, Jim cornered me and said he had to go to Bridgeport tomorrow, and wondered if I would go to Reno to fetch Genie back. I asked what in the world for, Jim laughed, and said, "He always goes in with his cousins, and he always gets drunk, and almost always he gets thrown in jail at the Reno rodeo, and if that happened the sheriff will call me tonight, he's an old friend of mine, so they take pretty good care of Genie. I am going to give you $500 in cash, because that's all they will accept. It usually costs about $250, unless he really broke something up". Jim handed me five new crisp one hundred dollar bills, which was more cash than I had seen in a long time. Well, we ate sage hen breasts along with a special treat that Jim provided. He had shot an antelope the week before, and we bar-b-qued an antelope roast, chucked full of garlic cloves and marinated in wine. Washed down with beer, it was all about as good as it gets. I was beginning to think I had died and gone to heaven. Every Cal Poly grad dreams of a job like this, I was the lucky one!

That night about 10, the phone rang, it was Jim, and sure enough Genie was in the slammer. So early the next morning I headed to Reno, about an hour and a half trip, but it took me a bit longer to find the jail. The jail was down town on Center Street, but due to the Fourth of July crowd, parking was not plentiful. Anyway, I finally found where I had to go, filled out the paperwork, reviewed the charges, which were considerable, including public drunkenness, brawling, breaking a police car window and a few other things. The bottom line was the bill for his release was $600! I tried to explain that all I had was $500, I showed them my wallet which contained no other cash, I didn't have a credit card, not that it would have done any good, and I didn't even have a check book. The officer in charge said that I would have to leave him until I could get another hundred dollars. I tried to explain that we all lived over a hundred miles away. In fact, we lived in California, which only Genie did, but that was close to the truth. "I guess my only opportunity was to come back next week, and you guys will have to keep him for the rest of the week", was my only response.

The officer frowned, said the sheriff was still out of the office, but he would go back and talk to one of the deputies to see what could be done. Well Genie must have known what the predicament was, because while we were discussing his fate he put two other drunks in the hospital. They tried to gang up on him and take his other ear off. What they didn't realize was that Genie had sobered up, and had his reflexes back in order, so in the scuffle, he bit an ear off of each of the other two ruffians. The deputy in charge had seen the whole thing, so he didn't blame Genie. Anyway, after a short discussion, they all agreed I could have Genie for $500. It would probably be a bargain for the operation of the Reno jail at the rate he was putting people in the hospital.

I got Genie out, and as we were walking down Virginia Street, past Harold's towards my pick-up, Genie said let's go in and have a beer. I explained how I didn't have a dime, and Genie had already said he had lost his wallet, which I am sure at that point didn't have any money left in it either. So, we took the long ride back to Coleville, after going through some shakes for about half an hour, Genie finally went to sleep. That night I gave Jim the paper work, minus any money. He couldn't believe it cost $500, but the paper work clearly showed that it did. When I explained how he almost had to go back the next day with another $100 he calmed down a bit. But when he read how Genie had taken the tomahawk out of the Harold's Club Indian display, and chased the men dealers around threatening to scalp them, he sort of understood why it might have cost $500. His only comment was "Damn, next year you are going to have to go with him, I just can't afford to keep this up"! Well, next year was a long way off and a lot could happen in between, but one thing for sure I wasn't going to accompany Gene Ramboux to Reno for the next Fourth of July - I could just imagine a bunch of one-eared Indians chasing me down Virginia Street.

On several occasions I had talked about going back to college to get a Masters Degree in some form of livestock production. I liked nutrition, and I was becoming ever more interested in range management. The University at Reno had a pretty well respected ag college, even though it was small. I didn't even know if they offered a Masters Degree. So one day in early July, Jan and I went to Reno. She wanted to shop and see the sights, and I was going to wander about the campus and see if I could meet anyone. She hadn't been to Reno. In fact, we hadn't been anywhere except to Gardnerville and Minden and once in a great while to Carson City since we had arrived at the ranch. Going down Virginia Street, Harold's Club looked to be about the tallest building Jan, or I had seen in a long time. I showed her the jail; she still didn't entirely believe the Genie escapade.

Jan wanted to shop for clothes, so I let her off with a prearranged meeting place. I went on up Virginia Street to the campus. It was summer, so parking was no problem. I wondered around the quad for a bit, totally impressed with the old buildings, especially Morrill Hall. The ag building wasn't as old, but it wasn't very new either. Inside, I looked at the directory, and noted that there were several departments, including animal science, range management, soils, economics, agronomy, biochemistry and home economics. I found the animal science office, and noted that a Dr. Cassard was the chairman. I walked in and asked if Dr. Cassard was in. An elderly lady asked if I had an appointment. I answered in the negative, but I wanted to know about educational opportunities. She asked for my name and said to wait. Shortly she was back and said Dr. Cassard would be pleased to see me now, so in I went.

Dr. Cassard was a very personable individual, probably about 45 years of age. I introduced myself, said I had just graduated from Poly, was working on the Fairfield Ranch down Coleville way, and was thinking about going back to school. He grinned, and replied, "Jim must be working you too hard". Well I didn't have the slightest idea that he

70

knew Jim, but it didn't take me long to catch on. Furthermore, he knew most of my professors at Poly as well. Dr. Cassard explained that he had most of his degrees from Davis, but he knew just about all the animal agriculture professors throughout California. He went on to say he was a sheep man, but that was simply his area of expertise.

I had indicated that I was interested in cattle, and possibly nutrition and range management, and finally I got to ask the most important question of all, could I get a masters. His reply was in the affirmative, and that I might even be eligible for an assistantship if my grades were good enough. I didn't want to pursue that subject any further right then, because deep down I knew my grades weren't going to be good enough to qualify for an assistantship. Anyway, he inquired if I would like to meet the nutritionist and the person responsible for range management, and I answered that I would love to. After a few quick calls he informed me that Dr. Robertson, the range manager was out in the field, but that Dr. Bohman, the nutritionist, was in his lab downstairs. He took me down to the basement, and into a lab, with lots and lots of laboratory apparatuses, some of which I recognized from biochemistry, and some which I had never seen before.

Dr. Bohman was a big and awkward man, both in his actions and his speech. It didn't take me long to recognize that he was a scientist through and through. I wasn't on a level to talk intelligently with him in any fashion, and it was soon obvious that I couldn't buffalo him either. So, I just listened. Finally he got around to asking me what my interests were, and I could see the combination of nutrition and range management interested him. He indicated that he would be happy to act as my advisor and help me put together a program, but the first thing I ought to do was apply, so they could review my transcript and see if I qualified for admission or not. That sent a chill down my spine, as I thought grades were only important as far as the assistantship goes. He replied, "No, we like to have students working on their masters to have at least a B average in their undergraduate work". I felt a sinking feeling, but he came back to indicate, if the student showed enough interest in doing graduate work, and their average was less than a B, the committee might let them in on some type of provisional basis. The hour to pick up Jan was fast approaching; I thanked both Cassard and Bohman for their time, and said I would think it over, and left. On the way home, Jan asked what I thought, I indicated that it would likely be a cold day in hell before they would ever let me in, and that I was pretty happy right where I was.

About two weeks after we had gone to Reno, Mr. Fairfield came to the ranch. He hadn't come up from Long Beach for quite some time. Dad had told me over the phone that his health was not good. And he didn't look well when I saw him. But he was happy, he always was when he was at the ranch. After a few minutes, he asked if it would be all right if he came by and had dinner with Jan and I tonight - I answered, "Sure, we always have plenty on the table". With that I made a hasty trip back to the house to tell Jan. Fortunately, she had a big roast ready to do, so it all worked out well. Anyway, about 7 that evening Mr. Fairfield came by. I offered him a beer, as that was about all the alcohol that we had, he said thanks, but the doctors had him on a "dry" diet at that time. I didn't inquire as to what the problem was, but he did enjoy dinner.

After dinner, it was obvious that he didn't want to leave - the house we lived in was small, the kitchen was off the front room, and there was one bedroom and a bath, not too fancy, but it met our needs. Anyway we sat in the front room while Jan did the dishes. Fairfield complemented me on the irrigation scheme that I had worked out for the alfalfa. He also asked what I thought about Antelope Valley and what was the best way to manage it. I gave him all of my ideas, because I was hoping that he would see fit to give me some more responsibilities, obviously with Jim's approval. However, I was pretty positive, that if we put in all the new techniques that I had learned in College, and included a good dose of common sense, I was more than positive that ultimately the overall ranch production could be greatly increased, perhaps doubled. We talked into the night about my ideas, Mr. Fairfield kept asking me questions about improvements. However, I had the distinct feeling he wanted to talk about something else, and after skirting the issue for a while, he abruptly changed the subject by saying, "Jim tells me you liked your visit to the University up in Reno". Well I didn't remember telling Jim anything; I did tell Dad that I didn't like the place. I started to answer, but he cut me off by saying, "I want you to go there. There's no future here: You stay around this place long enough and you will be just another potato picker". I sat there in stunned silence, not knowing what to say, kind of feeling my heart fall into my boots! He went on to say, "The place for you is at the University. You can't get enough education, I guess school starts sometime in September, you can leave the first of September, and I'll pay you for September and October. And, if your schedule allows, you can come back next summer and work again". I didn't know what to say, what if I couldn't get in, what then, a thousand thoughts went through my mind, and all I could do was look at him. I thought about Chubby, the Fee Lease, all the trips that I made back and forth between Fillmore and the ranch, the last year, rescheduling the alfalfa irrigation. I loved this life. I loved this place. What would happen to us - just thoughts coming far faster that the words, words that wouldn't come at all.

I didn't know if I had done something wrong, and if this was a polite way of being fired, but I knew that wasn't the case. Mr. Fairfield and his wife never had any children, never a son. I don't know how far his education went, but Dad said he didn't think it went past the sixth grade. Maybe he wanted me to have the education experience that he never had. I didn't know. I never found out. He just wanted me to go on to school, that was that. He excused himself shortly, as he said he was tired and needed some sleep before touring the ranch with Jim tomorrow. After he left, I just sat there, a few tears coming down my cheeks. Jan came over and consoled me; she said that she knew I could make it in graduate school. I knew that too, but that's not what I had on my mind right then.

It didn't take long for word to get around the ranch that I wanted to go back to college that fall. It never seemed to amaze me how everyone was so concerned about my education. I already had more college education than everybody on the OIL put together with about half the residents of Coleville thrown in to boot! I ordered copies of my transcript to be sent to Dr. Cassard. What a joke that would be! I also wrote him and told him how excited I was about the prospects of going to the University now that I had made up my mind. I figured we had better start this out as positive as possible, as there surely were enough negatives already without adding to them.

Slim was the first to congratulate me, and he added that he only wished his kids would have used me for an example. He cheered me up somewhat by saying that I would have a full supply of sage hen breasts as often as I wanted them. Jack and the rest of the boys didn't say much. Arnold wanted to know if I was going to play football. I tried to explain, but finally I just simply said that I didn't have any eligibility left. I guessed Genie's only thought was that I wouldn't have to drive as far to bail him out of jail anymore!

A few days later Jack said he had to fix some drift fences on the Walker River. They were letting a lot of water out of Topaz, so the river was high enough that we could get to them with the ranch boat. The "ranch boat" was a fourteen-foot aluminum skiff, with a seven and half horsepower outboard motor. The motor was worn out, and almost impossible to keep running. I imagined the reason why Jack wanted me to go was because he couldn't understand how to keep the motor running, much less start it. Mechanics was not his long suit! Shortly thereafter, he said maybe Genie and Arnold might like to go along also. I wasn't sure how four of us were going to fit in the boat, much less go up stream against the current, but I also got to thinking that maybe fixing fence wasn't the only thing on the agenda!

Well, the day came to fix the fence, it was in late July, and it was hot. I hooked the boat and trailer up to my pickup, threw in an extra five gallons of gas, plus some tools. Sure enough Genie and Arnold piled in the back, with Jack in the front. Genie threw in a box, but I couldn't see what it was. Jack had already put in the tools and wire that we might need. We launched the boat right above the old Hoyt Canyon Bridge. There was a clearing and a gradual slope into the river that Arnold had made years ago with the Cat. We threw in the fencing tools, and extra wire, plus a few posts. Jack and Arnold were sitting in the front, and I had the motor started, and was holding the boat against the bank waiting for Genie. He jumped in with the box he had thrown into the pick-up. It was a box of dynamite - I sort of stared at it, then looked up at Jack. He shrugged his shoulders, and said on one of the cross fences we sometimes need dynamite. I guessed I had never seen this cross fence, but I had driven alongside the river as far as I could, and walked all the way to where the canal comes in from Topaz, and I sure never seen any place where dynamite might be needed. I shrugged, revved up the motor and headed up stream, but I had to admit, that box of dynamite just didn't look copasetic to me. Besides we were riding mighty low in the water!

It took about an hour to get to the Topaz Canal, we had hung up on sand bars several times, everybody had to get out and push. There was really only one fence across the river that needed fixing, and that didn't take 30 minutes. So we headed back, the four of us, tools, wire, and the box of dynamite. That stretch of the Walker River is a relatively slow meandering stream, although it might well have been classified as a small river that day with the flow from Topaz. The banks were heavy with willows and underbrush, and there were occasional cottonwood trees. It was a hot lazy afternoon; we just sort of peacefully drifted back down the river. I let the motor idle, as none of us were in a hurry to get anywhere fast. We drifted around a big curve into a deep hole with a cottonwood tree overhead. It had to be pretty deep, because you couldn't see bottom, and the water was pretty clear. About that time a large; in fact, very large trout broke the surface. We all saw it, but Genie woke right up, exclaiming, "That's just what we been looking for"! "Now, turn the boat sideways over by the edge of the pool and I will catch that lunker", he continued. Jack got an immediate smile, and Arnold perked right up.

Now, I began to understand the need for the dynamite, as Genie jerked out a stick, placed the fuse in it, wrapped it all up, lit it and threw it right into the middle of the pool. Not much happened for about 15 seconds, then there was a muffled roar, the surface broke, and a water spout went about 10 feet into the air. Well, we didn't catch the trout, but several carp went belly up. The dead carp weren't a loss to anybody, then Jack broke in, "Genie, you either got to use more dynamite, or go to a shallower pool if we are going to have the luck we had last time". Arnold chimed in agreeing with Jack, but what the hell Arnold knew about dynamite, I'll never know. They all knew I liked to fish, and that I was the only one that had a fishing license, so I guessed that made me more legal than anybody else, or more correctly put, less illegal than the rest! Well, like I said it was a peaceful day, and we sure enough were a long way from civilization, so I guessed it didn't matter too much what we were doing. Besides we hadn't dented the trout population and nobody that I knew was going to get too excited about a few dead carp.

So we floated along until the next pool, which didn't appear to be as deep as the last. I idled the skiff over to the downside edge of the pool. Genie wired two sticks together this time, got them ready, lit the fuse, and skillfully threw it into the exact center of the pool. This time a much sharper boom went off, a whole lot of water got mixed up, and the spout went straight into the air a good twenty feet, and lo and behold about 15 dead fish showed up. I had placed the boat in the right position, all we had to do was just sit there and let them float by. However, all but two were carp, but there were two nice trout that would make a good dinner for one of us. Jack said, "You know the time is getting late, we need to do this right and get a mess of trout". I agreed, but I guessed I didn't understand the full significance of what "doing it right" truly meant! However, I got to admit I was getting into the spirit of this new way of fishing.

So I chimed up, "You remember where those two old cottonwood trees are? There was a big hole there. I think it's only about a half mile down stream". Jack and Gene agreed, Arnold was only along for the ride, saying he wouldn't eat fish anyway, just beef and sage hen for him. I fired the motor up and a few short minutes we were gliding into the pool by the cottonwood trees. It was a beautiful pool, one bank well shaded by a cottonwood, but there was a tree on the other side as well. They were old trees, appeared to be dying, but they still had some life. The pool, or the deep part of the pool was only about 20 feet across, but it was a long pool, maybe fifty yards long from the sand bar at the curve up stream to the sand bar where I was holding the boat on the low side of the deep pool. The water was about three feet deep where I had the boat, and it appeared to be three to five feet deep up stream to the next bar. Several carp were apparent, and while we were sizing the spot up, a five-pound trout broke the water in hot pursuit of a dragon fly. I guess that was all it took, because Genie proceeded to wrap all the rest of the dynamite into one big bundle, with one fuse sticking out. I don't know how many sticks he tied together, but it had to be somewhere between nine and twelve. I let the boat drift a bit farther down stream under a slow idle, I was beginning to get a mite bit nervous, what Genie had in his hands was a mighty big fishing pole! Well he lit the fuse, and threw it as far up stream as possible. I guess maybe Genie was also concerned, because he threw it a bit further than he intended to, sort of past the pool, right into the upper stretches, where I reckoned the water was no deeper than four feet. We waited for the usual fifteen seconds, and then it happened.

It's difficult to explain the exact sequence of events. They all happened almost simultaneously, but it was like in slow motion. First, the bundle went off; second the river parted, right to the river bottom. In fact it appeared to be about two feet below the old river bottom. The thought of Moses parting the Red Sea went through my mind. He didn't have anything on us - we did such a good job that you could have driven the whole OIL cattle herd through this gap, with only a few hooves even getting muddy! Everything went into the air, water, mud, rocks, and I suppose fish, but they were a little hard to discern at that point in time. The two stately old cottonwood trees just decided to give up living, simultaneously, they just laid down, each pointing away from the river, in opposite directions, as neat as you could imagine. I guessed our next venture was logging! Then reality began to set in; the first and most fascinating thing to watch was the tidal wave going back upstream against the current, that was making some gigantic white caps, but about then I also noticed the wave coming back down stream. It was several feet high, maybe five, and we had about a five-inch line between the water and the rail of the boat. I thought about trying to outrun it, but I had the boat pointing the wrong direction, sort of sideways. I wasn't much of a skipper, but I clearly knew that if I left our craft sitting as she was we would roll over, so my only choice was to take her head on - which we did. As we went over the top, Arnold started cussing or something, it was in German, so I couldn't really tell. Jack usually smoked cigars when he was working cattle, but he always smoked a pipe when he was doing something peaceful like we were doing today. As we went over the top of the wave, I saw the pipe leave his mouth with a loud rush of air; the pipe hit the water at about the bottom of the wave never to be seen again. It was his favorite pipe. Genie never said a word, but the grin on his face made me think that he was congratulating himself for being the best Paiute powder monkey in all Nevada.

Well, we survived the wave, but at the bottom on the other side we hit the bottom of the river, hard. It sent everybody flying but no one left the boat. Water came at us from all sides after that, but we were floating! Then everything that had gone up started coming down - rocks, mud, debris, and I suppose fish, although I hadn't seen any yet. The mud covered everything, the boat, all the equipment, and ourselves. But everything got pretty much back to normal, except the river began to turn white, and it wasn't from frothy water. There were fish, dead fish everywhere, all belly up and strangely silent, not moving at all, just drifting with the water, which had began to organize itself, and continue its slow meandering way down stream.

We were all mesmerized by our success. We hadn't sorted out the trout, but there must have been plenty, even if the ratio between carp and trout was ten to one, we surely all had our limits. Jack was the first to come back to reality, not a word about his favorite pipe; no he brought up another whole topic. In a little bit faster than his normal slow drawl, he said, "Boys, you know down at the far end of Hoyt Canyon, where the river goes under the bridge to Wellington, that little white house by the river, that's where Jack Humphreys, the game warden lives. Now it's going to take most of the night for these fish to reach that point, but they'll be floating past tomorrow morning. When he gets up, I'm going to be far gone". I guess the rest of us agreed, we didn't bother to harvest any fish. I put the skiff up to warp whatever, in fact, we never hung up on another sand bar between there and the bridge, just glided right over them. When we got to the trailer, I noticed that it hadn't been a complete failure. Under my feet was the better part of about a ten-pound carp. He didn't look as good as he did, but you could still tell he was a carp. Nobody wanted him, so I gently slipped what was left of him back into the river. Never did find the two trout we had placed in the boat from our second attempt at bomb fishing!

It didn't take more than a few minutes to get the boat loaded, cleaned and back into the potato cellar. Genie had already made arrangements with Jim to go see his ailing grandmother in Bridgeport for a few days. Arnold was going to see if Jim would let him go to town for a new pair of jeans tomorrow, and maybe stay an extra day or two. Jack said he had to move cattle at the upper end of Antelope tomorrow, and he needed me to go. I checked with Slim to see if he could cover for me on irrigation. "You bet", he said, "and what in tarnation was that boom about 4 this afternoon. I can't believe it was a sonic boom, it just didn't sound right. Boy it was sure a bigin, whatever it was".

I shook my head, saying, "I don't rightly know what it could have been, maybe they are starting to mine over in the Sweatwaters again".

"Yeah, I suppose, but it sounded more like down to the river", was his reply. It was at least 15 miles between the headquarters and the river as the crow flies. I suppose we were lucky that carp weren't raining down on the headquarters. The next day Jack and I rode the high country. I didn't see any marines, but I'll bet I could have sold a ton of carp if they would have been around. We stayed that night at the line camp, ate beans and steak. Jack was in a pretty good mood, but he did say he missed his pipe something awful. You know, I never heard another word about that event, not from anybody that was there, not from anybody in Smith Valley about dead fish or anything else. It's like it never happened. The only proof is those two cottonwoods. I'll bet they are still lying there to this day.

On August 15, I called Dr. Cassard to see if he got all my records, which he had. So I set up an appointment for the 17th to go to the University and see what my fate was. All the way in, my heart was pretty heavy. I didn't know what I would do if they wouldn't let me in. Maybe, Fairfield would let me come back to the ranch. That thought cheered me up, because that's where I really wanted to be. But it would be awfully humiliating to have to come back and ask. Why didn't he just let me have the option? It's going to be tough to look at Cassard when we go over my transcript. I didn't even want to think what Bohman's reaction would be. At least Cassard had a sense of humor. After getting on campus, I stumbled around for a while, building my nerve, what there was of it. Finally, I just went in, told the secretary who I was. Her answer was pretty short, simple and to the point, "Oh yes, Dr. Cassard and Dr. Bohman have been waiting for you, I'll let them know you are here". It kind of sounded like letting the firing squad know the next victim is here and waiting. Shortly, she ushered me into a conference room, where both gentlemen were sitting at a large table, with my transcripts spread out, along with the other information that I had sent in.

"Well, Terry, we have looked everything over, and I'll get right to the point, your grades simply don't qualify you for graduate school at Nevada", was Dr. Cassards firm welcome. Bohman sat there, kind of nervous, scratching his nose. I felt like getting up, thanking them for their time, and heading somewhere, anywhere but here. Cassard continued, "Your transcript seems really strange, you got A's in all the hard courses, biochemistry, your senior project, genetics, nutrition, most of your chemistry, etc., but you got mostly C's in your production classes, civics, and you even got one D in current affairs. How can you explain that"?

My first reaction was that I didn't want to, but I thought of all the options that I had been mulling over in my mind, none of which I liked, so I tried to explain. "Well, as far as the production classes go at San Luis, I always had to work to make ends meet. In fact, I worked 40 hours a week at a motel, the Sleep Off The Highway Motel. The only way I could make it work was to cut some of the labs in order to work. I didn't have a choice if I wanted to graduate. I guessed sacrificing a few grades in order to graduate was worth the price. Besides, I had built up a cow herd of over 50 mother cows, and as far as beef goes, I probably could have taught the course better myself," was my best answer. The frown on Bohman's face told me that maybe I shouldn't have tossed in the bit about being able to teach the class. How was I to know that my beef teacher had been one of his graduate students, a fact which I didn't learn until several years later, after which I had really sufficiently bad mouthed him. Bohman tossed in a comment at that point that sort of floated me out into never, never land, "Your grades in nutrition and biochemistry are impressive. I would allow you to enroll at Nevada as a provisionary, that means you are not a graduate student, you are just a student taking some additional courses. If after one semester, you do sufficiently well, I would support your candidacy for graduate school". I didn't quite know what he meant by a provisional status, although the way he was stuttering, I could well imagine! I almost shot back by saying that if I just wanted to enroll at Nevada for more classes, it damn well didn't require your permission, but realizing obtaining the Masters Degree was the real objective here, I thought better of it. Instead, I responded by saying, "That's a real opportunity. You give me the chance, I'll make good"! They both looked at each other for a quizzical moment, then Cassard asked, "How in the world did you get a D in current affairs? As a senior, if you read the newspaper or listened to the radio, you should have certainly gotten a passing grade". I didn't have the heart to tell him the whole story, but responded by saying, "It was hard, the teacher just didn't have my interest, I shirked off from doing what I should have done, and I earned a D, plain and simple".

The real reason I got a D in that course was another story however. I was right, I wasn't very interested in the class. It was at 8 in the morning, and with my schedule of working and doing studies at night, I wasn't my best at 8. I struggled to the mid term, which was ten true or false questions, of which I knew for sure the answer for four of them, which were all false. I reasoned with any luck at all if I guessed on the other six, I would get three of them right, which would give me a 70%, not bad. But then I remembered something another student told me, sometimes this teacher will give a mid term in which all the questions would be true or false, and seeing how I knew four were false, I marked them all false. I was the only one out of a class of over 200 that got a hundred percent on the mid term. I guess in hindsight it went to my head, because I didn't try very hard from that point on, thinking even if

I got an F on the final, the average between an A and an F would surely be a C.

Well my math was right, as was always the case, but my logic missed the point. When I took the final, which was 100 true or false questions, it was pretty obvious that they weren't all true or false, so I started guessing. Three days later the grades were posted outside his office and I got an F - total disaster, as I had to have this class to graduate, and it wasn't going to be taught until next year! I finally got in, by camping at his office door for the better part of the day, to plead my case. I said I couldn't understand how I got an F, after getting a hundred percent on the mid-term. He agreed, he couldn't understand either. I said something about the average, but he cut me short. "You must have missed the lecture where I explained how I graded, 75% of your grade is the final, 25% of your grade is the mid-term. You got 100% on the mid-term and 45% on the final. Now according to my calculations that amounts to, rounded off, 59%. You had to get 60% to get a D." I already had that much figured out, so I couldn't argue the math, instead I responded by saying, "I had the flu, I was getting over it, but it really affected my grades. I went from an A to a B in two other classes because of that. I have a job starting in about a week in Nevada. If I don't pass this class, my life will be pretty much ruined, as I will have to come back here next year just to take that class". Now, most of that was true, I did have the flu, and my grade did slip from an A to a B, in an education class, and it sounded pretty believable to me. He looked at me with a grin and asked, "Who is the president of the United States?" "Why Dwight D. Eisenhower, of course, and Richard Nixon is the Vice President", was my rapid response. "Well, I'll tell you what, you just got an extra point, which raises your overall average, rounded off, to a D, now get out of here and quit bothering me, and good luck in Nevada"!

Although I have enjoyed telling that story over and over through the years, I just didn't think then was the time to tell it, at least to Dr. Bohman. It didn't look like his sense of humor ran in those circles.

After a few more formalities, I shook hands, guaranteed Dr. Bohman that I would be there right after Labor Day, ready to go to work, and then I headed back to the ranch. That night I explained to Jan what had happened, it didn't come as a surprise, as I had long since warned her that a 2.7 grade point average wasn't going to get me into any graduate school, when at least a 3.0 or higher was required most places.

The last two weeks was spent tying up things at the ranch. I made a detailed graphic demonstration of the irrigation schedule that I had developed on the 500 acres of alfalfa I was irrigating for Jim and Slim. Slim didn't entirely understand it, but I assured Jim I would always be available to come back next spring and go over it with Slim. We had made several trips to Reno, found a small apartment for $75/month on Vassar Street, close to where it intersects with South Virginia. I tried to find something close to the University, but there was nothing that we could afford.

The last Sunday, Slim bar-b-qued a ton of sage hen. We all drank lots of beer, and told some tall tales. Nobody mentioned the fish. Jack said that Billy Wilson was slowly rebuilding his chicken herd, and the pick-up was still there, but now residing at the bone pile. I wanted the day to never end, I just wanted to savor the moment forever, but soon the sun was down, and tomorrow was a long day.

We had a U-Haul already at the ranch, so Monday morning, we all pitched in, and I was loaded by 10. As we pulled up the hill past Holbrook Junction, I felt a sadness like I had never felt before. I loved this place: The last six months had been the happiest of my life: I looked in the rear view mirror one last time. I secretly knew my life would forever be changed, and that I would never come back to this ranch, at least not on a permanent basis. I still remember the taste of the tears that were cascading down my cheeks.

GRADUATE SCHOOL

Reno was hot during early September of 1957. It didn't take long for us to get settled into the Holcomb Street apartment. Everything was close by, Safeway, a local drug store, department stores, etc. Jan was very pregnant and didn't want to work, so she pretty much stayed home. We had saved up some money from the ranch, as just about everything was provided there. I had a pretty good nest egg from the sale of my cattle, enough to get us through at least this first year. It was about two miles to the University, so I would have normally driven, but during these lazy September days, I chose to walk back and forth. I had promised Dr. Bohman that I would be there shortly after Labor Day, so I reported on September 4. As usual Dr. Bohman seemed to be nervous, but I guessed that was simply his manor. His first name was Verle, but I also guessed it would be some time before I would refer to him by that handle!

Shortly after exchanging pleasantries, he took me on a tour of his lab, along with introducing me to his lab assistant, Mike Wade. The rest of the day was spent familiarizing me with Bohman's operation, his research, what he taught in his classes, as well as his philosophy about nutrition, research, the University and life in general. It really didn't take me too long to figure out that both he and Mike were Mormon, in fact, devout Mormon. This would be quite a contrast to my previous place of employment! Actually, it would take me some time to figure out that the "employment" part of this arrangement just wasn't going to occur right away.

The second day, Dr. Bohman had planned an in depth revue of what he felt that I should do in the way of class work and how best to use my "spare" time. So, at about 8:30 A.M., with class schedule in hand, we started a process that would decide my future. It didn't take him long to outline the class work that he felt I would have to take. We primarily dealt with the first semester only, on this occasion. Bohman was not impressed with the quality of instruction that I had in science courses at Poly, so he felt that I should repeat some, mainly organic chemistry. Fortunately, he felt that I only had to take the lecture, not the lab, which amounted to just a three hour course, for three credits. However, he also felt that I should take physiology, which was a five-credit course, consisting of three lectures and two labs per week. Obviously, if one is to become a successful graduate student, completing original research that qualifies for publication, one must also have a command of statistics, obviously - three credits, two lectures and one lab. Also, seeing how I would be using the nutrition lab for some type of quantitative chemical analysis, I would have to take quantitative analysis, a three credit course in the chemistry department, consisting of two lectures and one lab. He didn't believe for a minute that my background in range plants in Nevada was adequate, so I would have to sign up for a special problem for one credit from Dr. Robertson, the range scientist. Also Dr. Bohman felt that I should be very knowledgeable about current affairs in animal science, so I would also have to take seminar, one credit, and make a presentation.

Well, all of this didn't seem too bad, just 16 hours of credit, I had taken as much as 24 at Poly. It looked like I would have only four afternoon labs, Monday through Thursday, and only about 12 hours of actual classroom work during the mornings, scattered over five days. I liked this schedule, because it looked like I might be able to clear out of Reno Friday afternoons, and be at the ranch early Saturday morning, to work through Sunday evening, and be back for Monday classes. Bohman soon brought me back to my senses; however, as he felt that to learn the nutrition lab, that I must complete a minimum of ten hours per week of helping Mike with the routine analyses. I briefly mentioned the concept of pay for this endeavor, but Bohman, with a hurt look about him, explained that money was a bit scarce, besides the opportunity of learning how to work in the lab should be viewed as an apprentice type of procedure. I guessed I understood. Bohman then proceeded to suggest that it would be to my benefit to start my lab training tomorrow, as classes wouldn't start for another two weeks, so that would give me time to really get acquainted with the lab. Then, with somewhat of a grin, he suggested that I might ought to spend my spare time in the library, researching ideas for my thesis project. He cheered me up somewhat by further suggesting that I might use that research to facilitate my seminar project.

Following our lengthy discussion about class work, Bohman felt that I should go meet Dr. Robertson and work out the details concerning the one credit special problem that I would be taking from him. And so, that afternoon I finally got to meet Dr. Robertson. He was a man of slight stature, seemed very laid back, but down to earth. He inquired about my range management knowledge that I gained from San Luis, after which he said, in his usual laid back philosophy, "not much!" So began my association with Dr. Robertson. Because of my lack of knowledge, he felt that my "one credit" special problem should include two things; first a plant collection of Nevada plants, including a fair representation of grasses, forbs and shrubs, consisting of a minimum of 50 species, and preferably 100, properly mounted and identified in a manor suitable for submission to the University herbarium, and secondly, obtain at least a grade of C on all of his exams. I mentioned that this might require me to attend some of his classes, and he agreed, that it would require my attending all of his classes, which occurred three time per week, but as a visitor, so I wouldn't be required to participate in class discussion. So, after my first day on the job I found out that in reality I was taking 19 hours of very difficult class work, was required to work an additional ten hours per week, gratis, and spend considerable time in the library. My mathematical ability shortly informed myself that this amounted to a minimum of 42 hours of actual classroom/library/work on campus each week assuming that I worked five hours per week in the library and each lab was three hours. I somehow suspected that Dr. Robertson's labs, being that they were scheduled specifically on Fridays, might last a bit longer than three hours. It appeared to me that becoming eligible for candidacy in graduate school at the University of Nevada might just be a bit more taxing than I had imagined.

That night when I got back to our apartment it must have been obvious that my day had been a bit perplexing. Jan inquired, and I told - and we both agreed - that life would be a lot different. Fortunately, we had a good desk in one corner of the front room, that offered a bit of protection. I designated this as my command zone, along with my father's ancient typewriter on a stand next to the desk. I could type easily 50 words per minute, so I was in good shape there. I made a point of having Jan get a bunch of tablets for note taking, extra lined paper for rewriting my notes, binders for each class, colored pens for drawing, and a half dozen other miscellaneous devices that I had never dreamed of using before; however, I could already see that going to college at Nevada was going to be a whole new and unique experience.

By the next morning I already had a plan laid out. I jogged the two miles to the "hill", as the people on campus liked to call their lovely institution, stopped for a brief rest at the restroom, and was waiting for Dr. Bohman at his office door by quarter till eight. He arrived about five minutes after the hour, and seemed obviously distressed by the fact that I was waiting for him. A short and to the point discussion followed about the ever increasing traffic between the city of Sparks, where he lived, and the University. I certainly understood things of this nature, suggesting that I might have to leave earlier than I planned due to the traffic on Virginia - he suggested that I should use Center, which was one way, and would obviously be faster than Virginia. Then I told him the way I wanted to work for the next two weeks, four hours each morning learning laboratory procedures, and four hours each afternoon searching the library about possible research areas for my thesis. By the time I finished, Dr. Bohman was into his usual stutter, suggesting perhaps it might be a bit better for scheduling if I went to the library in the morning and worked in the lab during the afternoon. I didn't bother to mention that Mike wasn't about quite yet; I guessed that had nothing to do with the change in my schedule.

So, off I went to the library, there were actually two libraries that I would be using, the agriculture library, which was a small-unmanned room on the third floor of the Ag building and the main library. I decided today to put my efforts into the Ag library, which in itself was an adventure. The Ag library was a long narrow room. All the ceilings in this building were twelve feet, including the library. Shelves were placed all the way from the floor to the ceiling on both sides of the room. A brass bar ran the length of the room on both sides parallel to the next to top shelf. An old, almost antique, ladder with hooks slid along on these brass bars, thus it was fairly easy, providing you were not handicapped physically or with age, to pull any book in this library.

The vast amount of the books were not really books, but bound journals representing the various disciplines in agriculture and related fields in biology. Usually, each bound set represented the year's publications for that particular journal. It didn't take me long to have a pretty good road map of the journals that were of interest to me - so I proceeded to pull down the oldest bound book of the journal of most interest, and start in. Fortunately, I had long since developed the knack of reading fast!

I was pretty sure that I wanted to do some type of research project involving the dietary habits of grazing cattle. This had always fascinated me, watching cattle graze, from my earliest recollections from Sulfur

Mountain, through my many experiences on the OIL. I had long since observed that cattle were very selective when allowed to graze freely. Cattle appeared to select the moister, succulent forage when it was available. It was my opinion that they normally would select grass; yet I had seen them eating forbs, and shrubs, especially on the winter range along the Walker River. Because of my interest, I decided to concentrate on journals dealing with animals and plants, of which there were quite a few. I concentrated on the journals dealing with animal science, agronomy, range management, ecology and forestry. It didn't take me long to realize that there was also a set of experiment station publications put out by every land grant college in the nation, including the University of Nevada, and these experiment station bulletins were also a source of information. I hadn't brought lunch, so I worked right through the lunch hour.

At one o'clock, I returned to the nutrition lab, where I encountered Dr. Bohman and Mike finishing their lunch. I couldn't really tell what Mike had eaten, but Bohman was just finishing his glass of milk, only it wasn't really milk, it was curdled milk, something he called buttermilk. I thought to myself what a Coleville coyote might think about the smell emitting from his glass of "fresh buttermilk". However, any buttermilk that I had tried you didn't have to strain through your teeth.

I showed him some of the articles that I had reviewed, but I had already decided around this gang it might be a good idea to play your cards a little close to the vest, so I only showed him about half of what I had reviewed. That seemed to impress him sufficiently that I had not wasted my entire morning.

That afternoon, I was turned over to Mike. Mike was reasonable, he actually was working on his masters in chemistry, so he didn't have too much on me. He briefly explained what types of analytical work he was conducting; primarily what was called the proximate analyses of feedstuffs that Dr. Bohman was using. Mike also analyzed a great deal of other tissue, including bone, liver, blood and hair samples from animals, but today we were going to deal with feedstuffs. My first assignment was to learn how to use the metric balance. Mike patiently taught me the metric system, and how a metric balance worked, and I patiently listened, not telling him that in biochemistry lab at Poly we had used the exact same balance on many occasions. After an hour he had me weighing out samples for dry matter determination, approximately 100 samples to the nearest one tenth of a milligram. It was easy work for me, my eyesight was excellent, and my hands were steady, two things required in using a metric balance. Mike figured it would take me the rest of the afternoon, as you had to weigh the small canister that was used for determining dry matter, empty, then with approximately one gram of the sample in it, the difference between the weights representing the weight of the sample. I had it done and calculated in about an hour and a half. Mike showed me the drying oven to determine dry matter in, as well as how to determine either extract, or fat, on the same samples the following day. With that it was approaching five P.M., so I decided to leave for home. That night I felt good - I could understand the library, and already had started my literature search for a project, and I was sure I could not only master the lab, but might enjoy it as well.

One day, after reviewing countless journal articles about all aspects of grazing, I decided to more thoroughly explore this little library. Material was stuffed everywhere, from the floor to the top shelf, at least ten and a half feet off the floor. There was only one window, and it was sealed shut. The door could be left open, but that didn't exactly improve circulation. If there was insulation between the ceiling and the buildings roof, it didn't seem to help much even on a September morning, so after four intense hours every day, one's mind did tend to wonder. I had been noticing, on an upper shelf, far in one corner, there were a series of open-ended boxes that appeared to hold maps, and I had noticed something about the State Engineer on the box labels. Finally, curiosity got the best of me.

In each box there were probably thirty to forty maps, mostly just one page. Each map consisted, more or less, of a single Nevada ranch. Most of the maps had been prepared on typical survey graph paper, showing each square to the nearest 40 acres. The privately owned land was usually colored red, or some similar color. The adjoining grazing allotment, or the area recognized as where the particular ranch's stock grazed was outlined in another color. Water sources were also identified, some by number, which I assumed was something recognized by the State Engineer. I finally counted 348 individual maps, but that didn't cover all Nevada by any stretch of the imagination. There was one container labeled index, which had a listing of individual maps, as well as a larger folded map of Nevada. All of the individual maps had been carefully drawn onto the large Nevada map.

I could only conclude that the Nevada State Engineer had requested, or worked with individual ranches to create these many maps. Almost all of them had a stamped date of around 1925. The more I thought about these maps, the more I came to the conclusion that these maps were the first effort on the part of Nevada to recognize individual ranch grazing areas, something that in 1925 no Federal governmental agency had undertaken. What really intrigued me is that the State Engineer was involved in this endeavor. His only claim in this process was water, and in this case mostly just livestock water. It seemed that livestock water, or the availability of it, might just be the factor that decided the range rights to federal grazing that these ranches had obtained, long before the development of the BLM.

This whole process wetted my appetite to learn more about how the range rights that became to be known as allotments were developed from a legal standpoint. Obviously, water, under the jurisdiction of the State of Nevada, was perhaps far more important in this process than the vast acreages owned by the Federal government, at least in 1925. I had a thesis to accomplish if I was ever going to get a Masters Degree, but the information gleamed from those multitude of maps didn't want to leave my mind very fast either. Somehow, I didn't think Bowman would share my interests on this subject, so it was best kept to myself for the time being. Nevertheless, the image of those maps, and what they represented, was always in the back of my mind. Over the years to come, more than once I would resort to those original grazing maps, to solve a question of rights, both grazing and water. They were, and will always be a treasure for Nevada.

By the end of the two weeks, I had reviewed about 200 articles concerning livestock and grazing in the library, and had successfully determined dry matter, ether extract, ash, protein, crude fiber and nitrogen free extract on those 100 samples of feedstuffs. Those constituents were what made up the proximate analyses of feedstuffs, and were the basis of all nutrition research, including balancing rations, determine milk production, gain and a host of other factors as well.

Registration was pretty simple. There were only about 2,200 students in the entire University, and there were only about 100 in the College of Ag, and only about ten of us graduate students. Oh, I forgot, only nine. I was just a student pursuing additional courses. I met a few other students during registration, but, at that point I was gradually beginning to realize that I was kind of an outsider, I didn't know much about Nevada, certainly including the University - therefore it was best that I do a whole lot more listening than talking. I got all of the classes that Dr. Bohman wanted me to take, even had a chance to see each professor before the day was over.

We registered on a Tuesday, so Wednesday was the first day of class - two lectures, organic chemistry and physiology. Organic was a large class, with mostly undergraduate students taught in the large lecture room in the Chem building. I could see it was going to be pretty much of a repeat of the organic I had at Poly, so I breathed easier on that one. Physiology, or more correctly animal physiology which was an animal science course, was taught by a real character, Dr. Weeth. I could readily

93

see this was going to be a fun class, many animal experiments, including some on ourselves. There was only five in the class, which was just the way Weeth liked it. Lab space was limited, as any more would have been crowded. That afternoon was our first physiology lab, measuring blood pressure, heart rate, and things of that nature. We not only did it to ourselves, but the lab was held at the Main Station Farm, located a bit south of Sparks; so, we did it to beef cattle, dairy cattle, pigs and sheep. By the time 5 P.M. rolled around we had done a pretty good rodeo!

That night I started a process that probably saved my academic butt, I recopied my notes. I not only recopied them, but they were done in detail, with added information from the text or anything else that applied. This helped me learn the information, but come test time I had a clear precise set of notes to study. It took me about as much time to recopy my notes, as it did to take the notes, but I sure learned a lot more. Even though it was about midnight when I finished, I vowed to continue this process until I had my Masters in hand. However, I did have to laugh at myself. In my illustrious four years of undergraduate studies at Cal Poly, I never once recopied notes, and further, hardly ever reviewed them. Guess that's why I just didn't qualify as a grad student at Nevada.

The next morning, Thursday, quantitative analyses was taught at 8, so there I was. This was just going to be a class designed to familiarize us with a number of different analytical techniques. There would be ten different analytical procedures that we would have to complete; each designed to analyze some substance for an unknown amount of a certain chemical or substance. The kicker, the instructor, Dr. Seim, alone knew the correct answer, and to complete the class we had to not only do the process, but had to come up with the right answer. Actually, my work of the previous two weeks in the nutrition lab did me well, as the first thing we were going to have to do was use the metric balance!

At ten o'clock I met for statistics. This was an animal science class taught by the geneticist, Dr. Kidwell. He was a wild man, short, stubby, glasses thick enough to pass for the bottom of a coke bottle. Kidwell didn't mince words. After about ten minutes his language led me to believe that he wasn't a Mormon. At least, I could feel at ease with him. And that afternoon was our first statistics lab - a lesson in normal variation of numbers. We got to use Monroe mechanical calculators, which I took to like a duck to water. By the end of the lab I was leading the pack, numbers had always fascinated me. I loved data, data of any kind - and that's what this class was all about.

We adjourned at 4:30, but Kidwell asked me to stay around afterwards. He wanted to know about my background at Poly and my work experiences, which all took about an hour to explain in sufficient detail. He had heard that I was the new kid on the block, but he wondered why I had chose Bohman as my advisor. I explained my interest in nutrition and grazing which he sort of took as OK, but then he asked the question - "Is it true that he didn't put you into grad school, that you just have to take courses for a year to prove yourself?"

I answered in the affirmative. Kidwell shook his head, explaining, "That's typical of that pompous carrot snapper!" I didn't quite know what to say, but I did have to admit that was the first time that I had heard a Mormon referred to as a carrot snapper! Kidwell went on to say, "When you and Bohman finally blow up and have had it with him, let me know. I have a place for you in animal genetics right now; and I'll go straight to the graduate dean to get you into grad school so that you can have an assistantship immediately." Again, I didn't know what to say, except to say thanks, but I really had my heart set on nutrition and grazing. But I did tell Kidwell that I loved data, it had always intrigued me, and that I would try in his class as hard as I possibly could - I would do my level best. I didn't want to get involved in the internal squabbles of the animal science department. So, I guessed I would just walk a fine line, and indeed do my level best. With that, Kidwell asked if I would

95

like to go have a beer at the Wal - and again, I really didn't know what to say, but a beer did sound inviting, a whole lot better than buttermilk.

Although I had been in Reno going on three weeks, I hadn't been to the Wal, or more correctly the Little Wal, or as the locals like to say, the Lil Wal. But it obviously was the University bar of choice, not only for the Greeks, but for everybody. I recognized several Ag students, and Kidwell was well recognized himself, obviously having been there before, as evidenced by the bar keep responding with, "Hi Jim, the usual". The usual was a can of Hams, so I took the same. We drifted over to a table, and Jim took it on himself to begin my informal education about the University of Nevada. He didn't like the President, a guy named Stout. Seems he was a dictator. He didn't like the Dean of the college, a person by the name of Jimmy Adams. "Ought to go back to Texas, only I hear he got run out of there years ago", was about all that was nice about Dr. Adams that he could muster. Kidwell obviously didn't like Bohman, but I gathered he had a general dislike of Mormons in general, so I couldn't hold that against Dr. Bohman too much. He did have a great deal of respect for Dr. Robertson, at least as a scientist. "He is the only one that collects good data that can readily be statistically analyzed", but he went on to say that he thought Robertson was a "sanctimonious ass". Needless to say, all of these descriptions were not fortifying my psychological stability concerning my immediate future. About then, two students came over to our table with more beer, but I bowed out. It was obvious that they knew Kidwell well, and that more "discussions" were going to occur - so I thanked Jim for the beer, headed out the door and down Virginia Street to home and copying my notes.

Friday came with a chill, in fact a near freeze, early for Reno. So I drove, which turned out to be fortunate in the end. Organic and physiology went off without a hitch, and at eleven o'clock, I decided that I had better go to Dr. Robertson's lecture, as I hadn't gone Wednesday, besides today was his lab. The class only had about ten students, I didn't know any of them, but assumed that they were all undergraduate

96

students. Robertson started the class off by saying that one way he graded was to give impromptu oral quizzes. He would try to ask each student one question each week, which if you got totally right would add ten points to the course total, which could be a thousand points, assuming you got everything right. That made me nervous to hear his description of these "oral" quizzes, as I never did very well at public speaking, especially if I had to know the facts, and it just didn't seem logical that you would try to BS Dr. Robertson.

Well, my nervousness got compounded real fast, as Dr. Robertson started by saying, "the first question is for the only graduate student in this class, Terry Hope, and the question is; the genus for sagebrush is Artemisa, now how many species of Artemisa are know to exist in Nevada?" Well my answer for that was pretty simple, "I don't know". I did know that there were several varieties of sagebrush, but how many existed in Nevada - that I plain and simple did not know!

His response was pretty direct. " I suspected you didn't know, but I did go over that information Wednesday when you weren't here." With that he went on with the next question to another student, and with that I sank pretty low in my seat. I made a mental note to never miss a Robertson lecture again, and to take better than average notes.

At about 11:30 I began to realize why he liked his class at 11:00, especially on Fridays, as the lecture, coupled with the lunch hour made for a 6-hour lab, providing of course, you quit at 5. Well that day we didn't quit at 5, it was closer to 7. As we went out towards Pyramid Lake and studied different plant communities until it got dark enough to where the plants were getting hard to distinguish. I came home with 20 pages of notes, and about 15 plants to begin the plant collection that we had talked about. Saturday was spent building a plant press, after scurrying around Reno to get the necessary parts. Sunday was spent copying notes and reviewing - I had survived my first week of "grad" school. Pretty much up beat on everything, with the exception of Dr. Robertson's pop quiz, a gentle reminder to attend his classes, even though I didn't legally have to. I remembered his words - if I wanted to pass his exams, it would require my presence in his classes - it sure seemed like a lot of work for one credit, but then I remembered, my mission was to obtain a masters degree - so on that basis I guessed it was all fair. And, I was sure of one thing, as the semester went on I would learn this game, if indeed that's what you would want to call it!

And I learned the "game". At Nevada, it really wasn't a game, unless you could call Dr. Bohman's getting me to work ten hours a week for nothing - but that wasn't even a "game". No - the University of Nevada, at least the pursuit of a master's degree in agriculture, was hard work. And I gradually began to realize, it was not only hard work, but if you were successful enough to complete the degree, you would be well educated.

The semester lasted from mid September, until late January, some 18 weeks, or 90 days of instruction. Outside of Thanksgiving, Christmas and New Years, there were no holidays, taken or observed. I had survived the initial academic shock, and by the end of six weeks, around November 1, I felt that I was in charge. I understood my classes, had done well on all of the intermediate quizzes, and was preparing both for midterms and my seminar. I probably had become what was to become known in future years as a "geek", head down, ass up, on the move with a book in front of my eyes at all time. Just how far I had gone that direction was well brought to my attention one late October Monday morning, when walking down the hall, Dr. Cassard stopped me by saying, "I saw Jim and his wife this weekend, they both wanted to know how you were doing, and I responded by saying you were fast becoming the best graduate student in animal science." My first reaction was who in the hell is Jim, but fortunately, that's not what I said. Instead I just looked at him for a minute; suddenly it dawned on me that he was talking about Jim Kilduff and his wife Barb. I got my composure back, and thanked him for the compliment, and, of course, inquired about them. Cassard responded by saying that they were fine, and getting buckled down for winter. Cassard went on to say, "Jim said that thanks to your new field and the irrigation program that you put together, this will be the first year that the OIL won't have to buy hay."

I responded, "that's great, tell them hi next time you see them, but I am almost late for class." With that, I ran to physiology. But later, I had to laugh; in the nearly eight weeks that I had been at Nevada I had almost completely forgotten about the ranch. But perhaps more importantly, I thought about Cassards comment to Jim, "you were fast becoming the best graduate student in animal science" - at least Cassard accepted me as a graduate student, that's all I really wanted, and I made a small promise to myself, that bit about being the best would just get laid away for the time being. Along about 48 credits of graduate work from now, and a successful defense of my thesis, I might just take that statement back out and cherish it, if it still applied.

By mid November, two things were rapidly approaching, mid terms and my seminar. Mid terms came first, and I was ready - they were all in the same week; organic, physiology, statistics, quant, and Dr. Robertson's special problem. I probably became unbearable at home - studied well past midnight every night. The Friday before midterms was also just about the time for Jan to give birth to our first child, and right on time off we went to Saint Mary's, to be blessed by a baby daughter early Saturday morning. Thank God for miracles, not only for the baby, but both my Dad and Mom were at the ranch all week long, so Mom was at the house when I brought Jan home Monday afternoon. Another small miracle occurred, my first mid term was not scheduled until Tuesday, it was physiology.

Mom stayed for about ten days. By that time we were pretty well put back together. I got A's on every mid term except physiology, got a B there, 85%. It was the second highest grade in the class, turned out no body got an A. Weeth graded on a strict 90- 80 - 70 basis, so I knew that I had to get 95% on the final to get an A. Seeing how I really hadn't gotten any sleep for the better part of 48 hours before taking his test I didn't feel too bad and I was pretty sure that I would get the 95 come January.

My seminar was scheduled right before Thanksgiving, Wednesday to be exact. Seminars were attended by all the seniors, grad students and staff in animal science. People came from other disciplines if the subject matter was of interest. I had long since chosen my favorite subject, a review of the literature concerning the various techniques that had been developed to estimate both the botanical and chemical composition of the grazing animals diet. I had reviewed at least 100 articles concerning this subject, articles from all over, Europe, South America, Australia, New Zealand, America, and quite a few from right here in Nevada. In addition to the University staff, the Agricultural Research Service, the research and science arm of the federal Department of Agriculture, had two range scientist stationed at Reno that both attended.

My seminar considered a review of the many methods, with about the last 15 minutes or so dedicated to an evaluation of the best techniques. And I wasn't very positive about any of them, because they all depended on some technicians ability to properly measure or evaluate some aspect of the process - and this introduced variability, variability at a level that I concluded was unacceptable. Dr. Evans from the ARS, Dr. Robertson from range management, as well as Dr. Kinsinger, Dr. Jensen from agronomy, as well as Dr. Bohman's work were all considered in my critical review. I had screwed up my courage to let it all hang out, but I had also done a whole lot of work. I had taken the liberty to reevaluate some of their data, using a different statistical method to estimate the sample size using these arbitrary methods, and it turned out the sample size necessary to properly sample the population was somewhere between 10 to 100 times greater than had actually been done. There were some pretty sour looks, but Kidwell about died laughing. But I answered all their questions.

Finally Cassard came to my rescue by saying, "the hours growing late, I believe what Terry has done was to open all of our eyes as to our own biases - he has pointed out in very real terms that we don't have good methods of sampling what the grazing animal really eats, and that's probably the number one problem here in Nevada, especially with some of the rumblings that we have all heard coming out of the Forest Service and the Bureau of Land Management."

The bell rang and I was out of there - off to physiology lab. But Dr. Weeth wouldn't quite let it lie - he had never liked Dr. Bohman, and was suspect of Jensen and Robertson. People with degrees from Davis were like that. So instead of starting to measure urine production of rats, we continued for a time a discussion of how to sample the grazing animal's diet. I had also been reviewing another whole area of literature, with the thought in mind of answering my own question - but I didn't want to talk about it just right now. After a 30 minute general discussion on the whole subject, Dr. Weeth concluded that somebody had to develop a simple way to actually get inside the animal and remove a freshly consumed sample of what the animal had consumed - and I agreed, but then I reminded Weeth if we were going to complete today's lab with urine measuring from rats, we had best get with it. Fortunately, he agreed, because I sure didn't want to participate in the current discussion any further at this point in time!

Weeth was right, somebody had to develop a system of directly taking samples from the grazing animal, and I tended to believe that somebody would be me. I knew a fair amount about the anatomy of a bovine, or what cowboys call cattle. Anyway, the bovine is a ruminant animal, that is they have four compartments to their stomach; the rumen, which is by far the largest, the reticulum the omasum and abomasum or true stomach. The existence of the rumen is the basic reason cattle are able to eat grass, which is high in fiber, and unable to be digested by normal stomach enzymes, such as we humans have. However, once grass enters the rumen, it is immediately attacked by jillions of bacteria, just like what happens in termites. The bacteria break down the fiber into usable products, and the unfortunate bacteria that wind their way down the digestive system are also digested. Anyway, the thought occurred to me one day, that if you were to make a fistula, or opening, into the rumen, it might be possible to sample what the animal was eating. It actually would be more difficult than that, because you would have to remove the rumen contents, then allow the animal to graze, then remove the freshly consumed material and analyze it. The idea seemed simple enough, but I was sure it would be more complicated than anything that I had ever attempted. However, it was my idea and until refined, I just didn't want to talk about it.

Rumen fistulas were not new by any stretch of the imagination. Scientist had been using small fistulas in cattle for years to study the digestive process, and the effect of different feedstuffs on that process. Even Poly had a fistulated steer, but the fistula was just large enough to insert a suction device for removal of rumen fluid. Actually, two professors at North Dakota State University, Schalk and Amadon, in the mid 20's actually perfected the technique of fistulating a bovine. Various scientists, usually with the help of a veterinarian, had perfected the technique over the years. In my "spare time" I had reviewed just about every article about fistulation that I could find. Nobody had built a fistula large enough to facilitate the removal of the rumen contents, but I thoroughly believed it could be done. I gathered up all of my information and went to the University veterinarian, Dr. Don Marble. After reviewing my information, Marble felt it would be possible to develop such a fistula, but his question was how in the world would you plug it. That would be my problem was my answer; but I had long been thinking how to do just that.

After Thanksgiving, I gathered all my notes, including those from Dr. Marble, screwed up my courage, marched into Bohman's office, and proceeded to tell him what I wanted to do for my masters program. After I finished the abstract of my research, I waited for the answer.

Young Tony Lesperance removing a freshly consumed forage sample form a fistulated steer in 1958. This was the first steer ever successfully fistulated with a large enough opening to sample freshly consumed forage. This steer was appropriately named Bronco Billy by Lesperance early on and lived to be 18 years of age. Bronco sampled forage over essentially all of Nevada, as well as a goodly portion of northern California. At least 15 thesis were presented at the masters level, having used Bronco in their research. Bronco was nearly lost at the Nevada Nuclear Test Range in 1962, but survived for many years. When he finally passed, Lesperance personally buried him on the University farm. And he later admitted he cried for some time afterwards. he often claimed that Bronco was the most amazing large animal that he ever had the pleaser of working with, and as he often said, 'Bronco was really a gift from God".

The usual stutter started, but Bohman agreed in essence, that if I could perfect the technique, and show that it really worked, it would make a first class thesis project. I had drawn a diagram of the plug I wanted to start with. It seemed to meet with his approval. He was enthused that I had Marble's blessings. "Well all I needed was some steers for starters", was my response.

Bohman countered, "Why don't you go see Jim Hunter out to the farm and find what's available."

I had gotten to know Jim well, he was auditing statistics, and I had been helping him just about every weekend. Jim was the herdsman out at the Main Station Farm. Jim never had enough help, especially during winter months, as he was feeding nearly as thousand head of cattle all together, and some days, like Thanksgiving, he had no help at all. I had been helping him some on Sundays, and other days when he didn't have anybody else; so we had gotten to be pretty good friends. So out to the farm I went, hunted Jim down, and proudly informed him that I wanted two steers about 4 to 5 weight, for my thesis project. Jim looked at me with a blank stare for a second, then began to laugh, asking had I talked to Verle. My response was sure, in fact he wanted me to come out and have you help me get two head lined out. "Well let me tell you the facts. Kidwell has every cow on this damn place involved in some crossbreeding program that I will never understand, but it's every cow. Bohman has every steer, the second it's weaned, tied up in one nutrition program or another. The economist are monitoring all replacement heifers for cost evaluation, and would have my head if I let you put holes in them. On top of that Dean Adams just made me sell every damned animal on this place that wasn't committed to a research project. Pete Test, the fiscal officer, just read him the riot act about how we were going to meet salaries along about May of this fiscal year if we don't have some income. Now Bohman knows all of that, so my suggestion is you go back and ask that fat headed Mormon just where in the hell he thinks two more steers are coming from?" Man, I was glad he got that off his chest with nobody as a sounding board but myself. Jim was usually smoking a pipe, but right now he looked like a steam locomotive pulling Donner. And, he was scratching his nearly baldhead - so I knew he was thinking, and if it were possible he would come up with something. "You know, let's jump in my pick-up and run down to the far end of this place, by the Jones Farm. I think there are two steers still down there. They ain't much, but that's all I got", was his encouraging remark.

So down we went to the east pasture, and sure enough there were two steers peacefully grazing fall pasture, although they both appeared a bit nervous as we started down the lane. One was a bronco-faced calf, kind or a roman nosed critter. The other was a pretty much straight Hereford X Angus type. But they were steers, and I judged them to be about 500 pounds. "How come you didn't get them shipped along with everything else", was my stupid response.

"Well you see it's this way. The biggest one, the one with the white face, well, he plumb jumped out of the loading chute, and while I was trying to stop him, the little one, the one that sort of looks like he got alkalied, well he kicked the shit out of me in the process. The trucker couldn't wait, and I had made a mental note that I was going to personally kill these two sons of bitches, but listening to what you have in store for them, that will probably be better", was Jim's fond response to the whole situation. And that was my first introduction to whom I fondly called Bronco Billy and Alkali Ike over the coming year. Neither Bronco or Alkali exactly knew their fate at that minute, but they might have taken some pride in the fact that they were destined to become two of the most notorious steers in Nevada history.

Jim suggested that due to the fact that I would be working so closely with these two beasts over the next few months that it might be a good idea to halter break them, and there was no better time than the present. So between both of us, his dilapidated pick-up, and his ever-faithful

Border Collie, Duff, we soon had them into the main corral. Jim had an assortment of halters in the barn, and I just happened to have my nylon catch rope with me. Jim asked, "Wouldn't it be easier if we put them in the chute first?"

My response was pretty practical, at least I thought, "Nope, let me drop this loop over their head, I'll hold tight, then you put the halter on". Jim always smoked a pipe, and on my response I noticed a bit of smoke erupt, which should have been indication enough that he didn't exactly like my thinking. However, as I have come to learn over the years, when I get an idea in my head, that's the way it usually is - I have even heard people say behind my back that I am hard headed.

Well, it was my way, and with little effort, I dropped a loop over Alkali's head. Although I didn't really realize it then, I would come to know that Alkali had the mentality of a mule, only he was a lot dumber. Once the loop hit his neck, he simply stopped, and with little effort Jim placed the halter on. After discarding the loop, he took the lead rope and proceeded to the nearest fence, only when he hit the end of the slack, Jim just stopped. With a surprised look, he turned around and put all of his weight into a mighty tug - to no avail. I walked over behind Alkali, twisted his tail into a knot, and put my shoulder squarely under the tail head, lifting him clear off his hind feet. And with that we drug, pushed and carried Alkali to the nearest fence where he got tied. And not once during that entire process did his two front feet ever move. I was pretty tired after that, and Jim must have been too, as we both sat down side by side. Jim matter of factly said, "You'll have to teach that lad to lead". My response was pretty much straight forward, "Yup".

After we got some air back, we both noticed that Bronco had gone to the far corner of the corral, tightly backed his butt into the corner, and was eying both of us straight on. I knew what Jim was thinking, all I had to do was look at his face. Even Duff knew what was in store, as he had quietly laid down under the pick-up, well out of sight. "Oh well the time is getting on so I'll catch Bronco up, and you put on the halter", was about the only response that seemed appropriate at the time. So I built a loop, let fly from about 15 feet, which was about as close as I could get to Bronco in my judgment. The loop settled on just as pretty as if it had been in the movies, Bronco never flinched a muscle or batted an eye, until I jerked down tightening the loop around his neck. In hindsight I guessed I shouldn't have done that, it seemed to kind of rile him. Bronco charged straight down the rope. When he went by me, he kicked out with a hind foot, squarely catching me in the shoulder, spinning me to the ground, but I didn't let loose of the rope, no way! Well with one down, he set his sights on Jim. He made the prettiest loop around Jim, so fast I don't think he ever knew exactly what Bronco had done, until his feet went out and he hit the ground. He hit it hard too, because out came the air, and the pipe, just like it was that day with old Jack Davis. I don't know what sort of affliction I must have that keeps causing people to loose their pipe's, but I seem to have it, whatever it is. Bronco made a pass over me, kind of dragging Jim by his feet. Duff wanted to help, but he must have known better, because he retreated to the far side of a haystack. Well, directly, Bronco got tired of this game, and that was good, because in another pass or two, he would have had us wound up like a couple of tops. I was thankful that he seemed to want to run clockwise around us. Changing direction at that time might have been critical.

Directly, Jim and I both untangled ourselves. He said, "Just lay there and don't let loose of that rope, I'll go over the fence, then you pass me the rope through the fence, and we'll get junior snubbed up". I noticed this sounded like a pretty good plan, even if it did leave me alone in the corral with Bronco. Jim snuck out, Duff peeked around the corner of the haystack, and I made a dash to the fence with Bronco in hot pursuit. But I was the quickest, and the pass of the rope from my hand to Jim's was perfect, and fatal, at least from Bronco's perspective. Jim was quick with the slack, because just about that fast, Bronco found himself tight against the fence, and no amount of struggling would help him now. We both sat down again for a spell. Shortly, I spotted Jim's pipe and retrieved it for him. I felt it best if we changed the subject for a bit, so I recounted how we had lost Jack's pipe, only his was gone for good.

Jim agreed to let the two steers loose in about an hour, and I countered by saying that I would be out every day and tie them up for an hour or so. I wasn't quite sure how I might accomplish that, at least by myself, but it sounded good. The next morning, I hobbled into the nutrition lab, Bohman inquired if I had gotten two steers yet. "You bet, getting them halter broken right now. I believe they will be ready for Dr. Marble to operate on during the Christmas break", was my somewhat overly optimistic response. Going to class that day was tough, because no matter how I sat, the bruises got to hurting pretty bad after about 15 minutes.

Well, no matter how bad the bruises hurt, I had learned a long time ago there was only one way to work with animals, at least cattle, you just had to love them no matter what! In the scheme of things cattle are not the smartest animals alive, however, neither are they the dumbest, far from it. They remember abuse a long time, so if you return the favor, you are just making life more difficult in the long run. I found with both Bronco and Alkali that a little rolled grain with molasses usually made them feel pretty sorry for abusing me, and they remembered that, and responded to it a whole lot better than the sledgehammer that I had in the back of my mind. Its funny about animals, we have lived with them and depended on them for eons, but most people just don't understand that you have to reward good behavior, doesn't make any difference if its your dog, horse or your steer that you are training to put a cannon size whole in his stomach.

My Dad was a good example. He was gentle and kind hearted, at least always to me. But I guess he didn't like animals, at least he didn't trust them. He was always warning me how one day they would really hurt me. Maybe it was just worry for my welfare, but I truly believe he just didn't trust animals. Once on the Fee Lease when I had my cows, one cow had developed a bag after birth that was simply more than the calf could handle. Nothing to do but milk her out. We didn't really have a very good chute, so I opted to rope her and restrain her against the fence, but this would require some help, so I waited till evening when he got home. "Come help me, I got a little chore with one of the cows," was my excited response. His answer was in the affirmative, so we both went down to the corral where I had her caged up with her calf.

A quick flick of the wrist and a dally or two and she was restrained. I gave the head rope to Dad, explaining that it was essential that he not let loose of it no matter what. Milking her was pretty easy, as her teats were large and firm. I was about half done when she started getting pretty nervous. The inevitable happened - Dad let the rope slip! I saw the disaster starting out of the corner of my eye, sat back and tried to rise up, but I was too slow.

Wam! She brought her head right down over the bridge of my nose. I knew it was broken instantly, not so much from the blood, but I could see out of my right eye that most of my nose was pretty much in front of that eye. I stood up, because I thought I might sort of pass out, but that was probably a mistake, because immediately on seeing my condition Dad yelled, "I'll kill that God damn bitch for what she did." I guess he meant it because just about that fast he was bringing back the rifle he always carried behind the seat of his pick-up.

"Wow", I yelled. "It wasn't her fault, you let the damn rope loose. Besides if you kill her, I'll just have to bottle feed the calf. Anyway, she's my cow and you don't have any right to up and kill her." My Dad hadn't hit me in years, however, I thought for a second, now just might be one of those times. Hopefully, if he did it would put my nose back about where it was supposed to be. I guess when he looked at me he thought better of the whole project. I suggested that maybe we had done enough milking for tonight, and he agreed. So after cleaning up it was on to Fillmore to see the ever-faithful Dr. Kerr to more gently put my snooze back in the middle of my face. But that evening Dad gave me a lot of his philosophy about animals. It all boiled down to when an animal hurts you, you hurt it back so it will remember next time. As I say, I learned a long time ago that negative discipline with animals is not very rewarding. Besides, Alkali and Billy really got to like their rolled grain with molasses, and as it turned out, they would earn every bite they got.

The rest of the semester before Christmas was pretty much spent just studying, working in the lab and the library, going to the Main Station Farm every day, playing with Ike and Billy - but at least that seemed to be paying off, as I actually had Ike walking behind a lead rope, and I could catch Billy up pretty easy. He even allowed himself to be led once in awhile, but he also was becoming pretty adept at tattooing my body on a pretty regular basis. Our plan was to do the operation between Christmas and New Years, Christmas came on a Friday, so we planned to operate, or do the first phase, the Monday after Christmas, with the second phase to be completed the following Monday. Classes didn't start until Tuesday, so it looked like all would fit. About a week before Christmas, I had Alkali and Bronco settled down to the point that I could move them from the Main Station Farm, to the veterinary facility at the Valley Road Farm, immediately adjacent to the main campus, and about a ten-minute walk from the Ag building. I borrowed Jim's pick-up, as it had a rack, moved both steers at once, it was all so easy compared to how things were as few weeks back. Dr. Marble came by to look the animals over after we had arrived at Valley Road, stating they were fit and ready!

We had decided to conduct a two-phase operation, cutting a portion of the flank and connective tissue out, then suturing the rumen wall to the flank. After this phase, a week would pass, allowing the rumen wall to heal, or adhere to the flank, then simply cutting the rumen wall out and closing the opening, or fistula, with a plug. I had done considerable research and thinking about the plug, but in the end, I manufactured my own creation. I had found some soft, flexible neoprene type material, that I felt would be flexible enough to use for the inside of the plug. Additionally, I had found some soft plastic type material that placed between the neoprene and the rumen wall should protect the wall from rubbing. This material seemed to be inert, and would not likely be digested by the ever-present bacteria in the rumen. I was going to use a plain piece of two-inch thick wood, fashioned to fit the hole, as the centerpiece to hold the fistula's shape. The outer plug would be a piece of hard neoprene lined with foam rubber. The whole apparatus was to be held together with a stainless steel bolt and wing nut. The fistula, or opening, was to be the size of a three-pound coffee can. I reasoned that a hole of that size into the rumen would give me plenty of room to remove the rumen contents.

The day of the operation was bitter cold, it had been minus twelve degrees that morning in Reno, but the operating room was warmed by electric heaters. Dr. Marble didn't have any assistants due to the Christmas vacation. Jim didn't have any help out to the farm, so it was just the two of us. I thought about asking Dr. Bohman, but after watching his cattle working ability on several occasions, I thought better of that idea. Besides Mormon's get mighty busy around Christmas. Dr. Marble agreed we would be better off by ourselves.

I optioned to do Alkali first, simply because, even though he was awesomely stubborn, at least he was manageable. We shortly had Alkali tied against a restraining wall, so that Marble could block the nerves on his left side. An animal's rumen lies against his left side, so that would be where a fistula into the rumen would be placed. Marble reasoned that if he blocked about six main nerves coming off of the spinal column, lying primarily between the shoulder and hips, we would have Alkali in a position where the incision should be pretty painless. He was right: After injecting the solution to block the nerve, we laid Alkali down on

111

his right side, and he was oblivious to pain on his left. Next we shaved and washed the area with antiseptic. I drew out the diagram, using the coffee can on the area that I reasoned would be best suited for the fistula. With a few adept strokes with a scapula, the flank was removed, exposing the rumen lining. It didn't take Marble more than 15 minutes to suture the rumen wall to Alkali's side, and with that we were done. We had Alkali standing and eating just about that quick. Of course, having not eaten anything for 24 hours prior to surgery didn't do much to diminish his hunger.

I had forewarned Dr. Marble about Bronco's antics, so at least he understood that there was a chance things might not go as well with the second calf. But Bronco seemed so subdued when we got him into the operating room that we both probably really didn't think it could go bad, especially after the success we had with Alkali. Well, we didn't have much trouble restraining Billy, nor did Marble have any trouble administering the blocking agent. In fact, we didn't have any trouble laying him down on his right side. I drew out the diagram, and Marble quickly made his incision. And, just like that the rumen wall was exposed. However, just about then, good old Bronco became his real self - Bronco Billy! He gave a mighty sigh, both of us stood there somewhat hypnotized by the events unfolding in front of us. With the sigh, he seemed to suddenly strain greatly against the ropes restraining him. This caused the rumen to sort of balloon out, in fact his rumen started coming out through the fistula. I dropped to my knees, and started stuffing rumen back into the cavity, but not as fast as it was coming out - pretty soon we had more than rumen, the rest of the stomach, all three compartments, followed by small intestine. No matter how fast I stuffed digestive components back in, they just seemed to come out faster. And if that wasn't enough, the rumen started swelling like it had helium gas in it! I wasn't sure, but I had visions of it simply floating away.

We managed to subdue poor old Bronco, but it seemed too late. Doc put more nerve block into him, and I continued to stuff. Finally, it appeared that we had gotten everything back in, and Billy was more or less subdued. Doc came to the conclusion if Billy were to have any chance, he would have to dump a ton of antibiotic into the body cavity before he sutured the rumen to the body. Fortunately, he had plenty so we dumped about a half-pound of several different antibiotic powders into him. Then we had the problem of suturing the correct part of the rumen to the wall. On several occasions during the struggle, the rumen had turned completely over, and on the outside it looked all the same. Finally, I found the reticulum, and I knew from anatomy, exactly where it had to go, so I positioned everything to the best of my ability, and Doc started making like a Singer sewing machine before Billy came back and realized how much grief we had caused him. Finally, we got all done, even got Billy back on his feet, and led him to where Alkali was, but he didn't seem very interested in hay. Dr. Marble made a prediction that he would be pretty sick within 24 hours and dead within 48. "Peritonitis will surely get him", was his comment. Bronco Billy had already amazed me on more than one occasion, and I had a sneaking suspicion that he just might do it once more. We cleaned up everything. Alkali had ate a bunch of hay, but Billy was just lying in the corner watching us, and not very alert at that. I told Doc that I would come back later that night, and check on them again the next morning, and let him know their condition. Well the next morning Alkali was ready for more hay, and Billy was on all fours, head high, plenty alert, and not particularly fond of seeing me, but he did eat some hay. It's an amazing thing, but Billy survived that ordeal, and furthermore, he went on to be the star of my thesis, and several more theses' as well. He traveled all over Nevada, did some amazing feats and lived to be nearly 20 years of age, but that's for another story, another day!

One week later, we recaptured Alkali and Billy, carefully cut out the exposed part of their rumen lining, exposing the inside of the rumen as well as its contents. I carefully inserted the plugs I had been preparing, although they both needed some modifying. After it was all said and done, the University of Nevada had its first two fistulated steers, not only steers with a fistula, but probably the largest fistulas ever done on an experimental basis. And furthermore, both patients were alive and doing quite well, thank you! It would be a month or so before I would actually use them to sample anything, but for the time being, I reset the plugs daily, and in general tended their general care. Both adapted, even Bronco seemed resigned to his fate, only occasionally kicking me, however, usually it was when I wasn't looking.

After Christmas vacation it was back to the books. The third week in January was finals week, and I was determined to get straight A's. I checked on Alkali and Bronco daily, but they just seemed to get better, of course a full ration of alfalfa hay wasn't hurting them. Alkali just kept his dumb composure, but Billy always eyed me when I came to feed. It was kind of like he knew his ordeal with me somehow wasn't quite over with.

Finals week came with the advent of one of the heaviest snowfalls in recent Reno history, eighteen inches on the ground. For two days I couldn't get my car out of the parking lot in front of our apartment. Our apartment complex was owned by one of the old Reno Italians, Joe Benito. After the second day I called Joe, mainly to see if we could get some snow moved. Joe didn't hear too good over the phone, or at least he didn't want to. I kept talking about moving some snow, and he kept saying it was too early to mow. I think Joe understood, but it was pretty obvious that he wasn't going to budge. Seeing how I had to start finals the following day, I shortly found someone with a tractor and a bucket, so at least I could drive to school. Jan said that I should deduct the tractor expense from our next rent payment, but knowing Joe I didn't think that would pay many dividends.

Reno, or more correctly Truckee Meadows, was settled by Italians, mostly farmers back in the Virginia City heydays. After the demise of

Virginia City, these old time Italian families survived by being frugal, and Joe Benito was no exception. Over the years I would come to know and work with many of the families, and I learned that they were all hard working, honest and yes, frugal!

I went all out for finals. Somehow, I had it in my head that if I got a 4.0 grade point average, that I might just be accepted into grad school. The thought of an assistantship had even entered my mind. But it was not to be. I didn't get the coveted 4.0. I got A's in 11 hours of class work, including the highest grade in the class for statistics. I was near the top in quant and organic. Perhaps, my proudest grade was an A+ from Dr. Robertson. I earned every inch of that one, and having over 200 plants in my collection didn't hurt. But my downfall was physiology. I had gotten an 85 on the midterm, and according to Dr. Weeth, I would have to get a 95 on the final to make an A, as he graded on the straight 90 - 80 basis, etc. Well, I didn't get a 95, no, I got a 93. Even though I got the highest grade in his class, it just didn't cut the mustard as far as he was concerned. There were only 3 B's given, one C and one D. Weeth knew how important an A was to me, because he started laughing and making comments when I picked up my exam. He felt that I placed way too much emphasis on grades, and not enough on learning, although he admitted that I probably learned more than any other student. I didn't argue, there really wasn't anything to argue about. Even though I probably would have agreed with Dr. Weeth, his perfect academic world really didn't exist outside of his classroom. Certainly, Dr. Cassard and Bohman didn't think that way. I challenged Weeth to give me anything but an A in any other class that I took from him. Although, I probably didn't have the slightest idea of how difficult that challenge might become, history proved that I, in fact, finally did win that challenge. All told, my GPA for the first semester at Nevada was a 3.7, and considering all of the other activities that I had been involved in, that probably wasn't too bad. Dr. Kidwell thought it was fantastic, Bohman thought it was OK, and frankly, neither Alkali or Billy seemed to care!

After my last final, which was Dr. Robertson's special problem, one of the range students asked if I would like to go have a picon punch at the Sante Fe. Now I had never had the legendary Basque drink, but I felt this might just be the right time. His name was Peio Echegoyen, a true Basque. Although his first name officially was Peio, the American version of that was just plain Pete, which everybody knew him by. Pete was a graduate student under Dr. Robertson, but he was monitoring the range class, just to sharpen his skills. Pete had gotten his BS at Nevada, but it was in general Ag, not range. Pete came from a ranch in northern Washoe County, north of Gerlach. He had gone back to the ranch for a year since graduating, but decided he needed a masters degree, so he came back to Nevada a year later. During the semester, we had gotten to know each other a bit, he told me about his parents ranch, I told him about my cattle operation in Ventura County as well as the OIL. However, we were both trying hard to make a showing at this grad school business, so neither of us had spent much time socializing, or at least I hadn't as I came to find out.

Anyway, we went to the Sana Fe, long a favorite hangout for the Basque population of Reno, as well as a significant number of Nevada students, regardless of ethnic background. And we had picons. It didn't take long to develop a taste for the drink, although I rapidly figured out you just sipped these, you didn't swallow them straight out, like I did my first high ball many years ago. Pete started out by paying me what I had to believe was a great compliment. "You are becoming a true Nevadan, and that I like", was his first comment after the initial swallow. Well, Pete and I were friends, but in my mind the friendship suddenly became a lot stronger. I guess I wanted to be considered a true Nevadan more than just about anything else in the world! I had to return the compliment some how some way. One thing I had noticed about Pete, was that the girls in our classes, or just at the University in generally, just seemed to pay a lot of attention to him. In fact right as we were talking, I noticed two young ladies at the bar giving him the once over.

So I responded by saying, "Pete, its my limited observation that ladies seem to be attracted to you. How does that work?"

He laughed, and said it was no big deal, but that led into a general conversation about sex with the opposite sex. Pete said he really didn't know how it worked, but he had long since become accustomed with the fact that members of the female sex did seem attracted to him. And, he added, "I don't see what's wrong with that. In fact, my old Daddy tells me it's a sin to cull any women without some kind of knowledge of them, at least as long as I am single. And, if you want to know the truth, I intend to remain single until I have sorted out the culls." Well, a second picon led to more talk, although, you just had the feeling with Pete, it was pretty straightforward.

I was fascinated by Pete's casualness towards sex. Most other young men my age that I had gotten to know either just didn't know, or exaggerated beyond belief. But to Pete, it just seemed to come natural. I was especially interested to find out how he developed not only the appetite, but the knowledge, because living 50 miles north of Gerlach, Nevada, much less going to high school at Gerlach, just didn't seem to me to be the background that would develop the expertise that Pete obviously had. But Pete didn't always live north of Gerlach, I came to find out. "Before Dad would let me go out with the bands during the summer, I often went to my uncles ranch down on the East Walker River, out of Yerington. They were my mom's brothers, and they trailed sheep way into the central Sierra, but they also irrigated a lot of land on the East Walker. My job was to help irrigate," he explained. There wasn't much water at his parents ranch, so irrigation was not a high priority. "I loved to irrigate on the East Walker, the fields were big, the water was a real challenge to control, kind of like what you talked about in Slinkard," he further explained.

"I don't know what this has to do with sex," was about all I could come up with as another Picon slid down.

"Well you see, it's kind of like this, when the herders came in, they would always offer to take me to town to celebrate; My Aunt and Uncle never knew what really was happening. There was a real "house" and bar on the north side of Yerington they liked to go to after payday. I never had any money, too young to buy a drink, so they would stand me for that. The first time they took me there I was only 13, so they all bet each other that I couldn't make it with one of the girls - I guess I fooled them, there were three working girls and I made it with all three before the night was over - and the herders had to pay for it all! Until I was about 15 or 16, they took me there once or twice or more every summer, and they always bought everything. They finally figured out that I was slowly breaking them, so they made me pay after that, but I quit going, because about then I had my first girl friend", the explanation left me somewhat dazed.

"You mean to tell me that you were going to a "house" several times each summer since you were 13?" was about all I could muster. "Yup, that is until I started dating Ruthie. She was a year behind me at Gerlach, but I could get rubbers over at Bruno's so I sure didn't see any reason to pay for it. Those herders at my uncle's ranch still haven't figured it out", and with that he bought another round of picon's! Pete started describing several situations that developed after he became a student at the University. By that time I had come to the conclusion that Pete had "fine tuned" his sexual relationships with the opposite sex. Seeing how the Sante Fe was packed with Basque at that point in time, I was somewhat leery to ask the obvious - is this an individual trait, or something in common with Basque in general? That question had to wait for another day.

Directly, after Pete's true confessions, he wanted to know about my escapades. I was afraid I had lived a pretty tame and boring life after listening to him. I wasn't very good at fabricating stories, so I told it like it was, my first encounter was in high school. Certainly not at Fillmore, the girls there were not very forward about anything like that. However, over at Newhall, a railroad town, things were a lot different. The high school there was called Willam S Hart, and it was loaded with pretty fast girls. Several of the older guys at Fillmore had girl friends over there, and it didn't take me long to catch on to that as soon as I was legal to drive at 16. I started going with a girl named Patsy, and it didn't take very long for the clothes to all come off. Patsy was fast, but it didn't take me very long to realize that this wasn't going to go anywhere, except possibly with a disastrous ending, and I was only 17. So that relationship didn't last very long! I went over some of the adventures at Cal Poly, mostly at San Dimas. But I could see Pete's eyes kind of turn green with envy when I mentioned that there were four all girl colleges within a 30 minute drive of the campus. I was kind of hesitant to describe the private dance we had with a group of girls from Claremont, so I eased into that one kind of gently. We had rented a large house, which was really a ski lodge during winter months, near the end of the road up Baldy. We set up a bar, had dinner catered, because it was going to be a long night. It all started over a casual bet that my old buddy, Tom Peltzer, made with one of the coeds from Claremont. After every dance, if the girl was so inclined she got to take whomever she was dancing with upstairs to one of the private rooms. Well, it all happened just about that way, and the girls were definitely so inclined! Anyway, describing that to Pete caused him to buy another round of picon's, but no matter what, it just didn't top his story about when he was 13 years old. Nothing could!

Finally, we both decided that we had enough picons. Tomorrow was another day, and registration for the second semester was going to be exactly one week away. Pete was headed to Gerlach, and I was headed home, but to be up early the next morning to start my first official test with Alkali and Bronco. So after a warm "good by" away we went. It's kind of funny, but somehow as we parted that day, I kind of had the feeling that Pete was going to be an integral part of my life for a long time to come. It was a warm feeling, because I liked the guy. You just couldn't help that, but it was something else, like our paths, and perhaps our destinies were just somehow intertwined. If I could have looked into the future that day, I am not sure what I would have thought, but certainly my instincts were true, only I just didn't know how true they were at that time.

Dr. Bohman and I had agreed that we would start testing the concept of using the fistulated animals to evaluate livestock feeds during the semester break. At that time the operations were approximately 30 days old, and Dr. Marble had agreed that represented sufficient time for the rumen wall to completely adhere to the flank and hide of the animals. My plan was to take about ten different feedstuffs, sample each feedstuff for analysis, then allow the animals to eat the feedstuff after the rumen contents had been removed. After consumption, a sample would be removed from the rumen also for chemical analysis. A comparison was to be made between the raw feedstuff and that obtained through the fistula, and if that comparison showed basically no difference, then we would be ready to sample grazed forage come spring. I had selected silage, grass hay, alfalfa hay, oat hay, four different grains, cottonseed meal, and a commercial supplement for the comparisons.

The semester break coincided with the last week of January. So, on January 25, 1958, the first test of my concept of using animals to sample livestock feed occurred. The animals were still housed at the small vet facility located at the Valley Road Farm adjacent to campus. However, there wasn't room inside to do the sampling, so I tied both Alkali and Billy to a fence, removed the plugs and started removing the rumen contents. I kind of knew how much there would be, so I had obtained two large buckets from surplus, each would hold at least 100 pounds of material. As usual, I did Alkali first. I could trust him to stand still. Of course Billy got to watch the procedure, so his mind was already working overtime. Removing Alkali's rumen contents was surprisingly easy. I had that done in about ten minutes. Once the plug was removed, I just slid the bucket next to him and started rolling the material out by hand. All of the solid material came out like a flash. However, there was about two to four gallons of fluid on the bottom. My physiology class had really helped in this process, because, I had learned to anticipate the fluid being there. So, I just slid a flexible one inch hose into the rumen cavity, allowed it to fill with fluid, pulled one end out of the rumen, slid it down into the bucket and allowed the siphon to go to work. I held the other end in my hand on the bottom of the rumen, kind of like a vacuum cleaner wand. In a few short moments Alkali's rumen was empty, and seeing how it was a bitter cold day and about to snow, I replaced the plug. Alfalfa hay was on the menu today, so a flake was placed in front of Alkali, and lo and behold, he promptly started eating it!

While Alkali was eating his hay, I proceeded to empty out Billy. He performed admirably, no kicking, no struggle, just as mellow as he could be! Once Billy started sampling the feed, I went back to Alkali, opened him up, removed a consumed sample of alfalfa, replaced the rumen contents and plug, and that was that. On to Billy, removed his plug, removed the sample of hay, and then a strange thing happened.

Samuel Clemens, or better known as Mark Twain, was the first person to really describe a Washoe Zephyr when he was editor of the Virginia City Enterprise. He described the Zephyr as being a darn right miserable event of wind, dust, boulders, sagebrush, and anything else not immediately tied to mother earth, sometimes mixed with snow, sleet, rain or other heavenly peculiarities, generally headed in a northerly fashion. Well, just as I had removed Billy's sample of consumed hay, and was properly storing it for future chemical analysis, the January Zephyr hit. This particular Zephyr was accompanied by a significant amount of snow, making it somewhat different from the classical

Zephyr as described by Twain. But what was particularly significant about this event was that when I returned to fill Billy's rumen back up, I was struck by the amount of snow blowing through the fistula and into the empty rumen. Billy looked like he was getting cold. But I was awestruck by the event. I was undoubtedly the first human being on this planet to actually witness a snowstorm occurring within the rumen of a ruminant animal. Unfortunately I had no camera to capture the event of the millennia(s). I had told everybody to stay far away this first time: I didn't know what to expect and I didn't need disturbances. That included the folks from Agriculture Information that wanted to photograph the historic event. Over the years I always have laughed about this event. I never really knew which was the most monumental, actually using a fistulated animal to sample his diet for the first time, or watching a snowstorm occur inside of a rumen. I have always tended to vote for the latter!

Even though this first sampling went without a hitch there was still much to learn. I had inherited a bunch of old one gallon unused paint cans for the fistula samples. I thought they would suffice, as I could place the lid on the can and pretty well seal it with one or two blows with a hammer. And, using a black grease pencil I could readily identify the sample by marking on the can. My plan was to sub sample the can, dry the sample for analysis, leaving the rest in the can for future analysis if needed. After I got Billy closed up, I took everything back to the lab where I had a desk. The samples were placed on the counter, but before I could do anything, Bohman came in and wanted to know how it went. I gave him a blow-by-blow description, including the snowstorm, for which he didn't seem the least bit interested. But he had a thousand questions about the process in general. It must have taken an hour or so to satisfy his curiosity. By then I wanted something warm to drink, so I set out to make my usual cup of instant coffee in a beaker heated by a Bunsen burner. That took another 15 minutes or so, and I probably took about 15 minutes to drink it. All told, the airtight cans had been sitting on the counter for about an hour and a half or so before I decided it was high time to get to work. Despite all the precautions that I had taken, it just simply never occurred to me that rumen fermentation of the samples would continue while the sample was in the airtight can. Well guess what, bloat was occurring at an alarming rate, and the gas had no where to go, until such a time as the internal pressure exceeded the lid's ability to hold it in, and it went. The roar was deafening - the lid hit the ceiling, bounced off some water pipes, made a 360 degree trip around the lab, creating enough havoc so that both Mike and myself found ourselves laying on the floor. I was reminded of the CO_2 cylinder going off years before. The concept of thinking you were dead was similar for both events. From that point on I learned to put an eyedropper full of a strong disinfectant into the fistula sample, stopping all further bacterial activity on the spot.

Over the rest of the week I sampled the remaining nine feedstuffs. The only difference was that on each sampling I had more and more observers. Most of the department wanted to watch; even old Dean Adams came out one day. Ag Info took lots of pictures, word got out to Reno's two newspapers, the Journal and the Gazette. They both ran features on the crazy grad student up on the "hill" putting holes in the sides of animals big enough to stick your head in. Somebody from the Animal Welfare Institute, or some such organization paid me a visit to make sure I was being humane. She was a middle aged lady that got right into the pen with the animals while I was sampling. I tried to explain how they might live indefinitely because of this rather than becoming hamburger, that didn't seem to help much. But Billy came to my rescue. She was slightly over weight, and had a long trench coat thing on. Well, she brushed up against Billy, the coat sort of went under his flank, and he did his thing. The standard kick to the side sent her sprawling into the floor of the pen, which was long overdue for cleaning. I offered to wash her off with the hose. She thanked me, climbed over the fence and left. I guess she was satisfied that I meant the animals no harm, as I didn't hear from her again for some time.

The best press review I had was from the student newspaper, The Sagebrush. Of all things, Pete was picking up some extra credit and trying to learn something about journalism, so he was covering anything of agricultural interest. Pete knew exactly what I was trying to accomplish with Alkali and Billy, and why I was doing it in the first place. Besides, he had helped me on several occasions, had learned well the temperament of both beasts. In fact one day Billy left a calling card on his ribs that took about two weeks to go away. So Pete did a great story, and he placed special emphasis on the animals and their nature. They did some great photographic work, even including placing a camera into the empty rumen of Alkali, and taking a picture looking back at me through the fistula. Even Bohman was impressed!

By the end of the week, I had 40 samples for chemical analysis, including twenty of the feedstuffs, and twenty of the corresponding fistula samples. Only ten feedstuffs were used, but on both animals, so statistically, I would have some chance to see if any animal variation occurred. However, by the end of the week, it was time to register for the second semester.

Needless to say, Bohman had already devised a plan for my academic future. It included the second semester of both quant and organic chemistry. Organic was still just 3 hours, but the second semester of quant was 4 hours, two lectures and two labs. Bohman also wanted me to take his nutrition lab, but the course description for the two-hour course was real similar to what I had already accomplished. He said that was OK, but that he wanted me to learn some additional techniques; however, in his good nature he indicated that the labs would not be formal, just whenever I wanted to do them, even on weekends. I thought that was real nice, because I could already see that there were insufficient afternoons in the typical week to satisfy all the laboratories he was going to have me signed up for anyway! I also was aimed to take physiology of reproduction from Weeth, three hours including one lab and two lectures. This was my chance to even up on Weeth for that damned B that I got in physiology. I had talked to Kidwell about teaching an advanced statistics course as a special problem. He said he would if I could get four other students. That was no trouble, Pete wanted to take it, and I found two other grad students that wanted it, one in econ and one in agronomy. There were two business majors from across campus that also wanted it, so Kidwell agreed to teach the course, two lectures a week for two credits. The real kicker was that Bohman felt that I still needed to be better in plant identification, even after collecting over 200 Nevada plants for Dr. Robertson. So I had to take what was called Systemic Botany, or more commonly taxonomy. That was a four-hour class, three lectures, one lab, and a plant collection of at least 100 plants! The catch here was that to properly identify collected plants they must be in the flowering stage, which just wasn't going to occur in Nevada until just about the end of the semester. So that meant I would be spending a lot of time over in the California foothills of the Sierra. And of course there was seminar and another special problem from Robertson. At least that was just a field trip across Nevada that occurred after finals.

All told my course load for the second semester was 20 hours, including six labs during the five-day week. But as I said, Bohman came to my rescue by allowing me to work the two labs for nutrition however I wanted to. Along with everything else I was doing, I kind of felt that what he wanted me to take was a bit heavy. Even the official University catalogue indicated that graduate levels were not to exceed 18 hours of credit per semester, and were normally 12 to 14 hours. When I pointed this out to Bohman, he promptly pointed out in the eyes of the University I was not yet a graduate student! Much to his credit he did point out that I would not be required to work the additional 20 hours in the lab as I had during the first semester. He felt the time needed to analyze the 40 samples that I had already collected for my masters thesis would do instead. And, so the second semester of my pursuit of the wily masters degree began.

The second semester was more of the same, with the exception that there just weren't enough hours in the week. The 100 or so plant collection for taxonomy required us to be in the Sierra foothills every Saturday morning as early as possible, usually returning to Reno after dark. Sunday was usually spent messing with Alkali and Billy and Monday through Friday was spent on class work, lectures, labs and chemical analysis of the collected samples.

I was pretty much holding my own for the first two weeks, but the world fell apart on the third week. The special statistics course that Kidwell had put together was meeting on Tuesdays and Thursdays at 9:00 a.m. We had met four times and were getting deep into multiple regression and correlations. I was eating it up, and probably had a better understanding than anybody else in the class. So we met on the third Tuesday, only problem instead of Kidwell in walks Cassard with a very grim look about his face. "Apparently Dr. Kidwell ran into some marital difficulties over the weekend, he has left the Reno area and returned to his home in Louisiana. He has indicated that he will not be returning to the Reno area in the near future, if at all. I have briefly discussed this situation with the staff, and no one feels qualified to take this class over for the duration of the semester. I am going to look across campus to see if any faculty member could possibly take up the challenge. At this time I don't have any other suggestion, unless one of you do." - End of report, wow, did I feel like my world fell apart or what!

I sat there in kind of stunned silence, then Pete leaned over and gave me his two cents worth. "You know what, I'll bet you could teach this class, you're a full lecture ahead of everybody else, you understand it better than all the rest of us put together - what say?"

He actually had a grin on his face as he was asking me the question! Cassard overheard him and responded, "It might not be impossible for one of you to sort of hold this class together, and perhaps with the help of one of us faculty we could pull it off so that you would not loose the credit." Everybody sort of pointed at me, but I knew better. I was already worked beyond belief, I didn't have time to prepare meaningful lectures about information which I had no prior knowledge. Besides it just dawned on me, I was not a graduate student in the eyes of the University! End of case! At that point Dr. Cassard asked that we all be dismissed for today's lecture, and he asked me to come to his office.

When I entered Dr. Cassard's office, Bohman was also there. Cassard started off by saying that he didn't believe there was anyone on campus that would pick up the course from an instruction standpoint. Bohman agreed. Further, they both agreed that I was probably the only one that could hold the class together and had the interest and knowledge to pull it off. I asked about pay, both responded that there just wasn't any available money. I asked about part of Dr. Kidwell's salary, both responded that they didn't have access to that, and likely it would be tied up for the remainder of the semester anyway. Bohman pointed out that I had to have the credit anyway for my graduate program to balance out at the end of next year. I started to say something about not being a grad student, but thought better of that. The thought of me teaching myself a course that was required to obtain my masters degree, when I was not a graduate student in the eyes of the University was difficult to explain to myself, to put it mildly. At least I will be able to grade myself. But Cassard threw cold water on that concept as well, "I'll let Dr. Bohman take charge of the class, he can do the grades and all of that stuff if you will coordinate the rest of the semester. It will be necessary for him to receive credit as being the instructor in the eyes of the University, you understand I am sure." Yeah, sure I understand, then the final crowning blow came when Bohman asked if I minded if he sat in on the class, as he just never understood some of the advanced statistics that we were going to be getting into. I could just about imagine me teaching the class, Bohman taking the class, Bohman making out the grades, and me getting less than an A. I guess about right then I thought for the first time some unkind words about Mr. Fairfield for getting me into this position to begin with. But Bohman had a way, for he offered the carrot that he was sure I would snap up; "If you can get through all of this, I'll definitely recommend you for grad status at the end of the semester, and I am pretty sure the graduate dean will approve it. Furthermore, if an assistantship becomes available, I'll recommend you for consideration." At that point I again remembered that my primary mission for being in Reno at that point in time was to obtain my masters degree - so I put thoughts of killing the S.O.B. temporarily on hold and agreed to teach the course, beginning Thursday.

I put all my effort into teaching the advanced statistics. Statistical Methods by George Snedicor was the text that we were using and it was fairly easy to follow. The rest of the semester was to be devoted to covariance, multiple regression and covariance, curvilinear regression, binomial and poisson distribution and finally design and analysis of samplings. I laid out a schedule for the remaining 12 weeks or 24 lectures. I talked with Bohman about tests and how to grade. He admitted that he wouldn't be qualified to grade the tests, and I indicated that I didn't want to either, so in our usual fashion, we finally agreed that I would write and grade the tests, and he would issue the grade based on my recommendation. At last I finally got it through my mind that I would probably get an A in this class.

The next two weeks were difficult to say the least. Highway 40 was closed due to snow one weekend so I didn't get to California to collect plants, which allowed me to get caught up in my studies. Quant was my biggest problem. The second semester was more oriented to mining students, most of the techniques were for various mineral ores, etc., and I just wasn't real interested in that, so I fairly well prepared myself to accept less than an A this semester. I was holding my own in the rest, and way ahead of the game in Weeth's reproductive class.

After having taught stat for four lectures I informed Pete that it was time to take me to the Santa Fe for picons. Furthermore, if he didn't,

I doubted that his grade in stat would qualify for graduate standing. He seemed to understand what I was implying so that afternoon we went to the Santa Fe. He kind of apologized for the predicament that I was in by having to teach the class, but he assured me that anyone else that would have tried to teach the course would have fowled it up so bad that no one would have learned a thing. As it was, he assured me that he was grasping the advanced stat concepts very well. In fact I had explained the whole concept of biological variation better than Kidwell ever had. And with that we had another picon!

I had to laugh about an experience in Weeth's reproduction class, and related it to Pete. We were studying semen quality, and the factors that affect it, so for a lab exercise, Weeth had all of us bring a sample of our own semen for analysis. Well, we all did. I don't know about the others, but mine was my own. Anyway, my semen ranked head and tails above all the rest in both quantity and quality. Approximately 90% of my sperm cells were alive and well. On examination abnormalities were nonexistent. One poor student found out that 100% of his sperm cells were dead, not only dead but badly disfigured. Most of the students ranged in the 50% area. Weeth proclaimed me a natural breeder. That's when I told Pete we should evaluate his semen - I guessed by his reported actions he would probably grade at 100% +, if that's possible! After a good laugh about all of that he started telling me about his new girl friend.

"Yup, as a matter of fact she lives just about in front of your house", was his teasing remark that sure wetted my appetite. Turned out she owned a bagel shop on South Virginia, which was in fact nearly in front of where our apartment was on Holcomb. I knew about the bagel shop, but had never been in there. Pete said he had stopped in there for lunch a few weeks back, was impressed by a lady that appeared to be running the show. They struck up a conversation, she asked him to come back after the lunch crowd was gone. He did. She asked him upstairs to her apartment. He went. She asked him to go to bed with her. He did

- and that's how Pete's new relationship began. Yup, we should have analyzed his semen! I did start noticing his pick-up behind the shop when I was home in the afternoon. I don't know how he maintained all of this and staying even with Dr. Robertson in his grad program. I had heard Robertson was a worse task master than Bohman. Pete was an amazing fellow to say the least.

Mid terms rolled around, I got 100% in Weeth's, didn't do so well in quant or taxonomy, but aced all the rest. I suggested that Bohman take the midterm that I had devised for the stat class. It gave me the greatest of pleasure to give him an 88%, especially when Pete and one of the business students both scored in the mid 90 range. Bohman reminded me that he was just sitting in on the class, and his busy schedule simply had not allowed him time to properly prepare for the exam. I agreed, but made a mental note that he would pay hell before scoring 88% on the final.

Alkali and Billy were fairing well, although I had not used them for some time. We were developing a pasture grazing study to further test them on during the coming summer. Dr. Jensen, the agronomist, had agreed to work with me, and was getting quite excited about the prospects of truly learning what grazing animals consume under different grazing regimes. Quant continued to slide, I was starting to hold my own in taxonomy, and had a plant collection approaching 100 specimens. And Pete and I drank picons at least once a week.

It was on one of those occasions in which a situation developed that would have profound impact on the rest of my life, although at that time that concept couldn't have been further from my mind. Pete and I were sitting at the bar sipping our second, when this squirrelly nerd student walked up behind me and said, "Excuse me, but aren't you the graduate student working with fistulated cattle?" When I turned to respond I almost laughed, for he wore clothes that seemed to come from the depression, had glasses twice as big as his eyes, carried a stack of books, and in general was about as far out of place for the Santa Fe as anybody could possibly be. Before I could respond he went on to say, "Your work is truly fascinating. It sounds like you are a true humanitarian, trying to help solve the coming world food shortage. I admire people like you. Perhaps I could help you sometime with your cattle, I want to be involved in things like that, not only now, but definitely in the future when I complete my studies." I didn't quite know what to say, and I sure wasn't going to offer to buy him a picon. I could see Pete grinning out of the corner of my eye, he must have known a whole lot more about this situation than I did, which was nothing. I mumbled something about how I enjoyed my work, and just wanted to get a job when my studies were done. Well the nerd spotted somebody else that he wanted to talk to, so with a fond ado, away he went.

By this time Pete was dying with laughter, so I asked for a bit of clarification. "That guy is from southern Nevada, down around Searchlight somewhere. His name is Harry Ryan, and in case you didn't know it, he is campaigning to become student body president next year. He probably figured out that as a grad student you can't vote, so he didn't waste too much time except to blow some smoke up your ass," was Pete's initial description of the nerd. "Thanks to my excellent reporting in the Sagebrush, you're a pretty well known fellow on campus, so it pays to be seen in your presence when you are running for student body president", was Pete's next epistle. Pete went on to explain how he didn't think Harry Ryan could win dogcatcher much less student body president. "He tried out for Sundowners last year, but during the fight, he got both eyes blackened and a tooth broke, and he didn't make Downers, not by a long shot," was Pete's next explanation. I had come to know the Sundowners, which was the men's informal drinking club on campus, and Pete would know, because he had been a Downer when he was an undergrad student, but he didn't actively participate anymore. Sundowner tryouts test your ability to handle alcohol, and if you more or less pass that test, and a few other grizzly details, they all go to the mountain to fight for or against accepting new pledges. Apparently in Harry's case, they were pretty much against him, as his sponsor was the one that hit him first and the hardest.

After listening to Pete's description of the events, it was beyond me how this guy could conceivably believe he could become student body president. But Pete explained, "Not everyone on campus loves the Downers. In fact, quite a few would vote for Harry just because of what happened. And a lot of girls feel sorry for the guy because of the beating he took, so I guess anything is possible. One of the reasons the Downers got on his ass so bad was because he portrays himself as a Mormon, at least when its appropriate. He has always maintained his parents are itinerant miners, what the hell ever that means. They are not only itinerant miners, in fact they are itinerant Mormon miners!"

I thought about that for a while as we were downing our third picon. I summed it all up by saying, "Well neither you nor I can vote, nor can Ike and Billy for that matter, and I expect that Bohman would really feel bad about a fellow Mormon attempting to become a Downer, so in other words, it's out of our hands." Pete agreed.

Spring in western Nevada is a fickle thing. It sometimes starts in March, but don't count on it. Early April can be so cold and windy it can only be considered cruel and inhumane. However, usually sometime after the 15th, spring actually starts to make an appearance. The fruit trees are in blossom, the daffodils are out, and the tulips are appearing. The spring of 1958 was typical, first warm, then cold, then warm, then really cold. It was one of those warm days, I had just finished teaching stat, when Pete yelled at me, "Hey, let's go to lunch, I'll buy." That sounded good to me, so all I wanted to know was where and when. "Quarter till 12, I'll meet you at the bagel shop on South Virginia", was the response. Well if I am going to eat right in front of my own house, I better call Jan, which turned out to be fine with her. I had been wanting to meet Pete's latest squeeze anyway, and a nice warm spring day seemed appropriate.

Well to say that I didn't expect to see what I saw is putting it mildly. Pete hadn't said much about Gina. Her name was Gina Winston, only that she was very friendly and awful playful. Well I didn't know about the latter, but she sure was a looker. About five eight or five nine, I guessed maybe 140 pounds, but a figure to carry it all and a lot more. Her topside was way past 36 D's, whatever the upper ranges were, I don't know. And they stood straight out, and it appeared without a lot of support. She had long light auburn hair, a waist I swear you could hold between your two hands, and legs that seemed to reach forever. I did a double take, she smiled at my obvious stare, which caused me to turn close to purple. Pete took it all in with a big grin. Gina came running when she saw Pete. I had never met her before, but Pete had told me her name and a little about her background. She originated in Burlingame, north of San Francisco; but as a young kid had come to Reno to make her fortune in and around the clubs. That didn't work well for her, however, it didn't take a guy named Joe Conforte long to find her. Joe ran the Triangle Ranch; a whorehouse located about 30 miles east of Reno, alongside Highway 40. Joe somehow convinced Gina that the road to fame and fortune went right through his "house", and she apparently bit. After about two years Gina had enough of being a legitimate hooker, so she cashed in her stake and bought the small but efficient bagel shop on South Virginia. And of course along came Pete. Well, Pete made the introduction. Shaking hands with Gina was an experience. Her handshake was very firm, but very warm - I could understand why Pete was where he was - real quick! Gina had a million different kinds of bagel sandwiches on the menu, along with lots of different imported and domestic beers. She pretty much ran the whole show, some help in the kitchen, one bus boy and one other girl helping with the tables. But Gina was everywhere, and it was obvious that most of the customers, at least the men, were there to watch Gina. She commanded attention. I didn't need to ask Pete how it was upstairs with Gina. The answer to that was obvious, both from his smile as well as her flushed color when she glanced his way. Imagine - right in front of my house! When we finished, it was closing in on one o'clock and my taxonomy lab, as well as a range lab for Pete, so goodbyes were brief. Gina's hand on my shoulder as we left gave me a whole new impression about springtime in western Nevada. Somehow, I had the feeling that I would see Gina again, wasn't sure where or how, but somehow. Funny how those types of feelings surface.

Another funny thing happened about then. Harry Ryan won the election for student body president - imagine that! He'll probably advocate for kicking the Downers off campus. Oh well, I was past student body politics; my mission was to obtain my masters. What wasn't so funny was a cheating scandal that involved quite a few students on campus. Seems like somebody got the keys to the history department and had been snitching exams before test day. Apparently a number of exams had been sold around campus, but somebody reported, and Sam Basta, Dean of Men, had a fit. Lot of keys got changed, some kids got the boot, but according to Pete, they didn't get the ringleaders. "You know what? I am hearing that Harry Ryan was one of the organizers of the exam ring. Basta's secretary, whom I know quite well, sort of hinted that it was Harry that turned them all in to save his own butt. Because Harry had won the election, Basta didn't give him the boot in exchange for the information on the rest," Pete concluded.

"Well it wouldn't surprise me. I don't really know the prick, nor do I care to. From what I have seen so far he is a kiss ass of the first order. I don't have much to do with Basta, being in grad school, but he strikes me as a hard ass. If what you say is true, I guess he felt not booting the student body president was the best, but I'll bet he wanted to. Too bad he couldn't find a way. Like you have been saying, Ryan is the kind of person that probably won't go away. Ha, probably twenty years from now, you and I will be sitting around lamenting over the fact that we ever knew him to begin with," I summarized with another picon.

Finals were approaching, Alkali and Billy were doing fine, again had their mugs on several regional publications. I think fame was actually going to Billy's head. He could really ham it up sometimes; then every once in awhile he would give me the old hind foot rake just when I wasn't expecting it. The day after finals we were set to go on Dr. Robertson's range field trip across Nevada, and the day after returning we had scheduled the start of our pasture grazing trials, which were scheduled to last all summer. But finals first.

Final week went so fast it was over before it started, or so it seemed. I really only cared about Weeth's class and I was totally prepared for it. In fact I got 100% on the final. Weeth complained to me that in his entire teaching career he had never given a student 100%. I muttered to myself there was a first time for everything Bud, but not loud enough for him to hear. I just took my A with a brief thanks and was on my way. An A in organic and nutrition lab as well as seminar. My seminar was a review of selective grazing, which would also be much of the literature review for my thesis. I politely gave myself an A in stat, and unfortunately was only able to give Bohman a B, as he scored in the low 80's on the final. He promptly informed me that he would be the final judge of the grades anyway. I slipped through taxonomy with a B by some miracle that I would never understand; however, the 150 correctly identified plants in my collection probably didn't hurt. But I fell to an already accepted C in quant. Robertson's grade would have to wait until the report for his field trip was completed. But for 19 hours I got a 3.3 GPA, quant had done me in, but I and a whole lot of other people knew full well that I should have gotten a lot more credit than a simple A for teaching the advance stats class. I was more than satisfied, although Bohman never understood how I could manage to slip to a C in quant. So after one full year of graduate class work, including teaching an advanced statistics class, and making good progress on a thesis, I had taken 35 hours of class work and obtained an overall GPA of 3.5. And still wasn't a grad student in the eyes of the University! I had made up my mind that immediately on returning from Robertson's field trip it was straight to Cassard's office and I wasn't leaving until I was an official grad student with an assistantship contract in hand.

We all piled into two old GMC travel all's and headed out for Robertson's one-week whirlwind tour of Nevada. Seven students, three staff members, two besides Joe, and one hanger-on. The students were a great bunch, including Pete and another grad student in Range, Bob Ferraro, who hailed from a ranch in Paradise Valley, our first night's destination. This was a no frills tour, sleeping bags, and food, as we did our own cooking. Down Highway 40, which was gradually becoming Interstate 80 in places. It was fast paced, the first day stops at Fernley and Mill City to review range research as well as a stop at Lovelock's lower valley to hear how the farm land was reclaimed after Rye Patch Dam was constructed. The first night we pulled into the Forest Service compound in Paradise Valley, long after dark. We had to cook, clean our mess, and write our notes, I was sure Robertson was going to demand an excellent report if an A was in the works. Bright and early we woke to see Paradise Valley for the first time. This is what I had always imagined the real Nevada to be, a beautiful valley surrounded by snow capped mountains, yielding numerous streams that irrigated hay lands for the winter-feeding of the cattle herds. And smack dab in the middle of the valley stood the little old historic town of Paradise Valley, which included two churches, a post office the Forest Service complex, one bar and small general store. We all agreed it was a beautiful sight. Outside of Dr. Robertson, none of us had ever been in Paradise Valley before. But he was well acquainted with the Valley. Before accepting a position with the University, he had spent considerable time here doing research about range revegetation. He worked for the Intermountain Forest and Range Research Station located in Ogden, Utah, but he actually lived and worked at a research station they maintained right in Paradise Valley on Lamance Creek. We spent the next two days touring his old research projects, as well as several ranches. As we headed back towards Winnemucca, I made a mental note that I sure wanted to see more of Paradise Valley, especially the surrounding mountains. The fourth day was spent on the old W.T. Jenkins outfit located north of Battle Mountain. "Cap" Marvel, his wife Louise and their three sons, Dick, Tom and John were our hosts while we toured from the headquarters up to and including the Independence Mountain Range north of Elko. That night we stayed at the BLM compound in Elko before heading to Lamoille and Secret Pass the next day, including numerous stops.

I became amazed at the knowledge that Dr. Robertson had of Nevada. He seemed to know the owners and operators of every ranch, as well as most of the history. That night we stayed at a ranch in Clover Valley. The owners offered to feed us, but Robertson assured them we were well equipped. However, he wouldn't let it come to a vote. The next day we headed for Contact, 60 miles north of Wells and a tour of the University Field Station, Knoll Creek. The next morning, after leaving Knoll Creek, it was back to Elko and Carlin with a long journey down the Reese River to Austin. The last night was spent at the Forest Service compound in Austin, then back towards Reno on Highway 50. All in all, we traveled nearly 1,300 miles, ranging in elevation from 3,900 feet to 7,452 feet, and made some 41 stops. After returning to Reno, I was amazed to find that I had accumulated two notebooks full of notes and several rolls of film. I was equally amazed at what I had seen in seven days - a goodly share of Nevada, from the Rubies to some of the driest ranges known to man, and it was all beautiful. Cattle ranches that ran thousands and thousands of cattle over hundreds of thousands of acres. Alfalfa fields that yielded four to five tons of hay per acre. Abundant wildlife, and streams demanding to be fished. Aspen and pine groves that defied description. Yup, this Nevada could indeed grow on a guy.

We hit Reno on a late Friday afternoon, I checked on Alkali and Billy, they were fine. Saturday and Sunday was spent organizing and preparing my report for Robertson. And Monday morning at 8:00 a.m. I was in front of Cassard's office door. He was late as usual, but not by much this time, he knew I would be there. After sitting down he suggested that he call in Bohman as well. So it was another 15 minute wait. When Bohman came in he was nervous, not that he wasn't always, so I immediately expected the worst. Cassard showed me a letter he had prepared for the Graduate Dean, suggesting that based on my GPA for the last year, as well as voluntarily beginning work towards my thesis, that I be granted graduate standing. He had sent the letter last week and further suggested that while we were all here he call the Dean to see if he had made a decision. The answer was affirmative; but I could swear I also heard something to the effect as to why had he (Cassard) waited so long, should have been done after the first semester. Oh well, I couldn't be sure, it just wasn't that clear.

After that Bohman started in by saying that they were prepared to offer me a teaching assistantship because of the outstanding job I had done teaching stat. "I thought a teaching assistantship was $1,800 per year, but a research assistantship was $2,400 per year", I quizzed. There answer was pretty direct, "You're right, but we thought you would like the more relaxed atmosphere of teaching, and it would only take you two years to complete your masters degree with a teaching assistantship", was Cassard's reply.

Well for the first time in my academic career at Nevada, I became mentally disturbed. I didn't really threaten mayhem, but I supposed I might have implied it. Between the use of some non-Mormon-like phrases, I was able to point out that I had already completed well over half of my course work, and probably had actually done over half of my thesis work. Then I began to explain that due to my efforts, and the temperament of Alkali and Billy, that the three of us had brought more positive publicity to the Animal Science Department as well as the Max C. Fleischmann College of Agriculture both on a local scale as well as a national one, than anything that had ever been done here since J.E. Church developed the still used snow surveying techniques in the 1890's. When I finished Bohman and Cassard looked at each other with the kind of a hurt feeling look, much like young bull calves have when they are let up from the ground after becoming steers. Neither

138

had much to say, except that they truly thought I would rather have a teaching assistantship, but since I insisted, they would draw up the contract effective July 1 for a research assistantship. Then Bohman added that since I would be starting my grazing trials in June, he had an extra $200 to cover June as well. That all decided, I went straight to Dr. Jensen's office to figure out when to get going. However, as I went up the stairs, I somehow wished that Kidwell would have been here to see that performance. He had always wanted someone to give those two eccentric academicians the what for.

Jensen had some small five-acre pastures at the Main Station Farm that we were going to use for sampling. These were mixed clover pastures. The plan was that we would use intact steers to fully graze the paddocks, but also use Ike and Billy to sample every other day. So I made arrangements to immediately move Ike and Billy back to where they came from. Upon arrival, Jim smoking his every present pipe came over to view his God calves, as he liked to call them. He was reluctant to say it, but he was impressed with their behavior, especially Billy's. He walked up to Billy and started scratching his back, and Billy responded just like he expected to be scratched, just couldn't get enough of it.

The next day was my first sample day, it worked like a charm. Took about 30 minutes to clean both out, another thirty minutes to sample, then about an hour to finish up. Jim let me use Duff, so getting them back into my temporary corral after grazing was a piece of cake. It took me less than three hours from the time I left the lab until the time I returned. That left plenty of time for sample preparation, as well as gradually finishing the analysis of the 40 samples I had obtained last winter. Jensen had already worked out a technique to botanically analyze the collected grazed sample, so that part of the project was out of my hair. During the summer we collected samples from five different grazing trials, all aimed at determining how selective grazing cattle might be. From the preliminary data analyzed by Jensen, they appeared to be plenty selective, in fact far more than any of us imagined.

139

I had finished the analyses of the 40 samples from my first study by early July. From that we determined that the only real contaminant of the collected samples was from saliva, then mainly just ash and phosphorus. It didn't take me long to figure a regression equation that I could apply to the grazed samples to eliminate that source of variation. By summers end, I had collected around 90 samples, basically used Alkali and Billy every other day. They never got tired, on the other hand they never got to keep what they grazed. I wondered if they would ever catch on. By the start of the fall semester I had half the analytical work completed with a goal of having all my chemistry complete by Thanksgiving. My literature review was already just about complete. I figured it would take about a month to complete all of my statistical analyses, which would put me to the first of the year. Writing wasn't my long suit, but still, with a little luck I planned to have my thesis in the first draft by March 15.

It's a funny thing how time seems to fly when you really get on top of a project. I think the first semester of my graduate career was the longest six months of my life. Since then, time was just picking up speed. Here it was, ready for the start of my second year, I could see light at the end of the tunnel, and it was approaching fast! Bohman didn't even bother to spend much time with me for class work. We both already pretty well knew what was required. I really only registered for three actual classes; comparative anatomy which was a five hour killer type of class, histology, two lectures and one lab for three credits, and physical chemistry, three lectures for three hours. In addition I had to take seminar, and three hours of credit for my thesis work, all told 15 hours. Comparative anatomy was the only tough class; the lectures weren't bad, but for the lab, we had to totally dissect both a shark and a cat. We had weekly lab exams, where various parts of the anatomy of either were pin pointed and we had to identify them. Each student had his own cat, so I used to take mine home all the time and have Jan help me identify parts. By the end of the course, she probably knew as much cat anatomy as I did. Besides class work, I spent as much time as possible completing the chemical analysis of my collected samples. I had all of the chemistry done before mid terms, so I was ahead of schedule. For relaxation, I would go to the Bagel shop with Pete about once a week for lunch. I loved watching Gina, especially around Pete, a real display of sex, on both of their parts. But they were having problems; I think Gina had other "friends". Sometimes she would suggest that Pete shouldn't be around that afternoon. It was probably just as well for Pete, as Dr. Robertson was starting to get a bit irritated with his lack of academic enthusiasm. One day, I suggested that we ought to take Robertson to lunch with us, and he might be a whole lot more understanding after meeting Gina. Pete said, "Yeah, and we might as well take Bohman so we will both be out on our ass!"

Pete's thesis was on studying factors that affected the establishment of crested wheat. Crested wheat was being used all across northern Nevada to rehabilitate degraded sagebrush ranges, but sometimes with variable success. The Bureau of Land Management had given Robertson a sizable grant to determine why the variability was occurring. He and Pete had set up a very sound study to separate out some of the factors, but Pete was having trouble with the statistical analyses, and Robertson wasn't much help. The University hadn't secured a replacement for Kidwell yet, so I was getting to help Pete with his statistics. Robertson had asked Bohman if I could help. Bohman's response was, sure he has time this semester, he's taking a very light load, besides we are paying him, at least that's what the secretary told me he said. I didn't mind, I enjoyed working with Pete; in fact, the more I worked with him, the more we became real friends. In the end we had to redesign his experiment, but the data he had collected was sufficient to allow us that privilege. True scientist might have frowned on what I structured for Pete, but we were just graduate students with a single mission in mind, obtaining the masters degree!

By Christmas I had completed all of my statistical analysis, and had actually started writing the manuscript. The data showed just how selective Alkali and Billy actually were. They selected clover over grass at every opportunity. When only grass was left, they selected the most succulent parts and species without exception. From a chemistry standpoint, these data showed that animals selected the diet that was highest in protein at all times. Although observations of this nature were in fact only preliminary in the big picture, they never the less were the first data of this nature that had ever been obtained by eliminating the bias of man; and they were significant in light of the fact that the selectivity was far greater than any had ever imagined or predicted.

The end of the semester rolled around and I got all A's, except a B in physical chemistry, but I didn't feel too bad about that because the Prof was another Weeth, he didn't give A's! Anyway my GPA for the semester turned out to be 3.8. Along with the A I had gotten from Robertson for the range field trip, my overall GPA was over 3.6. I thought about the discussion that I had had at the start of my program with Cassard and Bohman. I knew I could do it, but in all fairness they didn't; and I hadn't done much before coming to Nevada to make anybody think differently. I told Pete over a picon, I not only got the grades, but I kind of paid my dues also. He laughed and agreed, but reminded me that Robertson hounded him on a day-to-day basis a whole lot more than Bohman did me.

I hadn't used Alkali or Billy for collection since late summer, but they weathered just fine. Alkali hadn't grown much, but Billy was pushing 800 pounds. At least he had finally calmed down to the point that he only leaned on you periodically. However, they were the rage of the Washoe County school system. Hardly a week went by that I didn't have to give a demonstration of some kind or another. My favorite was with first and second graders. Alkali's fistula had enlarged to the point when he was cleaned out I could stick a small child's head inside the rumen. Didn't have many girl takers, but there just about always was a boy or two. One day a reporter from the Reno Journal was photographing the proceedings, and he got a shot of me holding this small boy up to Alkali, and all you could see was this body disappearing into the animal's side. My friends from the Animal Welfare League called again, along with several parents, as the picture really did look a lot worse than it was. One hysterical mother called Dean Adams and said the boy's head would likely be digested! Dean Adams didn't see the humor, so I stopped that practice. After all of this, Adams suggested that if we weren't going to use Alkali or Billy any more that perhaps they ought to be slaughtered. Bohman agreed. I reminded both of them of the article that came out of the confrontation with Animal Welfare, wherein it was clearly indicated that both Alkali and Billy would live to ripe old ages because of their work for science. If Adams and Bohman wanted them slaughtered, it would be totally their decision and they could answer the questions. Adams chewed on Bohman for allowing this to happen in the first place, then ordered him to make enough hay out of his, Bohman's, budget to keep the animals until they died of old age. Bohman's look was pretty serious, but I thought I was far enough along with my thesis, that he wouldn't dare do me in. That afternoon was pretty warm, so Pete and I took a six-pack of beer out to where Alkali and Billy were. We thought about pouring a beer through their fistulas so they could join in the celebration. However, in the end, they settled for some alfalfa hay and we drank the beer.

My final semester started in February of 1959. I took endocrinology for three credits from Weeth. He informed that I wouldn't get 100% this time, but I might get an A. I really only took one other class, range study techniques from the other range scientist, Dr. Kinsinger. Of course, there was the every faithful seminar, and the rest of my thesis credits. By now I was writing furiously, and Bohman was pretty much agreeing with what I was producing. In addition to my thesis, he wanted me to prepare two articles, one covering the techniques that were developed, and the second covering the grazing trials. Bohman was actually originally a dairy nutritionist, even though there weren't enough dairies in Nevada to satisfy the thirst for milk from more than a handful of Mormons. Nevertheless, he wanted to see the articles printed in the Journal of Dairy Science. Now writing a thesis was one thing, but preparing articles for peer review in a major scientific journal was far different. However, regardless of what Bohman wanted, my first and only priority was completing my master's degree, and above all else that required a thesis.

The last semester went by in a flash. Weeth was right, I didn't get 100%, but I did average 98%, which completed my challenge, I got A's in the rest of his classes. Range techniques was easy, much of it was based on elementary statistic. So for my final semester, I did finally get a 4.0 GPA. By late April, I submitted a semifinal draft for Bohman's approval. It came back looking like it had bled to death, but the corrections were more grammatical than anything else. I submitted a final copy for distribution to my graduate committee, which included besides Bohman; Jensen, an economist by the name of Glen Fulcher, and two at large faculty members chosen by the graduate dean. My final exam was scheduled on June 10, at 3:00 p.m., so I knew it couldn't last too long. The two at large faculty members wouldn't have known enough about my project in a hundred years to ask a meaningful question. Both Jensen and Bohman had already argued with me long enough to satisfy their curiosity. But Fulcher was something else. Dr. Fulcher was a socialist in my book. His contempt for Nevada ranchers using the federal lands for grazing of their livestock had come out loud and clear during Dr. Robertson's range trip across Nevada last year. He felt livestock should be greatly reduced or eliminated from grazing these lands. Nobody took him seriously, but he was asking some very difficult questions on my oral, and I wasn't quite sure how to deal with him. Oh, I had answers for his every question, but I also had to have his signature on my committee evaluation. Finally, Bohman for the first time in our relationship became my hero - he politely stepped between Fulcher and myself, and suggested that the questions in this oral exam should pertain to the thesis being evaluated, not to enhance

Dr. Fulcher's personal political philosophy - well put YEAH! With that Dr. Fulcher sort of grinned, and suggested that we should continue this discussion some day. I thought about that discussion with Jim Kilduff nearly two years ago, and momentarily logged the thought that Fulcher must be the epitome of what he was talking about.

At the end of the questioning, Bohman asked that I step out while the committee determined my fate. I knew I had passed, but there is always that nagging doubt at times like this. Anyway, I walked the hall for about ten minutes. Bohman stepped out, grabbed my hand, and proudly proclaimed that I had successfully met the qualifications for the Masters Degree from the Max C. Fleischmann College of Agriculture, University of Nevada. I shook everybody's hand, gathered up the comments written on the various copies of my thesis, promised Bohman that he would have a corrected final copy within the week, and that I would have two completed manuscripts ready for publication in the Journal of Dairy Science before the termination of my assistantship on June 30.

That night Jan and I celebrated, but not too much. We were both exhausted, so we just sort of counted up what we had accomplished. I had taken 60 hours of credit in two years, obtained an overall GPA of 3.8, taught an advanced statistics class, completed a thesis that would change the thinking of what cattle grazed forever after and would be the senior author of two peer reviewed scientific journals. Not too bad considering that I wasn't even eligible for graduate school less than a year before. "Yeah, and I can recite nearly a thousand different parts of the average alley cat", was Jan's response! With that we opened the champagne!

THE YOUNG PROFESSOR

It didn't take me more than two weeks to have my thesis ready for the necessary signatures and binding. I had been fortunate that we had located an excellent manuscript typist and she could fly. My thesis was only 79 pages long, but you had to submit five near perfect copies, four carbons plus the original. It was just about impossible for us to try to type anything of that nature on my Dad's old 1920 Underwood. It just wouldn't handle more than a carbon or two at best. I was also scheduled to make a presentation of my thesis at the regional meetings of the American Society of Animal Science, which was being held in Tucson that year. So between getting my thesis finalized, preparing slides for Tucson and a few other details, June went by pretty fast.

I had been keeping pretty mum about job opportunities. Several people, including Pete seemed quite concerned about my future. I had talked to Mr. Fairfield, but not about going back to the ranch; in fact, I didn't even want to do that. I just wanted to thank him for making me finally realize that education was important, and forcing me in that direction when I really didn't understand very much. I guess the reason Pete and others were concerned about my employment prospects was that Jan and I already had a year and a half old daughter, and she was awfully pregnant again. However, what I hadn't really discussed with anybody was the fact that I had already put in an application with the United States Forest Service, and between my background and academic training I was almost guaranteed a job, even in Nevada. The only problem with that is that I really didn't want to go to work for the Forest Service or any arm of the federal government for that matter.

I had also visited with Dr. Joe Stein on several occasions. Joe was head of the Cooperative Extension Service for Nevada. He had also indicated that he would like to hire me for a range/livestock position that he had created working out of Elko. I liked that idea a lot better than the Forest Service, but a lot of the Extension Service funding was also federal. I was also very aware of the fact that Dr. Bohman had received a grant from the Agricultural Research Service to study molybdenum toxicity, a livestock nutritional disorder that was very prevalent in western Nevada. Even though that money was also from a federal source, those funds would be totally under the control of the University. I was kind of surprised that Bohman hadn't talked to me about this project, because there was no one else that was really available and understood the system. I had suspected that he had someone else in mind, and to put it bluntly it was irritating me, so I just sat back and kept quiet. However, after considering all of the facts, I didn't really know who that could be anyway.

We went to Tucson on June 20; I rode with Dr. Stein and Dr. Weeth, as Bohman flew. It took us two days down, we were there for three days, and two days back, so it was June 27 before I showed back up on campus. At that point, I was employed for three more days, Stein had kept me informed of the status of the ARS grant and Bohman had yet to say a word. On the twenty ninth of June, I started removing my few possessions from the lab. Mike looked at me kind of funny and inquired if I had a job yet. I casually replied, "Yeah I got several opportunities, go back to the ranch, the Forest Service, and the Extension Service." I also had an opportunity to get involved in biochemistry research with an emphasis on statistical analyses at the Mayo Clinic. Dr. Harris, the nutritionist at Utah State University had heard my presentation at Tucson and knew of an opportunity at the Clinic. They had called and asked that I come for an interview in July, but I was still mulling that one over. The more I thought about it, I didn't really believe for a second that Bohman had anybody lined up for the ARS grant, and come July 1 he would be in a bind.

Sure enough, early on the morning of June 30, Bohman called me at home and asked if I would mind dropping by his office that afternoon. He was more nervous than usual, but proceeded to start telling me about the grant he was receiving as of July 1 dealing with molybdenum toxicity. He went through all the details, details that I was very familiar with already. I sat patiently and listened, although not once during this part of the discussion was a job ever talked about. Finally, after he explained how 32 head of yearling cattle would be involved in this study, and that blood, liver, hair and skeletal samples would have to be obtained on a regular basis for a year, as well as digestion trials run at least three times, he looked at me with that little boy hurt look that he had become famous for and asked if I knew of anybody that might be interested in the job. I inquired, "Wouldn't the job really start in two days?" The reply was yes, so I said, "No, I don't really know of anybody that would be available with that kind of background right now." I went on to explain how I already had several job opportunities, but I wasn't sure exactly which way I wanted to turn right now. With that I said that we had business to tend to and I had to be gone, so out I went.

That night Cassard called me at home and more or less apologized for Bohman. I laughed because I had long since figured Bohman out. Anyway, Cassard had heard about our late meeting, and had called Bohman into his office afterwards, and according to what he told me, he more or less laid the law down that Bohman would have to have somebody lined up for the job by 5:00 p.m., July 1, tomorrow, or he, Cassard, would not approve Nevada receiving the grant. The grant was for about $100,000, which was a whole lot of research dollars to put it mildly, so I was sure Cassard, as Chairman of the Department, did not want to loose it. I was pretty sure Bohman didn't either, but if he had somebody in mind for the position, that person was awful hard to see at that point in time. Cassard asked if I would mind coming to his office at 10:00 a.m. the next morning. I casually replied, "Sure, I am not doing anything tomorrow."

So 10:00 a.m., July 1 came, and I was waiting outside of Cassard's office. I could plainly hear some heated words, from both he as well as Bohman, but at the appointed hour the door opened and Cassard asked me in. On seating, Bohman asked, "We thought you might be interested in taking the job with the ARS grant and in fact heading up that whole program. If you are interested, we are prepared to offer you $400 per month."

At best, the ARS grant job was a two year temporary position. I already knew that either the Extension Service or the Forest Service would pay around $450 per month, so I looked at the two of them with about the sourest grinch mood that I could offer up, snarled something to the effect of thanks, but no thanks, and started to excuse myself. As I was turning around, I saw a look of great frustration on Bohman's face and a look on Cassard's that I read to be, "I told you so!"

Before I was out the door, there was a pleasant roll across the room, "Let's negotiate", from Bohman. So I said that I was on my way to sign a contract tomorrow morning, and really wasn't in a negotiating mood. "What's it take?" was Cassard's reply.

"Five hundred dollars per month, all the benefits that any professional staff member has and a rank of assistant professor, and the right to any permanent job opening on the staff that becomes available" as I started to exit the room.

"That's impossible", I heard gurgle from Bohman's mouth. I knew it was, couldn't have a rank of assistant professor on a temporary grant position, but the rest was all very possible.

"Now just a minute Verle, I think we can do most of that", was music to my ears from Cassard. I turned around, extended my hand to Cassard, and said I would settle on the title of Junior Nutritionist, whatever in hell that meant. Cassard shook my hand. There was a faint look of relief on his face. About right then, I realized for the first time that Bohman was tight, miserably tight, and in fact miserably Mormon tight, other than that he didn't have many problems.

So, on July 1, 1959, I became a Junior Nutritionist on the staff of the Animal Science Department, Max C. Fleischmann College of Agriculture, University of Nevada. Wow! There wasn't really time to celebrate. I knew this late in the year it would be hard to find the right kind of cattle. To make a good uniform group of 32, I would probably need at least 48. So off I went to Bill Behrens, the Extension Livestock Specialist, to enlist his aid, and out to the Main Station Farm to see my old friend Jim Hunter, the herdsman. Jim was relieved that I got the job. He could imagine all kinds of people ending up in charge of the project, none of them acceptable to his way of thinking. He also had a line on some cattle locally, here in the Truckee Meadows. Jim had built a beautiful feeding facility, where either a group of cattle could be fed, or individual cattle could be fed. We would need 32 individual pens for this project, and we would need them for a year. Fortunately, all of that was available.

Both Jim and Bill searched for acceptable cattle. I went with Bill to look at several sets of cattle in both Humboldt and Elko counties. But they were either too big, too variable, or something just wasn't right. I knew full well that if this trial was going to work, I would need a very uniform group of yearlings. In the end, Jim found exactly what I wanted, and it was right there in the Meadows. Ben Damonte, an Italian rancher who lived down at the south end of the Meadows had an excellent herd of pretty straight Hereford cattle. He had intended to keep the calves through the summer that year, but water was short in 1959, so he was worried about sufficient pasture. In the end Ben agreed to sell the calves to the University, but the price was about 10 cents over fair market for five weight heifer calves. Hunter soothed my feelings by explaining how Italians were; however, I had already learned that lesson.

All I needed to do next was find some grass hay, develop the right supplements, some of which would have added molybdenum so that we could study the dietary effects of the element. However, before the trial really started, I needed to determine how much molybdenum would make animals sick. Naturally occurring molybdenum at about 10-15 parts per million in grass would make cattle pretty sick. We had long since learned that when we tried to duplicate mineral effects, added inorganic minerals usually were far less effective than those actually in the plant tissue. Probably, they were closely attached to organic molecules, making them far more effective, and certainly that was the case with molybdenum. We shortly discovered that it took about the equivalent of 100 ppm of inorganic molybdenum to create the same toxic effects as 10-15 ppm of organic molybdenum by feeding different levels of inorganic molybdenum to young cattle.

I contracted locally for straight grass hay. It wasn't going to be harvested until about the first of August, but it looked like an awfully good stand. It was going to require about 150 tons of hay to feed the 32 animals for the full year. I was also busy preparing the supplements. We determined the approximate level of supplements that were to be fed, including the added molybdenum. We were also studying the addition of sulfate, as dietary sulfate level had a known interaction with the degree of molybdenum toxicity. The University did not have a feed mill at that time, so I located the necessary equipment at the I.H. Kent feed facility, located in Fallon, some 60 miles east of Reno. This necessitated many trips to Fallon to complete the preparation of the necessary supplements, but these trips were enjoyable, as I became good friends with the Kent family, something that I would come to appreciate in the coming years.

It's funny how the world just keeps right on going, regardless of what your individual status is. My Dad developed a full-blown case of Miners Disease, which caused him to frequently lose balance. Consequently, he could no longer do the type of work that Mr. Fairfield required. So, he left the employment of Fairfield after 16 long hard years with the man. My folks sold the Fillmore property, moved to Newport Beach in Southern California and Dad took up real estate. He also had a series of operations that more or less corrected the Miners problem, but his health would never again be as good. Fairfield developed the world's worst case of shingles that kept him pretty close to his home in Long Beach, and Jim Kilduff had a heart attack. Jim was back at the ranch, but he wasn't able to do much. Jack Davis was in charge of the cattle, and Slim took over the farming end. But you could see the end of the empire coming, and they all knew it. It wasn't six months later that the shingles got the best of Fairfield and he passed away, and within the year, Jim had a fatal heart attack. The ranch was split up and sold, with Slinkard going to the State of California for deer habitat.

When I heard that I felt a great deal of sadness, a tremendous amount of work went into making Slinkard some of the best cattle ranges in California, and it did nothing but help the deer. Now I could well imagine the cattle going, and the deer range never being as good as it was when it was run as a cattle ranch. I couldn't have imagined what Mr. Fairfield would have said about the State of California ending up with Slinkard for deer habitat. I once went to a meeting with him at the California Division of Wildlife offices in Bishop when deer were completely out of hand at Slinkard. He informed the State people that if they didn't damn soon get their deer under control, he would. He went on to say, "I'll mount two 30 caliber machine guns on the back of a 4 X 4, and when I am done, there won't be a deer left standing in Slinkard." It didn't take long after that before there were depredation hunts in both Slinkard and Antelope Valleys.

But now Fairfield was gone, Kilduff was gone, and California had the prize. Like I said, the world goes on, not necessarily in the direction that we would want. Fairfield's estate did do a lot of great things. They built a beautiful hospital in Meeker, Colorado, his and Jim's hometown. They also built a beautiful building in Santa Paula, California, for the Boys Club, with sufficient endowment to run it for a long time. As sad as I was at his passing, I guessed at least the next time I wanted to go on to more college, it would at least be my idea.

By September we had our molybdenum trial started. Daily feed consumption had to be determined, but only on a weekly basis. Animals were bled and weighed every month. Liver biopsies were obtained every three months, and a skeletal sample was obtained at the beginning, the mid-point and at the end of the 12-month trial. Blood samples were simply obtained by drawing 50 mls of blood from the jugular vein by puncture with a bleeding needle. Liver samples were obtained by a trocar and cannula inserted through the hide and directly into the liver. Actually, this method of obtaining a liver sample was more correctly called the aspiration biopsy technique. Skeletal samples were a different challenge, because nobody had ever reported any success in obtaining bone samples from live cattle. I solved that dilemma by having a large block available at the tail end of the livestock chute. I simply held the tail over the block, took a sharp hatchet, and with one quick blow I had an adequate bone sample. We just analyzed the ash, so the whole sample, hide and all was placed in the ashing oven. It worked like a charm. Subsequent samples were obtained by just working up the tail, or what was left of it. By the end of the trial, we had some pretty short tailed cattle

Digestion trials were difficult and very labor intensive. In this trial, we actually had eight treatments; so, one animal from each subgroup was selected at random for the first trial. Exact daily feed intake was measured, along with exact daily excretion of feces. Everything was sampled daily and composited for analyses. The plan was to run three digestion trials during the yearlong trial. After the first one, I didn't look forward to the others. At the last minute, based on some research out of New Zealand, we determined that we ought to determine energy balance as well as a normal digestion trial. To determine energy balances, as well as various mineral balances, total urine had to be collected in addition to feces. Fortunately, we had selected heifers instead of steers, so it was a pretty simple matter to insert a catheter into the bladder of the animals.

However, this also required the development of a urine collection device. I fabricated small inner tubes, by having the valve stem adapted to the outer curvature of the tube. We enlisted the aid of a local awning maker to fabricate a holding bag for the tube that could readily be attached to the harness that held the fecal collection sack. In the end, we had heifers that looked like they were from outer space, but the feed and water consumption remained normal, so it all worked.

After getting his degree, Pete had taken the range/livestock job in Elko that I had considered. He came to Reno every month or so, so we kept in touch. He and Gina were all finished, so we didn't go for bagels anymore, but the Santa Fe was still frequented, and a new Basque joint on Fourth Street, Louie's Basque Corner. His bartender, Manuel, could make the best picons I had ever tasted. Pete didn't let too much grass grow under his feet. He had established a number of trials of one type or another with ranchers in northeast Nevada. I had to ask, "And how many rancher's wives have you seduced so far?" A resounding none was the answer, "Do you think I am crazy?" However, it didn't take too long to find out that the office secretary and he were carrying on at a fast hump.

But Pete had other concerns. "You know, the BLM is making all sorts of waves about reallocating forage, and I don't like what I see and hear so far", he lamented. The Bureau of Land Management (BLM) actually controlled about two thirds of Nevada, with the Forest

Service controlling another major portion. Nevada was under federal domination to the tune of about 85%, or so. The BLM had grown out of the old Grazing Service, and had allocated forage, based on surveys, mainly before the war. I thought of those old maps I had found in the Ag Library when doing my original research. No matter what the problem, I bet those old ranchers were awfully happy they had seen fit to work with the State Engineer in those early years.

Forage was allocated to all the old-time ranches based on their historical use. This was done to prevent the continuation and escalation of the never-ending range wars. Now the BLM was trying to revegetate much of the degraded sagebrush ranges of northern Nevada, by planting crested wheat. In fact, they were using many of the techniques that were developed by Dr. Robertson and graduate students like Pete. But they were also talking about instituting better livestock grazing management, and resurveying forage availability, with an eye on readjusting forage allocation. However, the BLM had a long way to go, because some areas, like the Battle Mountain District, were just now being cleaned up. Pete was afraid that this process would not be well thought out, as though too many BLM employees were just not that familiar with the country. He was adamant that the whole process would not be beneficial to ranchers and the long-term stability of the ranching industry. I tended to agree, and briefly reflected on that night long ago when Jim Kilduff expressed these very concerns to me.

After another picon, our talk turned to what we had learned in college, and what in the hell we were ever going to do with all that knowledge. "you know, with what you know in range management, along with what I have learned in nutrition, as well as genetics, 'll be given the chance we could significantly improve Nevada's production of red meat", I concluded.

"I am in total agreement, discounting management blockheads, I am positive we could double, if not triple livestock production", Pete offered. "However, there is a small problem with individual ranch management, and couple that with the problems I see coming from the federal boys, and frankly, we will be lucky to hold our own in the coming years."

Pete's comments made me feel sad, maybe we had wasted our time going to college, but I couldn't handle that miserable thought. "I think we should devote our immediate careers to improving livestock production in the Silver State", as I ordered another picon.

"I agree" concluded Pete.

I had also heard some other things that bothered me, which I reiterated to Pete. The Ag. Econ Department had been conducting a series of in-house seminars, or what I guess you might call "think tanks". They were aimed at investigating how the federal lands in Nevada could be made more productive. I had always been taught that livestock grazing was just about the only profitable use of this vast landscape, and everything that I had learned to date had not changed that point of view. Sure, mining could come and go, but right then there wasn't much mining activity in Nevada. Even if it were to boom again like it did in the days of Tonopah, or even Virginia City and such places as Austin and Eureka, it would at best only affect a bit of the landscape. And no matter what, I just couldn't see tourism, or hunting and fishing ever offsetting the economic impact from livestock. In fact, livestock was so important that there were more cattle in Nevada than people, and Elko County was the second largest cow county in the United States. So, I was surprised to observe what was seemingly to emanate from these econ seminars.

"I am telling you those economic professors are looking at alternatives to livestock grazing on the federal lands", I told Pete. "The driving force seems to be Fulcher, remember him? He went on our range field trip", I asked Pete.

"How could I ever forget that son of a bitch. I took two econ classes from him. I believe he's a communist", was his terse reply.

"Well, I don't know if I would call him a communist, but he damn sure has socialist leanings. He is strongly advocating that the federal government must get control of the water on federal lands, even has gone so far to suggest that all water in Nevada should be under federal control. He feels strongly that the feds will never be able to control livestock grazing if they don't get control of the water, and he also feels strongly that the livestock industry is totally overgrazing the federal ranges at this point in time", I went on to say. We both agreed that federal domination of the water in Nevada would be a catastrophe for Nevada and states rights. As it was, Nevada owned and controlled the waters within her boundaries, like all western states. Pete went on to grumble more and more about Fulcher, which did not make me too proud about an event that occurred shortly after I signed on as a Junior Nutritionist.

"I've got to tell you about an experience that I had with Fulcher earlier this summer", I fessed up, "You remember Jack Jordon, that big Iowa farm boy that was in Ag Econ?" I asked.

"Yeah, I took several classes with Jack, I remember he was in the air force at Stead, in fact he damn near drowned up at Tahoe fishing. When he left the air force, he enrolled at Nevada. I think he was a year or two behind me", was Pete's response.

So, I told Pete about my experience with Jack and Fulcher, early in July, and I wasn't too proud of it either. For years, when I was working at the OIL, sometime each summer I would go fishing on the south fork of the Carson River. It was pretty easy for me to get to. I just went to the top of the ridge on the west side of Antelope Valley; there was a good road to the top. There was a trail that led off through a big group of pines, the locals called them the Jack Benny pines, for whatever reason, I never learned. Anyway, after breaking out of the Pines, it was a pretty straight shot down to the river. I always called it the South Fork, but some referred to it as the East Fork. Anyway, once you hit the river, it was good fishing all the way. About five or so miles upstream there were some of the biggest beaver dams that I had ever seen, and another three or four miles above that were some small lakes. This spot was really back in the Sierra's, and the fishing was unbelievable. I never packed fish out; I just ate what I couldn't release, and fished till I was tired.

"Well, last May, Jack asked me if I knew where there was excellent fishing, and I told him about my old fishing grounds on the South Fork of the Carson River. He went on to ask me if I would take him and a friend. I liked Jack, but I sure wanted to know who his friend was before I showed anybody this fishing spot", I related to Pete. "I was surprised that his friend was Fulcher, and I said I wasn't too sure about that. Jack suggested that if he could take Fulcher, it might be beneficial to his grade in Econ 405, which was the really hard senior econ class that econ students had to take. I knew better, but I finally agreed to take both of them", I went on to relate.

Well, I did take them both. It was beautiful weather, and the fishing just couldn't have been any better. We caught nothing but 12-to-16-inch trout. I think they are what they call Paiute trout, but it sure was fun. As usual I kept only what I damaged to bad to release, and Jack did likewise. We soon had more fish than we could eat, so I just sat down alongside the river and enjoyed the scenery. But I noticed Fulcher kept fishing, and I also noticed that he didn't throw very many back. That evening we had a good fish fry; I really hadn't paid attention to what Fulcher had. The next morning, I figured that we should head back about 10, because it was about a five hour hike to the car, and the following morning I had to be at the office. The limit in those days was 15. I guessed Fulcher wanted to take a limit home. After breakfast he said he wanted to fish a bit more. Well, when we got ready to throw our packs on, he had thirty trout altogether. Jack and I hadn't kept any, so Fulcher asked me if I would take his extra limit. My response was pretty negative, and probably about right then and there was when he and I began to agree to disagree. Anyway, Jack consented to pack the extra limit out, so Fulcher was legal. "Like I said I wasn't very proud of this event, but it kind of shows the type of person Fulcher is", I concluded.

Pete said, "Yeah, like I said, he is a God damned communist!" That was before I told Pete that Jack didn't get to keep any of the extra fish that he packed out for Fulcher.

Both Pete and I agreed that we had better keep our eyes on the developments on federal lands affecting livestock grazing but we also agreed that as a neophyte extension agent and a "Junior Nutritionist" there was not much we could do at this stage of the game.

Along about January of 1960, some six months after I had been employed by the University, Mike Wade got interested in starting his own testing lab. Mike was originally from Pocatello, Idaho, and he wanted to return. Actually, I always thought he was growing tired of the domination of Bohman, not only in his work, but I gathered in their particular Ward, to which they both belonged, that the domination spilled over into that category as well. At any rate, Mike had saved enough money to purchase a small on-going testing lab in Pocatello, so he made the decision to go home, which of course meant he was leaving the University. It didn't take Bohman long to come to me with his usual grin and inquire if I minded taking over the lab after Mike left.

The ARS grant job was a full-time position to put it mildly. Also, it was certainly my impression that Mike's position was also a full-time job, even though he was classified as technician. I indicated to Bohman that I would be interested in taking over the responsibility under one condition only, and that a new professional position be created which was a permanent position, and it be considered to be filled with an assistant professor level, with tenure track consideration. I further indicated that I would take over the responsibilities of the lab, along with continuing the ARS grant job, if I could do it under those considerations. As usual, Bohman became nervous, scratched his nose and said that's impossible. My response was, "OK, who is going to coordinate and conduct all of your chemical analyses?' which was about all Mike did. Over the next two weeks numerous meetings occurred between Bohman and Cassard, as well as other staff members. Everyone located on campus in Animal Science had Ph.D. degrees, with the exception of Bill Behrens, so I guessed that was somewhat the cause of all of this flurry of activity. Dr. Baily, Dr. Kidwell's replacement, was a real stickler on this sort of thing, being fresh out of Nebraska with a brand new Ph.D. in hand. Hunter, and some of the extension people like Behrens thought the predicament that I had placed the department in was hilarious. I didn't have time to even worry about my proposal, take it or leave it; I had a very difficult and interesting trial to conduct.

Along about February one, Cassard called me into his office to discuss the whole thing, at least this time Bohman wasn't there. He started by saying, "I want to hire you exactly like you outlined. I believe that you would be an immense addition to this staff. However, everybody is concerned about you not having a Ph.D. I don't know what your plans are, but if you could show that your intent is to obtain a Ph.D., and how you might go about it, I believe that I can convince the staff to support you obtaining this new position as an Assistant Professor." I had to laugh to myself, my world had apparently replaced Fairfield with Cassard, but in all actuality I was already one up on everybody.

When I had presented my paper in Tucson last summer, Dr. J.E. Oldfield, the nutritionist at Oregon State had said that he would love to have me come to Corvallis and work on my Ph.D. if I ever so desired. Shortly after the molybdenum trial got started, Jan and I went to Corvallis to visit Oldfield concerning his proposal. I went over the molybdenum work that I was going to conduct, and he felt that the

Graduate School at Corvallis would certainly accept that effort for a Ph.D. thesis. Additionally, I could take up to six hours per semester as a staff member while at Reno, so in essence it would only take one year at Corvallis to accomplish my Ph.D. When I showed the paper work from my visit to Oregon to Cassard, he indicated that was about all he needed. So, by March 1, 1960, I became an Assistant Professor and Assistant Nutritionist, even got a nice bump in salary to $600 per month, and it was a permanent position with the possibility to receive tenure. Again, I had to laugh, it had not been until July 1, 1958 that the University would even recognize me as a legitimate graduate student. When Pete came to town next, he, Jan and I went to the new Nugget, owned by another Basque, John Ascuaga, to celebrate with a fine dinner and show.

It wasn't long before I realized other academic requirements came along with promotional success. Dr. Charles Seufferle, an Economist by training, and currently the Dean of Instruction for the College, sent a message down to me that he would like to visit. I liked Seufferle, he seemed very reasonable, and very concerned about the welfare of the students. However, not having any teaching assignment tacked on to my contract, I could hardly understand why he wanted to see me, but up to the wheelhouse on the second floor I went.

"Good morning, Mr. Hope, may I just call your Terry?" he asked.

"Certainly" I replied.

"I really don't know very much about you, except that the scuttlebutt around the building is that you are a hard worker, willing to take on new challenges, and after reviewing your transcript while earning your masters, its pretty obvious you are a good student" he continued. "Because I think you are a good student, and I think you probably know quite a bit about Nevada agriculture, and I suspect you care about the welfare of students, I was wondering if you would like to participate on the College Admission team?"

Well, I didn't know how to answer that one, for sure, in my case the College Admission Team was simply made up of Cassard and Bohman. I didn't really want to go through that history, so I just simply asked, what is required?

"Not much, we get about 50 to 75 new applicants each year, mostly just out of high school. The Admission Team reviews each applicant, making sure they have a high school degree, that their grade point average is sufficiently high to allow admission, then make recommendations based on their test scores as to if they have to take remedial English and Math or not. Not much else. Why I thought you might be interested, it gives you a leg up on the new students, and it might give you some idea of possible part-time employees. I see your new job description, as well as running the lab for the likes of Bohman might well require you to have some additional part time help."

"It seems like you have me figured out as to job requirements. I am pretty sure you are right, I will need some help, and it's an excellent chance for students to both learn something academically, as well as monetarily", I concluded.

"Great, you will accept then? And if you do, I don't think the additional work will be overwhelming. I usually have about four staff members help me review applicants, starting in early spring, so no one reviews more than 15 or so applicants. We usually meet as a group, some time before high school graduation dates, so that we can notify the individuals of acceptance by this University for acknowledgement at their individual graduations. All told, it won't take more than 20 or so hours of work, and I'll bet you will enjoy it", Seufferle concluded.

Well, I thought to myself, if I am really going to be part of this organization, this is a good place to start. And I did, but my career in admissions only lasted for a few years until other obligations just made my participation impossible. But it did allow me the "leg up" just as Seufferle suggested, and it allowed me to find potential employees, as well as meet some mighty interesting folks, folks with long, long histories in Nevada.

Bohman had a thousand different projects going on, none of which were well coordinated. As I dug into them, I began to realize that there wasn't much that I could do without some help. Nevada was growing. In fact, the Animal Science Department had nearly doubled in student enrollment since my initial appearance. So, I suggested to Dr. Bohman that we take all of the funding for his projects, put it together, and create a separate fund for student laboratory assistants to work in the nutrition lab. For once, he agreed, and not even with the slightest argument. I shortly found two young ladies, both pursuing a degree in Animal Science, although they were both freshmen, to work in the lab. One was Jim Hunter's daughter, Virginia, and the other was from a ranch in Humboldt County, Allie Tipton. Within a couple of weeks, I had them both up and running. My commitment to them was simple - they got keys to the building, they could work as many hours as they wanted to, providing that they maintained at least a B average. Furthermore, they would become my laboratory supervisors in coming years, overseeing new students as work and funds became available. I promised them both they would make enough money to totally finance their education in Nevada, and it did. Both stayed with me until they graduated, and in fact Virginia even stayed around to get a master's degree.

Getting Virginia and Allie on the payroll freed up my time to sort out Bohman's projects, and it freed up his time to publish his results. This made us both happy. In addition to the molybdenum project, he had various grants to evaluate feed additives, and was also doing work with both fat and alcohol as livestock feed additives and had a significant grant from the Atomic Energy Commission to study certain effects of radiation on the test site. This was the project that Mike Wade had been working on, and had successfully completed his master's degree in. Mike developed a technique to measure strontium in animal tissue. The reason that strontium was of interest is that it is a normally occurring element in all tissue where calcium is present, such as bone. However, strontium is only present in minute amounts and at an almost constant ratio with the amount of calcium present. The problem with strontium was not really strontium as it normally occurs, rather an isotope of strontium, strontium 90. Strontium 90 was one of the worse isotopes to occur because of a nuclear reaction, as it had a half-life of something like 1,800 years. Thus, if you got strontium 90 contamination from an event, or even an accident, it was there for the rest of your life to put it mildly. I was fascinated by the work, although limited, that Bohman was involved in with the AEC. However, until I sorted out all the other projects and got the lab up to speed, I sure didn't have time to worry about the Test Site.

Bohman also had a variety of nutrition trials going on at the Knoll Creek Research Station located in northern Elko County. I had briefly toured that facility in Robertson's whirlwind tour of Nevada, but while there I had gotten to know the Station Superintendent, Clark Torell. Clark ran a tight ship: He had to keep Bohman organized, but he had four young boys and one stout wife, so help was available. I shortly called Clark after reviewing all that Bohman had going on. We couldn't work much out over the phone, but we made arrangements for me to spend a week at Knoll Creek as soon as possible. Bohman also had nutrition trials going on in southern Nevada in the Caliente area. These trials were financed by the Atomic Energy Commission grant, but according to my way of thinking they didn't have much to do with atom bomb testing, although the area of work was adjacent to the east side of the test site. A fellow by the name of Henry Melinde was in charge of the fieldwork there. I spoke with Henry over the phone, but it was pretty obvious that he wasn't really thrilled by what he was doing. I made a mental note that there would be problems with this area of work in the near future, and I had better pay attention.

The rest of 1960 was a whirlwind of activity. By the end of 1960, I somehow had accumulated six publications, so I was winning the "publish or perish" war. We now had two other lab workers in addition to Virginia and Allie. I was dealing with the Nevada Department of Fish and Game for a grant to study the relationship between mule deer and cattle, and Bohman was happy. Even Alkali and Billy were doing well, although Alkali's fistula kept getting larger, which worried me as it was becoming increasingly difficult to keep tightly closed. This made his digestive system inefficient, and he had actually lost weight, down to about 600 pounds. Billy, however, just kept getting fatter. Collectively, they ate about 7-8 tons of feed per year. Bohman bitched a bit about the expense, but whenever I mentioned Dean Adams, he would quiet down.

At the end of 1960, Cassard announced that he was returning to his native Texas to go into private consulting work. Dean Adams promptly replaced him with Bohman. I was glad I was where I was at now, because I don't think I would have wanted to enter Nevada with the GPA I had from Poly and face Bohman, both as the nutritionist and Department Chairman. It didn't take Bohman long to realize that being Department Chairman placed him in a whole new range of work. Along about May of that year, he came to the conclusion that he would not be able to continue his current teaching level, so he inquired if I would be interested in teaching the beginning nutrition course, Feeds and Feeding in the fall of 1961. I agreed, but not until he promised that I would have more funding for student labor. So, by the fall of 1961, or more correctly July 1, I was not only an Assistant Professor and Assistant Nutritionist, but I had both research and teaching assignments as well. It slowly but surely began to dawn on me; I was a real professor at a real institution of higher education and doing what I had always loved more than anything else, working full time with cattle. And, most important of all, I was in Nevada, and I was truly becoming a Nevadan! We now had two daughters, and of all things, Jan was again pregnant.

When Pete heard that I would be teaching the beginning nutrition class, he called and said that he would come to Reno and help celebrate. I needed more time to work, not celebrate, but with Pete, you couldn't really say no. So off for picons, this time at Louie's. Pete brought me up to date on all that he had going on in Elko and the status of the livestock industry. Although Pete was in a good mood, he didn't seem too positive about what the future held, at least for those operations using federal lands, which of course in Nevada was just about everybody. I told him about how Bohman had lightened up on me now that he was chairman. "At the rate you are going in a few years you will be the nutritionist", was his encouraging remark.

"Nope, that isn't my goal, I just want to spend another few years, get all these messes cleaned up, then I want to find something in private industry," which was really how I felt about then.

Pete indicated that his dad had been making rumblings about him returning to the ranch. Pete never really was thrilled about the sheep industry, but their ranch was gradually converting to cattle, so he was more inclined to consider returning. We reminisced about the two-year ordeal that we both went through to get our degree, then Pete reminded me of somebody that I had just about forgotten about, "You remember that Ryan guy that became student body president?" How could I have forgotten, so I reminded him of our one escapade into student politics.

When Harry Ryan ran for student body president, he ran against a student named Don Travis. Travis was in education, but he came from an agricultural background, so all the aggies backed him for the election. Another graduate student, Bob Ferraro, who was more into politics than either Pete or I insisted that we had to help Don, if for no other reason than we all were aggies. Bob was an aggie all right, in fact he came from a ranch in Paradise Valley. Bob also was working with Robertson, but it was on a project dealing with the revegetation of parts of the Humboldt River basin near Battle Mountain. Bob had this idea that we ought to put a sign on top of the old Ag building on campus, proclaiming to one and all that Travis must be the next ASUN president. I guess the reason that I got involved was because I had keys to the building, sometimes I think I will never learn.

At the appointed hour, near midnight, we all met at the rear of the building, alongside Manzanita Lake. I opened the door, and Bob, Pete and I made our way to the third story. There was a narrow stairway, through a closet, that went to an outside door on the roof, but Bob had made his sign on a 4 X 8 sheet of plywood, and at first, we didn't think it would fit through the closet. But with enough effort just about anything is possible, so we made it to the roof, and to the front edge of the building, where Bob had planned to put the sign. He had brought all of the necessary hardware, so in short order we had Mr. Travis's sign perched on the front edge of the building. We started to clean up and retreat, so that we could observe our handy work from the Quad level. Pete was starting to get nervous, and frankly so was I, but not Bob. He backed up a bit, and said as soon as we were done, he would buy a round at the Lil Wal. And with that he disappeared with a cracking, crunchy sound, followed by a sort of woosh as his body went through the roof.

We heard an awful thud, followed by a groan. "At least he still sounds alive", was all Pete could muster as we headed back down the stairs. By our reckoning he landed in the biology classroom, but the door was locked. We both were astounded to find that Bob opened the door as soon as we jiggled the handle. "Come in gentlemen, what took you so long?", was his half serious greeting. Bob had landed right on his feet in front of the front row of desks, on the hardwood. He said he went to his knees, kind of knocked the wind out of himself, but that was all of the harm. Those classrooms had a 12-foot ceiling, I remembered from my days in the library. Well, Bob was OK, but it did seem strange seeing stars through the ceiling. Pete took out his flashlight, survived the damage, which wasn't much, some plaster, some laths, some broken wire, and some old tarpaper and asphalt. We scrapped it all together into a pile, built a small cross out of two lathes, Bob wanted to place a sign saying here lies the remains of Harry Ryan, but Pete and I out voted him. In fact, all I wanted was out about then, and Pete wasn't far behind me.

Pete and I about died laughing every time we relived that story. Nothing really came of it, except, the President made Don pay for the damage to the building. Poor Don never knew anything about it, much less who fell through the ceiling. However, unfortunately our efforts didn't turn the tide, because Harry won the election. "You know, I never realized it, but Harry was in ROTC, and when he graduated, he went into the army as a second lieutenant", Pete brought me up to date "But I just read in the Reno paper last week that he got some big scholarship or something, and he will enroll at Hastings College to become a lawyer", Pete went on. I had trouble visualizing that guy as a lawyer, but Pete added, "I'll bet you right now that within five years of graduating, he will become active in statewide politics." I didn't want to bet Pete, because deep down I kind of suspected the same thing, and I remembered Jim Kilduff's warning, "Its awfully easy for us to send somebody to Washington that would be better off in jail"!

Pete had to head back to Elko, and I had to start getting geared up to teach in the upcoming fall semester. It's kind of funny, in primary or secondary education, it takes at least four years of intense education to prepare you for teaching. But at the university level all it takes is the right set of circumstances. I had never had an actual education class of any type, ever, but I felt that I would be a good teacher. I had lots of bad ones, and I made up my mind that no matter what I wouldn't fall into that category.

The molybdenum trial had been completed by mid summer of 1961, but it hadn't been easy. The trial required my presence on a near day-to-day basis, because if something could go wrong it would. But the trial was completed successfully, however, due to all the other activities that I had gotten involved in, the analyses of the data would take some time. At the start of the trial, I hadn't really figured out how much work would actually be involved, but I knew it would be plenty. In addition to taking care of the 32 animals on a day-to-day basis a significant number of observations would be obtained requiring eventually both chemical and statistical analyses. In fact, well over 6,000 individual observations were recorded including about 4,500 individual chemical analyses. Due to the fact that some of the chemical techniques had never been accomplished at Nevada, just the development of that phase of the study would take over a year of time. Although the ARS grant for this study was for only two years, it actually turned out that the results were not complete until 1965, or nearly five years after the start of the trial. However, with all the other activities that I was becoming involved in, the time frame didn't bother me, and it didn't bother the ARS, as long as I gave them updates every six months or so.

After learning that I was going to start teaching come September of '61, my priorities somewhat changed. To become prepared to teach the beginning animal nutrition course, Feeds and Feeding, I reviewed Bohman's notes to see what he had been covering. In addition to Feeds and Feeding, animal science students also had to take an advanced nutrition course, which was still going to be taught by Bohman. I didn't want to infringe on his territory, but it was obvious that the way he had been teaching, Feeds could stand some modernization. I chose to continue to use the same text, Feeds and Feeding, written by F.B. Morrison. The most recent edition was the 22nd edition, printed in 1956. Simply put, there just wasn't a better text for this course, even if the most current edition was already five years old. In addition to what was normally taught in Feeds, I decided that a lot better basic knowledge of nutrition wouldn't hurt anybody. A lot of students from other majors, like Agriculture Education and Economics took Feeds, but that was the end of the line for most of them. Also, Feeds was a junior level class, and it was my opinion that in addition to being a real "science" course, it should be a course that students wouldn't forget for a while. However, for me to teach such a course would require a lot of education on my part as well. So, a goodly share of the summer of 1961 was spent on a self-education course in both nutrition and biochemistry. I also promised myself that if I were ever to really become a true "Nevadan", then it was imperative that Feeds must relate to conditions in Nevada, so a lot of time was spent understanding how Nevada's farm animals, mostly range cattle, met their nutritive requirements. In that regard I got Pete and a couple of other extension agents to give me a crash course on how they viewed ranching in Nevada, at least from a nutritional aspect.

I also had scheduled a two-week trip to the Knoll Creek Station in August, before school started, so that Clark Torell could educate me on all that Bohman, as well as other researchers, had been doing. By the end of that two-week period I had become pretty well indoctrinated on the philosophy of the range research going on at Nevada, at least as to how it related to beef cattle. There was some agronomy research as well, but there was pitiful little water for irrigation at Knoll Creek, so the agronomic work was relegated to just plot work. Pete came up from Elko for a few days while I was there, as he was also not really familiar with the Knoll Creek work. Clark and his boys had done a masterful job of making Knoll Creek work, especially in light of the fact that his budget was totally controlled by Bohman and Robertson. It was obvious that very little was spent on maintaining the facility. Clark did just about everything that was needed, and if he couldn't make it, it better be available at surplus, or they would do without. It seemed strange to me that Knoll Creek, which was actually on loan from a local grazing association, only consisted of a few acres of ground for research, along with a grazing permit. All told, the Station could not support more than 50 to 75 cows, along with a few yearlings. Hay, for winter feeding, had to be purchased and trucked in.

Pete, who accompanied me on the Knoll Creek trip, felt that he could work cooperatively with ranchers in either Elko or Humboldt Counties, and actually come up with a more realistic setting for most of the research that I might be interested in. I tended to concur, especially in light of the fact that between Bohman, Robertson and Jensen, there wasn't a cow, or a blade of grass that wasn't already committed to ongoing research at Knoll Creek. However, I didn't go to Knoll Creek to start new research, just to understand what Bohman was up to. The night before Pete left, he, Clark and I sat up into the wee hours of the morning discussing the future of range animal research in Nevada. We all agreed it was of vital importance and somehow, Nevada had to get its hands on a real experiment station. However, as Clark pointed out, getting rid of Knoll Creek would be difficult. A local rancher, Ira Boise, who was also a prominent Elko County Commissioner, with eyes set on Carson City, seemed to take a great deal of pride in the fact that the University of Nevada maintained an experiment station next to his ranch. I casually observed that Ira also seemed to enjoy the use of the surplus D-8 caterpillar, as well as the Cat Road grader that belonged to the station. Clark didn't want to talk about that, and Pete thought better.

One week after returning to Reno, classes started, and I started teaching, Monday, Wednesday and Friday's at 10:00 A.M. The first lecture was spent familiarizing myself with the students, as well as explaining the class procedures to them. I could tell by the glances and raised eyebrows that the students were beginning to realize that this class might be a bit different, and very likely harder, than what the grapevine had led them to believe. I had eight students, all men, and from all over Nevada. Most were from ranches, two from both Elko and Humboldt counties, three from the Reno area and one traveling military veteran. We had quizzes every Friday, covering the information generated during the week. I didn't like the mid-term and final concept, so I opted to have four tests plus a final, as I felt with the amount of material, we would be covering more tests would give the students a fairer chance.

We didn't waste much time, jumped right into the chemical analyses of feedstuffs, and the digestive process in various types of farm animals. I introduced a lot of math, as well as chemistry, but my first quizzes were encouraging by the fact that all eight students were with me. However, you shouldn't let success go to your head. I liked to throw in a little philosophy along with the biochemistry and everything else. At any rate, I had developed a flow chart of where the feed for Nevada's approximately 700,000 head of cattle must come from. Nevada is 85% owned by the federal government, much of that land is managed by the BLM and the Forest Service. I explained how ranchers have the right to graze the forage from those federal lands, which in fact made up a large percentage of the nutritional requirements of these 700,000 head of cattle. Now Pete and I had had a number of philosophical discussions about this very point, and I was gradually coming to the conclusion that the ranchers' right to continue to graze these lands might someday be challenged. Certainly, the handwriting was already on the wall that that day might come sooner than later.

As I said, several of my students came from ranching families, so they were well aware of the fact that their parents grazed cattle on federal lands, although a fair value was also paid to the government for the right to graze these lands. But, as I said I like to throw out a little bit of philosophy, and I did just that. In covering this nutritional "flow chart", I casually mentioned that by the year 2000, that in all likelihood, grazing on these federal lands might be greatly curtailed, if not actually eliminated. Several students raised their eyebrows at that comment, but one came clear out of his seat, John Albisu from up McDermitt way. John demanded to know how I could make such a statement. I tried to explain that I didn't support this concept, but based on what I had been hearing, and certain things that were happening, I suggested that it was a distinct possibility. That didn't suffice for John, it was his position that we shouldn't even talk about such things, they were simply impossible. I promptly pointed out that politics governs federal things to say the least, and one day Nevada, and the other western states might not have the political power to protect livestock grazing on these federal lands. John was about to bust a gasket, but the bell rang so our discussion ended, or so I thought.

About a week passed, John had calmed down, as I was giving enough biochemistry to keep his mind off my philosophical discussions, but in my mailbox was a notice from Dean Adams that I was to appear in front of the College Academic Council concerning material that I was covering in my Feeds and Feeding class. And the appointed time was that afternoon at 4:00 P.M., upstairs in the conference room. Without any other knowledge, I assumed that this must have something to do with my comments concerning grazing on the federal lands. However, the timing, or lack of time led me to believe that it might be closer to the Spanish Inquisition!

Well, at 4:00 P.M. sharp, I appeared in front of the academic council. The council was made up of senior professors, Bohman, Robertson, Jensen, a soil scientist by the name of Larry Dunn, an economist, Edmund Barmettler and a few others that I didn't know at that time. Dr. Seufferle, the Dean of instruction chaired the meeting, but it was obvious that Dean Adams was the driving force behind this fiasco! At least Seufferle had liked me enough to put me on the admission team. I was pretty sure that I was expendible in Dean Adam's mind. And he started off by indicating that a complaint had been filed with the Council indicating that I was straying from the subject material in my class, namely I was not teaching about Feeds and Feeding, but was covering such things as the future of grazing on federal lands, a subject more correctly taught in such classes as range or possibly Ag econ. At this point I wasn't really taking all of this too seriously, so I jokingly asked what the penalty was if I was found guilty. I guess this sort of didn't amuse Dean Adams because he told me in terms that were pretty clear, if I continued such nonsense my teaching contract, in fact my entire contract would become null and void. "You're not on tenure young man, and as such you can be terminated without any further notice", was his terse response. Well, I doubted that, and frankly at that point I didn't really give a damn either, so I opened up with both barrels.

Without making reference to Fulcher, I pointed out how there were staff members, far more senior than I, right here in this building, that were already calling for a complete review of grazing on federal lands, with the possibility of livestock removal. I also pointed out what was going on in both the BLM and the Forest Service in regard to the future of grazing. Further, I pointed out how a major group of people right here in the Reno area, the Washoe County Sportsmen's Association, made up mainly of doctors, dentists and lawyers, an affluent and outspoken group with strong political connections, was calling for the removal of livestock along the entire eastern Sierra front, from Bishop, California to Susanville, California, including all of the area in Nevada, as being necessary for the preservation of the Sierra mule deer herd.

Then I read directly from the University of Nevada Catalogue, "Feeds and Feeding, Animal Science 303; a basic course surveying the dietary needs of farm animals. Lectures (3) to cover feeds, feed composition, digestion and metabolism of common farm animals and related species. Survey of sources of feedstuffs for farm animals common to Nevada and surrounding western states." Finally, I quoted the University of Nevada code and by-laws as they related to academic freedom. "Basically, the University describes academic freedom as the right to discuss anything related to the professor's area of expertise; in other words in my case, if I perceive that the major source of feedstuff available for cattle and sheep in Nevada, range forage from government controlled lands, is in jeopardy then I have every right in the world, as guaranteed by the

University's code and by-laws, to discuss that information, which is precisely what I did." With that I rested my case.

It was obvious that Dean Adams did not like problems. When John Albisu, or whomever, complained to him that I was discussing things which should not be discussed in my class, he perceived it as a problem. Certainly, it was not the first problem that I had presented the good Dean with, and I suppose, that weighed somewhat heavily in my disfavor. However, I trusted Seufferle, and I didn't think any of the senior professors would vote against me. Barmettler, the Econ professor raised his hand to be recognized. He was the one that I was unsure of, so I expected as Barmettler went so did my fate. I said a silent prayer to the effect that I sure to hell hoped he didn't share his colleague, Fulcher's, thoughts about livestock grazing on the Federal domain. The thoughts whirling through my head at that moment dealt with the travesty of having come so far in such short order only to lose it all simply because I said what needed to be said.

Seufferle recognized Barmettler and I held my breath. "I believe Professor Hope has raised a most valid point, a point that I have attempted to raise on several occasions in front of our faculty only to be put down. Hope is entirely correct, the winds of change are in the air, and that change does not bode well for our livestock producers. Believe me, if the right to graze federally controlled lands in Nevada is lost, we would not only loose our livestock industry, but ultimately there would be pitifully little reason to even support a College of Agriculture, because the livestock industry, the range livestock industry, is just about all the agriculture that Nevada ever has had, or ever well have for that matter. I congratulate Professor Hope for having the courage to have brought up a subject that is politically unpopular at this time, and I urge my fellow professors to fully support his efforts." With that Barmettler sat down, and I breathed a great sigh of relief.

Immediately Jensen, Robertson and Bohman, who knew me best of all, rose to support Barmettler, and nobody chose to speak in opposition. I had nothing more to say, Seufferle adjourned the Council, he and several others congratulated me on my presentation, indicating full support. Adams left, never saying a word. In hindsight, those events were instrumental in my teaching career, for I never thought twice about what I might lecture on again. For sure, I wasn't preaching revolution nor was I talking about things that did not relate to agriculture, but from that point on I wasn't afraid of the politics of the situation. And in hindsight I had to believe it had a great impact on the staff and the future of the College. It was but a few months before Dean Adams chose to retire, and I couldn't help noticing that some professors started getting greater class enrollments because their material became more controversial. And as far as John Albisu, I never said a word about this matter again. To this day I don't know for a fact whether he was the one that filed the complaint, nor did I care. In hindsight, there were still cattle grazing federal lands by the year 2000, although the total number was only about 50% of what it was in 1961 and the trend was definitely down. So, I was right, but also, I wasn't right, I probably just should have said by the year 2025, or possibly 2050, not 2000. As to Albisu, he got a B in my course, and eventually became pretty successful in McDermitt, but not in the livestock business, rather as a distributor of petroleum products. As to the family ranch, that was only diminished with time by the actions of the federal government over the years.

By the time the semester ended, February 1962, I don't know who was the tiredest, myself or the students. I overshot my goal to teach a hard but educational course. It indeed was both, but where I made the greatest mistake was on the final exam. Up to that point most of my tests had been pretty simple, at least from the standpoint of the type of questions, fill in's, true or false, etc. However, in the final I asked about twenty questions, and they were all essays. I had provided five pages for answers, which was totally insufficient. Some of the kids wrote upwards to twenty pages during the four-hour exam period, which I allowed to go for five hours. The problem for me was that my exam time was towards the end of exam week, and I only had about two days to post grades after all of the exams were turned in. To fairly correct an exam of this nature required about two to three hours on my part per exam. I finished in time, and the effort was worth it, although the scuttlebutt around the halls was that I got what I deserved. But so did my students, four A's, three B's and one C. But more importantly, I fully believed that I stimulated their interests in education; eventually two went on to graduate work, with both becoming themselves eventually professors. One became a veterinarian, two became very successful in business, and three returned to a successful life running their family ranches. Although there were always complaints at the time about the difficulty of my course, I noticed over the years those complaints tended to disappear, in fact after about twenty years of hindsight most of those that I maintained contact with seemed to feel pretty strongly that their kids needed teachers like myself, which in itself made the effort all worth while.

After Feeds was over, I had to get caught up on Bohman's work, as well as my molybdenum trial. I had also been pestering the Nevada Fish and Game Department that we needed to do some research to determine the actual relationship between deer and cattle. I fully believed that relationships were far more compatible than competitive, but I needed facts to make my case. I had been bending the ear of the big game specialists with the Department, Nick Papez, along with their public relation specialist, Dave Mathis and Gene McDowel. They seemed to agree a project that I envisioned was indeed needed, but nobody was sure where the money would come from, however, I was pretty sure it wasn't going to come from the College, at least not the lion's share. They liked the idea of using fistulated cattle to see what the cattle were eating, and we guessed that we could sacrifice a few deer in key locations to possibly attempt to see what the deer were consuming. However, a project like this had a lot of bridges to cross so it had to remain in the talking phase for a while.

Up to this point I still had Alkali and Billy, in fact we had used them several times in the Feeds class to demonstrate a number of points. However, poor old Alkali's fistula continued to get more difficult to maintain, which resulted in a weakened situation. He caught pneumonia during the winter of 1962 and no amount of antibiotics cured the problem. After he died, Jim wanted to have him disposed at the rendering works, but I said no way. He was born at the Main Station Farm, he lived most of his life there, and he died there. Along with Billy he had undoubtedly become one of the most famous beef animals in the history of the University, much less Nevada, so I wanted him buried on the Main Station! I didn't really want to get permission from Dean Adams about this, due to recent events, there was some question in my mind if he would side with me, I didn't want to bother Bohman, so I presented Jim with a pouch of his favorite tobacco and barrowed his backhoe and buried him myself. It's difficult to understand shedding a tear for a common crossbred steer, but that day I did. It was a cold February day, and a zepher was coming. After the hole was dug and I had carefully placed Alkali at the bottom, I reminisced about what an impact both he and Billy had had on my life. Sometimes it's just damned tough to let go. But anyway, I still had Billy, the only problem he had was that he now weighed close to a thousand pounds.

By March, I had just about caught up on everything, with the exception of the molybdenum work. Henry Melindy, Bohman's man taking care of his work on the test site announced that he was going to quit. Bohman didn't know what to do, but rather to continue the work, change directions or whatever. I suggested that, due to the fact that I had never been to the test site, it might be good for me to go meet with the AEC officials, review the work and look at our options. Bohman agreed. So, I made arrangements to fly to Las Vegas, and meet with the officials at their downtown offices. I didn't want to go to the test site; besides I didn't have clearance, which took some time. So, in mid-March, 1962 I flew to Las Vegas to meet with those people in charge of the monitoring work on the Site. Little did I realize that out of those meetings would come events, events that would forever change not only my life, but perhaps most importantly, how I would view the government, or at least those responsible for carrying out governmental functions. Events that would cloud my life and my thinking for the rest of my days on this earth.

ALL IS NOT WELL IN NEVADA
(AND UTAH FOR THAT MATTER)

It was hot, even for Vegas in March, over ninety degrees. It had been a cold, windy day when I left Reno that afternoon, probably about what we called forty-forty, forty degrees and a forty mile an hour wind out of the northwest. So when I finally walked out of the airport building at McCarran to the cab I about wilted. I had made arrangements to stay at the Plaza, where I was to meet with the AEC officials for breakfast. The Plaza was old, but clean. It was downtown so I didn't get to see the strip. However, I figured this wouldn't be my only trip to Vegas. Besides, in those days the strip was really just beginning, and was nothing compared to what it would become in time. Living in Reno didn't make me any more eager to gamble in Vegas, so after dinner and a drink watching the lounge entertainment, it was early to bed. I was up at 6:00 A.M., as our breakfast meeting was scheduled for seven.

There were three officials from the AEC, all basically in the monitoring division; Jim Fountain, project leader, Gary Smith, a veterinarian in charge of all animal work on the site, and Tom Brech, who, I pretty soon figured out did the work. Breakfast was cordial, mostly discussing my work with fistulated cattle, and what Bohman was trying to accomplish. The Atomic Energy Commission had a major office building right downtown, but the monitoring offices were in an adjacent high rise on Fremont. After breakfast Tom accompanied me back to my room, and then on to the monitoring offices. It was about nine when we all sat down for business.

181

The first thing on the menu was Bohman's work. Fountain indicated some displeasure, as the AEC had given rather sizable grants to Bohman with the intent that the cattle Melindy was working with over east of the site in the Delamar area were to be used to measure fallout. Instead, Bohman had emphasized work evaluating various supplements with these cattle. However, it was also his intent to monitor skeletal strontium as time went on. Since Mike Wade had left, little progress had been made on this portion of the project, and that was what seemed to be irritating Fountain. Fountain was unaware that Melindy was planning on leaving, and I didn't want to agitate him further so I let that ride for the time being. Dr. Smith, the veterinarian, chimed in that he saw little benefit for the AEC from what was coming out of Bohman's work. This led me to inquire as to what really was the objective of the monitoring division.

Fountain indicated that in all likelihood above ground testing was coming to a halt. It looked like President Kennedy was going to sign off on the treaty banning further above ground testing. The problem as he saw it was that testing was going to continue anyway, albeit underground. One of the problems that he freely admitted to was that satisfactory techniques to fully contain underground testing had simply not been developed yet. I gathered that underground tests conducted to date had not been all that successful, and probably had resulted in some degree of contamination. As I came forth with this philosophy, some grim looks occurred, with significant eye contact being made with everybody present but myself. I sort of said "Bingo", at least to myself. At this point Fountain made it very clear to myself and everybody else present that I had no security clearance, so some things at this time could not be discussed in my presence. I was a fast learner, so I suggested that based on my limited knowledge of the whole picture, I should simply make a proposal about what I could offer.

That approach seemed just fine, so I explained in detail the concept of sampling with fistulated cattle. I felt we could analyze the fistula samples for just about anything that the AEC might be interested in. I also suggested that if we kept the animals in an area of no contamination when not being used, that salivary contamination of the collected fistula samples should not be a problem, at least with isotopes, which I gathered would be about all these folks would be interested in. All three of them liked what I was suggesting, so I went on to explain a little bit about sample size, and even structuring a sampling grid for the areas of concern within the site. Fountain indicated that all information coming from collected samples would have to be critically screened before being released, which, of course, meant that for some time publications would be suppressed. I countered by indicating that a lot of the information, such as the protein and energy content of collected samples surely would not be classified, and could be published, which would, of course, would make Bohman happy. That brought out the smiles and even chuckles from both Fountain and Smith which I guessed didn't happen very often.

"What about statistical analyses on this type of information?" asked Smith.

And obviously, that was just the lead in I was hoping for. So after my standard fifteen minute seminar on my statistical knowledge and abilities, all agreed it sounded good.

"What we need from you is a firm proposal including sampling procedures, time frame, all that kind of information, including cost, and we need it within a couple of weeks. And in the meantime we will be authorizing your clearance," countered Fountain.

"What a minute, if we have Terry involved in the sampling, he will be in some damn difficult places, places even I am not sure I am authorized to be in, and if we get him to help analyze some of our other data he'll need a top clearance, M-3, or what in the hell ever they call it. What I am saying is that his clearance will have to be top flight, and you know as well as I do that can take 30 to 45 days," countered Smith.

"Wow", exclaimed Fountain, "You been watching too many English flicks on TV. I think M-3 is an English security classification, not FBI. What Terry needs will be what the agency calls 'Top Security'. Top Security is what civilians are issued when they qualify to basically have unrestricted access to the Site as well as data. It will be pretty hard to get that classification, but if Terry has kept his nose clean, especially while in college and during his tenure as a professor, it's possible. Assuming that his family's record is clean as well."

"I am not very old, I haven't done very much, my trail should be easy to follow", I responded.

Both Smith and Fountain laughed, "That's got nothing to do with it. They will be more interested in what your grandmother did," was Jim's response to my ignorance.

"Well another factor that we haven't considered are the animals. Right now I only have one fistulated steer, and I would guess that ultimately we may need six to eight. It will take me at least 60 days to fully prepare a fistulated animal for work, starting right now," I responded.

Fountain concluded, "Let's leave it at this. We like your thinking. We will make a commitment to fund your work starting right now, with the amount to be determined based on our acceptance of your proposal. What you need to do immediately on returning to Reno is to work up the proposal, go ahead and get the animals started. You have my personal guarantee that even if the project falls through, we will reimburse the University for the animals, because I think we need to have this type of biological sampling device on the site. Do you agree

Gary and Tom?" Nods of approval went around the table so I guessed it was a done deal. "One more thing, if we can work out all of the details will you give me your assurance that you will take a more active roll in Bohman's work, and do your level best to make it usable for us?" asked Gary. I assured them that would be no problem. Time simply had not allowed me to get any more involved at this data, but that would all change. Ed and Tom had to leave for another meeting, so Gary took me back to the Plaza and then on to lunch after a short tour of Vegas. However, I made him guarantee that I would be at McCarran for my 4:00 P.M. return to Reno.

Gary and I had a relaxed lunch, he told countless stories about major problems that they had at the site. Seems like the AEC wanted to establish full scale agriculture at the site, all for the benefit of monitoring. There was a beef herd, a dairy, a swine unit and a poultry flock. Nothing could be salvaged as usable food from any of these entities, they just existed to sample. Then Gary's mood seemed to change. He became somber and quiet, looked me straight in the eyes, then proceeded to say, "I hope I can trust you, that what I am about to say goes no further, but I think you are honest and I think you need to know a little bit more than you learned today so I am going to tell you."

"The military puts tremendous pressure on the AEC to conduct as many tests as possible. I don't know who really designs these tests, for what, for why or whatever, but the tests are numerous. To date, the vast majority have been above ground, although over the last year or two more and more have been underground because of the proposed treaty. It's my personal opinion that the underground tests to date may have been dirtier than the above ground blasts, because every single one has vented, and some have vented damn bad. Regardless, there's lots of contamination. Our unit is supposed to monitor that, but that's a joke because the real power people won't let us monitor where we should, consequently all of our data, what there is, gives a clean bill of health. That's what the military wants. Both Jim and I are very concerned about all of this, but our hands are tied by the higher-ups, so that's why we bent over backwards to get you involved. Your approach is new, and likely won't be under the scrutiny that we have been under. The bureaucrats in the military rarely catch on very fast, so you should have considerable freedom for most of the first year at least. Now, as far as I am concerned, this conversation never occurred. I'll totally deny it if you ever mention it. It's simply for your benefit, and perhaps, having a slightly better handle on it will help when you write your proposal. Now, I have to be at a meeting by three, so lets go straight to McCarran, it will get you there about an hour early, but that should give you time to get your notes in order. And don't worry about the clearance, we already have enough data on you for the Bureau to get started."

At that point I didn't respond to what Gary had said, but when somebody says something really significant I usually can remember it verbatim, and those words would stick in my brain for a long, long time. We just passed the time talking about Vegas on the way to McCarran, Gary never got out of the car. I just leaned over and shook his hand. And while doing so, I looked him straight away in the eye, and said simply, "Thanks".

It was an hour wait, an hour to Reno International and about a fifteen minute ride to the house, but when I got there I didn't know if I should tell Jan what I heard or just lay it away. I chose the latter, but I didn't really lay it away. That night as Gary's words went through my head for the thousandth time, I began to realize that I was stepping into a high stakes game and I had better play this one pretty careful, pretty close to the vest so to speak, and above all else, there had to be a fail safe mechanism. After listening to what I had listened to today, I had little doubt that the Test Site was highly contaminated, or certainly more so than the public had been led to believe. I also had little doubt that using fistulated steers would do nothing but show the whole truth, at least if they were allowed to do so.

The next morning I went straight to the Director of the Ag Experiment Station, Dr. Ray Ely, who was new on the staff. Adams had left, and a new Dean had not been hired yet, so it seemed appropriate that I go straight to Ely for both advice and approval. After explaining the proposed project in detail, Dr. Ely sat for a long time just contemplating. "Well, I suppose its appropriate that we be intimately involved in monitoring, after all, this is all happening in Nevada, and I suppose the possible ramifications could be rather serious. What are they doing about milk. There are some pretty large dairies in southern Nevada, I believe, although I haven't really had time to learn about that yet?" he inquired. Dr. Ely's interest in milk was logical, his background was dairy nutrition from Michigan.

"All I can tell you about the dairy situation right now is that they maintain a dairy on site as part of the monitoring effort. However, the dairy sits just north of Yucca Flat, and it's really up-wind for about 90% of the testing, if not more. I just don't think the dairy site gets much contamination. Most of their pasture and hay comes from the site, but again they are up-wind. Furthermore, the concentrates come from commercial sources. In short, it's doubtful if the dairy gets much contamination, which I might guess is somewhat by design". I should have thought better about that last little epitaph, it just slipped out.

Ely raised his eyebrows with a quizzical look. "Are you suggesting that they want the monitoring program to give the testing the green light?" was his response. I thought carefully before answering that, but my answer followed the lines that they just didn't really know how to monitor correctly, and I felt that's where we could make a big contribution

Then Ely surprised me by saying, "I'll bet that if we started monitoring commercially produced milk in southern Utah, of which there is plenty, it would show a significant contamination, especially with such things as iodine and strontium. Maybe, just maybe, if you could get your foot in the door, we could gradually get involved in a comprehensive region wide monitoring program. I have been reading quite a bit about what has been going on down there. I recently read a weather review, especially about the constant wind direction over southern Nevada, and I really don't like what I have read. Besides, some of my old colleagues at Michigan have been raising questions about all of this for some time." So Ely was in full agreement with my proposal.

"I'll clear all of this through Bohman this afternoon, and I'll suggest that I sort of take the lead in his cattle work over in Delamar. I don't think he will object, besides, I guess you know Melindy is leaving," I concluded.

Melindy was leaving, and filling his position, for what would likely be no more than one year might have been a very difficult project. However, Bohman had just taken on a new graduate student, Charles Speth, a native of Barstow, California, by way of Cal Poly, my old alma mater. Speth was married with three daughters, so I knew he was struggling financially. I suggested to Bohman that sending him down to Caliente to finish the cattle work could make a great thesis, as well as, going a long way to taking care of Speth's financial problems. Bohman agreed, so that afternoon we put forth a proposal to Speth, and he jumped, hook line and sinker.

Later that afternoon I went to the Main Station farm, specifically to see my old friend Jim Hunter about several more fistula candidates. "Yup, sure thing, this is a lot better situation than the first time you pestered me. At least I got some extra calves for you to choose from today, but of course by tomorrow they may be committed to something else," Jim responded.

I wasn't going to let that happen so we separated out five Hereford, six weight steers, put them into a special pen with alfalfa hay and water. "Charles Speth, the new grad student, will be out in the morning to start halter breaking them. I'll even supply the halters this time," I cheerfully submitted.

Hunter laughed, "Boy, you are really getting up in the higher circles of academia. A budget that can afford halters, that's something else," he caustically replied. I didn't have the heart to tell Jim that I didn't even have a budget for this project, and probably wouldn't for some time, but I had started to learn how to play the game, and somehow the halters would be there for Charlie in the morning, and what ever else might be required over the next few weeks.

I had been pretty much on a chase since returning from Vegas. There was plenty of lab work, but Virginia and Allie were staying even with all of that. The biggest problem I had was just keeping up with the paper work. The whole damn department only really had one secretary, and you just about had to have an appointment to see her. Virginia didn't realize it initially, but she was also gradually becoming a secretary as well as a lab assistant. Bohman didn't know, and I didn't care, the work had to get done.

My little wreck with Dean Adams and the academic council was still getting a lot of attention, especially seeing how within a week of that event Adams had indicated that he would retire as of June 30, and he had sufficient leave built up to take the rest of the year off. His departure didn't sadden many people. In fact, somehow I seemed to get a lot of credit for the event. Enough so that at the annual elections for Faculty Senate, held every March, I was overwhelmingly elected to the Senate. I wasn't sure where the time for that event would come from, but I guessed if I was going to really be a professor, I had better act like one. Fortunately, the Senate only met one afternoon a month, and being the new kid on the block, I probably wouldn't get appointed to many sub-committees.

It had only been about a week since returning from Vegas, when my Dad called me late one night to ask, "What in the hell have you done. Your mother and I had an FBI agent sitting in our front room yesterday afternoon for about three hours. Besides that, I found out tonight that your mothers parents and my dad have also been visited? You haven't become a damn pinko after going to work for that University have you?" I tried to explain, but Dad's hearing wasn't good since Minears disease and he was convinced that the feds were after my carcass. Besides, Dad was pretty conservative, and he was surely convinced that I would become a left wing liberal once I actually went to work for a university. Fortunately, Mom's hearing and rational was such that I was able to explain. I apologized for not forewarning them, but I really didn't completely understand what this clearance thing was all about in the first place. I just didn't believe that my parents and grandparents would be subjected to such detail, however, Gary had warned me. I made a mental note of paying a bit more attention to such details in the future.

After that call, I did have time to think about the possibilities a bit. Certainly, if they were going to question my grandparents, I wondered what my old high school friend, Harry Biggers, might have to say. I also could imagine how Dean Gibson might try to explain my fireworks display. As I drifted off to sleep I was wondering how the AEC officials would look at someone who was pretty much responsible for one of the largest unauthorized fireworks displays in the history of Southern California - oh well, to hell with them, if they can't take a joke!

The next morning I saw Charlie pretty early, but he didn't seem too happy. He was limping, had two bruised legs and some sore ribs. I inquired how the halter training was going, he mumbled something about maybe I ought to do that for awhile and learn something practical. I just grinned, it's not something that you really can tell someone about, just better to experience it yourself: and he was. However, I did have some fleeting memories about Bronco Billy in his prime. I doubted that Charlie had anything like that in his herd. Instead, I just told Charlie to hurry, because he was going to Caliente in about 10 days, and he had to have them trained by then. I left before he had a chance to respond.

Charlie did leave for Caliente by April 15, and the steers were pretty well halter broken. We operated shortly thereafter, and a week later the University was the proud owner of five new fistulated steers, and along with Billy, that made six. Life was getting better for me, as Bohman came up with enough money to hire some help to care for the new animals. I was able to grab a young animal science student by the name of Ron Lynch. Ron had a 4H background and wanted to be a vet one day. He took care of the steers on a daily basis for the next sixty days. Which allowed me to start to prepare a budget for the anticipated test site work. I had never really prepared a budget for this type of grant activity before, but in visiting with some of the older professors, it didn't take long to catch on. I figured we should sample for a year, on at least a monthly basis, which meant in addition to getting the animals down to the Site, I would also be going down every four weeks or so. The chemistry from our standpoint would be very routine, and we knew just about exactly what that would cost. However, my concern, which I really had not shared with Ely, Bohman or anybody else, was how to protect ourselves from what Jim Fountain had warned me about that day at lunch in Vegas. We had a biochemist on the staff that was doing a lot of work with isotopes, Dr. Cliff Blinco. So I took it upon myself to visit Blincoe and let him know what I was up to. He felt it would be a simple matter to determine background noise (radioactivity) on the samples, but as to individual isotopes it would be more difficult.

After thinking this through, I felt it might be a very good idea if we determined background activity, sort of as a protection against anything happening. So in the proposal, I briefly mentioned that all fistula samples after collection at the Site would be split in half, with half left at the Test Site Lab for detailed isotope analyses, and the half maintained by the University to be analyzed for proximate analyses, as well as phosphorus, calcium and strontium. Additionally, the University would determine overall background radioactivity on their samples. I'll admit in hindsight that the latter was in fairly small print, but it was in the project proposal.

After completing the proposal, and properly signed by myself, Bohman and Ely, off it went to Fountain. It didn't take a week and he called back to say that everything was a go, with the exception that he didn't think the budget was high enough. So, he was recommending an additional 10% overhead for the University, to cover any possible contingencies. No mention was made of the University doing any kind of radiochemistry, so obviously that was approved. Payment was to be made quarterly to the University, in advance, so needless to say, there wasn't much opposition from the University, especially seeing how the total budget amounted to nearly two hundred and fifty thousand dollars for a full years work!

By June I received notice that my clearance was ready, but it would not be activated until I went through some special training on site. The fistulated steers were ready. So, we made arrangements to ship the entire lot by commercial transport directly to the site. I made arrangements to drive to the site on June 25, which just happened to be my birthday. I was to meet Tom at the gate, and from there we would start my indoctrination into Test Site protocol.

The trip to Mercury was long and boring, even at 80 miles per hour. I had left Reno at about five A.M., in a department pick-up loaded to the gills with ever conceivable thing a fistulated steer handler might need, plus a whole lot more junk. Its about 400 miles from Reno to Mercury, the base camp, but it only took six hours, even with a gas stop in Beatty. Tom was to meet me at the main gate at high noon, but I was an hour early. Site security was under contract to a firm called Wackenhut Services, Inc., but just because this was a business contract didn't mean security wasn't for real. The main gate guards, including holstered 45's, were polite, but firm. I was told in no uncertain terms to proceed no further until my site escort arrived, at which time I would begin my indoctrination program. So I waited for the next hour in the parking lot. I guessed my steers, which were already supposedly here, didn't have as much trouble getting through security - well after all they couldn't talk.

Tom showed up promptly at noon, and by 12:30, I was wondering why I had showed up. Indoctrination included a series of briefing as to the physical definitions of the Site, staffing, purpose, etc. The only good part of this procedure was that Tom had to accompany me throughout, and he had heard it all before. After Test Site 101, we adjourned to Safety Procedures, which more than anything else was a series of lectures on how safe the Test Site really was. At the end of that lecture we were shown safety badges which only had to be worn in certain locations. These badges contained a film like substance which would capture radioactivity in the unlikelihood event that you were exposed to any activity while on site. At the days end when leaving the site, the badges were monitored, thus allowing the safe exit of the worker. I leaned over and asked Tom what happened if in fact your badge became contaminated to an unacceptable level. His hushed response was, "That doesn't happen, I'll explain later."

After Safety Procedures, my real test came when I was introduced to the AEC official in charge of security. He, Ben Johnson, myself, and Tom entered a small room with no windows, only the door. Inside was one table and three chairs, at least there was a chair for all of us. By this time I was thirsty and I had to relieve myself. Mr. Johnson didn't seem the type to care much about my personal needs, therefore I didn't ask. He was short, stocky, with a barrel chest, bald with a moustache, almost just like you would see in the movies. Once seated he pulled a series of folders from his briefcase. I could clearly see my name on the top of each, in addition was another name, such as Fillmore Union High School, Cal Poly, relatives, etc. After briefly thumbing through the folders he allowed, with a frown, "You seem to have a pretty clean past, most everybody gave you a plus. I see from this that shortly after your 21st birthday you registered Republican. I also notice that there is no indication that you ever were a member of any left wing leaning organization while you were in college. Are you still a Republican?"

My answer was yes, but I really didn't understand what that had to do with anything, although other than yes, I said nothing else.

I wasn't sure what Tom's reaction to all of this was. He was just staring at the floor. Next Mr. Johnson indicated that my activities while on site might cause me to see or hear things of great interest to national security, and that if I did, it became imperative that no further mention of anything of that nature must come from me. Because of the fact that this possibility existed, I would now be required to sign a form, of which the number I can no longer remember. However, before I had a chance to read the form, Mr. Johnson read it for me. Basically, he read me my rights, which at this time were, to put it bluntly, not much! The form simply indicated that release of any part of any classified information could be considered treason against the United States of America, thus any proven release of unauthorized information could result in fines, prison sentences and other possible penalties up to and including even possible execution. The thought whizzed through my brain that I was awful glad I had that little paragraph in my research proposal about the University of Nevada doing background radiochemistry work. At that point, Mr. Johnson indicated that if we were to proceed any further I must sign the form. I guessed then if I ever wanted to see my old buddy Bronco Billy again, I guessed I had better sign.

So I started to sign, but Johnson said, "Wait, we have to have five witnesses, so I'll call in three of the girls." In came three secretaries, which along with Ben and Ron, made five I guess. No explanation was required for the secretaries, who were all chattering amongst themselves. I guessed they were so use to all of this riggamaroe, they didn't need an explanation. Then Johnson clarified all of this for me. "Please stand at attention ladies. Mr. Hope is signing this document, making him solely responsible for any and all of his actions in dealing with classified information while on the Atomic Energy Commission's Nevada Test Site. Failure of him to comply could lead to severe penalties, up to and including execution." The fact that none of the ladies fainted, or even showed signs of faint at this point, led me to believe that this routine probably had happened before, likely quite a few times before. So I mustered up all my courage like a good soldier should and signed away. Funny how thoughts like that occur, but as I was signing, I wondered what the consequences would be for misspelling your name, even if completely by accident. It was signed by me, then ceremoniously by all five witnesses, lastly by Johnson himself. At which time he shook my hand, which was a surprise. "Welcome aboard Mr. Hope. I know something about your line of work, I was raised on a farm in Illinois," which was about all he had to say, as he and the ladies exited. I thought to my self, you pompous ass, you don't have the slightest idea about my work! Oh, how I wished I had the nerve to say what was usually on my mind! On the way out, the receptionist had all of the necessary documents, including an appropriate name tag. "Your safety badge will be issued to you daily by the monitoring group. I believe you have all other necessary information at this time. Good luck to you." I understood everything to that point with the exception of why she was wishing me luck.

As I exited the building, the positive feeling that I would now be able to relieve myself came over me, but it was promptly broken by Johnson storming out and yelling, "Terry, there's one more thing I forgot to discuss, wait while I go over it with you." My initial reaction was to run, but I knew that wouldn't solve anything, so I squared my shoulders as I turned to face him. "You will likely be in some very classified areas at first, so the director and I have concurred, and we feel it best that someone from internal security accompany you until you know all the ropes. I'll try to get you someone familiar with livestock so maybe they can help. In fact, I would go myself, but my schedule right now just won't allow it."

With that final comment, I said a silent prayer to God thanking him for the small favor. "No problem, whoever accompanies us, and I am assuming Tom will also be there, can help if they are so inclined. I look forward to it," I lied!

Before any other disturbances I told Tom that the nearest restroom wasn't close enough! That accomplished, on the way back to our trucks I asked Tom if this was the usual. "Yes, we all get a kick about his bit about Republicans. We have only ever brought in a few Democrats, but each one of them got a stern lecture from Johnson, to the point that they almost had to agree to switch parties. That fruit cake is a real conservative to put it mildly, and frankly, I think he is a phony. It's been rumored that he is gay, but packing that 45, I guess no one has the nerve to ask! And don't worry about internal security, we'll take an ice chest full of beer, that's probably all they will care about anyway. Rest assured none of those idiots are going to stick their hand inside of a cow's stomach!" That's all fine I thought to myself, but I could well visualize screwing up on this detail and Johnson himself heading up the firing squad!

After leaving security we traveled into the site, to the monitoring facility, located adjacent to their farm. The one thing that I hadn't done in my initial proposal was establish a sampling grid. Test site maps were classified, so I really couldn't establish a sampling grid until I cleared the final hurdle for security. We had all agreed to meet right after my "indoctrination", go over the maps, establish critical areas, and set procedures. The Nevada Test Site was large, even by Nevada standards, some 1,350 square miles or 864,000 acres. It was originally established in 1950, having been carved out of the old Las Vegas Bombing and Gunnery Range, which had been heavily used in World War II. What was left of the Bombing and Gunnery Range had since become known as Nellis Air Force Range, and provided a significant buffer between the Site and the city of Las Vegas.

Various government actions had enlarged the area, actually considerably in excess of the 864,000 acres. However, a large area on the northern border of the site was off limits to everyone, so atom bomb testing was not of consideration there. The northern site was a top secret research facility, managed by the Sandia Corporation. In those days no one knew what was going on there, but in time it became famous for hatching the Stealth concept of fighter and bomber craft. It also housed the infamous "Area 51", reputed to be the home of captured alien spacecraft, but, as I said, in those days no one knew what went on there, and we certainly weren't going to sample there anyway.

It seemed strange to study the maps, and realize how many tests had in fact occurred at the Site. Great paranoia existed throughout the country concerning the Cold War with Russia, and the possibility of nuclear attack. Fear raged, and rightly so, that how contaminated the world would become if a nuclear war erupted. However, right here in southern Nevada prior to 1962, some 198 test had occurred, mostly above ground. With the fear that the president would sign the proposed ban on above ground testing, some 96 additional tests had either occurred already in 1962, or were planned. Thus, we were supposed to monitor the results of 294 blasts, mostly above ground, and as I had already correctly guessed, those blasted off underground were even dirtier.

Most of the early tests had occurred in Frenchman Flat, and Yucca Flat, far more in the latter. The prevailing wind was from the west northwest, so by simple reasoning, the majority of the drift would be east southeast. However, climatological data that had been gathered also indicated that as the drift tended to leave the immediate site, the drift became more due east and eventually even started a more northerly flow. This all seemed somewhat a product of the season, probably greatly influenced by the presence of summer tropical storms coming up Mexico's west coast. Anyway, it didn't take long to establish a sampling grid. We would concentrate on the east side of Yucca Flat and the adjoining areas known as 3, 7, 9, 10, 11 and 15. I just made lines on a new site map, crossing these areas in both an east west fashion as well as a north south fashion. All told, once all the lines were in place, there were 196 intercepts. I then took 196 numbered tabs, placed them in a coffee can for random selection. I suggested that, since we had six usable fistulated steers, that we use four at any one time, sample on three consecutive days, once a month, Each sampling site was to be a product of the number we drew out of the can. Once a number was drawn, it would be discarded, so the same area could not be sampled twice. I laid all of this out like I knew what I was talking about. Actually, I kind of did, because I had put a lot of thought into it, and had gone over sampling procedures with anybody at Nevada that would listen to me.

It must have impressed the AEC folks, they all just stood there shaking their heads in agreement. I assured them that this method would pass muster with any bonafide statistician. I got to admit, it all sounded pretty good to me also, even if I was only 27 years old. Gary's only concern was that I write all of the sampling procedure up in detail, so that in my reports, that were due quarterly, nobody would question our methodology. Every time we started talking about this, Jim always seemed to get nervous. I didn't know if it was his habit, or if something was really bothering him.

By the time we had all of the sampling procedure laid out it was well into the evening. Both Jim and Gary were headed back to Vegas, but Tom opted to stay with me at the Mercury Hilton, which was the local handle for the camp sleeping quarters. Actually, the Hilton wasn't bad, nor was dinner at the cafeteria. There were movies, free, but I opted for bed, as we both wanted to get an early start tomorrow. Our plan was to go through a dry run for sampling, with the first actual sampling day to occur the following morning.

After a quick breakfast, we went directly to the farm where the fistulated animals were housed. They had only been there a week, but like always, there plugs needed refitting. Tom took to the process like he had been doing it all of his life, so that eased some of my fears. We gathered all of the necessary paraphernalia, tubs for rumen contents, sample bags, halters, lead ropes, tools, etc. The farm had a gooseneck stock trailer, and Tom's pick-up was equipped to pull it. Several horses also were housed here, but they were under the care of Dick Hostetler, affectionately known as the "Atomic Cowboy". Dick's job was to run some of the farm cattle directly through ground zero immediately after the dust had settled. Tom explained that this was a scheme, pretty much as a result of the military influence, intended to show just how little impact was occurring from these tests. "I don't know how Dick has survived this long, he's confided in me that his contamination level is off the scale. He's a bachelor, and I guess he feels it's really important what he is doing. I suppose it will get him one day, it sure to hell has affected some of the cows anyway."

I finally brought up the question that had been bugging me about the test badges that we were to wear. "Doesn't Dick have to wear a badge?"

"Well, now that you asked, you might as well get the straight answer. We use a special badge doing monitoring work, slightly different than what is worn by the typical test site worker. They are similar in every detail to what everybody else uses, but they are not numbered. The typical worker's badge is numbered, and he must check out every day, and the numbers must match or there's hell to pay. That way if a worker is contaminated, it is immediately known. The unions insist on that. In our case, and keep in mind besides our immediate staff and Dick, there's no one else that fits into this category. Oh, yes, you. Anyway, when we leave, we always go through our lab, where we have badge reading equipment. If our badges show a significant level of contamination, they are thrown away and we just put on a new badge. That way, there never is a problem when we go through our final checkout. Before we implemented this procedure some of us didn't get to go home for several days we were so contaminated. Usually, we don't have a problem, but on those days when we are too close to an event, or the aftereffects of an event, it sure simplifies the procedures."

I was dumb enough to ask how the final checkout people knew not to get excited about our badges not being numbered.

Tom chuckled, "Wackenhut runs the checkout, but remember, they are a private company that is here under contract, and the military runs everything, and I think Gary talked to you about that, so see, there's no problem!"

Dick showed us which horses he would let us use. He was a savvy cowboy, and I think he recognized that I knew my way around a saddle also. Two of the horses didn't look good, hair was falling out and appeared to be discolored. Dick explained that he had gotten a bit too close with them and they were hurting, but he fully expected them to recover, they had before. I asked how he survived so well. "Hell, I wear the most fancy protective suit you ever saw, and as soon as I come out the far side they wash me down with a solution that's fit to clean any Nevada whorehouse!" I thought to myself maybe it would be a good idea to at least fit the horses with some of the same material. Dick also showed and explained about the only horse trailer on site. It was old but usable, a double, but we would only need two horses anyway. "You won't be sampling when we have a test, and that's about the only time I use that beast anyway, so you are welcome to it. It fits a two inch ball, and I see your pick-up has a two inch ball, so you boys are all set to go. I'd like to come with you, but I am just too old a cowboy to learn about the insides of a live cow, besides, I kind of think there's something all haywire about what you educated people are doing with these critters." I guess it didn't make any sense to argue about driving a herd of cows through ground zero within an hour after a detonation. Sometimes I began to wonder if I was just too young to cope with this world, or if maybe I had just learned too much too soon. Tom came to my rescue, "Let's go have some lunch."

After lunch, we laid everything out for a final check, and everything looked good. "Our guide dog should be along any minute now," Tom ventured forth. I probably looked more than puzzled at this point, but Tom resolved my delirium. "Remember, Ben telling you yesterday that someone from internal security would accompany us until we are sure you are reliable."

"Yeah, I guess, I remember the first part, but I am a bit hazy about when I will be reliable" I responded.

"Well, anyway, one of those guys will be by this afternoon, I don't really know if they will accompany us or not, I kind of doubt it, but it's their call."

It wasn't long before the black sedan pulled up. Out stepped a person that I immediately determined that I would respect. He was about 6'3" or 4", probably weighed 225, crew cut, and fortunately, carried a grin from ear to ear.

"Hi Tom", he shook Tom's hand then headed my direction.

"Hi Mr. Hope, my name is Richard Jensen, just call me Dick, and I am from I.S." I couldn't help but notice his southern drawl even if he was crushing my hand. "I guess you know, I am supposed to monitor your activities while on site, but I'll lay it out. I have reviewed your complete file, and you are probably more reliable than 90-95% of the people on site. I trust you, we trust you, obviously the FBI trusts you, so we probably wouldn't normally monitor your activities." I waited for the other shoe to drop.

"But I've got to tell you, I was raised on a ranch in northern Oklahoma, went to Stillwater on a football and wrestling scholarship. I majored for two years in animal science before switching to political science and pre-law. I remember reading about fistulated cattle. When I saw your information and what your project was all about, I just about came apart. So, I guess, what I would like to know, could you just use an extra hand for a few days? It will get me out of the office before I rip somebody's head off. Maybe you can teach me something, and maybe I can help you".

"Well, we are stuck with two horses, but actually, these cattle are tame enough I don't really think we will need horses anyway. The only problem I see is I am not sure that fist of yours is small enough to fit through one of these fistulas. We only used a three pound coffee can for an outline!" I looked him straight on in a serious nature waiting for a reply.

"Oh, hell, I'll just pick them up on their side and shake them good and it will all fall out anyway", was Dick's quick response. I sensed we were going to get along just fine.

"Well, I sure don't have a problem with you going along. We can probably sure enough use the help. Besides you can spend the extra time explaining how the Sooners have beaten you Cowboys so bad the last few years," was my challenge.

"Well, now, I think I can explain that: but, lest you forget, we flat smothered them in wrestling. In fact, if you remember, we completely obliterated Cal Poly in wrestling," was Dick's response. True enough, Cal Poly had a fantastic wrestling team, but it sure wasn't the same caliber as those Cowboys. We made our final arrangements. Dick was to meet us at six straight up the next morning, and we were to be off to my site 87, located right smack dab in the middle of area nine.

202

After he left, Tom just about came apart. "Internal Security has some real jerks. I think there is only about six all together including Ben Johnson. The chances of us drawing Dick Jensen has to be a lot less than one out of six, especially if Ben had anything to do with it. Dick's the only one I can even be civil with. The rest of those pompous idiots drive me to drink. We are lucky to put it mildly". Well I hadn't met the rest, but if most were more like Ben than Dick, I opted to not go out of my way to meet them. Period!

The next morning at six straight up, Dick met Tom and myself at the farm. It didn't take us long to load Billy and three new steers. Getting the horses was a bit more challenging. I could see pretty quick that old Dick, "The Atomic Cowboy", Hosteletter wasn't a whole lot different than any of the other old time buckeroos that I had known over the years. The only two horses in the whole outfit worth a damn were reserved for him. The rest looked questionable at best. The positive side of it was that the nags that we were left with probably hadn't been exposed to sufficient radiation to kill us on contact, but a couple of them looked like they could kill you in other ways. Jensen proved to be a pretty good hand. He took one of my ropes and as pretty as you please he had the two best horses available to us ready for halters and loading.

"You keep that up, and I will consider hiring you as a hand", was my backhanded compliment.

"Well, if you knew the truth, I don't think you can afford me, but I sure love to work like this, especially on the fed's dime!" I couldn't top that, so with a quick check of all of our supplies, we were shortly off to area nine.

The Test Site is located in the northern stretches of the Mojave Desert, or what the plant ecologist like to call the warm desert shrub region. Actually, there is a surprising amount of grass on the test site, most notably bottlebrush squirreltail and galleta grass. There's lots of plain old sagebrush due to the elevation, 5-6,000', but there's also vast areas of low sage, mainly winter fat and shadscale. But, due to the many disturbances that had occurred because of the testing, there was a great invasion of annual forbs, commonly known as weeds. Chief amongst these was the likes of halogeton and Russian thistle. Whenever it would rain, which in the warm desert region might be anytime, but most likely in the spring and summer months, these annual weeds would become very green and succulent. Consequently, they would be the feed of choice, and the early summer of 1962 had been wet in southern Nevada, so our site was green with a cover of weedy growth.

Once we located a suitable site, the steers were unloaded, and tied to the side of the trailer. It didn't take more than a few minutes to show Tom and Dick the tricks of emptying the rumen of its contents. I let Tom do Billy, and Dick took the tamest of the new candidates. The other two new steers were a might bit fidgety, but they soon tamed to the procedure. Within thirty minutes, they were grazing, which left ample time for the three of us to pass a little bull ourselves.

I noticed that Dick did not wear the detection badge that both Tom and I had put on that morning, not that it really made any difference under the circumstances. However, curiosity had gotten the best of me again, so I asked. "We are immune, so we just don't bother to wear the damn things", Dick responded.

"How in the hell are you immune to this crap", was my dumb response.

"Well, obviously, we aren't immune in the strict sense of the word, but sometimes we have to do rather unconventional things, which would result in rather unconventional publicity if it became known. So, for the peace of mind of the base commander, we just go naked - no hot badge, no hot report!"

The steers were kind of off in the distance, so I opted to follow. "Let's just lead these horses and follow along and kind of head these critters towards that knob over there with those scrub junipers. I think if we let them graze around that knob and back towards the trucks we will have some pretty good samples", I offered in my best scholarly tone. So we just sort of drifted along, the vegetation wasn't real thick, and to get what I perceived as an adequate sample I figured would take about two hours.

The sun was starting to bear down pretty good as we approached the knob. Tom was lost in thought, and Dick was just plain happy to be here. "It's probably good to get out of the office and get back to what you knew as a kid," I ventured.

"Well, I am not in the office much, but the crew I work with, and I am generally with some of them every day, gets kind of old. We are all on loan from the FBI. In fact we really are a subdivision of the Bureau, as they oversee all of our activities. I am kind of the new kid on the block, and when I finish my law degree it's my hope to go straight into the typical type of FBI work. The other guys have all been around for a lot longer than I have. They sort of accept this kind of assignment as the status quo. Now Ben, he's a little different. I think he has ambitions of really finding something here, like an honest to god spy ring or something. I think he's hoping to pole vault from here back to the big time."

"Spies, now that's a spooker out here on the desert. I'll bet they'll have a hard time reporting what we are doing right now," I replied.

"Well I don't think they will be too interested in fistulated cattle, but they might be interested in the radioactivity results. The real problem is not out here, it's in Vegas. Vegas is a wide open town, with tourists from all over the world passing through every day, and that's where our work is. At any one time there, might be a dozen or more known Ruskys in and around Vegas. They are masters at picking peoples brains over cocktails, or seducing them with sex, or whatever. That's our problem, keeping track of the Ruskys, who they see, who they talk to, on and on. And if that's not hard enough, we know for sure that for every known Rusky, there's at least one more from the eastern block that's not known, and those are the ones that can do the damage." Dick went on to explain how they keep track of these various individuals, their activities, where they reside, and if they are collecting any actual information, how it is used. "It's probably not as serious as it sounds, but working for a guy like Ben Johnson, we have to really keep on our toes. He thinks that everyone in Vegas is a suspect," he concluded.

I offered, "Not if they are Republican, surely". A loud Oklahoma laugh clearly indicated that I had hit that nail on the head.

Our BS session had gotten us clear around the knob and back to within a hundred yards or so of the trucks, a full three hours had passed. "I think we have more than enough sample now. Let's take them back to the trucks. They all seem gentle enough, maybe we can catch halters by hand and save a rodeo," I directed.

"Shucks, I thought I came for a roping", responded Dick.

"You did your roping catching those nags. Lets see if we are fast enough to just grab a halter by hand." And we were. Billy was simple. He would come to you, the others once they saw Billy was tied to the truck, seemed to just want the same treatment.

It took about an hour, but sub-samples were obtained for analyses from the freshly consumed forage, placed in ice chests with dry ice for immediate freezing, and all of the old rumen contents were replaced, plugs reinserted, and everything was loaded. The first four samples of freshly consumed forage had successfully been obtained from the

Nevada Test Site. Back at the farm everything was unloaded, laid away in preparation of repeating the same process tomorrow. Dick, with the usual grin said, "same time, same place tomorrow"? Tom was good help, but Dick, because of his background, just made the whole day really go well. I was just thankful that he was coming back. I didn't know how long that would keep up, but as far as I was concerned, I hoped he would show up every time I did.

True to his word, Dick was back at six the next A.M. This time we were off further to the north and east, in fact to the north east corner of area 15. It was a much higher mesa than where we had been the day before, covered with some juniper and sage, with an under story of dried grass. The green weeds prevalent the day before were lacking here. We had the cattle turned out by 10:00 A.M., but I could see that sampling was going to be a bit longer today, due to the scarcity of forage. Tom wasn't feeling good, so he stayed with the trucks. Dick and I tagged along behind the steers, but we opted to ride horses this time. We ambled along to a high spot, where we could overlook most of the mesa. The steers were very relaxed, and just grazed peacefully. So we pulled up, let the horses graze also and passed the time of day.

Directly, Dick said, "I'll not be able to come out tomorrow, so you will be on your own. Having to watch over you is just so much BS, but you know how the agency is. I doubt if they will let me come out next month either, but I just wanted to tell you that this has really been interesting and fun. I called my Dad last night and told him that I had both my hands inside the stomach of a live cow. His only comment was that it sure seemed like a hell of a waste of tax payers funds. He still is wondering when I am going to come back to the ranch!"

I inquired as to what was so important that he couldn't play cowboy tomorrow? "Bus load of tourists from Europe will be in town tomorrow. We have to monitor them pretty careful, because sure as hell there will be a real honest to god Rusky or two on that bus. Also, we have been looking pretty close at an old couple that escaped from East Germany a few years back. They seemed to find their way to Vegas pretty easily, and we don't know how they support themselves. The gentleman has applied for work on the site twice, but both times we rejected him. We know he spends lots of time driving around, and we just found out that he has been frequenting the bars where a lot of the site construction workers drink."

"Sounds exciting", was my response.

"Not really, its just the routine day to day work that never seems to go away. We have interviewed so many people, I sometimes think that I must have talked to everyone in Vegas at least once."

That comment got me to thinking about a girl that I went to high school with, Nancy, the girl I admired so much, but hitting her in the butt with that chicken head pretty much ended any possible relationship. Anyway, some of the guys that I had gone to school with had told me that Nancy went to Vegas shortly after graduation. I didn't know if she was still here or what. I sort of imagined that she might have been a show girl, she certainly had the looks for it. So I asked, "I went to high school with a pretty special girl that I have been told now lives in Vegas. If its not too much trouble, could you locate her? I looked her up in the phone book, but there's no listing.

Dick grinned, "What are you trying to do, find an old girl friend in Vegas? She is probably way too fast for you by now!"

"Naw - I just wanted to see how she is doing and if her life is good, that's all. She was pretty special", I responded.

Anyway, Dick indicated that he would try to find her before my next venture to the site. All he needed was the year we graduated, as well as the school, and her maiden name. "I can likely get her social security number from the high school, and if she ever worked, in just about any capacity here, we will have some kind of a record, it won't take long. Besides, we have technicians back at the office that are trained in this type of work and half the time they are just sitting around on their fat asses!"

Time was marching on, the steers were getting tired of eating not much of anything as two of them had laid down on the job. So we opted to drift back towards the trucks, about two miles west. When we finally got there, Tom was sleeping solidly in the pick-up. We talked about dumping a bucket of rumen contents on him to wake him up, but thought better of it. He said he had the flu the night before, but I smelled the distinct odor of whiskey on his breath. Oh, well, Dick and I cleaned up the steers, processed the samples, loaded everything, then politely woke Tom. "Sir, could you drive the steers in the trailer back to the farm?", I inquired. I'll never forget the sheepish look on his face when he realized that he had slept through the whole process.

The next day, it was just up to Tom and myself, but we were loaded and on the way to Area 11 by ten. Area 11 was a beautiful site, lots of junipers, fairly abundant grass, a lot of little valleys, all draining to the east. We let the steers go by 11:00 A.M. Due to the terrain, we definitely would use the horses. So we drifted along behind them. Tom had never been in this area, and obviously neither had I. After a few ridges, we came into a broad valley, rimmed by junipers, but only to the crest, the rest of the area was very open. And, we were amazed by what we saw.

A whole regiment of military equipment stretched out before our eyes, jeeps, trucks, half tracks, cannons and probably 20 tanks along with a variety of other equipment. Neither of us could believe what we were looking at. The area covered by equipment probably included several hundred acres. It was all spread out, and heading the same general direction.

"Wow, I have heard of this sort of thing out here, but this is the first time I ever saw it", Tom exclaimed. I just sort of sat there in amazement. I had to laugh, the steers just grazed through the whole mess. Billy stopped and licked the end of a cannon barrel. What a time not to have a camera! We just rode along, peering into one vehicle after another. None appeared to be too damaged, although the paint was blistered. By the growth of the vegetation up through everything, I guessed that the equipment had been there for at least five years.

"I guess you noticed that all of the juniper stops at the ridge crest here. Must have been an aerial blast to test equipment. Every valley we have crossed today had juniper in it, except this one. Wow, the heat must have been intense", Tom pointed out.

I couldn't help but notice the tanks, the hatches were up on just about all of them. "I always wanted to drive a tank. I am going to climb in one and see what it's all about", I said, probably sounding like a teenager. Tom cautioned me about radioactivity, but I responded by saying, "Oh shucks, you'll just have to give me a new badge before checking out tonight" Tom's only response was an indifferent shrug. I tied my horse to a nearby jeep, and climbed aboard, through the hatch, and into the drivers seat. I never did learn what model the tanks were, but I presumed that they were probably pretty old, likely what we had before the war, or during the early stages of the war. I soon found that you could hand crank the turret, as well as the elevation on the cannon. I was having a ball!

"I don't think it's a good idea for you to be in that tank, especially without your shirt on. If you notice, all the padding on the back of the seat has been burned off, and that metal may be hot as hell", Tom cautioned. I had taken my shirt off, and I hadn't noticed that the seat had burned up. I was just having too much fun. But I heeded Tom's advice and slowly climbed out of my new found toy. Despite my fun,

I did learn two things from my brief stint as a tank commander. That night my badge was far too hot to allow me through security, so I got my first refill. The second thing didn't become obvious for about thirty years. But after age 60 I eventually had to have most of the skin on my back removed from basil cell carcinoma, or skin cancer. A lot of doctors told me that it couldn't have been from radiation, probably from being badly sun burned when I was a kid, but the scars eventually formed an arc on my back, very reminiscent of the back of a tank seat. Oh well - the things we do when we we're kids!

We got everything back to the farm by about four that afternoon, far too late for me to return to Reno. However, both Gary and Jim wanted to see me early the next morning in town at their offices. So that night I stayed in the big city, at the Plaza, and next morning was sitting at their office doors at eight sharp. They both arrived at the same time. We briefly went over all of the sampling. We now had 12 samples, all split in half, theirs frozen, identified and left at the farm under Tom's supervision, mine also frozen and identified, and packed away in my big sample ice chest with plenty of dry ice. Everybody seemed pretty pleased with the results, we had come and we had conquered!

Finally, Jim took out a folder from his brief case and said, "I have some old data here from the early days of the test site. I understand you are very good with statistics, and I was wondering if you might be interested in analyzing it for us, using whatever techniques you see fit?"

I looked at them somewhat questioning and responded, "Sure, I probably can get after it during the upcoming month, but what kind of data is it anyway?

They both looked at each other, which made me a bit nervous, and thinking to myself that maybe I really didn't want to do this after all. "It's some data from the old pig research, where they used pigs to measure the impact from ground zero out to several miles. I have looked at it, but it didn't make too much sense to me. I thought that your training might be such that you could make sense out of all of this. The people that took the data are all gone. No one around here knows anything about this at this point in time", Jim responded.

"Why pigs I inquired?"

Jim quickly replied, "Most of the physiologist that have been working with bomb impact have long since come to the conclusion that the pig is nearly the equivalent of the human in just about every regard except brain power. So, they make an excellent test animal." I thought to myself, at this point I might even question the brain power concept, but I let that one go for the time being.

I took the folder and briefly thumbed thorough the pages. There weren't a lot of observations, maybe a thousand or so, but less than a ten thousand. There was sort of a key at the front, and maybe with enough thinking I could sort the mess out. "Okay, I think I can do this, but what's the catch?" I inquired.

"Well there's no catch. We just want to know for sure what went on there. But you have to promise not to copy any of this. All of your stats, as well as any write-up must be given to me, completely, no questions asked, do you agree?" Jim responded.

"Well I guess I don't have a problem with that. I guess what you are saying is this is super sensitive or secret as the case goes, and probably best that no one knows that I have it or what I am doing, correct?" was my reply.

"Correct", they both responded in unison. I was dumb enough to accept this assignment with "no catch"; but I began to have visions of old Ben Johnson heading up the firing squad if I screwed up. With that, we all shook hands and I headed to Reno.

After about two days back in Reno, I finally had a chance to look at the folder full of data that Jim had given me. The key in the front wasn't much help. It appeared that some of the information was missing. There were a lot of observations taken of various pig criteria, none of which made very much sense to me. However, after several hours of trying about every combination, it finally dawned on me that the observations were taken on pigs at various intervals from ground zero. Further, pigs had been stationed at four quadrants, basically, north, east, west and south. Further study indicated that a group of approximately 4 pigs had been stationed at every intersect on each quadrant. Intersects appeared to be at every 250 meters, up to 5,000 meters. Thus, there were 80 sets of pigs, or approximately 320 pigs altogether. Observations were pretty simple; first, did the pig survive, and if so was it still in a working condition. It appeared that a zero for this observation meant that the pig didn't survive, and a plus meant that it did. Next, was a measure of external bleeding from some body orifice, but no mention as to the orifice. There were three observations here; no bleeding, minor bleeding, and profuse bleeding. Next was an observation taken one hour post blast, giving a general rating to the animal's well being, with rankings from zero to 10, with a zero indicating that the animal had succumbed to the blast, and a ten indicating no apparent after effects.

The final observation was a hematocrit, or measurement of the red blood cell content of the animals blood. These samples were taken at approximately one hour post blast. Samples were apparently taken from just live animals, or those live enough to have blood drawn. There was no rational for this observation, and it confused me. If the animal had suffered excessive radioactivity, or rems, as it was called in those days, it theoretically would not affect the blood for some time. However, who was I to question scientist dealing with atomic bomb aftermath. In addition, the weight of each animal had been recorded. The only information here was that the weight was pre-blast, but as to how long, I was left in question.

I categorized the data on a large data sheet, with ample space to plot the four quadrants, as well as the 20 intercepts per quadrant. Using a combination of "T" tests, and factorial design, I soon learned that there were no significant differences between quadrants, that is the total impact was the same, regardless of the direction animals were from the center. Zero's for survivability were 100% up to 1,000 meters, and about 50% for the next 500 meters. After 1,500 meters, most animals survived the initial blast. However, most animals showed profuse bleeding from body orifices up to 2,000 meters, and some bleeding after 2,500 meters and even much further. At one hour post blast, many of the animals that survived the initial blast between 1,000 and 1,500 meters had succumbed. Further, from 1,500 to 2,000 meters about 10% had perished one hour post blast. Two thousand meters is the equivalent of 1.25 miles, so I guess what these data were telling me that up to 1.25 miles from ground zero just isn't any place for human survival. From 2,000 meters to 3,000 meters, the impact may well make you wish you hadn't survived. Three thousand meters is nearly 1.9 miles. Considering the typical block in most cities is one tenth of a mile, that's 19 blocks in every direction of pretty horrible consequences.

The more I played with the data, the more intrigued I became. I applied correlation and regression every way I could, as well as just about every other statistical test that I could imagine. I hadn't done anything with the weight data nor the hematocrit, mainly because, they should be inconsequential. However, curiosity got the best of me. So eventually, I applied my factorial model to both the weight data as well as the hematocrit. I pounded away on my old Monroe calculator, grinding out the data, with my mind on other university problems. I did the weight data first, and initially, no differences appeared. However, my factorial model measured about every aspect possible, and suddenly a very significant difference jumped out in front of my face. Up to three thousand meters, pigs had averaged about 85 kilograms (190 pounds). However, from 3,250 meters on, they averaged 73 kilograms

(160 pounds). This I did not understand. I had to assume that the pigs were randomly selected, so a difference of this nature would be pretty difficult to achieve mathematically. In fact, the significance of the difference told me that the weights of the two groups of pigs were different, and that to make that assumption, the chances of being wrong were about one in 10,000. In other words, the two groups of pigs definitely weighed different.

As I studied these data, I began to wonder about the hematocrit. Surely, just because the two groups of pigs weighed differently, their hematocrits would be similar. So away went the many wheels in the Monroe once more. It took me about two hours to run the factorial design on the hematocrits. But, lo and behold, the same difference stood out, and just as significantly. Pigs stationed up to 3,000 meters had an average hematocrit value of 39%, while those pigs stationed at 3,250 meters and beyond had a hematocrit value of 46%. I was stunned, and had no answer.

I laid the pig data away for a few days, which was often a habit of mine. When I faced a scientific obstacle that I couldn't answer, or simply didn't make sense, I found that laying it away for a few days, often made the answer seem very obvious. However, after a week I came back to the data and no answer mystically appeared. There just wasn't an answer. My old physiology prof, Dr. Weeth, resided in an office directly above mine, on the second floor of the Fleischman Ag Building, so I thought I might pick his brain. I summarized my data down to a simple sheet, listing two groups of pigs; group A weighed 85 kilograms and had a hematocrit value of 39%, while group B weighed 73 kilograms and had a hematocrit value of 46%.

"Doc, I am going to ask you to sort out something for me, I have two groups of pigs that I have never seen, but these are the data. How do I explain the differences?"

Weeth looked at the data quizzically for awhile. "That's easy, somebody threw in a ringer on you; group A has a hematocrit of 39%, which would be very typical for pigs about ready to be slaughtered. Group B's hematocrit value of 46% just about wouldn't fly in pig physiology. The blood would likely congeal somewhere, so I think group B aren't pigs. A hematocrit value of 46% would be just about normal for men weighing 73 kilograms." With that, Weeth started laughing, "I am sure that doesn't solve your problem. I don't have a better explanation, but either the data is bad, or there is something else going on. It's just not normal for pigs to have that high of a hematocrit. Like I say, I think it's impossible."

At that point, I felt a general sickness coming over me. I thanked Weeth, and suggested somebody was pulling my leg. Back in my office, I sat in total stunned silence. I'll never forget the instant, the sickening feeling slowly coming over me. I just wanted to go across the hall to the men's restroom and throw up. It was more than I could handle. In fact I couldn't. Often, when things totally overwhelmed me I would seek answers from God. I was not a church goer in the typical sense, but I believed in God devoutly. During times when I really needed God, I always seemed to want to be by myself and climb the highest mountain around. I found that I felt close to God on a mountain. I could feel his presence. It gave me a chance to love and cherish His world. It would help me understand.

Within a few minutes after getting back from Weeth's office, I had notified the secretary that I wasn't feeling so well and I was taking the afternoon off. I drove south on U.S. 395 to the Mt. Rose turnoff. Within thirty minutes, I was at the Mt. Rose summit, high in the Sierra's, where I parked my pick-up. I had never been to the top of Mt. Rose, well over 10,000 feet, but there was no better time than now. There was no one on the trail. I ran as much as I could until I was totally out of breath. Then, I would walk as hard as I could. It probably took about two hours to reach the top. I don't know, I had lost track of time. A thunder storm lurked off to the south, with lightning bolts being thrown about. The wind was fierce, cool but not cold. A gigantic snow drift lay directly below me. I likened the lightning as a threat from God, mend your ways or else. I thought of many of the biblical phrases that had been drummed into my head by Reverend Korver, the preacher at the Fillmore Presbyterian church that I went to throughout much of junior and senior high school at Fillmore. I recited the Lord's prayer. I asked for answers, there were none. I hurt, almost beyond belief. I could not come to grips with what was going through my mind - the military had actually used human beings as test animals to measure the impacts of above ground atomic bomb tests. The awful truth of that made me drop to my knees and cry until I could no longer see. A bright flash followed by an almost immediate loud snap, brought me to my senses: a lightning strike had hit within a few yards, perhaps less than a hundred. It was like a message. You're still alive, go do something positive about what you have found out. The thought just seemed to come forth in an overriding manner following the lightning strike. I again fell to my knees, and recited the 29th Psalms from memory. I couldn't remember the last time that I had done that.

The storm had passed, the afternoon was wearing on. I stood, gazing down on distant Reno and Sparks with the cool wind blowing hard against my face. I could feel the tears slowly drying. I felt weak and shaky, but I also felt amazingly strong. I knew that I didn't want to traverse the trail down after dark, but I couldn't leave, not quite yet. I knelt down and prayed once again, thanking Him for what he had given, the beauty of the world that I had come to know and love, and most especially I asked to have the strength for what I knew lay ahead.

Dusk arrived about 500 yards from my pick-up. It was late when I finally got home. Jan had had a long day, and I had made up my mind I would not burden her with this problem. Our communication had not been good lately. So, it was just about impossible to describe what I knew, what I had been through, much less what I knew I surely faced.

Jan knew something was wrong. However, first, I couldn't eat, which for me was highly unusual. Secondly, I just couldn't seem to go to bed, and once I did, sleep was simply not on the agenda. I think it was one of the longest nights that I ever spent in my entire life. The next morning I was anxious to get to the office, but I was unsure of whether I really wanted to look at the data again. But it wouldn't leave my thoughts. So it was to work at about 6:30 A.M., and there, in front of my face, was the folder.

I wanted to review the data from 3,250 meters only. Before, I hadn't really paid much attention to it. From 3,250 to 3,500 yards, some bleeding was recorded in about 15% of the test subjects, from 3,500 to 3,750 meters, only 1% registered bleeding, with none past 3,750 meters. The only other measurement of significance was the measure of survivability, with rankings from zero to ten taken one hour post blast. From 3,250 to 3,500 meters the average score was 7.5 for all subjects, clearly indicating some degree of stress had been caused by the blast. However, there was some pretty big variability in these figures, from as low as 3 to as high as 10. I could only wonder what the condition of the subject was to receive a rank of 3. Again, there was no indication in the key as to what these figures meant, other than a zero indicated that the subject had perished during the one hour period post blast. Survivability increased rapidly past 3,500 meters, and by 4,000 meters, nearly all subjects scored 10.

After studying this information for several hours, the questions began to come forth. Who were these test subjects? Did they do it willingly? With full knowledge of the consequences? Were they prisoners? By 1951, the date of the first blast at Nevada, prisoners of war had been repatriated, or at least I thought. Were they domestic prisoners? I couldn't hardly imagine that. The logistics would be almost impossible. Surely some one would have known enough to get the information out. From 3,250 meters to 5,000 meters on the four quadrants would have covered eight intercepts, or 16 for the four quadrants, so a total of 64 subjects would have been required. Who were these people? I doubted that either Gary or Jim knew, or at lest I wanted to believe that at this point. I knew that early on, the military had conducted numerous tests with the initial above ground blasts. These included measuring the blast impacts on all sorts of facilities, from ordinary houses and office buildings, to, obviously military equipment, such as the tank I played with. There were lots of rumors that animals were also used. But, I had heard of nothing except pigs. Once the AEC really got into the act, I felt much of this type of activity had ceased, and testing followed a more orderly and scientific approach. Although I had to admit, whoever laid out this experiment clearly knew what they were doing from at least a statistical standpoint.

Two weeks had passed since I had returned from our original testing. So in a little over two weeks, I would be heading south again. I was determined to have a report prepared for Jim and his staff, and the report was going to include a complete analysis of the data, as well as a paragraph stating clearly what I believed to be the situation, namely humans were used for test subjects from 3,250 meters to 5,000 meters. The report wasn't long, just mainly summaries of the various statistical tests that I had run, as well as a brief statement as to whether the data indicated significant differences between various means existed. I really wasn't qualified to make any further observations. Probably, the area that I was best qualified to make a statement based on the data, was the comparison between those test animals that were used from ground zero to 3,000 meters (pigs), and those subjects (humans) that were used from 3,250 on. On that point, I felt very firm, based on the data that I had at my disposal. Unless somebody could come up with a better, and believable, explanation, I intended to firmly make that assumption in my report. However, my report was also going to be very scientific, and not include any personal philosophy on the latter point. The plain simple truth of the matter was that I couldn't come to grips with that point in a rational enough basis to deal with it anyway.

I wrote my report in longhand. I had made a promise to Jim, that I would not make a copy of any of the data, and he would receive my only copy of the report. So, instead of asking Mary, our one and only secretary to type it, I simply asked if she minded if I borrowed her typewriter during the evening, fortunately, for a picon at Louie's, she was agreeable. It took me several hours, but after one evenings work the report was done, and enclosed in a sealed, manila folder along with the original data, with Jim's name on the front. Other than discussions that followed, that was the last that I ever saw of the data, or my report. I had been true to my word, no other copy existed.

About two days later Dr. Blincoe called me and asked if I would drop by his office, which I shortly did. Cliff was not in his jovial mood when I caught him in his lab. "Those samples that you brought me from the Test Site, we have to talk".

His statement made me feel sick all over again. "What's the matter"? I sort of half light hearted responded.

"They're hot, too damn hot, where did you get them, under a bomb?" he shot back.

We reviewed the data, what there was of it so far. Of the 12 samples, he was about half done. However, the samples were running about ten fold over background. I was not a radiochemist, and I really didn't understand very much about radioactivity. But, I fully realized after looking at the limited data that the forage these grazing fistulated steers were consuming was pretty active. Probably two to three times what the folks at the Test Site would like us to believe. Cliff was always like a mad scientist, but today he was grumbling that the samples were too hot for his own safety. I knew that not to be true. Besides, he had plenty of isotopes in his lab that were a lot hotter than these samples.

"See, one of those radioactive signs you have over there? Just put these samples when you are done in one of your lead cabinets, slap a sign on the front and keep them. We may be asked to review. I suspect this will not please some people".

"Hope, you better not be getting me into something that I don't fully understand" Cliff groused.

"You saw the agreement, you are doing exactly what all parties agreed to, and that is, you will analyze all fistula samples collected on the test site for activity, a quarterly report will be prepared and submitted. Further, we, the University will never publish this information without prior approval from the AEC. However, as soon as you get this first month's data complete, I think it's a good idea that you prepare an initial summary from this first data so that I can hand deliver it to the boys at the Site. It should make their day", I concluded. It took Cliff about ten days to complete all of the analyses and prepare his brief report. So, I had two reports for Jim and Gary, neither one was what they probably wanted to see. It wasn't exactly what I wanted to present to them, but the facts were clear, and I certainly wasn't going to back down.

It was early August when I headed back to the site. I had called ahead, indicating that I would be at Mercury about noon, and that I wanted to meet with Jim and Gary. I indicated that probably Tom shouldn't be there. I wanted to clear the air on both reports before we commenced with our second sampling period. I was determined to deal with the "Pig" data first. It was still causing me considerable anguish. We had agreed to meet at their offices at the farm about 1:30 P.M., and just as I was driving up, so where they.

"Well, did you have any trouble getting in?", queried Gary.

"Nope, I think the Wackenhut boys almost know me. Anyway, when I flash my badge, they just grunt and wave me through", I responded.

We sat down around a small table that was in what could be considered a conference room. "I would like to cover the information that you asked me to analyze first. All of your data is here, there is a single copy of the report that you asked me to prepare. I did the best job of statistically analyzing these data that I could. But you have to admit there wasn't much information. As requested, I made no copy of the data, nor the enclosed report." Jim just looked at the folder and never opened it. Gary seemed to be getting a bit nervous. I went on, "The information is pretty straight forward, the pigs got blown to bits up to 1,000 meters and didn't do well for another 500 meters or so. In fact, up to 3,000 meters they were damaged by the blast. In fact I guess, everything that I analyzed was a direct result of the concussion of the blast. Any effect from radioactivity simply wouldn't have been measured at this early point. Now, a strange thing happens between 3,000 and 3,250 meters from ground zero. Up to 3,000 meters there is nothing to suggest that the test animals were anything but pigs. However, from 3,250 meters on that does not seem to be the case. In fact, there is a very significant change in both weight and percent hematocrit starting at 3,250 meters, which suggests to me that pigs were not used from that point on. Although limited, the data you gave me clearly suggests that human beings, likely young males, were substituted from that point out to 5,000 meters."

Neither Jim nor Gary said anything at that point. They just sort of hung their heads and looked at the table. Ed was the first to speak. "We didn't want to cloud your thinking. We sort of wanted you to come to whatever opinion you came to completely independently. But we have both been through the same ordeal. We found these data in an old file. We have never been able to find who authorized the study, or anything else for that matter. The key to us was the hematocrit values also. We both have felt men were used, and like you said, it starts at the 3,250 meter range. Our problem was that neither of us believed what we saw. So, we both agreed that another person ought to look at this information and come to a third opinion." I didn't bother to tell them how it affected me, for all I knew maybe it did the same to both of them. Perhaps they climbed to the top of Mt. Charleston to clear their thinking.

"Well, it's needless to say that I found this information extremely upsetting. I really can't imagine anybody placing human beings in harms way like this, at least not intentionally so. Who were these poor slobs that nearly got blown up, and in all likelyhood suffered extreme radiation, perhaps even lethal radiation?" I asked.

"We don't know for sure, but we have been led to believe it was military personnel; perhaps young soldiers returning from Korea. We can't find any verification on any of this. Believe me, you aren't going to get an answer from any military brass. Some of the brass that was here throughout the '50's are still here, but they are right under the base commander, and they are about as tight lipped as anybody you will ever see. I can assure you that nobody associated with the AEC conducted any such tests. If they had and I knew about it, I would attempt to make it public, even if it cost me my job", Jim concluded. "And I totally agree", added Gary.

As we talked, it became obvious to me that both Jim and Gary were probably as upset and disgusted about these historic events as I was. At that point in time, there seemed little more that I, or we, could do about these events. They could have occurred up to ten years previously: the records had been destroyed, with the exception of the information that we had in front of us. Without any more to go on, a public inquisition would probably be foolish and likely be viewed as coming from a bunch of whackos. And so nothing more came of Jim's strange manila folder. However, it's sufficient to say that for the first time in my young life, I began to look at things a bit differently. Although I loved my country, my government, and was a student of the constitution, I also realized, for the very first time, that all is not necessarily as it seems. I would carry the hurt from this experience for the rest of my life, but it would be many, many years before I finally realized the truth of what occurred during the early days on the Test Site.

After digesting the first report, I presented them with Blinco's analyses of the twelve fistula samples collected thus far. Both Jim and Gary raised their eyebrows instantly. Jim responded, "This is not a surprise, our measurements suggest that contamination on the east side of the site is quite high, regardless of what our military friends say. What do you think Gary, should we show this initial report to the brass, or just wait until the first quarter report is complete?' Gary laughed as he replied, "You know Major Treadwell. He's our primary contact Terry, right under Colonel Moore, the Base military commander. Treadwell about blew a gasket when he finally got it through his head that the University had the right to analyze their half of the samples for activity. If we hadn't had our legal counsel explain to him that the contract was binding, he probably would have found a way to stop you dead in your tracks. He may anyway. But to answer your question, I think it might be appropriate to let them see these data. They will sooner or later. I am satisfied that these are not an artifact, but probably represent just about what is really going on. Hell, he might as well blow another gasket. He's going to sooner or later anyway."

I responded by saying, "If he is going to blow, why not let him blow after I have another 12 samples. Give me three days from today, and I'll have them and be on my way." "Good idea", Jim and Gary booth agreed in unison.

So, the next morning, Tom and I headed out again with our traveling circus. Only this time, Tom had a helper. The plan was that I would discontinue coming to the test site after three months, as we all felt with some help Tom would be able to handle sampling from that point on.

This was certainly fine with me, as I had not grown to like this place anyway. Tom's helper was a young man by the name of Jason, from Vegas of all places. He liked cattle and horses, so he fit right in. He had already studied the plugs, and refitted some in my absence. So, the process was no stranger to him.

Our first morning's efforts were in area nine, not far from Yucca Flat. From our vantage point, I could look back and see numerous "inverted cones" from recent underground tests. It was obvious the days of above ground testing were coming to a close. There had been a fury of activity to develop adequate underground facilities for testing, but to date, these had not been particularly successful. The equipment didn't exist to drill a big enough hole for device placement, that likewise was deep enough to prevent venting. Consequently, most blasts had vented. It was my belief that the underground tests probably greatly eliminated the airborne cloud of radioactivity that was surely contaminating eastern Nevada and southern Utah. However, when venting did occur, I also believed that a great amount of highly contaminated strata from the depths of the hole were deposited in the general vicinity of the test, probably up to a half mile or more on all sides. This material, coming primarily from rock, would be fairly high in nutrients such as calcium and phosphorus, as well as a great number of micro elements and probably even some heavy metals. Nutrients sprayed on vegetation in this manner have a tendency to be taken up by the plant in two ways, directly from the leaves, as well as much like a topical dressing of fertilizer. The only problem, a lot of these elements got converted into their radioactive isotopes as a direct result of the blast. Consequently, I suspected that much of the contamination that Blincoe had found was a direct result of the venting of these underground blasts, not above ground testing. If this were the case, today's test should be sky high, as I could see about twenty apparent inverted cones from my observation point. I wondered around on my horse looking at some of these "cones". Some were rather minor, perhaps only ten to fifteen feet across and a like number of feet deep. Some, however, had really vented. They were maybe 100 feet across and perhaps 150 feet deep. I shuddered to think of the tremendous blast that would have made such a hole in mother earth.

I pretty much let Tom and Jason do the sampling, I just stood back and kept out of the way. Tom had long since mastered the fistula trade, and it was obvious that Jason was going to be good at it also. I noticed that he was extremely gentle with the animals, far more so than Tom, and that pleased me. I never liked to see animals handled roughly, especially ones that you had to work closely with such as these fistulated steers. By noon, sampling was complete and we were back to the farm and all cleaned up by no later than two o'clock. Just as we were finishing, Dick Jensen drove up, looking like a lonely cowboy.

"Damn, I wanted to come out and meet you guys at six this morning, but I had to run all over Vegas chasing some wild tale about spies, all false alarms again, as usual, but it caused me to miss being out here. Sorry, I really wanted to come and play!"

"Well, we hired Jason to take your place anyway, and he turned out to be a pretty good hand. You weren't missed", I quipped back.

"Well, just for that comment, I might not share with you what I found out about your old girl friend", Dick shot back.

"Hell, she was never my girl friend! She was too good for that. I just wanted to know how she was doing", I responded.

"Well, my report is she is doing fairly well. She married a vet about eight years ago, started a family, but it looks like she and her husband moved back to your home town a couple of years later. I knew the agent in charge in Ventura. We went to the academy together. He told me that they are working on her family's orange ranch", he concluded. Both Tom and Jason had been listening to this conversation with some interest, so Dick really loaded it on at this point. "However, I feel that I must warn you, before you go sniffing around there you better understand that she didn't marry just any vet. This guy is a highly decorated vet from both the War, as well as Korea. He's an expert with small arms, and he knows how to disable, and kill for that matter, by hand. So, whatever designs you had on this young lady, my advice would be go the other direction." With that Tom let out a big guff haw, and Jason was trying not to openly laugh, but had a grin from ear to ear.

I kind of felt the red creeping up both cheeks as I tried to explain I only just wanted to know how she was doing. "Yeah, sure, sure, we know. You wouldn't even consider talking to an old flame, even if she were a show girl on the strip," Dick just kept pouring it on. I could see this wasn't going any place fast, so I just dummied up. But I felt good that Nancy was married, especially that she had gone back to her family's ranch. Las Vegas was no place for a girl like her, especially if she was raising a family.

The next two days sampling went off without a hitch. I just more or less went along for the ride. In fact, each day I took one of the horses and cut about a tenmile circle around where the sampling was occurring. I never ceased to be amazed at all that I saw. Craters from above ground testing: craters big enough to put a small town: in, vents from underground tests, remnants of structures, equipment that had been subjected to testing, on and on. The amount of work that had gone on at the test site since its inception 11 years before was essentially beyond belief. I could only guess what this must have cost us American taxpayers, but I rationalized that it must have been necessary to keep the Russians at bay. I didn't like to think about the testing that had included humans. The emotional impact of that knowledge was slowly coming down to a point that I could deal with it at least in a rational manner: but I could never accept it; and it would never leave me. Well, I got out of Dodge without further problems. I could only imagine what this Major Treadwell might be like. I supposed that I would probably get the pleasure of meeting him next trip. I supposed, in my thoughts, as I headed north of U.S. 95, that he would probably bring along Ben Johnson as his hit man!

Well, my worst suspicions about below ground testing were confirmed. It took about two weeks, but Blincoe showed me the results from the samples we got from area nine, where all the holes in the ground were. They were about twice the level as any previous samples. I guessed it was better to poison the test site (and a few people like myself!), rather than contaminate the whole of Utah. I had Blincoe prepare an additional report when he was finished with this set, attach it to his original report, and I added a short summary. Now we had the results from 24 samples, nothing had changed, in fact the last 12 samples actually averaged higher than the first 12 samples, but that was primarily a result of the area nine samples. I guessed if this Tredwell guy was going to blow a gasket, I might as well help him make a clean shot!

September also represented the start of school, and I would be teaching Feeds again. The University was registering during the first week, with classes starting the second week, so I had scheduled the September sample date for the first week in September. About three days before my blast off, Jim called, and said that I had better come a day early. Treadwell was going berserk and we had to meet with him. Gee, he hadn't even seen the latest samples yet, but I agreed, and indicated to Jim that I would have an updated report, but I also warned Jim, Treadwell probably will grow less fond of me after I coughed up the latest. Jim cautioned, "This is not a laughing matter, the military answers to no one. They will play hell stopping this sampling process, but guys like Treadwell are not to be taken lightly."

I thought a lot about Jim's comments as I again headed south. I was sure that the military didn't want the knowledge to come out that contamination was anywhere near where the data was indicating. I also thought a lot about the data that I had analyzed for Jim. I supposed that

Treadwell would get plumb excited if he had the slightest knowledge that I had access to that information. As I was thinking this process through for the hundredth time, I began to kick myself for not having retained a copy of that information. A copy, retained somewhere only known by myself just might be a valuable card to play. Well, I was good at poker, and I guessed that I could bluff that one if I had to. I could just imagine the anguished look on Jim's face if that knowledge came out.

As planned, I arrived at Mercury a day early, passed the "pecker checkers" as I had grown to call the Wackenhut gang and drove straight to the office at the farm. Only Jim was there. He indicated that it probably wasn't appropriate for Gary to attend this meeting. "They want to meet with you on a road north of Yucca Flat. We call that the Yucca road. There's an intersection out there with the road that goes west to Paiute Mesa. I am not sure why they want to meet there, but I informed Major Treadwell that I would attend the meeting. That didn't set well, but under no circumstances would I allow you to meet with the military on sensitive issues without the AEC being present." I didn't say anything, I just sort of looked at Jim. He never carried a side arm, and he probably wouldn't know how to use one anyway.

I sort of joked, and was probably slightly more than half serious when I said, "I have noticed that old, thirty-ought six rifle in your office, don't know why you keep it there, but I am beginning to feel like I might want to borrow it."

"Well you can't. We just keep it for animals that must be destroyed, but you're not authorized to carry a firearm on the Site under any circumstances. Now don't get up tight, Treadwell's never killed anybody here yet, at least not as far as I know. He's just a mean and disagreeable ass as far as I am concerned. Now let's get going, or we will be late" The "at least not as far as I know" comment was really comforting. I liked Jim, but he was a bureaucrat through and through. I suspected there were lots of things that happened on the test site that he didn't know about.

It was about 25 miles out to this so called intersection. We took Jim's official AEC car, a Buick Roadmaster, which was one of my favorite automobiles. It purred right along, even had air conditioning, so the ride was in comfort. The Yucca road north went in a near north/south straight line. We cleared a juniper covered ridge, and headed down a long alluvial fan to the valley bottom. Coming out of the east was another road heading towards the Mesa. The Mesa road didn't appear to have a good gravel cover, as I could clearly see the dust from two vehicles heading west on it. They were about the same distance from the intersection as we were, but they appeared to be traveling much faster. "I suppose that's Treadwell. Sometimes, he brings a whole entourage, which I guess he is today by the looks of things", Jim summarized.

Treadwell beat us to the intersection by about a minute or two, so the dust had settled by our arrival. Despite the two vehicles, there were only two of them, both in uniform. Jim got out and approached Treadwell. The Major didn't offer to shake any hands. He just indicated that the person in the second vehicle was a Sergeant Stafford. The Sergeant gave a right smart salute to Jim. I immediately noticed that both Treadwell and Stafford carried side arms, and Stafford also had a rifle of sorts mounted against the front window of his sedan. Jim started by saying, "Major, and Sergeant Stafford, let me introduce Terry Hope, as you know he's from the University of -"

Before he could finish, Treadwell cut in, "Yeah, I know his pedigree. Remember I reviewed his file as well." With that, Treadwell turned, put his hands on his hips and approached me head on. He was not a big man, but certainly larger than me, probably 5'10", and likely 180 pounds. I judged him to be tough. His neck muscles were standing out. His hands were large. I stepped back, but only a half step, then I realized that I had better hold my ground. He almost ran into me before he realized that I wasn't going to back up, which clearly surprised and agitated him.

"You either got to be the dumbest son of a bitch that ever stepped foot on this facility, or you got brass balls the size of 25 pound cannon shot. I never knew anybody in academia that had balls, so I believe you to just be dumb."

"Now, stop this nonsense Major. This type of conduct is simply not necessary, I'll - " Jim tried to intervene.

"Stay the fuck out of this Fountain. This is between this little asshole and me", exclaimed the major. As this was happening, the sergeant moved over somewhat alongside Jim, whose face was now ashen grey.

"Now I am going to tell you and I am only going to tell you once. I detest what you are trying to do. I hate people like you. We work our selves to death, taking every risk in the world to protect the likes of you from the enemy. Yet you show up without a care in the world, and phony up some data trying to prove how we are putting the whole western world in jeopardy. We ought to send the likes of you to Russia to see just how you might like it over there. I saw your first set of data, and that was enough. I don't want to see anymore. As far as I am concerned, however you want to fix it is fine with me: but it will be fixed. Or else! You know, you little bastard, people have died in wrecks on this facility, in fact people have died in wrecks right here at this intersection!"

I hadn't said a word, nor had I moved an inch. My arms were hanging loosely at my side, but I could feel the temperature rising. A side ways glance at Jim clearly told me he was of no use. Besides the sergeant had all but restrained him. So, I guessed it was up to me. I had seen my Dad handle some pretty tough people in the oil patch, but frankly I had never been quite in this position. I really didn't know how to respond, but I wasn't going to back down to this jerk, no. No matter what!

I turned away at the conclusion of his final outburst, and sort of looked across the playa. The Nevada landscape never ceased to amaze me. God had made it spectacularly beautiful, even in its driest form, and this valley was no exception. The sky was a turquoise blue, nearly beyond description. A few silky white clouds seemed to be just laying, with no purpose, against the blue. The way the ridges undulated to the valley floor was done with a flourish that no sculpture or artist could ever capture. You could see the heat waves rising against the distance ridges. As I stared, of all things, about a half mile or so away, a coyote ambled across the playa. I could only wonder what thoughts were going through his brain at this time. It was God's world, and it was being offended by mankind, and this I found extremely irritating.

I turned slowly to again face the major. By now his face was near crimson. "Sir, I will ignore both your comments as well as your language. But, I will tell you as an officer of the United States Military, I find both to be extremely unbecoming. However, for your information, there is sound reason to be doing exactly what I am doing. Sampling the vegetation of this facility, in a fairly scientific manner, to attempt to determine exactly what the ramifications of the actions of people like you have been over the last ten years or so is reason enough. And so far, I find that you have pretty well contaminated this facility. Now, to you and your mentality, I am sure the end justifies the means, but I would remind you that just slightly over 15 years ago we concluded the most horrible war that mankind has ever fought, all because one person, and his followers, believed without exception that the end justified the means. I have no doubt that the atomic bomb is now an essential weapon. It indeed is probably the only way in the world we can neutralize the Russian Bear, and I have no doubt that continued testing of atomic weapons is absolutely necessary for the survival of the free world. Now I am just a scientist, not a politician, nor a military man.

But my job here is to begin to get a handle on what has happened, and I suspect in due time, when we have sufficient data, we will find, that indeed, this facility has been unnecessarily contaminated, and likely we will also find, that this contamination will impact the long term health of test site workers. And furthermore, I also suspect that in due time we will also find that the health of a vast number of innocent civilians off site, throughout eastern Nevada and southern Utah will also have been impacted. And this says nothing about the innocent people that were used as test subjects on this facility in the early days. Now, as you know, our agreement clearly states that the University can publish none of these data without AEC approval, and likely that will not come for a number of years, if ever. But I will tell you this Sir, if you ever as so much as approach me or any person involved in this ongoing research again in a manner similar as to how you just approached me, then I will do my level best to see that somehow that data becomes public, if for no other reason than to see that you and your type are forever buried. Now, I will tell you once and only once, I am a patriot. I love this country beyond belief and I would gladly give my life for it if I so had to. And, if I must die in some phonied up automobile wreck out here on this facility so be it, but I will assure you that copies of all data that I have collected, or have been provided to date, will surely find their way into public consumption if that happens. Now, Major Treadwell, Sir, I really have nothing more to say to you. I must get on with my sampling tomorrow, and for that matter the two days that follow. If you so like, you certainly can accompany us, who knows, you might even learn something." I thought about a final sentence, something like - And Sir, for your information, I also hate bastards like you. But I thought better, I just didn't want to descend to his level.

There was stone cold silence. The Major's eyes bored holes right through me, but he said nothing. Sergeant Stafford had backed away from Jim, and was just looking at his feet. I guessed Treadwell was either going to hit me, or ventilate me with his 45 where his right hand was resting, or just shut the hell up and back out. I bet on the latter and that's what happened. As he headed towards his car, he stopped once and said, "Remember, none of this is to be published without AEC approval. We'll hold you personally responsible if it gets out, let's go Sergeant". And with that, they were gone in a cloud of dust. Jim looked exhausted, but he was not pleased about my statement about test subjects, "You promised me you didn't keep a copy of that information."

"I didn't", I countered.

Our ride back to the farm was slow and labored. Jim began by apologizing for the military, but I said forget it. He countered with several experiences where Treadwell had dressed him down in a similar fashion. I inquired why he took it, but about all I got back was the distinct feeling that Jim was scarred to death of the guy. "He's actually slapped a couple of AEC employees, but he's never really hit anybody to my knowledge. He has also threatened to shoot, in fact, he threatened to shoot Gary, and that's why I wouldn't bring him today", Jim continued.

"Hasn't anybody turned him to his superiors, whoever they might be?" I asked.

"Yeah, and that hasn't worked very well either. After Gary and Treadwell had their encounter, Gary did file a complaint with my permission with Colonel Moore, the base military commander. Moore fired back a memo for everyone to read, with a copy to the head of the AEC, basically saying he backed Major Treadwell in any and all actions that he felt necessary to take in order to keep the base mission on course. And of course, the base mission is to test atomic devices of one kind or another. Like he said, accidents have happened. You got to understand, people like Gary and I are career bureaucrats, with few short years before full retirement, five years in my case. So we don't have much fight on incidents like this. All that can ever happen to us is to be big losers, or worse. I don't see how we can win."

I didn't have much to say for the rest of the way, but I did a lot of thinking, thinking that literally lasted for the rest of my life. I began to realize how a bureaucracy works, and how it could become so complacent. Just don't rock the boat - don't complain, don't rat, don't even think, just attend. And if you do so in the proper fashion, you will be rewarded with a fine retirement package for your final days in this world. And for the first time I realized that maybe the military wasn't all I had been led to believe.

I had always held the military in the highest regard. That was a product of my mother. Every male member of her family had been a military officer at one time or another. Mom tried to enroll me in the New Mexico Military Academy at the start of the Korean war, so that I could go to war as an officer, not an enlisted man. I was only about 14 when that happened, but I would have no part of it. In fact, I flatly said that I would run away if forced to go there. Mom was extremely strong willed, and the next few days had been a test of wills beyond belief, but I didn't go to New Mexico, nor did I have to run away. I guessed my belief of the military had always been a picture of G.I. grunts slugging it out through France in mud up to your knees, and I guessed if I ever went into the military that's exactly where I would be. Thus far, my experiences on the Nevada Test Site had somewhat distorted that concept.

I felt sorry for the likes of Jim and Gary, not so much for their situation, but that they lacked the courage to stand up for what they knew was right. It was hard for me to imagine a job being so important that you would literally compromise your very beliefs just to keep that job. Bureaucracies were really a new thing, not very many of these agencies existed before the war. The ones that did were still small enough that individual incentives still counted for something. I could clearly tell that I didn't like what I was beginning to see in, at least this bureaucracy. I could readily believe that it was a growing and incurable phenomena.

By the time we got back to the farm, both Jim and I had regained our composure. "Let's just forget this incident ever happened. It was just so much B.S. as far as I am concerned", was my suggestion. I could see Jim sort of breathing a sigh of relief as he nodded in the affirmative. There wasn't much more to do for the rest of the day, and I didn't want to stay in Mercury. So I told Tom that I would see him at six in the morning, but I was going to Vegas for the night. I toured the strip, but didn't really want to stay in a joint. So, it was back to my original rest stop, the Plaza. I ate an early dinner, my favorite when out, chicken fried steak and mashed potatoes with gravy. And I opted for an early bed, but sleep didn't come real fast. As the night wore on I thought long and hard about the many events that had occurred since I had come to Vegas. It was now September 8, and my first trip to sample had been on my birthday, June 25, just 79 days ago. And in that short time an awful lot that I had come to believe in, accept, or just simply take for granted, had come under attack. And, I was just 27 years old, probably far too young to really make any sense out of it.

I had set the alarm for 3:45 A.M., as I wanted breakfast, and it took over an hour from downtown to the farm, but I made it by six. Tom and Jason had beat me by about five minutes, so they had started to load things. Just as I started to help, Dick Jensen also drove up.

"Mind if I tag along today, got nothing better to do."

I responded, "Hell ask the boss, I have been demoted to just an observer."

Tom laughed, "Yup, we can always use another grunt." However, I couldn't help but notice the side arm that Dick was packing.

When everything was loaded, Dick suggested that he take his car as there were some things that he wanted to talk to me about. As we pulled out, he started, "Well, I already heard about your little set-to with Treadwell yesterday. A Sergeant Stafford happened to tell one of my "good" contacts about the events of yesterday. Seems Stafford hates Treadwell, but he thought my contact was a safe person to vent his frustrations on, which he was. Anyway, my contact called me, so I ran this Stafford guy down last night and he told me the whole story. It sounds like you pissed the good Major Treadwell off, in fact, probably better than anybody else has ever done. Stafford thought you were staying at Mercury last night, but I found out you went to town. Anyway, we know Treadwell went back to Mercury last night, and my guess, he was looking for a piece of your ass, in fact, probably all of it. So, for the rest of your time on the Site you are under my supervision. That's a direct order from Ben Johnson. Even though Johnson's an ass himself, he hates, and fears Treadwell. Turns out Johnson thinks you are OK, and he said its my ass if Treadwell so much as harms a hair on your body. So that's how you get an extra hand for the next three days."

I really didn't know how to respond. I liked Dick, but I didn't like the concept of him baby sitting me. I knew I could hold my own with Treadwell, but then I thought about the ridiculousness of that idea. Treadwell wasn't the kind of guy to make a play on a level field to begin with. Suddenly, I liked Dick sitting next to me, especially with a pretty fancy long barrel 38.

It was a pleasant day, with no problems whatsoever. We were sampling on a high plateau, to the south of Frenchman Flat, the view was superb. Dick and I took the horses, leaving Ron and Jason on foot. I quizzed Dick how a guy like Treadwell could ever get where he was now in the first place. "He was a highly decorated vet from the war. He fought with Patton, and everybody that I ever knew that fought with Patton felt we should have continued right on to kick the Bear's ass. We didn't, but guys like Treadwell become paranoid about the Ruskys. He probably believes, without question, that the free world's future is totally dependent on us building more and bigger bombs than them, and faster. So, he looks at a guy like you as somebody that is muddying up the works, and in his mental frame of mind, if you've got to be wasted to keep things on track, so be it. The end justifies the means."

"Damn, this is like something out of the movies. I thought when Bugsie got wasted here, hit men were going out of style. Now I find a United States Major has taken over the assignment, the only problem is that it appears that in this case I am the hitee".

Dick laughed, "Well, I wouldn't worry too much. I think he would be satisfied just giving you a black eye. I kind of got the impression from Stafford that you are probably the first person to ever call his bluff." Well, I didn't worry. I'd had black eyes before, and I would have them again, but it never came from major Treadwell. In fact, I never saw the gentlemen again, perhaps thanks to Dick. We stayed pretty close for the next three days. I left my pick-up at the farm, and I rode back and forth with Dick. Sampling went off without a hitch, except for the last day.

The last days sampling was to be done in the far northwest corner of area 15. Jason reported in sick, so it was just Dick, Tom and myself. The area was dotted with many junipers, sometimes almost in groves. Additionally, there were several large inverted cones, as well as a number of smaller ones. We turned the cattle out. I was still recommending that we always use Bronco, and three of the five other steers. Bronco just seemed to know, having now been sampled so many times. I felt that you could just turn Bronco loose, and he would kind of keep the other animals in line until it was time to go home. So, we did turn them loose amongst the trees and we shaded up. After sometime, Tom saddled up and drifted out to see what was going on. In about half an hour he was back saying they were about a mile away, shaded up like us, but he stirred them up and they returned to grazing. I suggested that by now they probably had good samples, so it was time to finish the day.

Tom and Dick rode the horses, I just ambled along behind them as we journeyed down through the groves of juniper. As we broke out, the steers were in the open scattered over a flat about a quarter of a mile away, but I only counted three. We all noticed the discrepancy about the same time. I scratched my head, especially as now I noticed the missing critter was none other than Bronco Billy himself. I suggested to Tom and Dick that they head out in opposite directions and I would think about this predicament. I was sure he wasn't far away, and oh how right I was! About two hundred yards off to my left was a large inverted cone, or at least by the berm it had left, I judged it to be large. A horrible thought occurred to me, but then I realized that Bronco couldn't be that dumb, or could he?

I ambled over to the cone, peered over the edge, and there was Billy, smack dab in the bottom, about 50 feet straight down, munching peacefully on tumbleweed that had blown into the pit. My heart sank, because I really had no idea in the world how we could ever get him out of here. I whistled for the boys, and they both came at a gallop, with me standing on the berm, the whereabouts of the fourth steer was no longer a mystery.

Dick's only comment was, "Shit, he's a goner." Tom agreed. I stood there looking at Billy, he was just peacefully munching, oblivious to his predicament. Tom only made matters worse, "The bottom of those cones are supposed to be hotter than hell. We have been told repeatedly to never go down one." Dick was upholstering that long barreled 38. All I could think of was how faithful Billy had been once we got the kinks worked out. Somehow, the thought occurred to me that I wasn't going to leave him on the Test Site, dead or alive. Billy was going back to Reno with me, regardless. He was too good for this place.

"Put your God damn pistola away. We ain't shooting no steers today", I yelled.

"Well what plan have you got? The nearest helicopter is in Vegas, and it would take a week to get clearance for that", responded Dick.

"Well for an Oklahoma cowboy, you must not know everything. You guys go back to the trucks and get all of the ropes that you can possibly come up with, I think there are probably at least two lasso ropes, and in the horse trailer, there's a long cotton rope. I'll jiffy down there and explain to Bronco how this is going to work". Dick and Tom looked at each other and shrugged as they rode off. I wanted to go down with Billy to see how soft the material on the sides was, and it was plenty soft. I more or less slid to the bottom, the only problem being, there wasn't room for Billy, much less me. But, when I hit, we seemed to make room somehow for each other.

Billy had a pretty good halter on already. It looked like it would just about hold his weight, so we were in luck there. I headed back up, then I fully realized just how difficult this was going to be. For about every step I took up the side, it felt like I was slipping back about a step and a half. And it was hot in the bottom of that pit. I choose to believe it was the desert heat of southern Nevada, and not radioactivity. But I did make the mental note that I would likely wear a new badge to get out tonight. By the time I made it to the top, Dick and Tom were back, and they had rustled up plenty of rope.

"OK, here is what we are going to do. First, pull those cinches down as tight as possible, we can't loose a saddle. I am going to take the best nylon rope we got and tie these two horses together by their saddle horn's. Let's leave about five feet between them. You guys take the halter lead ropes for both horses and just hold them steady while I rig this up". I actually sounded like I knew what I was doing. The horses were gentle, and for whatever reason we had taken the two stoutest horses available today. Once they were securely tied together, I took the cotton rope and tied it to the mid point of the lasso rope between the horses. The lasso rope was a long one, 30 feet, so I had been able to make three complete loops to tie off the cotton rope on. I threw the rest of the cotton rope over the berm. "Now back both horses up to the berm, as far as you can, but Lord's sake don't drop a horse in that hole, or we will really be in a mess", I again commanded with authority. Once this was done, I headed over the edge again and down to my old buddy.

I tied a stout bowline to Billy's halter, and yelled up to start leading both horses away together until we got the slack out. "OK once we start, just keep going slow and steady, don't let them back up no matter what happens. If I yell to stop, that means we got to rest, but don't back up whatever you do."

And the circus started. I could tell Billy wanted to go home, and it seemed like he knew this would work. He headed straight up the side, but he weighed a thousand pounds and no way did he have the strength to do anything but just hold his head up. I watched as the rope grew taunt, and his neck stretched out, but it did enable him to take a couple of steps. Just don't fall down old buddy, I prayed to myself. Once I finally got his hind feet out of dead bottom, I got squarely behind him and put my shoulder squarely into his ass, and yelled with all of my might, "Keep going!" It was slow, but Billy never fell. We had to stop a time or two as both he and I were exhausted. I had to laugh about putting my shoulder to his ass. Under these conditions, I probably wasn't pushing more than 50 pounds, but it did help stabilize him. Once we were half way, the going seemed to get easier. I could see the edge of the berm, 20 feet, 15, 10, and finally 5. Billy could just about see over the edge, but he was getting awfully wobbly. I shouted, "One more big jerk" And that's what happened. Billy went over the berm, fell flat on his side, both horses looked about dead, I laid down besides Billy.

"I can't believe we did it, your right, this Oklahoma cowboy sure to hell didn't know everything. I never seen nothing like this before, and

I sure to hell hope I never do again." Dick looked at his watch, and grinned when he said, "It probably didn't seem like it to you, but from the first pull until you all cleared the berm, it took 45 minutes of non stop pulling." No wonder Billy and I were a bit tired.

We didn't get home real early that night, but we did get home. And sure enough my badge didn't pass the test. Tom checked me out, and said he had never seen one that hot before. "I think it was from sweat, not radioactivity", was about all I could muster. I thanked Dick for all he had done, "I don't like being baby sat, but it probably wasn't such a bad idea for the last few days." I left word that within a week I would have somebody down for Billy. I'll be damned if he is going to stay in this hell hole. Treadwell would likely use him for target practice. Early the next morning I headed up highway 95 and never looked back. I didn't want to go straight to Reno, but I sure to hell wanted out of southern Nevada.

I never wanted to go to the Test Site again, but unfortunately to see the project through, I did have to go to Vegas at least once a year, or more. If we could accomplish business in Vegas and not go out to the site, it was just fine with me.

The only other noteworthy from that trip was that Billy's sample from the bottom of that hole registered higher on the contamination scale than any other sample we ever collected on the Site.

By the time I got to Tonopah, I was tired. The events of the last few days had really caught up with me. So I said to hell with it, got a room at the Mizpah, and spent the afternoon at the bar. I didn't want to drown my sorrows, but I just wanted to contemplate what all had happened. As the day wore on a few old miners struck up conversations with me which I thoroughly enjoyed. This was old Nevada, the Nevada I had grown to love in a few short years. One asked me what I was doing in Tonopah. "Been down on the Test Site", was my response.

"Oh, that's a bad place, bad for Nevada, bad for us miners. I hear there's so much radioactivity down there everything underground will be contaminated - soon won't be safe to be underground south of Tonopah!" was his comforting response. "Sure hope you didn't get hurt, your too young to have to deal with that", he added. I tended to agree, but probably not for the reasons he might have thought.

In the Mizpah bar, if you sit at just the right spot, you can watch the sun go down over "T" mountain. And I did just that, contemplating how fortunate I was to live in Nevada, and to have known, no matter how briefly, the real Nevada. I would willingly vote to give Las Vegas, and the rest of southern Nevada, including the Test Site to California or Arizona. They could fight over it. Just let me have Tonopah north!

The next morning I still didn't want to go back to Reno. So I headed down Highway 6, towards Ely, for about 15 miles. Then north to Smokey Valley. I wanted to cross over the Tequima range, through the old town of Manhatten, then on to Belmont. Belmont was the first county seat of Nye County, but it had long since been a ghost town. I had spotted a place called Morgan Basin on a map of central Nevada, and that's where I really wanted to go. I got to the Arcalarius Ranch in Smokey Valley, asked directions. Found I had to back track a bit, but I was at the head of Morgan Basin, as far as I could drive by noon. The road ended at a trail head to the top of Table Mountain. I could see the rim rock about 2,500 feet above me, but below were dense stands of aspen, with some intermediate pines. I figured I could be to the top in two hours, but it took nearer three. But it was worth it. The top of Table Mountain was a garden spot beyond belief. Not over 10,000 feet high, but it was solid meadow, interspersed with aspen groves. There were a few cattle but deer were everywhere. I sat on the edge of the rim, looking across Monitor Valley at nearby towering Jefferson, and far to the north, both the Toiyabes and the Tequimas. I just wanted to sit and take in God's world. I wanted to distance myself from everything that I had learned and saw at the Site. I wanted my Nevada to always be just like I was experiencing at that point in time. But try as I could, the nagging feeling kept creeping into my thoughts that I had better enjoy the moment. Strange things were starting to happen in Nevada, probably not in the too distant future either. Things I didn't believe I would like. I was back to the pick-up about an hour before sunset, so I hurried up Monitor Valley, eventually taking Pete's Summit back over the Toquemia Range to the Smokey Valley highway and Highway 50 to Austin. That night I stayed in a motel in Austin, had dinner at the International, listened to some old buckaroos talk of yesteryear in Nevada at the bar, and how things were going to hell in a handcart. I had to laugh as I listened, for these old gents didn't have the slightest clue as to how lucky they really were. Their Nevada still existed and would for quite a few more years. The next morning I finally faced up to the fact that I had to be in Reno.

For many years I never really learned the whole truth about the Test Site, and likely I never will. But these things I did learn in due time. There was contamination from above ground testing and it was significant. The small communities of Caliente and Pioche and Panaca, as well as the many isolated farms and ranches in eastern Nevada paid a stiff price for this contamination. And so did the nearby towns in southern Utah, Saint George and Cedar City. In some areas cancer, often in the form of lukemia, but just as easily breast cancer or stomach or whatever, were often four times the national average or more. However, reporting was poor, and often times these facts were not known until much later. Birth defects were elevated. There were many studies, but essentially the government never did a thing. Workers on the site paid a stiff price, especially many of my AEC friends. Charles Speth eventually died from leukemia, even though he only stayed a year in Caliente. Like many, he came down with lukemia around 1980, twenty years after the fact, and was treated with massive blood transfusions. The only thing that they didn't realize in 1981 or 1982 was that the blood was dirty, carrying AID's. So he, like many, got the double whammy, and when your immune system is already shot, getting dirty blood can cause the worst of deaths. Charlie's family could have gotten help if they could have proven he was on the Site at one particularly dirty event. But the University conveniently destroyed all of his travel records, so his family received no help. Charlies death was a particularly sad event for me, but that is another story to tell later.

I didn't really know the final chapter of the Test Site until nearly the year 2000; And those who were the mystery people in the experiment I analyzed for Jim and Gary. We can thank the internet for solving that riddle. The internet had allowed people from all over to communicate, and that's how it was all got put together.

Soldiers were used in the tests. They just did what they were told, not knowing the consequences. Gradually, over the years they became aware of the consequences. Survivors asked questions, but they got no answers, until the internet became a viable tool. Through the internet, they found each other and learned what happened. A good example is Herbert L. Stradley, currently Pennsylvania State Commander for the National Association of Atomic Veterans.

Stradley indicates that only one man from each company within the military were selected for the Test Site, so you never knew where your buddies were from, or what happened to them afterwards. And this process greatly discouraged or made impossible future communication between the soldiers. Stradley was only 20 when marched onto the Test Site He wasn't worried, after all, in training classes they were told, "Don't worry, it takes 27 rems to kill you and 35 rems to make you sterile". The young trainer also assured Combat Battalion A, "This is not a haphazard maneuver. The radiation may be high, but you will be moved out before you have time to develop radiation sickness." Not knowing what a rem was, Stradley and 2,450 other soldiers marched into the desert in the predawn darkness of April 25, 1953. The men hunched down in trenches were ordered to keep their heads down and then charge forward towards ground zero after the explosion.

Federal scientist in charge that April morning expected the blast to pack a nuclear wallop equal to 24,000 tons of TNT, roughly double the size of Hiroshima. Stradlley was in the first trench, about 10,800 feet (3,270 meters) away. The bomb went off at 4:40 a.m. Those in the rear of the trench say they saw the bones of the men in front of them, like a three dimensional X-ray. Stradley said, "Then the earth shook like a bowl of jello." The force of the explosion slammed Stradley against the bottom of the trench. "I busted my nose", he says. Actually, the blast threw a nuclear punch equal to 60,000 tons of TNT, more than double what was expected. After the blast, as ordered, the men leaped out of the trenches and moved towards ground zero. Birds fell out of the sky for an hour. In addition to the soldiers, there were animals there that were being used in experiments. "The ones above the ground were not there anymore, only chains that held them, some of the animals that were below ground were either dead or had blood running from their nose, ears, and rectum. As the men charged ground zero, they heard radiation monitors shouting warnings. "They said it was too hot, to get out of there", he said. After running to safety, the men stood in long lines to remove the radioactive dust from their uniforms. "Decontamination was some guy standing with a broom brushing the dust off of you and that was it", Stadley remembers. By the end of 1953 Stradley's gums bled extensively, and his teeth fell out. In 1989 Stradley developed extensive stomach cancer, from which he still suffers today. Stradley has spent years petitioning the government for help, not only for himself, but the approximately 200,000 other servicemen that were exposed to radiation. He has not been successful and concludes, "Bottom line is, it's a stall tactic till there's nobody left. When there's only a few of us left, they'll make it a big thing."

In 1951, the AEC, Public Health Service and the Department of Defense knew that exposure to radioactive materials was a deadly threat. In 1951, every aspect of nuclear testing was controlled by the AEC. But the military wanted realistic results in atomic exercise. To get that the military concluded the men would have to be "stressed". They wanted the men to be placed ever closer to the atomic blasts so they could learn how to conduct atomic warfare on a future nuclear battlefield. To do that, the Defense Department would have to wrest control from the AEC. By early 1953, the Pentagon had done just that. From then on, whenever a nuclear test involved battlefield maneuvers, field commanders would be responsible for the placement of their men, not the AEC. And so it goes.

The AEC never authorized the University to publish the radioactive data collected from the fistual samples, although several years data was obtained, analyzed and written up. Years later, the AEC did publish their version in a federal publication, but to their credit, the results paralleled that which the University found.

In searching the web, I never found contact with any survivor from the study that I analyzed. But only a handful of men were involved in that study, while some estimates place total troop involvement at the site at as much as 200,000.

After learning all of these facts, the same sickness or depression or more likely guilt seemed to come over me that came over me that day so long ago when Dr. Weeth said, "These results are from people, not pigs". I could have done so much more to warn people about the dangers of radiation. I knew it had spread far to the east, I just never fully realized just how much, nor how far. I knew men were involved in experiments at the Site. Yet, I never attempted to find the truth for nearly 40 years. At least President Kennedy signed the Limited Test Ban Treaty on August 5, 1963, disallowing any further above ground testing. I always believed our efforts had some hand in that. And of course, the Comprehensive Test Ban Treaty went into effect on September 24,

1996, disallowing any further atomic tests. Nevertheless, I could have done more, and that thought will never leave.

It was a sobering experience, almost more so than I could ever explain, or even comprehend for that matter. It made me realize that as much as I had grown to love Nevada, there were parts of the Silver State that just weren't so very good. It began to make me realize that a state that is 86% controlled by the federal government is just that, controlled by distant bureaucracies that had very little to do with the real Nevada, regardless of the circumstances. I had often heard the phrase "Military Industrial Complex", the Test Site was one such place, a place for people like me to stay far, far away from.

ACADEMIC LIFE

I didn't discuss the Test Site with anybody at the University, except Blincoe. I simply indicated that he should keep testing the samples as they came in every month. A report had to be prepared quarterly, but it must be at my doing, actually Cliff was not authorized to even see his own data in this case. He knew that the samples came from the test site, but other than that he had no knowledge, and after my experiences, I assumed that was the best way to keep it. Other than that, no one knew on campus anything about what had happened, except Pete, and he lived in far away Elko.

Pete knew that I had been to the Test Site; we had discussed it over the phone once or twice. He also was perceptive enough to readily ascertain that my experiences there hadn't been totally pleasant. So it wasn't long before we found ourselves at Louie's drinking picons and telling stories. I told him my story about Treadwell, Dick Jensen and the rest of the AEC crew, but I never said a word about what I had learned about the early tests involving humans. I simply could not deal with that. Pete loved the Treadwell story. It was now worth a laugh, but somehow, it didn't seem so funny that day out on the playa.

"Damn, I would have loved to see the expression on his face when you let it all out," Pete exclaimed. "I wonder if people really have died out there," he went on.

"I suspect there have been "accidents", although I don't know how you could prove it, and what would happen if you did. Likely you might be the next accident", I suggested.

After two more picon's, the talk turned to what Pete had been up to. "I decided to learn to fly. I am single, and that's not going to change. I have the money, and there is no better time than the present. There's an old boy at the Elko airport that flew all during the war, Ralph Scott. He's wild, but good and he told me that he could make me into a good pilot, if I paid attention enough."

I laughed, "Can't you get around to all of your women fast enough by car?"

Pete didn't seem to think that was so funny. "No, that's not it. I have to come to Reno every few weeks for some damn meeting; besides, Elko County is mighty large, I go from Owyhee to Wendover, to way south of Carlin and both sides of the Ruby Mountains. Now the County Agent down in White Pine County, A.Z. Joy, wants me to start coming down there some. I just decided that I am going to start flying." I knew A.Z. He was from Texas originally, and in my opinion he was a good county agent. There was lots Pete could learn from A.Z., so I was pleased to hear that.

Pete also conjured up the idea that he was getting to know all the ranchers pretty well. "You know what? I'll bet you that there is at least ten ranches, or ranchers, in Elko County that we could set up trials with for testing products that might be beneficial to their operation in one way or another. If you can come up with the industry cooperation, product, money and whatever, I believe we can come up with the cattle to do the test. A lot of these ranchers have individually identified their cattle with numbered ear tags; most of them have scales that we can probably even get individual weights on. I guess most of this would be during the winter feeding period, but it sure offers some possibilities.

You can do the statistical work, write up the study, and we will both be famous!" he concluded.

I had plenty of work going on, but his concept sounded intriguing. Besides, I readily knew that I needed to do something to get the Test Site out of my mind. "I don't think it would be any problem to get products to test during the winter period. There's several new growth stimulants coming out on the market that need to be looked at for our type of livestock production. There's some new forms of urea for a source of nitrogen for the rumen that seem to work. In short, there's probably half a dozen products out there right now, all we need to do is contact their reps and tell them what we can do," I responded. And so, with a final picon, we decided to go to work on product testing. Pete would locate willing cooperators, where we had sufficient numbers and control   I would locate industry reps that might want to sponsor research in Nevada, and together, yes we might get famous!

The selection of a new Dean, the replacement for Jimmie Adams, was progressing. The senior professors, one from each department made up the selection committee. Several potential candidates had been interviewed, but the committee chose a fairly young range weed specialist from Wyoming. He had been at the University for some time, and he was a native of Wyoming. His name was Dr. Dale W. Bohmont. Bohmont was offered the job, and he accepted, so he became the new Dean and Director of the Max C. Fleischman College of Agriculture, University of Nevada, July 1, 1963.

I had missed Bohmont's first visit to the campus, but I didn't miss his inaugural day on the job. He had scheduled a faculty meeting, so I attended, to see what the new man was all about. I figured, not having a Ph.D., but doing the work expected of Ph.D.'s it might behoove me to understand his philosophy. It didn't take long to learn that he expected things to be full speed ahead!

Bohmont was straight to the point, he expected work, he expected publications that meant something, he expected good teachers, he expected enrollment to go up - in short he expected positive production. Quite a change from Jimmie Adams! Although it wasn't discussed by him, I kind of read between the lines and guessed that he didn't like problems either, at least problems that someone else caused. At least, he and Adams were alike in that regard. I made the decision that not having a Ph.D., I would give him a wide berth for the time being. I also guessed that in due time we would get to know each other pretty well. I could produce with the best at this college, Ph.D. or not, that I knew for sure.

However, not having a Ph.D. was worrisome to me. The molybdenum trial had been completed, and nearly all of the statistical analyses were nearly complete, at least complete enough so that I had been able to present some partial versions of the work at several regional meetings, as well as having presented one part of the study at the national Animal Science meetings in Chicago. I was also keeping Dr. Oldfield, at Oregon State, informed of my progress. In addition, I was attempting to take 3-5 hours of academic work every semester to whittle away at the required classes to obtain the Ph.D. goal.

I guess Bohmont knew more about me than I did about him. He hadn't been on campus more than a month when he dropped by my office out of a clear blue sky. "Say, I have been reviewing some of your work and it looks like you get around the state about as well as anybody", was his informal introduction. His sudden comment as he walked through the office door caught me off guard, but not for long.

"Yup, I have been working from the Test Site to Knoll Creek and just about every where in between", I responded.

"Well, I note that you don't have a Ph.D.. What are you doing about that?" he asked. I explained the molybdenum work, and my

252

association with Oldfield at Oregon State, which seemed to satisfy that immediate problem. "What do you see as the number one problem that this College faces today?" he asked.

That was easy, "An adequate field station. This College needs an actual operating cattle ranch, including a BLM or Forest Service grazing permit, preferably both. If we are ever going to solve some of the complex problems that the livestock industry in this state faces, much less the West, then we need to be dumped squarely in the same position the ranchers are in. The only way to do that is to obtain and operate a real ranch."

Bohmont appeared to totally agree with my philosophy, "Let's start looking towards that goal. I don't know how to get there yet, but once I get to know the legislature, and the politics of this state, we'll accomplish that goal."

With that, Bohmont left my office about as quick as he entered. I decided right then and there that he was a man of action, and that my level of production, with or without a Ph.D. would be recognized. However, I also made note of the fact that the first thing he asked was where was my degree.

Money for research was always a problem. I had wiggled my way into a couple of regional research projects, but the funds from that source were never enough to really accomplish much. Besides, any monies I got from those sources seemed to always go through Bohman's hands one way or another. We got a lot of money from the AEC for the ongoing work at the Test Site which covered a lot of problems, but it was only going to last so long. Grants were out there for specific problem areas, but there wasn't much for range livestock research. I was constantly searching that aspect for possible areas where I could apply for grants, but I hadn't been real successful yet. I got to thinking about Pete's comments about product testing. I hoped he knew what he was talking about by saying that there were ranches out there that we could use. I decided that it might be best to check him out. So I arranged to make a fast trip to Elko to call his bluff.

We took a whirlwind trip through Ruby Valley, Star and Clover Valleys, up to Contact and finally over to Independence Valley. We visited about ten ranches in two days, met with some of the backbone of the Nevada livestock industry: the Marvel family, Cap and Louise and their boys; Stanley Ellison; Lloyd Sorenson, both stout Mormons, but even stouter rancher: the Wright brothers; Hillary Barnes; Peter Marble; some of the Filippini clan; the Dahl family; the Neff family; the Hoopers; more names and places than I could keep tract of. One thing for sure, Pete, between his own ranching background and his Basque heritage, was on a respected first name basis with all of these old time ranching families. And it was obvious, at least with a little imagination, that he was right. There was research potential of some kind or another on just about all of these ranches.

We both returned to Elko after the second days travel. We had a few drinks and dinner at the Commercial, and, we summarized what we saw. "I think we could probably work pretty well with most of these folks, if we can keep the projects simple, straight forward, and offer some kind of guarantee that we won't negatively affect their production. We can supply the ear tags, whatever product we are testing, and anything else that is required. We can do all the work. All they have to do is let us have access to the livestock, usually just twice, at the start and at the termination of the project", I summarized.

Pete indicated that he could bring an extra horse trailer over from his father's ranch north of Reno, and he would keep a couple of horses at the stock yard for our use. "And you know what else? We can use Dad's ranch for both sheep and cattle. Besides that, I know of about a half dozen other ranches we could probably get access to in northwestern California, in the Susanville/Alturas area", Pete threw in for the clincher.

"Wow, we'll have to get to know some extension agents in California before we completely loose our head", I cautioned.

"That's OK, I have already met some of them, and they are dying to do this type of work. They just don't have anybody in the California system that will show the type of leadership that you and I can show them," Pete countered.

"Well, maybe, just maybe, we will have the ranches to work on, but we still have to get the products to test, and a little money to go along with it", I cautioned.

"Look, every company developing livestock products has a field rep. I have met some of these guys. They are invariable rounders. You make contact, get them here and we'll show them a time they will never forget. Remember, we can take them to some of the biggest ranches in the world; run their asses off all day on some horses, back to Elko or Winnemucca at night for a Basque dinner with plenty of drinking and gambling. If they so desire, we can even give them a guided tour of the local houses! We can't lose", Pete summarized as only he could. Well, I couldn't top that, so I agreed. I would return to Reno, construct a letter to go out to appropriate companies, generally outlining what we had to offer from a research standpoint, and then we would see what might happen.

I made the proposed letter as attractive as possible, extolling the virtues of actually conducting research on operating cattle ranches versus the more confined concepts associated with research stations. The letter was sent to a variety of animal pharmaceutical houses, feed supplement companies, and just about anybody else that I could think of. I shared a copy of the letter with Bohman, Ely and Bohmont. Bohman, being the confirmed basic scientist, felt it was an unwise area to be venturing in to. "You will never have the control over the subject animals that's

255

necessary to conduct meaningful research," was his dismal evaluation. Ely was more optimistic, however, I suspected his enthusiasm was somewhat driven by the fact that the Experiment Station was going through some very trying fiscal times.

On the other hand, Bohmont thought the idea had great merit, "Get those guys here, I think you could sell just about anything to anybody with your enthusiasm. I'll help anyway I can, just let me know. Having to go to the rancher as a basis for conducting our research will give me a powerful tool in the legislature to get funds for buying the ranch we need." That was about all the administrative support I needed, the letter went out.

It didn't take long to get replies. However, the discouraging part was that the first ten or so said it's a great idea, but their funds for product testing was limited at this point in time. They would, of course, supply us with complimentary amounts of their products for demonstration purposes. Finally I got two encouraging responses, Dow Chemical Company and Commercial Solvents Corporation.

Dow Chemical was developing a new source of nitrogen for ruminant animals called biuret. Urea had long been used as a source of nitrogen, to act as the building block for protein under feedlot conditions. However, when urea was tried under range conditions, where protein is often the limiting factor, it either didn't work, or proved toxic and occasionally fatal. The theory was that the nitrogen in urea was released too rapidly and couldn't be assimilated into protein by the rumen bacteria under the lower levels of nutrition often associated with western range conditions. The extra release of nitrogen, if picked up in the blood stream could be fatal. Biuret on the other hand appeared to offer a much slower release of nitrogen. So theoretically, it could be successfully used as an eventual source of protein on protein deficient ranges.

Commercial Solvents Corporation had discovered a product called resorcylic acid lactone, or more commonly called zeranol, that when administered to steers under feedlot conditions improved gain and efficiency as much as 15%. Stilbesterol had been used by the industry in a like manner for a number of years. However stilbesterol was an estrogen like compound, and fear was mounting that stilbesterol residues in beef could actually be carcinogenic. Consequently, there was considerable interest in developing alternatives to stilbesterol, and zeranol was the leading contender, but its use had only begun to be investigated. The opportunity to conduct numerous field trials under a variety of conditions was apparently of significant interest to Commercial Solvents.

It wasn't long before field reps from both Dow and Commercial Solvents made appointments to come to Nevada. Dow's rep was a large animal veterinarian by the name of Dr. Jack Anderson, and he was first on the scene. I had been discussing the concept of what we were attempting to do with Jim Hunter, both because he was a trusted friend, and he had a lot of savvy about how to handle livestock under less than desirable conditions. Jim thought the idea of using Dow's product, biuret, offered a lot of promise. He knew a lot of the ranchers in Humboldt and Elko Counties that we might be eventually be working with, and he had already met Pete. So Jim was chomping at the bit to go with Dr. Anderson and myself when we headed east to hook up with Pete.

The most beautiful time in Nevada is October, and October of 1963 was no exception. A cold spell in September had turned the aspen groves golden brown to almost a blood red. The east slope of the Sierra probably was never more spectacular. As Dr. Anderson and I left the Reno airport, the spectacular beauty of the Sierra was about all he could talk about. Anderson had grown up in the Rockies, but now he worked out of the Dow offices in Dallas and as he put it, "I get to see damn little of the real country anymore!" Well, I was going to make sure he got to see plenty of the "real west country" now. We spent one full day on campus, as I wanted to be sure Dr. Jack, as I began to call him, met all of the administration. The following day, Dr. Jack, Jim Hunter and I headed east to Elko to meet with Pete for lunch before really heading out.

It didn't take long to figure out that Dr. Jack indeed fit Pete's description of a "rounder". He was full of stories, mostly about ranches he visited, frequent wrecks with livestock and or people. Most stories were underscored with either alcohol or women, more frequently both. But he was a good storyteller, good enough to keep me in stitches for the five-hour drive to Elko. Jim got to laughing so hard that he completely forgot to smoke his pipe, and that was a rarity.

It didn't take Pete long to warm up to Dr. Jack. Pete had a way of sizing people up pretty fast, and he had Dr. Jack figured out by the time we sat down for lunch. Pete had us set up for a private lunch at the Stockmen's. He had brought in two ranchers that really didn't have the right facilities for us to do any kind of research at. But what he had brought in was the President of the Nevada Cattlemen's Association, Hillary Barnes, and Stanley Ellison, an outspoken critic of the BLM and the Forest Service. Lunch went well, I wasn't sure whether the cowboys were trying to sell something to Dr. Jack, or Dr. Jack was trying to sell something to them. Either way it went well, especially in light of Stanley being a devout Mormon and not saying a word about the three martinis that Dr. Jack downed.

After lunch we headed east and north, up to the Boise ranches near Contact. Ira Boise was an Elko County Commissioner, so that exposure didn't hurt. The Boise Ranch was one of the large ones, running from near the Idaho border down towards Wells. They ran on some of the best Forest Service land in Nevada, the Jarbidge Mountains, as well as some of the better BLM land. Ira was pretty conservative, but Dr. Jack warmed him up as he commented about the quality of his cattle.

After Boise's, we headed south down towards Metropolis with a stop at the Bill Gibbs Ranch, then on into Wells and Star Valley. Pete had three stops scheduled in Starr Valley. The Star Valley ranches were generally smaller, but that wasn't all bad. In general, the smaller ranches offered a lot more control over cattle. The final stop was the Frank Hooper Ranch, and before that visit was over, I began to realize that the Hooper Ranch probably offered the best chance to do "meaningful" research as suggested by Bohman. Their corrals were such that you could readily sort and work individual cattle. Their scales lent themselves to weighing individual cattle, and most importantly, Frank Hooper took a liking to Dr. Jack.

We were back to Elko by seven P.M., but there was no quiting in either Pete or Dr. Jack. Jim was admittedly tired, so was I, but I thought better than admit it. We went to the Dinner House, a Basque joint, for dinner and drinks. Pete introduced Dr. Jack to picons, and I wasn't sure there would be an end, but tomorrow was coming. Jim had already folded his cards. I opted for bed about ten. Pete volunteered to take Dr. Jack gambling. I reminded them that breakfast was to be at six, as tomorrows journey was to be mighty long.

Pete had laid out a long trip for the next day. Up to Independence Valley for a quick visit with Cap Marvel, one of the Wright boys, then through the ghost towns of Tuscarora and Midas, then take a back road into Paradise Valley. I hadn't been into Paradise since being a graduate student in Dr. Robertson's range class. Pete had gotten to know Kirk Day, the long time Humboldt County Extension Agent, and he planned to meet us at our first stop, the Bull Head Ranch. Representatives of the McLeary Ranches were to meet us at the Bull Head as well, and as I came to find out, they had lunch catered there for us as well. It was noon when we hit the Bull Head. Dr. Jack was still talking about the Marvel operation, as he couldn't believe the size of their combined cow/calf/yearling and sheep operations. But it didn't take McCleary's two cow bosses long to explain what a really big operation was and how to run it.

Frank Loveland and Lynn Kimball told it just how it was; running twenty thousand mother cows from wintering in Paradise Valley, through the Little Humboldt in the early spring, out to the Owyhee Desert for much of the summer, as well as keeping the cows high in the Santa Rosa Mountains where possible. It was truly one of the largest ranches, and with men like Loveland and Kimball running the show, it worked like a well-oiled machine.

Later that afternoon we visited two of the smaller Paradise ranches, the Lyman Schwartz and Johnnie Ferraro Ranches. Lyman was a graduate of the Ag College at Nevada, so he was a strong supporter of the type of work we were talking about. Of course, Johnnie's son, Bob, had gone to school with me at Nevada, so Johnnie was also interested in what we had to say. Kirk Day was married to one of the local ranching families, the Bogie's, so he was also interested in seeing that some of the work be accomplished at least in Humboldt County. To say the day was a success would be a vast understatement. By the time we headed to Winnemucca, Dr. Jack couldn't wait to get started.

Pete had laid out the itinerary about as well as it could be. We stopped at the Gem Bar, long a favorite watering hole for picons, followed by more picons and Winnemucca coffee with dinner at the Martin Hotel. Pete had inquired if I thought Dr. Jack would like a tour of the circle. The "circle", was Winnemucca's world famous red light district, located just about three blocks from the center of town, at the end of Baud Street. The circle comprised of five pretty lively "houses", each stocked with four to six lovely ladies. I wasn't sure, when I answered Pete's question, but I figured it was a pretty safe gamble, based on Dr. Jack's ability to drink and some of his stories. What the hell, he didn't have to sample. After all he might just enjoy a drink or two, and polite conversation with the ladies.

Well, it was a gamble that paid off. In fact it paid off big time. Dr. Jack had no idea prostitution was legal in Nevada, much less that a place like the "circle" even existed. I suggested after parking in front of the Star, that we take a little walk. It just wasn't a good idea to leave a University sedan parked in the circle. Dr. Jack asked why we weren't going into the Star. Pete responded, "Hell, Doc, its a pretty evening let's just take a short walk and enjoy the moment." Dr. Jack agreed, but he did look puzzled. Jim had lit his ever-present pipe, and I thought I could see a little more than normal amount of smoke coming out, in fact there were sparks. It didn't take us more than five minutes to round the corner and be faced with the bright lights. The circle is a pretty good example of positive advertising. Each place has a picture window, and the ladies display their attributes, as they urge you to come in. Penney's was the first house we stopped in front of. Dr. Jack just stood there for about a minute without saying a word, and then it came out, "God almighty, this Nevada is the most amazing place I have ever been to in all my life, let's go in!"

We went in. In fact, we went in all five houses. Dr. Jack buying a round in each, whiskey or beer for the four of us, sugar water for the girls. After leaving the last house, Dr. Jack turned to me, asking, "Well, now that we have sampled the population, which house has the best quality in your opinion?" Now that was a tough question to answer. By then I had listened to so many girls tell me stories that I had lost track. But it did seem that the three best houses were the Cozy Corner, My Place and Penney's. So that's what my score was. Pete and Jim seemed to agree, but Dr. Jack resolved the problem. "Well, I liked that little girl, Shanna was her name I believe, at My Place, so let's settle down there for awhile.

So into My Place the four of us went. It didn't take Dr. Jack more than about a minute to chart the course. "Here, I'll put a hundred dollars on the bar for you boys to buy drinks with. Shanna and I are going back to talk things over." Pete looked at me like maybe we had bitten off a mite bit more than we could chew, "Damn, beer's fifty cents, a whiskey is a dollar, sugar water is a dollar, the most expensive champaign maybe is five dollars. That C-note will last us all night, does he expect to stay in the room all night?"

My response was pretty simple and direct to the point, "Damn if I know, but let's get to work, we got a powerful lot of drinking to do."

And, we did a powerful lot of drinking, and Dr. Jack did a powerful lot of fornicating, at least that's what I guessed he was doing. Shanna was just the first, there were three other girls on the line as well, and sooner or later all three of them disappeared with Dr. Jack. Each time he emerged he would inquire if our money was holding out. It was. The first time we were down about fifteen. The second time about twenty-five, and so on. By about one A.M., we still had twenty-five to go, but that's when Dr. Jack got really serious, two and three at a time. Well, along about four in the morning, we finished the hundred dollars. Dr. Jack stumbled out just about right on cue, "Damn, I just can't believe this Nevada".

It would be pointless to say that the next day was anything but long. Kirk Day had agreed to take Pete back, so it was just Jim, Dr. Jack and myself on the trip back to Reno. Jim slept the entire way, Dr. Jack dozed some. I drank coffee, but we did make it. Dr. Jack had to catch an early morning flight the next morning, but as we parted he indicated that as far as he was concerned, Nevada was the place to really test biuret. "I'll place twenty thousand into the College by the end of the week for openers. You write the projects up, I don't care what it costs, just treat me fair, and I'll cover whatever it takes. We have budgeted close to a half million dollars for field testing biuret, and as far as I am concerned, most can go to Nevada."

Well, as I watched him board the United flight to Denver, I guessed the gamble paid off. In fact, it paid off more than I could have ever expected. The relationship between Dow Chemical and the University of Nevada was firmly entrenched from that point on for many years. Money was made available for a steady stream of graduate students, resulting in numerous publications. We not only put biuret on the feed additive map, but we undoubtedly made Dow a lot of money. The money the University received made me a very legitimate professor at Nevada. Dr. Jack liked to come to Nevada about twice a year to review the work. Sometime he would bring some of his cronies, and sometimes we would have to introduce them to the circle as well. Dr. Jack's ability to drink, much less everything else, never ceased to amaze me. But he was also equally amazed at my ability to drink whiskey, especially when we were at the circle. I guess he never realized that I was a frequent enough visitor that the girls had long since learned that when I brought a guest in that I got sugar water too!

Fortunately, the folks from Commercial Solvents were a lot more sane. Their home base was Terra Haute, Indiana, and I always presumed that local religious influences were such that the Commercial Solvents gang was pretty straight shooters, not that Dow wasn't also. But they were equally impressed with what we had to offer at Nevada, so it wasn't long before they had stepped up to the plate with a pretty handsome offer to start a myriad of field tests with zeranol. The type of testing that Commercial Solvents wanted done seemed to lend itself more to smaller, more confined operations. With Pete's help we had made good contact with extension agents in California. So, that's where a lot of their work was accomplished. In order to keep peace in the academic family, it was obviously necessary to work cooperatively with California's Ag school, located at Davis. But as it turned out that presented no problem, as Davis was so top heavy with basic research, that our offer to initiate some field tests was well accepted with the ranks of their extension staff. We worked particularly close with two county agents, Cecil Pierce, located in Alturas and Carl Rimby, located in Susanville.

We also started working closely with Jim Clawson, the State Livestock Extension Specialist housed at Davis.

To facilitate this cooperative effort, I got Bohmont's blessing to establish a sort of revolving "chair", specifically designed for California extension personnel to come and spend time at Nevada on sabbatical leaves. Clawson, Pierce and Rimby were all able to take advantage of this opportunity during the decade of the sixty's; which, of course, always gave me an extra set of hands, resulting in more publications.

As I said, the Commercial Solvents boys liked Nevada. We probably ended up running nearly a hundred tests of zeranol under a wide variety of field trials, as well as some under very refined research conditions. The financial support offered by Commercial Solvents rivaled that of Dow Chemical in the end. We put zeranol on the map. In fact, it is still marketed today under the trade name of Ralgro. It is essentially the only approved growth implant on the market, as stillbesterol, and all the other estrogen based implants have long since been removed.

The monies that we received from both Dow and Commercial Solvents built a research machine that was second to none. It wasn't long before I had more graduate students under my direction than the rest of the department put together. Not having a Ph.D. didn't add to my popularity with the rest of the staff. Professional jealousies were starting to emerge. I ignored them for the most part, but I began to suspect that if left unchecked they could cause problems in the coming years. Little did I realize just how correct that notion would become.

Accomplishing all of the field trials was difficult under the best of conditions, and those conditions didn't usually exist to begin with. Probably, it could never have been done to begin with, but Pete held true to his word, he learned to fly. About as quick as he learned to fly, he bought a plane from his instructor, Ralph Scott. It was a Piper PA-18 Super Cub, equipped with a hopped-up 185 horse power Continental engine. Ralph Scott didn't spare the details, the plane could fly! A Super Cub is designed to successfully negotiate tight spots, and between Scott's training and Pete's nerves of steel and quick reflexes, it would get into some tight spots indeed! The only problem was that a Super Cub could only seat two people at best, one in front of the other. Two people just about used up the pay load, so other than a few ear tags, perhaps some implants and necessary paperwork, I didn't get to take much in the way of supplies unless I wanted to drive.

Pete took to flying like a duct takes to water. The Super Cub had sufficient power that he could just about land, or take off anywhere, as long as the field was flat, or the road was straight, at least for 100 yards, especially in light of the hopped up engine. The first few times that Pete showed up by air, I had driven to the project. It wasn't that I was afraid to fly with Pete, but the landings seemed to cause me some apprehension. I had come to know Pete as a great athlete and he obviously had nerves of steel. So after a time or two that caused me to drive for many hours, I began to think more seriously about his proposal to fly me to our field trials whenever possible. Probably, all I really had to do was close my eyes on takeoffs and landings. I was pretty sure that I would thoroughly enjoy the view for the rest of the trip. And sure enough, pretty soon I didn't even close my eyes. However, Pete always had me looking for telephone and power lines when we came in, and that was sufficient inducement to cause me to keep my eyes open! Ralph had outfitted the plane with wire cutters on the landing gear and rudder, so Pete really didn't worry too much anyway. To the best of my knowledge, we never had to see if the cutters worked, but we did come close to some phone lines on more than one occasion.

Pete was always telling me about their ranch in Buffalo Canyon, which was about 75 miles north of Reno as the crow flies. When we got into the Zeranol work he offered up his Dad's sheep as a possible field test, so that was inducement enough to go to Buffalo. Pete had flown to Reno for an extension meeting on a Friday, so our plan was to fly up to Buffalo early Saturday morning, establish the trial Saturday, then he wanted to show me his parents range on Sunday, before returning to Reno. It sounded like an exciting trip, so early on a spring Saturday morning we left Reno and headed north at about 10,000 feet. It was a spectacular trip, with the crest of the Sierra's to the left, the Virginia Mountains beneath us, and the vastness of Pyramid Lake to our right. Far to the north, the snow-clad Mount Lassen began to take shape. As we left Pyramid Lake, we went northwest across the Smoke Creek Desert, a vast playa that once hosted a desert lake. Off far to the right, I could see the Black Rock Desert, Nevada's largest playa, and at the south end of the rugged Granite Range, stood the small, but historic town of Gerlach.

We were headed directly into Buffalo Canyon, which drains the Buffalo Mountains to the south and into the Smoke Creek Desert. The Buffalo Mountains were not particularly high. In fact, the highest point is Poodle Mountain, right at 7,000'. But the Buffalo Mountains, like all of northern Washoe County, is less dominated by the rain shadow from the Sierra than the mountains from Reno south. Consequently, they receive more annual precipitation. This accounted for some mighty good grasssland that Pete's family had taken advantage of for many generations at the Buffalo.

"This will be a little tricky landing here. I've only done it once. We don't have a runway, but the road's got a good straight stretch of about 100 yards if the wind is blowing right", Pete casually brought me back to my senses. Fortunately, Mrs. Echegoyen had done a wash that morning, and we could tell by the clothes on the line that the wind was blowing gently from the west. "Good, with no more side drift from the west, I think I can bring us down right as that last curve straightens out, then throttle down as fast as possible, so we can make the last turn upright", cautioned Pete.

"I don't see any lines, so if you don't mind, I'll just shut up and close my eyes", I cheerfully responded.

"No, don't close your eyes, you got to keep me clear of that cedar tree on the right. I meant to cut it down after last time, but it just about catches my wing tip regardless - so just make sure I am going to clear it", Pete shot back.

My only response was, "Oh Shit!" Well, we lived for another day, but as I climbed out of the plane, I could see some green spots on the wing tip. I guessed I had cut him a mite bit too close. "Say, if you want, I'll be happy to cut that cedar down before we take off tomorrow. Of course it will be on your side then so maybe it's best left standing."

Pete's only response was, "I'll get you an ax".

Pete's parents were even more Basque than Pete if that's possible. Marcelino and Honorine Echegoyen were their God given names, but fortunately for me, they went by the handles of Marty and Reene. Marty had been born at Buffalo, and I gathered his father had as well. His grandfather had come from the old country, worked as a herder until he gathered up enough money to homestead, which he did right there in Buffalo Canyon. Pete's mother, Reene, had come from up Jordan Valley way in Oregon. Marty was a died-in-the-wool sheep man, but Reene, unlike most Basque women was very outgoing and truly into horses and cattle. Consequently, the Echegoyen's had both cattle and sheep, as well as quite a bunch of brood mares under the sharp eye of Reene.

After lots of "hello's" and the usual seven course Basque mid-day meal, we set out to accomplish what I came for, a field trial with zeranol on baby lambs. Marty had kept back a small band of about 500 ewes with fairly new lambs. "We'll just keep this bunch here in the Buffalo Hills this summer, that's about all that damned BLM will let me run here on the home range anymore. Just think, Grampa used to run five bands right here, and year around". Well that pretty much told me how the Echegoyen's felt about the BLM!

We sorted out about 100 lambs for the trial, ear tagged them and implanted every other one with zeranol, with each being weighed on a small platform scale. We also had to dock all of them as well as castrate the male lambs. And the Echegoyens being Basque did it the old fashioned way. "Don't worry, you will catch right on. It's simple, and I promise I won't laugh", explained Pete. Well it was, the lambs were thrown on their back in a cradle about waist high. After you had a good hold on the little critter, you spread his rear legs, cut a slip off the bottom of the scrotum, sucked the testicles out with your mouth, then gently bit them off in a kind of sawing motion. After release, the testicles were spit into a bucket, because nothing was wasted on a Basque ranch. The only thing that really bothered me was about the third lamb that I finished I looked up to a grinning Pete with camera in hand. I was sure at some appropriate meeting I would get to see that picture, probably along with about a hundred other people.

It took us a couple of hours to complete the trial, then Marty proudly announced that we needed to finish the rest of the lambs since we had done such a good job so far. Fortunately, two of his herders showed, so we had a lot more help for the remaining 400, which only took another two hours. In our strange world I learned that young herders were no longer Basque, they were now Peruvian. "Kids from the old country want too damn much money, besides these Peruvians got a lot more ambition", explained Marty.

It was about six o'clock when we finished, and I was so tired that I could hardly stand up. But Reene grabbed me by the arm and said, "You got to come see my horses, you will love them". Well, I guess it was OK, but I sure hoped she wasn't proposing a ride. I could imagine a "short" ride around this outfit would probably be more than I could handle at this stage of the game. Fortunately, we just looked. Reene knew her horses, that was obvious. She had about twenty brood mares, mostly quarter horse or quarter horse thoroughbred crosses. "I was raised on quarter horses on the ranch where I grew up, but we cover so much territory here that I like a bit of thoroughbred in them. They might not be as fast on the draw, but they are still going by sundown", she explained. For the most part they were indeed stout looking horses, long legs, strong quarters, good flowing lines. There were a number of colts and yearlings that she had been working with. "I break all of the ranch's horses myself. The men, including Marty are too rough, and they leave a mark on a horse for the rest of their lives. The horses I break turn out just as good, and they are a hell of a lot more dependable when you get into a jam. They don't have a mean streak in them", she further explained.

"Yeah, that's true, all except that stud you caught", added Pete.

"Oh yes, I'll have to show you my Charger, he is going to be our new stud".

So around the barn we went to see the stud. Charger was a big horse, all over. He was not only tall, but he was just plain big all over, kind of like he had some workhorse in him. His color was unique, dark, almost a tint of red. In fact, as he moved about in the corral and the sunlight hit him just right there was a distinct dark red hue to him. He had a long mane and a long tail, but they were dark, nearly black. He had four white socks, and a white blaze down the middle of his nose. I couldn't really determine what breed he was, so in order not to display my ignorance, I just marveled over his size.

"I expect you are wondering what Charger is and where did I get such a critter", quizzed Reene.

"Well, the thought did enter my mind that he doesn't look like your typical horse, at least on this spread", I countered.

"I'll have to tell you about him. One day, I was looking for lost cows, way over on the Paiute side of the Black Rock, there's lots of mustangs over there, and they sort of don't care when a single rider ambles through. Anyway, I was working up the east arm of the Black Rock, and had passed several studs and their groups. Suddenly, this little colt, full of piss and vinegar, runs out of a draw, right past me. He didn't appear to be a member of any group that I could see, but he surely must have been. His markings were beautiful, exactly like you see today. But what impressed me was his muscling, unlike any mustang that I ever saw, certainly not anything on the Black Rock."

"Well, anyway it was late that night when I got home, had to ride clear back to Andy Jackson's place north of Wallipie, where I left my pick-up and trailer. The next day I told Marty that I wanted to catch the little fellow. He thought I was crazy, but about a week later, Marty and I took two of the best cowboys all the way around to about 5 miles south of the Paiute Ranch, as far as we could go, and started riding. It took several hours, and we probably saw a thousand mustangs, when I spotted him right above the Point. We all moseyed up to him, he was more curious than anything; the first throw dropped a loop right on his head. He fought some, but after a few minutes we fashioned a halter out of the loop and just led him back to the trailer. So that's how he got to Buffalo", she concluded.

Reene went on, "I just didn't have the heart to geld him, he seemed so proud of his masculinity. I fed him good, started working with him when I reckoned that he was about 18 months old. He took right to the saddle, and I was actually working him with cattle when I guessed he was about two. He has turned out so good, that I want some colts out of him. So rather than buy another pricy thoroughbred stud this year, we are just going to use him. We named him Charger about a year ago, the only problem that I have ever noticed is that he is getting a bit hard to handle since we turned him with the mares."

"Yeah, and Mom, now that he has figured out he is a stud, he's dangerous. You have already admitted that yourself," Pete threw out.

"I know, I know, even your Dad worries about me riding him, but nobody else is going to ride him ever, so we will just be good friends, and I am sure he won't ever hurt me." Reene concluded.

Well, we all agreed that Charger was some kind of horse. But I couldn't help but notice as we walked away, Charger ran to the far end of the pen, and looked at me out of the corner of his eye. I could detect a nervous look coming out of an eye that seemed to turn flame red, and I couldn't help but notice the nervous muscle spasms in his neck. For sure he was more horse than I would ever want to handle, with or without his balls.

It was getting on towards dusk, we all adjourned to the house to hear Reene announce, "It's Saturday night, and I don't cook for the boys tonight. So I fixed some leftovers from the noon dinner, you can just pick and choose what you want." I breathed a sigh of relief, because I was just too tired to eat anything more, even if I could have. It was early to bed for me. I was sure this bunch would be expected to be at breakfast by 6.

I was right. At six sharp we all set down to a breakfast of ham, scrambled eggs, fried potatoes, biscuits, gravy and lots of hot coffee. "Dad, Mom, as soon as we are done with breakfast, I am going to take Terry all around our range in the plane. I'll probably end up over around the Point, so from there its straight back to Reno, I've got plenty of fuel," Pete announced. Well, that sounded fine with me, I had never really seen the northern Washoe country, but I made a mental note of suggesting that I might cut down that cedar tree before we took off.

Marty beat me to the punch. "You know, I think you are crazy flying that wore out piece of canvas all over the west, but one thing I am going to do before you take off is cut that God damned cedar down first. You two kids were so awe struck with the country yesterday that you never noticed that your right wing nicked that tree on the way in."

"Oh, Dad, we didn't hit that tree, your just imagining things," Pete responded. I wasn't going to get in the middle of this, but I was damned positive that we did hit the tree, I didn't need any more proof than I already had. So after a mighty friendly Basque hug from Reene, and a bone shattering hand shake from Marty, with the promise that I would return as often as I could, we were off with the dual roar of the plane and Marty's chain saw laying the cedar low.

We headed north from Buffalo, over the mountains and across Duck Flat, paralleling the California border about 5 miles to the west. "We run both cattle and sheep all the way up here to about ten miles south of Via and the Powers Ranch. I don't know if you ever met Powers, he actually headquarters over in Surprise Valley, but a few years back he was Lieutenant Governor of California. I think about the time Earl Warren was Governor or sometime in there. He was a hell of a good neighbor. I never really knew him, that's when I was pretty small, but Dad sure talks highly of him," Pete explained. "I don't know what for sure they call these mountains north of Duck Flat. They are really a northern extension of the Granite Range, but we always called them the Pinto Mountains. That peak you see off to your left is Hays Canyon Peak, its about 8,000' high, lots of springs, aspen and Mahogany," Pete continued.

We flew northward for another 30 minutes over what seemed to be a never-ending expanse or rolling hills, isolated stands of cedars, mahoganies, and occasional groves of aspen. The sun was right so that the glare from water stood out everywhere. And there were still snow drifts on the north side of the higher hills. We finally broke over a small flat valley, with a much larger valley to the north. "This is about the end of our range, its called Boulder Flat. We just went over our northern most line camp, we call it Home Camp. See that pond down there, its Boulder Lake, may not look like much, but that's some of the best trout fishing anywhere up here," my tour guide continued.

"I am going to swing to the east, go over to the Calico Mountains and the High Rock country, it's pretty wild." All I could see was miles and miles of low rolling hills. "See that rise to the north about 20 miles, that's Badger Mountain, and that rise to the south, about the same distance, that's Fox Mountain. I think Fox is about 8 and Badger is about 7,000', but they are both plenty good range. Badger is not our range, except by mistake, but we use Fox plenty hard," Pete continued. "We're going to come up on to a drainage that heads east. It's pretty gentle at first, but it drops into a steep canyon, way too narrow for us to fly in. That's High Rock Canyon, and the early pioneers that left the emigrant trail at Winnemucca went right up through High Rock on their way to Oregon. Part of the Applegate cut-off. There's all kinds of pioneer writings on the rock walls down there, really something."

As we left High Rock Canyon, High Rock Lake, the recipient of waters flowing from the Canyon appeared. Pete informed me that it might look good now, but it gets dried up every summer. A short hop over the Calico Mountains and we emerged over the northwest arm of the Black Rock Desert. "Look to the north at the end of the flat, there are a bunch of springs and a meadow there. They call that Soldier Meadows. There's an old cavalry fort there that was built to protect the emigrants after the Paiutes killed too many," Pete explained. "We're going to take a short hop over the Black Rock Range, and then down the east arm of the Desert to Black Rock Point, where Mom told you about catching that useless mustang yesterday. Watch for mustangs. They're all over this country, ruining the range," Pete concluded with an explanation point. Pete was right, there were horses everywhere.

But I was more interested in the country, off to the left coming far from the north was the Quinn River, which actually had its start way over in the Santa Rosa Mountains. On the other side of the Quinn was the Jackson Range highlighted by the ominous head of King Lear Peak. I could see ranches on the edge of the Jackson's, and I knew they belonged to the DeLong gang. I had already met some of the DeLongs. In fact I had several of their kids in school, simply put, tough, very tough people. "We're coming up on Black Rock Point, right around on the west side you will see a pond. It's fed by hot springs, great swimming. I'll dip low and you can see an old remnant sheep wagon. Dad always told me that was his grampa's first wagon, but I think he's pulling my leg. At any rate it's plenty old." Pete went on. "We're going to pull up to about 8,000', head towards Gerlach and Reno, but that's pretty much our range. Dad runs about 4,000 sheep, four bands, still, and our cow herd is up to about 600 pair. Its big country. The crews are out all the time as you could guess. My folks love it, and I guess one day it will be mine. Don't guess I'll have any brothers or sisters at this point!"

And so that was my introduction to the Buffalo Creek Ranch and the Echegoyen's. I was able to get back there on many occasions, always to be welcomed almost like a family member. The Echegoyens were proud of Pete. He had gone to college and even got a masters degree. Now he worked for the University. I sometimes wondered why they didn't want him home more, but I guessed they thought he was aimed at a better life in the meantime, but surely they knew that one day he would have to take over the reins. Pete had mentioned that there was no estate planning. So I knew it would not only be a big challenge when that day came, but after Uncle Sam got through taking his chunk, the financial burdens would also be there. But that was all another day. For the time being Pete and I both enjoyed doing exactly what we were doing. He was becoming an excellent county agricultural extension agent, and I hopefully becoming and good university professor.

The late 1950's through the early 1960's were the years representing the greatest numbers of mule deer in the state of Nevada. From the earliest records of fur trappers, wagon trains, turn of the century livestock operations, right up until World War II, mule deer had always been a fairly rare commodity in Nevada. In fact, so rare that the mere sighting of a mule der was worthy of note in the press. The explosion of deer numbers that started during the decade of the forty's and continued until 1961 or 1962 was of extreme interest to people like myself. There was a great deal of discussion as to why this might have occurred, but science had no clear-cut answer. I discussed this phenomenon in my class work, and had been predicting that when the pendulum began to swing the other direction there would be an outcry from the public, especially in light of the rapidly expanding population in both Las Vegas and the greater Reno area, that grazing livestock were causing the demise of the deer herd.

Well, it began to happen after 1962 and 1963. Deer hunter success ratios began to taper off. Despite the fact that more deer tags than ever were being sold, success just couldn't be maintained. And right on schedule, those that like to hunt the most, and probably knew the least about the subject, including doctors, dentists and lawyers, began to blame livestock grazing. Several sportsmen's groups voiced vicious attacks on livestock producers for their "rape" of the range causing the destruction of their cherished deer herds. A basic knowledge of population dynamics would have predicted that the rapidly expanding deer numbers would eventually surpass their environmental constraints, regardless if livestock were a factor or not, but that group just didn't have that knowledge. They made a lot of noise, and because of their professional standing, they made a lot of political noise.

I had long been interested in the relationship between deer and livestock. It was a natural area of investigation for a person with my background. I had been pestering the Nevada Fish and Game

Department for several years about the funding of possible research but it had fallen on deaf ears. However, the growing controversy about the supposed competition between deer and livestock started to create a little bit more interest. I had a good "in" to the department. Dave Mathis had headed up public relations with the Fish and Game Department. However, after Bohmont's arrival he had made the decision that the public relations efforts of the College needed to be greatly expanded so he created new positions in the tiny Ag Information Department. One such position was news editor, and Dave had successfully applied for the position. Dave was an old time Nevadan from Ruth, the home for the copper mining employees of Kennicott's giant copper mine at Ely. In fact, Dave was a third generation Nevadan, well versed in rural history. Conflict was no stranger to Dave. His maternal grandfather had been a victim of the eastern Nevada livestock wars of the 1880's. He was murdered, reputedly, by henchman of a land baron that would eventually become governor of Nevada. Since coming to the College, Dave had become very interested in my work, especially that utilizing fistulated cattle. So with Dave's help, I once more decided to make my case with the Fish and Game Department.

We approached Nick Papez, head of Game and Gene McDowel, who now was head of Publicity for the Department, and eventually would become a highly respected Washoe County Commissioner, with some novel ideas. My thesis was summed up in a few short words, "If there is indeed competition between mule deer and grazing cattle, it should be easy to prove. We have the ability to sample what cattle eat by using the fistulated steer. I believe by sacrificing a few deer and examining their rumen contents, using the techniques we have developed, we should be able to readily tell what plant species deer are consuming. Doing this in key areas several times a year we should be able to pretty accurately determine if there is competition between the two species, or if, in fact, they are quite compatible." Both Gene and Nick seemed to like the idea, but Gene was quick to point out that the number of deer sacrificed must be kept at a minimum. I tended to suggest the best way to handle that aspect was to keep the publicity of the number more at a minimum, rather than the number. But I countered, "You are already trapping deer every fall for a few key measurements, age, weight and condition. Why not get some samples from these animals, at least blood, and possibly hair, for a comprehensive chemical analyses that should tell us far more about the status of the herd health than what you are now getting." That offer seemed to create enough interest to finally talk about how to finance such an operation.

Nick volunteered the fact that the Department had a surplus of funds from what was called the Pittman-Robertson Act. He went on to explain, "The Pittman-Robertson Act was created by Congress in the late thirty's. An excise tax was created on sporting arms and ammunition, with a percentage of that going back to the individual states. The funds can only be used for wildlife enhancement, primarily big game enhancement. Furthermore, they must be matched. We have been able to come up with some state funds to meet the match criteria, and that is how we have been getting most of our wildlife management areas. If you could come up with some funds from the University, I believe that we could legitimately use Pittman-Robertson funds to match." I wasn't overly impressed, as I assumed that by "match" they were referring to a 50-50 match. The concept of coming up with enough of my precious University dollars for such an arrangement just wasn't appealing. However, Nick immediately brought me to my senses, "Yes we could match what you could provide, and a match is on a three to one basis. For example, if you could come up with ten thousand dollars, we would match it with thirty thousand dollars."

I never blinked an eye, "Yes, I just happen to have an extra assistantship that we have not committed yet, and I believe the value of that is about seventy five hundred per year, considering overhead, staff time, etc. Additionally, I could probably come up with another seventy five hundred from my general research fund, so that would make fifteen thousand dollars per year. Now based on what you just indicated, you would match that with forty five thousand dollars, so that we would have an annual budget of sixty thousand dollars to work with, is that right?"

"Yes, and we certainly have forty five thousand in our present match funds."

So started the Ruby-Butte Deer Herd study, the largest scientific study of any deer herd ever conducted in the United States. Originally, as the name implied, the study was to be conducted in an area stretching from the east side of the Ruby Mountains in Elko County down to Butte Valley in northern White Pine County. However, the scope of the project seemed to increase almost logarithmically with time. Soon, we were conducting studies from Mount Wilson in southern Lincoln County, to the northernmost reaches of Elko County westward to the top of Washoe County bordering both the states of California and Oregon and down south to Esmeralda County. Basically, a site of particular interest would be identified. Graduate students would conduct a botanical survey of the area, then three or four deer would be sacrificed, rumen contents removed and sent back to the lab for analyses. Immediately thereafter, other graduate students would bring in fistulated steers to sample the cattle diet in the same local from where the deer were sacrificed. The resulting comparisons began to give us some idea of the respective diets of the two species grazing similar areas. Generally we tried to sample any one area of interest at least three times yearly, with some areas being sampled more than one year.

Needless to say, as the project grew in scope, it became more than I could handle by myself. Paul Tueller had recently been employed by the Department of Range Management as a range scientist. Paul was from Pocatello, Idaho, but had gotten his masters at Nevada the same time that I did. Our courses parted there, as he went directly to Oregon State to obtain a Ph.D. in range. I was glad to see him return, and was more than happy to turn the range portion dealing with deer over to him.

In addition, to the sampling of diets, we also somewhat expanded the winter trapping of deer. Generally, deer were trapped within the confines of the original scope of the Ruby-Butte study area. Traps were mechanical devices holding nets, baited with alfalfa. Once sprung, nets fell on the animal, and then technicians would subdue the trapped animal, which was weighed, with a variety of observations taken as to condition, etc. Additionally, a 50 ml sample of blood was obtained from the animal for subsequent analyses back at our laboratories. Trapping was a unique experience, somewhat analogous to rodeo competition in the bull-riding event, sometimes even more so. Usually at least ten traps were set in any one area. Usually, at least five would have deer every morning. Our goal was to trap at least 250 deer every year, and this was accomplished for the several year duration of the study. Later, we did expand the trapping study to include some areas on the east flank of the Sierra, generally in the vicinity of Reno. It never ceased to amaze me, but after trapping thousands of deer, no real serious injuries ever occurred. However, we all got lots of bruises, strains, black eyes and other superficial blows.

The Ruby-Butte study grew to almost astronomical proportions. Ultimately the study produced about twenty successful graduate students, about half in Range under Tueller and about half in Animal Science, under my direction. All told there were at least 50 scientific publications that came out of the study. Additionally reports were given in scientific circles throughout the United States and the World. Tueller traveled more than I did as a result, going to Australia and Africa. My exploits were mostly in Canada, where I became a consultant to the Province of British Columbia dealing with the Queen's Land, comparable to our BLM or Forest Service. In hindsight, the Ruby Butte study made me a legitimate scientist, Ph.D. or no Ph.D.

One thing that the Ruby-Butte study did, was to vastly increase our herd of fistulated cattle. Eventually, I took five to the Nevada Test Site, and they stayed there, with the exception, of course, of Bronco. Bronco became important in the early stages of the Ruby-Butte study. He seemed to train animals better than all the rest of us put together. However, he was also increasing in stature, over 1,200 pounds. So he became difficult to transport, especially into some of the more remote areas. He also had difficulty walking under some of the extreme conditions that we were working in. We finally made the decision to retire Bronco, back to the farm, to be held strictly as a display to the many Washoe County school kids that were constantly having field days there. His picture was in the paper a lot more than mine, but that was OK. As far as I was concerned, Bronco Billy had earned his place in the history of the University of Nevada.

Billy survived as a public idol for several years, but along about 1968 he finally succumbed to a combination of old age, and constantly loosing too much energy out of an ever increasingly difficult fistula to close. I personally dug the grave for Billy, right along side or where Alkali was buried. People thought I was crazy, but after he was buried and no one else was around I sat down between their respective graves and just plumb cried my eyes out. A lot of people had been responsible for me being where I was then, a successful professor with a great career, my parents, Jim Kilduff, Mr. Fairfield, maybe even Bohman, but in a way, Alkali and Billy had been as much responsible as anybody. They worked with me, they cooperated, and they never gave up, even in some damn difficult times. I would miss Billy, more than any other animal that I had ever known. It was kind of a closing of a chapter of my life.

A successful professor, especially one without a Ph.D., not only had to do a good job teaching as well as conduct meaningful research, but he had to take an active role in the academic community. Basically, this meant that participation in committees was essential. This aspect always puzzled me, for it seemed that administrators were hired to run the University, and staff was hired to teach and do research. However, most professors that I knew seemed to have the philosophy that they were pretty knowledgeable about how a University should be run as well. Often, their version did not necessarily agree with that of the administration.

I had been involved with the Faculty Senate almost from the beginning, but in the eyes of my colleagues, I was never a very good senator. The problem stemmed from the fact that in controversial areas, areas that seemed to pit the faculty against the administration, I almost invariably sided with the administration. This problem didn't cause too much concern among the Agriculture faculty, but I sure wasn't very popular with the Liberal Arts faculty. I just never could understand how an English or Political Science professor could understand more about running the University than could the President. What really confused me was that some of these very same English and Political Science professors eventually got promoted into administrative positions. Then they seemed to understand even better how to run a University, but, often as not, it was from exactly the opposite standpoint that they had been espousing as professors! My inability to truly understand all there was to know about institutions of higher education would ultimately lead to my demise as a professor, but that is another story and far into the future.

My "zeal" for committee assignments didn't stop with being on the Faculty Senate. I was also interested in scholarship, as it hadn't been so very long ago that I was a financially struggling student myself. Bohmont was also interested in scholarship, having discussed the College's lack of a good scholarship program at a faculty meeting. After listening to his concept of what a scholarship program should be, it didn't take my enthusiasm and imagination long to drop a short note to him concurring with his view as well as suggesting some additional concepts. My concerns were rewarded with by his promptly placing me on the College Scholarship Committee, not only as a member, but as Chairman. At that time the College had an enrollment of approximately 150 full time students, and we had sufficient scholarship monies for about ten scholarships of a thousand dollars each. Some scholarships were based on an annual gift from a donor, while others resulted as interest from a secured investment. Both Bohmont and I agreed that we should set as a goal at least 25% of the Ag students should be on scholarship, and more dependence needed to be placed on monies resulting from secured investments rather than annual donor gifts. Based on an estimated annual return of 5%, this basically meant that an endowment of approximately $750,000 needed to be obtained.

Between some "creative accounting" accomplished by Bohmont and Pete Test, the chief financial officer of the College, we already had the equivalent of $250,000. My challenge was to raise an additional half million dollars, not easily accomplished in the 1960's! My committee barnstormed a number of ideas, but in typical academic fashion, most, if not all, of their ideas were from fantasyland. Plain and simple, no one was going to give us the money.

A new concept had been entering the livestock industry in those years, which was especially exciting to Nevada ranchers who customarily sold their cattle as calves every fall. This concept included the retained ownership of representative cattle from a ranch, so that their progress through the feedlot and ultimate slaughter, including carcass characteristics could be evaluated to help the rancher with his genetic improvement. This program had not entirely caught on in Nevada, but it was creating excitement. I have long since forgotten who suggested the idea, Bohmont, somebody from the Committee, or myself, but the concept came forth that perhaps the College could run such a program, in which a rancher would donate a typical calf, or calves, to the University. We would then feed the animals to slaughter, providing the donor with both feedlot performance and most importantly, carcass quality. The cost of the program would be covered by the value obtained from the sale of the carcass, with the excess to be placed in an endowment to support scholarships.

The College had a brand new slaughterhouse, and I suggested that a small research facility located on the banks of the Truckee River near Pyramid Lake, called The S BAR S would be the ideal place to feed the calves. The S BAR S already had working corrals and unloading/loading facilities. It didn't take long to build a simple but functional feedlot. Bill Behrens, the state livestock extension specialist, was placed in charge of the program as far as conducting the feeding and slaughtering portion of the program including reporting of all results. However, the major portion of the program was the recruitment of calves from the several hundred ranches scattered throughout Nevada. I felt that this should be the Dean's job, and fortunately my Committee agreed. So, on behalf of the Committee, I prepared a nice letter, explaining how he, Dean & Director, Dale W. Bohmont should compose a letter to be directed toward every livestock operator encouraging their participation in a new College of Agriculture Scholarship program to become known as "Calves for College". Well, I thought it was a good idea.

It didn't take but a day to see a whole new side of Bohmont. In fact, just a day after I dropped his letter into the campus mail, he burst into my office, uninvited. "Buddy, when you have an idea, you come to me to discuss it. You don't write me a letter, unless you're looking for a new job!" I really didn't know what to say at that point, so I took the wisest course possible, just sat behind my desk, staring at his dark glasses. That route didn't work very well either. "OK, I'll grant you I should write the letter, but somebody else is going to see every one of these ranchers as a follow up, and somebody else is going to have to collect these calves; and I, damn well, don't have the time. Seeing how you have time to sit behind your desk, apparently doing nothing, you'll do it in your spare time!"

Ouch!

The Calves for College campaign began, and it was a success. Every year, for the rest of the decade of the '60's I would work through the extension agents in every one of Nevada's 17 counties, arranging to meet ranchers to encourage their participation. Every fall, once firm commitments were made, I would head out with the College's livestock truck, picking up calves from Searchlight to Jackpot to Denio to Beatty. It was an experience that I will never forget. It probably was an experience most of the ranchers won't soon forget either. We had fed out well over 1,000 head of donated cattle by the end of five years, built an endowment of several hundred thousand dollars, returned invaluable information to ranchers all over Nevada, and put hundreds of students through the College. By the end of the 60's, student enrollment had grown from 150 to nearly 500 full time students, much of it attributed to the success of the agricultural scholarship program; and Calves for College was the backbone of the whole program.

One fine early winter day, I think it was 1968, Pete, who had been on campus for a variety of extension meetings came by about five and invited me to join him at Louie's for our usual picon. Well, as usual, one led to two and two led to three, but we were maintaining. We had been discussing just about every aspect of life in Nevada, when Pete brought up the recent elections. He was saddened on how the rural elections had gone: he was grumbling on how agriculture was continuing to loose its clout. "And if that isn't bad enough, just like I told you ten years ago, that God damned Harry Ryan won't go away." I looked at him kind of funny, because I hadn't thought about Harry in quite some time, in fact not since the last time Pete brought the little runt's name up. "Yup, he done got himself elected to the Nevada legislature, an assemblyman from Las Vegas," he informed me.

"You're shitting me! Damn, he can't be old enough. I am 33, he can't be over 31 - that's impossible," I concluded.

"No, made quite a name for himself: he's been Clark County's public defender," Pete said.

"Well, I don't see how in the hell being public defender would ever make you popular enough to be elected in the first place. Course, Clark's pretty damn liberal. Maybe he defended the mayor's son from a cheating scandal."

Pete laughed, "Yup, that's a good one. If any one would know the ropes on that deal, he sure to hell would." And three picons led to four.

To be a successful professor, you had to be on at least one campus wide committee, not including the faculty senate. Most of the committees dealt with academics, professor's rights, libraries, fringe benefits and a multitude of things, that as far as I was concerned, we hired administrators to take care of. But one committee was of interest, Intercollegiate Athletics. As far as I was concerned, athletics was a very legitimate place for the University to be active in. Unfortunately, Nevada had been a bit too active in at least football back in the late 40's and early 50's. They became nationally ranked. However, one thing led to another and the whole program collapsed. In fact, Nevada did not even field a football team for one year after the dust settled. Gradually, athletics were coming back, and there were lots of folks in Reno that thought athletics should come all the way back. But, the 1960's were a lot different than the 1940's or even the early 50's. The National Collegiate Athletic Association, or the NCAA, was now in charge. To come back at the level some of the alumni were pushing for, including the local newspapers, would have only resulted in sanctions. So, my interests were to build a sound, but defendable, program. Getting on the Intercollegiate Athletic Committee was not a likely spot for me, as most members were long standing professors, all holding the Ph.D. degree. But I had done a lot of favors for Bohmont. So, I decided he owed me one. A short visit with the Dean resulted in a phone call to then University President, Charles Armstrong, resulting in my being appointed to the Committee.

The Intercollegiate Athletic Committee, consisting of about 5-7 members, met once a month with then Athletic Director, Jake Lawlor. Even then Jake was a legend, having played basketball when he was in college, coached some of the most successful high school basketball teams ever in Nevada at Virginia City. Finally, he rose to the level of basketball coach at Nevada and he turned out some barnburner teams that were nationally ranked. Jake was probably one of the finest men I ever met at Nevada. Nothing rattled him, he had done it all and he had seen it all. Jake and I spoke the same language, he didn't have a Ph.D. either. Nevada competed in the Far Western Conference in those days. It was a laid back conference consisting mostly of state colleges from California, but it sponsored football, basketball, track and baseball. Jake was adamant that was about all Nevada could afford and not get into trouble with the NCAA. He also knew that as Reno grew, the pressures would become unbearable to advance to more competitive conferences. The alums like to read about Nevada, not necessarily just in the local newspapers.

Jake realized that the pressures to upgrade athletics would be placed first and foremost on the football program. Nevada had a beautiful, but very small stadium on campus. But, it only seated a few thousand fans. As those pressures mounted, I also became chairman of the Athletic Board, and NCAA representative for the University - and Jake was nearing retirement. So between us, with considerable help from the University and the Legislature, we slowly but surely moved toward the goal of a new stadium. It was not only accomplished, but ultimately the new stadium would be expanded to meet the needs of a nationally ranked football program, but that took many years.

As Chairman of the Intercollegiate Athletic Committee, or Board as most liked to call it, I was always amazed at the nature of the staff members that wanted to be on the committee. The President made the final selection based on the recommendations of the Faculty Senate. Some members of the Board were there because they had a very "purist" attitude about athletics. Their position always centered around the concept that intercollegiate athletics was purely amateur, and that no incentive, such as tuition wavers, or athletic scholarships, should ever be offered. Other members felt that whatever Nevada was offering in the way of financial aid was totally inadequate. We should take steps to immediately upgrade to play the likes of USC and Notre Dame. Jake had long since instilled in me the ridiculous idea of both positions. Intercollegiate athletics might still be considered amateur, but it did cost a lot of money. The trick was to balance the expenditures with gate receipts and what the alumni could raise, and most importantly not break any NCAA rules. So, my job was to get both sides to agree and meet somewhere in the middle. There were a certain number of Board members that fell into the middle, but, more often than not, they represented a group that really didn't have an opinion, mainly because they didn't understand the situation to begin with. This group represented my biggest problem. They often represented the swing vote on critical issues: they were easily swayed: so my problem was to keep them squarely in the middle. These were often young professors that seemed more in awe of their academic standing than what their obligations were to this Board.

Typical of this bunch was a young political scientist with a brand new Ph.D. by the name of Joe Crowley. Joe simply didn't know why he was on the Athletic Board, but I guessed God or the President must have known. Joe would come out with some academic dissertations about athletics that would drive me up the wall, and likely would have got Jake to retire, if he hadn't already done so. But my patience prevailed, even though Joe was a card carrying Democrat. If I knew then what I was to learn in the future, my reaction to Joe might have been significantly different.

When Jake did retire, I was sad to see him go. He was replaced by former football coach Dick Trachock. Dick was brought out from Pennsylvania in the old glory days of Nevada football. After graduation he remained at Nevada, eventually to become football coach. Dick came from hardheaded coal miner stock, and he still possessed all of those traits. By the time Dick became Athletic Director most of the athletic program was set in concrete, pretty firm and growing slow but steady. I didn't stay on as Chairman, or even as a member for but a few years after Jake retired. We all missed Jake. The program he developed did well for Nevada for many, many years. Jake's wisdom and guidance eventually resulted in the largest indoor pavilion in northern Nevada being named after him. The Lawlor Events Center ultimately played home to some of the best basketball played in Nevada, and the United States, but that occurred many years into the future when Nevada's athletic fortunes finally became big time indeed. I have often thought back that the most enjoyable committee that I was ever on was indeed the Intercollegiate Athletic Committee.

In hindsight, the decade of the sixty's were some of my best and possibly worst of times. I was productive, probably almost too productive, and that was part of the problem. By the end of 1968, I had been able to amass 78 publications, more than some professors were able to complete in a lifetime. Yet I was only 33 years old. I had turned out eight successful students with the M.S. degree, and had five more under my direction, which was more than the rest of the Department put together. But my attitude was not good. I was becoming increasingly disenchanted with my fellow professors, with or without Ph.D.'s. They could find more things to bitch about than I could imagine; hours they worked, the administration, faculty rights, academic freedom, and now the Vietnam war. I admit I wasn't a fan of the Vietnam war. In fact, I wondered out loud why we were there in the first place. But we were, and a lot of young American lives were placed in harm's way, many to pay the ultimate price required by this nation, including some students that I considered my very own. I could never bring myself to bad mouth the military, our government, presidents Kennedy or Johnson, and my heart and prayers went with those that had to serve.

One day, when Pete was in town, we were sitting at Louie's having our usual picon, when a semi truck eased past on fourth street, or Highway 40 from San Francisco heading east to Salt Lake or wherever. This particular semi had a lot of steel boxes on it; in fact five high, three wide, and eight deep counting the trailer, for a total 120 boxes. We were both just looking at the truck when Manual, the bar keep, stated, "Yup, that's the third this afternoon. Each box has a body bag, straight from Nam".

The thought was sobering to say the least, and from that point my attitude about Vietnam changed forever after. I might not agree with what was happening, but for whatever the politics were, there we were, and there went 120 young men that paid the ultimate price. From that point on I became an outspoken critic of those that protested the war, be it violent or verbally. Several times at faculty forums, I spoke strongly in support of our troops, much to the chagrin of some of my elders. You could philosophically, and certainly politically protest the war, but you better not say anything about the troops. They were my heroes!

I guess my attitude about academic life in general just wasn't very good. I frequently found myself uttering cutting remarks to other professors. Perhaps I was jealous of their Ph.D. degree: perhaps, I was just becoming intolerant. More than one of my colleagues that still had some patience with me took me aside and suggested that I had to become more tolerant. But when I knew what they were being paid and what they were producing, it was difficult. Sometimes, I could envision making the whole bunch mad enough where they would rise in mass and actually attempt to eliminate me. It was an amusing sidelight to imagine such things. Little did I realize that one day my vision would essentially come true!

I did a lot of growing up in the sixty's. We bought our first house, had three daughters in school by the end, and began to find out how difficult marriage can become if not everything is functioning smoothly. I became active in politics, mostly because of the College and Bohmont. He frequently shoved me into meetings with the legislature, as well as, governor's meetings regarding college budgets. I got to know Governor's Sawyer, and Laxalt, having participated in discussions with them at various times. I learned the halls of the legislature, lobbying for college funding before every biannual meeting of the legislature. I met legendary legislatures like Carl Dodge, John Fransway, Floyd Lamb from the Senate side and Norman Glaser, Bill Swackhamer, Roy Young, and Lawrence Jacobsen from the Assembly. I hadn't yet met Nevada's senators, but I frequented the offices of Walter Baring, Nevada's perennial lone vote in the House. But other aspects made me grow as well. Life is created and life ends. I experienced the joys associated with the birth and development of our three daughters, and, sadly enough, I experienced the darkness of sudden and tragic death.

Jim Hunter and his wife had long lived in housing located at the Main Station Farm. His duties there required near constant presence. But Jim was getting up in years, so he requested, and received permission to move out of the Main Station. He, and his wife Ida, had purchased a small parcel of land, out in the country north of Reno, and they were building their dream home there. I would see Jim several times during the week. So, I lived a blow-by-blow description of the slow, but steady, construction of the Hunter adobe. Late, one Saturday afternoon, he was returning to the Main Station Farm from the construction site, less than a half mile from home, when he went through a country intersection, not seeing or realizing that a car was coming from the other direction. The collision caused Jim to be thrown from his pick-up; and when the dust settled, it was resting squarely on top of him. He was killed instantly.

Even though I was in my thirty's, I had never lost anybody close to me. Grandparents that were distant and old, yes, but nobody that was close on a near daily basis. Jim had shown me many kindnesses during my years at Nevada. His patience with me, in hindsight, would probably be in the legendary category if all knew about it. Jim was my friend, a friend that I could always talk to, no matter what the subject was. He clearly understood my frustrations with the faculty, for he shared many himself. He shared the high points and the depths that I sometimes sank to. His wisdom and support had become one of my mainstays, far more than I ever realized or acknowledged until he was gone. It was most difficult for his daughter Virginia, who was still working for me. It was difficult for his wife, Ida, an Austrian whom he married during the War. And it was difficult for me. For the person that I could always look to for support and understanding, council and comradeship, was taken away without a word - just final. The darkness of death seemed to surround me. After the funeral, I did the only thing that I knew to do and that was climb a mountain. Immediately after the burial was complete, I left for what was becoming my favorite spot in all Nevada, the Toiyabe Mountain Range. My excuse was to check on field trials, but the real reason was to get away, try to understand.

I went to the Reese River, where it crosses Highway 50, then down south, or up the River. The Reese is a real phenomenon in Nevada; it flows from the South to the North, where it intercepts the Humboldt, just west of Battle Mountain. I made it clear to Cow Canyon, from where it's about a forty-five minute walk down to the Reese. I camped on the River that night, and early the next morning I started my trek up the Reese, finally topping out at the head of South Twin River, which flows to Big Smoky Valley and the RO Ranch. The pass itself is right at 10,000', and it's was still nearly 1,800 feet of vertical climb to the top. The footing was good, but the air was mighty thin, but it did help clear my head. It's probably ten or twelve miles from where Cow Canyon intercepts the Reese to the top of Arc Dome, the highest point in the Toiyabes at 11,788'. It took me six grueling hours. Arc Dome, like many of Nevada's highest peaks had been used during the Civil War to send messages with mirrors, the ruins of the Union soldiers camp were still present, barely. But the view from Arc Dome is spectacular beyond belief.

It was a clear day and to the south west, both Boundary Peak, Nevada's highest point of elevation at the north end of the White's was stark against the skyline, as well as the distant back of the Sierra's. Immediately to the east was the rugged top of Mount Jefferson, and beyond that stood Table Mountain and the Monitors. I could clearly see several ranges past Table. Far to the east stood the distant outline of what I believed to be Wheeler Peak, Nevada's second tallest peak, located on the Utah border. I was literally looking at the entire state of Nevada, from California to Utah, rugged beauty beyond description. As I sat there, Jim's life with me sort of unfolded: from the first days, Alkali and Billy, the day Billy upset him and he lost his pipe, his ever faithful dog, Duff. Jim was my friend, and really, he had been much a source of strength. But yet in my heart, I knew Jim would not ever want me to miss a step because of what happened. One of his favorite saying when we worked cattle, as a cow or calf was being released, "You're on you own now, bud. We got you this far, the rest is up to you". I somehow could hear him saying the same to me. Indeed he had a great deal to do with getting me this far, and the rest was up to me. I would miss Jim, not only now, but much more in the future, as my life with the University would take a turn that made me realize just how much I missed him.

The cool air at nearly 12,000' was beginning to make me realize that I had better get off this mountain. Going back to the pass to South Twin, then all the way back down the Reese would have put me at camp after dark. So, I choose to dive right off the west side of Arc Dome. It probably wasn't anything for a mountain climber, but it was plenty steep for me. I came down with a ton of rocks, shale, sage, and anything else that happened by my grip, but down I came. It wasn't long before I ended up in a draw with running water that flowed directly into the Reese, which I could see was just a couple of miles away. I hit my camp about an hour before dark, just in time to catch two big German Brown's for supper. Life was good, but I had learned that life was also precious and it could be every bit as hard as it was good. As I sat and watched the last of the coals die, I realized that I would grow up and I would comprehend all that I had learned, but once again I also realized just how important God had become in my life. For I also had heard Jim say on several occasions, "I think I will talk to God about getting a bit more strength, the problems I face exceed what my mortal self can handle." I could only think, "Amen, my friend, God speed."

The second death that occurred in my life happened the following year. Although not as close as Jim, it was in time every bit as traumatic, and in some ways would impact my life forever after.

The call came in at about 10:30 p.m., in mid August. Although I was half asleep, I could tell instantly it was from Pete. His voice was steady, but I could also tell he was under great stress: I knew that before he got the first sentence out. "Dad just called, Mom's missing. She had that useless mustang out today, somewhere in the High Rock area looking for cattle. They found her pick-up and trailer, but she was nowhere around. They found that about an hour ago, and they, I guess the Washoe County Deputies, are searching by pick-ups tonight. Dad is frantic; there is no one at the house, except two of the cowboys. I'll head out in the Cub about 3 A.M. tomorrow morning. That will put me into Reno at about 4:15. I'll have to fuel up, then head to the Ranch. Terry, I need help: I'll need a spotter, can you go?"

This all happened pretty fast, but as I lay there I couldn't really think of anything that was absolutely essential for tomorrow. Classes wouldn't start for another day or two. There were some college academic committees that I was supposed to go to over the next day or two, but they would probably do just fine without me. In fact, the rest of the committee might just be relieved. "Sure, you bet. I'll bring my binoculars. I'll be waiting at the commercial lounge by 4:00 a.m. sharp.

I can stay as long as you need me," was my response. By then I was wide awake, wondering what might have happened.

I could still remember the blood red look in Charger's eyes that day in the corral. That horse gave me the willies, but Reene seemed to have him in complete control. The High Rock country included hundreds and hundreds, probably even quite a few thousand square miles of near wilderness. She could be anywhere, bucked off, down with a broken leg. The possibilities were endless. Hopefully, she had matches. You could probably see smoke for 50 miles in that country. I had reset the alarm for three, so that I would have time to grab a bite and a cup of coffee before leaving. Tomorrow would probably be one of those long days you never forget. It didn't seem like I had ever gone to sleep, but the alarm woke me. It didn't take more than ten minutes to be out of there. Jan wished me luck, and as I went out the front door, I responded by stupidly saying I'll probably be back tonight.

Little did I realize, but my return would not be that night. I hadn't been in the airport commercial lounge more than 15 minutes when I saw the Super Cub banking in from the east. It probably was the smallest plane to land at Reno that day, but for sure, it was headed on a brave mission. Pete was a mess. It was obvious that he never went to bed, but he was in control. It didn't take more than twenty minutes to get everything ready to depart. "You know, it will only be about 6:00 a.m. when we hit Buffalo Canyon. It's not real light, you think we can land?' I quizzed.

"Yeah, I been thinking about that all night. I called Dad, and they will have two or three pick-ups with their headlights on to light the road. I think we'll be OK," was his comforting remark. I didn't say anything, as it was obvious Pete was worried out of his head. It would be ironic to have Reene ride into camp, only to see us draped over some nearby landscape. I didn't need to think about things like that. So, I poured us both a cup of coffee out of the thermos that I had brought along. In the meantime, I studied distant lights on the ground, trying to guess which possible ranch they might represent.

The sun was breaking in the distant eastern horizon as we cleared the north end of Pyramid Lake. I couldn't really see the lake, but enough light was bouncing off the flat surface that I could make out the shoreline. I figured it would take about thirty minutes before we would be down into Buffalo Canyon. It didn't look too good from where I was sitting. But whatever else, our situation wasn't likely near as bad as that of Reene Echegoyen. I couldn't seem to get her picture out of my mind. She was pretty, very pretty, especially considering the hard life she had led. My mind was working overtime imagining all sorts of predicaments. I could only guess what was going through Pete's mind.

The sun had risen maybe 5 degrees above the horizon, but I could begin to see a bit of the landscape. I recognized the Smoke Creek Desert from our previous trip, but again it was flat and I was sure radiated some light. The mountains straight in front were a black blob. Somewhere down there was a windy road in a crooked canyon that we called a runway. Damn, I wondered what my mother would be thinking about right now. "Maybe we ought to circle out here for ten to fifteen minutes?" I asked the pilot.

"No, we are OK. I can see Buffalo from here. I'll flick on the landing lights in a minute or two so they will know to fire up the trucks", Pete cheerfully responded. About then I guessed he must eat a powerful lot of carrots, because over his shoulder, Buffalo appeared to me as a darker blob within an already very dark blob.

Sure enough, four sets of headlights switched on at the same time, all pointed generally in our direction. They even appeared in a fairly straight line. I wasn't sure that I had much to be thankful about right then, but I did remember Marty sawing down that cedar tree. This would be mighty tricky if we had to dodge that as well. Pete throttled the Cub back, dropped the flaps, and down we came. I will admit that I could actually see land, and even make out some objects such as trees. Well, he couldn't see me sitting directly behind him, so I guessed it didn't really matter much if I closed my eyes or not. More flaps, suddenly full throttle, the little Cub shook from stem to stern. I opened my eyes long enough to see a set of headlights go by about five feet from my side. There was a sharp thud, followed by an even bigger bang: back into the air we went: she slipped sideways, and I could tell by Pete's neck he was fighting it as hard as he could. Another set of lights, we hit again, but this time we were going slower and only came off for a second or two. I never did understand what all that plane had for brakes, but whatever it consisted of, they all got applied. "Hang on, we ain't going to make that curve, so we'll swallow some brush and a few rocks," he yelled. I felt us leave the edge of the road, thank God the barrow ditch wasn't very deep. I thought we might flip, but Pete was able to bring her back towards the road. The plane shuddered real hard as the prop chewed up a hapless sage plant. After that we just idled down, and taxied right up to the house. I don't mind admitting that I peed my pants, but it was dark, and there were more important things to worry about.

As I climbed out, Marty was hugging Pete, and yelling at him at the same time, "You crazy Son of a Bitch, if it ain't bad enough that Reene's lost, you crazy shit head, you damn near killed yourself and Jim as will." I didn't know who Jim was, but I wondered if Marty had any concern for myself. However, it didn't take a second to learn that Jim was Jim Sweeney, a Washoe County Deputy Sheriff, chief of Search and Rescue. "Boy, that was the damndest landing that I ever saw anybody make. It would have been perfect, excepting your left wheel knocked one of my red lights off the top of this rig," exclaimed Jim. Oh, I see, we didn't hit the ground that first bump, it was the sheriff's rig. Wonder how they will explain that was a meandering thought that went through my muddled brain.

A quick inspection of the plane indicated no damage, she was tough all right. The next stop was the house for a quick breakfast and coffee. "I thought I would have two civil air patrol planes here by nine o'clock, but we got a plane down in the Sierra. So, all we have is four ground rigs besides mine," Jim started off. "I think Marty needs to stay here. We'll have a ground radio here in a bit that will be powerful enough to reach just about all of us. Anyway, it will always reach the planes, and they can relay to ground. Between five ground rigs, we should be able to cover every road in this part of northwestern Nevada by sundown. Pete, you know this country better than all the rest of us put together. Your Dad feels she was in High Rock. What do you think? I guess after this morning's show, that Cub must be powerful enough to get right down and dirty, probably even into the Canyon, if you had to."

I could feel the urge to pee again, but this just wasn't the place or time. "Well, I have ridden with her enough to know her thinking. Since Dad called last night, I have pretty much mapped out in my mind just about where she would have headed. I know where the cows would be, especially the strays. I guess it sort of depends on how far she got. She could be a mile from her rig, or she could be fifty, but she's out there someplace. Maybe, she just got unloaded, and is hoofing it. Riding that useless mustang stud about anything can happen," Pete summarized.

Pete had several fifty-gallon barrels of aviation fuel at the ranch, so I pumped while he inspected. "Damn, the sage didn't hurt the prop a bit, which I was afraid would be our major problem. But Jim's light was fastened pretty good. We bent the wheel a bit out of alignment, but nothing looks cracked. She'll probably vibrate a bit taking off, but that's about all," he concluded. Well, on this rough road, I doubted that we would notice a vibration very much. Jim, Marty, and two more deputies that had just arrived in trucks gathered around the Cub as we got ready.

Marty came up to Pete with a bear hug, and obvious tears in his eyes. "I am prepared for about anything, but I know she's all right. She's too damned tough to let something like this get to her." He turned to me, and I got the bear hug, but it was OK. "God I am glad Pete has a friend like you: God bless you both: you've got to be his eyes today. It will take all of his wits to keep that bird in the air, so you got to do the looking."

The sun began to light the road as Pete turned the Cub back down the canyon. Within seconds we were airborne. With a thousand feet under us, Pete leveled out and headed in a general northerly direction. "There's a corral in what is called Smokey Canyon. Smokey drains into High Rock Lake from the south. The corral is actually in Humboldt County. Last night about dark, one of the deputies found her rig at the corral. That's not unusual, because if she was going to cover the country between High Rock Lake and the north end of the Granite's that's where she always started from. The Calico Mountains are east of Smokey Canyon, and they are a rugged pile of rocks - no cows there for sure. So, I think we'll start at her rig, go directly west for about twenty minutes. I'll try to maintain an air speed of eighty knots. That will cover more than I think she would have ever ridden looking for cows. After twenty minutes we'll turn south then back east again. I'll try to fly parallel runs about half mile apart. By noon, six hours, we should be about ten miles or so south, maybe to just about Fox Mountain. We'll be low on petrol. So, if we haven't scored by then, we'll dip back to Buffalo, gas up, then do the same maneuver north this afternoon. We should see something."

We crossed over the corral in Smokey Canyon, and sure enough there was her rig and fifth wheel stock trailer, with the tailgate down, just waiting for its rider to return. With that we headed west on our first run. "I am going to look as hard as I can, so I don't have much to say unless I spot something," I yelled in Pete's ear. His affirmative nod indicated approval. I tried using binoculars, but the ride was just too bumpy. I found I could use them for a second or two, but no longer, and to just observe the landscape they just didn't work. My eyesight was excellent, always better than 20-10, so I just put them to work. I tried to look at both sides, but I soon realized that if I always studied to the south on each run I would probably cover the country better. There were lots of horses in this country, but they were almost always in bands. There were occasional studs that had been run out of their harem by the new kid on the block. I could remember that dark red, almost a blood red tint to his dark body, and I figured that would stand out no matter what. Unless there had been a total wreck, it seemed that he should still have a saddle on somehow. My mind wandered from each rock outcropping to the next, from one unnamed draw to another, from one water seep to the next, finally we made our first turn to the south, then back to the east. There were roads and even isolated ranches, or line camps. The deputies had gotten the word out late the night before, and now every available rider in north Washoe was out. Occasionally, we would see one, or one of the deputies, Pete would always dip low, wobble the wings in response to the wave. I knew Reene was well liked, but the further we flew, the more riders I saw. They must have come from all over.

We droned on for countless miles, nothing but the vastness of the Nevada landscape, rolling hills, sharp outbreaks of rocks, occasional aspen groves around a green spot, cows raising dust, bands of mustangs, deer and antelope, but no Charger or Reene - just the great Nevada outback. I looked at my watch: it was after eleven. We had been airborne over five hours. Pete and I hadn't exchanged a word for several hours.

"How's the fuel?" I hazard.

"Enough for about 45 minutes or so. We'll hit Buffalo at twelve," was the only reply. At eleven thirty we concluded a leg heading west, about a mile north of the crest of Fox Mountain. From there we headed southwest toward Poodle Mountain. Pete got a bit more air under us, but we both continued to search as hard as our eyes would allow. Thirty more minutes and we were into Buffalo for a smooth and uneventful landing. If the damaged wheel caused us problems, I couldn't feel it. Marty was waiting, but he already knew that our efforts had been fruitless. Pete had kept up some chatter with the ground base and the other stations, but nobody had any luck.

"I know you will want to get right back up, so I had sack lunches made with some thermos bottles with lemonade, if that's OK?" Marty offered. Pete was pumping gas, and I said that's great. There were several deputies there. Everybody was trying to keep everybody's sprits up. I could tell Pete didn't want to talk, just get back in the air, so that's what we did.

After a quick fueling, a sack full of sandwiches and a thermos of lemonade, we were headed northeast again. It was about 2 p.m. when we made our first swing back toward the west, this time flying about a mile north of the Smokey Canyon corral. Pete seemed pretty sure that Reene had not crossed to the east of High Rock Canyon, so for the afternoon we used the canyon as our eastern reference point. Our tracks continued to take us north and west. Each pass showed us nothing, but more country, a few cattle, bands of horses, an occasional rider, but nothing else. I could tell by Pete's mannerisms that he was becoming more and more discouraged. He had doubted that she would be north, and the further we went, the more he felt we were dead wrong.

It was close to 5:30, we were north of Yellow Rock Canyon, when Pete turned around saying, "This is bull shit". I know she wouldn't have gone north, much less this far north. I am going to lift up about a thousand feet, make a big arc over towards Soldier Meadow, then head southwest towards Buffalo. That should put us down before dark. Up a thousand feet or so should be smoother, try to use those binoculars and cover as much country as you can, OK?" I already felt like my eyes were abut to drop out of my head, but I nodded an affirmative, and said a silent prayer that we would be back before dark.

I found that if I raised my self off the seat slightly, sort of using my knees and legs as shock absorbers, I could use my binoculars fairly well. I scanned the country north, clear to Badger Mountain, and south, back to where we had made our last pass. There were lots of horses, but they were the grays, browns and buckskins that all mustang bands appear to be from that distance. I was sure Charger would stand out. I had never forgotten his unique color. I was positive he would appear very dark from the air. No matter what, he should still have something on. I had noticed that Reene used a full rigging, including a double cinch set up, with a breast band. That saddle wouldn't come off easy, no matter what. But I just couldn't even imagine a horse that looked like Charger, much less actually seeing one. As we gradually changed directions from easterly to southwest over Soldier Meadows, the Black Rock Range and Paiute Peak fell to my left. I watched along the edge of that massive hunk of rock, but no horse would be on the side, so I concentrated on the Desert, and back toward High Rock Lake.

"I don't want to go down the Black Rock, the Deputies have covered that by truck. We'll head over to Smokey Canyon, then on down South Willow. When I get close to the mouth of South Willow, I am going to hop over the Granite's, then make one more arc to the north up Crutcher, over towards Cedar Canyon, then back toward Buffalo. Should put us down just about dark," Pete continued. I began to imagine another landing on top of a deputy's pick-up, but I had to concentrate on the landscape in the meantime. We were about halfway between Crutcher and Cedar when I spotted an abnormally dark horse, standing on a ridge all by himself. He was about five miles south, in a lot of cover that I couldn't make out, but I guessed it to be cedars. I tapped Pete on the shoulder and pointed. He saw what caught my attention immediately, and wheeled to the left.

We came in low, very low, over the ridge. Pete had maneuvered around to the south so that we could get a better view. We literally flew right up the horse's butt. He was a single stud, but at a few hundred feet, even though he had some markings similar to Charger, including his general color, he definitely wasn't Charger. After nearly ten hours of flying it was the only lead we had, even as false as it was. Pete uttered only one comment, "Shit", as he headed again back towards Cedar Canyon.

The light was getting difficult, as the sun was setting far to the west, over the ridge of the distant Sierra. Mount Lassen stood out against that distant skyline, but the ground below us was nearly black. We topped over the ridge of the Buffalo Mountains, and down through Buffalo Canyon, past the house surrounded by several deputy vehicles and some other cars. Lights were coming up the canyon, so we had to clear the cars out whatever else. I guessed we really only had about ten minutes of light left. Pete got a hold of the base station, requesting the road be cleared and a little light might help. He wheeled around, heading north again right up the canyon. We were down about as low as possible, full power, full flaps and down we came. There were lights, but now everybody was back from the road a bit further than they were this morning. Pete hadn't been flying that long, but either Ralph Scott had taught him well, or Pete was a natural, perhaps a bit of both, as it was about as smooth a landing as possible under the circumstances, no deputies vehicle, not even any sagebrush. Everyone could tell by the grimness of our faces that no questions need be asked. The extra cars belonged to families. Although Marty and Reene only had one child, Pete, they both came from large Basque families, and they were all descending. At least food would not be a problem.

I hadn't been on the ground more than five minutes; in fact I was still trying to stretch my legs when Jim Swenney drove up. Pete and Marty had already gone into the house. I was just walking around trying to get the cramps out. "I need to see you for a minute Terry. I may have some bad news," Jim said as he approached. "I was just coming up the canyon when one of my deputies called in. He had been driving down the Soldier Meadows road when he stopped to take a leak. He said he was just about where Willow Creek crosses the road, he had finished, but just happened to walk around the back of the car and noticed something that didn't look right. All he had was his big flash light, and the batteries were low, but it clearly looked to him like a horse had come down the side of the hill above the road, crossed the road, and headed out into the desert. He claims that by everything that he could see, it appeared that the horse was dragging something. He followed the trail out into the greasewood as far as his light would allow, but he was sure he saw blood several times. It was just too dark for him to go further."

"Christ, if that damn mustang has drug her out into that greasewood, she's done. Fact, probably already was done by the time he got to the road," was about all I could muster up.

"Yup, I don't know what to do. It's fruitless for us to search tonight. The road down the east side of the desert, down past Hardin City and Double Hot Springs is treacherous. In fact I got two rigs stuck over there someplace right now. Both those guys walked back across the desert to the Soldier road, and were picked up by Deputy Vest, but that was after he found the trail. The guys that got stuck and walked back never cut any trail that they recognized, but it was dark and they maybe didn't even see it," Jim continued.

"Well, if he's dragging her, maybe with a little luck he got tangled in some greasewood. The worst thing we could do would be to spook him tonight. If she's still alive, she might make it until daylight. My bet would be to go in, have a council, but, but my vote is for an early morning go. Mobilize your forces down the east side. Pete and I fly down towards Double Hot Springs. Pete showed me where the old ghost town of Hardin City is from the air. About there a horse could cross the Black Rock Mountains pretty easily. You know they found that nag just about straight across the mountain from Hardin City, from the way it was described to me," I concluded.

"Well, if she was drug that far, there's no life left now. Lets go in," Jim concluded.

As long as I were to live, I would never forget the look on Marty's and Pete's face as Jim laid out the news. They clearly knew what the consequences of being drug were to begin with. Where Deputy Vest had found the trail was six to eight miles from where the corrals and Reene's rig was. The greasewood out in the flat would cut you to ribbons, if she had survived to that point to begin with. No matter how much they wanted to go, both Pete and Marty realized there was nothing that could be done that night. Pete was physically so tired that he knew he had to have some sleep if he was going to fly in the morning. It would be nearly a 30-minute flight from Buffalo to where Willow Creek cut the Soldier Road, including taking off, so it was agreed, Pete would go to sleep, I would service the Super Cub. We would take off by car light an hour before sun-up. Jim was calling back to Reno for a new crew of Deputies to leave immediately in several four-wheel rigs, and start from both ends, one crew to come down from Soldier towards Double Hot Springs. The other to head out to Black Rock Point, across the playa from Gerlach, and head north toward Double Hot Springs.

We were up at three, aunts, uncles and cousins had a full breakfast of steaks, eggs, gravy, homemade bread made into toast and gallons of hot strong coffee ready and waiting. Jim indicated that two loads of deputies were ready to leave Gerlach, as soon as it was light enough to see the Point across the playa. Two other groups of deputies were already past Willow Canyon, on their way to Soldier, so they could head south towards Double Hot Springs. Jim said he and Marty would go on over to Gerlach, then up to Andy Jackson's place. From there they would head across the playa directly to Double Hot Springs. According to Jim, all you had to find was a blue teakettle out in the flat, head due east and you would drive right into the springs. It didn't look like Jim and Marty had ever slept. I guessed they could find the blue teakettle. Pete had slept. I checked on him several times during the night and he was sawing logs. Our plan was to leave Buffalo by about four thirty, fly straight to Willow Creek, then head down the Playa. I didn't know what to expect, but if Charger was heading down the flat, and was indeed dragging something it would leave a track once he cleared the Greasewood and was on the Playa proper. We figured if we were to Willow Creek by quarter till five, it would be just about light enough to see.

We were wrong. Quarter till five was too dark, so we circled for about 15 minutes before the light was satisfactory. The Gerlach group of deputies had already left town and were on the Playa heading toward the Point, which was a drive of nearly thirty miles. It was flat as a pancake until you crossed the Quinn River Ditch, and that could get pretty dicey. The second group of deputies was already to Soldier, and they were starting south. Marty and Jim were just leaving Andy Jackson's place. The playa is flat, in fact, so flat that you can see the curve of the earth. I suggested that we fly a lazy "S" type of pattern, generally heading south, and about ten to fifteen feet off the deck. My hope was that by being this low we just might get lucky enough and pick up a track. From Willow Creek to Double Hot Springs is about 15 miles as the crow flies, but we weren't exactly flying like a crow. About six to seven miles down the playa from Willow Creek, the brush pretty much is all gone due to the extreme alkalinity. However, the salty crust is soft, and clearly displays any kind of track. Unfortunately, due to the fact that the water at Double Hot Springs is the only dependable water on the east side of the playa between Soldier and the hot springs at the Point, there were a lot of tracks.

Gradually, as we headed further south, one set of tracks did seem more prevalent, it was shod so it wasn't a mustang. Furthermore, there was the faintest sign of something dragging, but at 60 miles per hour and ten feet high, I just couldn't clearly make out what I was looking at. The further south we went, the harder the surface became, so the track was becoming less discernible. "Can you land this crate here?" I shouted to Pete. With nothing more than a nod, he set her down. We both scrambled out and over to where the track was apparent, but there was little to see. It appeared that a shod horse was heading south, and it appeared that on his left side, something was dragging, but whatever it was, it was leaving only a slight imprint, certainly not what a drug body would leave. "You know, that is the only clearly shod track I have seen today: at least, that I could say for certain was shod, and I knew that long before we came down. If that is Charger, we need to find him, and maybe we can get a better idea of what happened," I proposed.

"Yeah, but I don't like my chances. She's not here for sure, but I don't know what else to do right now. This horse is going in a pretty straight line, seems to be heading towards the Springs. These tracks look to me to be at least a day old, I just don't know what else to do right now."

"Look, let's just lift off, start going straight towards the Springs, if there's another animal on the playa, we could see it for miles. That damn Charger may just be heading back towards where you guys caught him, down around the Point," I offered.

Pete snapped back, "Don't include me in you guys. I never wanted her to have anything to do with that nag to begin with. If I had my way, his balls would have come off a long time ago."

We were airborne and within sight of Double Hot Springs within minutes. We could see Jim's rig was already there, and Pete had him on the radio. "We think Charger has gone past here, maybe to the Point. We're going to take a quick trip around the point, then back over the mountain and we'll land at the Springs, go from there if we don't see anything, so sit tight, OK?

Jim responded by saying that there were shod tracks at the spring, one recent set only, but, "You'll be on your own, both of my boys got stuck about a mile north of the Hot Spring at the Point. The dummies drove down through a draw and hit black gumbo. They are both bottomed out, and it sounds like a Hughie will be about the only thing that's going to lift them out." Sure enough, about a mile north of the Hot Springs there was two Washoe County Sheriff's pick-up, up to the fenders, with four men standing around wondering what to do. We dipped our wings, waved, but there wasn't much else we could do.

"They are too muddy to ride back in this rig," was the only comment Pete made. In about five minutes the Point was right in front of us. We flew right over the pond and the old abandoned sheep wagon that Pete had pointed out on our first trip, but no sign of Charger.

It was a couple of miles clear around the Point. There's two old small dry lakebeds on the point a few feet higher than the playa, but again no sign of Charger. Pete eased the Cub around the southeast corner of the Point, and headed up the east side of the range. We hadn't gone thirty seconds when I hit Pete on the shoulder and pointed nearly dead ahead. There stood a big dark horse with a saddle. I wasn't sure, but I thought I could see something hanging from his left side. I pointed off to our right at a large flat white area, that beckoned for us to land on. Pete agreed and immediately set the little plane down. We climbed out, binoculars in hand, and with that aid it was clearly Charger, and indeed there was something hanging down his left side.

"Look, just let me walk over there. I don't think you should go. If everything is OK, and Charger will let me, I will unsaddle him and just turn him loose, unless you want to kill him. He looks dead tired. I kind of think that I can catch him." Pete looked like he was going to throw up, for he had also looked with the binoculars and he clearly saw something hanging from Charger's left side.

307

He slumped to his knees and started sobbing, "I can't go over there. Don't kill him. Just turn him loose and bring everything back. I know what's there. I'll be OK by the time you get back."

I knelt down alongside Pete, put both my arms around him and simply said, "I'll do my best."

As I approached Charger, he looked exhausted. I reckoned he had come sixty or seventy miles, probably much of it dragging Reene. His front was badly cut, probably by a blind charge through greasewood. In a way, I couldn't help but feeling sorry for him. The look on his face seemed to say it all, like he knew he had done something horrible wrong, and that he must pay the price. I eased up to him real slow. He was nervous, but never offered to run. What was left of the reins were hanging down, and once I had a hold of them, he quieted down somewhat. I really didn't want to look at what was hanging, but if I was going to remove the saddle I had little choice.

Her leg, and what was left of her pants protruded grossly from the stirrup. It looked like the ankle had been broken. In fact, many times. I eased the back rig loose, then the front, pulled the saddle towards me and to the ground. Next, I eased the bridle off, and slapped it across his rump. I hadn't noticed until then, but he had a decided limp. Charger went to the nearest ridge, then turned and watched me, never moving after that. Fortunately, the blanket Reene had used that day was a Navajo blanket, folded in half. I laid it out flat, then rolled the saddle over so I could work her foot and boot out of the stirrup. There were horrible scratch marks on the boot and on the edge of the stirrup. Obviously, she had almost made it, but all I could imagine is that about every time she grabbed the edge of the stirrup a hind leg caught her, or her head hit the ground or more likely a rock. How long it lasted was anybody's guess, but no matter what it hadn't been quick. Her ankle, foot and the boot were such a mess, that I didn't think I would ever get it out of the stirrup. But finally it came. I laid the leg out on the blanket as best I could. The knee was broken, most of the upper leg flesh had been ripped away. The femur head had pulled out of her hip, and again only God knew where, but I guessed it had been quite a few miles ago. I carefully wrapped the leg in the blanket, thought about taking the saddle back first, but didn't.

Pete watched the whole thing, and obviously knew what I was bringing back. He was sitting down alongside the Cub when I got there, holding his head. I laid the blanket package down in front of him, sat down alongside. We put our arms around each other, didn't say a work and just cried and cried and cried and cried, until there were no tears left. I could only imagine the horror and terror that she must have gone through. After sometime I stood up, walked back to the saddle, threw it over my shoulder. When I got back, Pete was holding the blanket, but he hadn't opened it. I gently removed it and stuck it under the back seat where I sat, then turned to Pete saying, "I think if I climb in, there is enough room to put the saddle on my lap, then let's get back to your Dad and Jim."

Pete just sat there looking at the saddle, "I bought that for Mom with some of my first pay checks when I became an extension agent. In fact, it took about the first three months worth, got it at Capriola's in Elko, made especially for her, just the way she wanted it." I noticed that he was holding the left stirrup, kind of rubbing the scratch marks. I didn't need to say anything, nor did he. Pete was far more knowledgeable about something like this than was I. He clearly knew what those scratch marks represented.

As we took off, Charger was still standing on the ridge, just watching us - he probably didn't understand this any better than we did. The flight to Double Hot Springs only took a few minutes, but seemed an eternity. Pete was obviously shaken to the core, and I could only imagine how Marty would react. As the plane slid to a stop, both Marty and Jim came running. The look on Pete's face told them all they would need to know. After I got out, I pulled the blanket package out, walked to Jim and said, "You best take this with care, it's probably all that remains." There were tears in his eyes as he gently placed it in his rescue box behind the cab. Marty and Pete flew back to the ranch together. I rode back to Gerlach with Jim and caught a ride back to Reno with a deputy.

The funeral was undoubtedly the largest that Gerlach ever saw. It was held in the high school gymnasium, with her remains, or what there was of them buried in the town cemetery. Governor Laxalt, also a Basque was there. Congressman Baring, and Senators Cannon and Bible were also there. Every agricultural association in Nevada and California was represented and I swear every Basque for a thousand miles, much less their families, which were indeed sizable. It was a hot windy day when she was buried, not a pretty day by any imagination. But it was a Nevada day, the kind every Nevadan had long since learned to tolerate, and even sometimes cherish.

The remainder of Reene's body was never found, the speculation was that coyotes had made short work of it. Many people searched, but to no avail. I heard over the years that Charger stayed on the east side of the Black Rock range, going from the Point to as far north as the Paiute Ranch. He never joined up with a band, just remained a single lost mustang out on the Black Rock.

The events of Buffalo Canyon didn't make me a better professor. In fact, if anything, they made me more difficult to get along with. I knew the effort that Marty and Reene had put forth to make their ranch work, and every time I saw a professor sitting on his useless tailend, drawing a phenomenally large salary, I became more difficult to get along with. I wasn't even sure what the connection between the two were, but it was a feeling that I was having ever more difficulty dealing with. I figured that I had a choice, get a Ph.D, and become a true professor, or get the hell out. I wasn't yet ready to take the latter route, but I also figured that if I was going to get a Ph.D., I needed some help, in fact lots of help.

I knew Dean Bohmont was the only individual that understood me, and much less would listen. So, I marched into his office one fine summer day in 1968 and bluntly asked, "Dean, how do I get a Ph.D.?" As usual, when he was bothered by something that had not captured his immediate interest, his replies were curt to say the least. "Well, go to school," was his helpful answer. It took me a few minutes of soothing of ruffled feathers to get to the core of my problem, which, bluntly put, was money. We now had three daughters, all in school, and just about every dollar that I earned was required to support our family, including buying a house. "Look, plain and simple, I think that I can finish the requirements at Oregon in one year, but frankly, I don't have the finances to take a year off, not with the size of family that I have", was how I explained my predicament. I was kind of hinting at a sabbatical. However, I knew equally well that sabbaticals were given to further scholarly goals, not complete the academic requirements for a Ph.D.

"You know, you have lots of imagination, how can we take steps to increase our class size in agriculture? My problem with the academic dean's council is that the liberal arts colleges all complain that they have to teach classes for the professional schools, such as agriculture. The English department is the worst complainers of all. All they do is bitch about agriculture, how they have to teach beginning classes for the dummies in Ag, and don't have time left over to do their research, although for the life of me, I don't see how an English prof can do any original research," Dean Belmont went on. "If you could figure a way to increase class size, I could probably figure a way to get you a sabbatical."

I always was a sucker for carrots, and this one dangling in front of me was all it took. "Tell you what, if you gave me a sabbatical so that I could go to Oregon State for a year, I would research out the information that I needed to teach a new course that I have been thinking about. I would call it "Animals in Man's Ecosystem". I have been working on the outline, but there's not enough information in our libraries to get the job done. I would like to trace the history of man's involvement with animals from the very beginning, starting with the bible, and show how dependent man has always been on animals. Bring it right up to the present. And I thought about showing how, for example, meat is produced today. Take a cow, show her getting bred, calving, castration and branding, weaning, growing and fattening, slaughter and cutting and preparing the various cuts. Show it all with the same animal. Have it as a class, elective, promote it and offer it campus wide. I'll bet that I could get an enrollment of over 100 students, and teach it fall and spring."

Bohmont's eyes lit up like a slot machine at Harold's Club that just came up with a jackpot. "Boy, would I like to have a class that had greater enrollment than any English class - that would get those damn monkeys off my back once and for all." I had been toying with such a class, but certainly at this minute, it suddenly took on a dramatically new level of importance. I could clearly see my ticket to Oregon. "Tell you what, put together a proposal for this class, get it to me. I'll see what kind of interest that I can generate with some of my friends in the other professional schools. If I can get their support for this kind of class in Ag, I probably can get their support for you application for a sabbatical leave. They will all know that you are going to go to get a Ph.D., but that will just be a sidelight. Your going to develop a class taught in a professional college that will attract loads of liberal arts students. They'll love it," Bohmont concluded.

It didn't take me but a week to put together the class outline. And within two weeks, I was preparing a sabbatical leave application, but that proved to be a bit more difficult. I got a lot of friends in academia, outside of Nevada, to do some creative thinking on the subject, and in due time a sabbatical leave application took form, supported by outstanding academicians in about every western state, including the University of Nevada. Animal scientists in other institutions clearly saw the advantage of offering such a course, but nobody currently taught a course remotely related to what I was talking about. And I had not been letting any grass grow under my feet since completing my masters at Nevada. Every semester I took at least one class if possible. By this time I had accumulated some 40 additional hours including calculus, German and about 25 additional graduate hours in various biology courses.

One cold January day in early 1969 I received a letter from Dr. Ed Miller, the current president of Nevada. I knew what the letter was, but it took a few minutes to screw up enough courage to open it. But there it was- congratulations for being selected for a sabbatical leave for the 1969-70 academic year! I had a lot going at that time, and for sure I just couldn't drop everything for a year. But luck was with me. I had an excellent graduate student doing some of the deer - livestock research. He was a native Nevadan, Basque, and a product of the ranching industry. In fact he grew up in Paradise Valley. His name was Ray Ansotegui, it didn't take him more than 30 seconds to respond to my question concerning his filling my position for one year. It was a done deal just about that fast, and the next day he started learning the ropes. He was well along in his thesis, he understood the lab, and he had taken my course in Feeds and Feeding, so he could teach that as well. He knew Pete. In fact, I guess they were related somehow, but Pete had already agreed to help with all of the fieldwork in my absence.

I also didn't want to forget that I would have a class to teach come the following year. So I started my picture taking campaign that spring with cows calving. I took several when they were pregnant, and then finally calving so that I would be sure that I had one to follow all the way through. My plan was to show the same cows being bred in about three months. They were all Hereford, so nobody would really know that when they saw a picture of a Hereford bull mounting a Hereford cow, then that cow being pregnant, and finally calving, that, in fact, the bull breeding the cow was not actually the sire of the calf being born. Nobody, that is but me, and I wasn't telling. I would be around through branding and castration, but it was up to Ansotegui to get pictures of weaning, pasture and finally the feedlot. I would be back from Oregon before slaughter.

It was an exciting time for me, there wasn't really enough time to get everything ready, but I was coming close. Then I got a call from Dr. Bob Raleigh, an old friend. Bob was the Superintendent of the Squaw Butte Field Station in eastern Oregon, out of Burns. Bob wanted to know if my schedule would allow for us to move from Corvallis to Squaw Butte the following summer. "If you can come out here, we'll make you a visiting professor, be able to pay you a stipend, and you and I can co-author a chapter in a book that Dave Church is writing." Dave was one of the nutritionist at Oregon, working under Oldfield. I had to take a god awful academic load at Oregon, but I wasn't really scheduled to take classes the following summer, as there were none that were being taught that would apply for my Ph.D. during the summer. I planned to just take my thesis credits during summer, and possibly a special problem. I had a lot of annual leave accrued, so I talked the administration into allowing my sabbatical leave to start on June 15, 1969 and run to August 31, 1970. With my annual leave I would leave around July 1 for Corvallis, which would allow a lot of time for library research. Everyone agreed that was a good idea, so that was our plan.

It was June 1 before I knew it, but everything seemed in order. We had been able to rent a small house near campus, enough room for all of us, as I wasn't planning on spending much time at home. The Department had been happy to see me finally come to Corvallis, and they made office space available, including a desk and filing cabinet.

Corvallis, Oregon, is a beautiful area during the summer and fall months. I was ready to start my library research right after July 4, and classes didn't start until October 15, so I had over a 90 day shot to prepare the course Bohmont had me agree to. I was damn well going to keep up my end of the bargain. Five days in the library for about ten hours a day was about all that I could handle. So every weekend we explored Oregon, mostly the coastal range and the coast. It was vastly different than Nevada, but it was a refreshing change. And every Monday, going back to the library seemed a bit easier.

Registration was around October 12, and classes started on the fifteenth. From that point until around May 15, 1970 I just put, as the saying goes, my head down and my ass up and never looked back. It was probably the hardest year that I ever put in in my entire life, but when it was over I had successfully negotiated my way through 47 quarter hours of graduate classes and obtained a 3.9 grade point average. By far and away the hardest class I had to take was biochemistry. Dr. Oldfield somewhat compounded my situation by insisting that I take an advanced biochemistry class that was normally the biochemistry class the Ph.D. candidates in that field had to master. The normal biochemistry that Ph.D. candidates in nutrition had to take was somewhat easier. However, Oldfield was bound and determined that I would not only get a Ph.D. in animal nutrition, but that I would have a Ph.D. minor in biochemistry and plant ecology as well. The tradeoff was that I didn't have to show fluency in two foreign languages. My German background was sufficient because of the classes that I had taken at Nevada, and for the first time in the history of Oregon State, a knowledge of basic computer language was allowed to be substituted for a foreign language. For the last few years at Nevada I had been working with the mainframe unit on campus, developing formulas for my nutrition work, as well as following much of the data from my field trials. This had required a pretty advanced knowledge of the old punch card system for writing individual formulas, and I had mastered that pretty well. That's how I ended up in advanced biochemistry at Oregon. The only two B's that I received there were in the fall and spring quarters of biochemistry. During the winter quarter I got an A, and along with everything else got a 4.0 for the quarter.

From around November 1, until probably the middle of March, you never saw the sun in Corvallis. It was always foggy and drizzly and a desert rat like myself just didn't take very well to all of that. I really didn't believe the weather stories when I arrived. Everybody asked where my umbrella was, but my prompt reply was, "I never owned one, and I sure ain't going to get one just for this year." There was a ten-minute break between classes, and that's about all that I did was go to classes, and most of them weren't real close together. When the rains came in November, I found that even with a raincoat, I was drenched at the start of each class. By the end of the class I would just about be dry, then away we would go again. After about a week or so of this drenching/drying regime, I began to feel not so very good. The infirmary diagnosed me as having an advanced case of strep throat, so with a couple of penicillin shots and a hand full of pills, I marched off to buy an umbrella.

The other problem was fog. By their winter quarter it was dark by 5 p.m., and I had two classes that lasted until 6. One night I came out of class to be greeted by fog sufficiently thick to cut with my pocketknife. It took me a few minutes to find my pick-up, but it was only a few yards behind the Ag building. The problem was to find my way home. People had been telling me to be sure to know my way in the fog - you had to observe the little things, like abnormalities in the curbs along the way, things like that. Well I hadn't paid much attention to that nonsense, at least not up to that point, but that night when I had difficulty finding my car it took quite a few tries and several hours before I got home. The next morning I searched my way, noting every abnormality in pavement, crosswalks, curbs, or anything else that would help me find my way. I was, as they say, learning to enjoy Corvallis!

But as beautiful as the Willamette Valley is in the spring, by May 15, I was ready to head to Squaw Butte. Dr. Raleigh had things all set up for us, including a beautiful house on the Station. And, along with several other projects, we wrote a chapter for Dave Church's book on animal nutrition. We also enjoyed that part of Oregon, traveled frequently to the Steens and Hart Mountain, both massive uplifts, not really bonafide mountain ranges. We fished the Donner and Blitzen River and Wildhorse Lake, high in the Steens, catching some of the largest trout I had ever seen.

One day on top of the Steens, I turned the radio on in my pickup to see what stations I would receive. And right there at 630 KHZ was KOH out of Reno. For the first time I realized just how badly not only I, but our whole family missed Nevada. As tough as Nevada is, the driest state in the union, noted for gambling, divorce, and the mafia, I loved it beyond description, but for reasons that few understood. What most people never knew, Nevada was also the most mountainous state, depending on how you counted them, somewhere around 108 distinct mountain ranges. It also had the greatest elevation difference between its highest point and its lowest point of any state that didn't border an ocean. It supported ecological zones from alpine to the harshest of deserts. It had the only glacier between the Sierras and the Rockies. Its history was as colorful as any state, far more than most. And it had the vastness of desert valleys too numerous to count, often supporting no permanent inhabitants. But mostly, I thought about the Nevadans that had been so important in my life; Jim Kilduff, the people at the University that had faith in me early on, the ranching families that I had the good fortune of meeting all over the State, Pete and his family that I had come to respect and love dearly. I thought about the tragedy that they had endured. I thought about Jim Hunter, a million thoughts went through my mind as I listened to that distant radio station. But most importantly, it was a Nevada that our family had to come to love. It was a Nevada that I knew in my heart that I could never leave, no matter what my course might encounter over the coming years. It was, in fact, my Nevada.

We returned to Reno for good in late August, 1970, in time to get the girls back into school, as well as get myself prepared for the coming academic year. My new course, The Importance of Animals in Man's Ecosystem, wasn't going to be taught until the spring semester, as I still had a number of photographs to complete prior to teaching. All I had to complete for my Ph.D., was provide Dr. Oldfield with a final version of my thesis, then defend it and my goal would be achieved. Defense of my thesis would be fairly simple. No one in this world knew more about molybdenum toxicity and copper nutrition than I did. As far as the statistics were concerned, I could hold my own with the best - it was just a matter of time. So in the fall of 1970, I was on top of the world, full of piss and vinegar.

I hadn't been on campus a week, when Bohmont's secretary called me, saying he had an emergency and needed to see me right away. That's the problem with Bohmont, he could care less until he had an emergency. There's nearly 100 professional staff in this College, why me? Those and other less than productive thoughts were whizzing through my head as I swung through his door.

"How was your year? Ready to get back to work after your vacation?' was his cheerful inquiry. The "vacation" part didn't set too well, but I mumbled something about the year was fine and the classes were excellent. "Let me see your degree, after all the trouble we had with you over the years, I think I'll put it on my wall." That's what I loved about Bohmont, he had a way of inserting the knife, then really turning it just right so that you got the full impact. I tried to explain that the degree wouldn't come for another year or so, and, of course, he already knew that. I was also pretty sure that my academic standing wasn't what he really had on his mind.

"Tell you what, I have a great opportunity for you. Bill Behrens has accepted a sabbatical leave for this year. In fact, he has already gone. I was thinking that if you took over his duties for this year, it would really broaden your educational background. The experience would be phenomenal." There's no question, Bohmont could make a living selling freezers to Eskimos. But I already knew Behrens was gone. In fact, I had talked to him last June before he left. He had asked if I might be interested in assuming the duties of State Livestock Extension Specialist while he was gone. My answer was a flat no. Mainly, I knew that I would have too much catching up to do, along with finishing my thesis and getting ready for my new course. Bill had responded by saying, "It's probably just as well, Bohmont wants to bring in one of his old cronies from Wyoming, a guy by the name of Tim Johnson. He just retired from the Extension Service. I only met him once or twice, but he's typical of people from Wyoming, he's a windbag of the first order. But he's old enough that I don't think he can screw things up much in one year." However, during the last week I had heard that this Johnson guy had a heart attack and simply was no longer available.

So, I responded to Bohmont's kind offer concerning my immediate future, "What happened to your boy, Johnson: thought you had him all outlined for the job?"

"Oh, I got to thinking about him, he's good, but his health isn't so good, and the rigors of Nevada, especially in this position would probably be more than he could handle. This job requires somebody that's young and has lots of ambition, somebody like yourself" was his response.

I guess we weren't supposed to know about the heart attack, but the young and ambitious comment did start to massage the ego a bit. But then reality set in. There was no way I had the time. "I don't think so Dean. I have to get ready for the course that I promised to teach this spring. Got to teach Feeds this semester: got four grad students to direct, and you know as well as I do you rule this joint by the publish or perish theory. So for me to do what you want could be fatal, doesn't make sense."

"Listen, I got you promoted to Associate Professor two years ago, and that was without a Ph.D., which was an all time first in this institution. If you take this job, finish your Ph.D. by the end of next year, 1972, I promise that as of July 1, 1973, you will be a full professor. If my calculations are correct, you will have just turned 38, which would make you the youngest tenured full professor in the history of the University."

As I said the S.O.B. could sell freezers to Eskimos, but I had the uneasy feeling that I just might become an Eskimo. "You know, being State Livestock Extension Specialist would be a great experience, I agree. But just who in the hell is going to do my job. You got somebody lined up for that?" I questioned.

"Frankly, no, that's somewhat your problem. You already have more grad students than anybody else in the College. You used grad students to cover for you when you were vacationing in Oregon. As clever as you are, I can't help but believe that you will find a way," he concluded.

I knew Bohmont well enough that when he was in a tight spot he would get downright mean to get his way. I also knew that the College was spread a might bit thin. Ranchers had a lot of political influence in Nevada. In fact, the legislature was well represented by the industry, in fact the whole government of Nevada had a strong livestock influence. I surmised that unhappy ranchers probably equated to pressured academic administrators, especially the Dean of the Max C. Fleischmann College of Agriculture. So, I figured that I would get Behrens job, and at this point it probably didn't matter rather I wanted it or not. Bohmont had taught me well - I figured he respected himself, so he must respect his tactics.

320

"Tell you what Dean, I'll take the job, starting tomorrow at 8 a.m. sharp, but with a couple of small conditions. You know that the way I have run my research projects with outside funding, place about 20% or so in a contingency fund to cover the unexpected? Well, this is unexpected, so you will need to place about $15,000 in that fund to cover the extra time required of grad students to cover for me. Behrens travels a lot, but it's on a routine basis. I'll have to travel every bit as much, but it will be interrupted and irregular, so what ever his travel budget for the year is, mine will be 25% more. And his sedan is worn out. I don't want a sedan, I want a new, brand new, Ford three quarter ton pick-up, and it's got to be a four-wheel drive. Now, as clever as you are, I know none of that will be a problem," I responded as I left his office.

Later that day, Phyliss, Bohmont's secretary called, "You know, if it had been anybody but you, you would have been fired because of what you said. Dr. Bohmont has to leave town for a few days, but he said to make sure $15,000 was transferred to your account, he asked Pete Test to have a new pick-up, as per your specifications, as soon as possible. I guess your travel budget will be augmented, but Extension's budget has been in a mess ever since Dr. Stein retired, but I am sure that will be taken care of as well." I apologized if my actions caused her any discomfort, but it went without saying that I sure didn't need to offer an apology to Bohmont. "That's OK, he did leave the office a bit disgruntled, but he'll recover. Actually I thought the whole thing a bit funny," she cheerfully concluded as I hung up.

And so started my career as an Extension Specialist. I soon learned that if extension personnel spent as much time working as they did going to meetings, they might actually accomplish something. Additionally, as most of their money came from the federal government coffers, the regulations were so restrictive that they couldn't have accomplished something, even if they wanted to. Up to that date, I had been somewhat critical of the extension effort in Nevada. Pete had tried to explain some of the problems, but I also noticed that Pete didn't seem to let the problems interfere with his performance. I soon learned that the feds had yet to develop a rule that Pete hadn't already figured out how to outmaneuver, or simply break. I decided that I would follow his example, because even for a year I wasn't going to let this nonsense restrict my efforts to become the best professor Nevada ever saw.

With help, in fact, lots of help from graduate students, we managed to teach Feeds, keep the nutrition lab going, keep the field trials going, keep Calves for College going, and on top of everything else go to countless meetings all over Nevada, dealing with countless problems facing the livestock industry. By October, I had already put 10,000 miles on my new pick-up. Bohmont was groaning, because he had promised a near new pick-up to Behrens when he returned from Australia. At the rate I was going, this rig would be worn out come July.

I had set up a series of meetings with livestock producers in every single one of Nevada's 17 counties, including even tiny Story County. I worked through the local extension agents, but what I wanted to find out was just what were the industry's most serious problems, and of those, which ones could the University truly help with. For support, I had asked Pete to attend as many of these as possible. However, that invitation went out to every single extension staff member that had anything to do with livestock. It soon became obvious that there were lots of problems such as; disease, state brand inspection laws, labor, the list went on and on. However, there was one overriding problem that invariably surfaced, yet no one could really put a hand directly on it. That problem was the federal government.

Nevada was, and is, mostly owned by the federal government. Although the federal government in the final analyses is nothing more or less than an extension of the citizens, the bureaucracies that carry out the assumed mandates of the citizens sometimes get a bit carried away with their supposed, and very real, power. And therein lies the problem. For of Nevada's 70 million plus acres, the federal government controlled about 61 million acres, managed primarily by the Bureau of Land Management and secondly, the United States Forest Service. The nine million or so privately owned acres consisted of the townships, dominated by Las Vegas and Reno, checkerboard land along the old Union Pacific right of way, and the private holdings in the few agriculturally irrigated valleys, and the isolated ranches. As the western livestock industry developed, it simply was not generally in the best interests of the ranches to own grazing lands. First, it was free for the taking in the early days. More recently it cost a minimal fee from the management agencies. The only real incentive to own land, at least in Nevada, was to tie up water, and water was the key to everything.

The earliest pioneers understood the importance of water, so the typical land ownership pattern for a Nevada ranch showed some base property where the headquarters and adjoining hay fields were, and then scattered 40 and 80 acre parcels which had long since been filed on wherever there were springs, stream or other live sources of water. Consequently, over the years the vast majority of Nevada's "outback" simply remained in federal ownership.

Grazing of these unclaimed acres had been occurring since the earliest of days, certainly since the Civil War. Renegade livestock operators had caused problems, wars between sheep and cattle people periodically occurred. Problems of this nature resulted in the creation of much of the forest reserve, claimed by the Forest Service around the turn of the century. In fact in Nevada, as well as some of the other western states, the vast amount of the forest reserve was created at the urging of livestock growers, so that grazing could be more uniformly and fairly regulated. The federal government attempted to control livestock grazing on the remainder of the range through the old Grazing Service, but it wasn't until the passage of the Taylor Grazing Act and the creation of the Bureau of Land Management in 1934 that grazing started to become truly regulated. Then it took another 20 years to get everything under control. In fact, it wasn't until about 1955 that nearly all BLM districts were clearly defined. Existing ranches were granted access to grazing on historical lands, based on their deeded properties and water rights. Gradually, this complicated process evolved, and by 1960, ranches all understood and knew their grazing rights on federal lands. They were charged an annual fee for this right, so much per mature animal per month, or what became known as an animal unit month. Grazing on adjoining federal lands were clearly considered a property right, as ranch holdings were taxed, by all of the various federal tax schemes, with those considerations. Additionally, it was not uncommon for ranchers to pay for improvements on these federal lands. Consequently, the ranching community considered these properties much as their own, or at least the forage it produced.

However, by 1970 times were changing. The BLM districts were starting to make noise about overgrazing, and that the animals must be reduced in number or complicated grazing schemes developed, and sometimes both. These concepts were beginning to cause great concern among the ranching community, and this concern came out loud and clear in my meetings. It was difficult to truly get a handle on these problems, because, in fact, they had yet to really occur. However, the threat was ominous. I thought about some of the seminars that I had sat through nearly ten years before, where Dr. Fulcher and some of the other economists discussed ways that the land management agencies could implement to gain better control on what they perceived as "their" lands. Invariably, after each meeting discussions would last until the wee hours of the morning on this subject. The ranchers were scared. They could see their way of life, a life enjoyed usually by several generations, probably coming to a close. They didn't know what to do to stem the tide of change.

Pete and I both had enough range management that it was pretty clear to us that the problems could be greatly curtailed through good range management, perhaps even to the point where more forage than ever would be available. But sound management was not being proposed. True enough, a vast majority of northern Nevada had been reseeded with crested wheat. In fact, an area equivalent to the size of Elko County had been reseeded by the federal government, often with rancher participation. The problem was the management policies of the BLM that were forced on the ranching community was simply not the way to protect these reseeded areas for the long haul. In the meantime, the areas not reseeded continued to decline, or at least that's what the BLM said.

Other complicating factors were occurring. There had always been wild horses in Nevada. They came with civilization, and they had been managed by the ranchers at an appropriate level ever since. Then one day, a Reno secretary, by the name of Velma Johnson, got agitated about the routine gathering of horses. Velma loved horses, especially wild horses. She set out to develop some particularly ugly and incriminating pictures of the gathering of wild horses. These were pictures of true "mustangers" in action, not ranchers. Mustangers were in Nevada, but represented a small minority of those involved with the management of wild horses. "Mustangers" only captured horses for one purpose, dog food. Velma's next step was to enlist the aid of grammar schoolchildren, nationwide to call a halt to mustanging. It wasn't long before Wild Horse Annie, as Velma became known, got her way. Although it wasn't until 1971 that Congress passed the Wild Horse and Burros Protection Act, it was pretty clear in 1970 that wild horses were going to become a big problem. The federal government was going to manage the horses, and AUM's would be set aside for their use, at the rancher's expense.

The ranchers problems would go on and on, but it was clear where federal lands were involved, they were not completely in control of their destiny. Although the courts had ruled that a grazing allotment on federal lands was a legal right for the fee property it was associated with, there were those that were agitating that it was not a right, but merely a privilege, and as a privilege, it could be taken away as easily as it could be granted. Therein lied the problem.

As the meetings progressed across Nevada, it became ever clearer that if the University was going to truly help this industry, it had to have a ranch of its own, a ranch with a federal grazing allotment, with water rights, hay fields and all of the other things that made a ranch what it was, as well as creating the very problems, the headaches and heartaches that the industry continued to cope with. I was convinced of the need for a ranch many years before. Pete and I had talked about it on numerous times. But after the survey of the Nevada beef industry that we completed during late 1970, I was absolutely positive. Right after January 1, I scheduled a meeting with Dean Bohmont concerning field stations. I had summarized a report on my county activities and had it in his hands a week before. "You've got the legislative session coming up. It's going to take extra financial help to purchase a ranch. I don't know a better time than now to go for it," was my cheerleader effort.

"You've got to have a ranch for sale before I go to the legislature for funds. Our budget's in place now. About the best that I can do is go for a commitment supporting the concept of buying a ranch. We'll go for the money if and when we have one in our sights. Roy Young, the legislator from Elko has promised to help on such a resolution. You need to have Pete work on him in the meantime," Bohmont responded. Well Pete worked on Young, and during the legislative session, Bohmont worked on the legislature, or so he took credit for. I put together as many facts supporting our need for a ranch as I could imagine, and several times I got to present them to both the Senate finance Committee as well as the Assembly Ways and Means Committee, the two money committees.

It wasn't long after that Pete and I were sitting in the upstairs lobby waiting for Bohmont to get off the phone so that we could take the next step in getting a ranch. I had a funny story to tell Pete, "Well, I finally ran into your old buddy, Harry Ryan. Bohmont had me testifying in front of the Assembly Ways and Means Committee, of which he is a member, about this ranch business. Well, I had lots of questions, mostly good, but good old Harry appeared to be sleeping throughout. There was a break after my testimony, and I talked one on one with several Assemblymen. As I was leaving, I ran into Harry outside the hearing room. He looked at me kind of funny. He has developed a very arrogant look and manner. Anyway, he stopped for a second, then said, "Aren't you the kid who use to stick your hands inside cows stomachs all the time?". I paused for a second, his comment just plain hit me wrong, but I maintained. Anyway, finally I answered, "Yup, that's me. By the way, aren't you the kid that was involved with that scandal about history tests?"

Pete looked shocked at what I said, then started laughing, "Good God, you didn't, that's too good to be true. Christ, Bohmont would kill you, he's got his nose up those legislators ass all the time, but I'll bet even he would see the humor in that one. I hear everybody hates Harry, but I also heard he wants to run for the Nevada Senate next time. I told you, he won't go away."

Phylis, the Dean's secretary yelled at us, "The Deans off the phone, go in." Bohmont was in a good mood, full of jokes and his eternal optimism about how we were making progress on getting a ranch. I didn't quite see it that way. It seemed like we were doing an awful lot of talking without any action. So I ventured forth, "Well how are we ever going to ever have one in our sights, if all we do is talk about it?".

"Good point, I have been thinking about this and it's time to form a ranch search committee. Let me think about that for a few days. Lets go over it next week," he concluded. And so it went. Within a week, the College had a ranch search committee consisting of Bob Thomas and Leslie Stewart, both successful ranchers from Paradise Valley, Bill Davidson, a rancher from Ely, Ira Boise, a rancher from Contact, north of Wells, and Harvey Barnes, a rancher from Lee. In addition to Bohmont, Ed Jensen from Agronomy, Joe Robertson from Range, and Bill Champney from Ag Econ and myself were to serve on the committee in an ad hoc manner. Bob Thomas was to serve as chairman. I liked the committee, as two of the voting members were from Paradise Valley, which to me was the logical location for a station. It was centrally located, closer to Reno, had nearby National Forest lands and probably represented a Nevada ranching area better than anywhere else. Bill Davidson clearly knew the Ely area was simply too far away and he was pretty level headed. Harvey had been one of my first students, and usually agreed with my philosophy, and he respected Pete. Even though Pete was the Elko Extension Agent, he liked Paradise Valley. The stickler was Ira Boise. He lived across the way from the Knoll Creek facility, and clearly could see no reason for moving anywhere else. "If you need more cattle, get more cattle. If you need more grazing land, work out a deal with the Salmon River Cattleman's Association. They will deal with you," was his standard reply. Even though more grazing land for the Knoll Creek facility would end up in Idaho didn't seem to bother Ira one bit. Furthermore, Ira was a county commissioner, had been for years in Elko, and as such he carried a lot of clout, even clear to the legislature. Ira could out argue Stewart and Thomas. He would dominate Davidson, and Harvey didn't dare become too vocal about moving out of Elko County. So I could see that this committee would have some problems. But, we started meeting, and it wasn't long before a list of ranches became available.

A lot of ranches were hurting financially, and when the word went out that the University was ranch hunting, a lot of places went on the sale block, albeit a might bit too high. My number one choice was the Gavica/Zatica Ranch located in Paradise. It consisted of several thousand deeded acres, an excellent water supply, had both BLM and Forest Service grazing permits and tremendous potential. It supported a herd of about 400 cows, but with little imagination, I could see that figure being doubled. It wasn't long before I learned not to let my emotions get too high on anything in this racket, because I was about to get introduced to old fashioned Nevada politics, along with regional jealousies and petty differences too frequent to mention.

A significant group of cattlemen within the Nevada Cattlemen's Association began to question why the University should have an operating cattle ranch to begin with. "The University shouldn't be in competition with private industry," was a complaint that I seemed to hear more and more. I suspected this philosophy came from Ira Boise, but I was never sure. Roy Young said he would support the University, but the Gavica/Zatica ranch was too much like a show place, too costly. "Can't go against Young, got to have his support," muttered the Dean. Next was the Cerri Ranch, also located in Paradise. At least this one was not a show place, but it had too much deeded land and not enough grazing permit. We looked at ranches all over Nevada, but no matter what, there was always a problem. We even looked at the Red House unit of the Maggie Creek Ranch, located north of Carlin. There seemed to be great support for Maggie Creek, and it looked like it would fly. Ray Knisley, a long time Lovelock rancher strongly supported the University's acquisition of Maggie Creek, and Ray was a personal friend and long time advisor to Mike O'Callaghan, whom currently was Nevada's Governor. With that support, it looked like a sure deal until local ranchers became convinced that the removal of that much property from the Elko County tax rolls would be too much hardship for the county to bear. So, Commissioner Boise convinced Assemblyman Young, who immediately put pressure on the legislature and the Board of Regents - and so it went. The sad thing for the University is that the Maggie Creek Ranch sat squarely on top of what was to become known as the Carlin Trend, the largest gold producing load in the history of the United States, and one of the very largest in the world. It would have ultimately been worth countless millions to the University, but for local politics.

Along about January, I decided that ranch searching wasn't too fruitful. In fact, I wasn't even sure the ranching industry deserved for the University to have a ranch. The industry knew the problems they would face. Maybe they thought they could handle it better than the University. Sometimes I wasn't so sure any of us could handle the problems that were coming down the road. Besides, I had two immediate monumental problems facing me. At the start of the spring semester, February one, I had to start teaching my new class, and later that spring, April, was the Junior Livestock Show. The only thing unique about this year's Junior Livestock Show was that I was to be in charge. I had never even been to one in years past!

The new course was a success beyond comprehension. One hundred and twenty five students from every College of the University registered. There wasn't a classroom in the College that could handle that load, so it was moved to the nursing auditorium, which sat 100. We literally had twenty-five hanging from the rafters. The highlight of the course was my picture sequence of a cow coming in heat being bred and on through to a family finally sitting down and eating the resulting beef. I even had some die hard vegetarians register that informed me it was done well. I followed the Bible, the history of the astrological charts, the earliest history of the taming of animals for work, food and pleasure. We followed the changing laws involving animal welfare in this country. Finally, with the help of several national organizations, a list of everything that is used in day to day life that comes from some form of animal life was presented, including the world of medicine. It was a fun course. It sure made Bohmont happy, as it was by far the largest Ag class ever taught and went a long way to creating an average class size that could hold its own across campus.

The Junior Livestock Show was a story in its own. Fortunately, I had two graduate students that grew up in livestock shows. Dave Bruce came from McCarthur, California and graduated from Chico State with a degree in Animal Science. But in addition, Dave had been involved in livestock shows all his life and he knew all the tricks. So I gave Dave an honorary title, Executive Assistant, 1971 Nevada Junior Livestock Show.

He loved it, even if he did most of the work. I also had as a graduate student Ron Hathaway from the Willamette Valley in Oregon. I had got to know Ron when I was working on my Ph.D. at Corvallis. He eventually ended up at Nevada. Ron also had an excellent background in shows. But my greatest support were the old time Italian families in the Truckee Meadows. The urban sprawl of the Reno/Sparks area had retired many of these folks from active agriculture, but not their love of the livestock shows for their kids and grandchildren. Early on with a leaders conference, I pleaded my ignorance, but promised that I would do everything possible to make the show a success if they gave their all, and that they did. The Damonte, the Curti, the Capurro the Landa, and the Cassinelli families to name but a few made me look like a genius, as the 1971 show topped them all at that time. The show lasted all week, with most judging occurring on Friday and Saturday, with the auction sale following on Sunday. Grand Champions were named Saturday afternoon in front of a packed house at the Washoe County Fairgrounds Events Center, but the sale the following Sunday was a sight to behold.

The committee had done its work. Buyers representing just about everybody and every entity were present and ready to bid. The sheep were first, and they set the stage. John Ascuaga, sole owner of the Nugget in Sparks, one of the areas largest casinos, was of Basque heritage from Idaho. And John always bought the Grand Champion lamb. Earlier, during one of our ranch search meetings, I suggested to Ray Knisley that it would be great publicity if Governor O'Callaghan out bid John this year for the Grand Champion lamb. Ray agreed, not because Governor Mike needed any more publicity, he was very popular. But there was a lot of speculation that Mike was going to run for the United States Senate, and buying the Grand Champion lamb wouldn't be too bad of a shot.

The bidding started at $25 per pound for a lamb that weighed 115 pounds. A whole bunch of people were bidding, but unfortunately

John was out of town on business, but his executive assistant was very obvious. Knisely was to bid on the Governor's behalf, but he never moved a muscle until the bid flew past $50. People were dropping like flies, Asquaga's man was still in at $65, thought he had it aced at a bargain, going once, going twice, then Ray nodded and it went to $70. From that point on it was obvious that O'Callaghan had made a commitment, buy the lamb. Ascuaga's man looked grey at $90. Knisely went to $95 without a quiver, except in his right index finger. There was a great sigh from the Ascuaga camp, but $100 came out. Again not a quiver from Knisely, $105. I thought Ascuaga's man was going to cry. Ascuaga had never failed to buy the lamb in previous years, but we were reaching dizzying heights for 1971. In their discussions, I was sure Ascuaga never dreamed it would go this high. His man was quite sure that he wasn't authorized to bid anything like this. Yet, Ascuaga had never failed to buy the lamb -- $110. And again, without any movement except the slightest twitch of that right index finger, and without any change in expression, the auctioneer yelled we have $115.00. All eyes moved to the Ascuaga camp, but it was obvious it was over. Going once, going twice, SOLD, to the Governor of the Great State of Nevada, the Honorable Mike O'Callaghan for $115.00 per pound, the Grand Champion Lamb from the 1971 Nevada Junior Livestock Show! There was thunderous applause, standing applause. It was all going through my head too fast to figure, but later I learned a young 12-year-old girl from Fallon took home a check for $13,225.00. And that set the tone for the rest of the sale. Afterwards, I often wondered just what would have happened if John Ascuaga had actually been there. Who knows, we might have still been bidding!

In the aftermath of the show a call came into my office, direct, "Terry, this is Mike, thought I should call to give you cutting instructions for my lamb." I about tipped over, but quickly realized that the Governor was a man of business. Besides, I guess he wanted his lamb for real, all $13,225 worth of it.

So I rapidly took his instructions. He was busy, and was hanging up when I shouted,"Hey wait a minute, just wanted to thank you. You know your bid made the show."

"Thank Ray, it was his idea, besides it was his money. He thought if we did that, it might make the day. He said you earned every bit of it, he's been telling me about the University's attempt to buy a ranch, and all that it has put you through. It's his way of saying thanks, got to go - take care." And with that a click. I sat there, like so many other times over the years. How amazing Nevada truly is. Sometimes your worst enemies are your best friends, sometimes your best friends are your worst enemies, and sometimes, like now, you just never know until after the fact.

Behrens returned from Australia in July. I happily relinquished my duties as State Livestock Specialist. I had a thesis to finish and defend, and I planned on doing that before December 31, 1971, which meant along with my teaching and research schedule I had plenty to do. I gave up on the ranch search, not because I wanted to, but there was simply no more interest, and there wasn't even a remote chance anything was on the horizon. I just concentrated on what was directly in front of me. I was anticipating the day when someone, anyone, would have to address me as Doctor.

I was immersed in academia, no politics, no frustrations. In fact I found that I wasn't even really interested in the problems facing the livestock industry. Pete informed me that I probably would be like the rest of the staff once I had the Ph.D. in hand, dumb, fat and lazy. Maybe at that point, he wasn't too far from being right. But as usual, Bohmont would end that illusion!

"Come up to my office, I want to talk to you about something," was the message on the other end of the phone. Obviously, I knew it was Bohmont, but it would be nice if the arrogant S.O.B. bothered to identify himself.

"What's cooking?" was my short response as I seated myself in front of his elegant desk.

"What do you know about the Gund Ranches?" he put to me.

"Well, not much, frankly. I have been on his ranch at Lee, it's beautiful. I understand he owns one in Grass Valley, you know where your friend Molly Knudtsen owns a ranch. But I have never been on that ranch. For that matter, I haven't ever even been in Grass Valley. I do know that Al Stenninger is the overall manager on the Gund properties. You know Al, his brother is Mel, the publisher of the Elko Daily Free Press," which about summarized my knowledge of the Gund properties.

"OK, well George Gund is going to be here tomorrow. He wants to talk to me about gifting the Grass Valley property to the University. His accountants will also be here at the same time, and from what he says they are looking at maximizing the gifting process. So, we will have to put a value on the gift, as high as possible, but defensible from an IRS standpoint. Apparently, they would like some kind of value by tomorrow. I called Molly, she didn't seem to have much nice to say about the property. According to her, the only thing of value is the fact that the place has a great big hot springs. She felt it was a much better ranch when the Walti family owned it. She thinks George has had it six or seven years, but her opinion is it has gone down hill ever since."

"Well what did he pay for it originally? How many dollars worth of improvements has he put in place since? How big is the allotment? Must be all BLM, there's no Forest there. How many deeded acres? How much hay land? How many cows does the property run?" were the list of questions that I could have stayed with for another 15 minutes or so.

"Friend, that's exactly what I called you up here for. I knew if anybody could get those answers for me by one o'clock tomorrow it was you."

I had already learned, the hard way, that when Bohmont called you "friend", he did not necessarily mean it. "Well I got several other things going on today. I have to teach two classes tomorrow. You are asking for a lot of material on damn short notice," I replied.

"Look, your the person that's been agitating for a ranch for a field station. You may get this one free which beats any other option we have looked at yet. I am sure it won't be up to your standards. That's too damn bad. Maybe we can sell it in a few years and get what you want, who knows; but I'll be damned if I am going to throw this opportunity away just because of your presumed busy schedule. If somebody offers me 2,800 deeded acres with an attached grazing permit, I am not saying no! Now, I need those answers, and I need them before noon, tomorrow. And furthermore, your are in charge of this project hence forth. If we get the damned property, I am putting you in charge of managing it. Understand?"

"I guess there would be some reallocation of my time commitment if I take this project on?" I gingerly asked.

"NO!"

And so began the most challenging and exciting activity that I ever undertook as a University of Nevada professor. I had no idea of the trail it would lead me on or the ramifications. However, even in hindsight would I had done it differently? The answer to that is a resounding no, just as loud as was Bohmont's. I returned to my office a bit tipsy from all that I had just heard. I had much to do, many phone calls to make. But first, I broke out the Nevada State Map I kept in my top desk drawer. I figured I had better learn where Grass Valley was, and just how in the hell to got there to begin with.

THE RANCH

A quick review of the Nevada highway map confirmed my worst fears; Grass Valley might have been nowhere! It was located in just about the exact geographic center of Nevada for whatever that was worth. It straddled the Eureka - Lander County line, two of the weaker counties in Nevada, and not dominant in the livestock industry. It was accessible by 50 miles of dirt road from U.S Highway 50 to the south, and 50 miles of mostly dirt road from U.S. highway 40, or Interstate 80 from the north. Realistically, the only supply center was Elko, 100 miles away, at least half by dirt road. I could quickly see why I had never been there. I had been on all four sides of Grass Valley, but never to Grass Valley, nor even close. It suddenly appeared to me as the great unknown in central Nevada, if not all Nevada.

As I sat there looking at the map, a certain sense of panic seemed to overtake me, so I did the predictable, rapidly dialed the Extension Office in Elko. Fortunately, Pete was in. "What in the hell do you know about Grass Valley," was my less than friendly hello.

"Which Grass Valley," was Pete's equally less than friendly response, "You know there's more than one, in fact I think there might be three or more."

"I mean the Grass Valley in central Nevada, the one that lies between Reese River and Pine Valley," I fired back.

After a short laughter Pete sarcastically inquired if I had a field trial scheduled there.

"No, but we may be inheriting a ranch there," I patiently replied.

"That's a joke, you can't get there half the time, the roads are washed out every spring, snowed shut every winter, and so alkalied up during the summer that I hear cars routinely disappear. Other than that, I suppose it's a pretty nice place. Might I inquire just which ranch the University is inheriting? Surely can't be the Grass Valley Ranch. Molly Knudtsen owns that, even though she is a regent, I am sure she isn't giving it to the University."

"No, Pete, its a place originally called the Walti Ranch. George Gund currently owns it, and he may wish to gift it to the University," I responded.

"Well, I guess Al Stenninger is his man, that's about all that I know. That place is so remote that when I fly to Reno, I purposely fly a bit to the north just to avoid going over it. High mountains on both sides, lots of thunderstorms in the summer, and blinding snowstorms in the winter. And, if I ever had to set a plane down, Grass Valley is just about the last place that I would want to do that!" concluded Pete.

"You don't know any more than that," I gingerly asked.

"Nope," was the terse reply.

"Well, Bohmont wants me to set a value on it by tomorrow noon, apparently both Gund and his account will be here, so I got to learn all that I can in about the next twelve hours if I am going to have time to prepare any kind of a report," was my position summary.

"Tell you what, I'll try to grab the nearest rancher, jump in the plane, make a low level pass before dark. You be at home or the office tonight?" Office, I replied, and with that I imagined that Pete was out the door.

I guess my next hope was Al Stenninger, whom I only briefly had met once or twice before. And luck was with me; Al was in his Elko office. After pleasantries, I inquired if he was aware that Mr. Gund would be on campus tomorrow to discuss gifting the Grass Valley property to the University. "Yeah, sure I knew that. I convinced him that the only way he could make that property work was to gift it to a charitable institution of some kind for the maximum tax right off. It's nearly an impossible operation for us to run in conjunction with the Lee property. It's at least a three-hour drive, one-way, between the properties under the best of conditions, and that only occurs once or twice a year. The Grass Valley property is high, too damned high, over 5,000'. It should be run like a desert operation; only it's in a winter zone. We have developed two extensive alfalfa properties, however, with the elevation, late springs, and early falls, we have never gotten more than two cuttings. The range is horrible, greasewood on the flats, and the mountains are so steep that we can't keep cattle up there more than one or two months. Got two good water wells, and a hell of a hot springs that's the best skinny dipping pond in all of Nevada. Oh yeah, there's only one house that's inhabitable. But other than that I think it would be a great place for the University," which sort of summarized his thoughts.

After listening to that tirade, I thought about asking Al what he really thought about the ranch but thought better. Al had a master's degree in range science from somewhere, but I always suspected for some reason or another he didn't like the University of Nevada. I was pretty sure that he was one of the outspoken critics of the University obtaining a ranch field station in Elko County, primarily because of taking the property off of the tax roles. And I agreed that was a legitimate gripe.

But apparently it wasn't a problem in Grass Valley politics, at least not yet.

"Well, could you briefly give me a rundown on the ranch's assets, so that I could help prepare some parameters for Mr. Gund's accountant, as well as the University," I hesitantly inquired.

"Well, I guess I could give you some background data, but remember, the University is setting the gift value, not us. IRS always audits Mr. Gund, and I am sure that this value will have to be defended. Furthermore, they would look rather dismally on the fact that I as a Gund employee set the value," Al lectured.

"I understand all that, all I want to know is about what was paid for the ranch originally, improvements, I'll figure the rest.

Al agreed, and went on to explain how there were originally two ranches, the Walti Ranch, and a small operation owned by an individual simply known as "Doc" Allen. "I think we paid Doc about $70,000 and Mrs. Walti got about $175,000. You can check those values, Allen's property is in Lander County so that information would be in the Austin Courthouse, and the Walti property is in Eureka, so that would be in the Eureka Courthouse," Al begrudgingly offered.

"OK, What about improvements?" I inquired.

"We put in two water wells, one at the Allen Place, one at Cold Springs, south of the headquarters, improved about 80 acres of alfalfa at Allen's and put in about 120 acres at Cold Springs irrigated with wheel lines. We also fenced off about 80 acres of pasture below Cold Springs with hog wire for a wiener trap, that's probably the major improvements," he continued.

"I guess that's probably what I need to start with, I'll work with the economist on staff to come up with realistic values. Oh yeah, I guess I need to know if electricity is to all the wells, and I need to know the ranch telephone number," I dumbly asked.

"Terry, you need an education, maybe this project will help you get that. There is no electricity in Grass Valley, the closest that commodity exists now is about 75 miles, and the telephone number is Grass Valley toll station number 2, which you can activate by dialing the store in Crescent Valley. Their number is Crescent Valley toll station number one. And that can be activated by getting the Battle Mountain telephone office and asking for Crescent Valley Toll. By the way, you and the McClusky Ranch people get to maintain the telephone line from the store. If you get this property, you will be the proud owner of the longest earth ground telephone line left in the United States. I thought you knew all of this. Why don't you have Archie Albright help you?"

Well, I should have known better, the Stenningers, both Mel and Al were long known for their ability to make people like me seem dumber than they already were. Ten cents worth of common knowledge would have told me there was no electricity in grass Valley. As to Archie Albright, the Lander County Extension Agent housed at Austin didn't offer me too much hope. The staff veterinarian, Earl Drake and I had just concluded a three-day tour with Archie. I didn't think anything of it at the time, but our tour completely circled Grass Valley, but we never once stepped foot in the valley. Besides it took a couple of fifths for Archie to complete that tour for us, so I wasn't too sure he could help with my problems. With that, I thanked Al for all of his help, suggested next time I was in Elko I would opt for lunch, and politely hung up.

My next stop was Ag. Econ. My old buddy Glen Fulcher had long since left Nevada to bigger and better things with the BLM. But a new economist by the name of Bill Champney was on staff and he seemed reasonably knowledgeable about ranch values. So, a quick conversation with Bill got me what I needed, at least for beginners. The problem was that the value of Nevada ranching properties had been escalating during recent years, a fact driven by things I didn't clearly understand, but it didn't have anything to do with the actual cash flow being generated by ranches.

I guessed it kind of started with Bing Crosby. Crosby, in the late forty's bought a ranch north of Elko known as the PX. Theoretically, he bought the ranch in an attempt to teach his three sons something about practical work and life in general. Based on the continuing escapades of the lads, one would have to conclude that his program hadn't been overly successful. Anyway, everybody that was anybody knew about Crosby's Nevada ranch. And therein lies the problem. It wasn't too long before Jimmy Stewart bought the Wine Cup, northeast of Wells. Shortly, Wild Bill Elliott bought a ranch in Ruby Valley, south of Elko. But he was probably a lot better at acting in westerns than running a ranch, as it wasn't a year or so before Wild Bill left town owing a few bills. But he sold to Joel McCrea, who stuck around with some success for quite a spell. And on it went. If you were a stud in Hollywood, you owned a Nevada ranch. It didn't take long before the promoters and ranch real estate brokers caught on to that, and ranch values started to escalate.

Ranches were always valued on their carrying capacity, or animal units. Each producing cow is an animal unit. So, for a 500 cow ranch, which would also include horses, bulls, replacement heifers, milk cows, chickens and perhaps a stray pig or two, the value of the ranch would be divided by 500 to achieve a value per animal unit. Conversely, if you knew how many cows a ranch would run, it was pretty easy to place a basic value on the unit. Generally, the higher the ratio between deeded property and federal property would raise the animal unit value, while the lower the ratio would create the opposite. Also, generally ranches in northern Nevada brought a higher value per animal unit than did ranches in southern Nevada, all other things being equal. By 1970, a realistic value per animal unit, considering a basic annual return on the investment would have been in the $500 range. However, between Hollywood and the promoters, the value in fact had been drifting towards $1,000.

Pete and I, over picons, had on many occasions lamented about this disturbing trend. We both agreed that literally no Nevada ranch could even operate if the federal agencies finally outlawed the use of federal lands for grazing, a fact I had predicted ten years before, and was becoming increasingly possible as time went on. That didn't bother the promoters, and I knew it would come into play in my attempts to maximize Mr. Gund's gift value. But it still bothered me, for if the feds jerked the carpet, the typical Nevada ranch might be worth just about nothing, except for what one could cart off to the local sales yards.

I was just starting to figure out some values when the phone rang. Pete's cheerful voice was on the other end. "Couldn't find anybody to brave the wilds of Grass Valley, so I headed south about three this afternoon. I flew the whole valley, from Cortez Pass, clear down the side of Callaghan, over Grass Valley to Bates, up the east side over the Simpson Park range. After I got up to McClusky, I made two low level passes down the valley. There's a ranch about five miles out in the flat off of the mouth of McClusky Creek. It looks like there is an alfalfa field there, but I couldn't see any water, or cattle for that matter. Couldn't even see any hay put up, but it did look like a producing field."

"That would have been the Allen Ranch, which is on the northern border of the operation," I added.

"There's lots of brush, I would guess mostly greasewood, between the Allen Ranch and the main headquarters. There appears to be a large spring at the headquarters, lots of water appears to be coming from near the base of the mountain. There is a large meadow below the headquarters, but it's probably closer to a swamp as I could see water

343

over most of it. There was only one car at the headquarters. On my second pass I saw a woman coming from the barn, she waved, and she looked like a hippy. Didn't see anybody else. South of the ranch there are some meadows, but they looked pretty alkali from the air. Five or six miles south there's another alfalfa field with three-wheel lines. There was a pretty good stack of hay there, and there appeared to be a spring or two in the fields. South, there's cattle on the flat, but it looks like mostly greasewood. There's a band of what appears to be low sage between the greasewood and the mountain, but I didn't see many cattle there. Altogether, between the Simpson Park range and the flat I didn't see 50 head of cattle."

"Well, what do you think, is it an operating Nevada cattle ranch?" I inquired.

"Well, back in the homestead days it was an operating ranch, I have heard that Mrs. Walti and her two boys made a good living there for many years. But today, at least from the air, it looks like a run-down ranch owned by an absentee owner, and run by a tribe of hippies. I am sure that Al Stenninger probably doesn't want anything to do with this piece of alkali and greasewood, course he was never one to get his hands dirty to begin with, and you would have to get your hands dirty on this chunk of real estate no matter what. What I can't figure out is why in the hell did Gund ever buy this to begin with. I hear he has enough money to buy Nevada, just can't understand what he saw in Grass Valley."

Well, I couldn't answer that question right now. So, after digesting what Pete said, I thanked him profusely, hung up and went to work. I tried to ignore the run-down condition that Pete described, but I knew just about what I would find, if and when I finally ventured into Grass Valley. Then it struck me, all I had heard so far was about the run-down condition of everything, nothing but greasewood, and likely worse. The irony was who in the hell had the nerve to name this place Grass

Valley to begin with. Maybe it was the hippies smoking grass. No that couldn't be, because in my office I had a 1934 wall map of Nevada that even then labeled it Grass Valley, and that was before hippies were invented.

Gund Ranch cowboys preparing to move the cow herd to another pasture.

So, as my pencil went to work, I tended to ignore Pete's comments, instead I headed towards a sort of fantasy land, a land that I knew in my mind really didn't exist at this time, but a land that I was sure could exist, given the opportunity. There was an existing BLM permit for 4,800 AUM's. The ranch proper consisted of 2,800 deeded acres. Additionally, water rights existed to irrigate about 200 acres of alfalfa, 75 acres of grass, and another 100 acres of pasture. I had gleaned these figures from Bohmont, Al and the BLM whom I had contacted earlier in the day. I reasoned that cattle would be outside for eight months; so 4,800 AUM's was sufficient feed for 600 animals. I assumed these would be all cows and bulls, with a bull for about every 30 cows or so. This meant that, for arguments sake, the ranch would run 580 cows and 20 bulls outside. Again, I assumed that around 20% of the cows would be replaced every year with replacement heifers, 116 head, which would be kept inside until they became cows. So, 600 mature cattle and 116

345

heifers added up to 716 head. That many cattle would require nearly 1,100 tons of winter feed, if we only had to feed for three and a half months, December one through March 15. Surely, with a little work, 210 acres of alfalfa should produce 1,100 tons of hay. Wait, that's over 5 tons per acre, probably can't do that in Grass Valley, so we will have to buy some hay. I worked it from every angle possible, and theoretically, I finally came to the assumption that the Gund Ranch in Grass Valley, Nevada should be considered a 550 cow outfit, and be valued at $800 per animal unit, for a total gift value of $440,000. The night was late and I was satisfied.

Well, the next morning was not good. Mary, the secretary, was in a foul mood. Guess my graduate students hadn't been keeping up with their extra curricular work. And Mary wasn't going to type my report, that was for sure. There weren't any extra typewriters in the department, and our typewriter at home was on the fritz. So, I went up to Phyllis, Bohmont's secretary, and pleaded my case. God was smiling on the second floor of the Ag building, because in about an hour I had a typed report, corrected, with zerox copies. And it looked better than Mary could have done anyway! I gave Bohmont three copies, kept one for myself. It wasn't more than ten minutes later when my phone rang. "Hey, this is a pretty optimistic report, lots of facts and figures. You will have to explain it though, because I think you got this value jacked up about as high as possible. Remember, you got me in to this mess, and if the IRS steps in, you will have to represent the University, along with counsel of course."

I thought to myself as I listened to Bohmont, how in the hell did I get us into this mess? But I thought better, and responded, "The place should have the ability to run 550 mature cows because of what they have done. Maybe $800 is too high for Grass Valley, but there's lots of ranches going in the neighborhood of $1,000 anymore, some good ones are asking $1,200, so I think $800 is defendable."

Bohmont's response was almost predictable, "Friend, you are going to get that chance. Be in my office at 1:15 this afternoon." Click! As I sat there, I wondered if he ever said nice things to his wife. Even though the majority of the staff didn't like me, we all had one thing in common, we were all Bohmont's friends, well at least that's what he said.

Well, I was there at 1:15, in fact I had been waiting out in front since 1:00. Mr. Gund's accountant was about as expected, three-piece grey suit, glasses, very brisk in his comments. Probably still knew where his first dollar was. But George was a surprise; I wouldn't have guessed in a thousand years that he would look the way he actually did. Short, stocky, probably not over 5'6", I would guess 175 to 185 pounds, and with dark black bushy eyebrows. He wore plain clothes, Levi's, plaid shirt, work boots. I shortly learned some things, however, that rapidly caught my attention. George had left his home in Cleveland that morning, flew to San Francisco, picked up his accountant, flew to Reno - all of this in his own Lear. The pilots were waiting at the airport, a cab delivered them to the Ag building. As I listened to their itinerary, I began to realize that George Gund must be a man of extreme wealth, although sitting there with him in Bohmont's office I wouldn't have guessed such ever, if all I had to go on was his appearance.

It was obvious that the account, a Mr. David Gist, had already studied the report. He started dissecting it in detail, but according to my calculations he couldn't have seen it more than 5 or 10 minutes before I walked in. He didn't question the biology, just the math. But between his shifty eyes and his pocket calculator it didn't take him long to determine that I was correct, at least in that department. "George, what do you think, will 550 cows hold up if, and when, we are audited by the IRS?" was Gist's first question.

"Well, I would certainly think so, especially if the University says so, they have put a lot of time and effort into determining just what the ranch will produce, and if that's what they say, that's good enough for me," was George's matter of fact response.

I began to have a very uneasy feeling in my stomach. I suddenly realized that in all likelihood, Mr. Gund wouldn't have known if his ranch would run 50 cows, 500 or 5,000 for that matter. The important point to him was that he had a ranch, and he was gifting it to the University. Now Gist's outlook on the world would be different. He didn't know any more than George did as to what the ranch would run. But I could already tell that he liked the $440,000 tax deduction, and I had to presume if Gist was happy, probably George would follow suit. The only person that had a problem was me. I said 550 cows and $800 per cow. And I could just about see the whole thing unfolding before my eyes - it would be me that would have to prove my figures correct, first as factually as possible, and secondly, justify it all to the IRS. As I sat there I had visions of Bohmont yelling his foolish head off at me how I got him in court. I could see Al Stenninger just about dying laughing. And I could imagine just about how irritable this Mr. Gist might become when he had to inform Mr. Gund that they had a significant tax problem with the IRS, because they had vastly overestimated the value of the ranch they gifted to the University. Of course, he would be quick to point out that the value presented to the IRS was solely dependent on the University's own appraisal. Yeah, I wasn't feeling really good at all, but to myself I had to laugh. Just last night I had to look at the map to see how to get to Grass Valley to begin with.

The meeting didn't last much longer. As George and Gist were leaving, George indicated that he owned the Cleveland franchise of the National Hockey League, and if I ever wanted to watch them play, he would send the Lear out. I thanked him, but right then hockey wasn't a priority on my mind. As the door closed, I spun towards Bohmont saying, "Christ, you knew damn well I have never seen this place. That was a preliminary report, based on three phone calls, and my imagination, nothing more, nothing less."

Bohmont laughed, "Look, I already told them no one knows more about the value of a Nevada ranch than you. I told them that you can look at a ranch for a few hours and nail the value to the penny. Besides, you will have a year or two to make it produce before there's an IRS audit. I'll bet right now that given two years, you will exceed your own values."

As I left Bohmont's office I couldn't help wondering if he really believed I was that good, or that was a polite way of saying I had better be that good. In either case I had a problem. The choice was pretty simple - send out the alarm and stop this nonsense before I get in over my head, or make that ranch, that I had yet to see, be every bit as good as I indicated it was. Thinking back over the years, I always seemed to take the hard road. Maybe it was my ego, maybe I was just plain stupid. But I knew one thing, I never did have a very good reverse gear. So, the answer was pretty simple. Somehow, we were going to make a very difficult ranch work. The only other real problem I had is I didn't clearly understand just exactly who the "we" were.

The next morning was a Thursday, and every other Thursday, I went to Fallon to weigh cattle that I had an experiment at the Fallon Station. John McCormick had long been the superintendent of that station. Several years before he had approached me about establishing a small feedlot there so that we could evaluate different cuttings of alfalfa hay. John had pioneered the concept of changing Fallon hay production from the customary three cuttings per year to four. And he was convinced that the fourth cutting was of sufficient quality to far outweigh the additional harvest costs. Our feeding trials had done nothing but substantiate his theory. In addition to measuring hay quality, the feedlot, which had twelve pens, housing four animals per pen, also proved invaluable in product testing. Our usual procedure was to start a trial with calves weighing about 500 pounds and take them to slaughter at the University facility when they cleared 1,050 pounds.

It was a typical beautiful fall day in Fallon. The cottonwoods were turning, it was cool, perhaps cold by some standards, but there wasn't a breath of air, and the sun shone so bright that it was a shirt sleeve day. John didn't help us weigh cattle anymore, as he was getting up in years and his health was a problem. But John was always there giving me his philosophical view of life in general and the University in particular. I always listened carefully to John, he was no dummy, having obtained a Masters in Public Administration a number of years ago from Harvard. John's two helpers always assisted in weighing, Clarence Carpenter and Izzy Barrenchiea. Clarence was a young lad, new to the ag game, but Izzy was an old Basque who knew not only Nevada, but just about everybody that ever lived there. I had brought my own pick-up this day, which had a camper shell. And it was full of camping gear, because I didn't have the slightest idea of what lay ahead. And, as it was Nevada Day weekend, I didn't face class until next Monday.

As we began weighing, I explained how I was going further east, not back to Reno, when weighing was complete. I explained who George Gund was, and what he might give the University. I could level with these boys, and I did. "I don't know a damned thing about Grass Valley, or the old Walti Ranch, but I guess over the next few days I'll learn.

Izzy laughed, "Yeah, you'll learn alright, you'll learn that is a mighty big country."

I looked at him quizzically, "Izzy, you know that country?"

"You bet, my grandparents lived in Eureka, and when I was a little guy, I stayed with them a lot. I started buckeroing when I was about twelve or thirteen. I rode for old Peter Damele, long since dead. He had a string of ranches, all around Roberts Peak, Tonkin, JD and I believe Three Bar. I rode all of that country, not much in Grass Valley, but we got over there some." Izzy went on to describe the good grass that was on all of the mountains in Central Nevada, and how on most years they just simply wintered on the flats. "It was good cattle country in those days, even a lot of sheep. But I hear it gone to hell since the drought of the 60's," he continued. The drought of the 60's had indeed been extreme, especially in Central Nevada, driving many ranches out or nearly out of production. I could well imagine that between the drought conditions and over grazing, plant communities had likely changed in their makeup, and definitely not for the better.

The old sage, John, had been standing next to the scales as we weighed, listening to my discussion and Izzy's response without saying a word. "You know, since you started this feedlot, a lot of good things have happened to this station. I attribute that to you, and Bohmont's faith in you. But this ranch you are talking about is a lot different thing. It's going to cost a lot of money to get started. And it's going to be a year or two before you begin to show any appreciable income, much less any kind of positive cash flow, which probably will never happen seeing how its the University. I hear what these other professors say behind your back. Most of them don't like Bohmont, and if the truth were known they like you even less. You have shown them up, shown them for what they are. But remember they all have tenure, so in a way there's not much that can be done about all of that. You're going to get very involved in making this ranch work, I can see that coming. Which means you will be in Grass Valley, or somewhere in between most of the time. You know as well as I do, they will think you are getting an unfair portion of the budget. It's probably going to be all right as long as Bohmont remains Dean, but heaven help your poor carcass if he ever tips over."

I listened to John's words very carefully. He was right. Bohmont wouldn't always be here, and it was predictable that the faculty backlash to a can do guy like Bohmont would likely result in the next Dean being a piece of Melba toast. "I have thought a lot about this, you're exactly right. I figure I got no more than five years to get this ranch organized, then I got another five years to make it attractive enough for enough professors to do research there that it will sustain itself, with or without me or the Dean."

As we finished weighing the last steer, Clarence, Izzy and John all shook my hand and wished me well on this new venture. "Don't forget, you gave this Station a shot in the arm with this feedlot. Just remember the road to Grass Valley goes right through Fallon and right past this Station."

I responded, "Don't worry John, coming out here every two weeks to weigh these steers and watch these animals grow is about the most peaceful thing I do. I'll not soon be forgetting that."

As I climbed into my pick-up, Izzy had one last bit of advice, "Watch the high country, those boys out there know how to ride and rope, mark your calves before they go out."

As I took the back road past the Fallon Naval Station on my way to Highway 50, I thought long and hard about what John had said, as well as Izzy's last comments. I would be stretched thin, no doubt about that. As to rustlers, well I guess I would just cross that bridge when and if I ever got there.

Highway 50 travels clear across Nevada, from South Shore at Tahoe, through Fallon to Austin, Eureka, Ely, finally hitting Utah and on to Delta. It was a two-lane road, traversing more mountain ranges than you could count on all of your fingers. In fact, if you count Spooners coming out of the Tahoe Basin, you will go over 12 mountain passes before you finally get to Utah. I had been told by some old timers that in both the winters of 1948-49 and 1950-51, you had to put on chains on every single pass to make it all the way. But times were changing.

Constant improvement to Highway 40, which was systematically being replaced by Interstate 80 had resulted in nearly all of the trans-Nevada traffic opting for the northern route. This made Highway 50 a very peaceful route of travel, but it was also adding to the slow but steady strangulation of towns such as Austin, Eureka and Ely, as well as the old stage stops every 25 miles or so that still clung to life selling an occasional beer, hamburger or tank of gas.

As I headed east, I started to make mental notes of the stations that were still in existence. I could well imagine that I, or a lot of people that I might be sort of responsible for, would be making this trip. It looked like help was about every 25 miles or so, and it would be in my best interest to make sure I was well accepted at all of them, especially in light of the fact that no telephone service existed between Fallon and Austin. The first place east of Fallon was Salt Wells. Salt Wells was supposed to be an old freight station on the way to the mines of Central Nevada. It didn't look like the station had changed much in the last 100 years or so. And it only had limited facilities, just food and drink, no gas. I had stopped at Salt Wells once or twice over the years, an old couple ran it, serving mostly Mexican food, but they did a good job of that. Salt Wells sits right on a vast playa, a playa that acted as home for Nevada's only existing salt mine.

At the far end of the playa, and slightly north of the highway sat Sand Mountain, a gigantic sand dune that was the winter recreation spot for sand buggy enthusiasts. Next came Silver Zone summit, then down into Frenchman's Flat, another vast playa. Frenchmen was of interest, as it was home to one of the most active bombing and gunnery sites for the Fallon Naval Air Station jet jockeys. More times than not, as you crossed Frenchmen's jets would be blasting up the mountain to the south. And right in the middle of the playa sat Frenchman's, a well-known hamburger, beer and gas stop. It was owned by a young couple that claimed to be direct descendants of the original Frenchman, a person by the name of Labeau. The story was that he was an early day

353

pioneer that settled this part of Nevada. He was supposed to have lost his children, and sure enough, not far from Salt Wells there is a grave in the playa that has become a shrine for his children, a grave that local legend claims hold the Labeau children. At least, Frenchman's had gas.

About fifteen miles past Frenchman's Highway 50 intersects with the road that goes south to Gabbs and Lunning. Another station exists there, called Middlegate, again, hamburgers, beer, and maybe gas, depending on circumstances.

Three miles past Middlegate, the road forks. Old Highway 50 continues in a westerly fashion, traverses two summits before hitting Austin. Carrol Summit, nearly 7,500 feet high, was always difficult to maintain during winter months, and was the frequent area of tragic accidents. In the 1960's the Highway department moved Highway 50 to Edwards Valley and over New Pass Summit, which was over a thousand feet lower than Carrol Summit. The new highway was actually two miles longer than the old one, but it probably saved fifteen minutes, and many lives. In the process of moving the highway, they also moved the old historic station that was at East Gate to a new location called Cold Springs. Cold Spring was about thirteen miles past Middle Gate, and as it turned out it was just about half way between Reno and the ranch, so in due time it became one of my mainstays. You could get a good meal at Cold Springs, more than a hamburger. They had a good bar, and a dependable supply of gas. An old couple, John and Mary, owned and operated Cold Springs, and they had owned and operated East Gate for many years before the Highway Department moved them. John was an old time Nevadan, and many times over the years he solved central Nevada problems, both political and physical, that I often just didn't have the background to solve myself.

It was a long haul from Cold Springs to Austin, some 47 miles of nothing but pure and beautiful Nevada landscape. Just about all unfenced, and as I was soon to learn, the home to numerous cattle and wild horses that seemed to love to bed down on the warm asphalt on cold winter nights.

Austin was the "queen city" of central Nevada, if there was such a denomination. Once home to over twenty thousand tough miners, it still lingered on as the county seat of Lander County and home to maybe 500 souls. But Austin had motels, restaurants, bars and gas stations, in fact several of each. Austin sort of stayed drunk, there weren't enough tourists to keep the town's four to five bars open, so they just resorted to serving each other. But Austin was a friendly place, at least providing you had a miner's philosophy. And I kind of fit into that philosophy, not only then, but it grew on me over the years, so Austin was always very good to me. After Austin, it was six miles over Austin Summit, 7,500 feet high, to the county road to Grass Valley.

The road to Grass Valley was poorly marked, but I was prepared for it, having long since studied the map. It appeared that it was about 50 miles to the Gund Ranch, all gravel road. As I left Highway 50, I stopped a few feet on the county road, just to contemplate. It had been a little over one and a half hours since I left Fallon, and I had traveled 110 miles. The road north intersected Highway 50 at the bottom of a valley, heavily timbered with pinion trees. A trickle of water persisted in the bottom, although nearly dry that fall. I sat there for a few minutes, both enjoying the beautiful quiet and scenery. But the overpowering thought on my mind was, if I head north on this road, in all likely hood, my life will be forever changed.

I didn't have any choice at this point, so why worry. A mile up the road I passed the old Stressley Ranch, owned by two bachelor brothers, a not uncommon trait in Nevada. In fact, the Walti's were the same way. The mother and two boys ran the ranch until the ranch was finally sold. I guessed marriage on these remote ranches had been tougher in the old days. Two miles past Streesleys, another old ranch existed, but I didn't know who owned it. I did note that both of these places had live streams running through them, even in late October. That, at least, was an encouraging sight.

As I left the last ranch, the road arched up over a large flat area, dominated mostly by grass with very little brush. Dead ahead, rose the hulking mass of Mt. Callaghan, well over 10,000 feet high. Off to the right appeared a small ranch, possibly just a line camp, I couldn't really tell from that distance. After about five miles I topped a ridge, and there in front of me was the vastness of Grass Valley.

Grass Valley was a miniature Great Basin. Everything that drained into the valley eventually reached the bed of a Pleistocene era dry lake or playa. Its name, not that meant much, was Pleistocene Lake Gilbert. From this vantage point the playa glimmered far in the distance. Far to the north, over 50 miles, stood the rigid silhouette of Mt. Tenabo, marking the north end of the valley. The valley was guarded to the east by the Simpson Park Mountains, named after the first government surveyor, to cross central Nevada. The Peaks of the Simpson Park's rose to 9,000 feet. And in the west the valley was guarded by the Shoshone Range, topped by the mighty Callaghan. Across the north end of the valley stood the Saw Tooth Range, a rugged and near impenetrable extension of the Shoshones. And right in front of me, although still ten miles away and fully a thousand feet lower stood Molly Knudtsen's Grass Valley Ranch. Although Bohmont wanted me to stop in today for a visit, after all Molly is a Regent you know, I had far too much on my plate to be sociable. I couldn't help but wondering, however, as I viewed her ranch, which appeared as a small town from this vantage point, if all that was worthwhile in Grass Valley didn't already belong to Molly.

It didn't take more than 15 minutes to come from the ridge, that offered the view of the entire valley, down to the valley floor. I immediately noticed Molly's fields off to my left that were covered with Hereford cattle. She was well known for her purebred herd, and it was pretty obvious that her commercial herd wasn't too shabby. I also couldn't help but notice the neat haystacks, stacks that represented several thousand tons of hay for the coming winter. Shortly I crossed Steiner Creek, coming off Bates Mountain, the southern terminus of the Simpson Park Range. And Steiner was still running water at this late date. I had been told that Steiner was good at fishing in the upper reaches, but that would have to be for another day.

As I left Molly's ranch, the vegetation turned from grass to brush and shortly to Greasewood. The vegetation reminded me of the edges of the Black Rock, and I couldn't help but thinking of Reene Etchegoyan and the terrible tragedy that ended her life. I could well imagine the same sort of things occurring in Grass Valley. Ugly thoughts that I didn't need right now. As I made my way up the valley on what seemed to be a never-ending road, I thought I could see distant Cottonwood trees against the base of 8,481 foot McClusky Peak, the highest point in the northern portion of the Simpson Parks. I also noticed, the further north I went the poorer the road became, I guessed nobody in Lander County thought it was important to get to Walti's from this angle. Soon I passed a dilapidated windmill to my left. It looked far beyond the working stage, but I also noticed water standing in a basin around the well. At least the water table wasn't far below the surface, a fact undoubtedly accounting for the vast field of greasewood I could see as far as the eye could go. Finally, I rounded a bend and a fenced field appeared, a real field with actual grass. And above it was an alfalfa field, with three-wheel lines, all connected with a main line to a water well directly opposite the road. I sort of shied away from looking at the greasy cat diesel which was the obvious source of power. Further, I noticed a cabin at the mouth of a canyon coming off the side of McClusky, then a cabin in a meadow with cottonwood trees below the road. I couldn't help but think of possible living sites for who in the world was ever going to do the work. I also couldn't help but notice the fences. They were truly antique if there was anything of such a nature in the world of fencing.

Very old wire, more or less supported by what appeared to be century old juniper posts every 20 feet or so.

Finally, I topped a rise that presented my first view of the ranch headquarters. A corral made of willows, an attached barn made of native stone, a dilapidated three-sided shop covered with tin, some missing. Several outbuildings in various states of decay, and the main house, surrounded by a few square feet of nearly dead grass. I also couldn't help but notice a beautiful stone structure immediately above a grove of cottonwood trees. And immediately under the cottonwood trees was an immense pond, surely the best skinny-dipping site in all Nevada, well or at least Central Nevada that I had been told about.

I stopped before entering the headquarters just to view and contemplate. My map research had shown that the road that I was on continued north, past Mt. Tenabo, and the old ghost town of Cortez, down through Crescent Valley, ultimately to hit Interstate 80 at Beowawe. From there it would be a short drive of 250 miles back to my safe confines in Reno. The tendency to be a professor and let problems lay until someone else came along was overwhelming at that point. What I had seen so far was discouraging at best. There was nothing here but a few old buildings, some worn out equipment, and hay fields that on first appearances would at best produce only a few hundred tons of hay if that. I thought about my model. I thought about $440,000. I thought about the IRS. I thought about being a full professor. I thought maybe if I went back to Reno and told Bohmont he could keep his full professorship, just leave me alone and let me do what I want to do. A million thoughts went through my head, but my overwhelming desire and common sense told me to just keep driving and never look back. But, alas, I never did have very good common sense, and I told them that I would do it. Everything that I had accomplished at the University so far had been uphill, against the odds, and accomplished mostly by just plain hard work. And somehow, I guessed this wouldn't be any different, just more of the same. So, I turned left, and idled into the headquarters.

Earlier in the week I had finally been able to make telephone contact with Richard Dilbeck, the resident manager, and inform him that I would be on the premises Thursday afternoon. I had used toll station telephones in Nevada already, as they were not all that uncommon. However, getting to the Gund Ranch required two toll stations, first the Crescent Valley store, and then having them throw a switch to activate the Grass Valley toll line. It worked, but barely. The static was horrendous, but Richard had assured me that later in the evening, after dark, the system worked much better.

As I pulled into the yard, stopped my pick-up, and climbed out, the first thing to catch my attention was the constant, although somewhat muffled, boom - boom - boom, the ever-present sound of the Wittie generator, the ranch's only source of electrical power. As I stood there, a young and attractive woman came towards me from the house. "Hi, I'am Pam Dilbeck. You must be Terry Hope," was her cheerful greeting. Although she was dressed somewhat along the lines of what might be considered a sixty's generation hippy, I quickly judged she really wasn't. Although, I had to laugh to myself, as I could readily see how Pete came to that conclusion, drifting by at 100 feet in the air. "Yes, I am Terry Hope, and it's a pleasure," as I extended my hand for her firm handshake.

"Rich is at Allen's watering cattle, but he should be here shortly. He said to make yourself at home until he gets here," with that she turned and looked to the north. "Oh, there he is now," she responded as we both watched a dust cloud coming from a distant grove of cottonwood trees, that I had already determined was the Allen Ranch.

For the next few minutes, I wondered around the various ranch buildings, if indeed they could be considered as such. There were two shop type buildings, at least three sided, with roofs that appeared to be somewhat watertight. The barn was a classic, made entirely from native stone and massive juniper posts holding the roof up. The roof was made from willows and rye grass, covered with tin. There were three windows, two on the south side, one on the north. Swinging doors allowed access from either end. Inside the barn was tight, when the shutters were closed on the windows, I could well imagine that it was pretty weatherproof. Two old ranch horses stood in a small, attached corral, part of the larger corral system, all made of willows and juniper posts, tightly bound together. I noticed a large water trough centrally located. The other buildings were hardly noteworthy, with the exception of the round rock building housing the ever-noisy Wittie.

I could hear the approaching roar of a well used ranch pick-up, minus a muffler, which announced the arrival of Richard Dilbeck. He stepped out with a smile from ear to ear, hand extended, for what turned out to be a very firm shake. "Howdy Terry, welcome to Grass Valley!" Although sincere, it was kind of like, well here it is, it's all we got! Rich took me on a whirlwind tour of the facilities, explaining the pros and cons of the barn, corral, chute, scales, sheds, Wittie, etc. I soon learned that this was indeed a hot water ranch, in fact that's all they had, which was mighty nice in the winter, but as he explained, "Its sometime tougher than all get out to get a cold drink of water around here during the summer months."

We journeyed up to the rock corral by the cotton woods, which was obviously an old sheep facility from bygone days. The hot springs probably emerged in the center of the corral, although not evident now, Rich explained, "Snow melts off this spot as fast as it falls, I am sure that's why the old timers built this corral where its at. Below the corral, a spring emitting what I guessed to be 400 gallons per minute came out of a crack in the ground. The water was far too hot to put your hand in for more than a second. Over the years, two ponds have been created below the spring. The vast majority of the water by passed the ponds, going on to the swamp below the headquarters. "We allow just enough water into the first pond to make the water just right for bathing. The water flows from the first pond to the second pond, which is much cooler and just right for swimming. The only problem is that somehow a leach population has built up in the cool pond, and they are vicious. A few minutes in there and they will be hanging all over," he cheerfully explained. A small dressing room sat immediately above the hot pond, with a wood stove. "It's great in the winter, build a fire, undress, dive right in. I have been in at twenty below, head frosted solid, yet was warm as toast. Just got to move fast when you get out," he continued to explain. I was beginning to understand that the hot pond might indeed become a valuable resource if the University actually ended up with this disaster.

"Look, it's getting late, lets go to the house and have something to drink, Pams' got a big dinner planned. We can talk about the ranch, then tomorrow I'll give you a complete tour." I couldn't have agreed more, and right then something wet sounded awfully nice. The house was comfortable inside, all the furniture was old, but neat. Curtains were on all the windows, and all the windows even had glass. A screened parch insulated the back or east side, and an open parch covered the west and south side. The kitchen was very functional, with ample room for a big table that Rich invited me to sit down at. "The house is heated with hot water from the spring, that's all we have ever used, don't even have a wood stove in here," as he cracked open two bottles of Bud. "I have a long line, several hundred feet in length buried near the surface out in back for cold water. If we don't use it much it gives Pam cool water in the sink, but not much more. We have it plumbed to the toilet and the bath, so that we can take baths if we don't want to go to the pond. Walti's always had an outhouse until a few years before they sold it to Gund. Then they put in a flush toilet, but I don't see how they stood the hot water. When I moved in, that's the first thing I fixed, got some cold water."

As the evening wore on, I listened with keen interest of Rich's description of the various ranch attributes, or lack thereof. I gathered spring run-off was not only marginal, but simply didn't occur for many years. Rich had suggested installing some pipes to the mouths of the various canyons, but the Gund people never spent the money. He indicated that possibly six canyons produced sufficient water to warrant the placing of pipe from the canyon mouths to nearby potential meadow sites. He reasoned that a fault line existed along the west slope of the Simpson Park Mountains, intercepting essentially all water reaching the canyon mouth. That was not an uncommon trait throughout central Nevada, and I had noticed that remnants of a not too distance fault line did indeed exist at the base of the mountain. He talked about the Indian Ranch, far to the south, close to Molly Knudtsen's spread, property that I was unfamiliar with at that point in time. Rich felt there was great potential to increase alfalfa production at the old Allen unit.

Finally, I asked what their plans were. "That depends on what the University intends to do. Al Stenninger thinks the University will simply sell this property once it's gifted. If that's the case, I will look at other opportunities. If the University were to keep the ranch, we would like to stay on," Rich summarized with Pam in obvious agreement.

"Well, I can't answer your question right now, that's for sure. It will probably take six months to complete the gifting process, then I would imagine the University will attempt to sell the property, as it fits none of the criteria for a field station. However, I kind of think it will be difficult to sell, because we just may have put too high a value on the gift. If we can't sell this property at 90% of the gifted value, we will create all sorts of problems, not only for Gund, but definitely for the University," I concluded.

The conversation drifted on well into the night. Pam served a dinner fit for any ranch, a large beef roast, baked potatoes, gravy, home made bread, topped off with milk fresh from their cow and a chocolate cake. I also learned, too my amazement, that both Pam and Rich had graduated from Chico State College, one of California's many state four-year universities. Rich had a degree in General Agriculture, and Pam a degree in Biology. They were intelligent, highly educated, but just didn't want to live in the crowded city, or even close for that matter. I could see that they loved this setting, and moving would be hard indeed.

Although my pick-up was well equipped for nights like tonight, complete with a mattress and bedroll, Pam insisted that I stay in their guest bedroom, which was a special treat. Not only was it well decorated, but the old iron bed had a mattress made from goose down, and a quilt that would have worked at the North Pole. I gently drifted off to the constant boom - boom - boom of the ever-faithful Wittie.

The morning broke early, I was up at 5:30, walked up to the hot pond, even contemplated a dip, but thought better. Breakfast was bacon, eggs, pancakes, fried potatoes and coffee. "You know, both Pam and I have to tell you, we thought you were a devout Mormon, because Al told us everyone in Ag at the University was. We had talked earlier about a drink, wondering if you would imbibe or not. We decided to just offer a beer and see what would happen. When you drank those beers last night, as well as coffee this morning, we came to the conclusion that you are not a devout Mormon, at least."

I could do nothing but laugh as I responded, "Well, you are somewhat right. My immediate boss is devout to say the least. But I have avoided the plague so far, generally consider myself a protestant, beyond that I don't take sides. As a matter of fact, I feel a lot closer to God sitting right here in your kitchen than I do any church in Reno. The only way I could get closer would be to climb to the top of McClusky."

Rich's smile indicated relief, but he followed my comment by saying, "I'll do you one better, we'll go around the back side of the Simpson's and drive to the top, or nearly, of McClusky."

After another cup of coffee, we were off in my pick-up. I inquired if the ranch had any equipment, and I quickly learned other than two old Alice Chalmers tractors, one a 1946 model and one a 1939 model there wasn't much else, other than the Wittie. "I even use my own pick-up, they pay a small mileage fee for that, and of course they let us use ranch gas for going to town," Rich informed me. I made a mental note that at least I wasn't going to have to contend with a lot of old junk; the junk was all in the bone pile above the headquarters. It looked like to me that if it moved, or could be loaded, Gund's people had already hauled it off to Lee. This place was just about clean, except for the Wittie, and two old Cat diesels for pumping water at Allen's and Cold Springs.

Rich directed me to Allen's first. There appeared to be only about 70 acres of producing alfalfa there, although in my calculations I had figured, and been informed for that matter, that the acreage was 80. But it was alfalfa land, no question about that. The only obvious problem was that the well had been pumping lots of sand, a symptom of an old cable tool drilled well, approaching the possibility of collapse. From Allen's, we went up McClusky Creek to the Baumann Ranch. McClusky was a live stream and even had some trout, according to Rich. We stopped at the Ranch, met Walt and Jeanette Baumann, descendants of the first pioneers to homestead here. Walt's brother, Ernie had stayed on over the years as well. Ernie was a World War I veteran, and obviously knew the local history well. The Baumann's son, Jim and his wife, Vera, were in town that day. The Baumann Ranch was in a beautiful setting, with McClusky Creek running right by the house. Mrs. Bauman had gardens, lawns, and flowers in every possible location. It was as beautiful as any park I had ever seen. And it was obvious that the Baumann's were genuine neighbors. After leaving the Ranch, we topped McClusky Pass. "This is usually closed with snow by the middle of November, and the County won't open it until April on most years. So, we have to get our cattle from the other side of the mountain no later than October, or face some risky situations," Rich explained

From the Pass, we took a seldom used dirt road, clinging to the side of the mountain, topping the Simpson Parks directly over what Rich called Potato Canyon. A short walk got us to a vantage point near the top of McClusky, where not only the Ranch was totally visible, but a lot of Grass Valley. The view was spectacular, but I also began to realize that Grass Valley was a miniature Great Basin, and squarely in the middle of the Great Basin itself. Ringed by mountains on all four sides, all run-off, when it might occur, went directly to the shimmering playa if not intercepted in a pasture or hay field. The playa proper was oval in shape, perhaps ten miles long by five miles wide, representing possibly over 100,000 acres of an absolutely flat hard pan of clay and salt. Starting with greasewood that surrounded the playa, just about every possible plant community, up to sub-alpine existed from the 5,600-foot elevation of the playa to the top of Fagin Mountain at 9,147 feet, far to the south.

After leaving the top of the mountains, we journeyed back the same way we came, to and past the ranch. I couldn't help but notice a small tin covered rock building about a half mile south of the Ranch headquarters. "That's the High Place. Lloyd High lived there for years. He was a World War I vet, that homesteaded a forty-acre parcel there, somehow Walti's just never acquired title to the property from the government. Apparently High found it in the courthouse, filed on it and set up camp. Eventually, he and the Walti's got along, as he worked for them for many years. I guess about ten years ago, he moved to Crescent Valley, and Walti's bought his property. If you look at the mouth of Potato Canyon, there's another cabin, and that was High's as well. He called that his summer cabin, and the one we just passed his winter cabin."

Rich pointed out every canyon that had water potential as we traveled south, Potato, Sheep Corral, Pine, Moonshine, and finally Big Canyon. "Big Canyon runs a perennial stream up in the canyon. Walti's always planted a few trout in there, but I haven't seen any there in the last year or two". The next canyon south was Hiller. "Doesn't run as much water, and from the mouth of the canyon, its probably three miles to the nearest field," Rich explained. "The next three canyons aren't ours, Underwood, Wood and Trail. They are tied to a water-based allotment, but I don't know who has it, so we just graze it anyway. Nice basin at the top of Underwood, full of aspen," he continued.

Finally, we left the Grass Valley Road, heading in an easterly direction. "Wanted to take you to Indian Ranch, Gund owns about a section of land up there, has a nice meadow, stream and a beautiful old log cabin." We slowly wound our way through a solid stand of pinion, finally topped over a ridge, and there in front of us was a beautiful meadow and cabin. The cabin was well-equipped, wood cook stove, table, chairs and totally tight. "The guys from the other side, Three Bars, Ferguson, Sante Fe, Ackerman, and even Benny Demale, from clear down at Dry Canyon use this cabin in the fall when they gather this side. They always shove ours back from the other side, gather theirs, then head home. We all work together to keep this meadow from being grazed until then, that's why it looks so good this late in the year. This is where my gathering really starts. We meet Benny and the boys here, separate, drink a bottle of whisky, then all head home in different directions. I head down Salt Marsh to the flat, Benny heads over the top to Ackerman, the rest head north to Park Canyon, then over the top to Shagnasty Basin, then to their respective ranches. Been some powerful parties here," Rich explained. And I could well imagine.

However, I cautioned Rich that I didn't think Mr. Gund's gifting included the Indian Ranch. However, I would assume that it would still be managed by the Ranch, regardless of who actually owned the property. Rich tended to agree, "I think George really loves this place, usually comes here at least once a year, loves spending a night or two here all by himself".

After the Indian Ranch, we headed back to the headquarters. Pam had an early dinner fixed, as it was my intent to head to Reno before dark, but not the way I came. I wanted to see the rest of Grass Valley, Cortez Canyon and Crescent Valley. I apologized for not knowing more about the immediate future of the ranch, but I assured Rich and Pam that if they wanted to stay, there would be a job until at least when the ranch was sold, if and when that ever occurred. They appreciated my concern but opted to keep every option open for the time being. They were very honest, as they clearly indicated that Molly Knudtsen was keeping a job and house open for them if they would go to work for her. After firm handshakes and good-byes, I headed north, past the historic ghost town of Cortez, down through Cortez Canyon, past the operating gold mine, one of Nevada's few, at the mouth of the canyon, and on through Crescent Valley. I wanted to stop at the store to see how the telephone switching operation worked, but the store was closed. Once closed, the store kept switched to the Grass Valley line for the rest of the night. On those nights that that chore was forgotten, Grass Valley did without.

As I hit the freeway north of Beowawe I started the 250-mile journey home with many thoughts on my head. I mentally reviewed the field station criteria determined by the search committee; (1) centrally located in relation to the livestock industry, (2) sufficient deeded lands associated with federal grazing rights, (3) access by public road, (4) electric power available, (5) adequate irrigation, (6) good domestic water, (7) adequate housing, corrals and barns, and (8) convenient to the University. Probably one, sufficient deeded lands associated with federal grazing rights was the only criteria that the Gund Ranch met, if that. The rest were a joke. But, as I drove west, I reasoned who in the hell thought these up anyway. It went without saying that I had been part of that scam, but I began to realize that my head must have been in the clouds, or maybe better, up my ass! The rest didn't really know what a University ranch should do to make it successful. So, I mentally tossed all the criteria out the window. And I concentrated on that view from the top of the mountain. A totally enclosed basin, a miniature Great Basin, with all the problems associated with agriculture anywhere in Nevada; too little water, too short a growing season, poor grazing, difficult terrain, dependence on federally controlled land, the list went on and on. A questionable telephone system, and having to generate the ranches' own electricity were just not that bad, something a lot of ranches had to put up with. Accessibility would be a problem. It was obvious there were winter days, when going to Grass Valley just might not be possible. But most research, at least plants, soils and related areas are conducted during the spring and summer, so that didn't pose a problem. The livestock, well, we would just have to overcome that part. As I neared Reno, I had already come to the conclusion that the Gund Ranch just might be the best possible place for the University in all Nevada. No one in their right mind would ever argue that it was anything but tough, probably the toughest environment conceivable. But the Ag College had always been considered soft by agriculture in Nevada. Make the Gund Ranch go, and that assessment would go out the window. And I believed that I could make it go!

I had a heavy teaching schedule Monday morning, but by Monday afternoon, it was time for my report to Bohmont. I didn't really know just how to approach this, because after a long weekend I was beginning to truly believe that the Gund Ranch was perhaps indeed the chance of a lifetime for the University. However, even with my enthusiasm, selling this idea would not be easy. For the time being it would be just as well if no one else saw the place. Other professors didn't look at things like this quite like I did.

"Well, tell me what you found out," Bohmont cheerfully inquired as I eased into the chair in front of his desk.

I thought for a split second, should this sound good or bad. Well to make it good would be a bald face lie, and I was never very good at that, so I opted for bad. "Its a nineteenth century ranch, it never made into this century, except the two alfalfa fields that have been put in, along with the two water wells. There's hardly a fence that could be considered adequate, the corral is adequate simply for working cattle, but poorly designed for anything that we would wish to accomplish. Hardly any surface runoff presently reaches the meadows, consequently there are hardly any meadows. The barns, sheds, etc. are minimal. Presently, there is one habitable house, although there are a couple of cabins that perhaps could suffice on an interim basis. The road from the south, as well as the north occasionally drift shut with snow. On a wet spring it looks like the road could wash out in several places. There presently is a generator sufficiently large enough to handle one house and a limited shop. The telephone barely works. The range is tough. The flat is mostly greasewood and bud sage, which cattle don't like. Whoever coined the name Grass Valley for that alkali flat must have had a diabolical sense of humor. The mountain has good grass, and there are good springs, but it is extremely steep. The only possible criteria from the search committee that this property meets is the fact that it has some private property, and an adjoining grazing permit on federal property. About the facility, there's not much more that I can say."

Bohmont look perplexed at first, then he started turning a bit red. I braced for the onslaught. "You mean you put $440,000 on a ranch that, after listening to your description, we probably couldn't sell for $220,000?"

"Yeah, its a great deal for Gund, I guess you noticed how pleased the accountant was. And, if you will calm down long enough to listen, I truly believe its a great deal for the University," I offered, and I offered it boldly, as I had long since learned that the display of fear only convinced the man that he was even righter than he thought to begin with. And

369

right then I was pretty sure that Bohmont had visions of eliminating me from his life.

"OK friend, you got about three minutes to explain," he threw my direction.

"Well Dean, its like this, even if we could sell the ranch for say, $300,000, that's not enough to buy what the ranch search committee has wanted. Further, every time we look at a ranch, the locals get nervous, in fact now there is a significant portion of the Cattleman's Association that is questioning why we should ever own a ranch. So my feeling is we shouldn't sell this property, and valuing it at $440,000 almost guarantees that." In hindsight I could just about guarantee that the last statement would infuriate Bohmont, it sort of sounded like I had forced the issue over his dead body. I was right.

He blew. I sat there and took the verbal abuse for about ninety seconds worth, which, if you really try hard, is just about as long as you can hold your breath for. After he quit for a second, I leaned forward, put both of my hands on the edge of his desk and started in, "Now, if you can remain calm enough for a few minutes, I'll tell you the rest of the story. I don't believe for a second that buying the picture perfect ranch, even if we could, will ever produce meaningful results. We'll just sit there and look pretty while wasting taxpayer funds. However, the Gund Ranch is almost like a picture perfect laboratory of the Great Basin. Admittedly, its facilities are minimal at best, but so what, in time they can be improved. What this ranch has in natural resources to work with from a research standpoint probably exceeds all the places all together we have looked at so far. It is a natural laboratory, with every problem that any ranch has, in fact all ranches in Nevada put together have. We couldn't have bought a better natural laboratory if we paid millions. Sure, it's going to be a gamble, and we might even fail. But, if the University of Nevada can make a go at the Gund Ranch, they will forever win the respect of the industry, the legislature, probably most of rural Nevada, if not all Nevada."

Bohmont looked puzzled, but at least the red had left his face. "OK, but where is the money coming from. Because of the enrollment growth we have been having, we are strapped." I knew money was limited, but it seemed like I should be able to make the case that the ranch could be run on an enterprise basis for some time, requiring minimal input from the University's coffers. I also knew that I would be placed in charge, total charge, so my salary was already paid for. Going in this direction would likely impact my research career for the next few years, but the price would well be worth the sacrifice. I began to lay out a minimal management plan that could be put in place relatively easily, probably minimizing the outflow of money, and gradually letting the facility regenerate itself. I explained my position, and Bohmont clearly understood, both the good and the bad.

"I know you can handle it, and you have enough graduate students that it probably can work for a year or so, but your professional career will suffer. You know how the vultures are around here, they'll gather up your goodies as soon as your back is turned."

My response was simple, "Yeah, but I look to you to protect my backside every bit as much as you look to me to get the job done, right?"

He agreed, and further added, "Our immediate problem is that we must go through some formality of trying to sell this place. The University lawyer indicates that can't occur for at least another 150 days at a minimum, which puts into March, late March 1972. The nature of the wording in the gifting process is such that we have to advertise it, so there will be legitimate bidders. If anyone comes within 90% of the gifted price, then we have a problem. If not, we maintain ownership for the time being, and at that point you got a ranch." OK, so we both agreed, I would indicate to Rich Dilbeck that the place would be on minimal status until next March, at such time, it would be decided what direction to go. We both agreed, if Dilbeck wanted to leave, I would find a watchman to maintain the facility for the winter. And Dilbeck wanted to leave, as Molly Knudtsen had offered him a job and he accepted. But Rich was true to his word, he did find a suitable watchman, none other than his father.

I had one more speech up my sleeve that I wanted Bohmont to hear before I exited. "Look at it this way, I believe the Walti's never could run more than about 300 mother cows, including Doc Allen's place. And I'll bet they never weaned anything, at least at eight to ten months of age, that weighed over 400 pounds. And I will further bet their calving percentage never excited 70%. So simply put at best, they produced 42 tons of marketable beef annually, including heifers that weren't to be sold but kept for replacement. Now just suppose that 42-ton figure is correct, and represents a long history of the productive capacity of the northern half of Grass Valley. Now let's suppose the University comes along, uses some good and sound techniques, including better nutrition, better disease prevention, better genetics, better water utilization, better cropping procedures, better range management, and suddenly started producing not 42 tons of marketable beef annually, but as much as 84 tons of beef or more each year, what do you think the cattle folks would say then?"

"If you could do that, and not break the College, much less the University, it would surely catch everyone's eye to put it mildly."

"I can do that, but only if you don't mix the operating cost of the ranch and the research cost that will surely come about if this does become an Experiment Station in due time", I responded.

"That's a bold statement, and I won't forget it, just in case you have taken a step too far this time", Bohmont concluded.

You got to love the guy, I thought to myself as I exited the wheelhouse.

Another trip was made to Grass Valley, getting the senior Dilbeck settled, making sure ample diesel was in place for the Wittie and so on. I left Grass Valley on a cold November day, with snowflakes beginning to fall. It was a beautiful scene, a scene I found I was becoming attached to, which was not a good sign. I had to get these thoughts out of my head until March. You never knew, some idiot might just come forth and offer $440,000 for the joint.

I had other priorities now anyway. My teaching schedule was heavier than ever. In addition to Feeds, I was again teaching The Importance of Animals in Man's Ecosystem, to well over 100 students again. Additionally, due to the increased number of graduate students, I was offering a grad course called Range Livestock Nutrition. All told I was teaching 7 hours of academic class, even though my contract indicated my time was divided 40% teaching and 60% research.

For the rest of my time during the winter, evenings and weekends, I spent finishing my thesis. By January 5, I shipped a final copy to Dr. Oldfield for his review, and it came back two weeks later essentially approved. My final exam was scheduled for February 25, and I was in Corvallis on the twenty fourth, ready to go. There were seven people on my committee, all had been provided a copy of my thesis two weeks before. Three members were from the Animal Science Department, one from Range, and one from Human Nutrition. Additionally, the Graduate Dean had appointed two to represent the University at large, one from Philosophy and one from Fisheries. My exam took most of the day, my thesis was difficult to explain, and that took about four hours. Every member was expected to ask questions about the thesis, my academic classes (they all had copies of my transcript), and questions at large. I had no problems with my thesis and class work, the problem came from the Philosophy Prof, who just didn't understand how I could only spend nine months on campus and get a Ph.D.

Dr. Oldfield patiently explained how that was all possible, and furthermore how it was approved by the Graduate Dean. That said, the Philosophy Prof. decided that he would find out how much I knew about Oregon. I guess he figured, even though I only spent nine months there I had better know my geography. Fortunately, I did, every extra hour in Oregon had been spent traveling around, and the summer at Squaw Butte provided the opportunity to see east of the Cascades. He was a self-styled expert on the Steens, and he did not know that I had spent the summer at Squaw Butte. So, when I successfully named the Lahonton Cutthroat trout as the nearly extinct trout species in Wildhorse Lake, he gave up. After being excused, and nervously pacing up and down the hall for about fifteen minutes, Dr. Oldfield came out and shook my hand, "Congratulations, Dr. Hope." It all seemed so easy, and almost anticlimactic, but there it was, my union card was finally in hand! And true to his word, after letting Bohmont know that he was now to refer to me as Doctor Hope, he put forth my name to be considered for Full Professor, which in fact did make me the youngest individual to ever receive that honor at the University.

The bid opening was set for March 28, 1972. I had continually been reminding Bohmont that if no one bought the Ranch, we would have to start irrigation by no later than April 15. He kept mumbling something about getting a budget set up with Pete Test, the fiscal officer. When I asked Pete, he would mumble something about the Dean not notifying him yet so there was nothing he could do. And he would continue, there were no funds available until July 1. I knew how much diesel would be required to run the pumps until July 1, but nobody wanted to listen to that anyway. I asked about harvesting hay, Bohmont answered, "Get a contractor". I replied, there are no contractors available. He replied, "See Lingenfelter." Jim Lingenfelter was in charge of equipment for the College. His response was, "Let me see your budget." And, finally, March 28 came about.

Pete was in Reno for a meeting, but he dropped by my office before the bid opening to let me know that we would have picons after work. That sounded good, because I was sure that afternoon would be a fiasco. More or less, I was right. A lot of people showed up for the opening, although only two bids were submitted. Several ranch realtors in the Reno area had tried to get buyers; chief among them was Jack Utter, long known as a wheeler-dealer. The first bid came out of nowhere, from a Fallon hay farmer, and it was for $250,001. The second bid was one of Jack's boys, and it was a bit healthier, $325,111. The University Lawyer promptly conferred with Bohmont after the second bid was opened, then announced, "No bid was sufficiently close to the University stated value of $440,000 for the gift, consequently, the University will maintain possession of the property for the time being".

I had positioned myself at the back of the room during the opening, not talking with anyone. As the room cleared, I didn't move. I just wanted to observe what everybody was going to do. I had to assume I was in charge of the facility. I had no indication of how the budget would occur, much less what it might be. And, in my opinion, the water wells had to be ready to function in about 15 days, which meant fields had to be drug, motors had to be serviced, ditches cleaned, and pipes repaired as needed. And somebody needed to arrange for diesel, about 10,000 gallons. Bohmont went out one door, Ely, who was now in charge of research and experiment stations went out the other door. Pete Test walked past me looking at the floor, but I did notice a slight roll in his eyes. The only one who would even acknowledge my presence was Jim Lingenfelter. He came over and sat down, with a grin from ear to ear and offered, "Well, now professor you really got your tit in a ringer this time."

Jim could be the most sarcastic son-of-a-bitch in all of Nevada when he chose to be, and now was such a time. But I knew I would need Jim's expertise, so I bit my tongue and politely asked, "I guess you will be available to help me run down equipment, because I do believe that I will be needing some."

Jim and I spent a few minutes going over what was at the ranch, and what was needed. I had a list of all models and serial numbers, and tomorrow I was going to get filters, oil, grease and everything else to service motors with. There was enough old junk to make a suitable drag to pull behind one of the Alice tractors. However, on about June 15, by my reckoning, I would have to start cutting hay. "I need a usable swather for mowing, and a pull behind bailer, probably only need a two-wire baler. Also, I have my eyes on an old 6 by 6 flat bed Dodge army truck at surplus. If I had that and a side mounted elevator, along with a slip, I think I could get hay to the yards. Now that's not much of a request, should be easy to accomplish." Jim came from a ranching background, and clearly realized that what I needed had to be obtained. He took pity, and in a rare moment of seriousness said he understood and would help to his utmost ability. I thanked him, and said I guessed I had better sit down with Ely, Bohmont and Test to see just how this was all going to work. However, the hour was approaching five, and none of the administration wheels seemed anxious to talk to me so I thought, well if it isn't any more important than that, I'll be around in the morning, maybe.

Pete was waiting in my office when I got there. "Well, it sounds like the University appreciates you like always," was his welcome.

"How's that?" I responded,

"I already heard about the opening through the grapevine. Several agents were in the room, and they all said the look on your face said it all, when all the deans walked out without saying a word to you. I can just imagine, it's your baby now, Terry!" he explained.

"I think its time for a pecon," was about all I could muster.

376

We mulled over the whole process, only it got better after about two of the Basque national beverages. There wasn't much more that either of us could say at that point. The University now had an operating ranch, almost, only no one really realized how you pressed the start button to get the operation rolling. "Well, I know it's all up to you. The rest of the faculty would winter kill out there. I don't think Bohmont and Ely really understand what you, and ultimately, they, are going to be up against. But in time, it will all get figured out," Pete lamented. We just bull shitted about life in general for a bit, but I had the feeling there was something fairly important that Pete wanted to tell me.

And it finally came out. "You know ever since Dad had that heart attack last year, he just hasn't been doing very well. In fact, he has never gotten over the loss of Mom, and I suppose I won't either for that matter. Anyway, Dad has been wanting me to come back to the ranch, and I guess he really needs me. He has plenty of help, but the constant war with the BLM is getting him down. We're just about out of the sheep business, and now we are down to less than four hundred cows. He's just worn out, completely. So, I have made a firm decision. I am going to give the University a sixty-day notice, really till July 31; I have enough leave to make up the rest. But then I am gone - back to the ranch."

I sat there in stunned silence, not really knowing what to say. I had become so used to Pete being involved in everything that I did, I guess I just assumed that he would be there forever. Now starting this damned ranch business, and not having Pete just blew my mind. "What the hell am I going to do? You're my ace in the hole. I knew I could run that place, it went without saying that I had your expertise behind me. Christ, now I'll probably really screw up, and it will be all your fault!"

Pete laughed, "You will do just as well without my help. You got this ranching business just about figured out. You will make some mistakes, all of us do, but in Grass Valley, probably no one but you will ever know a mistake was made. The trick is never making the same mistake twice. Now ever since we were graduate students, I have watched you, and you have made some mistakes, but I have never seen you make the same one twice. I got all the confidence in the world. And I'll bet you right now that God forsaken piece of real estate will be a show place within ten years."

I didn't need picons to build self confidence, and deep down I knew Pete was right. "Well, just make sure you are by your phone every night, because I believe there are still a few things that I have got to learn," I muttered as we finished our last one.

Early the next morning I had a general meeting of all my graduate students, as well as the lab help. All told I had five graduate students on assistantships, three more just working towards a degree on their own, and three lab technicians, all part time students. All these kids had kept well appraised on the situation, and most had indicated more than a willingness to help on the ranch if it came to that. I explained what had transpired the previous day in regard to the bid opening. I tried to explain what probably would happen next, although I wasn't exactly sure myself. I was scheduled to meet with the Dean and Dr. Ely at 9:00 later that morning, and I guessed that I would know more after that. But due to the time constraints, I wanted everyone that I was responsible for to understand that schedules might be changed pretty fast, and pretty dramatically. Furthermore, I let the graduate students know that henceforth, a certain amount of time would be required for "practical experience" at the Gund Ranch, assuming my assumptions became correct.

It was obvious from the onset that nobody was in a good mood. Dr. Ely, normally a very good-natured individual, had the appearance of someone that had just been severely chastised. Pete Test was not smiling. Bohmont was not smiling either, however, his dark glasses hid his eyes, which for my immediate frame of mind was likely a blessing. I positioned myself in a chair closest to the door, Pete and Ely were sitting closer to Bohmont's desk, and he, as usual was sitting behind his desk like the president of a big corporation. My presence was requested at nine, but it was obvious that the meeting had been in progress before my arrival, which did not ease my anxiety.

"Good morning, Professor. We have been exploring possibilities on how to get ourselves out of the jam that you have created," was Bohmont's warm welcome.

I could feel the red going up both sides of my face, as well as the hair on the back of my neck sticking straight out, a sure danger signal. I could have cheerfully torn Bohmont's head off at that point, but I had also learned that the best way to handle the man was to utterly avoid his caustic remarks. "Good morning, Dr. Ely, morning Pete," I cheerfully responded with a casual nod towards Bohmont.

"OK, let's face it, we now own a ranch that we can't get rid of. Terry tells me there are things that must be done shortly to protect the value of the alfalfa fields. I don't know what else must be done in the next few weeks, but whatever it is, it had better not cost money. Terry, before you were gracious enough to honor us with your presence, we went over finances. Here's our problem, it is illegal for the College to spend Hatch funds, or any Federal funds without having previously budgeted for them. Due to the fact that we found out yesterday that we must manage this property, we have little recourse until July 1 to do anything but minimize expenses. Actually, it will be difficult to spend any federal money prior to next November one."

I thought to myself enough is enough. "Well, first I guess I should apologize for missing the first part of your meeting. However, the note Mary delivered to me at five last night was that I was to be in this office at nine this morning, which, according to my watch, I was present at about two minutes before nine. As to the financial crises that "I" have created, I presented an estimated budget last October based on the fact that I never believed for one second that the University could sell this property for anything close to the appraised value. I do not think it is, or was, my responsibility to have created the budget for approval based on what I presented to all of you some nearly six months ago." As I concluded, I suddenly felt sorry for Dr. Ely, because I was sure that now it would all be his fault because he didn't budget for the crises.

Bohmont shot back, "Hope, if you hadn't placed such an absurd value on the gift, we could have sold it yesterday, and not had this problem."

As I said, enough is enough. "You're right, we could have sold it if I had placed a reasonable value on the property, but if we had sold it for the high bid, $325,111, where would we be? Tell me, is $325,111 going to buy the ranch we want? No way, and furthermore, we are never going to buy the ranch we want, it's a political impossibility. Let's face it, the Gund Ranch is as close as we are ever going to come to having a ranch. My suggestion is that we all quit pointing the finger and let's make it work. Either that or let's quit talking about a ranch to begin with. If we can't run this property, how in the hell are we ever going to run a real ranch, because then we would be in front of God and every cattleman in the State of Nevada, and let me assure you, not all of them are supporters."

My little sermon seemed to work. The finger pointing stopped, Bohmont looked at Ely saying, "Ray, Terry's right, let's make it work. You and Pete will have to find whatever it takes in the way of money to keep him going until July 1. From July to October 31, we'll have sufficient state funds. But let's incorporate some of our federal funding after October 31, but now's the time to start planning. Now, I have another meeting to go to, so I'll leave it up to the three of you to make it work. Good luck!"

I had to teach from ten to noon, so we agreed to meet after lunch in Ely's office. At least, I anticipated, this meeting would be minus the cutting remarks. I also knew that Pete and Ray would have to scramble to come up with whatever funding would be required. Clark Torell, who had moved from the Knoll Creek Field Station to the Main Station farm after Jim Hunter's untimely death had long since agreed to help me. Unfortunately, Clark's health wasn't good, so other than moral and psychological help, Clark wasn't going to buck bales of hay, or anything else for that matter. However, between myself and graduate students and other lab help, I felt that I could keep enough people at the ranch to get the irrigating done, and the first cutting of hay put up prior to July one. As I reported this to Ray and Pete, there seemed to be a great sigh of relief.

I guessed the financial status of the college was a mite bit worse than I understood. "I'll need camp rate per diem for three to five people per day until June 30. I'll need about nine thousand gallons of diesel. I'll need two used pick-ups from surplus. I'll need a six by six flat bed that's at surplus. I'll need a pull behind two-wire baler, a swather, a truck-mounted elevator, and a stack elevator. I have enough personal tools, except a welder and an oxy-acetylene torch to get by for the time being. All that adds up to about $16,000. I'll probably need another four or five thousand more to service everything properly, as well as make the main house usable as a camp. Better make it $20,000 to be safe." The euphoria that had been created by my assessment of labor rapidly vanished by the mention of $20,000.

But Pete knew the budgets, and he definitely knew where the money was, "You have over $50,000 in your general research budget that you have built up from all of your commercial grants. Would you object if we borrowed that money to run on between from now until July 1? Frankly, there's not that much money available from the rest of the College put together."

I thought to myself, oh now I see, this God damned ranch was my fault to begin with, now I get to finance it as well, but as usual I thought better. I trusted Ray, as I knew him to be a very honest individual. One glance at him was enough, "Sure, what choice do we have, go ahead and transfer the money, but I should make you guys sign a personal note just to make sure it transferred back about July 2!" A few nervous chuckles ended the meeting.

After his tenure at Caliente tending Bohman's cattle near the Test Site, Charles Speth returned to Reno and completed his Masters Degree. As I was elevated from the position of being in charge of the lab to an Assistant Professorship, Charlie was hired into a technical position that was created from the funds from my previous position. Charlie had no designs on obtaining a Ph.D., he was totally happy just working for the Department, doing mostly nutrition research, primarily directed by Bohman. However, over the years he had become increasingly interested in what I was doing, and because of my work being the primary source of any available funding, he had worked ever closer with my efforts, including teaching. So, for the remainder of the week, it was agreed that Charlie would take over the teaching responsibilities of my three classes. And I was off to the Gund Ranch.

Mr. Dilbeck had wanted to go back to his home in Chico, California as of April 1, so as he left, I arrived. I had previously brought out a refrigerator for Mr. Dilbeck, the rest of the kitchen requirements, primarily a propane stove, were already in place. But on this trip I also brought a ton of used kitchenware, pots, pans, iron ware, plates, cups, glasses, silverware, and as much food as I could imagine. I figured we needed enough to cover anywhere from three to five people, and I wasn't the kind that liked to do without. After laying everything away I turned my attention to the Wittie, because electricity seemed a good place to start. It was nearly sundown when my service was complete, and I restarted the monstrous single cylinder machine by slowly spinning the gigantic flywheels. Throwing the decompression lever made the machine fire on the first turn and she never missed thereafter. The house was warm, but the night was beginning to cool, so with a gentle turn of the main valve, the radiators throughout the house immediately responded to the surge of hot water. I cooked a big "T" bone steak in butter, made a salad to go with refried beans and French bread. But first I made a bourbon and water.

After dinner and dishes, I adjourned to the front porch with a hot cup of freshly brewed coffee. There wasn't a cloud in the sky, the moon had yet to put in an appearance, but countless millions of stars twinkled, some so close it seemed as though you could reach out and touch them. As I sat there, my first real night at the Gund, a thousand thoughts went through my brain. Was I really doing the best thing, probably not, not at least for myself if that was my number one priority. But I truly believed that the very way of livestock production, not only in the Great Basin, but throughout the west, would be in jeopardy during the coming years. And if institutions like the University of Nevada didn't step forward and prove beyond a doubt that livestock grazing of the federal lands was not only good from an overall economic standpoint, but was equally important, perhaps even more so, from an ecological standpoint, then I, and much less the university, had failed the people it was supposed to be serving. The more I thought about this concept, the more I realized that regardless of the obstacles, I must never fail.

As I sat there, my thoughts turned to Grass Valley. From the porch, almost the entire Valley could be seen, at least in the day. Tonight, all I could see was blackness. Then it occurred to me, not a single light, as far to the north as I could see, as far to the south, and straight to the west, clear across the flat to the tips of the North Shoshone Range, probably an area of well over a quarter of a million acres, and not one other living soul other than myself. I had enjoyed solitude on many occasions, but usually only for brief periods. But here, in the middle of Grass Valley, the solitude was almost overwhelming. As I sat there almost becoming intoxicated by the moment, the solitude was broken briefly by the distant howling of a coyote, in turn to be answered by another. It was their valley too, and perhaps tonight they were passing messages back and forth as to the newcomer. I supposed they were wondering if I would be good to them, and likewise I was wondering if they would be good to me once we had cattle here. But that would be another day. As I sat there listening to their gossip, my thoughts drifted back to that day long ago on the Test Site, when Treadwell and I locked horns. I remembered that lone coyote casually strolling across the playa as Treadwell and I stood toe to toe with so much emotion, apprehension, even hate radiating between us. I didn't think of the Test Site much anymore, but I had kept track of my friends there. And predictably, one by one they had died, always from cancer. I thought of those unnamed people that had been forced to face squarely at the above ground event, and what that had undoubtedly done to their lives. I guess a lot of what drove me was the haunting thoughts from that experience. I wondered how many of them would have cherished a moment like I was now enjoying. Sometimes I felt guilty for having even survived the Test Site, sometimes I felt guilty for not having done more about it. As I sat there that night I thought at least if I can make this place work, I'll make it a tribute to you, all of you, whoever and wherever you are, for what we did to you.

Jim was out early the next morning with a pick-up and trailer load of goodies. He had scrounged several beds, a sofa and chairs for the front room, table and chairs for the kitchen, as well as a ton of supplies for the motors. It was my goal to have the two big diesels serviced and running by nightfall, and we did. We changed oil, oil filters, fuel filters, as well as serviced air filters, greased all drive lines. Amazingly enough the batteries which had been stored at the headquarters were still usable. We had to jump from both pick-ups to get the critters started, but the generators were working, so it didn't take long for the batteries to be charged. I was amazed at the amount of water pumped from either well. At Allen's, we just let the water run down the main ditch, but after an hour or two, a meadow below the alfalfa fields was pretty wet. At Cold springs, we let the water run out the end of the main line, again onto a meadow. By sundown, we shut everything down, but I was satisfied that the diesels were in good working order. We both joked over the looks on Ray and Pete's face if we had to report that a Jimmy diesel, worth several thousand dollars, was shot, but that was not to be the case.

Jim had planned to return to Reno, but on my promise to cook and share my whiskey, as well as a trip to the hot pond he rapidly rescinded. And that night I learned one of the real joys of Grass Valley, the old Wallti Hot Pond. Lying there in chest deep water, as warm, if not warmer than a bathtub, it didn't take long for the pains of the day to evaporate. The stars of the night before were big, but lying there in the pond looking straight up at God's universe was a sight I would not soon forget. Of course, an occasional swig on my rapidly diminishing bottle of whiskey didn't make the stars any smaller.

The next morning Jim was off, and I set to work to build a meadow drag. Fortunately, Jim had also brought out a small electric arc welder and an oxy-acetylene outfit. There was plenty of scrap between what was at the headquarters and the nearby century old bone pile, so it didn't take me long to have a drag laid out ready for welding. The welder required 220 volts, which the Wittie could put out, and the shop was wired for 220. However, as I struck my first arc, the old Wittie belched black smoke and made a sound akin to what I thought must be an elephant fart. But it didn't quit, and I soon learned to strike my arc carefully and make it count. Repeated striking's would make the Wittie dance like it was close to its end, and I didn't want to imagine the look on my leader's face if I blew that machine up. In fact, I had already learned that single cylinder Wittie's were at a premium, basically no longer available and even some of the parts were becoming scarce. So the Wittie had to be protected at all costs. I well imagined in due time a larger generator would be required, but for the time being this was it.

By nightfall I had a drag constructed and ready for my first flight the next morning.

It was my plan to service the most usable Alice early in the morning, hook up the drag and head for Allen's. It was about ten when I hit the Allen turnoff from the main Grass Valley Road. Suddenly I noticed a pick-up heading at me from the north, the first vehicle that I had seen in four days, other than my own and Jim's. It was Walt Bauman from the McClusky Ranch. Walt had a grin from ear to ear as he pulled up alongside the Alice. "Hi neighbor, been meaning to come down all week, as I heard you were here. Looks like you are starting spring farming." I was a little embarrassed, as somehow it seemed that a Ph.D. from the University ought to be driving a bit more sophisticated tractor and drag than a 1946 model with a home built drag, but somehow I knew Walt would understand, and probably in his eyes I ought to get credit for doing exactly what I was doing. "Say, how in the hell you getting back to the ranch, once you get down to Allen's?" he quizzed.

"Well, I guessed I was just going to head back cross country. Don't guess it's more than three or four miles," I answered.

"Tell you what, I got to drop some salt to those cows up north. It will take me maybe 45 minutes, I'll come down and take you back to the ranch, your pick-up must be there?" That sounded good to me, so I headed down the Allen road, and was soon on the first field. All the fields had been heavily grazed the previous fall by the Gund cattle, so there was plenty of manure to level out along with the occasional gopher and squirrel mound. The drag worked perfectly, but the old Alice could only pull it in low, so I figured my speed and drag width would account for only about three acres an hour. Between the alfalfa fields and the meadows, it looked like Alice would be working hard for the next three weeks.

I hadn't made more than a few passes around the first field when Walt showed up. "Say, it's about dinner time, why don't you ride up to the house with me and eat with us. Soon as we are done, I'll run you back to the ranch, guess no one will miss you." I had to laugh, nope, no one will miss me, not today anyway, besides I had already heard that a lunch, or dinner as Walt described it, prepared by Jeanette was well worth the effort to get there. And I had been told right. Stew, salad, homemade bread, followed by homemade pie put me into a frame of mind to spend the rest of the afternoon in the hot pond. "Say, I hope you wont mind if Walt and I occasionally use the hot pond?" Jeanette asked. Being as I was in charge, and I had just consumed as good of a home cooked meal that I had ever tasted it didn't seem too unreasonable to let the Bauman's use the hot pond whenever they wanted to.

"Nope, help yourself. We'll be having some young bucks out as of tomorrow, and they probably won't be bothering with clothes, so just knock first," was my answer.

Jeanette laughed and had to admit that over the years they had mistakenly barged in more than once when not everyone was properly clothed. "Yup, saw George Gund himself once, buck naked," she continued.

"I had to kid Jeanette, that was the most expensive bare ass she will ever see," Walt added. I could tell I was going to like my neighbors. After "dinner", even though I didn't feel like it I drug fields until dark. And after Jeanette's "dinner", I really didn't want much for supper, just a sandwich, no hot pond, no star gazing, just straight to bed.

Clark was to bring two of the graduate students out Sunday, and after I showed them the ropes I was heading back to Reno. And, right on schedule Clark and his entourage arrived at the headquarters, one o'clock sharp. John O'Brien was an outstanding grad student from Davis, and Harvey Elg, although pursuing a more moderate approach for academic excellence, had graduated from Chico State. John was a city boy from California, and Harvey had been raised around Susanville. However, even in his wildest dreams, Harvey had never seen anything like Grass Valley, nor needless to say had John. Clark's first comment on arrival was, "I'll have to keep a close eye on these lads once you're gone. Looks like, by the glazed stare on their eyeballs, that left unattended they could wander off and get lost in this wilderness." I had to laugh, be pretty hard to get lost in Grass Valley, but the look on their faces told it all. The vastness was, simply put, totally overwhelming. By three I had Clark and his boys pretty well outlined for the week. It was 225 miles back to Reno, the first 50 by dirt road. But in 1972, Nevada had yet to succumb to the modern philosophy of a speed limit. So, in daylight I could make Reno in three hours. Nighttime travel had already taught me that anything over sixty was tempting fate, as well as the lives of more than a few cows and mustangs.

My first stop Monday after lectures was a meeting with Ray Ely and Pete Test. "OK, we got everything going pretty good right now. I'll have the sprinkler lines functional by this time next week. Start irrigating by May 1. Right now, it doesn't look like runoff from the mountain canyons will be an option this year, just been too dry. But we'll still have some good pasture. I am guessing that we can put up about 500 tons of hay. That should be enough for 250 head of cattle through the winter. I would suggest that we take in some pasture cattle this summer. I think we could pasture around 400 steers on the deeded land, the meadows, and the hay aftermath this fall. I think I could get about $8 per month, that seems to be the going rate. We'll just take non-use on the BLM permit. Between surplus heifers from here and Knoll Creek, there should be around 100 head that could be transferred there this fall. I don't know if there would be another 150 cows available or not, but whatever we have, I would suggest get transferred out there, so that we can get a cow herd started." Both Pete and Ray seemed in agreement.

Pete had already figured out that the pasture cattle could generate nearly $20,000, and that put a smile on his greedy face. "Maybe we could sell some of the hay, right now its bringing $60 per ton. You're going to put up $30,000 of hay according to your figures," he continued.

"Who, selling alfalfa hay in Grass Valley is not an option! You would never get a trucker back for the second trip; the road is just too rough and rocky. It's going to be tough enough just getting cattle in and out until something can be done about the road," I cautioned. "Right now, we had better start planning on what goes into effect as of July 1", I continued.

Ely gave a large sigh, looked at Pete, then said, "Your right, lets get it down on paper so Bohmont can't chew our ass like he did last week."

I thought to myself that I was the only one that continually got the ass chewing, but the look on Ray's face suggested the favor evidently got passed around. "Here's what I think we will need; a full-time position for a manager, enough part-time funds so that I can hire at least three students for the summer. Jim Lingenfelter has already located the haying equipment that we'll need for this year, all used, and all together won't cost over $7,500. But that place will have to have a decent diesel tractor, about 75-horse power variety, and four-wheel drive. And we have got to have some kind of a cat dozer and a road grader. Jim can locate all of that through surplus properties. I don't think it's reasonable for the University to have employees in Grass Valley during the winter months and not have heavy equipment available for snow removal. Historically, on more than one occasion, that place has had over five feet of snow on the ground for more than a few days."

I could tell by their expression I had better slow down. I was pretty sure that I was projecting expenses a lot faster than they could find the money. "OK, I agree on your labor and equipment needs. But for the time being I need two projections from you so that I can keep your

389

friend, Dale, satisfied. First, I need to know what kind of gross income this place will produce when it is in full production and when will that occur, and secondly, when can the staff start doing research there?" Ray asked.

My friend? I could have made a comment on that suggestion but thought better. "OK, let's just start as of July 1, this year, 1972. Give me five years, and I will have a herd of 550 cows. I think without some major breakthroughs, that's about all that we can expect. Right now, our economist tells me that the statewide average gross income from a beef cow is $400 per year, probably $350 in central Nevada. I think we should be able to beat averages but let's hang our hat on $350 for the time being. But for 550 cows, that amounts to over $190,000 of income annually. But I'll tell you right now at the Gund Ranch, if that figure is to be obtained, we'll have to produce considerably more hay than is possible right now. But the potential is certainly there to accomplish that. As to research, the potential is there right now. Certainly, it's there for range research. I would like to get a better handle on water and forage production before I commit to hay and pasture research. Livestock research, other than general comparisons such as breed and cross breed comparisons, etc. had better wait until we have a real herd. That's about as close as I can come to answering your questions right now."

I could tell Pete liked the $190,000 figure. "You know, this place could almost carry itself once it's in full production. Considering the diesel requirements, labor, and everything else Terry has described, I believe $190,000 will almost cover it. Hell, that's a thousand times better than we do on any of our other field stations," Pete summarized.

I cautioned, "The trick at the Gund is to keep things in just that perspective. If you ever let this become like your other field stations, it will eat this college alive, financially. Everything this administration does in regard to the Gund has to be predicated on the assumption that this is an operating ranch, where research and demonstration can be accomplished, as long as it doesn't interfere with the operation." For the rest of the afternoon, the three of us finalized an operating budget for fiscal year 1972-73. I was satisfied that it would cover our needs, allow the ranch to gradually get back into production, and ultimately not show such a negative cash flow as to cause undue criticism from throughout the faculty. One thing about a land grant university, there are no secrets. I was sure the ranch budget would be scrutinized by each and every professor. And I was equally sure that the vast majority of them would fully believe that my efforts were being funded at their expense.

By weeks end I was back in the Gund. Clark and the graduate students were headed back to Reno and had accomplished dragging all the fields at Allen's and were started at Cold Springs. My goal by Sunday night was to have the three-wheel lines in place, straight and tested for leaks or other problems. And again, I was on my own for the weekend, the girls were too busy with school activities to come with me, besides, I had made arrangements with Speth to again teach my classes through Wednesday. And by Sunday night I had the wheel lines ready to begin irrigation. Some sprinklers were missing or broken, but some spares had been left in the shop from the previous operation.

Clark was back on Sunday night, bringing a new graduate student of mine, John Coote. Coote had graduated from my old alma mater, Cal Poly, but as of yet hadn't adapted to graduate work. I was reluctant to allow John to work on the ranch, I was keeping this as an award for being good students and John hadn't shown that capacity yet. But, hopefully, a few days of fresh air in central Nevada would cause him to excel academically. Monday morning, we headed John towards the Alice and her obedient drag. John groaned when he saw the size of the meadows below the Cold Springs alfalfa field, and he became even more discouraged when he realized that the old AC would only pull the drag about as fast as he could walk. "Don't worry, you got enough gas to last

391

all day, and as you go round and round you can memorize last weeks lectures in your head", was my cheerful farewell as Clark and I headed to Allen's to burn ditches.

It was hard work, mostly from sun-up to sundown, thankfully only about 12 hours in April, but by the time I left on Wednesday, Allen's was ready to start irrigation, and John had the meadows drug and was started on the Cold Springs alfalfa.

I had started worrying about places to live. We were scheduled to hire a manager as of July 1, and the only livable place was the main house, and we were all camped there right now. A small room existed on the end of the shop, and I reckoned it would hold at least two bunks. Meanwhile, Jim Lingenfelter had procured, by means unknown to me, a small camp trailer, with at least a self-contained kitchen.

I had been eyeing the old High Place that Rich Dilbeck had shown to me on my first visit. Although dirty, I reckoned that it would serve me in the coming year as my "home away from home". Lloyd High had done a good job when he built his house after World War I, probably around 1919 or 1920. Although it had only one room, with a lean too structure on the back, it was tight. The walls were built of native stone, some cut for square corners. The floor was built about six inches off the ground with rough-hewn two by 12 lumber. The windows were all intact as well as both the front and back doors. The ceiling was non-existent. Open beams allowed access clear to the roof, made of old-fashioned corrugated iron. Some kind sole had long since piped in warm water from a nearby hot spring. Additionally, a small gas range still existed, and best of all, in the lean too on the backside stood a gas refrigerator, all in working order. And to top it all off, attached to the open ceiling joists was a gas line servicing three gas operated ceiling lights. And if all of that wasn't enough, an old Montgomery Ward wood burning stove stood by the main entrance door. I had found an old double bed frame at the main house that I confiscated, so in reality, all I needed to make my new house was a mattress, kitchen table, chairs and a few utensils, pots and pans. The High Place even had the remnants of a lawn around it, and I guessed with a little sprinkler I ought to be able to not only have a lawn, but flowers and a garden as well. Home Sweet Home.

I had conned Jan and the girls to accompany me during my next weekend trip on the basis that we were going to make the High Place livable for all. So, with a pick-up loaded with wives and daughters, and a small trailer with mattresses, plywood, tables and chairs, kitchenware, cleaning equipment and a bundle of energy we all arrived. The first order was to douche the entire place out. I rigged up a hose off of the line servicing the sink, and started to wash down the inside, from top to bottom. Swabbing the floor was not too difficult, as the excess water just went down through the cracks between the planks. Between Ajax, detergent and a variety of cleaners, years and years of grime gradually disappeared. By noon, the place was presentable, but we opted to have a snack lunch under the nearby cottonwoods. It wasn't long before our youngest daughter, Tina, ventured back into the house. Shortly, the peace and tranquility of Grass Valley was broken by an ungodly scream emitting from our new quarters. As we ran through the door, Tina was exiting in a fashion that knocked several of us down.

She was near hysterical but did manage to blurt out something that sounded like there was a boa constrictor in our new home. Sure enough, once inside, there for all of us to see was not a boa constrictor, but an uncommonly large Nevada bull snake, I guessed about the four to five foot variety. He was casually draped over one of the rafters, his head hanging down about six inches, beady eyes glaring at whoever had the nerve to disrupt him from his home. I could see how Tina, all 3'9" of her, might have mistaken the critter for a boa constrictor. Between a shovel and broom, I gradually coaxed him to the floor and out the back door. "Aren't you going to kill him," Jan asked with eyes almost as large as Tina's. "Nope, he's our friend, probably lives in those rock walls. As long as he's around there sure won't be any rattlers, much less pack rats," as he slithered off into the nearby sage. It took awhile to convince everybody that the high Place was indeed livable, but I was thankful that if old King Boa did have a mate, at least it had decided not to show up that day.

By nightfall we had the place livable, a double bed in one corner, a couch along side one wall that made into a double bed, kitchen table in place with four chairs, frying pans hanging above the sink, a cupboard full of china, another cupboard full of canned goods, and spices, the refrigerator stocked. And most especially, I had worked two sheets of plywood onto the rafters at the north end of the place to act as a loft for the girls sleeping quarters. A rapidly built ladder, consisting of two 2 X 4' uprights, with steps made of attached 2 X 4's, serviced the area. An upstairs window existed on the north side of the building, situated so that as the girls went to sleep, they could view the landscape to the north.

That night we had steak, beans, salad, French bread and a special cake that Jan had made for the occasion. And Jan and I celebrated with a glass of wine. Before going to bed I cautioned the girls not to be nervous if they saw moving lights in the distant Saw Tooth range at the north end of the valley. Legend had it that the ghost of an old miner still prospected the Saw Tooth's at night, with the aid of his lantern. Sure enough at about eleven, long after we had all gone to sleep, another scream split the peacefulness of the night; "There it is, I see it, you see it Tina, you see it Linda, look its moving again," shouted Lisa. As I drifted back to sleep again, I began to realize that Grass Valley would leave its imprint on all of us in many, many different ways.

Between myself, Clark and the graduate student brigade, we had a hay crop in place by the middle of May. I had my old buddy, Dave Mathis, draw up a brochure advertising the luxurious life at the Gund. He titled it "Summer Excitement, Fun and Sun at the Gund". Dave was an excellent artist; he had drawn a shapely young cowgirl standing under a beach umbrella offering a large soda to a stout young lad attempting to dig a fence posthole. Copies were run off and placed at appropriate places around campus. I soon had more takers than spots, but at least summer help didn't seem to be too much of a problem. A young student, by the name of Charlie Watson, that already had one degree, but was wanting more approached me about both he and his girlfriend coming out for the summer. He suggested that she could cook for the crew if they could live in the main house. The fact that they weren't married didn't bother me too much anymore. After all I had survived the University throughout the decade of the sixty's and had seen just about everything imaginable already. So a little cohabitation between agreeing parties didn't faze me a bit. We had made arrangements to provide a camping per diem rate for the students, so by paying that to Charlie's girlfriend so that she could buy and prepare food it would work, besides she could make a bit of money herself. I did think that it might cause some explaining to Bohmont, but until he knew, the actual truth wouldn't hurt him one bit, besides my summer crew would have meals!

By June one we had Charlie, his live in, and five stout young lads prepared to tackle the haying and irrigation, and the graduate brigade could go back to being graduate students for the time being. Lingenfelter had acquired a used twelve-foot swather, and an old pull behind a two-wire baler. True to his word, he also acquired the six X six flat bed truck from surplus, a side mounted hay elevator, as well as a regular stack elevator. Clark had constructed a slip to pull behind one of the old Alice tractors. With a new sickle, and several spares, the swather was also ready. And, on June fifteenth we started cutting hay.

It didn't take me long to realize that at nearly 6,000 feet elevation, and very cool nights alfalfa windrows don't dry very fast. Fortunately, in the historic ranch "bone pile" most of an old pull behind rake existed. With a bit of work, it was soon functional, so each window was turned about a half a turn, and twenty-four hours later they were just right for baling. The first day I wanted to bale during daylight hours so that I could clearly see what might go wrong. The baler was about as cantankerous as you could imagine, but with patience it would work, only occasionally missing a knot. Unfortunately, I was about the only one that had the patience to put up with the beast. Amazingly enough, little, other than the occasional missed knot, went wrong. The only problem was that you just couldn't force much hay through the machine, or it would jam. The two wire bales weighed about 70 pounds. I could kick out a bale about every 30 seconds, which amounted to about four tons per hour at best. I could see that the better part of this summer was going to be spent pulling this old international baler, so I had better get used to the thump, thump, thump constant thump!

With a little experimenting, we soon learned that we could slip about a ton per load, while the six X six was good for about two tons per load. Hauling hay kept four lads pretty busy, one driving, one stacking. Each crew stacked the hay when they reached the stack. The truck with the side mounted elevator worked like a charm, but the slip was a hoot. It took a lot of practice between the driver and stacker, but just as the stacker set his hooks in a bale, we soon found that a bit of extra throttle at just the right time helped the stacker swing the bale on to the slip. Too many throttles, or a heavy wet bale, usually resulted in the stacker laying flat on the ground, still attached to his hooks while the old Alice and driver went merrily on their way.

Bohmont hadn't made up his mind if we should stock the ranch at this time or not, but I had. I had searched for someone with enough stocker cattle to harvest all of the deeded land, including the meadows, as well as possibly the hay field aftermath during the coming fall. Bohmont was talking about selling the hay, but I knew we could never get a hay hauler back to Grass Valley a second time, and Lingenfelter flat said he wouldn't do it. So, I had convinced Clark Torell to hide every available female animal at the Main Station, based on the assumption

Bohmont would finally see things my way and we would have cattle at the Gund this coming fall.

We did find stocker cattle, but it didn't quite work out the way I planned. There just weren't a lot of stocker cattle available in the fall of 1972, besides, anyone knowledgeable about Nevada didn't seem to readily see the advantages of summering a bunch of yearling cattle in Grass Valley. But it didn't take me long to find cattle. Through the "grapevine" I heard about a professor at Berkley that had wanted to get into the cattle business and was looking for good Nevada pasture. It didn't take me long to have the good Dr. Jason Donaldson on the phone. It turned out that Donaldson was some kind of a political scientist at Berkley. It didn't occur to me then that being a political scientist at Berkley was a long way from being a successful cattleman in Nevada, but in hindsight I freely admit that it should have caused me some concern. However right then I needed cattle, and Donaldson was about the only source that I had found. The fact that he agreed to the then exorbitant price of $9 per head per month might have been further proof that he was more into Berkley academics than cattle, but I was already counting the money. I told him that we could handle at least 400 yearlings under fence, but he could only come up with around 350 head. They were to be all yearling steers, properly branded and straight down from Montana. I was pretty insistent on northern cattle, as I had long since learned that it's always safer to move cattle south, never north, unless you enjoy doctoring cattle. Everything else seemed in agreement, including the $1,575.00 advance check on deposit representing half of June's grazing fee. Cattle were to be received between May 30 and June 2.

And, right on schedule, four semi's each carrying 85 to 90 five weight calves arrived on June 1. We were well set up to receive cattle. The loading chute was old, but sturdy. From the chute, the caves were to go into the main pen which held the largest water trough at the headquarters. I reasoned that the cattle had likely offloaded around

Ogden the night before and would have been on the trucks ever since and would be pretty thirsty. Well, at least in hindsight I was right on that point!

As the first rig pulled up to the chute, I noticed that the driver was wearing dark glasses, and seemed to have a bit of trouble landing his rig. After he finally got it in place and stepped out, I distinctly noticed the aroma of whiskey. I didn't say anything, as it was obvious that his mood seemed a bit bent towards the bad side. "God damned road, this is the worst hell hole I ever been in my entire life. Probably half of these crazy ass Mexican steers got broken legs," he growled at me as he began to open the trailer door.

I kind of let the "Mexican steer" bit go right by me, chalking it up to a driver that hadn't wanted to go down a 50-mile dirt road, full of alkali pits, rocks and other assorted obstacles. And the whiskey breath? Well, let it slide for the time being so let's get these steers unloaded. I was positioned between the truck and the chute, making sure the chute doors stayed in place, so I couldn't really look at the steers as they came out. Besides, protocol is such that the driver is always responsible for unloading his rig, compartment by compartment. But I could see enough of the critters as they flashed by, and they didn't look exactly like my version of a Montana steer, or what I had perceived they should look like.

It didn't take long to unload each truck, in fact probably 45 minutes after they arrived, we had 350 steers in the corral. I still hadn't taken good luck, I seemed to be more interested in the condition of the drivers. They all had dark glasses, they all smelled of whiskey, and they all looked hung over. "You boys look like you had a tough night, where in the hell in Utah did you find booze?" I casually asked.

"Utah, we weren't in Utah. Me and the boys hit Vegas about ten last night, no place to unload, so we just shut things down for about four hours and had a few drinks, let the calves stand. It had been a long haul from El Paso, besides we had to wait there about six hours, because where we picked these calves up, they hadn't finished branding yet."

I never said a word, just stood there and looked at this yard bird. Montana steers, my ass. These calves probably just came out of old Mexico, crossed the border somehow at El Paso, went through some kind of a brokerage yard, branded to Donaldson's specifications, sent straight to Nevada, nonstop, except for a short driver R and R stop in Vegas. Well, there wasn't much I could do then, except get these drivers out of my sight before I lost what was left of my fragmented temper!

As the trucks pulled out, one of my lads yelled, "Hey, the steers just broke down the corral looking for water." Sure enough, they had drunk the main trough dry, which was fed by a line only delivering a slow trickle. My guess was that about half never got a drink, and they were starting to have that crazed look that only water-deprived cattle have. "Christ, don't let them get out. They will go clear to the Rio Grande looking for water before they stop," I yelled. Fortunately, there was an irrigation ditch that came from the hot pond and ran alongside of the corral. It didn't take but a few minutes and we had it diverted directly through the corral. The water was still warm, but drinkable, albeit a bit muddy. But for Mexican steers, water's water, they weren't likely to complain about the mud. Then I noticed something unique. In addition to Donaldson's new brand, backwards D Bar on the left ribs, there was a multitude of other brands, some on the hips, some of the ribs, some on the left, some on the right, not too many that were similar. It began to dawn on me that Professor Donaldson didn't know much about cattle, and that some slick talking cattle dealer had unloaded on him, big time. It wouldn't even have surprised me if the cattle were hot.

Ron Torell, Clark's son had just come to work a few days before on our summer "Fun in the Sun" campaign, looked at me and said, "I think we have got problems boss."

399

"No shit", I responded, "All the way from El Paso. Branded, loaded, driven for probably 36 hours, no feed, no water, it's a wonder any of them are alive. I guarantee you, we will have a shipping fever break within two to five days, so get ready."

But right then I was headed for the phone and aiming to give Professor Donaldson a piece of my mind. And strangely enough, I was able to ring right through to his office on the Berkley campus. It was one of those conversations that I would never forget.

I started by saying that we had taken delivery of exactly 350 head, we counted them off the trucks, and we all agreed, 350 steers. Then I enquired as to where these calves came from.

"Well, out of New Mexico. The buyer I have been working with indicated that he was having some trouble coming up with a uniform group of 350 steers but felt that he found just the right set of calves down New Mexico way, somewhere.

"I thought you said they were coming from Montana?"

"Well, I said that was maybe my first choice, but we just couldn't find what we wanted."

"I thought we discussed why I wanted these calves to come from up north. I think I remember talking about stress, sickness, shipping fever, things like that."

"Oh that, that wasn't important. My man assured me that these calves from New Mexico will do fantastic on Nevada grass, probable gain two, maybe even two and a half pounds per day all summer, likely even into fall."

"Oh, I see. Well, I guess your "man" must be pretty knowledgeable about Nevada grass."

"You bet; I trust him explicitly. This is the first time I have ever dealt with Raul, but it's easy to see he is a man of integrity. Assured me these would be a uniform group, all from the same ranch, all similar. How do they look?"

"Like a piece of Mexican shit. These cattle are from south of the border, probably from all over Sonora. They were worked in El Paso, loaded on trucks for a straight through haul, only problem, your drivers stopped in Vegas for a little relaxation. When we unloaded, your steers were so thirsty they tore down half my corrals. I doubt that your "man" explained what a shipping fever break can be, but it will be a miracle if you can avoid that. Now, without going back and reading the fine print of our contract, I am informing you that you have two immediate choices. First remove these cattle from the Gund Ranch within 48 hours, or secondarily, all health-related topics in the contract are henceforth null and void. I will immediately purchase the necessary drugs at your expense. No amount of loss will be our responsibility; all provisions concerning death loss are null and void. In other words, your cattle are here, plain and simple, and at nine dollars per head per month. We will charge you for all drugs; time spent doctoring and any other health related expenses. By the way, as soon as I hang up, I will type a letter to cover these points, and it will be hand delivered to the University lawyer by me tomorrow morning."

Donaldson had been trying to interrupt me during my statement, but to no avail. "Now see here Hope, you are not dealing with just anybody. I am a professor, full professor at that, at Berkley. I will not tolerate being treated in this manor. I think you are trying to hoodwink me, probably to cover up for your own ineptness. What did you do, lease out the good pasture to somebody else, now you are trying to put mine on something less than good, probably outside on the BLM?"

"First of all, Donaldson, I am a professor too, in fact a full professor with tenure for what in ever the hell that means. But you invalidated our contract, because if you carefully read it, you will note that under the heading Source, it specifically states that the cattle must originate from north of the Nevada state line, and they must all wear the same brand at time of purchase by you, unless approved by me before hand. I can assure you that this bunch of long legged, lopped ear cross bred cattle from some place south of the border would never have been approved by me before or after having seen them. Now, as the contract states, payment will be within ten working days of the mailing of the monthly bill. At the end of June, I'll mail your first bill. Additionally, it will have an accounting of all veterinary expenses. Furthermore, so that there can be no confusion, I'll send you a picture of each dead calf, as soon as that occurs, along with the severed left ear. I'll forward ears under separate cover. Now sir, I have much to do today if your calves expect to have any grass before sundown. By the looks of their ribs and hollow bellies, I would imagine that's something they haven't seen in about 48 hours or so. Goodbye!"

I never gave Donaldson a chance to respond, my comments were good enough for me. By the time I had hung up and gotten back to the corrals it appeared that the calves had watered up, but they were sure enough bawling for some feed. "Best saddle up two horses, let's move these guys south to the wiener trap at Cold Springs. You will have to go slow, let them eat, don't excite them, whatever else happens. If this bunch of orangutans split, they'll probably just up and head for Sonora," I cautioned the lads. It took a couple of hours, but between all of us we got all 350 into the wiener trap, about five miles south of the headquarters. The wiener trap was solidly built, one of the better things that Al Stenninger had built under his tenure. "We'll hold them in here for two days, plenty of feed and water, hopefully they will calm down. I am going to town tomorrow to get plenty of antibiotics and sulfa, and I probably better see the University lawyer, because I am sure that idiot from Berkley can't believe any of this mess is his fault - but before we are finished, it will be a mess. Two days from now we'll move them back to the pasture by the corral, so that we will be ready to start doctoring calves," I concluded. Everybody agreed that the plan made sense, although besides myself, and possibly Ron, I wasn't quite sure what any of these lads knew about our "mess". Guess they were just trying to make me feel good.

The next morning, about as early as I could get away, I was in Bohmont's office explaining what had happened. "Thought you knew better than to deal with anybody from Berkley," was his comment.

Reminding him that he signed the contract, not me didn't help much. "Well, at least you wrote the contract right. Donaldson doesn't have any wiggle room. The information you have on the trucks, their numbers, etc. should allow us to document they weren't off loaded, so at least if Donaldson wants a war, that part will be with the truck lines," which was about as good a compliment as I could expect today from Bohmont. "I'll take all of this to the lawyer; your notes are good enough to explain everything. I suppose you will be seeing Dr. Drake shortly and heading back?" he questioned.

Dr. Drake was the station vet, having come from private practice in Colorado, dealing primarily with feedlots. And I knew Drake well enough that he would be the best source of help for our pending disaster. "Yup, I am on my way, I want to be back there tonight and watch those babies pretty close for the next few days - see you," as I exited his office.

"How in the hell did you ever get yourself into a pickle like this? I thought the Gund Ranch was going to be used for research or something like that," Drake asked after listening to my story.

I didn't have time to explain the events of the last year, instead I just said, "Look, I am trying to make this place go without any budget or anything else. Sure, I probably made a mistake taking these cattle on, hindsight's awfully good in that regard, but somehow, I have to generate income. And you know what? That's not the first mistake I have made, and I'll bet my bottom dollar it sure in the hell won't be the last! Now, if you have a better idea on how to make this place work, I would love to hear it, in the meantime I need answers, what do I do and how do I best do it? I am very afraid that I am going to have a whole bunch of mighty sick calves in two or three days."

Drake looked at me a bit sheepishly and answered, "Your right, trying to make this ranch go with the support you have from this faculty is a tough job. And you're probably the only one here with guts enough to try the job. We all sit around making fun of you, but I sure don't see any of the rest of us out there trying to make it go, me included."

"Thanks, I appreciate your understanding, but right now I need your best advice," I countered.

"OK, you need at least 500 doses of penicillin, 500 doses of combiotic, and I think five mls of either would be a good dose for this size of calf. You also better get at least 500 boluses of sulfa. And you will need a four cases of electrolyte. It's best to give that intravenously, but it can be injected directly into the peritoneum cavity with a long injection needle. There's not much you can do to prevent the break at this point, if they are going to get it, they already are coming down. In the meantime, keep them calm, keep them on good grass with plenty of fresh water; a running stream is better than a trough. Keep the treated calves separate if possible. The first symptom will be listless calves, slight hump to their back, no appetite. Next, they will get runny eyes, and finally snotty noses. By the time their noses are snotty, they will be pretty sick with elevated temperatures. Treat them daily until they start to improve. My schedule is busy as hell, but I'll do my level best to come out in a few days and help. In the meantime, good luck!"

As I left his office, I looked back and said, "Thanks Doc, I appreciate the advice, and I sure appreciate your understanding."

After a short trip home, I was heading towards Austin. But I had an ice chest full of penicillin and combiotic, a sack full of sulfa boluses, four cases of electrolyte, extra ropes, intravenous infusion apparatuses, peritoneal needles, sacks of disposable syringes and needles, just about anything and everything that I could think of.

And sure, enough just two short days later Ron and I were wondering through the calves, when we both spotted a particularly ugly long legged crossbred steer with a humped back and sort of slobbering from the mouth. And from there it went downhill, fast. For the next three weeks about all we did other than irrigate and put-up hay was treating sick calves. I swear we treated everyone of the 350 head, but the actual number was just about half. Most required two treatments, the bad ones three times or more. And we weren't always successful. Eventually 13 died of the disease, but all things being considered that probably wasn't too bad. As I indicated, the left ear of every dead calf was removed and sent to Donaldson. At first, I usually sent two in each box, directly to his Berkley office, along with a request verifying that he received the box. It didn't take long before he called Bohmont demanding that I quit sending ears, so I did, sort of. From that point I just sent one per box.

It was over by July, in fact once it was over, the calves looked pretty good, and actually appeared to be gaining some weight. Donaldson showed up in mid July, he called and said he was coming, so I made sure I was there. "They look horrible," was about all the good he could say. I inquired if he had seen them before, and of course I knew he had never seen these calves until that day. He didn't want to answer, except to continue to say that based on Raul's description they sure looked horrible. "I don't think we will pay you the full cost of grazing based on the contract. I haven't decided what to deduct, but it will be significant," he added.

We were both leaning on a fence viewing the calves. I never moved a muscle, just continued to look out over the claves, and for a while I just sort of ignored his comment. Finally, I offered, "You might want to reread that contract pretty carefully. You will note under Financial it pretty well spells it out. Payment is due ten days after receipt of the monthly billing. If we haven't received payment by the following first of the month, I have the option of filing an adjuster's line, which allows me, some thirty days later, to begin selling your cattle to satisfy the debt. Furthermore, upon the final day of grazing, when your trucks show up, you will have in my hand a full payment for the last month's grazing charges, including any and all other miscellaneous expenses, before I allow the cattle to be loaded. Now, since you have opted to leave the cattle here initially, and we have successfully doctored all but thirteen, I will live by the exact letter of our mutually signed contract, which means at the earliest possible time, if you miss a payment, renege or anything else, I'll begin to sell these calves, and apply the proceeds to what your debt is. You will also note in the contract that if things get to that point, I have the option to charge for my services in selling your cattle to satisfy the debt. Now being a full professor, with tenure, in good standing at the University of Nevada, you can well imagine that my hourly rate will be fairly high. And I might not sell them real fast." We both continued to stand at the fence staring directly ahead. Finally, Donaldson turned, walked towards his car, climbed in, fired it up and headed south, not in another word, not anything. And that was the last time I ever saw the man.

We kept the calves until mid October. And all the bills were paid on time. His "man" Raul came to supervise the loading, which was just fine with me. Raul was a likable man, always with a smile. He was a half-breed, and I surmised, just as capable of doing business on either side of the border, in Mexican or English. I hadn't counted the calves, just figured there were 337 head, considering that we knew 13 had died. Well, when we loaded, we could only count 335, two pairs of shorts. The calves had gone out once or twice during the summer, but I was pretty sure we had gotten them all back, but apparently, I was wrong. When we finally accepted the fact that we were missing two, I said to Raul, "Well I guess those two hombres must just have gone back to old Sonora, where they came from to begin with." Raul looked at me a bit nervously at first, then just about died laughing. That said it all.

After everything was loaded and the trucks had headed down the valley, I invited Raul down to the High Place for a shot of whiskey. As we touched glasses, Raul said, "You know, I would have treated that son of a bitch a whole lot better than I did, but his arrogance just got to me. He hates Mexicans, when I told him my mother was full blooded Mexican Indian, in fact Apache he just looked down his nose even further. That's when I decided I would get him a set of calves he wouldn't soon forget. I am sorry if it caused you some trouble, but he should stay at Berkley, not in the cattle business."

I had to laugh, "Well you not only taught him a lesson, but we had an iron clad contract, and I didn't give an inch, in fact there is even a clause allowing for 1% loss other than death, so those two missing calves will be his loss, not ours."

"Salute, compadre," Raul held up his glass to me and I did likewise to him. I never saw or heard of Raul after that day, but every time I ran into an arrogant professor, and there sure are plenty, I always thought of him.

That wasn't quite the end of the Donaldson matter, however. After it was all over, he wrote a letter to then Nevada President N. Edd Miller, outlining in some detail just what an unwholesome crook I was. His major thesis seemed to be that he was hopeful that people of my despicable nature were not really representative of people in Nevada, much less professors at Nevada. His final comment seemed to question the wisdom of the University in promoting me to the full professorship level, much less ever granting me tenure and professorship status to begin with. Miller showed me the letter, along with a great deal of laughter. He suggested that my portrait should be hung in the Nevada honor Hall, located in Morrel Hall, with the label, Head Honcho, One Tough Customer. I thanked him but suggested he might hold on to that honor, probably in a few years I might really earn it. He also showed me his response letter to Donaldson, which basically said that he, Miller, would like to have a few more on his staff than had my character. That set pretty well with me. He even sent a copy to Bohmont, and that sat even better.

Fortunately, as August drew to a close and my lads had to head back to school, we also finished the haying. And our final count was nearly 400 tons of good alfalfa in the stack and another 200 tons of grass as well. Not as much as I had hoped for, but probably more than we had any reason whatsoever to expect. I had plenty of other problems, but fortunately, a week before I had paid Bohmont and Ely a panic visit, as some things had to be resolved.

"Look, things are going great at the Gund, putting up lots of hay, the pasture cattle are doing good, and the place looks great, but in a week or two, all my help leaves to go back to school. I have been suggesting that we need a permanent position, probably two. We just can't wait any longer. We can't sell our hay, you will never get a trucker back twice, even Lingenfelter says he won't haul it as his truck and trailer won't last. We're going to have enough hay to winter at least 200 head of cattle. But what's really bothering me is how the hell are we going to finance this whole adventure. We just can't continue indefinitely like we are doing now," I pleaded with the three of them, Bohmont, Ely and Pete Test.

For once Bohmont came to my rescue, "Your right Terry, we have taken your figures and been reworking them. And it looks like your figures are just about right on. I agree we can't sell hay, probably can't even afford to haul it out. So, we'll feed it to cows there. But your right, that takes two full time men. So, we have put together a schedule for hiring, both a foreman, and a support technician. The foreman's position currently pays about $12,000 per year, while a technician's position pays around $10,000. Pete has the exact figures. You can throw in housing and anything else you can get away with except beef. They can have gardens, chickens, we'll provide a milk cow or two, whatever you want. How you get these people is up to you, we have been able to cut through the red tape in that regard, so it will make your life a bit easier. I have talked to Clark, he says you have some females already lined up, we think we can jar loose about a hundred bred females and 50 open heifers, but that will depend somewhat on your friends Bohman and Bailey." I could imagine that whatever those two professors allowed me to take would be at least twelve years old, have broken mouths and caked udders, but beggars can't be too busy.

"The finances?" I asked.

"Yes, we are immediately transferring $50,000 to the Gund account. I have asked Pete to set it up as an enterprise account, money in, money out. We expect you to run a business, and fully realize at first that you will be operating at a negative cash flow. Pete will explain." And Pete explained, "Any purchase over $50 will require a signed purchase order by either Bohmont, Ely or myself. We'll issue you a number over the phone in emergencies up to $1,000. Any purchase over $1,000 will have to be accompanied by a signed purchase order. And of course, for purchases under $50, you can continue to simply use the small purchase order book that you are already authorized to sign. But I noticed a couple of times this summer you used the purchase order book at the same store twice or more on the same day, and it looked like it was for the same item, which suggested to me that you were trying to circumvent the system. I won't tolerate that kind of crap in the future."

Again, Bohmont came to my rescue. "Its OK Pete, I am sure Terry did his best under impossible odds, and I am sure he won't purposefully try to circumvent your system." I could see Pete was boiling, Ely was laughing, and Bohmont was trying to calm everyone down. And I did once or twice circumvent the system, on a Saturday, buying parts in Elko, when I was damn sure that I couldn't have reached anybody in Reno anyway. Then Bohmont concluded, "We understand it's a difficult position that you are in, that's why we are willing to work with you, to do whatever it takes. The system we have outlined is workable, and I am sure you can make it work. But Buddy, let me tell you that if I get wind of you trying to go around us, you'll have to answer me personally!" That final sentence from Bohmont kind of restored my faith in him and the system.

And as luck would have it, it wasn't two days later when Rich Dilbeck called me up. "Hey, I hear all of your college students will be leaving and you will be by yourself again." I agreed but indicated that I now had permission to hire a foreman and a cowboy.

"That's good news for me. I love working for Molly, but I can't stand her husband, Bill. And that's who I really work for. I would sure like to be considered for that opening if possible."

It didn't take me more than a New York second to respond, "Well sure, the jobs yours if a thousand a month sounds OK. You will have all the benefits, health, retirement, and you can have chickens, a garden, we'll provide a milk cow, just no beef, unless of course we accidentally kill one now and then. You got the big house; I'll even spend a little money fixing it up if you want."

410

And just about as quickly Rich responded, "I'll take it and I can be there by September 15. I even know of a damn good hand here that would jump at the other position if that's possible."

"Well let's wait a bit on that, but the jobs yours, I'll make that commitment right now."

Clark and I worked out a schedule so that one or the other of us would be there from the day that the lads headed back to school, until the 15th when Rich was to arrive. But on the last day the students were there, we kind of had a surprise party for everyone at the high Place. Jan had made a big cake that was decorated with barns, farm animals, tractors and everything else imaginable, with "Best Wishes from The Gund" written across the top. Somehow, I had managed to get the cake to Grass Valley without destroying it. We had lots of ice, soda pop, beer and even a shot of whiskey or two. The boys had worked hard, even Charlie and his live in. She had done a good job cooking for the boys, and best of all, everyone had gotten along. I would miss these kids; they never grumbled, worked just about six and one half days a week and did everything they were asked, usually more. We had a good summer, and they all deserved a little bit of fun.

True to his word, Rich was moved in and ready to start work on September 15th. The night before, as the sun was going down, I sat in front of the High Place contemplating just what we had accomplished in one short summer's time, and where it might all go. We had managed to put up the hay, some 600 tons of hay. Despite all the problems, we had grazed nearly 350 yearlings inside all summer, with feed left over, and even took in about $13,000 for our efforts. And now I had a budget that seemed workable, with the opportunity to survive on my own ability. And I had one full-time employee, with the promise of another, which would make my life a lot more enjoyable. But most importantly, the University finally had a ranch, albeit somewhat lacking in certain areas, but with seemingly unlimited potential. The Gund

Ranch was here, and as far as I was concerned, it was going to go a long, long way.

THE GUND RESEARCH AND DEMONSTRATION RANCH

Control over invasive browse plants, such as sagebrush, was established early on at the Gund Research and Demonstration Ranch. Thousands of acres of vegetation were improved for both livestock and wildlife at the Gund utilizing aerial application of the appropriate herbicides.

Cattle – a cow ranch just ain't worth a damn without cattle! And that was my immediate dilemma. Bohmont was understanding, but as he delighted in saying at times like this, "Buddy, it's your problem, you and your friends, Bohman and Bailey will have to solve that one". In a way he was right, Bohman and Bailey had long standing research projects involving mature cows at the Main Station, which was just about the only option available for me. I did have two groups of crossbred heifers involved in a project that Clark Torell and I had been working on, Brown Swiss crossed on Herefords and Red Poll crossed on Herefords. The Red Poll cross would work well at the Gund, but the Brown Swiss would never make it under the harsh conditions that Grass Valley offered. Fortunately, the crossbred heifers had all been bred back to Hereford bulls, so at least they were pregnant.

Lengthy meetings, pleading, almost including bribery hadn't resulted in either Bohman or Bailey releasing any of their cattle to me. And I understood. They had sure things going; about all I represented to them was nothing but a fast talking promoter. In the end, I was able to move 100 crossbred heifers, all bred, about 75 aged Hereford cattle, mostly with broken mouths, and about another 15 head of miscellaneous junk females. About all I could hope to get out of the 50 Brown Swiss crosses and the aged cows were one or two calves at the best. Hopefully the majority would be heifers.

Bohmont did authorize me to buy 10 bulls during the winter months, so that in the upcoming spring breeding season, at least that wouldn't be a problem. I was also able to pick up two old Holstein dairy cows from the University dairy. So, by November 15 Jim Lingenfelter had delivered 187 assorted female cattle to Grass Valley. I was proud to put it mildly, but Dilbeck's only comment was, "These sure don't look like the typical cattle that I have been used to in Grass Valley!" I responded by muttering something about how he didn't understand research yet, and I looked to him to make these animals produce.

At least we had horses. When Rich Dilbeck left to go to work for Molly Knudtsen earlier in the year, he left his three horses at the ranch, and they were there waiting on his return. In the meantime, I had purchased a steady old cow horse, half Thoroughbred, half Quarter horse. He stood tall, maybe nearly 17 hands, but I liked him because he showed me that he could travel, maybe all day and half the night. Somehow, I seemed to think that might be the most important criteria for a horse in the coming years.

Dilbeck kept muttering about how feeding was going to be an awful lot of work for one person, seven days a week. My response was that I would be out every weekend and help, so he and Pam could leave once in a while if they desired. I didn't want to exercise my option of hiring another technician to the first of the year, if possible, so the carrot that I offered Dilbeck was that he could hire the cowboy that he had told me about as of January 1. In the meantime, somehow, I had to squeeze out enough money for some equipment, as I couldn't see going through another summer like the last one as far as hay harvest went.

And with the help of Pete Test and some creative accounting that I never clearly understood we were able to purchase a new 65-horsepower four-wheel drive Massey Ferguson tractor. In addition, I made arrangements to get a Hesston hay stacking system and feeder for delivery prior to next summers haying season. I felt the stack hand system of making a three-ton loaf made more sense for our situation than anything else possible. Additionally, we placed an order for a new 14-foot Hesston diesel swather. The old swather we used for the first year was just about done. We had welded the header up so many times, that it probably was starting to break just because of the welding rod weight! And Jim Lingenfelter, true to his word, obtained an old, but usable cable D-8 caterpillar dozer, as well as a Caterpillar D-12 road grader.

So, I settled into winter, just about fully equipped, and more than enough feed for two hundred head of cattle. We also settled into a routine, where I spent weekends at the ranch, weekdays in Reno, teaching my usual three classes, and trying to keep track of several graduate students. On a lot of weekends Jan and the girls went to the ranch, but their activities were such that as often as not they were too busy. It was a tough schedule, but we had made the commitment to make it work, and it was working.

But just making the ranch work was only the beginning. Nobody else shared my optimism, but I could clearly see why this facility could one day become the major agriculture and environmental research center in the Great Basin. My challenge was how to accomplish that.

"Dean, we got a ranch, but outside of my monies, I haven't seen much enthusiasm being expressed by the faculty to join my parade", I lamented in a winter meeting.

"Well, so far you have told me you are the only one that you will allow out there to do livestock research, so that eliminates Animal Science", Bohmont responded. "Further, you have let it be known that it's too early to consider any kind of irrigated forage research, and I suppose that includes soil work as well. As you have so bluntly put it on several occasions in faculty meetings, you feel the Economists live in an ivory tower, so I don't suppose that they are very enthusiastic about coming to your rescue, so that just leaves range research."

He was right; I probably had cut my throat in regard to most of the faculty. "You know, I just received an evaluation from the USDA concerning USDA agriculture range scientists that are housed here. This evaluation suggests that if we want to keep these scientists, and their budget, in Reno, they need to get more involved in Nevada range research. Maybe you need to take your hat in hand and go see those people. They could sure bring you some instant credibility."

The Agriculture Research Contingent (ARS) of the USDA that was housed on campus was mainly involved in range research. Three scientists headed up that effort, Drs. Evans, Young and Eckert. Eckert

416

was involved in other Nevada projects, so I didn't want to bother him, but I knew Jim Young might just like working at the Gund, and if he had their leader's blessing, Dr. Evans, I just might get lucky. I had known Jim for a few years, as he had got his Ph.D. at Corvallis shortly after I had, and I knew him to be a serious scientist, but totally interested in the ecosystem of the Great Basin. Besides, he was raised on a cow calf ranch in northern California, so I was also pretty sure that he knew something about livestock production.

It didn't take long to schedule a meeting between myself and Evans and Young. They were polite, listened and asked a few questions as I laid out the history of the ranch, at least as I knew it, went over what maps I had been able to put together so far, and summarize about where we were now, after six months of operation.

"What's your budget?" Evans finally inquired. With that I choked a bit, mumbled something about how the place was going to be self sustaining after a year or two, and indicated that for the time being the research funds that went into the operation were mostly from my product testing efforts, as well as one regional range livestock research project that I was head of.

Both responded with some laughter, but finally Young broke the spell, "We were pretty sure that was about how the situation was. The rumors we have been hearing is that you have even rustled some stray cattle to make ends meet."

"Not quite that bad yet, but the thought has entered my mind as an alternative management style during the coming grazing season," I responded. Actually, my fear was that the reverse of that option wouldn't in fact happen, but I wasn't sure Evans and Young were quite ready for that scenario just yet.

"You know Jim, this just may be the opportunity we have been looking for. Our unit administrator has been crying that nobody is doing range work where it's integrated between private lands and federal lands. This Gund ranch would sure give us that opportunity", Dr. Evans noted. I didn't need much more of an opening than that, so after about two more hours of suggesting all that could be done, as well as what I could or would be willing to commit, we had a deal.

A so started a marriage between the Nevada Agricultural Experiment Station and the USDA Agricultural Research Service, a marriage kind of consummated at the Gund Ranch so to speak! Jim Young was a scientist through and through. There was no aspect of vegetation in Grass Valley that he was not interested in. The Ranch had 2,800 deeded acres, of which probably no more than 500 acres was irrigated, sub irrigated, or could be considered anything but typical Nevada rangeland. I wanted it improved, improved to a point to where it would positively impact our livestock production - as simple as that! And how could we better manage the surrounding BLM lands that comprise our grazing allotment?

Well, it didn't take a week for Jim to arrive at the Gund. For the first venture I offered up living quarters at the High Place, with shared cooking when I was there. Most of the first week I was teaching in Reno while he trudged from the alkali playa to the top of McClusky Peak and traversed essentially every canyon in between. He was overwhelmed with all that he saw, and intent on overwhelming me as well on our first encounter after his initial survey.

"Grass Valley is virtually a miniature Great Basin in every regard. It has every plant ecosystem from the harshest saltiest environment able to support only the absolute minimum of vegetation to essentially a sub-alpine community on the upper end of the aspen grove on top of Shagnasty", he exclaimed with only the kind of enthusiasm that a dedicated scientist has when he has truly discovered something new.

Only in this case, Jim had discovered the greatest natural laboratory in the Great Basin, and I could only agree. He was putting into words the very thing that I had suspected, even known, from my very first visit. Only Jim was putting it into scientific words, words that the scientific community could understand. I also felt pretty sure he was putting it into words that those responsible for budgeting, at least at the USDA level, would understand far better than anything that I could express.

The USDA budget year, like all federal budgets, runs from November 1 through October 31, so at this time, mid-winter, we were a full nine months before any meaningful budget changes could occur. But Jim and his fellow workers had other resources that they could draw on, not only personnel, but a thing that immediately caught my attention, a thing called surplus properties.

Jim's right hand field man was Allen Bruner. Al had gotten both his B.S. and M.S. degrees at Nevada in range, studying under Joe Robertson. I had Al in my first Feeds class, he turned out to be an exceptional student. Al was a navy veteran, and he was actually older than I was. But his best trait was that he was an avid student of Nevada. And it didn't hurt that he was also a licensed contractor in addition to his duties with the ARS as a scientist. So, Al came to the Gund ranch, and the first thing he said was, "Where can I help the most?" It didn't take me long to take advantage of that offer!

True to his word, Jim let me review the surplus properties information that USDA had. My immediate concern was housing, because outside of the main house, a small bunk house without running water attached to one of the shops, the High Place, and a semi usable camp trailer that Lingenfelter had stolen from God only knows where, we didn't have a single place to park anybody outside of a bed roll draped over a sagebrush plant. It didn't take long to find two portable office units, including bathrooms, and kitchens that were available back east. Between Al's construction ability, and Jim's enthusiasm it didn't take long for us to put together a plan on where and how we could use these facilities. And, in short order, mainly due to Jim's unique knowledge of how to cut through USDA red tape, our request was granted. So Lingenfelter headed east, somewhere around Rock Springs, Maryland with his Peterbuilt tractor and flat bed to bring to the Gund what was to become the beginning of our "Science Center".

And true to my word, come January 1, 1973, I had Richard Dilbeck go ahead and hire his own cowboy, or what we more correctly knew in University vocabulary, a "Livestock and Feed Technician, Grade II". That turned out to be a mighty fancy name for Dwight Anderson, but it didn't bother me, and I guessed it didn't bother Dwight either, but come to think of it, I don't suppose he ever saw it. Although Dwight was only a little over twenty, he was from the old school. I never did learn who raised him, he kind of suggested it was himself, but whoever did, they did a mighty fine job. Dwight had spent a year on the rodeo circuit, and nearly was voted "Rookie of the Year" by the Association. But he had tired of that action, and now just wanted to be a cowboy and ranch hand. And the Gund Ranch was all the luckier for that! He came fully equipped, pick-up, trailer, horse, saddle and everything else that went with it. And best of all, he didn't mind living in a bunk house that was periodically the playground as well as the mating ground for some mighty healthy mice and an occasional rat or two. Fortunately for all of us, Pam Dilbeck didn't mind feeding Dwight for a little extra purse money.

By spring, things were looking up at the Gund. We had branded our first claves, with a mighty big NX on the left ribs. NX stood for "Nevada Experiment", but some of the crew began to call it "Nevada Exempt", based on some of the shenanigans that we had pulled off to collect necessary tools equipment or other essential items. I hounded every surplus property facility between Salt Lake and San Francisco as often as possible. Any stray merchandise on campus or any of the other field stations became fair game as far as I was concerned. My attitude simply put was, "use it or lose it". It didn't always work like it should have, but sometimes I actually got away with it. Although campus security did have to come retrieve an older pick-up once. My version was it showed up at the ranch, and nobody came to get it back. Buildings and Grounds version was someone stole it from campus. However, in the report B & G did note that it had not been used in several years and they thought it wouldn't start. Funny what you can accomplish with nothing more than a set of jumper cables, some starting fluid and ten cents worth of knowledge about how to hotwire a vehicle!

In April, once the road was passable for Lingenfelter, he showed up with the first shipment of the "Science Center", Bruner showed up to put it together, and Jim Young showed up to direct the operation. Now Jim was a great scientist, don't get me wrong on that point, and he was about as personable as anyone could be. But around a construction site, just look out. I didn't fully understand that at first, but Bruner cautioned me that despite Dr. Young's level of intelligence, out in the field, "Things seem to happen." Brunner added, "We call him Jungle, kind of short for Jungle Jim. I don't really know who coined the handle first but believe me it fits." Al went on to describe a number of near disasters that had befallen Jim, most kept me in stitches, even despite the near demise of Dr. Young on a number of occasions. Typical was the time he was doing range research on the side of a mountain from his pick-up. He had come to the typical old wire gate with a wired-up latch. It was on the side of a hill, so Jim parked, got out and struggled with the gate. Just as he finally accomplished the task, he looked up, and lo and behold, he was face to face with the pick-up, of which different versions have it that the parking brake either didn't hold or it was never set. Regardless, the pick-up exited the field with Jim and the gate in tow. Shortly, Jim managed to extradite himself from the moving mess, but watched in dismay as the pick-up, a federally owned vehicle, with the wire gate in tow disappeared into eternity by flying off of a cliff. With a chuckle, Al went on to say, "We never really knew what upset Jim the most, the broken ribs, or having to go back and build the ranchers gate, or having to explain to the feds how he destroyed a ten-thousand-dollar vehicle. Guess all three equally upset him!"

After a lot of bruised shins, hammered fingers, and bumped heads, all suffered by, predictably Jim, we finally got the "Science Center" up and going. We positioned the two units in an "L" fashion, about 75 feet from the High Place. With extra hot water, I was able to establish a fair lawn in between. All told, the "Science Center" consisted of two bedrooms, with two single beds per room, a bathroom with shower, basin and toilet, a kitchen and one small office and one general room that could be used for any number of purposes but would also accommodate up to ten to twelve people comfortably for meetings. And Bruner had constructed a covered porch from one end to the other. Perhaps best of all, by tapping into one of the many nearby hot springs, we had hot running water inside. And, we even had built a nearby cesspool by digging a pit about 10 feet deep, lining the sides with railroad ties, as well as covering the top with ties. After placing about eighteen inches of dirt over the top we called it good. Bruner, in his usual quizzical mood asked, "When do you suppose somebody will finally drive over the top after these ties are all rotten and fall in?"

"Probably not till long after you and I are gone," I responded,

"Hell, just blame it on Lingenfelter, if he hadn't absconded with that backhoe from wherever he did, we couldn't have accomplished this to begin with!"

By April 15 we had nearly one seventy-five calves on the ground, branded, cows and calves vaccinated, and ready to turn out. Our adjacent BLM range covered maybe a hundred thousand acres, but none of it was fenced. I reasoned that the old cows, and the Brown Swiss cross heifers might not go to far, but the rest were likely to end up pretty far afield by next fall. I had already discussed this with all the neighbors, the Bauman's to the north, Filbert Echemendy to the east,

Benny Demale to the southeast, Bill Knudtsen to the south and John Filippini to the west. Collectively, the range covered by these operators covered a few million acres, and as I said, there were essentially no fences. "Oh well, open the gates boys, I can see these cows want some green grass." And I kind of closed my eyes as out they went. And the ten Brangus bulls that we had just purchased were following in hot pursuit.

The next few days the boys did a powerful lot of riding. Fortunately, Rich knew the range, and where cattle just likely would go, assuming that they knew that to begin with. Our problem was we were dealing with two hundred or so cattle, not counting calves, that didn't have the slightest idea what sagebrush was, much less that in order to survive until we found them next fall, that they might even have to eat some. In fact, as I liked to observe over the next few years, "There wasn't one damn animal that even knew where one damn water hole was to begin with!" But somehow it worked, but frankly I never completely knew for sure how or why.

I had only seen Pete once during the winter; he was pretty busy at Buffalo, learning all the ropes of running his dad's spread. But around May first, he called, just while I was finishing up my finals. "Let's meet at Louie's about five." I didn't need much more of an invitation than that! Pete wanted to know about how my "ranching" experience was going, so with the help of a picon or two, it all came out. Pete about died laughing over the Jungle Jim stories, and completely understood the total anxiety I had felt as I watched the cattle go out the gate. "Don't worry, Basques are hardly ever rustlers, and when they are, they will be so good at it, you won't really know." Somehow, that didn't help my anxiety. Pete went on to talk about Buffalo and how things were going for him. "Dad's heart attack was worse than I realized. I kind of think he has been having more minor ones. Just sits on the chair out front, kind of like he used to do when he was waiting for Mom to ride back in after a long day. Only Mom's not never coming back now." With that we both sat at the bar in silence, reflecting on those recent events.

"I don't really know what to do", Pete finally broke the silence, "Went to a BLM meeting the other night, and it's clear, we are now out of the sheep business rather we like it or not. Damn feds, I believe in another ten years it will be the same for the cattle. There was a little weasel environmentalist that kept butting in on how cattle were destroying the natural beauty of High Rock Canyon, as well as all the markings the Forty Niners left. Think his name was Charlie Watson or something like that. Said he represented an outdoors coalition, whatever in the hell that is supposed to be. But the point is, the damn BLM listened to him more than us ranchers. I see nothing but trouble for the north Washoe country, guess maybe it's the same everywhere."

I responded by saying, "That's kind of what I am liking about Grass Valley, haven't seen an environmentalist yet."

"Yeah, Christ, you would have to go look in the mirror to see anybody out there to begin with." Pete responded as he ordered another round.

"Say, not to change the subject, but have you been following the political career of that jerk, Harry Ryan?" Pete quizzed.

"Yup, sure have," I responded, "Seems the Nevada Assembly just wasn't good enough for him, now he is the senator from Clark County. Remember that talk we had several years ago, that one day that squirrelly guy would be governor? Well, by my reckoning, he is dead on course."

"I suppose when he is governor, he'll be an environmental governor?" Pete asked with a mighty sourful expression. That comment caused me to take an extra-large swallow of picon.

"Well, the point is, when he runs, and I promise you that day will come, people like you and I had better damn well get involved!" I concluded. As I sat there studying why the surface of a picon always seems to be in motion I contemplated just what kind of mischief Harry Ryan could cause if indeed he ever became governor. "Remember how he tried to kiss my ass that day when he wanted to know all about fistulated cattle at the Little Wal?" I asked.

"Yup, sure do, he was all excited about you being a humanitarian because your research would somehow solve the coming world food crises. Shit, I wish I could see his expression now if he knew what you were up to. Hell, you haven't solved the world food crises. Right now, you're just trying to figure how you ever got into Grass Valley, much less how to get out!" Pete concluded with a burst of laughter that nearly tipped him over from his bar stool.

"Careful stud, your sick sense of humor is likely to get you bucked off that stool, besides, you don't have your spurs on."

"Yeah, I better rein up here, Hey Manny give the professor and me another round. You're an important person now Hope, full professor and all. Hell, you're probably rubbing elbows with the likes of Ryan!"

Pete was starting to rub me just a little bit the wrong way, but I had learned that sometimes Basques in general, and Pete in particular, tended to get a little obnoxious after several picons. But patiently I responded, "Well, as a matter of fact I did see him a few months back. Seems Bohmont wanted some extra money for some reason or another. Anyway, he told me that I had to testify before the Interim Finance Committee as to how the cost of research has suddenly skyrocketed. Course he blames me for everything, so to make peace with him I agreed. Well anyway, somehow Ryan was on the Interim Finance Committee. Usually, only senior legislators are on that, but somehow there he was. So, I did my thing. He drilled me with some asinine questions that didn't have anything to do with anything, including did I ever went to Nevada. He obviously didn't either know me or didn't want to admit that he did. When he asked if I went to Nevada, I felt like asking him if he knew anything about that cheating scandal."

"Oh God! That would have frosted his balls, you already accused him once, a second time of reminding him about his college activities outside of academia might have caused poor Harry too just finally tip over – probably missed the chance of a lifetime. Well, thanks for reaffirming my faith in the world. I was afraid that when you became a full professor, you might become somebody real important. I can see that's not the case. What time is it anyways?"

"It's six, why?" I inquired.

"Cause, I got to go see Gina, promised I would be there at six," Pete responded.

"I thought you and her split the sheets, so to speak, when you went to Elko," I asked.

"Well, more or less, she always has several friends, and once in awhile I drop in."

"Oh, I see. Strictly plutonic in other words."

"Easy Hope, you're surrounded by all those new and eager co-eds, and now you are starting to sound jealous just because I got an old friend."

"No, no, just thought you and she had gone separate ways. But keeping in touch with an old friend like Gina would have its rewards," I responded, still remembering that soft sexy voice and touch of her hand from years before. Maybe I was jealous! "What she wants, anyway?" I inquired.

"I don't know, maybe just me, but I think she really wanted to pick my brain about some kind of project. Anyway, I got to go."

"Keep a dry one, and I'll see you whenever", I cheerfully responded as we went our separate ways.

Fortunately, the next morning all I had to do was correct tests. After the previous afternoon with Pete, my head hurt a mite bit too much to be giving a lecture. In fact, I had noticed the last two or three times that Pete had come to town, I seemed to suffer plumb miserable headaches. It got so bad that I even went to see my long-standing Doc, Noah Smernoff.

You couldn't pull the wool over Smernoff's eyes, so he pretty soon figured out that my headaches were nothing more or less than too much booze. Smernoff was a card carrying Catholic from the old school, so he didn't cut me much sympathy, much less understanding. Doc had cut his medical teeth as the company doctor in the old copper towns of McGill and Ruth in eastern Nevada. In hindsight, he probably had to deal with enough Bohunks from Serbia to spot any known type of hangover, and it probably caused him to forever frown on the pleasures of alcohol.

Well, anyway, he promptly sized my head problem up, "You know, if I still smell booze on your breath when you're here complaining about your brain problems, I can only surmise that you drink too damn much. Besides, you're 40 this year, if my records are correct, so my prescription is pretty simple, stop drinking, especially, if you want to live past 50!" I wasn't one to suffer hurt feelings very often, but I could honestly say that Doc cut too quick. I had always prided myself on being able to drink anyone under the table and walk away just about as sober as I showed up in the first place. Well, I could probably still do that, but I did have to admit the headaches were getting a little tough. Maybe I should just switch to wine, yeah that would probably be OK, besides I was getting tired of those damn picons anyway.

Well, my head still hurt, and the pile of tests in front of my face wasn't getting any shorter. I was pretty well known for being rough on grading, so being hung over wasn't going to particularly help any body's grade point average. I hadn't been at this unenviable task for more than about 30 minutes when my semi sleep state was rudely interrupted by my phone ringing. "Hey professor, come up I want to talk about the Gund." CLICK! Didn't that lousy son of a bitch ever have any manors I thought to myself? Me with a hangover, a stack of tests sitting in front of me that have to be graded by tomorrow A.M., so that I can gather up my stuff and get to the Gund, so that I can make sure irrigation is going right. And he wants to talk. Crap!

"Yeah, what do you want", I grumbled as I barged into his office.

"Hey, you look a little under the weather, what's the problem? Can't keep up with all you bit off?" Bohmont cheerfully inquired.

I just sat down, frankly, my head hurt too bad to take issue. I chuckled when I responded, "Nothings wrong much, I kind of think I am coming down with the flu, hope I don't expose you", as I faked a cough.

Sometimes in hindsight, I wonder why Bohmont just didn't throw me out of the University. I guess one reason he didn't was because, first I never allowed him to get the best of me, and secondly, I met every challenge he threw my way. In fact, I usually tried to always throw one back his way, just for good measure. Today was no exception. "Say, I talked to George the other day, he wants to know how his ranch is coming," Bohmont responded.

"His ranch? For Christ's sake, I thought it was ours now," I shot back.

"Well technically, you're right. But he did indicate that if the IRS had a problem with your valuation, he might be willing to take it back."

Suddenly my headache went from the mild hangover type to a full force and effect magnitude ten thumper. The kind only a properly placed bullet to the brain can cure, or a good old-fashioned fist fight. "Take it back after I have put my heart and soul for 18 hours a day, for seven days a week, without a day off for the last 18 months. You can go to hell, George can go to hell, the whole God damned world can go to hell as far as I am concerned. It ain't going back!"

"Easy Professor, you don't ever want to forget that technically I am your boss, and if you hadn't been doing such a good job, I would have fired you long ago, simply because of your rotten attitude," Bohmont jabbed back.

I could see that this conversation wasn't going to go too far, besides, even I had to admit that if I wasn't so hung over, it probably wouldn't have occurred in the first place. "OK, I apologize. Trying to get my tests corrected today, so that I can get out there tonight and make sure our irrigation is going right tomorrow," I meekly responded. "So maybe the best thing to do is to invite George out early this summer, say next month, perhaps around June 15, and let him see for himself how things are going on his ranch. My bet is that he will be impressed by all that has been accomplished."

"You know, that wouldn't be a bad idea. Maybe you could put together a sort of field day, we could invite George, and possibly some of our rural legislators. I would like them to see what we are accomplishing at the College. I can just about guarantee that we will have a hard time in next year's legislative session with all the new faces. Tell you what. You make all the arrangements with Ag Information, get some invitations made, put together a pamphlet describing all that you have accomplished, what research results you have to date, you know all that kind of stuff. Plan for a good lunch, I would suggest some kind of bar-b-que, maybe ranch steaks, whatever you can come up with. I'll make up the invitation list and take care of that end. I am late to a meeting, so I have to run. Keep me informed," as he stormed out his office door.

As I stumbled back towards my office, a myriad of thoughts flew through what was left of my brain, most of them were not very good. One centered around throwing Bohmont out through his second story office window. Actually, that was a good thought, although I will have to admit, again in hindsight, that that kind of practice ultimately would nearly lead to my total demise. But today, I decided it might be best to just concentrate on getting my tests corrected. Driving to the ranch tonight, I would concentrate on how to turn mere survival into positive results, including research results.

Well, we did have a field day at the Gund Ranch, and it was a dandy. As usual I decided that the only way to deal with Bohmont was to do him one better. I didn't worry about the invitation list. I knew for sure that he knew a lot more important people than I did, so I was sure that legislators, regents, and whoever would arrive along with George. My part was to put on a show. And I had determined that if he wanted a show, I was damn well going to oblige him. But the show part I kept to myself as much as possible. There were only hints to it in the press releases and that's about all anybody ever saw before show time.

Bohmont was true to his part of the bargain. They all came. He personally picked up George Gund at Austin airport. George's private jet had flown out from Cleveland that morning. Other Ag administrators were responsible for delivering the rest. And, we were in luck, the roads were passable. Governor O'Callaghan sent his regrets, but about three of his top staff people were there to represent him. And Senator Paul Laxalt sent his regrets as well, but his top Nevada aid was present. Congressman David Towell, a Carson Valley native, was in Nevada, and drove himself out, along with the University purchasing agent, Jim Jeffers. Snowy Monroe, the State Senator from Elko showed up with a carload of Elko County cattlemen. Bode Howard, the Humboldt County assemblyman, as well as Roy Young, the assemblyman from Elko also showed up. Three University Regents were there, including Molly Knudtsen from right there in Grass Valley, as well as Fred Anderson from Reno and Harold Jacobson from the Gardnerville/Minden area. Both John Marvel, President of the Nevada Cattlemen's Association and Elias Goicoechea, President of the Nevada Woolgrower's Association showed. And the surprise of all was University President, N. Edd Miller. President Miller showed up driving his personal car, along with most of his office staff. I had kind of invited President Miller, we were pretty good friends, as he always like what I had tried to accomplish on the Faculty Senate, as well as the Faculty Athletic Committee. Besides, I knew he and Bohmont didn't always see eye to eye, so I thought his presence might liven up the day.

We had spent the better part of the week cleaning up the High Place as well as the ARS "Science Center". The lawn in between the two facilities never looked better, and the adjacent cottonwood trees were in full bloom.

Chris Collis, an Ag student that I had taken a liking to had offered to help coordinate the lunch. Chris wanted to become a graduate student in a year or so, and he wanted to do a thesis at the Gund. Chris was from Ely, his dad was a White Pine County Commissioner, and knew several people in the Ely area that were famed for their bar-b-ques. And fortunately, they even brought all their equipment. All I did was supply the meat, something Bohmont never figured out. As people arrived, they were greeted with the aroma of giant roasts and loins being slowly spit bar-b-qued over open hearths filled with Nevada mahogany. And

I had gotten Mrs. Baughman, from the McClusky Ranch, to prepare some of her famous breakfast cakes. We kept them hot in the High Place oven and brought them out to be served on a table under the cottonwoods, along with freshly brewed "cowboy coffee", for which I was responsible. I had also got a group of Cattlewomen from over around Eureka to prepare beans, salads and garlic French bread to go with the main meal. And as people arrived, they were greeted by these ladies, dressed in their Cattlewomen aprons, with coffee and cake in hand!

I had told Bohmont he could have the floor from our official 10:30 start until 11:00. I knew he would want to introduce everybody, and let the politicians say a few words. I wasn't disappointed.

By 11:15, it was time to start the science show. I had ignored Bohmont's remark about showing research results. Frankly, at this stage of the Gund Ranch we were still in a survival mode and research was about the last thing on my mind. So reportable research results were somewhere between the moon and Grass Valley, likely much closer to the moon. But I did have my ace in the hole, Jim Young my ARS range scientist. Now Jim had research going on all over Nevada, and he even had actually started some plot work right here in Grass Valley, albeit still very minimal. After explaining my predicament caused by Bohmont's remark concerning research results, Jim had said relax, he had enough results already that would be interesting, and if he talked really fast, probably nobody would actually figure out that what he was talking about hadn't actually been accomplished in Grass Valley, at least not quite yet. Well, Jim talked fast, with authority and above all else convincing. When he finished 30 minutes later even, I wasn't sure that what he was talking about hadn't actually taken place right under my nose here in Grass Valley. At any rate, everybody had a lot better appreciation of what it took to turn Nevada brush land into pure stands of grass. I couldn't help muttering to myself at the conclusion of his talk that the theme for the Gund Ranch should be that we will "put the grass back into Grass Valley"!

I still had one more trick before lunch was served. When Bohmont informed me that we were going to have this field day, we had already turned out the cattle on the BLM, in fact about thirty days before. On that I kind of breathed a sigh of relief, because our "herd" at this point wasn't something you would actually want a bonafide Nevada cattleman to necessarily see, at least at this point. But it didn't take me long to come up with a plan. "Rich, you and Dwight got to go back out and find the ten best pair of cows we have for this upcoming field day. I spec, they'll mostly be those Red Poll cross heifers, as a group they look pretty good. And bring back the best Brangus bull you can find."

Rich did not look happy on hearing my idea, "Do you know how much work we have to do to get ready for haying, not counting irrigating? It will take us a week just to find them. We'll probably have to bring in the whole herd, then separate them here." I could see Dwight was looking at the problem from another angle. I was sure he would a whole lot rather ride than irrigate, and the smile he had on his face confirmed my suspicion, despite the bitching from Rich.

Now I still had a hangover from my drinking bout with Pete a couple of nights before, so I didn't have much patience with Rich's problems. "Nope, that's the way it is boys. I want the ten best females with calves here by this time next week, with the right bull. Tomorrow, I have to go back to Reno, but I'll be back bright and early Saturday morning to help. Got no choice in this matter, and that's direct from Bohmont, not me."

We did get in ten good heifers, with calves at their sides, and a good Brangus bull. And I had some mighty bloody shorts from a ride further and longer than even I had contemplated! We put the heifers in our best pasture, one which we planned to hay, but right now some outstanding females were worth more money to me than some potential hay on down the road. By the time of the field day those heifers almost looked like a show string, and they had really gentled down. I had prepared Rich and Dwight to hold the stock in the main ranch corral until I had given them the sign to bring the bunch down to the back side of the High Place when they saw my sign. About 15 minutes before Jim was finishing his talk, I blinked my lights from my pick-up towards the corral, about a half-mile north. And as Jim was finishing, the boys had the group about one hundred yards away, moseying through some lush grass.

As soon as Jim finished, I stepped up to the mike, "Now right before lunch I want to quickly show you some typical Gund Ranch females. These heifers all calved about 75 days ago, this is their first calf, and I suspect they are just about to come into heat. They are out of grade Hereford mothers, and some beef type red poll sires." I didn't have to say anymore. My lads just let them drift by the fence, the heifers were more curious about the people than anything. The calves actually acted like they were on parade. Cameras came out right and left, I could plainly hear nothing but positive results. "Yup, the University is finally really on to something. Those look as good as anything that I have on my place," a grizzled old Elko cattleman uttered.

And then the ultimate thing happened. Early that morning Rich had warned me that he thought one of the heifers was coming into heat, and wondered if he should hold her back. I responded in the negative, as I didn't believe for a second that one of these heifers was going to cycle that quick, even if we did have her on the best feed in Grass Valley for the last 30 days. But luck wasn't with me, or was it?

Just about the time they all got right opposite the High Place, I noticed the Brangus bull did get right behind the heifer in question, and she even looked like maybe she had been ridden, but I didn't believe it. Well, it didn't take long to make a believer out of me! Suddenly the heifer stopped dead in her tracks. The bull gave a mighty lurch and came down directly on top of her. He harpooned her with a tool that I swore was at least 36 inches long. She grunted; he farted as he fell back to his feet. The ladies gasped, the gentlemen gawked, and the real cattlemen all exclaimed it was almost unbelievable to see a heifer come into standing heat so soon after calving, especially in a setting like Grass Valley. And I didn't waste a second, "Gosh, I apologize for that, should have known better, these girls have been cycling pretty hard the last few days. Anyway, that's pretty typical of our herd, wish we had more of them in to show, but most are pretty far up in the mountains right now, these were some of the tail enders going out. So, we held them back so that you all could have a better idea of what we are trying to do. Thanks for your attention, but right now I am getting powerful hungry, and these Ely boys seem to think the meat is ready. Let's eat!"

And it probably was the best meal ever served in Grass Valley. Chunks of beef, done to perfection over mahogany, salad, beans, roasted garlic French bread, any beverage you wanted, and home-made pies for dessert. Tables and chairs weren't exactly a long suit of the Gund Ranch, so people just sat wherever, the porch on the Science Center, the banks under the cotton woods, the lawn. And I didn't hear too much complaining right then. Grass Valley is sufficiently far away from anywhere that I figured most people had to get up by 5, and be on the road at 6 to be here by 10 a.m. So, they had been going for a while and they were hungry.

I grabbed a plate of food, and just drifted off by myself to watch. It wasn't long before John Marvel, President of the Cattlemen's Association, sidled up alongside with his plate full of vitals. "Hell of a show, I am impressed, say, didn't you come to the "25" with Joe Robertson about 15 years ago?"

"Yeah, it was about '57 or '8 if my memory is correct. Met your dad and Mom, brothers Tom and Dick. Matter of fact you guys put on quite a show that day also," I responded.

"You know, I rode this country some when I was a kid. We trailed sheep down through here some, so I got to know the lay of the land, met the Walti's, Doc Allen and all the rest. This is a tough country, very tough. The cattle you ran by today sure aren't typical of what was here twenty years ago, and I am not sure they are typical of what will work here today. And I wasn't going to say anything but finding that first calf heifer that was hot was either as stroke of luck, or some masterful planning on your part."

I was savvy enough to realize that I wasn't capable of bull shitting John Marvel. So, I had carefully put a large chunk of meat in my mouth, causing me to chew for a bit before I thought up the right answer. About then, it occurred to me that the right answer was the plain truth, no matter how much it might hurt my pride or anything else. I laughed a bit before responding, "Well, you're right, they're not typical. We had already turned out when Bohmont came up with the idea for this field day. Me and the boys must have ridden a hundred miles to bring back those ten heifers and their calves. But we did get them, and they likely are about as good as we have. As to that one coming in heat, they told me early this morning that it looked like one might be hot, but I said don't worry. Frankly, I didn't believe for a minute one of these heifers would be coming back so fast. I just about gasped as loud as some of those ladies did when that bull mounted her. But you got to admit it was quite a show!"

John laughed, "Yup, it sure to hell caught a lot of people's attention. And about then it dawned on me what you probably have gone through to get this place this far along. Hell, you haven't been here hardly a year, and as far as I can see you and your "boys" have accomplished a lot, especially from the University standpoint."

"Thanks for the compliment, I'll sure enough pass it along. But if you can, I am sure the boys would like to hear a compliment of that nature directly from you, they done all the work, not me."

"Well, I expect they have done a fair amount of work, but none of this would have ever happened if you hadn't put forth the effort to acquire a ranch to begin with. You probably didn't realize it, but I have followed your efforts over the last few years, and behind the scenes I frankly didn't support this "ranch" concept that you were spouting. I kind of thought you were just trying to promote yourself, typical of just another young ambitious professor at the University. But this place is different, it's a challenge, and I can begin to see you are really trying to accomplish something that will really help our industry."

At first, I didn't really quite know how to take John's remark. There sure enough had been a lot of opposition to the University acquiring a ranch, I didn't for sure really know where it had all come from, but now I was more clearly beginning to understand. I couldn't really help but agree with John, I hadn't really supported a lot of places the University looked at either, certainly some of the fancier places we likely would have ended up making a mess out of if we had got them. So, I just added, "Your right, no matter how many mistakes we make here, at least we can't go down, we can only go up. I believe this is the best place for the University, if for no other reason than that. But I also believe that eventually this place will become the ultimate laboratory, not only for the livestock industry, but just about all aspects of studying the Great Basin."

"I got to go do some politicking, with all of these legislators here, I got to get the Cattlemen's viewpoint in. But before we quit talking, there's something I want to tell you. I graduated from the University, so I kind of know the staff, at least their philosophy. Most don't have the ambition to get off their dead ass. Somebody like you comes along and really tries to do something. The old timers won't like that. So, a bit of caution, you are going to rattle some cages, they won't like that, and someplace down the road they'll try to do you in, mark my words. But I'll also guarantee this, if you keep up this kind of work, the Cattlemen will be squarely on your side if the issue ever comes up."

"Thanks John, I appreciate those words very, very much," as I stuck my hand out for a firm handshake, eyeball to eyeball. And that began a friendship that lasted for a long, long time.

I promised Bohmont that he could have some time after lunch to make announcements and introductions, including George Gund. George said how happy he was to have donated the ranch to the University, and how he was sure it was going to have a great future. As he was talking, I couldn't help but think that any day now, we would be getting a notice from the IRS requesting documentation concerning the valuation of Mr. Gund's gift. I was sure hopeful George would be just as happy that day as well. Gund concluded his remarks by saying that if he ever had realized that the ranch had this type of potential, he would not have gifted it to the University in the first place. I kind of winced on that one, because when that comment got back to Al Stenninger, and I was sure it would, there would be hell to pay!

I had requested about thirty minutes of time after all the dignitaries had got done talking. Just wanted to wrap up the day, thank everybody for coming, and so forth. But I really hadn't given too much serious consideration as to what I really was going to say. I had made a large map, showing the Ranch boundaries, fields, the lay of our BLM permit, water sources, and so forth. The map had been made really for my own use, but it was big enough so that everyone could see it. Like I say, I hadn't really made up my mind what to say, but as I listened to George and the rest talk about how wonderful the University was to venture out on this new experience in Grass Valley, I thought why not? Like John Marvel had said at lunch, I probably already had everybody at the

University pissed off, or would have soon enough anyway, so why wait any longer. No, now was the time, and now was the time to do it right. Well, I did!

I had kind of had had fantasies, for lack of a better term, about this moment, so I was pretty well prepared, other than the fact that I had never practiced this speech. Somehow that didn't seem to bother me. I stepped up to our homemade podium, pinned my map to the side of the High Place, and started in.

After a short "thank you" for all of those that had driven so far to come and see the Gund Ranch I started in. "You know, I think the livestock industry in this State has a problem, it's nearly totally dependent on federally owned land. We all know the statistics, Nevada is owned by the federal government, in fact to the tune of 87% or so. This concept has worked for nearly 100 years, worked damn well. But everyday we hear more and more environmental outcry as to how grazing cattle are running the federal land. Now, we even have the BLM preparing environmental impact statements to even justify livestock grazing, in fact the very first one will cover the lower half of this very district, the Tonopah Unit of the Battle Mountain District. I am afraid that all that is going on will not bode well for the future of the Nevada livestock industry. It strikes me that much of this potential problem could be eliminated if, using the Gund Ranch as an example, we were able to acquire sufficient federal property adjacent to the present private property, and develop it to a suitable level to support our basic cow herd. This would protect the economic future of the ranch, place far less pressure on the surrounding federal range, and hopefully satisfy the concerns of the environmentalist." Although I knew that in the early days of the Grazing Service, the precursor of the BLM, there had been congressional intent to do the very thing I was suggesting, in fact even on a much larger scale. I also knew that the livestock leaders responded to congress that they couldn't afford to own the land, because it wouldn't generate sufficient income to cover the taxes. But I thought the time might be coming when the livestock leaders might be receptive to what I was suggesting, at least from a research standpoint.

"I believe its possible to take ten to fifteen thousand adjacent acres to our deeded properties, develop them with our present knowledge of range improvement, perhaps drill a well or two to produce more forage, but eventually have a self contained unit that would support our basic cow herd of say 500 cows. We then could use our surrounding range permit on federal lands to sort of put and take the extra cattle, extra heifers, extra cows, yearling steers, whatever. This would greatly reduce grazing pressure on the adjacent federal lands, should improve range conditions, and most importantly, hopefully get the environmentalist off our back."

At that point I paused for a second, attempting to judge the reaction. I could see there was a lot of confusion, but that came as little surprise, my attention was really focused on John Marvel. This plan, if it were to succeed would have to have the support of the industry, and as their president, I was primarily concerned by his reaction. And it was plain that he liked my plan. So, without a moment's hesitation I pointed to my map, generally outlining the area that I had in mind to acquire, namely the area between Allen's and the Walti, with extra land to the south thrown in for good measure.

"You will note there are six canyons coming off of the Simpson Park Mountains to our east: Potato, Sheep, Pine, Moonshine, Big Canyon and Hiller. All of these canyons run good water during the spring months, but only in the best of years does this water reach our meadows. There's not much question that relatively recent seismic activity has created faults that consume 90% of the water coming out of those canyons. By building pipelines from above the fault lines, approximately at the mouth of the canyons, I think we would have the opportunity to greatly enhance both our grass hay production, as well as our meadows. Additionally, on the alluvial plain between the old

Walti property and the Allen Ranch there would be a section or two that could be developed into very productive alfalfa land if we were to drill an additional well or two."

Now I was having fun. I was not only letting my imagination run wild, but I was truly enjoying the reaction. Ray Ely, the Assistant Dean in charge of field stations, and Pete Test, the College fiscal officer were standing slightly behind Bohmont. Ely normally was a jovial person, just about always with a smile. It was now gone. Pete was starting to sway from foot to foot, and his normally dark Italian complexion had turned a crimson red. Bohmont looked perplexed, as he turned and whispered something to both Ely and Test. I could only imagine what that might be. But why stop now?

"If this station is to become the model for all research within the Great Basin, then we will need some permanent facilities, including housing. As you all realize, we are not adjacent to the freeway, shopping or schools for that matter. So, to attract good technicians, and even researchers in future years we'll have to have decent housing. We need better corrals, better shops, better barns, but all that will come with time. If we can create the enthusiasm to accomplish what I am talking about, then I firmly believe that all the other problems are solvable." I sort of stopped on that point to measure the reaction. It was pretty swift, and it was pretty positive.

Molly Knudtsen, our neighbor twenty-five miles to the south was the first to respond. "What Dr. Hope has outlined is a truly remarkable effort to help the livestock industry, and what I really like is his interest in the environment. As an armature archeologist, and a genuine ecologist, in addition to being a long-standing Nevada rancher, I can only applaud his ideas, and I can assure you all as a Regent I will support the concept to the utmost of my ability." Regents Anderson and Jacobson followed with similar supportive statements. The scowls on both Ely and Tests faces became more obvious. However, Bohmont was quick to seize the opportunity, as he realized, as the regents went so would he, regardless. And the legislators supported it, and so did Congressman Towel. Wasn't much more to say.

People gathered around my map, discussing, pointing and carrying on in general. Marvel came by, shook my hand and said he would be in touch. President Miller congratulated me on a fine day, and a most ambitious program, "Its obvious you have strong support in the College, keep up the work, and good luck!" I said a silent prayer thanking our Devine Being that President Miller was not returning with Ely or Pete Test. As the crowd thinned, I sort of stood off by myself. I realized Bohmont would have to get it off his chest, and I had long since learned the quicker the better. Sure, enough he finally spotted me standing alone over by the cotton woods. He strode over with a smile and said in a voice loud enough for anyone standing remotely close to hear, "Great show professor, congratulations." However, as he shook my hand and moved closer, much closer, he said in a very low voice that only I could hear, "You son-of-a-bitch, you ever do that to me again, and you will be lucky to survive as a livestock feeder in this institution, no maybe a janitor."

"Easy Dean, I have been trying to tell you for a month of Sundays about all of the advantages that this place has. After talking to John Marvel today, it just seemed to be the opportune time."

"Well, the least you could have done was to give me a copy of a report before you made your talk. At least I could have answered Pete's questions a little better."

"Gosh, you know if I had ever written a report, you would have been the first to get it. But as a matter of fact, five minutes before I started, I really wasn't at all sure what I was going to say. As a matter of fact, I started cold turkey; stopped, looked at Marvel, saw he liked what he was hearing, so away I went. Actually, most of what I was talking about just came out from that point on. As far as the pipelines, when I turned around and looked at the map, that was probably the first time I ever really thought about pipelines."

Bohmont looked like he really didn't believe me, and granted, I had given him sufficient reason over the years to always have a certain question. But this time it all was pretty straight arrow. "Well, OK, I guess, right now I haven't the slightest idea of how all this will be accomplished. Nor do neither Pete nor Ray for that matter. Maybe that's not important right now. But I'll give you fair warning, I have got to go to D.C. tomorrow, so I wouldn't advise you to come to town for a day or two. You got those two gents sufficiently mad at you to bar-b-q your nuts for breakfast tomorrow morning."

"Well, have a nice trip to Washington. Actually, I have to irrigate for the next few days. It will be next week before I am back on campus. But I'll be by, got several other ideas, including we need something better than the Gund Ranch for a name. Be thinking about that. After today we are legitimate, and we ought to celebrate with a better name. Maybe that would make Ray and old "money bags" a mite bit happier.

"Good idea, and congratulations again, you either really woke this College up, or you have forever pissed them off. Either way, you'll need a bit of luck to get to where you want to go. On the other hand, I think you have been living on luck for a long time. See you next week."

Bohmont was the last to leave; George Gund had caught a ride to Austin airport earlier, so he left by himself. As his dust settled, Rich and Dwight showed up after finishing evening chores. They were both still in a state of shock, as I hadn't discussed any of these plans with them. Come to think of it I hadn't discussed them with anybody else either, course, I hadn't really even thought about them through myself. Rich was still laughing about what had transpired at the barn, "I was milking, Dwight was feeding the horses, those boys from Elko stopped and wanted to look at the corrals and such. I told them to help themselves. After about five minutes they came back in shaking their heads and wondering how in the hell you were ever going to accomplish what you were talking about with no more facilities than this. I told them not to worry, these facilities were so much more modern than what we had one year ago that there was no telling where we would be in another year. I heard them muttering as they walked, one of them said that he knew for a fact that the barn had been built before 1925. I didn't have the heart to tell them that Emil Walti told me the barn was built sometime around 1885."

I couldn't help but laugh, just guessed my so-called "optimistic" attitude was catching, which I couldn't do anything but thank the boys for. "Here, we had this little bar for those that wanted to hang around for awhile. Got two bottles of whiskey left, I'll split them. You guys go home and have a good drink with me. I am going to pull up a chair myself and have a tall ice-cold whiskey and water, and just watch the sunset. You all were great, that old Brangus bull harpooning that heifer made the day as far as I was concerned."

And with that I made myself a tall drink, sit back and watched the sunset over the distant mountains. I always had a tendency to push myself into something bigger, and not necessarily better. And I usually did it with a minimum of forethought, sometimes none. I was pretty sure that someday, I would likely just push myself right off the end of the plank, but I guessed I would deal with that if and when it came. Right now, I had to figure out how to buy 10,000 acres from the federal government, much less find five or six miles or so of pipe. I kind of wondered how much that many miles of pipe would cost. It pleased me to think that maybe Pete was thinking the same thoughts at that very instant.

In hindsight the Ranch would have many more field days, most with well over 100 people in attendance, and from all over. We would have field days that would display new concepts of all phases of agriculture; we would have proceedings with abstracts of twenty or more projects all being carried out at the facility. We would have field days where almost as many airplanes would land at our airport as we had cars on that first field day. But we never had a more successful field day than our very first one on June 15, 1974. And I don't ever recollect a more beautiful sunset, or a better highball than I enjoyed that evening!

I had to be back in Reno early Monday, a week after the field day, to make sure everything was tied down right in the lab, and all the grad students had their summer assignments correct. After that, I journeyed up to Bohmont's office to see how the view was from the second floor. "Hello Professor, got lots of compliments from our field day last week, even Miller called over saying what a great thing we got going here in agriculture." I didn't raise the issue about "our" field day, and I didn't inquire about the mental health of either Ray or Pete. But I did want to know what we were going to call the damn place if nothing else.

"Been thinking about a name?" I inquired.

"Yes, I think it ought to have the name Great Basin in it, and also something indicating both agriculture and ecology," he responded enthusiastically.

"Well, I don't. I think out of respect for George, and the fact that he may still eventually gift us with additional property or other valuables, we need to recognize his name. Also, over the weekend, I did some reading out of one of your federal handbooks, I think its called Guidelines for Spending Hatch Dollars, or something like that. The point is there's definite guidelines on spending research dollars, they must be spent on research. But there's a broad category for some of the funds related to Extension, much more flexibility. I see the word "demonstration" used rather frequently, and the thought occurred to me that for the foreseeable future, whatever we do from the College standpoint is going to be a whole lot more along the lines of demonstration than research. So, in order to keep us both out of jail for misusing federal dollars, I kind of like the name "Gund Research and Demonstration Ranch."

I hadn't really thought the whole thing through, in fact the name research and demonstration had come to mind about the time Bohmont was expounding on the importance of ecology. In fact, if true to form, I fully expected him to throw my suggestion out with the dishwater, or whatever. "Hey, you know, that's a great idea, and you're right, it would get me off the hook with Pete. He has been yelling at me that we can't do some of the things that we have already done, but you're right, the Smith-Levor funds associated with certain aspects of Extension would be totally legal to support some of your demonstration projects. Hey, Pete, come over here and listen to what the Professor and I have come up with."

I had a momentary urge to jump out the nearest window. I still could visualize the plain ugly scowl on his face as I was going over my plans last week. Knowing Pete, I doubted that he had gotten fully over that as of this moment. I was right. "Well, hi, Prof., or should I call you the Prof. that broke the bank at the College of Agriculture?" he slurred at me as he entered the office.

"Pete, I got a great idea. I think we should change the name of the Ranch to the Gund Research and Demonstration Ranch. This will help us fund some of the Professors projects through the use of your Smith-Lever funds for demonstrational purposes."

"Christ, Dean, we already have over expanded the use of the Smith-Lever funds as it is. We have more Extension Agents spending more money today than this College has ever supported. Now you want me to throw these funds into a bottomless pit out in Grass Valley? Forget it!

It can't be done, those funds are committed for the next year regardless of what you want or say."

I was kind of sitting low in my chair, but I could have told Pete that he made a fatal mistake. I learned a long time ago you never point blank tell Dean Bohmont "it can't be done". And I was right one more time.

He exploded out of his chair in a near total rage, "Friend, I am telling you right here and right now, transfer 25 grand of Smith-Lever funds to the Gund Research and Demonstration account, under a heading called Demonstration. I don't care where you come up with the funds from, or whose ox you gore. I want that done by five tonight, and I want a complete account to set up for both research and extension funds established under the account name Gund Research and Demonstration Ranch. You understand. And I'll remind you right now I am also acting Associate Dean and Director of the Agriculture Extension Service, so you don't need to waste any more time conferring with me on how you are going to do this."

Pete just turned and slowly exited the office saying in a low tone, "Whatever is right boss!"

But Bohmont wasn't through quite yet, "Phyllis, send Ray in right now. I want to get him squared away before he gets any more confused on this subject".

I could tell by the way he yelled for Ray, that Phyllis didn't really need to relay the message; it could have clearly been heard down to the far end of the Ag Building. "Dean, I got an awful lot to do today, would it be OK if I got on my way?" I meekly inquired.

"Yeah, that's alright. Just don't bring me anymore of your problems for me to resolve today. Seems like every time you come up here everybody gets all upset."

447

As I slipped down the hall, I was kind of glad that the Smith-Lever thing had become his idea. Everybody on the teaching and research staff already hated me for stealing their funds. I still had some friends left in the Extension Service, so they sure didn't need to think this was my idea.

As I walked past the Animal Science office, Mary stuck her head out and asked what in the world that I had caused upstairs. "The yelling was so loud that Dr. Bohman got up and closed his office door," she reported.

"Oh nothing, we were just discussing budgets," I responded.

"That must have been some kind of discussion. I never heard Pete and the Dean go at it like they just did. It must have been pretty wild, at least from the sound. Now, poor Dr. Ely is in there getting grilled. Oh, by the way you got a visitor in your office."

I didn't know if I should just walk out of the building or actually go to my office. I could well believe my "visitor" was the first of many extension agents, all wanting a piece of what was left of my ass. Well, I was only part right, it was an extension agent alright, but at least at this point only a former agent.

"Well, I already heard all about your field day. Sounds like you tipped them over good and proper this time. I came by to help you celebrate, take you to lunch at Louie's and have a picon or two."

"Thanks, but my doc said that you are bad for my health, can't have any more picons, but you sure to hell can take me to lunch."

Over lunch I told Pete briefly about the field day and he responded by telling me what some of his old cowboy buddies from Elko had to say. "They say you're crazy, but maybe just crazy enough to actually get the job done. They all told me that was the first field day any of them had ever attended where a bull sticking it to a cow was the featured event."

"That was somewhat by accident. But if I had it to do over again, don't think I could have done any better. You should have heard the ladies gasp, there were several from here at the University. I imagine that was the first time they ever saw anything like that."

As lunch progressed our talk drifted through the field day, my encounter with the Dean this a.m., and Nevada life in general. Finally, as we were sipping a Winnemucca coffee, Pete said he might have some real news. "You know the East Gate ranch out on old Highway 50? Well, I am thinking about buying it."

"Wow, that's great. Yes, I know that ranch pretty well, been all over it. Actually, I even thought about taking a run at it myself about a year ago, but I just don't have the capital. But I did go all over it. Saw all the grass on top of the Destoyas, the lake on Smith Creek, all the fields, and that is some kind of winter country down towards Gabbs."

"Well, as I am sure you know, it is in foreclosure. Production Credit holds the paper, and they just haven't been able to do anything with it. Peers to me that there is too much against the property. Anyway, in talking to them I offered to cash them out at about fifty cents on the dollar, never dreaming they would go for it. But I guess they are getting tired of looking at another non-performing asset, as they like to say, so they said let me see the color of your money. Went home, went over it with Dad, and he said go for it. Don't think he wants to move, but he knows we will eventually get squeezed out of Buffalo, and I am sure he wants to see me keep going somehow. He kind of knew the ranch as an old crony of his owned it before the depression and Dad had actually

449

been there a time or two. Anyways, to make a long story short, with the signing of a few papers, I'll damn near be a neighbor of yours."

I thought to myself, well not quite. I already knew that it was about a hundred miles from our headquarters to the Campbell Creek headquarters, and that was on the east side of the Desatoyas, and East Gate itself was on the west side. However, there were only two ranches between, so we would just about be neighbors. "That place will easily run fifteen hundred cows, where are you going to come up with that many?" I inquired.

"Well, that's the beauty of this deal. Nobody's gathered cattle this year, and nobody really knows how many are there. They will guarantee 500 cows; they hold the paper on everything. We have to buy 500 cows, but I flew the place all last week, and I counted nearly a thousand, so that pretty well makes the cows fifty cents on the dollar also."

"Well, keep a bunk house open for me. The way things are going here, I may well get canned within a year. Besides that, the place is way too big for you to run by yourself. I heard those miners down Gabbs way like to eat free beef. And you know those Indians over at Yumba never paid for a cow in their lives."

"Yeah, I already figured all of that out. You're right, I will need some help, that ranch is big, in fact it's about five times as big as what we have at Buffalo. But I just couldn't help but marveling about all the feed, grass every where, and where there ain't grass, there's good shrubs, bitterbrush up high, shadscale and whitesage down low, feed everywhere."

"With this new ranch, all you need now is a wife," I volunteered. "Time to marry Gina."

"Wow stud, I haven't lost my head that for. But funny you should mention Gina, because if I buy this ranch, I may start helping her some."

Will that peeked my interest to put it mildly, "Last time I met Gina, she was making beagles on South Virginia Street. Somehow can't imagine you cooking beagles?"

"No, its not quite that simple. You know how that Naval Air Base east of Fallon has been expanding? Well, it seems that the flyboys have been causing some trouble with the local folks in Fallon. So, the Commander approached the County Commissioners a while back and inquired if the County might consider an option of legalizing prostitution. I never really thought about it, but Fallon is about the only town in northern Nevada that doesn't have a house or two, outside of Reno, where it's illegal by state statue."

"Yeah, I guess you're right, I never thought about that either, but come to think of it I have never heard about a house in Fallon, sure enough, one or more everywhere else though. Never heard it wasn't legal in Churchill County. That's a new one on me!"

"Well, anyway I guess about six months ago the County boys thought better about their anti-vice statutes, and voted it down. Guess they decided to legalize prostitution in the County, but any houses had to be at least ten miles out of the city limits. The sheriff, a guy by the name of Banovitch knew Gina, asked her to come to a Commission meeting and make a presentation, if she were interested. Guess he knew she had worked for Joe Conforte at the old Triangle Ranch before Bill Raggio had it burned down. Well, I'll be damned if she didn't go out to a commission meeting, make a presentation, and the boys gave her a license just like that."

"So, where's the house going to be?" I asked, laughing at how I imagined Gina doing a number on those commissioners.

"Well, that's the beauty of Gina. She had it all figured out before hand and had made an offer on that old place called Salt Wells. You know where it's at, you drive by it every time you go to the ranch."

Indeed, I did, and my curiosity had about gotten the best of me in the last month or so, because suddenly there had been a lot of construction going on there, and for the life of me I couldn't imagine why anybody would be wasting money on Salt Wells, it just wasn't going to fly as a restaurant or bar. But as a whorehouse, well that might be a whole other subject.

"What's neat about Salt Wells is that its only a mile back to that old, graveled road, called the Beach Road, I am sure you have seen that as well. Anyways, the Beach Road is a straight shot, nearly from Salt Wells to the Air Base. The commissioners got so excited about the whole deal, especially seeing how the drunk fly boys wouldn't have to be driving through town anymore, that they even promised to considerably upgrade Beach Road, just for Gina."

Again, I could well imagine her sexy smile, her big boobs, and the way she dressed. "I'll bet she had those commissioners literally eating us of her hand. I know a lot of people in Fallon, I got to find out the local scoop on this, it should be great," I concluded. "By the way, you said you were going to be helping her, you got enough money to buy Middle Gate and finance a whore house also?"

"No, no, she has some partners, but I don't know who they are, and she hasn't told me. When she heard that I might buy East Gate, and would be traveling back and forth, she got really excited and said I could help her get her girls back and forth. I never knew it, but there's some stupid Nevada law on the books about a madam not being able to provide transportation to and from the house for the working girls. Guess they're just supposed to show up. Salt Wells is ten miles out of Fallon, and Fallon is not exactly the travel hub of northern Nevada. She thinks with a little scheduling I'll be able to pick girls up in Reno and bring them back when I go back and forth."

I sort of looked at Pete dumfounded, not really knowing what to say, "I kind of figured you would be flying most of the time not driving."

"Well, that's probably right, but there's an old strip at Salt Wells, and she's going to get that fixed for fly in "guests"."

I was still dumbfounded, "If she can't get the girls there by law, I still don't see how you fit in. She can't pay you; you aren't part of the operation, you are doing this for a favor?"

"Well, as a matter of fact, she can't pay me, but she said if I would help her get this started, there would be "favors."

I rolled my eyes back, thought a bit, then added, "Holy shit Pete, you're going to be the biggest rancher in central Nevada, and you're going to be a pimp on top of it. Only in Nevada! Despite my doctor, I think maybe its time for a picon after all!"

Well, I didn't heed Doc Smernoff's advice for the rest of that day, and, once more, I paid the price. But seeing how my best friend was going to own one of the biggest ranches in central Nevada and have the run of a whore house on top of that was, after all, just a little bit more than I could handle. However, despite Pete, my world had to go on, I had laid the groundwork for the Gund Research and Demonstration Ranch, and now it was totally up to me to make it work, even if my head did hurt a mite bit!

"Look Dean, I know that I laid a lot on the line the other day at the field day, and with more thinking, I fully believe all of that can be accomplished. However, first, some other things got to be accomplished, we got to survive, and we got to do some serious planning," I added, during a lengthy meeting on a hot July day in Reno. I hadn't really had the opportunity to talk to Bohmont, or Ray Ely and Pete Test for that matter since our June field day, but today was that opportunity, even if it was because of the demands put forth by Pete and Ray. "I haven't found the pipe we need, and for that matter, I haven't even had the chance to look. There are some other matters that must be addressed first."

"Pipe large enough to carry what you are talking about will cost several dollars a foot, and you are talking about 25 thousand feet, or more. That might amount to a quarter of a million dollars, and despite all your bull shit, that money doesn't exist," Pete shouted. I was thankful that I hadn't seen my Basque friend the day before, because at least I didn't have a hangover, and I could see that this meeting might require a clear mind if it were going to be successful.

"Look, we can't even start planning pipelines until such a time as we have clear title to the water in those canyons, including the point of diversion. That means we have to have a certified water engineer do a survey, establish points of diversion, show place of use, and on top of that it all has to be approved by the State Engineer," I continued.

"How long do you think that will take?" questioned Bohmont.

"It will take at least a year, if we were starting today. But they should be uncontested, so at least we won't have that obstacle," I answered.

"Well, have you secured an engineer yet?" Bohmont continued.

"No but I have talked to the same one that did our work on our Truckee River rights for the Main Station, and he felt he could do the whole thing for less than $10,000. And that means all you have to do is authorize it, because for services of this nature it doesn't have to go out to bid," I shot back.

Pete started to say something, but the look on his face suggested that the sentence must have gotten caught in his throat cross ways. Ray almost looked like he was agreeing with me, then finally Pete got it out, "Well at least, if we have to have a survey, like Hope says, it will take a year, and then there's no guarantee. No reason to get anxious about pipe until we know for sure we will be needing some."

"Yes, you are exactly right on that Pete. In fact, I need to do about a week worth of work myself, to be fully satisfied that where I want to divert the water will be OK. As it is, just about all the diversion points will be on BLM land, but there are remnants of old irrigation ditches there that should give us a vested right, so I don't think the BLM can say much."

"Well, it sounds good to me, Pete, you and Ray draw up the necessary paperwork to get Terry an engineer and lets get going on this project. Now what steps have you taken to get 10,000 acres of BLM land?" Bohmont quizzed.

"Nothing, except doing a lot of reading in the library. There's only one-way that we can accomplish this, at least that's what my research shows. We don't qualify through any kind of homesteading act, including the Desert Land Entry Act. Besides, none of those acts, even if they would still work, would get us anywhere near 10,000 acres. But there is an act, name escapes me right now, but something like public purposes and recreation act, which allows public entities to obtain significant parcels of land for public purposes. It's usually been employed to gain land around land locked cities for projects like schools, sewer plants, etc. To the best of my knowledge, it only been used around Las Vegas, Henderson and some of the other fast growing towns in southern Nevada, again for purposes like I just mentioned. However, the words demonstration and research are used as legitimate purposes, and a university is certainly a legal entity, so I know it is theoretically possible to get 10,000 acres through this act," I summarized.

"Don't our congressional representatives have to initiate a request of this magnitude?" Bohmont asked.

"Yes, I would imagine it would take a regular congressional act, signed by the President, to transfer this amount of land, with or without the support of the BLM. So, I would imagine that we would have to have our Congressman as well as one of the Senators introduce appropriate legislation." I concluded.

"That's not very good, I am kind on the outs with either Senators Cannon or Bible right now, and Towell never seems to impress me, even though he did seem pretty enthused at the field day," Bohmont puzzled.

"Well, again, let's not get into a rush. Sure, as all get out former Governor, Paul Laxalt will beat Bible in the upcoming election. You have good relations with Paul, I know that for sure, and I am not entirely a stranger to him. And right now, I'll bet my bottom dollar, Jim Santini will beat Towel, even if Jim is a Democrat. I went to school with Jim when I was getting my master's here, and I am sure he would support this concept. So, I am saying that a year from now, we will have both a Senator and a Congressman that would be very supportive of enacting legislation of this nature. In the meantime, we had better be sure we have the support of the BLM."

"You know, I think you are right Terry. I don't know Jim Santini, at least yet. But I sure know Paul and I am positive he would be supportive, even if we had to run a few sheep to satisfy him. No, you're right, let's just wait until the elections are over, then let's see which way the wind blows. In the meantime, you're probably right, we had better make sure the BLM is supportive. That probably had better start with your District manager in Battle Mountain, what's his name anyway?" Bohmont asked.

"Gene Nodine. Actually, he just recently transferred here from Burns, Oregon. I actually met the guy that summer I spent at Squaw Butte, I think he is OK," I answered.

"Well, OK, I guess we know what we have to do. In the meantime, you have a ranch to run, Professor, let us know how we can help," Bohmont concluded.

As I left the meeting I kind of had to laugh to myself. I was betting that neither Ray nor Pete went along with Bohmont's concluding remark. But I didn't want to bore them with details, so I hadn't thought it necessary to inform them that I had just found, and purchased, at Surplus Properties a used Quonset hut. Only cost $500, so it was well within my discretionary fund limit, even if it would take Lingenfelter two trips with the Peterbuilt. I hadn't really thought how we were going to reconstruct the Viet Nam relic into a cookhouse and dining commons, but I figured with Al Bruner, just about any construction project was possible.

Well, Bruner wasn't as conciliatory on the Quonset hut as I imagined, "Hell no, I won't put that bucket of bolts together, that's up to you guys. But if you do by chance get it up, I might consider finishing the inside, assuming you got electricity and water to the damn thing!" was his less than enthusiastic remark. Well, that's OK I thought to myself. I knew Rich and Dwight would jump at the chance, especially after I told them that's what they would have to do anyway.

And Lingenfelter wasn't really enthused about bringing it out to begin with. "Have you looked at that mess? There's parts laying everywhere, bolts and nuts lying loose and rusted, no directions, I am not even sure what all belongs to your great purchase", he bellered after viewing my "purchase" at Surplus.

"Relax, big guy. All you have to do is bring it out, we'll put it together, and if there are extra parts, we can always find a place for them," I responded.

"Christ, the Dean sees me hauling this mess out, I'll probably get fired. You probably should be, just because you wasted the money buying it to begin with," Jim concluded.

Well, miracles happen, although it did take a couple of months. By late 1974, we had a 30-foot by 50-foot Quonset hut standing, all finished, with electricity, water and sewer stubbed in. And Al groaned when he saw the finished project, "I didn't really agree to finish the inside off into a kitchen, bathroom and dining commons did I?"

My only comment as I went on my cheerful way was, "Yup!" But I didn't worry about Al, in fact, he had become about as enthused about the Gund as I was. And he knew every bit as well as I did that the day would come when we would need a cookhouse, dining commons and meeting room. Al's only problem was that he was such a perfectionist that he wanted to build it from the ground up, but that sure wasn't in my budget!

Nineteen seventy-four was a far easier year for me than 1973. We were fortunate to obtain a great group of summer employees, mostly from the University, and between Rich and Dwight, things just went well. Instead of irrigating, putting up hay, or whatever, I was able to really zero in on planning and building what in my mind would one day be the premier field station in the Great Basin. And I had two major projects to plan for, pipelines and how to acquire 10,000 acres.

We all agreed that not much could be done on any kind of land transfer until the upcoming elections; however, it was full speed ahead on the water rights. I had spent considerable time studying the six canyons that we wanted to bring water out of. All had remnant ditches; clearly indicating at some distance point in time water had successfully been transported out of the canyons and down to the nearby meadows. However, with time those systems had failed, likely because of seismic activity along the front of the Simpson Park range. But it was pretty obvious where the pipelines should start, which would be the points of diversion, which also coincided with the start of the historic ditches. To take the water to the appropriate places in the nearby fields would require a total of nearly six miles of pipe, assuming relatively straight lines could be maintained once the pipes left the canyon mouths. The points of diversion were all on adjacent federal land, managed by the BLM. However, Nevada water law is pretty clear, and we were not suggesting any change of points of diversion, simply replacing ditches with pipes. That fact, coupled with the fact that no adjacent landowners existed within many miles led us to believe that protests would be inconsequential. Even the Reno based water engineer that we had retained to do the surveying as well as file the necessary forms and paperwork agreed to that. "This is a great plan, and there are simply no complicated factors," Ross Dikins, a highly regarded engineer from Smith, Dikins and Pearson commented after his first review.

It took me about a week to show Ross what my thinking was, and for the most part he agreed. From that point it was up to him to do the surveying and map making. My problem was to find a pipe. Any kind of new pipe was out of the question, as nothing in the 10 inch plus category could be found for less than several dollars a foot, and for at least 30,000 feet of pipe, that put me way out of the ballpark. As the summer wore on, I became increasingly discouraged, there was nothing available from surplus, either federal or state. And I studied every bankruptcy auction from the Pacific to Mississippi.

Late one fall night I was reading trade journal want ads under the gaslights of the High Place, when suddenly a small item under surplus caught my attention. "Vitrolic surplus pipe, 40' lengths, good condition". The ad listed a telephone number in Prineville, Oregon. I didn't have the slightest idea what Vitrolic pipe was, much less what it might cost, but at that point one more telephone call didn't seem out of line. I wasn't going to try that call from the Gund, as that was about hopeless, but I was going back to Reno early the next morning to teach, so, I carefully cut out the ad and put it in my wallet.

"Hello, I am calling about the ad I read in the Farm Journal about Vitrolic pipe."

"Oh yeah, got a ton of it, how much you want anyway."

"Well, none until I know what Vitrolic pipe is and what size it is and what condition it is in, much less how much you want for it.

"Well, Vitrolic pipe is steel pipe designed for "quick coupling" using a clamp set up. Its surplus straight from Nam, it's all eight inches, inside diameter. They tell me it was used for water distribution to their camps in Nam. Price is variable, depending on how much you want. Mostly, it's in pretty damn good shape, all things being considered. Surely worth a dollar a foot, unless you want the whole pile."

"How much you got?"

"Don't rightly know, hell of a big pile though."

"A mile, five miles, ten miles, give me a guess."

"Don't know, never counted the joints, already sold nearly hundred joints and the pile don't look a bit smaller."

460

Talking was going too fast, and by his tone I was beginning to figure the whole thing was a sham. "So how much you asking?"

"Oh, probably a dollar a foot, maybe a bit more. Or you can make an offer on the whole pile.

I couldn't figure out if this guy was being cagey, just plain dumb or whatever. However, a dollar a foot was better than anything I had seen yet. Eight-inch pipe was a bit smaller than I wanted, but at this point beggars couldn't be choosey. "Well, I guess I know where Prineville is, better give me directions from there, maybe I'll come look at it," and I left it at that after getting directions.

I left the Gund, mainly because I wanted to figure the best way to haul pipe from Prineville Oregon to Grass Valley. Besides, I had always wanted to take the Winnemucca to the Sea Highway, which generally left Winnemucca in a northwesterly direction, transversing southern Oregon before hitting U.S. 395 at Lakeview. From there it was a short 250 miles up the eastside of the Cascades to Prineville. And Prineville wasn't much, kind of looked like Oregon's answer to Appalachia; it was obvious my guy wasn't the only junk dealer about.

I finally found the address, but the pipe wasn't readily obvious. However, through the pines, not much was obvious. Suddenly I remembered why I hated Oregon, at least central and western Oregon. Damn trees so thick you couldn't see a mountain if your life depended on it. But it didn't take much time before an old timer in bib overalls followed by a less than friendly hound showed up.

"Yeah, I am the guy that called last week about the Vitrolic pipe."

"What took you so long? Oh, I see, you're from Nevada, sounded like one of those flat landers from over in the Willamette Valley."

461

I let that one slide, I just wanted to see the pipe, and it had better be good after driving nearly 500 miles just to get here. "OK, lets see your pipe."

I followed him around a dilapidated barn, down a dirt road through the pines, and suddenly there it was. A near mountain of pipe, laying in every conceivable direction possible. I guessed the mountain to be nearly 10 feet tall, maybe several hundred feet long, and no telling how wide.

"I kind of thought this pipe might be stacked, like a regular rack of pipe. How the hell do you get it out?"

"That's up to you, but if you buy enough, maybe I could help."

"How many joints in this pile."

"I already told you; I don't know."

After walking clear around the pile and doing my best to estimate, I felt confident that at least a thousand usable joints existed. At 40 feet per, that was 40,000 feet, or 7- 8 miles. I swallowed hard. Tried to downplay the number of feet, while commenting that with that much rust, couldn't weld successfully to begin with

"There not in very good shape, I see some holes, and it looks like a hell of a lot of rust inside."

"That rust will come right out, and you can close the holes with an arc welder just like that."

Yeah, I thought to myself. Hit it too hard with your arc, and you will make a very small hole very large in about a microsecond.

"Well, I need a lot of pipes, and I wanted 10 inch. But if you give me a fair price, maybe I will take the whole pile."

I could see a noticeable jerk at that offer, besides, I couldn't see any recent tire tracks on the dirt road, and so his story about selling 100 joints recently seemed questionable.

"Hell, I wouldn't let the whole pile go for less than twenty thousand, well maybe fifteen."

"Nope"

"I got ten in it myself, so it ain't going for less."

"I'll give you five grand for the whole pile, clamps and gaskets included."

I figured he was hurting; it was beyond me what this old timer was doing with the pipe to begin with. He certainly wasn't your average junk dealer. Somehow, he had got hold of this pipe, he probably didn't know how or why, but I was pretty sure he needed cash, and probably wanted to see the pipe go.

"Well, I got to get some money. Seven thousand five hundred dollars, cash or certified check, maybe we have a deal?"

I stuck my hand out, "Yup, tell you what I'll do. Here is a brand new, crisp hundred-dollar bill. It's yours; nobody else looks at this pipe from here on out. I'll have a truck here within the week to start hauling. You will get a thousand-dollar check from the University of Nevada every time we get a load, and I'll hold the last thousand until we have it all. The hundred is yours to keep as long as this deal works, but if it falls through, I'll be back to get the hundred." I could kind of feel him wince in his handshake on the last words, but I was pretty confident I

463

had his number. "Also, you'll have to help my driver load. Probably have to have two men, and my driver tends to get a little grouchy if things don't go right."

"Wait, helping load wasn't really part of the deal."

"Neither was that hundred," I countered as I was reaching for it.

"Well, OK, I guess my nephew can help, and we got a loader that works sometimes."

It took me ten hours to get back to Reno, so bright and early the next morning I was in Bohmont's office. "I believe I got close to 40,000 feet of used eight-inch steel pipe, located in Prineville, up in Oregon. The guy took $7,500 for the whole work. Don't trust him, so I want to pay him about a thousand each trip, hold the last thousand or fifteen hundred until we have it all. It'll be a fairly easy haul for Lingenfelter."

"Well, as usual you don't do anything by the rule book, but you do get results. I'll OK everything, but I am sure Pete and Lingenfelter will scream their damn fool heads off," Bohmont concluded. I couldn't do much but concur.

"Christ, Hope, I can't authorize a purchase of this nature, just based on your word. Besides, the University won't issue a check every load like you wants," Pete Test said in a voice sufficiently high enough to be heard several offices away. He continued in his usual excited somewhat Italian accent, "Hope, you're going to be the ruination of me, I just can't continue to let you do this kind of flagrant violation of University purchasing regulations."

"Say Pete, Professor Hope found his pipe and for a lot less than what we thought it would cost," Bohmont cheerfully explained as he stuck his head into the accounting office.

464

"Yeah, sure, I'll get it taken care of Dean," concluded Pete. By then I was out of the office, hopefully faster than the dagger that I was sure had been aimed at my back.

"Look, you miserable bastard, I am not going to Prineville to bring back junk pipe, not even once, and you want me to go up to maybe eight times? Besides, my rig will never get clearance in either California or Idaho and I sure as hell don't know how else you're going to get there." Lingenfelter exclaimed.

"Oh, its OK, I have already checked with the Oregon patrol, you can get a permit that will be good for six months in Lakeview, all you got to do is go straight from Nevada to Oregon, just take the Winnemucca to the Sea Highway. Bohmont thinks it's a great idea."

As I was crawling into my pick-up, I distinctly hear muttering about that God damn Dean, he couldn't even drive a rig if he had to, much less over Doughty Grade. Well, anyway, apparently Lingenfelter knew about Doughty Grade, a grade on the Winnemucca to the Sea Highway, that would make just about anybody nervous, but he said he was the best, so I was taking him at his word.

It took about a month and a half; we got a load every week, couple of times twice a week. But in the end, we had stacked in neat racks, some 1,115 joints of usable 40-foot X eight-inch pipe, plus gaskets and couplers. At $7,500 for the works, not counting transportation that came to a little less than seventeen cents a foot. Finally, even Pete said it sounded like a good deal.

And it was a good deal, likely the best I had ever made to date for the Gund. Now all we had to do was wait for Ross Dikins to get all the paperwork to the State Engineer and get his go ahead. Soon we will be laying pipes.

Everything seemed to be going very well about right then, but the invariable call from my good friend Dale Bohmont always could tip the scales very rapidly. "Professor, you remember sometime back you placed an astronomical value on the Gund gift, something like $440,00 or thereabouts?"

"Yup, what's wrong now" I asked?

"There is a letter here from Mr. Gund's account, that David Gist, you remember him? Well, just like I predicted, the IRS is questioning the gifting value of that amount. The letter implies that they may need some help in justifying that value, and if we can't, then you will have a very big problem on your hands."

You had to love the guy, totally predictable, and I was sure, just like he said, I may have a big problem. Not really, ranch prices had escalated since the gift, and now that it was generally accepted as an experiment station, not a ranch, the value would surely stand. All I had to do was construct the letter for Bohmont to send to Gist and his lawyer friends explaining the facts. How the hell would the IRS know how to value an Experiment Station anyway?

"Here is what you do Dean, rewrite this letter that I have roughed out, explaining with the improvements in place, the property would easily be valued in excess of a half million dollars from a ranch standpoint. However, the value of the gift was basically impossible to accurately account for in the first place, because this property was essentially the only property available in the State of Nevada to establish a range ranch type Experiment Station, which we have done, know known as the Gund Research and Development Ranch. As such, I would conservatively place the value of this property at two million dollars today. It is essentially irreplaceable from our standpoint. We were looking at ranch properties before Mr. Gunds generous gift became available which would have cost the University several million dollars."

"Dr. Hope, frankly most of the time you scare the hell out of me, and now is just one of those times. How in the hell do you think you can convince the IRS that that dried up piece of alkali could be worth two million dollars, yet as you have proven to me a thousand times, you just ride on your blind luck, and date with a great deal of success. Tell you what I am going to do. I will let you write the letter, and I will let you sign the damn thing. You will sink or swim, I am just getting too damn tired of stepping up to the plate to bail you out one more time. Hopefully, for your sake, your luck will hold one more time."

So, OK, I wrote the letter, with a cc to Bohmont. And it got me an invitation to a mighty fine address in downtown San Francisco to justify my continuation of being a professor at Nevada.

Gund's San Francisco headquarters was on about the tenth floor of a downtown building on Market Street, and it was impressive. Gund wasn't present; Gist and three lawyers, long since forgot their names, and two squirrelly looking gents from the IRS. Everyone had a copy of my original letter, as well as my map, outlining all the improvements to date, as well as anticipated ones. I had prepared a brief outline of the values but had been very careful to only talk in generalities, as in this meeting, I sure didn't want to get tied to something I couldn't defend.

The questions weren't tough, as it appeared that the two IRS nerds just were not familiar with the concepts surrounding a land grant university, such as Nevada. I made the point, because the University was a land grant university, that it had a legal obligation to assist the agriculture industries of the state of Nevada, and certainly Nevada's number one agriculture product was cattle. Therefore, we legally had to have an experiment station dedicated to a range of livestock production, regardless of the cost. I explained how we had a ranch search committee,

467

consisting of highly respected livestock producers, just couldn't find the right property, all the ones we looked at were well in excess of a million dollars, and they didn't fit the bill.

I explained how I had appraised the property, coming up with the $440,000 figure. "I just used standard appraisal techniques, exactly as any appraiser would have done. I appraised it as an ongoing operational ranch. However, if I had appraised it as the potential experiment station that it now is, I would probably have placed a much higher value on it, probably between three quarters and a million dollars. No other property, to our knowledge in all Nevada, had the potential to accomplish that goal."

I tried not to wince when I saw the look of frustration, maybe even anger, on Gist's face when the three quarter to a million-figure drifted by his beady eyes and sniffing nose. I doubted that old David missed many dollars in his efforts on behalf of Gund, and a million was a lot bigger tax deduction than $400,000 or so. But, if my gamble worked, they at least would get a legitimate deduction of $440,000, and that was way more than their original estimate.

Well, the gamble worked, the IRS approved the gifted value of $440,000 for Gund without question. I didn't even remind Bohmont that I guessed I could keep my current position for a bit longer, probably just best to let that one go. I did enjoy the trip to San Francisco, even if I had to pay for it myself.

It's funny sometimes how things work out. You can have a project where the obstacles seem insurmountable, yet when it's all over and done with, suddenly everything just sails through, and all you can do is ask yourself what you were so worried about. I guess the IRS fiasco was kind of that way. Other times you might not have a care in the world, you're just sailing through, you got it made. Then suddenly, your whole world falls apart. My pipeline project was one such event.

I had just finished teaching my ecology class when the phone rang. It was Phyllis, Bohmont's secretary. "You better get right up here; the Dean is pretty upset." I didn't bother to ask who he was upset about; it went without saying, it would be me. My only problem was that this time I didn't have the slightest idea what my problem was.

"Hi Dean, Phyllis said you wanted to see me," I cheerfully announced as I casually strolled into his office.

"Buddy, you told me there wouldn't be a damn single problem with your pipeline project. Well, guess what, you got problems, and this is the kind of problem that can get us all."

I could tell he was mad, in fact probably as mad as I had ever seen him. I couldn't imagine what the problem might be, except one thought did creep into my head, ownership of the pipe. I always wondered if it might be hot – I was beginning to imagine the headlines in the Journal; Local Prof indicted on charges of fencing stolen property --! When suddenly that fear went out the window.

"Look, I have here a response from the State Engineer, simply says your application for six pipelines to divert waters of the State of Nevada for beneficial use has been temporarily denied. We are attaching a protest from the BLM in regard to your application. Until this matter is resolved we are withholding your application. If the matter can not be resolved, your application will have to be resubmitted, however, due to the nature of the BLM protest, it would be unlikely that the State would override their protest and grant your permit."

The words reviberated through my head, much like a ton of tin cans being dropped in a cement floor in an empty metal building. I was stunned; just about the last thing imaginable had happened. My first reaction was to blame Ross, but I knew that was hopeless, this buck pretty well had to stop with me, and my big mouth.

"You have no idea what this will cost me. When the word gets out that we spent $7,500 for junk pipe, another $5,000 to haul it from Oregon, much less nearly $10,000 in surveying, map preparation and filing fees, only to learn that it would be impossible to ever get our hands on the water to begin with, the Council of Deans, much less the President will make me the laughingstock of the University. You better figure a way to resolve this situation, or you will be lucky to end up being a lab technician, which is where you should have stayed to begin with."

Yeah, I could tell he was really mad. I had yet to say a word, in fact about right then I was thinking about not saying anything, maybe it would be best to just look dumb, and actually, being a lab tech was not the end of the world.

"Why didn't you know that the west side of the Simpson Park Mountain Range was declared a Public Water Reserve by President Hoover in 1927?"

Oh, now I began to see where my problem was, I just didn't do my history, didn't know what old Hoover did eight years before I was born. Christ, don't say a word, just hang tough and think. Wait a minute, those ditches are a hell of a lot older than 1927. The State has vested rights – there's a hell of a mistake.

"OK Dean, I admit I didn't say a word to the BLM, but I believe there is a mistake, and give me a few days, I believe that I can get your project back on track. If not, maybe we can build a big barn with all that pipe." He didn't see the humor in that, either, or proceeded to inform me in words that I wouldn't forget for a while that the God

Damn project was mine to begin with. I wanted to say that if I got everything fixed and the pipes worked, would it be his project then?

I snuck out of the second floor the back way. Being pretty red around the ears, I didn't feel an encounter with Pete Test would be good for either of our presently semi-healthy conditions right now. Besides I had to do some quick research and thinking. The first place I went to was the library to find out just what in the hell a public water reserve was to begin with. That didn't take long.

The Public Water Reserve Act was set up when concern was expressed that the early cattle and sheep barons were establishing control over all the waters throughout the west. The fear was expressed that pioneers migrating west, or simply moving about the country would not be able to acquire water for their stock, or oxen, or even themselves, so various appropriate areas were set aside as public water reserves, forever making those waters available to the public. I had a little trouble understanding how the pioneers were still wandering around Grass Valley in 1927 when the Simpson Park Reserve was set apart. Oh well, maybe my friend Gene Nodine could explain that.

"Hi Gene, this is Terry Hope at the University. I understand you protested our water filings at the Gund Ranch," I meekly spoke over the phone.

"Yes Terry, I had to, our resource people in Reno are really sticklers about that, and your applications for points of diversion are not only on public land, but they all fall within a Public Water Reserve. We are bound by law to not allow water within a public water reserve to be tied up for any use, other than that which benefits the general public."

I kind of wanted to say that I hadn't seen a covered wagon coming up the valley lately, but finally thought better of that approach. "I guess I don't fully understand the concept of this public water reserve. I kind of thought that the old ditches that the Walti's had build would have superseded that act by some point in time?"

"Well, for your benefit, I kind of thought that might be the case also, but our resource people really researched the facts, and they can't find any indication that those ditches were ever built prior to 1927, so they denied your application."

Oh boy – I thought the State Engineer was the one that denied the application, not the BLM, they just opposed it. I kind of remembered once somebody telling me to watch out for the growth of the bureaucracy. There was a lot I wanted to say about right then, but I figured maybe to ask for help was the best approach. "Say, Gene, would it be possible for you and some of your resource people to come to the Gund and better explain this public water reserve concept to me? I think I had better understand this pretty well before I put my foot in my mouth again."

"Sure Terry, I am sure I could get some of our group from Reno, as well as my resource people from here and meet with you to explain this whole thing. I think if you had a better understanding of the Public Water Reserve Act it would make you feel better about this whole situation. Sounds like a good idea, we'll be looking forward to the opportunity."

"Great, I'll have a big pot of coffee ready for when you all show up. Let's see, today's Friday, how about next Tuesday at about 9 in the morning.

I thought about those old maps I had encountered in the Ag library years ago when I was doing my initial research for my master's project. Unfortunately, the Walti's never filed on anything with the State Engineer in regard to their assumed grazing allotment, much less water rights. Nor had Doc Allen, even though the Baughman's had.

So factual data wasn't too plentiful. Even though I could substantiate when the Walti family made the original homestead, early '70's, I had never found anything factual information concerning dates, water applications (all was vested) or anything else for that matter. But I knew one thing beyond any reasonable doubt, and that was that those ditches were a hell of a lot older than I was. And the water reserve was only seven years older than me. I had to figure out a way to prove that point beyond question.

The thought occurred to me that I had better talk to Ross before I went any further. After all, he should have known about the Public Water Reserve, and maybe he might have a bit more history on those ditches.

"Ross, did you know that the BLM protested our filings?"

"Well, no, at least not to a couple of days ago. I talked to one of my good BLM contacts, and he indicated that they had sent in a protest. I asked him on what basis, and he responded on the basis that the BLM was never going to let your request for 10,000 acres of public land to be transferred to the University happen. And their first line of defense was to not let you get your hands on the water."

"I understand the water reserve, but those ditches are a lot older that the reserve."

"I agree, but I can find no published documentation on those ditches anywhere. Furthermore, the only surviving Walti is in the Philippines on some sort of a religious adventure, and no one has a current address. Without his testimony, you have a problem. You got to find some way to prove the ages of those ditches, no other way. I'll help you anyway I can, but that's the bottom line. And as adamant as my BLM friend was, its going to take something bullet proof, because I think thy have made up their mind, that transfer is not going through!"

473

I kind of wanted to meet the BLM folks at Sheep Corral Canyon for some special reasons. First of all, the best-defined remnant ditch from yesteryear was at Sheep Corral, and there was good fresh stream of water there, just right for making old fashioned cowboy coffee. Sure, enough about nine in the morning the bureaucrats showed up, three cars worth, two out of the main office in Reno and one from the Battle Mountain District.

Gene was an OK kind of guy, at least for a BLM employee. However, the bunch from Reno didn't look like they had been out in the weather much. Earrings, ponytails, and ill-fitting slacks just didn't add to their demeanor. Will, I played the part of a good ranch host. The coffee was good and hot, with plenty of fresh cream and sugar. It was a cold winter morning, so the coffee went over good. After introductions, Gene covered the Act in good fashion. I acted like I enjoyed the lecture, including the fact that Grass Valley was much better off having this Public Water Reserve at our back door. After Gene was done, I was subjected to a few snide remarks from the Reno nerds, but again, being the gracious host, I just smiled and agreed. Finally, it was my turn.

"This has really been informative, and I appreciate your efforts no end. However, I just can't seem to understand what the difference is between me taking water out of this stream into this ditch that we are standing on or putting it directly into a pipe at the same location."

Gene appeared that perhaps I was trying his patience, but once more he attempted to explain to my limited mentality why I basically couldn't put it in the pipe, or even in the ditch for that matter, "Terry, its pretty simple. This reserve was created in 1927. Simply put the water on this side of this mountain, including all of these drainages was reserved for public use, not the use of any individual, including in this case the University."

474

"Well, OK, then I guess the Walti's were illegal to put water in these ditches to begin with, is that right?"

"Yes, they were, but the BLM just wasn't well enough organized to do anything about it then."

"OK, now I understand, the Reserve was created in 1927, the BLM was created around 1935, and the Battle Mountain District was finally created about 1955, last such district created in the U.S. Then I guess sometime prior to 1955 the Walti's built these ditches, which at that point in time were just plain and simple illegal."

"Yes, I think that's a fair assessment of the situation."

"Alright, but suppose the Walti's had built the ditches prior to 1927, would that have made them legal?"

"Yes, it would have, if they would have filed on these waters with the State Engineer, but there is no record of that ever having happened, so they were still illegal if that were the case."

"Alright, now let's suppose just for the sake of argument that these ditches were built prior to 1905, which of course as you realize is the cutoff point for vested water rights, then would these ditches have been legal?" I could see Gene starting to get a bit uneasy, like maybe he suddenly thought I might know more than he had given me credit for.

"Well, theoretically, you would be right, if the ditches had been built before 1905, then even your application would be legal in the eyes of the BLM. However, our resource people have done considerable research in this matter, and we can find absolutely no indication that the Walti family ever built these ditches anywhere close to that time."

I kind of wondered what possible research they could have accomplished to make that statement. I had never been able to find any written information to substantiate that point in time, and obviously nor had Ross. Old Emil Walti, who was probably 40 years older than me, had told me that his grandfather had built all of those ditches with a mule and a Fresno. Grampa Walti apparently died at age 96 around 1910. Course, that's merely hearsay, probably not usable information for BLM standards, but I did have another option.

I had chosen Sheep Corral for one additional reason. Squarely on a very man-made ditch bank, the prettiest little pinion tree was growing, and I kind of felt that tree just might make my case.

"I guess what you're saying then, is that pinion tree over there by our coffee fire must be less than forty years of age, because obviously by where its at, its younger than that ditch bank." I could see by Gene's face that he might just realized that he had been had. For I believed he knew enough pinion ecology to probably know that the tree in question was a lot older than 40 years of age. However, the Reno nerds hadn't quite caught on yet, at least as evidenced by their faces.

I had put a brand-new chain saw in the back of my pick-up, covered with a tarp. Previous to anybody showing up I had successfully started it with one pull. And to maximize the effect of the lesson I was about to teach, I prayed it would start with one pull, once again. I was successful.

Before anybody could realize what was happening, I had the saw at full roaring throttle biting into the pinion trunk about an inch above the ground. It all happened in seconds, the tree lying on its side, a nice stump very visible, and the saw safely back in my pick-up just about as quick. All done just in case anybody wanted to count rings.

The uproar was outrageous. One of the Reno nerds claimed he had police powers and could arrest me on the spot for destroying government property. I got right in his face, "Bud, I just exercised my right for ditch repair and cleaning, this tree was going to obstruct the flow of water. By the way, if anybody wants to count rings, here's a magnifying glass." I could see Gene was beaten by the expression on his face. But one of the nerds insisted on counting rings, so I said, "Be my guest, I'll have another cup of coffee while you count." I was really pretty sure the tree would be at least seventy-five years of age, if not a hundred, based on my research of the previous day. I had cut down a number of pinions elsewhere and counted rings just to be sure. Fortunately, the BLM never found my research site, as it was all on federal lands as well.

After several attempts to count rings, it was agreed that the tree was approximately 95 years old, making it born around 1880. "Guess that makes this ditch legal after all," I concluded.

Nodine didn't have much to say, except that he would be sending a letter to the State Engineer the next day removing their protest.

"All six canyons?"

"Yes", as he climbed into his car and headed towards Battle Mountain.

Telling Bohmont was kind of anticlimactic. His response was along the lines of good, I knew you could take care of the problem. As I left his office, I mentioned something about the fact that I was glad that the President wouldn't have to fire him for wasting taxpayer dollars. If the look on Phyllis's face meant anything, I probably would have already been dead.

We didn't get any pipelines that winter, because we had a real winter. In fact, we didn't make much progress the next summer because there was just too much going on, and frankly we were still recovering from winter. But within two years, we had five pipelines, four of them serving meadows, which greatly increased our hay production. The fifth line eventually served our agronomic plots, as well as the house for the agronomic technician. Time would eventually allow us the chance at finishing the sixth line. Couldn't hardly ever look at those pipelines without thinking of the expression on Gene Nodine's face that cold winter day when he finally figured out that I had completely out maneuvered him.

Someone once told me that winters in central Nevada are sometimes difficult. However, with our headquarters located at about 5,700 feet in elevation, I had already prepared ourselves for the worst, or I assumed. The winter of 1974-75 started off pretty typical. By Thanksgiving, we had some snow on the mountain, it had already been down to zero once or twice, but all of that was to be expected. By December, I was finishing up my class work, and the deep freeze had set in so there wasn't any need for me to go out every weekend. Besides we had enough hay to last to mid April, and we were legal to turn out by March 15, so things seemed pretty good. My time was better spent in the library getting ready for my pitch to newly elected Congressman Santini as to why the BLM should give us about 10,000 acres.

We had a big family Christmas in Reno, and everybody was pretty busy for the holidays. However, I had decided that a quick trip to Grass Valley sometime between Christmas and New Years was appropriate just to make sure everything was OK. I had been able to get a hold of Rich on our antique phone system. Although it had snowed, he assured me that the road in from Austin was clear. So, after lunch on Wednesday, I headed out.

It was pretty obvious that it had snowed all right. Highway 50 was icy from Fallon through Austin, so I didn't clear Austin Summit until about nine that night, but I was in luck, because the Grass Valley Road had been plowed out. I stopped at the intersection to relieve myself, then I finally realized just how cold it really was. Didn't have a thermometer, but it had to be well below zero. Well, the road was plowed, and I was pretty sure it would be all the way to the Grass Valley Ranch, and from there I knew I wouldn't have a problem.

The road was icy, so I slipped my Ford into four-wheel drive, and started thinking how nice a warm fire in the High Place would be. Hadn't gone more than two miles, when a bend in the road seemed to come up a bit faster than I anticipated. I knew all the maneuvers for ice, but when your inertia is sufficiently great it really doesn't matter how good you are at driving on ice. The turn was to the left, but the pick-up just seemed to want to go straight. As I watched the freshly plowed berm come up from the right, I realized that we would hit, but I had hit snow berms before, and other than scattering a little snow, nothing serious ever happened. However, this berm seemed a little different, kind of like it was made of concrete.

For a second, I thought we were going over, but finally my trusty Ford 4X4 3/4-ton pickup righted itself, and gradually slid to a stop. There was some snow powder on the window, so I couldn't really see exactly where I was, so I just opened the door and stepped out. I was dumbfounded, but the ground was no longer where it should be. In fact, when I finally hit the ground, it was directly on my back, with an awful thud to my head. I had the feeling the ground was several feet from where it should have been. Also, as I lay on the icy road and looked up, I could make out the outline of my pick-up against the stars, and it seemed several feet higher than it should be.

In due time I collected my wits, managed to get a flashlight, which seemed like climbing Mount Everest, and surveyed the situation. Sure, enough, the road had been plowed, and all the snow had been plowed into a berm on the right side of the road, probably a three to four feet high berm. We hit it, slid right on top of it before grinding to a halt. And the berm was frozen just about as hard as the concrete that I thought I would hit. And the most amazing thing about the whole incident was that the pick-up was perfectly balanced on the berm, and no wheel was closer than three to four inches to reaching anything, snow, ice, or much less roadway! So much for four-wheel drive.

Damn, it was cold, but I did have enough clothes, jacks and tools to do about anything. However, chipping at the frozen berm with a shovel proved futile. I thought about walking back to Highway 50, but it was the loneliest road in America, and traffic wasn't very heavy tonight, in fact I hadn't remembered seeing a car since Fallon, and that's nearly 200 miles ago. No, I did this, I will fix it. Then I remembered that I still had the chain saw that had done Nodine in earlier. And I was right in the middle of a forest of pinions. And this was Forest Service land, so at least I wouldn't make the BLM any madder.

After due consideration, I figured that if I could knock down several tall pinions, clean them up, I could make a sort of wedge, which in due time should get the damn truck off the berm. Well, it worked, but it did take more trees than I figured on. Guess I finally cut down twenty or so, but along about 5 a.m. we hit solid ground. I don't know if that open spot in the forest is still there, but it sure enough remained open for as long as I traveled the Grass Valley Road. I suppose the Forest Service would have thrown the book at me, but by springtime when they finally showed up, the evidence as to my involvement would have been pretty minimal.

Rich showed up at the High Place around seven, and I was still drinking coffee in a feeble attempt to get ready for the day, even though I never had hit the sack.

"Hell, you look like you had a mighty long night in Austin. Didn't know there was enough nightlife there to keep you up that late. Did you get any sleep?"

I didn't say a word, just went to the cabinet, pulled out the bottle of whiskey and poured us both a shot in our coffee. "Well, you might not believe this, but this is what happened," It took a couple of more coffees to get clear through the story, but it was a good one, one that lived for a long time in the annals of the Gund Research and Demonstration Ranch.

The snow seemed to just keep coming that winter. Every few days there would be another half to a foot, and no thaw was in sight. Before long, sufficient snow existed so that the road from Austin just couldn't be kept open any longer due to drifting. So, I could only access the Gund by I-80 to Beowawee, then south through Crescent Valley, up through Cortez pass to Grass Valley. That added about a hundred and twenty five miles, one way, to my usual twice-weekly trips, but at least I wasn't stuck in a snowdrift, or so I thought.

Despite the cold and the snow, our haystacks were sufficiently large, that we had hay through March, besides we could turn out by March 15, and my experience was such that snow on the flat was always gone be the first of March. However, by January 15th, the bottom fell out of the temperature, first it hit ten below, then twenty, and by around January 25th, we broke the record for Grass Valley at −35 degrees below zero, Fahrenheit. At that temperature, diesel motors get pretty hard to start, in fact about impossible. However, our saving grace was the hot springs. Every night we took water hoses and placed them around the tractor motors, with hot running water, so the following morning, starting just wasn't a problem. We did, however, build some mighty big ice fields where all the water drained out. The faithful old Wittie just kept humping away. Don't know what we would have ever done if it had died in the middle of the night – guess from that point on we just might have done without electricity.

One Friday night I made a mad dash to the Gund with John Coote, who had now finally become a legitimate graduate student. We came in from the north, so it was long after dark when we hit the High Place.

The thermometer read −18, and it seemed even colder in the High Place. So, the first order was to build a roaring fire in the wood stove.

"John, there's kindling wood in the lean too out back, throw a bunch of it in the stove, also there is a can of diesel out there as well, throw some of that in so we get warm, I'll start unpacking our grub and stuff. Be careful, there's a can of gas also, there both labeled," I cautioned.

I was unloading stuff, nearly stumbling over John each trip, as the wood stove was right alongside the front door. I had had John as a graduate student for a bit longer than normal, a slow learner, but by now he pretty well knew the ropes, or at least I thought. Brought him out this trip to see how he liked the cold weather, sort of part of my grad student training program so to speak. I had already figured out that John wasn't a rocket scientist, but I thought he could at least read.

"OK, I got this thing ready to go where is a match," he asked.

I reached over above the range and handed him a box, from which he promptly struck a match and threw it into the stove.

KABOOM! The blast knocked both of us off our feet, as we were standing directly in front of the open stove door. There was a bit of resulting fire about the High Place, but not bad all things considered. Lost count, but I believe three mice flew by in various stages of being on fire. I just hoped that the big old bull snake that lived in the walls would survive, he was too damn valuable.

As things slowly started to come to order, I noticed John was missing most of his hair, about the only damage I suffered was my mustache got shortened up a bit, and a brand-new Pendleton shirt was a little bit on fire. Other than that, we were fine.

John's first response was, "By golly, I think I got the fire going."

Well, he was right, but the fire outside the stove was growing at an alarming rate as well. However, a few shovels full of snow and we pretty soon had most of the fire in the right place.

"Damn, Boss, I think somebody switched cans on you."

"Look again, John, the can you used says gas, G A S!"

"I guess your right, it sure looked like diesel to me."

"We may have you take remedial English before you finish your master's program," was about all that I could offer at that point.

It took about an hour to warm the High Place up and get everything back to order. By then the outside temperature had dropped to –25, so a big fire was required. At that point there wasn't much else to do but get out the whiskey bottle. I guess in hindsight we were lucky to not have been badly damaged, but the blast must have been so fast that it just blew right past us. After a couple of drinks, I began to laugh looking at John's lopsided crew cut, most of which was missing from the left side of his head. He got to laughing too, because he claimed my mustache was awful lopsided. The High Place didn't have the luxury of a usable mirror that night, so all we could do was laugh at each other. Don't suppose the mice much appreciated our antics!

By February, I still couldn't get to Grass Valley from the south, and the snow was starting to melt on the north, so that road was washed out about as much as it was good. Somehow we kept going, but if every winter was going to be like this, maybe Grass Valley wasn't such a neat place after all. But even at that I still had more to learn about snow.

Along about the last of February John Marvel called, "Say, you always have to go through Battle Mountain now, how about stopping in your next trip, some things I want to pick your brain on." John and I had met several times since the field day, so I enjoyed seeing him, and his lovely wife, Willie. They were both graduates of the University, so we had much in common, besides Nevada livestock. John's ranch was at Dunphy, about 25 miles east of Battle Mountain, which left me about a hundred miles to go to get to Grass Valley.

John was becoming increasingly concerned about the upcoming Environmental Impact Statement concerning livestock grazing in the Tonopah Unit of the Battle Mountain District of the BLM. "I don't like a lot of what I see in this first draft, have you reviewed it yet?"

"No, frankly John, I just haven't had time, but I suppose I should."

From there our conversation pretty much centered about if I would be willing to take a lead role on behalf of the Nevada Cattlemen's Association in reviewing and making comments concerning the upcoming document.

"Of course, I'll review it, and make a prepared statement. That's perfectly within my rights as a livestock professor at the University. Besides, the nature of this Impact Statement may well dictate our future research efforts at the Gund."

The evening was wearing on, it was already 10 p.m., and I had a hundred miles yet to go. But Willie thought better, "Terry, you had better just stay here tonight, we had another good snow last night, and that road up through Cortez Canyon could be pretty snowy and icy."

But my usual thick-headed self came through once more, "Thanks Willie, but with four-wheel drive I am sure I won't have a problem. Besides. I promised my boys that I would be there bright and early tomorrow morning, as we got to make sure we have enough hay to finish this winter that never seems to want to quit."

"Well, I think its dumb to be taking off this late at night with the kind of winter we have been having, but I suppose you are as thick headed as John, he would do the same!"

As I exited, John gave me a wink as, I guess, acknowledging Willie that he was indeed just that thick headed as well. It was cold, about zero, but the freeway was absolutely clear, and you could see stars by the millions. At least it wasn't snowing. From Dunphy, it's only a few miles to the Beowawe turn off, then about 45 miles of pavement before the gravel starts at the mouth of Cortez Canyon. It probably had been less than an hour before I started up Cortez, which is not a long canyon, but the elevation does rise about a thousand feet before getting into Grass Valley.

As I started up, I did notice more and more snow, finally the road was covered, but there were several sets of tire tracks visible. However, I also noticed the further I went the more the wind was blowing as well as some snow. About halfway up I hit a fresh snow drift, about 12 – 18" deep, but at thirty miles per hour and in four-wheel drive it didn't slow us down a bit. There were several more drifts, each a bit deeper, with the last one almost stopping me. I was starting to get a bit concerned, as I had never seen drifts this big in the Canyon, except right at the crest of the Canyon. I reasoned that with the wind coming out of the southwest, there could be a fairly large drift there. And the problem with that drift was that you could never see it until you were right into it because of a bend in the road. I was sure I could make it, as the blown powder hadn't had the opportunity to freeze, and so far, it was relatively light.

So, I upped my speed to about 45, rounded the corner, and there she was, the mother of all snowdrifts! It was far too late to stop, so I just stepped on the throttle as hard as I could. Closed my eyes and prayed for the best. For awhile it kind of felt like we were floating in slow motion, but finally it definitely felt like the pick-up had stopped, but the wheels were going, at least I was pretty sure that was the case. I let off on the throttle, put it in neutral, turned on the windshield wipers to clear the snow so that I could assess my situation. Nothing happened, that seemed strange. I turned on the dome light, I could see the wipers, but they hadn't moved a bit. I also noticed that the window was solid snow, solid enough that I couldn't see my headlights. That also seemed strange. I thought to myself that my next move was to open the door, step out and see how badly stuck I was. The door handle worked, but I couldn't open the door, now that seemed really strange. So, all that was left to do was roll down the window. As I did a ton of snow fell in on me, but after I got it down, I could at least see stars, so I knew I wasn't completely buried. But when I shined my flashlight out, I realized that I wasn't really far from being completely buried either.

The only way out was through the window. The crash had packed the snow in the immediate vicinity of the pick-up to a degree that I could more or less walk on it, but a few feet away, and you would fall in, and it was about four feet deep. I finally made it to the other side of the drift, and I finally got the whole picture. I had actually made it to the center of the drift, perhaps a bit more than halfway. However, the impact had pushed snow completely over the top of the truck, and the snow on both sides had settled in so tight that it was impossible to open either door. In front of me towards Grass Valley, there didn't appear to be over six inches of snow on the road. I just lacked about ten feet of making it.

Oh well, it really wasn't that cold, not a cloud in the sky, and the moon had come up, so on the fresh snow, I didn't even need a light. All I had to do was to get back to the back of the truck, retrieve the shovel and go to work. It was twelve straight up.

It's funny how heavy a shovel of snow, even powder can get after an hour or two, or even how sweaty you can get even if it is about zero. It took nearly four hours to reach the front of the pick-up, but I knew I wasn't finished yet. Even in four-wheel drive on this slippery surface the snow would have to be moved mostly from the sides before this glacier would release my truck. And by 6 a.m. I was on my way.

I just got the High Place warmed up when Rich drove up about 7:30. "Say, didn't I hear you drive by about an hour ago? I thought you were coming in last night. What the hell did you do, have a big time with the girls in Winnemucca? Your sure enough look like you did."

"Remember last month when I made you that coffee after spending all night down Austin way? Well, I did the same God damned thing last night on Cortez Summit! Here drink up."

"You know what? I almost came looking for you last night when you didn't show up by ten. Pam talked me out of it, said you're a big boy now, surely can take care of yourself. I agreed, specially as warm as the bed was."

Rather than kill Rich I thought more about Willie's comment about being thick headed. She may have had a point.

By the time I headed back to Reno, Lander County had plowed the drifts, but they still looked menacingly like they could blow shut again at a minute's notice. On the way back to Reno I started to wonder if maybe some of my opposition had a point after all. "Too damn isolated, especially in the winter," I had heard those words many times from my colleagues, and right about now, maybe they were right. However, it wasn't like me to admit that somebody was right, especially after I had told them they were wrong to begin with.

Two days back in Reno tended to make snowdrifts seem a thing of the past. Besides, a late afternoon call from Pete saying he would meet me at Louies around 5 reduced the perils of Grass Valley down to nothing more than a great experience to talk about.

"What brings you to Reno? Besides, driving from Buffalo to East Gate should cause you to miss Reno," I inquired, as the first picon gently swirled in front of me.

"Well, I needed some supplies, there's not much at East Gate, except a lot of cattle someplace, and I still haven't figured that out yet. Besides Gina just about has Salt Wells open, and I am supposed to pick up her first girls tonight. She has a house here in Reno, and there supposed to be there about seven. I promised I would deliver them by nine tonight safe and sound."

"Your really serious about running girls for her! When you told me that last month, I thought you were just bull shitting me. Christ, my best friend, not only from college, but ever since, turns out to be nothing but running girls for immoral purposes. I can't believe it. God almighty, what would Joe Robertson say, what would Verle Bohman say, what would your mother say? Wait, forget I said that!"

"God damn it, get off my ass. This is a legitimate operation, I already told you that. I am just taking the girls out as a favor for Gina. Besides, outside of dropping them off, I got to be at East Gate tonight, because I am interviewing potential cow bosses at about six tomorrow morning. Now, if you didn't have your nose so out of joint about my helping Gina, I would offer to meet you at Salt Wells one of these days and show you around. Gina still remembers you, says she sees your name in the paper all the time."

I didn't know rather to feel sorry for Pete, or maybe I was actually jealous of his good fortune. I knew for sure in short order, Pete would know his way around Salt Wells, especially if Gina was really going to give him "favors" for delivering her girls. I didn't understand why Pete never thought about marriage. I knew for a fact that there was a whole string of girls from the University that would follow him anywhere, given the chance. I guess he just liked to play the field, and now with Salt Wells at his disposal, his field was pretty big.

"How do you like this winter? You must be getting lots of snow at East Gate; we sure have it in Grass Valley. I can't even begin to get in from the Austin end, got to go clear to Beowawe, then south through Crescent Valley, over 250 miles more driving, round trip," I offered as an intelligent way to quit talking about Salt Wells.

"I am going to the East Gate headquarters tonight, but that's the first time in a month or so. Been going to the turn off to Gabbs and going to Gabbs Valley. I got a little camp trailer down there, got two cowboys down there, we're still gathering for a final count. I'll bet there are at least two feet of snow on the ground right above East Gate. Haven't been to the other side, Campbell Creek, but I heard there is more snow over there."

"How many cows you got gathered for the count so far?"

"Well, I think I told you the sale was contingent on 500 cows, and when I flew it last fall, I thought I counted close to 1,000. However, so far, we only have about 675 actual cows in, but we got at least 100 long yearling steers that there was no mention about in the sales agreement. Don't know what might happen there. I think there is still another 400 cows some place. I will fly it again next week, but I think what happened, some of those cows were still on the Smith Creek/Campbell Creek side of the ranch, and when all this snow started hitting, they just drifted south. My bet is some of them will be clear down on that RO country, clear to Tonopah flat, warmer there and hardly any snow. It'll sure enough make for a big gather this spring though."

Well, I could see another headache coming on, but I had to tell Pete about my pipeline stories, as well as outfoxing Nodine on our water applications. The best part was my snow stories, Pete loved it when I did something that really made me look dumb, and both of those episodes didn't exactly add to my intellectual stature.

"I can't imagine anybody being that stuck in the snow, not once, but twice, and in the same winter to boot. That's the problem with you Californians, you'll likely winter kill when a real winter comes along."

I kind of thought this was a real winter, and calling me a Californian, instead of complimenting me on how I survived, much less got myself out kind of hurt my feelings. "Well, its 6:30, you got to go pick up your whores at seven and deliver them to the madam, safe and sound. I guess that doesn't really qualify you as a pimp, but there must be a name for somebody that delivers working girls. You know what that is?" I inquired.

"Well, I am going to ignore all that crap, I'll just leave it at this, when I show you around Salt Wells, you'll be talking out of the other side of your mouth then. Of course, you are being married and all, you'll just have to listen to my version of how things work there. Your right, I got to go. Don't get stuck in another drift!" With the usual handshake we left, and just to make it seem right, it was snowing.

Fortunately, our earth ground telephone system worked best in cold weather, so I was able to keep pretty close on things, long distance anyway. Don't know why the snow hadn't knocked the poles down, but so far, the system was intact and working amazingly well. According to Rich's count, we had enough hay to hold everything until about the 25th of March. At that time, we would have enough hay to feed the replacement heifers, horses and bulls, as well as cows that hadn't been calved yet. But the main bunch of cows would have to go out between March 20th and 25th, which meant we would have to brand

and castrate by March 15th. I kind of shuddered at that, because that meant that I would not only have to go out again, but we would be looking at least two long days, and about all I could imagine was it was going to keep right on snowing.

Besides teaching three courses, running the lab and shepherding graduate students, I just wasn't up to starting a new project. So, I told Bohmont that I wasn't going to start on the land acquisition project until summer. And that was probably just as well. As predicted, both Paul Laxalt and Jim Santini had won their elections, but I could tell by the press, that both were already just about over their heads. Hopefully by summer, at least Jim would have time to hear my story. Bohmont didn't like my delay, but when I told him how difficult things were with all the snow he mellowed and understood my predicament.

We got the cows and calves worked right on schedule, and it was even fairly warm. And out they went on the 25th, just like Rich wanted, even though green grass seemed a bit scarce. However, within two days they were spread all over the flat. At least right then there wasn't a problem with water.

However, that night after finishing the cattle I felt abnormally tired, and I felt like I was getting a fever, kind of a strep throat kind of fever. My old nemesis from rheumatic fever seemed to show up every time I pushed too hard, but usually a quick shot of penicillin from Doc Smernoff took care of the problem. Only this time Doc was 250 miles away, and I didn't fancy driving to Reno tonight, or tomorrow for that matter. With a fever of 103 or so sleep was limited. But as I lay in bed sweating it occurred to me that right here on the Gund, we had bottles of penicillin, and syringes as well, so what's to worry? As I finally drifted off to sleep, I had pleasant visions of easily inserting a needle into my ass and administering the life-giving elixir the next morning after breakfast.

Well, it didn't take long until the next a.m. to round up the necessary equipment. The only problem was the smallest gauge needle that I could find was 16 gauge. I never paid that much attention to Doc Smernoff, but I was pretty sure what he used was probably a 22 gauge, or smaller needle. In comparison, the 16-gauge needle looked like the blunt end of a telephone pole. I was beginning to have visions of failure, simply because I wasn't sure that I could watch this process, but on the other hand I damn sure didn't understand how I was going to get a shot of penicillin into my ass without watching what I was doing. Maybe I would just swallow half a jug and see if it would work orally.

In due time I got everything set up, stripped down in front of a small hand mirror that I had recently purchased to facilitate my shaving, and watched with anticipation as my hand, steadily and surely, brought the syringe and needle against the lily-white tissue of my right buttocks. Nothing happened! I pressed harder and harder, still nothing. No matter how hard I pressed it wouldn't penetrate, just pushed the skin and flesh into a deeper and deeper hole. Now I realized why we always hit cows hard and fast when we were vaccinating them. But I just couldn't bring myself to do that to myself, something just shorted out – but my temperature just kept going up!

Finally, I came to the conclusion that I wasn't going to do this by myself, at least not with a 16-gauge needle. "Rich, come over to the washroom with me, I need some help," I pleaded.

"What the hell you need in the washroom, plumbing's all fixed, I saw to that last week."

"Just come over here and give me a hand. I'll show you what when we get there."

"OK"

"I need a shot of penicillin, and because the smallest needle this God damned ranch has is 16 gauge, I just can't get it done by myself. Now here, you take this syringe, I'll drop my pants and bend over and grab hold of the wash sink. I want it in my left butt."

"OK, hold tight, because I think I am going to have to hit you pretty hard. Pam, come quick and watch what I am doing."

I heard the back door slam, so I guessed Pam was going to get to watch despite my objections. Right then getting that shot was of prime importance, regardless of the nature of the audience,

"Ready?"

"Yeah"

"OK, here it comes."

"Oooh, shit, you killed me."

"Naw, you just got a shot of penicillin, relax. I ain't never even seen a cow carry on like this". In hindsight I had to admit the shot worked as good as any that I had ever had. And for the rest of her stay at the Gund, Pam would always remind me how white my butt was, especially when I was out of sorts, or she needed something that I didn't understand the need for. Well, at least she didn't see it the next day or two, because it sure wasn't white then. Biggest damn radiating bruise I ever saw! I did make a point thereafter to always have my very own very private stock of at least 20-gauge needles.

Easter was in early April, and that coincided with a week's break in college, so a break from teaching gave me time to go to Grass Valley and do some intense planning. The University schedule didn't coincide with the public-school schedule, so Jan and the kids didn't come to the ranch for spring break, which probably was rather fortuitous, all things considered.

I had gone out on a Monday morning, still the long way, but I was getting anxious to try the Austin route, as I had heard that some people had finally gotten through. On the way out the weather forecast was calling for an increasing chance of snow throughout central Nevada, in fact by the time I got to Battle Mountain, the radio was giving snow alerts every fifteen minutes or so. However, the sky was clear, except it did look dark to the south, but it was far too warm to snow. The road was clear all the way to the ranch, which allowed me to spend the afternoon going through all the fields with Rich. At about five we returned to the High Place for a cup of coffee, as the temperature seemed to be dropping pretty fast. By the time I had coffee built a cold hard wind had come up from the south.

"I don't like this weather, in fact it scares me," commented Rich.

"I understand, after this winter, we just don't need any more storms, but I don't think this will amount to much. Probably more a thunderstorm than anything, maybe it won't snow at all," I speculated.

"I don't know, I think I better get up to the headquarters and get the chores done before this thing breaks wide open. See you in the morning."

After Rich left, I stepped out and looked to the south, and it didn't look good. In fact, the southern half of the valley wasn't visible, just a big black something. I knew it couldn't be dusty, as it was too muddy for any amount of wind to kick up anything like that, so I assumed it was just a great big thunderstorm. Well to hell with it I thought, so I stoked up the fire, put a potato in the oven, and got ready to cook a big juicy "t" bone, but first a bourbon and water.

It was just about dusk, I was ready to put the steak in the frying pan, when a big gust of wind rattled the High Place almost to the point that I thought the roof was coming off. A quick look outside confirmed my worst suspicion, it was an absolute blizzard. By the time my steak was done, the wind had died down, but the snow was still coming, at least now straight down. By eight o'clock there was at least six inches of new snow on the ground and still coming. So, I built the fire up as much as possible, jumped into bed and decided to get a much needed night's sleep.

At about six thirty the next morning I finally woke up to the beginning of sunlight. It seemed awfully bright, so I staggered out of bed, looked out the window and just about fainted. The sky was crystal clear, and the sun was breaking over Simpson Park on the damndest sight I had ever seen. Snow, snow as far as the eye could see, couldn't see anything but snow, nothing else showed. It looked to be about 36 inches, or more, of snow as a matter of fact, just about even with the windowsill. Didn't appear that there was much I could do about anything right then, my pick-up sure wasn't going anyplace, I wasn't going anyplace, so I just decided that a breakfast of beacon and eggs, with toast and coffee sounded a whole lot better that going out and coping with one more snow in this God forsaken hell hole of a place.

Fortunately, I had enough wood stored in the little lean too on the back of the High Place to get me by for a few days, so with a roaring fire, hot coffee, beacon frying in the pan, and fresh eggs being cracked, the morning really didn't seem too bad, providing one didn't look outside. I had just finished eating what in my opinion was one of the best breakfasts that I had ever had, when suddenly there was a hell of a clatter at the door. I couldn't believe anybody was there, because I was even concerned about making it to the outhouse, which wasn't more than 25 yards away.

But when I opened the door, sure enough there was Rich, although he was hard to recognize in his parka and wool cap. How he got there was immediately explained, when he stepped out of his snowshoes so he could come through the door. "Well, I ain't got no snowshoes, so I am not going very far today," I said in amazement, as he staggered through the door.

"Checked everything around the house and barns, just to be sure there wasn't anything serious broken. Looks like we survived as far as that goes. If it wasn't for these snowshoes, I couldn't have even made it to the barn. I would say we got a good 36" on the flat, and there's some drifts up on the road that are about five to seven feet deep."

It began to dawn on me that I was maybe a little bit more than snow bound. "Suppose the telephone is down?"

"Oh hell, it went with the first gust of wind about six last night," Rich responded. "Did you stay up and watch it last night?"

"Naw, I was probably asleep by 9, but there was six inches by then."

"I went to sleep about midnight, but by then I had never seen it snow that hard, couldn't see 50 feet."

"Where's Dwight" I asked.

"That poor bastard. When I was feeding the horses, he actually made it from the bunkhouse to the barn. He was muttering something about going back to Texas as soon as the road cleared. He saw my shoes, asked if I had anything else. So, I got him my cross-country skis, and finally got them on him. He got about ten yards, tipped over, then couldn't get back up. We had a hell of a time even getting the skis off of him. Got him back to the bunkhouse. Brought him a pot of hot coffee, but he said he had a bottle of whiskey, was going to drink the whole thing, and he knew that by the time he came too, the snow would all be gone, or maybe this was just all a bad dream. Anyway, to make a long story short, he isn't going to be about, but I don't know what he could do anyway."

"We got plenty of diesel for the Wittie, about the only thing to do is keep the stock in the barn fed, guess there is enough hay in the barn to last a few days?"

"Yeah, and thank God for hot water, at least we aren't freezing up,"

"Hell, I can't go anyplace, impossible to move my truck, don't have snowshoes, and sure as hell I am not going to try those cross-country skis after hearing what they did to Dwight. Our cows are scattered over a half million acres, so they sure enough are on their own for the time being. Right now, I think the best thing we can do is pray for a little warm spell, except if it gets too warm, we'll drown!"

"Well, I better be getting back to Pam, she was pretty nervous when I left her to head down here. I see you got your rifle, if you need anything, fire a couple of shots over the headquarters, and I'll try to get down. We sure will have you up for dinner tonight, but I'll be damned if I can figure how to get you there. I am going to try to fire up the D-8 and start shoving snow around up there, if I get far enough, I'll be down to rescue you. The road grader would be useless in this mess."

I couldn't do much but agree, right now, the outhouse was about the biggest obstacle that I cared to challenge.

I did have some magazines to read, and I did have some bookwork in my briefcase, so I could at least keep occupied for a while. My biggest immediate fear was that the whiskey bottle was just about empty, and right about then, the town seemed a long way away!

By one in the afternoon, I had read everything that was worth reading, rearranged everything in the High Place, and was contemplating either going to sleep, or maybe going outside and building a snow castle. My euphoria, however, was suddenly broken by the sound of an approaching plane, right over the High Place. I stepped out and watched what appeared to be a brand-new Cessna 180 make a banking turn to the north and begin another low approach over the High Place. I got out into the snow as far as I could go, the 180 dropped almost to roof top level. Just as it came over the ARS Science Center, something came out of the plane. It appeared to be a box, with a long cloth attached to it, which appreciably slowed its drop. Whoever was flying, knew what he was doing, as the parcel hit right in the center of the lawn, between the Science Center and the High Place. Four feet of snow sure helped to break the fall as well. The 180 circled around twice, while I struggled to retrieve the parcel.

It was a package all right, with a giant beach towel attached. Well wrapped too. "Open immediately" was written all over it, and I guessed who ever was flying around in circles wanted me to do just that. Inside the box, with a ton of packing material, two items emerged, one a letter, and the other a fifth of Jack Daniels. The letter soon explained it all.

"Thought you might be getting dry. Wave if you don't need help. Lay down in the snow if you do. I'll call Jan and let her know. Signed, Pete, P.S. See you at Salt Wells." With that I picked up the bottle of J.D., waved, as he made one lower pass slightly to the west. This time, he rolled the plane a bit and I could clearly look into the window and tell it was indeed Pete. But what I didn't understand who was the passenger? With that they roared off to the southwest and the general vicinity of East Gate. All I could think of was how lucky I was to have a friend like Pete. I didn't know about the airplane, I could swear it was brand new, sure looked it anyway. I was glad for the note about Jan, as for the time being, we were pretty much isolated from the rest of the world. As I looked at the bottle of J.D., I wondered what the hell Pete would have done if I had laid down in the snow!

By the end of two days, we had most of the snow cleared away with the D-8, at least around the headquarters, and I could actually drive from the High place up there. There were some giant size snowballs, some nearly ten feet high. We could see cows with the binoculars, at least from on top of the barn. It looked like they were in little bunches all over the valley. Cows are tough creatures, and as long as they have water they will survive, or even snow for that matter. But it was warming up rapidly, so I knew water for the cows wouldn't be a problem. Most of the snow was gone within a week, but we still couldn't go anyplace, as the roads were impassable. Finally, I set out with the road grader, heading north, fixed about ten washouts, when I ran into the Lander County Road crew heading south. So, after an extended Easter vacation I finally headed back to Reno, my first concern was who in the world taught my classes, and what did they taught. And my second was to catch up with Pete and thank him for the bottle of J.D., much less his concern.

As it turned out, Charlie Speth picked up my classes, so the kids didn't lose much. Pete had not only told Jan what had happened to me, but he got the word to Bohmont as well, so the University knew I hadn't gone south. But that early April snow wasn't the end. We had three more snows that April, two about 18" and one about 12". All told that April, we had nearly 90 inches of snow, and along with the 75 that we had already had for the first part of winter, it made for a grand total of 165 inches of snow for the 1974-75 winter. Probably a record for all time!

But that winter was also a good lesson for me in that first of all, turning cows out by March 15 was risky at best. We needed to plan for enough hay so that cows would never go out before April 1, and perhaps even April 15. It also made me realize that we needed a better means of communication, as the old earth ground line was all right most of the time, but in periods of storm it was unreliable. If we were really going to have a major field station, with more than a few employees, the risk factor would be simply too great not to have adequate communications. Those would be matters of priority that would have to be taken care of shortly.

And of course, that winter of isolation didn't help my popularity with the faculty. It was being said pretty routinely in department and faculty meetings that the Gund truly was inaccessible, and consequently should not become a major field station. Some were even suggesting that it should be sold for all of the above reasons, and a thousand more, that I cared not to respond to. It was this feeling of dissent by the faculty that lead to my near total alienation. My attitude was that I made it through the winter, what was their problem. Besides, most of them, even if they were involved, would only be out in summer months. Outside of Charlie Speth, and Ed Jensen, the agronomist that was contemplating some upcoming plant trials, I had no friends, and it really didn't bother me. I knew what Nevada agriculture needed; I was positive of that. Besides that, I also knew Bohmont believed exactly the way I did, although sometimes I think he would have felt better if we had held our meetings incognito or something to that effect.

I didn't have time to worry about the faculty, I had to figure out how to get 10,000 acres. Santini was going to be in Reno in early June, so I had set up an appointment with him through his Reno staff. Jim was a Democrat, but about as conservative as a Democrat could be. He remembered me from school, although he was an undergraduate when I was a grad student, so we ran in different circles, but we had shared beer at the Little Wal. I showed Jim my maps, showed him what I thought we could use, read the Recreation and Public Purpose Act details to him, and explained about how much support that I thought we could get from the Cattlemen's Association as well as the Woolgrowers.

"You realize what you're asking for is the biggest parcel of BLM in the history of Nevada to be kicked back from federal ownership, to at least in this case, State ownership?' Jim questioned.

"Yes, I guess this is much bigger than anything that has been done before, but I believe it's totally justifiable," I responded.

"I don't have any question about that! Ought to give the whole damned BLM back to state and private ownership as far as I am concerned. Tell you what, let me think about this whole package for a week or so, then let me take it to Laxalt, once I really understand what you want, it will be easier for me to explain. I am sure he will want to start concurrent legislation at the same time as I introduce a bill in the House. And of course, they will have to be essentially similar. Also, the University will have to pay something for this transfer. What has been happening in the past, on unimproved rangeland, not adjacent to someplace like Las Vegas, their appraisals have been running around $50 per acre. On a large tract of land like this, I would imagine it would be less than $50, but that's not up to me for sure."

So began what I assumed would be a simple task of preparing appropriate legislation, getting the necessary votes, having a presidential signature, paying the BLM perhaps as much as a quarter million dollars, then go about building a truly great experiment station. To say I did not understand the complexity of the situation would be a gross understatement. For sure, Ross Dinkins had warned me, but after getting Nodine to back off, what more could they do? Preparation of appropriate legislation in both the House and Senate was very simple. However, shortly, the BLM indicated complete agreement and support for the request, but that several obstacles would have to be overcome to clear the way for title transfer. Things like the Antiquities Act and the Endangered Species Act would have to be dealt with first. And assurances had to be provided that no current mineral reserves existed, and no other title problems existed. And of course, public use, such as recreation would have to be dealt with. Things that in reality common sense should be able to handle, but in the bureaucratic world, I was soon to learn that common sense did not prevail, at least as far as I was concerned.

"I just about laughed so hard seeing your miserable ass buried in snow it's a wonder I didn't crash," laughed Pete over our usual Picon.

"Well, I can't do much else but say thanks, because I sure wasn't going anywhere right then, and for sure, I had no way of getting word out that we were OK. Besides that, bottle of J.D. was mighty welcome, as my bottle was just about down to the last shot or two. Say, who in the hell was in the plane with you, and was that your plane to begin with?"

"Well, as to the latter, that's a Cessna 180, and I just bought it. It's used, but only 5 years old, and it only had a thousand hours on the books. Bought it from Reno Air with essentially a new guarantee. As to the former question, that was Gina, spent the night at Salt Wells, when we heard how bad the snow out Austin way was the next morning, I decided I better have a look see. Figured a California dude might winter kill, you know. Anyway, when Gina heard what I was going to do she wanted to go, and it was her bottle of Jack Daniels, so you owe her a big thank you, not me. The towel, well that was from Sidney, oh, aw, she and I spent some time together that night. When Gina saw how pathetic you looked standing waist deep in that snow, she said that she should have put something special in that box with the Jack"

"OK, I see, you landed at Salt Wells with a load of fancy girls from Reno, and Gina gave you a favor in the form of this Sidney. She white or black? And what in the hell was Gina going to put in the box."

"Well, seeing how your being so God damned jealous and crude about this whole thing, you'll just have to find out what color Sidney is

502

when you thank Gina. By the way, next time your ass is under snow, I might just have a tendency to let it cool down a bit. And Gina never told me what she was going to put in the box, but I would guess it was a free pass, that's her style."

"Look, I have already bought four rounds of picons, as a partial thank you. I ain't jealous, and crude is my nature. Guess I should have asked, instead of what her color is, was she good. Could I sell the pass"?

"Well Sidney was good enough to keep me entertained for eight hours and no, you couldn't sell the pass, because she writes your name on them."

I knew better than to say anything at this point. I firmly believe that when God created Basques, he somehow gave them an overdrive gear in their sexual transmission. Pete had screwed every girl possible at the University. I knew that he had probably screwed enough ranchers' wives while masquerading as an Extension Agent in Elko, that for his own safety he had to leave. Well, at least he couldn't harm too many people at Salt Wells. But I did have a small wonder about coming to my rescue after playing all night. Probably a miracle I didn't have to rescue him.

"Say, you know I got Santini and Laxalt working on our land transfer. Trying to get 10,000 acres, won't that make the Gund something when it's all completed?"

"Yeah, but I already heard through the grapevine that the BLM is going to fight you all the way."

"Not what they said, besides I whipped them on the water already."

"Well, you remember Lester Sweeney? We went to school with him. He now works out of the Carson District, which is East Gate's district.

Anyway, Sweeney is my range con, if you can imagine! However, he told me about your attempt to grab public land, and he thinks the big boys are never going to let it happen. However, with Paul on your side, I'll admit you got some clout. My Basque friends all tell me that if Regan ever gets elected, Paul will be his V.P. Wouldn't that be something, Vice President Paul Laxalt. We Basque would stay drunk for a year!"

Five picons, and I had to teach class at eight the next morning. "Well, thanks again for checking on my welfare. Say, what in the hell would you have done if I had laid in the snow?"

"Gina didn't know what I had written on that note. If you had lain down in the snow, I would have just told her that you truly were a crazy son of a bitch, and that was just your style. Still would have flown back to Salt Wells. Don't know what I would have done then, guess called the National Guard."

Summer came faster than usual, and classes ended when it seemed that I still had much to teach. We got a good summer crew of students, and we had more graduate students than ever. Jim Young's range research had really taken off, he now had two summer employees at the ranch in a new house trailer, and Bruner was busier than ever. Everybody had to cook for themselves, except Dwight. He still got to eat with Rich and Pam.

But I was getting nervous about our land transfer. I was definitely worried about artifacts, both historical and pre-historical. There had been several homesteads at our end of the valley that had long since failed, but they were still very evident. As far as pre-historical artifacts, they were everywhere. In fact, I was amassing a very nice collection of arrowheads myself.

In discussing this with Jim Young, who was far more knowledgeable than I on this subject, he also agreed that it was a problem. "You know the best way to deal with the BLM on an issue of this nature, is to make them an offer they can't refuse. If we could put together a program that would support antiquities research here in the valley, and give them the credit, they would probably roll over, at least on this point,"

"Yeah, but how can I possibly do that. When I go to Bohmont and tell him I need a full-time archeologist, he will likely just shoot me. If he doesn't, you can bet Ely and Test will," I lamented.

"There's an anthropology group that works on campus, more or less. They have some grant money, if we could find something unique out here to create enough interest, they might throw in."

"Well, what do you mean by unique, hell, there's arrowheads everywhere."

"No not just arrowheads, we need something different, something unique."

"Gosh, I remember once last fall I was chasing cows over across the dry lake, on a beach ridge way over there, and I came on a ton of worked rock. It was everywhere. Almost looked like axe heads, they were maybe eight to ten inches long, real crude, maybe two inches wide. I think they were all made out of basalt. I don't really know what they were, but that was something different."

"Sounds like mastodon points to me, although I would doubt that. Mastodon points would suggest that Indians were here nearly 10,000 years ago, and that's about 7,500 years more than present day philosophy. However, if by chance those were really mastodon points, that's probably all it would take. Could you find that spot again?"

"I don't know. When you're chasing cows, you don't pay a whole lot of attention to where you're at. But I think given time I might. It's probably worth a try, but like you say, they are probably nothing. On the other hand, I am not going to get an archeologist by asking the College of Agriculture, that's for sure. Tell you what, I am going out tomorrow, things are pretty much under control, maybe if I have the time, I'll saddle up and mosey over there to see if I can find that spot. It will take all day though, it's at least 20 miles one way, and it's about impossible to get any closer than the ranch itself."

Things were beautiful, not only at the Gund, but all of central Nevada. The extreme wet winter made the whole area look like a Garden of Eden. And things were running incredibly smoothly at the Gund, so I indeed had the opportunity to go arrowhead hunting, or perhaps better said, mastodon hunting. I loved collecting arrowheads, so whenever I was riding and not chasing cows, I tended to keep one eye on the ground for the tell-tale sign of chips. Yup, this trip would be a little longer than usual, as the dry lake was brim full of all the snowmelt. And I had long since learned that you gave the lake a wide berth with a horse when it was wet. The alkali silt around the edge of the lake had no bottom when it was wet, more than one horse had met its end by bogging helplessly down in that mud. I started out about seven, told Rich that if I wasn't back by nightfall, I would build a fire so he could come rescue me. A prospect which didn't seem to thrill him.

I had ridden about three hours, covered probably 15 miles, as that old thoroughbred cross had either a trot or lope gear that he seemed to be able to maintain indefinitely. I had found one spot of chips with about a half hour worth of searching did yield one nice tip. But my mission today was to find a spot that I had been at last year, a spot I never paid any attention to begin with. And on a greasewood flat of several hundred thousand acres, there wasn't much to make one spot any different than any other spot. I did remember the stones were on a gentle ridge, however, on the west side of Grass Valley in the general vicinity of where I was, there were probably 50 gentle ridges all running towards the dry lake, products of erosion over the ages.

I had probably covered thirty ridges by noon, and my eyes and my ass were both getting tired. My horse was also getting thirsty, but that would have to wait, as the nearest water was many miles away. We ambled over one more ridge, and there it was just as I remembered. Without a close look, they would just appear as basalt rocks, and with that the only thing unique about them was that they just shouldn't have been there in the first place. Basalt rocks have to have a source, and this area was far too flat for them to have been washed in. And on close examination, they definitely had been worked.

I rode the entire area and learned that the vast majority of the rocks occurred on about a 50-acre site. I rode a mile in every direction, and could find no other rocks. Next, I gathered up five that I felt were representative of what existed, marked the sites where I removed stones. Finally, I took careful aim across the valley in several directions, sort of triangulated my position, so that next time maybe I wouldn't wander around for half a day. Besides, I could just about imagine what kind of nerds these archeologists would be. Getting lost on the flat with a group like that didn't sound like something I would like.

It was just about dark when I finally pulled up to the corral. I don't know which was happier, me or my horse. Dwight strode over and asked, "Where in the hell have you been all day. Rich and Pam had to go to town, and as he was leaving, Rich said to watch for you by dark. Never said one word about which direction you rode. I figured you were on the mountain, and I was about to drive down the valley looking for your."

Well, Rich said he never worried about me to begin with, guess he just proved the point. "I rode across the flat looking for some special types of Indian artifacts. Ever see anything like this?"

"What's so special about that rock, just looks like another rock to me."

"No, no. Look at this edge, it's been worked, see the flaking."

"No, but maybe when you go down to the High Place and poor me a drink of whiskey, I'll be better able to see what you are talking about."

"Come on, I'll pour us both a shot, but I don't think you will ever make an archeologist."

About two days later I got back to town, and my first stop was the ARS offices and Jim Young. "Well, here they are," as I laid the five stones on his desk.

Jim stared at the stones without saying a word for what seemed like an eternity. Then he carefully turned each one over, closely feeling each edge. I could tell by his demeanor, that something powerful big was going through his scientific brain. "Hope, in one second of time, so to speak, you may have rewritten the archeological history of the Great Basin."

"In other words, you think they are mastodon points?"

"I am no expert by any stretch of the imagination, but I do know some experts that can answer that question. But unless I miss my bet, yes, they are mastodon points."

"I'll leave them with you, show them to the experts. I guess if they are interested, we need to make some kind of an arrangement so that I can get off the BLM's antiquities hook."

"Give me a week, I'll have an answer."

About then, Ray Evans, the ARS leader walked into Jim's office, and of course, Jim had to go through the whole thing of mastodon points with Ray. Ray was polite, but I don't think he was overly interested in Indian archeology. But he did have other thoughts on his mind. "Are you going to have a field day again this year?"

"I don't think so. We did so good with that one last year, I thought I would just let it rest for a year. Got lots of things going, but we, nor you guys, have anything really new yet to talk about."

"I understand, probably just as well. As you are aware we are putting in for a significantly larger budget for range research because of the Gund. It's a large enough increase that in order to justify it, some of the top ARS people want to come out from D.C. and inspect the site. We thought that if you were having a field day, we could coordinate their trip with that. However, maybe it's better that we don't involve a field day. If we all came out and you could spend a day with us going through all of your ideas, I think it might really help sell the program."

"Sure, be glad to, just give me a few days notice, and we can probably do about anything you would want. Throw a bar-b-q, hell we could even take them skinny dipping in the hot pond."

That caused Ray to sputter a bit, but he finally got it out – he just didn't think these folks would be up for skinny-dipping, but they would probably love a bar-b-q after a long hot day in the field. I wasn't exactly sure what Ray would consider a long hot day in the field, but if that's what they wanted, I was damn sure positive I could give them that too.

Jim was right on one point, the mastodon points, and it didn't take a week. In fact, it was only a day or two after I had left the points with Jim, when my phone rang, and suddenly I was talking with Jonathan Davis, who I shortly learned was associated with both the Anthropology

Department at the University, as well as the State Natural Heritage Department.

"OK, what Jim showed me was astounding, if in fact it came from Nevada, and I might add, if it did come from Nevada, you are already in violation of several State and Federal acts simply because you picked them up to begin with."

With that I began to think that already maybe I wasn't going to like this Jonathan guy, but for openers I was going to ignore the threat of the federal pen, "Well, what the hell, for openers there's a ton of those broken rocks out there, so I didn't figure anybody would miss a few. Besides, Dr. Young asked me to bring him some examples, and if they looked good to him, he thought you would be really excited. Oh yeah, in regard to moving the rocks, if you look closely, you will see a very small number in ink on one side. That number coincides to the exact site, and position the rock occupied before I removed it, which I amply documented on site, as well as with photographs."

"Ok, ok, calm down, I was only kidding. Young assured me that you would have documented everything to begin with. And by the way, those aren't rocks or even broken rocks. Even with limited examination, I am positive they are what we archeologist call mastodon points. Although crude, they were definitely sculptured by aboriginal man, maybe five to seven thousand years ago, the age we can only guess at now. But they were used for slaying giant animals such as mastodons, that's why the name. Now, as for the location, if they indeed came from Nevada, you will have had a significant hand in rewriting the archeological history of the Great Basin."

By this time, I was beginning to think this Jonathan guy was maybe all right, even for an archeologist, so I decided to level, "Well, you will have to trust me until you see the site for yourself, but I can assure you that they came from the very heart of the Great Basin. In fact, right in the middle of Grass Valley, about 75 miles north of Austin and about 75 miles south of Beowawe, as the crow flies."

"How soon can we see the site? Jim says it's on the University Ranch, and he already told me it was Grass Valley. We have done work before in Grass Valley, so I know it's big, very big. You know, it's funny, but in our earlier work, we didn't find anything dating back further than maybe 1,500 years at the outside. However, I always felt that there was a good chance that the first major discovery of truly ancient man in Nevada would be found in Grass Valley. We just never found it, but in two weeks, you can't cover very much of Grass Valley."

"Well, today's Wednesday. I usually go out every Friday afternoon, after my last class, so that's the day after tomorrow. I don't have anything specifically planned for Saturday, so, if you could come out Saturday morning, we can take the whole day. It takes at least four hours to get to the Ranch from Reno, and after we meet, it will take another two hours to locate the site. I never have driven to it, but I found the remnants of an existing two-track road, less than a mile from the site. And I took some pretty accurate coordinates last time, so I think I can locate the site and drive right to it with my pick-up, its four-wheel drive. There's not much to distinguish the site from the surrounding several million acres, other than some broken rocks."

"I'll be there by 9 a.m. May bring somebody else."

And so, it was. Just as he said at 9 straight up in rolled a brand new one ton Ford pick-up, fully equipped for the out-back. I couldn't help but notice the state license plate and wonder how these archeologists could get that kind of money and we had to subsist literally off of "borrowed" equipment at times. Such was Nevada.

Jonathan was no surprise, in fact just about what I had expected. Medium height, grey beard, not very well trimmed, and long grey hair, unkempt, at least no earrings, but definitely a "free spirit". After a quick handshake, he introduced me to his buddy, Bob Erickson. Turned out Bob worked both for the State as well as himself. Had a consulting firm located in Silver City. And he had the appearance of a square shooter. No long hair, clean-shaven, no beads, etc. After a few more pleasantries, Jonathan looked at me sort of quizzically, and asked, seeing how they had been on the road for over four hours, if I minded if they had a beer. "Of course not," I responded. Out rolled a giant ice chest, which contained beer, seven-up and a bottle of bourbon. Again, he looked at me with that same sort of quizzical look, "Could we interest you in a soda pop?"

"In Grass Valley, on the Gund Ranch, which I run, if you want to drink beer, I'll be mighty pleased to drink a beer with you, not soda pop!"

"Gosh, OK, I apologize, but Jim said you were Mormon and never drank, so I didn't want to offend you."

As I reached for the beer, I thought to myself, that God damned Young, always a practical jokester probably had these guys set up from the beginning.

"Well, you can tell Jim the jokes over, but one of these days I will be evening up a bit for that one. Hope you two dudes didn't take all this too seriously, but for clarity, no I am not a Mormon. And maybe after you see the site, we'll just sit down and drink that bottle of bourbon."

"Let's go," they both said in unison.

"Wait just a minute, I am sure Jim indicated there's more to this than just seeing this site. We have an application into the BLM for a transfer of 10,000 acres of their land to the University under the Public Recreation Act, and that requires an archaeological clearance before that occurs. You see the site, you do the clearance, at no cost to the University."

At that point Bob Erickson took over the conversation, "Are there any spring mounds on the valley floor?"

I wasn't exactly sure what he meant by a spring mound, but there was an elevated site that always seemed to be wet and sometimes ran water. It was off the mouth of Potato Canyon, so I decided to answer yes.

"You have a back-hoe?"

"Yes"

"You dig it out according to our specifications?"

"Well, I guess so, why?"

"Because we need some other data to verify the age of your site. We can use pollen data to do that, and spring mounds are the best place to find pollen data. And if you dig that spring mound out for me, I'll do your archeological clearance, and for free."

About then Jonathan started laughing, "Got to watch Bob, he'll snooker you every time. He already agreed with Young to do the clearance. As we came in we saw the spring mound at the mouth of Potato Canyon, so he just wanted to be sure you would help him dig it out."

I looked a little embarrassed, and felt even more so, so I decided we had better get going before I gave away any more of the ranch. "Put the ice chest in the back of my rig, jump in, open me another beer, and if you both will be quiet for awhile, I'll show you Grass Valley.

513

And so, with little more than a hand shake we started a decade long cooperative agreement between the Gund Research and Demonstration Ranch, the Anthropology Department of the University, the Nevada Historical Society, the State of Nevada as well as the BLM. The mastodon points proved to be the real thing. Although we never found a mastodon carcass in or around the dry lake as predicted, we did eventually find a lot of other long since deceased species that surely took more than a point or two to bring down. Eventually the archeological detectives determined that early man had arrived in Grass Valley as much as ten thousand years ago. And the pollen data indicated that Grass Valley was a much different place, much wetter and much colder. Spruce forests were dominant where now nothing, but juniper and pinyon existed. Vast wetlands existed around the lake that was several hundred feet deep, where now only a dry lakebed existed. Eventually the program developed into a look at the more historic aspects of Grass Valley, including a dig at the old mining town of Cortez, located at the north end of the Valley. The emphasis there was on the different ethnic factions that did the labor, including Chinese, Italian, Serb and Spanish. And they documented the history of all the early homesteads that with time became the deeded property that we knew as the Gund and Allen Ranches. And true to his word, Bob directed the effort that cleared the lands involved in the transfer to the satisfaction of the BLM, and I might add, at no cost to our budget.

I loved the archeological work, was totally fascinated by it, and helped every time I had a few spare minutes, which wasn't very often. Whenever Jonathan or Bob were in the Valley, or their helpers, they always brought me up to date on what their latest finds had been. Eventually, the archeological program was always featured at out Field Days, and was the enticement for University sponsored programs from far and wide. In a way, it always amazed me how such a program could have developed from nothing more than a wild ride across the plain chasing some cows!

It wasn't long before Ray Evans got in touch, "Say, we have scheduled for mid July for the brass from Washington to tour the Ranch, I think it will be somewhere between the fifteenth and twentieth. I think there will be three from Washington, one from our regional office in Berkley, plus Jim and myself, so that makes six. Think we can pull off a bar-b-que for that many?

"No problem, I'll bring out all the food, just be sure you pay me. What about lunch?"

"We plan to stay in Austin the first night, have breakfast early the next morning. I'll have the International prepare sack lunches. After our bar-b-que, we will go on to Battle Mountain, spend the night there and then back to Reno for the rest of our work."

"Damn, I thought we were going to go skinny dipping in the hot pond!"

"No, no, no. I told you that these gentlemen are simply not up to that, they wouldn't understand. I am afraid you and your cowboys would be just a little on the wild side. Remember, these people live in Washington, they all have Ph.D.'s, and probably they would feel more at home with the Queen of England than here." Ray lectured me. Well, I thought to myself, we'll see.

Well, quick enough the middle of July came, and I got the word, and just like Ray said, there would be six all told. So, I bought the vitals, and at the last minute an extra fifth of scotch, just in case. After due consideration I chose scotch over bourbon because, if as Ray said, they would feel more at home with the Queen of England than me, scotch just seemed more appropriate. Besides, I had plenty of bourbon in the High place for special occasions.

I was waiting beside the road, at the south end of the ranch with my usual set up, sage brush fire, large pot of boiling cowboy coffee, sugar cream, cups, and spoons. It was a right fine setting, even for me. And soon enough the dust was boiling up on the horizon. It didn't take 15 minutes before the big government van pulled up along side my pickup. As they piled out, seemed like more dust came out than they had raised. Everyone looked a bit tanned.

"Air conditioner didn't work, had to leave the windows down," Ray muttered. "And Jim drove too fast besides," he concluded.

As I looked at the sorry mess, all I could say was, "Welcome to Grass Valley!"

Then I began to size up what I had on my hands. As introductions were made, the first thing I noticed was that everyone had a Ph.D. or some such degree that required the formal introduction as Dr. so and so. Couldn't help but notice that I was just plain old Terry. Oh well, I did have to admit that it didn't seem too logical to find somebody with a Ph.D. out here building a big black pot of coffee over a sagebrush fire, least not right in the middle of what surely looked like the largest desert valley these dudes had ever seen, And they were dudes – two had some sort of bush safari hats, kind of like I remembered from the old Tarzan movies. Two had khaki shorts, with knee socks. One had a scarf wrapped around his neck that I would have been proud to wear, at least in winter anyway. After quick introductions I poured coffee for everyone. Styrofoam cups had to work for China, but everything else was up to snuff. As soon as coffee was over, out came the notebooks and cameras – and questions. It was pretty obvious that these boys had never been on a western cattle ranch, in fact I felt pretty confident in concluding that they had never been in the west. Course the exception was the one from Berkley, but I would have guaranteed that he had never been over the Sierra before, except possibly by air.

"Yes, we do brand all of our cattle, its necessary because of rustling. Yes, we do castrate all of our bull calves within two months of birth. No, we don't bite them out, that's just for sheep, we use sharp knives. Yes, it's cold here in the wintertime, often –25 to –35. Yes, it snows, sometimes several feet at once. No, there are basically no fences, except around the ranch proper. No, the cattle don't really know how to stay just in this valley, they will go over the mountains on either side of Grass Valley and drift into the neighboring valleys, sometimes 50 miles or more from where we are standing. No, they don't eat the greasewood except sometimes in the early spring. Yes, there are mountain lions, in fact many. Yes, coyotes often kill our cattle. No, it's not against the law to kill coyotes."

Finally, everybody got a picture of me. The biggest mistake I made so far was to just wear my standard fare, work boots, levis, T shirt and baseball hat. If I had only known that I was going to be so well photographed, I would have really duded up. Finally, the questions stopped, the coffee pot was drained, and the morning part of the tour, which fortunately didn't include me, was about to start. There was one more question. "Where is the nearest bathroom?"

"Right the other side of the van. See you after lunch," as I hopped into my pickup. I had decided that if they were going to eat dust anyway, they might just as well eat mine too.

As directed, I met the safari about one that afternoon for the cattle tour. It didn't take long to see that apparently either we hadn't gotten enough sleep in Austin last night, or the rarified atmosphere of Grass Valley was starting to make folks drowsy. And if that wasn't difficult enough, these folks were definitely not animal scientists. But the tour went well. I took them to the high country so they could see that there was actually grass in Grass Valley. We saw lots of cattle, and while doing so I tried to explain our crossbreeding program, and which crosses were working. After the mountain we saw the fields, the heifers, the horses, the corrals and just about everything else that I could think of in the way of raising livestock in a place like Grass Valley. Finally, Ray said, "I think these gentlemen need a bit of a rest, and maybe splash off their faces with some cold water. Terry, it's now nearly 5:00, maybe we could have dinner ready by 6:00 or so. If we get out of here by 7:30, we can be to Battle Mountain by 9:00, as I am sure we will all be tired."

Two thoughts hit me simultaneously, first, I'll be damned if I knew where they were going to get some "cold" water to splash off their faces with. I have been here five years now, and I sure to hell never find any. Secondly, the schedule sounded like I got to cook and wash dishes too.

I went down to the High Place, washed up with hot water, poured a nice bourbon and water, using some carefully guarded ice cubes, threw a bottle of bourbon and the prized bottle of scotch in the pickup, along with an ice chest of some more carefully guarded ice and headed over to the Science Center to start the fire. Ray was breaking out some prepared salad that looked like it might be older than a day, had put potatoes in the oven and was acting very official. I got the fire going well, but Jim almost knocked the whole thing over, before I asked him to stay away. The three from Washington and Dr. Berkley were all sacked out. I took Jim over to the car and poured him a bourbon and water, with ice, and all he could do was mutter, "Thank you," over and over. I gathered it had been a long day for him as well. I asked Ray if he thought his boys would like a drink before dinner, but he didn't feel it was proper, this being state and federal property and all. Then he got a bit flustered and said, "I did get a bottle of fine wine for dinner. I guess under the circumstances it would be OK. Split between seven of us, it can't hurt too much."

Damn, I thought to myself, a bottle of wine split seven ways isn't going to wash much dust down anybody's gullet. Well, if we are going to have wine, we better have garlic French bread as well. "Hey, Ray, I got a loaf of French bread over at the High Place. Why don't I get it to go with these steaks?"

"Great idea."

I didn't tell him about the garlic bit, but I just happened to have some garlic and butter made up from the night before, so it didn't take me but a shake to have the loaf sliced, buttered, and ready to go on the grill.

Soon, the steaks were sizzling, smoke was flying, and I had made Jim a second highball unbeknown to Ray. The boys couldn't stand the smell of the sizzling steaks, so soon they were all standing around trying to make polite conversation. Ray was busy finishing the salad and setting the table, I turned the steaks for the last time, the bread was hot, and the potatoes were done. Another Grass Valley feast was upon us!

"Come on in everybody. Terry has the steaks ready, everything is all served, so all that is left to do is to open this bottle of wine and let's toast to a beautiful day and the future of our research."

I could hear something like "Hear, hear" coming from the boys, and I could also hear quite a clutter coming out of the Science Center. "Jim, where is the cork puller?" was next.

"What cork puller?"

"The cork puller I told you to buy."

"When did you tell me to buy a cork puller?"

"Why, just last week, don't you remember?"

"No!"

I could see this was going to get ugly, and I had a puller in my pickup, just for special occasions. And there were several in the High Place as well. But I thought it would be better of offering my services just right then. Anyway, I was just the chef and dishwasher, but I did have to admit that a devious plan was beginning to formulate in my demented brain.

"What are we going to do?"

"I don't know!"

"We have to open this wine."

"Terry, do you have a wine cork puller?"

I could see Dr. Berkley getting a bit nervous. Coming from Berkley, I could just about guarantee that he wouldn't mind for a second having wine with dinner. The three from Washington looked perplexed.

"Oh hell, give me the bottle. I'll show you how we open wine bottles here in Grass Valley," I exclaimed.

I grabbed the bottle from Ray, went to the glove compartment in my pickup, pulled out my Buntline 22 magnum pistol, grabbed my handkerchief out of my hip pocket and wrapped the top of the bottle immediately below the cork. I took my time, as I was watching six sets of eyeballs bare down on me like I was some kind of kook, completely out of control. I put the bottle on the edge of the bed of the pickup, grabbed it with my left hand, kind of making a "V" between my thumb and index finger, laid the end of the barrel in that "V", took a big breath and waited for the reaction.

There was pandemonium, but I could hear Ray above all else, "God Terry, don't do that, you will likely kill yourself."

What the hell, I needed to help my reputation, besides, I had always wanted to do this just to see what might happen – so I pulled the trigger. Now a 22 magnum makes a fair amount of noise. When it's fired in tight quarters, which we were kind of in being between the Science Center and the High Place, it makes an even louder noise. However, I learned when the end of the barrel is tight against the top of a wine bottle, it makes a really loud noise. And that's just what happened! But amazingly enough, when the smoke cleared, I had an intact bottle of wine in my hand, minus the cork, and a bit of glass that used to hold the cork in place.

As casual as I could be I handed the bottle to Ray as straight faced as I could muster, and said, "Lets eat."

I thought Dr. Berkley was going to throw up, and I thought two of the Washington crowd were going to feint. But I just started serving steaks and asked Ray to begin pouring wine and talking about how good the meat smelled and how good Ray's salad tasted. Dinner went well, all things being considered, but it did take a few minutes for everybody to digest what they had seen.

Towards the end of dinner, I commented on what a wonderful day it had been, and how pleased I was to meet everybody. "Soon as I get the dishes done after you guys leave, I am going to the hot pond and go skinny dipping. Got a brand-new bottle of scotch to open." I figured that should just about put the frosting on the cake, and it did.

Just about that quick the head Doctor from Washington said, "Ray, why in the hell are we going to Battle Mountain tonight? I see enough beds and blankets here for all of us. Why not bed down here, besides, I quite frankly would much rather go to the hot pond with Terry, and maybe he would let me have a nip of his scotch. What do the rest of you think?"

There was unanimous agreement, although I did hear Ray mutter something about a confirmed reservation or something like that. I had figured that the ARS program needed a financial kick in the butt, and after my little bit with the wine bottle before dinner and a good dip in the hot pond, without clothes, and perhaps a nip or two of scotch, that maybe these guys could just give it that kick.

Well, we went to the hot pond, my bottle of scotch got killed, and from all that I could ever gather, the ARS program, at least for the Gund Research and Demonstration Ranch did get a kick in the butt. Two things for sure did come out of that evening. First, it took the better part of a week to dig all of the glass splinters out of my hand, and secondly, some years later, when I was at a meeting at the USDA in Washington a young bureaucrat came up to me and asked, "Are you really the person that shot the top of the wine bottle off out in Nevada a few years back?"

"By God son, I can't tell a lie, I am the one, and by gosh I did it!"

"People have been telling that story around here ever since. I didn't really believe it, even though I must have heard it a hundred times. I am going to tell my kids tonight when I get home, I actually met the man that shot the bottle top off!"

I guess it's the things legends are made of, but I freely admit I never tried that stunt a second time!

It was a hot August day in Reno, a Wednesday, and I had just about finished all the bookwork, or at least all that I cared to do right about then. My pickup was packed, as I planned to be heading to the ranch in about 30 minutes for a couple of hard days of corral building. And just about then the phone rang.

"What the hell you doing this afternoon?" Pete's ever pleasant voice drifted over the phone.

"Well, in about 30 minutes I am leaving for the ranch, why? Where the hell you at anyway?"

"Buffalo, but the Cessna is warmed up and I am out of here in about ten, got to stop in Reno to pick up some cargo, then on to Gina's. She's pissed at me because I never brought you in after last winter, she's convinced you probably got your weenie froze off in all that snow."

"Well just tell her its OK, but she doesn't get any more proof than that."

"No-no, you don't get off that easy. I figured you were heading out this afternoon. I'll land there before 5, and I promised her you would be stopping by to get her gift!"

"No-no yourself, I don't have time, pickup's loaded and I plan to start on the new artificial insemination corral tomorrow morning, bright and early. I don't need a hangover."

"Look Bud, Gina would have not only called out the national guard for you last winter, she would have personally made the Governor drive the first vehicle if she really thought you were in danger. Now plain and simple you are showing up if I have to run you off Highway 50 in the process, if for no other reason than just to thank her for her concern. Now if you are embarrassed for showing up in a Nevada cat house through the front door, just drive around in back, you will see a service entrance, and we'll be waiting for you. Let's see, its 3 right now, if you leave in thirty minutes, you will be there by 5:30. Meet the girls, let Gina make sure your all there, have a drink or two, your out of there by 7. Hell, its light till 8:30, you'll be damn near the ranch by dark!"

I thought to myself, yeah, a drink or two, with that God damned Basco, one never had the opportunity for just a drink or two. But I had to admit my curiosity about Salt Wells had been building ever since I first noticed the reconstruction. And I don't mind admitting I was curious about Gina. Hadn't seen her up close in over 15 years, I was wondering how she had weathered. And it probably goes without saying that I was curious about Pete's favorite girl, Sidney, much less the "cargo" he was picking up in Reno.

"OK, I'll be there about 5:30 or so, but one light drink only, I got a long day tomorrow."

I always loved the afternoon drive to Grass Valley, especially after I cleared Truckee Canyon. From Hazen on, you could smell the alfalfa fields, and it always seemed cooler when the green was close. As usual Fallon was all a bustle at 5, the Fallon Navel Air Base just seemed to keep growing all the time. I often wondered who would win in the long run, the military and development, or the Fallon farmers. I really didn't like contemplating that thought too much, because my gut reaction was that I already knew the answer to that one. As I cleared Fallon, I began to wonder if Pete would be there. I would surely look like a fool barging in through the back door acting like I knew exactly where I was, when in fact I didn't know jack shit. Oh well that's Nevada.

I eased up in front of Salt Wells and I couldn't help but notice there was only one car parked in front, must be a slow day. I followed the service road around to the back, breathing a sigh of relief when I noticed a familiar Cessna parked about a hundred yards away on the runway. Parked, screwed up my courage and knocked on the service door.

"Come on in stud," was Pete's warm welcome as he handed me a drink that wasn't light. I was in a back room, close to the kitchen. Tables and chairs suggested that meals might be served here.

"Saw you drive up and figured you would be scared to death to come in, but you made it, so come on in. Gina's dying to make sure your OK."

I followed Pete through a hall and into a room that was classic whorehouse. Red velvet wallpaper, hanging chandeliers, beautiful overstuffed matching couches, chairs and love chairs. The walls were lined with pictures of beautiful ladies, some somewhat naked, but all well done. I had a feeling that I was sinking into a carpet that more closely resembled a solid field of red clover than any rug that I had ever seen.

"Hey Gina, Terry's here, come check him out."

A slight rustle caused me to turn, and there was Gina, coming straight towards me, with the same infectious smile that I remembered from years before. As she approached, I couldn't help but notice the tight-fitting slacks that suggested a skimpy set of panties underneath. Her blouse was open far enough to see cleavage you could fall into, and there was no hint of a bra. I suppose she was laughing all the time I was staring, but it didn't slow her advance.

"God, Terry, you're a sight for sore eyes. I was so damn mad that day at Pete. Shit, he just laughed at you when we flew circles around you in all that snow. I was sure you would freeze to death. Come here, let me hug you, I just want to assure myself your OK."

Well, a hug from Gina was something else. If I would have been a little bit shorter, I was positive that I would have suffocated in those enormous breasts. Her midriff and thighs were pressed tight against me along with everything else.

"I just want to make sure you are all right," as a warm kiss came down.

Well, I guess I was all right, because in this embrace it didn't take long for everything to start working. As I pulled away a little embarrassed, Gina laughed, "I think you survived, at least it feels that way!"

"Pete, take Terry to the bar, get drinks for all of us and introduce him to the girls."

I followed Pete into the bar feeling completely out of place. And the bar was as much a class act as the rest of what I had seen so far, looked like it must have come around the Horn to San Francisco for the gold rush. Everything was mahogany or oak, I knew not which, but it was impressive. You could sink in the red carpet to your knees. There were an abundance of deep chairs, couches and other structures, obviously designed to make the customers feel at ease, and just as obvious to facilitate the "developing" relationships between customers and the girls. I had never given much thought to what a "plush" whorehouse might really look like before, but this left little doubt in my mind from that point on.

"OK, Copper, Terry and I usually drink picons, but the last time you tried to make me one it was a disaster, so I guess we'll go with more standard cocktails, ditch all right with you Terry?"

Copper was of Jamaican extract or something like that I recollected. Her skin color was indeed copper, only enhanced by the long shinny black hair hanging down over her shoulders. And the "see through" bra and thong like panties didn't hurt either.

"Terry, you can go fly a kite. You damn well know that I am not the bar tender, Alicia has that job, I am only helping her tonight cause she is sick, and I am off duty. So, I am not paid to be able to fix your Basque national beverage to begin with."

I sat there in amazement wondering what her costume would be if she were "on duty", but I could only speculate on that one. "Yeah, a ditch is just fine," I finally got around to responding.

There was just Pete, Copper and myself, as no obvious customers were at the bar. However, off in the distance I could readily see two long halls, with several doors on each. No telling what was going on down there. About then, Gina flowed into the bar. "Pete, get me my Champaign, you know I don't like that rot gut whiskey!"

Pete immediately instructed Copper on which Champaign to pore for Gina. Once full, Copper slid a fancy Champaign glass towards Gina.

"Let's toast." She held her glass high, "Here's to old times. I often think about Reno and my beagle shop. You two were like little boys, well at least Pete was. Really can't speak for you Terry, but I suspect you would have been like a little boy too."

Watching Gina's statuesque form, I probably would still be pretty much like a little boy, but it didn't faze Pete. He put an arm around her waist, took a swallow of his drink and replied, "Yeah, but I am not like a little boy anymore."

"Oh Pete, quit bragging. Besides we are supposed to entertain Terry tonight." With that she reached for a small brass bell on the counter which emitted a sizable noise as she rang it. "Girls, lets have a line–up for Terry."

I started to say something, anything, but the red coming up my throat and over my face seemed to squelch that idea. Besides, the line-up had started as four statuesque ladies paraded towards me. I probably made a complete ass of myself as I stared in awe as they came forwards. Each could well have been a centerfold out of Playboy.

"Hi, my name is Sherrie," the lead girl warmly informed me. That was quickly followed by, "Hey Terry, I am Ginger." And as Ginger was introducing herself, she bent forward, so that her loose fitting blouse, if you could call it that, fell away, completely exposing her breasts. "Hi baby, my name is Sidney." And then I remembered Pete talking about Sidney, and I could suddenly understand why. The last girl came forward, put her arm around my neck, rubbed her torso against mine and gently whispered, just loud enough for everybody to hear, "My names Terry also, and I'll bet we would make a perfect fit."

I didn't have much to say at that point, just more or less stared at what was standing squarely in front of me. Then Gina proudly asked, "So what do you think of my girls?"

"Fantastic, beyond my imagination," I was able to gargle out as I took a big swallow of my drink. I could see Pete about to burst forth with his usual Basco laugh.

"You might be interested to know that Ginger is here on a sabbatical leave from Stanford. You, being a professor and all would probably have a lot in common, right Ginger"?

It didn't take Ginger long to explain that her pre law curriculum was simply costing more than she had, so the extra income she was making during her semester off, should just about clear the hurdle for her. And then it was Sherrie's turn, "I am going to enroll at Nevada next semester myself, taking social sciences."

I was having difficulty responding sensibly, without biting my tongue or something, so I just went along with the flow. But I was beginning to realize that Gina's was not only a class act whore house, but the "ladies" were something special as well.

"Well, they are beautiful ladies, and they are very experienced in the things that will bring you pleasure. Now, I have already told them about how bad I felt seeing you in all that snow last winter, so the first trick is on me. And to make this a bit more fun, I am giving the first girl that turns that trick a special bonus."

"Halleluiah, the professor is going to get bred. Drinks for the house." as I watched a "C" note leave Pete's wallet.

I backed against the bar, as all four girls surrounded me, all talking at once on what they expected of me, and probably all equally anxious to collect Gina's special bonus. All I could think about was that I was never this far in over my head, even when I took my Ph.D. orals.

I had been saved by the bell on several occasions in my life, but what followed was a classic. As I was standing there not knowing what to do, but admittedly enjoying every second, the peace was shattered by a loud buzzer.

"Damn, girls, it sounds like we got company. Well, the offer still goes for Terry, but we better welcome whoever is at the door." With that, Gina strode to the front door, deftly unlocking it and welcomed three very young but professional looking gents.

Just as quick as my personalized line-up had occurred, the four girls were all over the trio. "Jet jocks from the Naval base," Pete muttered in my ear. "They won't last long so you still get your choice."

Well, Pete was right on one point, it wasn't long before Sherrie, Ginger and Terry were disappearing down the hall, flyboy in hand. Sidney had obviously wanted to talk, or do something, with Pete, as she had come back to where we were standing and draped her lithe body all over him. With that it didn't take me long to explain to Gina how much I appreciated her concern for my welfare, and how beautiful and desirable her girls were, but because I had a load of parts desperately needed at the ranch (more or less a lie) and that I simply had to go. "But I'll sure accept a rain check if that's agreeable?"

"Well, my word is my bond. The first trick is on me for whenever you stop. I'm sure Pete will see to that, won't you Pete?"

"You can count on that Gina," and with that I started for the back door. But not before Sidney gave me a hug and a kiss on the check, followed by a hug from Gina.

"You know, I will always remember the both of you when you were students at the University. You were both so young and innocent; it kind of makes me feel wholesome that I had the fortune of knowing you then. Those were good days." I could see sadness in her eyes, almost a tear. I suspected in actuality her life just wasn't that good, despite all the show.

I suddenly felt sorry for her, and as I left, I gave her a real hug, saying, "Hey, you're not only beautiful, but to me you have always been honest and straight forward, and that's really all I care about. You're a very special lady."

And with that I was off to the ranch. I thought long and hard about Gina and her girls, about prostitution in general. It was probably a dirty business, but it was going to exist, regardless, and at least in Nevada it was legal and regulated. I thought about Pete. Contemplating if he would ever settle down and maybe start a family. And I couldn't help laughing all the way to Grass Valley, for in fact I was quite sure that I had been saved by the bell.

It was unbearably hot for Washington, especially for October. I had been here several times before, and I had felt humidity, but a late season tropical depression was working its way up the coast, pushing heat and humidity in front of it, and it seemed like it was all descending on D.C.

"Well, we have the House version just about ready to submit, it looks good to me, at least. The Secretary of the Interior indicated that they would not oppose it, although I am sure they still have some questions," Santini summarized.

I had been requested by Jim to come to D.C., just to go over the final details of the House Bill, as well as Senator Laxalt's Senate version. "Those BLM bureaucrats drive me up a tree. They have just about nit-picked this bill to death. I think, thanks to your help, we are just about ready. I never met this Nodine guy, but I have been told by some higher-ups in the Bureau, that you about did him in by chopping down that tree to make your point. I guess he had bragged clear up to the Director, that the BLM would never lose control on 10,000 acres of their land. Apparently, he let all his objections hinge on the water, your tree trick ended that. However, I was told that he wanted to press charges against you to the fullest extent of the law for destroying government property, even had the Nevada State Director in his camp. Fortunately, cooler heads here prevailed."

Well, I hadn't heard that version. Never had thought about how much a pinion tree might be worth to the feds. I supposed under some circumstances, it might be quite a bit! But the tide was turning on Nodine. He had irritated so many users of the Battle Mountain District, that I heard he was going to be given a lateral transfer to the Moab, Utah District. That kind of sounded like a death verdict to me.

"You know, I really love the University, and getting this land transfer is one way I can really help to promote the University of Nevada. Of course, it wouldn't have been possible if you and Bohmont hadn't dreamed this thing up to begin with, much less all that you have done to make it work. But I must warn you, I don't think we will get all 10,000 acres. My guess is about 8,000. Even though you have done everything possible, I am sure they will want to remove something, likely from the southern end, just to let me and Paul, along with everyone else, know that they are earning their money."

I had always suspected as much. To counter that possibility, I had originally included two to three thousand acres on the southern edge of the transfer that really weren't too important for what we wanted. And I had extended the line into the dry lakebed a bit further than was realistic, just for the same reason.

"Well, don't worry about the loss of a few acres, as we have discussed many times, its my opinion what they will want to keep is some brush land that I don't really want to begin with. Just don't let them touch those acres between the original Walti Ranch and the Allen Ranch. That's what's really important!"

"Got you, I have at least one good contact in Interior, and he keeps me pretty much informed on what the BLM's thinking is. However, rather than have me go over this with Paul, I think it should come directly from you. He knew you were here this afternoon, they wanted you at his office by around 4:30.

It didn't take long to walk from the Rayburn House Office Building to the Russell Office Building, even if the humidity now exceeded the temperature, which wasn't exactly cool. I had never been to Laxalt's office, much less the Russell building. But it didn't take long to recognize what House Representatives frequently complained about. The Senate confines were definitely better quality!

"Good afternoon, Dr. Hope", a most attractive receptionist greeted me. "Come right in, Senator Laxalt is currently on the phone, but as soon as he is off, he wants to visit with you. May I get you a refreshment, or a cup of coffee in the meantime?"

"No thanks", I responded. I felt a little dumb, because her natural grace and beauty simply had caught my attention. Here I was, in Senator Paul Laxalt's office, one of the most powerful senators on the hill, and I was mentally comparing his attractive receptionist with one of Gina's girls. I couldn't help but thinking that they both had the beauty and the brains, but how far apart their respective worlds were.

I was deep in thought about this perplexing problem when suddenly my world was shattered, "The senator will see you now, Dr. Hope."

Laxalt's office was decorated, nearly wall-to-wall, with Nevada pictures. Most offered different versions of the sheep industry, mostly with a Sierra Nevada setting, reminiscence of his Basque setting. Directly behind his massive desk was a beautiful fall photograph of Marlette Lake, the legendary home base of the Laxalt clan.

"Come in Doctor, its great seeing you again." His strong handshake hadn't been dulled by years on the Potomac.

"Well, I am about ready to introduce Senate Bill 917, which simply put, will transfer about 8,500 acres more or less of public land to the University of Nevada, thanks to your hard work."

"On behalf of the University, and probably more importantly the people of the State of Nevada, thank you for all of your hard work. One day the Gund Research and Demonstration Ranch will be the research jewel of the Great Basin, no doubt about that," I offered.

"Don't thank me, remember, although nobody recognizes it anymore, we're elected public servants, here to protect the needs of the public which we represent. You did all the work, cleared the archeological sites, wrestled with the BLM. I even heard you are beating down the State Engineer in regards to water rights. No, you have taught the cowboys and even us hardheaded sheep men a thing or two on how to get things done. Its I who must thank you."

"Those were kind words, Senator. I'll personally relay your remarks back to Dean Bohmont. This was as much his idea, and a result of his hard work as anyone's," I lied.

"You're a busy man, and you have come a long way. So, lets get to work and go over the Bill, so it's to your satisfaction."

For about the next thirty minutes we went through the bill, the legal descriptions, the maps and all the rest of the paperwork necessary to get the ball rolling. And it was all in order, actually to perfection. "My staff took all of your documents, boiled them down to this, and I am supposing that it meets your expectations, by the fact that you haven't told me to go to hell yet."

I could only laugh, "No Senator, its great, and I am not going to tell you to go to "hell", nor would I ever, regardless, I have far too much respect for you and what you stand for to ever say that" I added.

"However, there is one question that I have, its in the last paragraph, where it states, if the University ever decides to sell the property, the transfer lands denoted in Public Law ---- (currently Senate Bill 917), will automatically revert back to the Federal Government. I don't understand exactly why that is in there. For the life of me, I can never imagine the University selling the Gund Ranch, not now at least."

"I am not surprised you asked me that question. I have spent a bit of time studying you, because it intrigued me as to why you left the comfortable confines of the University, literally to place your very professional life on the line, to make the Gund Ranch go. I think deep down, you're more of a cowboy than a professor. But I have to say this, for a cowboy, you have a damn fine brain. I believe the Gund Research and Demonstration Ranch represents you, far more than the University of Nevada. And as such, one day you won't be there. Chances are, your replacement won't have your enthusiasm, or ability to crack the tough problems. And likely, the University will gradually lose interest, distance is too far, on and on, all of the very problems you have so successfully fought. Ultimately, in a tight fiscal period of time, some amazingly bright University administrator will put together a white paper dealing with what the Gund Ranch actually costs, and how much it could bring to the Universities coffers if it were sold. So, to combat that, and make your efforts more secure, I think the final version must have that safeguard in it. I have talked it over with Jim, and, although House Bill 5350 currently does not have that concept contained, he is more than willing to include it. Frankly, in clear and definite terms, I have an inherent distrust of any and all university administrators. As far as the University of Nevada is concerned, the current bunch there are the damnedest bunch of rascals I have ever had the displeasure of dealing with. I don't trust any of them."

"Well, I can't argue with that, but frankly, the thought of selling the property sometime after the transfer occurred, would be beyond my comprehension. Fact is, I had never even thought along those lines. But I have to admit that it would be awfully discouraging to pick up the paper ten years after retirement only to find the University was selling the property."

We exchanged a few more concepts about the Gund, the western livestock industry, and conservative politics in general before I departed. And as I left the receptionist gave me a slightly sexy smile and the slightest of winks. Yeah, what a vastly different world we can all find ourselves in.

I never got to personally see Senator Laxalt again, not about the transfer, nor any other matter, although we corresponded frequently. But for many years to come, I would often get a chuckle about the last sentence in Senate Bill 917. It took some time, but eventually Senator Laxalt's words about the "damnedest bunch of rascals" would ring very, very true.

It was a cold winter day; I had just arrived at the Ranch late on a Friday after a full day of teaching. It had taken an extra hour to get from Austin, because of snow and drifts up to three feet deep, but at least I had made it. No sooner had I got the gaslights on and a fire started in the wood stove, when Rich drove up.

"What the hell you doing up so late, come for a bite off my jug?"

"Well, that's not a bad idea, we better both have a drink, because probably what I am going to tell you, you won't like very much. Course on the other hand, it may make you happy as hell."

I didn't like what I had heard, so I thought before the bad news broke, whatever it might be, we both had better have a shot. My supplies included a new bottle and some ice cubes, so it didn't take but a second to have two extra tall, double strength Jim Beam highballs sitting on the kitchen table, directly under the gas light. And the fire was starting to put out lots of heat, so things didn't seem too bad, yet.

"Pam and I been doing a lot of talking. We sure as hell enjoy being here, and working for you. But I don't enjoy those assholes from the University. Every time they come out here we have to wet nurse them one way or another. And I probably shouldn't say this, but they always talk behind your back. Now hear me out. I would love to stay here forever, but I sure enough can see the direction this thing is going. There's going to be all kinds of professors running around here within a few years. This place will change forever. Hell, probably sooner or later you're going to get fed up and quit, and then where would I be?"

That was the second person that had brought up the subject of my quitting recently, which frankly, was the furthest thing from my mind. "Don't worry about them talking behind my back. Actually, I am pretty used to them talking right to my face anymore, and they don't even say nice things then. I can understand your concern for the future, and yes, you're right, it will likely get worse. You have been a great employee, and I would hate to lose you, but it's your decision, and I'll support you whatever direction you want to go. But for right now you have a job as long as you want it."

"Thanks Terry, but I am pretty sure Pam and I have made up our minds to go north. She knows a vet that works at Washington State, and he has offered her a job starting next July 1 if we'll move up there. What we would like to do is take a week or two off in February, go find a place, and see what job opportunities I might have, then move up there in June. That's more than six months away, so that will give you time to find replacements for us."

"Us" hit me a little hard coming right out the chute. "By us, I guess you mean you and Pam?"

"Well, not really. Dwight said he couldn't take it without me, so he goes when I go."

"Oh, I see." With that I slowly drained the tall highball and made one a bit stronger.

"Well, I guess I had better talk to Dwight in the morning and get his version straight. Anyway, I'll mix you another drink, you move to northern Idaho or Washington, you'll never have another drink in a setting like this, so you might as well enjoy it."

We reminisced well into the morning, or at least until my new bottle was empty. True enough, I could never have gotten done what had been accomplished in the few short years we were here without the likes of Rich and Dwight, and Pam as well. But I had already had secretly known that they would never fit in when the Gund became a full-scale research station. I wasn't ever going to bring the subject up, because I knew sooner or later this conversation would occur. And I would sure as hell rather have it come from them, than me. It was only going to be a matter of time before Dwight would cold cock a loudmouth professor, and I could only imagine the grief that scenario would bring forth. And I had figured one day Rich would give me about a week's notice, instead I was lucky, he gave me six months.

It hadn't been more than two days since Rich had dropped his bombshell when a strange meeting took place. I had been working on a new artificial insemination facility all day, but had knocked off about 5 to have my customary bourbon and water and contemplate the baked potato and broiled rib steak that I had planned for dinner. Just settled down with the bourbon when a strange pick-up pulled up in front of the High Place. A short stocky man emerged, and inquired in a very noticeably German accent, "Are you Dr. Hope?"

"Well, by gosh, I am. How may I help you?"

"Allow me to introduce myself. My name is Eckhard Wehmeir, and I am a geographer/geologist from the University of Stuggart,"

"Well, by your accent, I must assume that you mean the University located in Stuggart, Germany?"

"Yes, yes, you are correct. I have always been intrigued by the Great Basin, both the Geography and the Geology. I am currently on leave from the Geography Institution, researching the Great Basin. Someday, we would like to bring a class of our graduate students to study the Basin, so that's what I am doing here, investigating."

"Well, you are in the heart of the Great Basin, in fact this valley is just like a miniature Great Basin. That's why the University will one day have a great research facility here."

"I know. I had the good fortune to run into your neighbor, Dr. Knudtsen. She tells me she is a member of the University's governing Board. And she told me to come see you, as you know as much about the Great Basin as anybody."

"Well, those are kind words. I do know something about the Basin, but I am not a geographer, much less a geologist. Say, I feel like a fool sitting here with a drink and not offering you one. Would you care for one?"

"Yes, what is it you American's say when you go to the bar? Give me a ditch?"

"Well, that's about right. I can do that."

The good Doctor Wehmeir visited for several hours, in fact I even had enough steak and potatoes to cover for his dinner as well. He picked my brain about anything and everything about the Basin that I possibly knew, from pre-historic through what our ultimate plans were. Before he left for Austin, his base, he asked if I thought the Gund could sponsor a field study for his graduate students one day.

"Sure, as long as it doesn't cost us any money, we're on a very tight budget."

"Oh no, no. I already have a grant from the German Commission for Foreign Studies, as well as the Geography Institute at the University. We pay for everything. I just wondered if it would be possible to spend a few days here studying your valley, your mini-Great Basin. Perhaps you could be so kind to spend a few hours with us, departing your knowledge, your expertise. I want our students to be exposed to everything, even, what you say, being a buckaroo?"

With that I had a good laugh, and of course, my answer was in the affirmative. We desperately needed new and good publicity, and I couldn't imagine anything being as good as attracting students clear from Germany.

"So, your boys are quitting, what's their problem can't stand you?" Bohmont asked.

"No, its not me, but the rest of the chicken shit professors you have working for you sure to hell haven't helped," I shot back. "Besides, they are giving me six months which is a hell of a lot better than anyone around here would expect."

"Well, seriously, you're right, I am sure its not your fault, and I suspect your assessment is not too far from the truth. Why in the hell don't you just move out there and run the thing from the ground up? This driving back and forth to teach, and act like a professor one day and a cowboy the next is going to kill you sooner or later. You probably don't think that of me, but I do worry about the schedule you keep, not only the schedule, but how you keep from hitting a cow on Highway 50 at 100 miles an hour is beyond me."

"Well, we have thought about moving, and yes, it would be far easier. But right now, there isn't even a trailer available, and won't be, if we replace everybody we need to replace, and get the agronomic technician you promised. Our youngest daughter will graduate from high school this spring and she plans on going to the University, so from that standpoint it would work. But you know as well as I do, the day I move out there, and you're not watching my backside, this outfit will hang me out to dry."

"Only over my dead body."

"That reminds me, two people, including a United States Senator have talked about the day that I won't be involved with the University anymore. What in the hell is going to keep you from getting fired sooner or later? You have already ran three presidents of this institution off. Sooner later, Custer, they are going to get you too, then where in the hell will I be?"

"Once there is sufficient opposition within this University, I'll be gone, that's for sure. But right know I have strong support among the Council of Deans, and in fact it's probably more likely that I will become President than be fired. Time will tell. But let's get back to your problem, why don't we build a house out there?"

The conversation about building a house at the Gund was causing me concern, concern that started the second the words came out of Bohmont's mouth. Sometimes I felt Bohmont didn't understand the political ramifications of some of his decisions. I was pretty positive that even if I chose to move to Grass Valley, the faculty would look dimly at me living in anything other than a double wide, at best. There was no way financially the University was going to contract out the construction of a house in Grass Valley. The only way it could ever be built was to build it ourselves, and I sure wasn't going to do that. I supposed Al Bruner could, he was a craftsman, and still maintained his contractor's license. Al had been working over at the ARS lab lately, so I decided to pay him a visit.

"Hi Al, when you coming back out to the Gund?"

"Soon as Jungle Jim has another project for me, or you lose your head and want something fancy built."

"Well, that's what I wanted to talk to you about. Would it be possible to build a house at the Gund, say by you?"

"Oh sure, in fact Bohmont was talking to me about it last month. Suggested that maybe I might draw up some plans in case we decided to go that direction."

A feeling of either fear or rage began to overcome me, I couldn't rightly say what it was. But it was pretty obvious that I wasn't entirely in control of what happened at the Gund. The thought of building a house at the Gund, when in fact in six months I might not even have any employees, was disconcerting to say the least.

"How in the hell could you build a house in Grass Valley? Outside of Lingenfelter's semi, we don't have a truck big enough to pack all the material out to begin with."

"That's no problem, I can haul just about all of the stuff with my pick-up, and Buildings and Grounds have a couple of flat beds if we would have an especially big load."

"I suppose you already have this house designed?" I quizzed.

"Well not entirely, I have been going through a lot of my trade journals looking for ideas. I would like to build something very heat conservative and take advantage of the hot water for heating."

"Oh, I see, well, when you get some firm ideas give me a call."

542

I didn't want to discourage Al, but it was all beyond my comprehension. We were struggling financially; Nevada was starting to grow population wise, which was causing the University to slowly change priorities. Not that agriculture wasn't important, but in the eyes of the University it was becoming less important. And I was going to get a new house! Usually, when things became overwhelming, I would call Pete for a picon or two, and that's precisely what I did!

"So Dwight and Rich want to leave, well that doesn't surprise me. They been good and dependable ranch hands, farmers, and irrigator's, as well as cowboys. But I could always tell that when the professors started showing up they began to get nervous. Totally out of their element."

"Yeah, I know all of that, but where in the hell am I going to find somebody to replace them with?" I questioned as the first picon went down.

"Well, if anybody at the University would know, it should be you. You have taught every kid that went through that place for the last 15 years. What about this year's seniors? They will graduate just about the time your boys want to leave. That Torell kid has worked for you on and off since starting college. Doesn't he graduate this year?"

"Yeah, but he is married, and his bride is expecting. He would be plenty good, sure enough, but Grass Valleys a long way from the hospital."

"Actually, if our operation was a little bigger, I wouldn't mind hiring him, but there's no way East Gate and Buffalo can afford a man of his caliber".

"Pete. If you hired a foreman for East Gate, you wouldn't travel back and forth as much, and what in the hell would Gina's girls do without your shuttle service, much less your special services?"

We contemplated that fate over a couple of more picons, and I patiently listened about Pete's latest lady friends. "So how's Gina anyway?"

"Hell, she is as sexy as ever, always wondering when you're coming by again. She said you're welcome to just visit, but asked me to remind you there's still a free trick for you whenever you so desire.

"Well tell her thanks, she's definitely a special lady, I might visit, but I'll keep the free trick on the books for the time being. Not to change the subject, but Bohmont wants to build a house, and we have even talked about me moving permanently to the Gund."

"Whoa, partner, that will sure enough piss the folks off. I could only guess about what some of the problems you'll have then. Shit, the University and the ranching industry have finally agreed on something. In both their eyes you're an over paid ranch manager, if not now, that sure as hell will happen when you move out there permanently."

"Yeah, I probably know that better than you, but if we are ever going to make the Gund Research and Demonstration Ranch the center of learning for Great Basin studies. I don't think it can be accomplished by me driving back and forth on U.S. Highway 50 five times a week."

"Well, this 'center of excellence' dream you have had may materialize in time. But you got to remember, times are tough in the livestock industry right now. Calf prices haven't been this low in years. The BLM is flexing its muscles to the point that there isn't hardly an operator that hasn't taken a hit. And here the University, which has the highest paid ranch manager in the history of the state, is now building him a mansion. And you expect the industry support!"

"Well, when you put it that way, no I wouldn't expect their support. But what we are trying to accomplish by maximizing production on private lands, and resolving some of the conflicts on federal lands, ought to make them want to support us all the way. I would hope they could see it from that standpoint."

"Of course, the more intelligent ones do, and they support you all the way. But there is a lot of negativisms right now in the industry. I hear it at every meeting. Hard times bring out the best and the worst. Right now, anybody slopping at the public trough is a target for the negative crowd. And in their mind, you're definitely slopping, regardless of how hard you work, a fact I clearly recognize by the way."

Picons were far more appealing than continuing the present line of discussion, which frankly I found quite depressing. So, we drank some more picons, not really contemplating the price that would be paid tomorrow. But it did bring to light one more area of concern that I wanted to bounce off Pete.

"You aware of how large Vegas is getting?" I inquired.

"Yep, its well over a million, supposed to hit two in another ten years or so."

"I read a very good analysis of the Las Vegas Valley and there were many problems last week. At their present rate of growth, they are projected to have a real water problem sometime after the year 2000. Their allotment of water from local sources is dwindling, and so is the Colorado. They are going to have to go looking for water elsewhere, and I think they have their eyes set on Lincoln and White Pine Counties. Some bright local politician is saying that if they bought the eastern Nevada ranches, dried them up, shipped the water to Vegas, their problems will be over with."

"That's a hoot', Pete countered. "Christ if the legislature allowed that to happen, I guess us cowboys would become just about worthless!"

"Well, its something to think about, I'll guarantee you that. However, Reno isn't home free either. They are currently using about every drop they have, and yet the area just continues to grow. Remember, right after we graduated, we had the drought of the mid '60's, and Reno had a building moratorium, because the Truckee was dry. That could all happen again, only difference there's twice as many gullets to swallow water now, then back then".

"Why are you bringing this water thing up anyway," Pete asked?

"Well. It just seems to me, the more successful we can make agriculture, the safer the water for agriculture is. I think that is the concept that is driving me the most at the Gund these days. We have to demonstrate to the good folks across Nevada that water for agriculture, and the preservation of our present environment is absolutely important for Nevada's survival. And if that means the promoters in Vegas and Reno have to pull in their horns a bit, so be it", I concluded.

"Well, that's a tall order stud, but I suspect you are right, even if you are looking ahead more years than either of us will be around to enjoy".

"Say, not to change the subject, but I heard your old friend, Harry Ryan is going to run for Attorney General. And I'll bet if anyone would ever steal water from agriculture to make Vegas grow, I'll bet it would be good old Harry," Pete announced.

"Well, we both agreed that he will be Governor one fine day. And since when the hell has, he been my friend?" I shot back.

And with the general depression the thought of Governor Harry Ryan brought forth, even Manny, the bar keep joined us in downing some more picons.

It didn't take long for Bruner's schematic of the ideal Grass Valley dwelling to take place. It was to be a relatively small structure, 1,200 square feet on the bottom, including a two-car garage. The structure would be two and a half stories, built into the side of a hill, located due south of the High Place. All told, the basic structure would be built of cement block, utilizing massive beams over the second story great room, with two bedrooms and a bath on the third level. The bottom would be, in addition to the garage, a washroom, an additional bath and bedroom. Bruner never ceased to amaze me on his creativity, and he had outdone himself on this occasion.

"Al, you have really done something here that looks great, what do you think Professor, well this look great at the Gund or what?" Bohmont quizzed.

"Oh yeah, for sure it will look great, I just hope not too great, we sure don't need bad publicity right now," I responded.

Al looked puzzled at my remark, "This will be an innovative, heat efficient home. I would think it would be a model for any ranch, don't see how a University project of this nature can cause bad publicity."

"The professor has a point, Al. He doesn't want to draw attention to himself, where he lives, much less what he gets paid. Right now, the average Nevada rancher looks at the professor more as a ranch manager than a professor. They all believe professors get paid too much money, and they will damn sure believe our ranch manager gets paid too much," Bohmont responded. "However, I like your idea to set this up like a basic research or demonstration project. Fits right into the scheme of the Gund. You'll have to keep precise records so that we can respond to any and all requests for information. If this is presented as a demonstration ranch house, typically designed for any ranch, it should sell well and keep the professor off the hot seat."

"How long is it going to take to build and what is it going to cost?' Bohmont asked.

"Depends on labor. If I do it all myself, working at the site say 2-3 days a week, haul everything myself, I would guess two years. My salary, materials, I am not sure; the average cost today for a house is around $65/square foot. This house, counting the garage will have 3,000 square feet, so that's $150,000. But I have minimized construction costs with this plan, used block for the basic structure, which is cheap, used giant beams for the support of the top floor over the great room, kitchen and dining room. All told, I'll bet that I can come in under $100,000."

I was wondering where another $100,000 was coming from, but my quizzical thoughts were interrupted as Bohmont yelled, "Hey moneybags, come in here and let's figure out where Terry is going to get the money to build his Gund Ranch palace."

Pete Test walked into the room, looking a little blacker than normal; however, I didn't really believe that he had heard of the latest scheme yet. But it didn't take Bohmont long with all of his exuberance to explain to Pete what a wonderful idea that I had come up with.

And it didn't take Pete long to respond. "Christ Dean, first of all we don't have a hundred thousand dollars laying around, and even if we did, this would require at least Board of Regents approval, and I would guess the Governor will want to have legislative approval. We have had enough damn trouble getting doublewides for Hope every time he wants to hire someone new. You can't do this!"

I knew the response, almost by heart.

"OK, friend, you don't have to preach to me on what I must or must not do. Remember, your job is to find the money to support the projects that this College deems important, nothing more, nothing less."

Black turned blacker.

"Yeah, you forgot one important component of my job, as recognized by Congress when dealing with federal funds. That's to not only find the money, but more importantly it's to balance the budget. You can't spend federal dollars when they're not accounted for by previous design, and you can't spend more federal dollars than you have to begin with. I can assure you both factors are in effect here. Furthermore, I don't plan on going to jail because of your or the Professor's wild ambitions."

"Ok, Ok, calm down, we'll spend state dollars, or the income off of the Professor's cattle."

I was starting to get one of those pecan size headaches; in fact, I really hadn't gotten over the one from my last visit with Pete to Louie's.

"Your state budget is broke, and the money from the Professor's cattle has already been spent twice over," Test shot back.

"Alright, everybody, relax, no more finger pointing, we aren't going to break any federal or state laws, we're just going to build the Professor a house one way or another," Bohmont responded.

"May I say something, no I'll say it anyway, without asking. First of all, it was never my god damned idea to build a goddamned house to begin with. There are probably a lot more priority items than a house. For the last 5 years I have done very well with the High Place, I have even noticed some of you have enjoyed its hospitality. If my wife and

I decide to move out there, we would be very comfortable in a double wide. However, someday, when this place grows to the point where a resident superintendent is required, it would be nice to have a good house to entice somebody new to live in the wilds of Grass Valley. Right now, I don't know when that will be, but at the rate we are going, I'll either resign, or get fired because of your blunders, likely sooner than later."

Well, that pissed both the Dean and Test off, so they jointly started in on me that the whole mess was my fault to start with.

"You know, to quote you no more than 30 seconds ago, there wasn't to be any more finger pointing," I casually said.

Somehow that brought some humor to the situation, as everybody, including Al, who had yet to say a word started laughing.

"You know Dean, your right, decent living quarters are a priority item. We have a bit of money in contingency; can squeeze a few thousand dollars out of the general fund. If we could convince ARS to continue to pay Bruner's salary, it might just all be possible. But I am positive you will need Board of Regents approval," Pete concluded.

"I could approach it this way, even though we have two bonafide residences on the Gund now, we have an upcoming personnel crisis, and it's our opinion that in order to solve this crises, long term, we need to build permanent housing. We just don't want anymore doublewide trailers; they don't stand the harsh climate of Grass Valley very well. This is just simply part of our ongoing construction of the Gund Research and Demonstration Ranch. We can do it in house, but the final product, plans, costs, etc. will be available to the general public, just like the results from any research project."

I could readily tell when Bohmont was happy with his concluding statement, he always had a smirk of satisfaction, it was very obvious right then. And the wink from Test resembled a Mafioso Don's parting kiss of death.

"Well, its pretty obvious we are going to build a house. In the end, it will be my responsibility, and Al's, to make sure we follow whatever the rules are. So, we will need to know your rules, explicitly! I'll start working with Al so that we have a better idea of what this will cost, so that you have some decent figures to present to the Board. In the meantime, I got to go give a lecture, then grade some tests, so that I can be ready to leave for Grass Valley at 4 a.m. tomorrow morning, thanks." And with that I walked out of the administrative offices, which to my way of thinking was slowly becoming my one-way ticket to hell.

It was about a week later that Pete called on a Thursday afternoon. "You going to Grass Valley tomorrow?"

"Yeah, the usual run, leave here about 4:30 or so, why?"

"I need to see you, stop at Gina's, I'll be there by 5, or 6 at the latest."

"Can't"

"Why"

"Because my wife and daughters are going out for the weekend. I am sure Gina would be the perfect host under the circumstances, but it probably just wouldn't be the right atmosphere for the girls."

"Damn, you're getting to be a prude, but I guess I understand. So, I'll tell you now on the phone what my concern is. I went to a board meeting of the Cattlemen's Association yesterday, the research sub-committee. They raised a lot of questions about why the University is competing with commercial beef production interests at a time like this. I tried to explain what all your doing, and the benefits that the industry will one day receive, not only the research, but the relationship with the BLM. It was a tough discussion, no votes were taken, but by my count, at best, you would have won six to five. There's twelve on the research committee, but only eleven showed up. I am sure it won't end with that. You know how cattlemen are, can't see past the nose on their face most of the time."

"Doesn't surprise me, I suppose when they learn I am building a mansion they will really get upset."

"Christ, no mention was made of a house. You wouldn't have gotten six votes if that had happened."

"Well, I have the support of the original ranch search committee, and John Marvel and that bunch. However, I realize that there are a lot of new voices in the industry, younger guys, and not many of them went to the University, so I don't know most of them very well. I am kind of getting to the point that I am not really sure I gave a damn anymore, that's probably a dangerous place for me, but so be it. Thanks for the information, and I will think of you when we fly past Gina's. See ya."

It was about a month later when Bohmont called me to go over the request to the Board of Regents for building the house. It was short and factual, well at least to a point. "Your request states we will build a 1,200 foot structure, nothing more."

"That's correct, 40 feet wide, 30 feet deep, built with cement block, walls fully grouted with rebar all the way. Solid structure."

"Dean, the structure may be 1,200 square feet in dimensions, but the final product will have 3,000 square feet within. Basically, three stories, or as Al says, two and a half."

"Well, I don't want to confuse the Board, I'll think they will go for 1,200 feet without a hitch."

"What do we say when they find out it was actually 3,000 square feet, not 1,200, and sooner or later they will?"

"You raise a valid point, what if we say 1,200 square feet, then later on in the dialogue we say three stories?"

"No, that makes it sound like a 20 X 20 foot structure, with 400 square feet on each of three levels. The only structure resembling that in all Nevada is Stokes Castle at Austin, and nobody has lived in it since the turn of the century."

"Well, as usual you're right, but I still think we'll call it a twelve hundred foot structure, then later talk about the unique design Bruner has come up with that allows three bedrooms, three baths, a great room, dining room, wash room, full garage, all in one structure."

"Just make sure everybody understands, because I fully believe one day, this whole ridiculous mess will become my fault."

"Professor, you need to be more optimistic, maybe you have been working too hard, had a vacation lately?"

Well, sure enough Bohmont got full Board approval to build the house. Wasn't even a meaningful discussion, not even the cost of the house. Regent Knudtsen, our next-door neighbor forty miles to the south, stated that it would eventually become the shining jewel of Grass Valley. I didn't read the rest of the article in the paper, that was enough for me.

One major obstacle remained before starting to build the house, and that was the budget. I had requested a meeting with Bohmont and Test to iron out these details, as Al was ready to start moving dirt.

"Ok, we're ready to start building, but I haven't been given a budget, or how to proceed."

Both Bohmont and Test looked at each other like the other one knew the answer. Neither did. "I thought you had set up a special account for Terry's house, Pete?" Bohmont asked.

"No, I haven't set up a special account for Terry's house, because you haven't precisely told me where to get the funds," Pete responded.

"But you listed several accounts when we discussed this last month."

"I suggested several accounts, it takes your directive, or Ray Ely's directive before I transfer any funds."

"Boy, you sure can make the red tape work to your advantage when you want to," snapped Bohmont.

I stepped back, but Pete's patience prevailed, fortunately not his temperamental side. "I suggested using some funds out of the general fund, and if we are lucky, there will be a fair amount in contingency, if nothing major happens for the rest of this year. However, you already had me transfer quite a few thousand dollars our to the general fund, for your service center you are building in Fallon, so right now we can only come up with about five thousand dollars."

"Well, that's a start, transfer that to the Gund account, label it special construction. Oh, by the way Terry, so we don't call undue attention to this, I think it best you just have Al use a purchase order book, and don't write requisitions. Less people see it that way, you know less talk."

"You mean, I am going to build a house with a fifty dollar limit on a purchase order book?"

"Yeah, and I don't want to see you use more than one fifty dollar number for any one vendor during any one twenty four hour period," Pete through the dagger between my eyes.

"Well, I stole half the things to get the Gund Ranch going to begin with, I guess I'll steal the other half now. By the way, what do I do when I use up the five thousand dollars, stop?"

"Be reasonable Hope. When we get to that point, I'll find more money to put into the account, or maybe you will find more cattle," Bohmont concluded.

As I walked out of the office, I clearly heard Test say something about "pity the poor neighbors".

Sometimes strange things happen. After Al got started in the house, for reasons beyond my wildest comprehension, things just started going better. Al didn't mind using the fifty-dollar purchase order book. Life to him was one big challenge to begin with, and the more challenging the better.

That spring I talked Ron Torell into taking Rich's job. He had only two conditions, first, we had to spend some money to fix up the old Walti house where Rich and Pam had been staying. And that was easily accomplished in two weeks time with all of us pitching in. Even accomplished the whole job with a "cleverly" written purchase order that no one ever questioned. And Ron wanted to bring a friend of his who had also just graduated from the Ag school, Ken Conley, from up Gerlach way. Both were married, so the population of Grass Valley was starting to grow.

And livestock prices were improving, so there was less and less talk about the University "competing" with private enterprise. But the situation with the faculty didn't improve at all. The more dollars that went towards the Gund, the more bitter the faculty became, no matter the fact that these new dollars were coming primarily from grants and other projects that I had obtained and was responsible for.

Sometimes those projects came out of a clear blue sky, sometimes they were the result of hard work, and sometimes they were the result of the unique attributes that the Gund had to offer to begin with. In particular, one grant that had lasting impacts on the Gund Research and Demonstration Ranch materialized simply because we had an adjacent mountain range that supported drainages that produced water. That proposal came from the Kettering Foundation, a foundation that was involved in a whole lot more than cancer research, as I was shortly to find out.

I had just finished teaching my nutrition class, when Mary buzzed me saying there was a strange sounding man inquiring if he could talk to me, "Says he is from some sort of foundation, can't really understand him very well."

"Hello"

"Hello Dr. Hope. My name is Ryhid Nanjamir and I am with the Kettering Foundation. I am told that you are in charge of a research station called the Gund Ranch, and that it has large mountains that have excellent canyons producing water, is all of that correct?"

Fortunately, he talked slowly, so that even in his broken English I could understand him reasonably well. "Yes, that's correct," I responded.

"We have developed a high head hydro-electric arc nitrogen generator designed to produce nitrogen fertilizer, using only limestone and the atmosphere. Water from the generator, will be used as a vehicle for calcium nitrate distribution to suitable crops. It is our hope that we can find a suitable site to test both the machine and this concept of nitrogen fertilization. If we can successfully test this concept, similar units will be manufactured on a somewhat larger scale and shipped to Nepal where nitrogen is in very short supply. What we need is a source of water for the high head generation system, obviously a high-pressure pipeline, as well as a suitable place to test the nitrogen fertilizer. Would you have such a site, and would you be interested?"

First of all, I could understand the accent; he must have been from Nepal to begin with. Secondly, my native intuition told me that the Kettering Foundation likely had lots of money. And I could rapidly visualize that this project would require lots of money. So it didn't take long for me to respond, "Yes, we have such a site, and yes, we would be very interested in such a project."

And I was right on both counts. Dr. Nanjamir was from Nepal, although pretty much American educated, at least as far as college. And the Kettering Foundation had lots of money. Money enough for not only the generator, but a nice building to put it in, but money enough for a high pressure pipeline to deliver water out of Sheep Corral Canyon and replace the old metal line we had already installed, money enough to hire a technician to conduct the research, and money enough to buy a new double wide for the new technician to live in. It was the biggest grant we had yet to receive at the Gund, and it proved ultimately to be both a highly productive project from a publicity standpoint, but in a way it also made us truly a legitimate research organization.

Ultimately, the generator proved itself very capable of delivering calcium nitrate to the adjacent agronomic trials. However, in the fairly alkaline soils of the Great Basin, calcium nitrate proved to be less effective than it would be in the more acid soils typical of Nepal. Nevertheless, the high head generator system was the hit of our annual field days, and on more than one occasion it received national recognition.

After two years of testing, the project was moved to Nepal, and we were left with the pipeline, the doublewide, agronomic plots and a technician. It took little convincing of my old friend Dr. Jensen, that the agronomic plots were very worthwhile to continue with, so, or course, we would need to keep the technician. He agreed, and ultimately Dean Bohmont agreed, but Pete Test never really understood. And so it went, Bohmont almost always agreed with whatever expansion plans we had, at least if they made academic sense. Poor old Pete Test was always left with the job of finding the money, a task he really didn't relish.

"Hope, you have got to come up with some concrete plans of what we are going to do with the transfer lands, assuming Congress will finally get off their dead ass and get the legislation passed," Bohmont yelled.

"Well, I have been doing a lot of thinking about this, and I do have some ideas that will be novel to say the least. But like any good idea it will take some money. However, if we want to keep the BLM off our ass, I think it imperative that some really good ideas come forth that will accomplish exactly what we sold this project for, namely taking pressure off the surrounding public lands," I countered.

"Well, lets get them on the table and take our best shot."

"First of all, I think we can assume that the transfer will go forward. As you know, Laxalt's bill, Senate Bill 917, passed last fall. In fact, I just got the final version sent to me last week, and here, I made a copy for you. Senate Bill 917, passed unanimously by the United States Senate, October 27, 1977. And I just talked to Santini. He says all the differences are ironed out on the House version. He claims that their version, House Bill 5350 will be passed within the month. And he thinks President Carter will sign the legislation within a month of passage. You ought to plan on attending that signing." I could readily see that Bohmont concurred with my suggestion. Well, he was the Dean, and I sure as hell didn't need the publicity.

"Anyway, this brings us back to your question, what to do? I have held tight to the block of land between the Allen Ranch and the Walti Ranch. I asked for way more land to the south, knowing full well that the BLM wouldn't feel good about this whole thing if they didn't whittle our request down some. And I think they are whittling to the south, where there are some archeological values, and other interests. Hopefully, they will leave the block of land I am talking about alone. We can squeeze out a full section there, 640 acres, which is a lot of land in one block, and its pretty good soil throughout."

"Now, what I am proposing will be controversial, and I will definitely need your help politically, especially with the State Engineer. Because what I am going to propose will require a whole new concept on state water law, but I also can't find anything illegal. I have been doing a lot of studying on these pivots that are starting to go in everywhere. Normally, you drill a well, hook up a pivot, and you get water right for a full quarter of a section, 160 acres, even though a pivot actually only irrigates about 135 acres. However, let's suppose the pivot was movable, then you could use the pivot to help establish 160 acres of, say, a range grass such as crested wheat. Then you could move the pivot to another 160-acre field to establish a crop of fall rye for hay, which would require a late fall irrigation, and then irrigation from mid March to early May, which should be enough to grow a plenty good hay crop of rye. Then after early May, move the pivot to the 160 acres of alfalfa for irrigation until September, when you go back to the rye fields."

"Professor, if there is any way possible to upset the State Engineer, you'll find it," responded Bohmont. "You know as well as I, even if you could move a pivot, which I think is basically impossible, Roland Westergard isn't about to approve such a controversial idea as this."

"Well, on the first point, you are wrong. I have here a brochure from the R. M. Wade Company, located in Portland, that features the very thing we are talking about, a moveable pivot. Looks simple as all get out. And secondly, I thought we would call this place the Gund Research and Demonstration Ranch. I really believe all you have to do is approach Westergard with the idea that this is experimental. Let him chew on that for awhile, have him issue us a special permit, based on research concepts, which such a policy exists in the Engineer's book on how to do things. Until we all see if its works, if it is economical, and so on, he doesn't have to go any further. If it works, and there is real interest, then let him take some of the credit for this novel idea."

"So, if I understand you correctly, we will have to drill a well, provide I assume a diesel motor, seeing how you don't have electricity, put in a mile or so of twelve to sixteen inch pipeline, and on top of all that buy a pivot."

"Yeah, that's about right, but maybe its not all that bad. Wade has already told me that if we were to actually get this approved, they will sell us the pivot at 10% lower than their cost, which is a real bargain. And Lingenfelter already has located a suitable Detroit Diesel for ten cents on the dollar at Army Surplus. So, the only two full fledged costs will be the well and the pipe."

"And I suppose you will help me present this to Pete, so that we can find the money legitimately?" he asked.

"No, that's your job, I don't get paid enough to take those kinds of lumps. I'll write up the proposal, but it's up to you, the administration, to figure out how. But I'll say this, if we could do this project, it sure would help out the public relations problems."

560

"Well, I can't argue with you on that one. If we could stretch the amortization of a well and pivot over 640 acres instead of the customary 160 acres, every farmer and rancher would be at our doorsteps. I got to hand it to you Hope, it's a brilliant concept, but selling it will be a monumental problem."

"I think you need to be ready to go with it immediately after the President signs the transfer. We'll get a lot of good publicity from that, and after the work that Laxalt and Santini have put into this project, don't see how Westergard can turn us down right then," I offered. "Santini assures me that Carter will sign the bill within thirty days of clearance of the House version, assuming it is identical to the Senate's version."

I wasn't totally wrong with my optimism, Santini got unanimous House approval for House Bill 5350, on April 18, 1978. And strangely enough, less than 30 days later, May 12, President Carter signed Public Law 95-278, which allowed the University to formally petition the BLM to transfer 7,796 acres of Public Lands to the University of Nevada. But even at best, the wheels of bureaucracy move slowly. It took more than three hundred days before the BLM got around to doing the very thing that they swore, in private, that they would never do, transfer the land to the University. But they really had no cards left to play; however, even at that they still saw fit to remove four more acres from the petition, I guess just to let me know that they really did have the last word. However, they did transfer 7,791.61 acres of BLM land to the University under patent number 27-79-0048 on April 5, 1979. And all the saber rattling about how costly the transfer would be sort of blew out the window as well. We got the whole thing for about $5 per acre. The only comical part was that I never did figure out where the 4.39 acres in question where.

"Hope, when you move to the Gund, how do you plan on taking care of your classes?" Bohmont quizzed. "How many classes are you teaching right now?"

"In answer to your first, I don't know. In answer to your second, I teach 'Importance of Animals in Man's Ecosystem' twice a year, three class hours per week. I teach 'Feeds and Feeding', a four hour class, three lectures, one lab, every fall. I teach 'Range Livestock Nutrition' a grad class, and a three-hour class every spring. I teach 'Nutrition Research Techniques', also a grad class, two hours, every spring as well. Additionally, Bohman has been making noise about me beginning to teach his 'Animal Nutrition' class next year. And the Home Economics College has requested me to start teaching a human nutrition class in a year or two."

"How in the world do you expect me to replace you, your teaching a heavier load than most professors that are at least 50% teaching, on your contract, your only 25%."

"I thought it was your idea that I move to the Gund."

"Never mind, we have to get serious about this. If you move, we have a problem, because we will have to hire at least another staff member, and this College doesn't have enough money to replace you and cover all of your exorbitant plans for the Gund as well. Who is going to run the lab?"

"Bohmont, I have been doing it all myself up to this point. You want me to move, but I can probably keep this up for another year or so. However, sooner or later I am going to be picking myself up out in the sagebrush. I'll freely admit I can't keep this schedule up forever, without missing a turn, sooner or later."

"I know, I know. The administration is keenly aware of the problem. We feel you shouldn't continue to do both jobs, it's not fair to you or your family. We're not wanting to send you to Siberia, but we all feel the greatest potential this College has for truly international recognition is the Gund, and we feel equally committed to the fact that you are the only one on the staff that can make it go. Even all the department chairs agree on that."

I thought to myself, yeah, shipping me to the Gund, permanently, is likely the least of all evils in their mind. "Well, thanks for the nice words, but I seriously doubt if all department heads really wish me the best."

"You know, you would do a lot better in this institution if you took a more positive attitude,"

"I thought that comment was pretty positive, actually."

"Ok, I am not going to argue the point anymore. After July 1, you will be transferred to the Gund full time, your title will be changed to Superintendent. You'll still retain the Full Professor status, and of course, you will still be tenured. I am instructing Dr. Bohman by memo to put together a plan to pick up your teaching assignments without additional staff. This is the only way we can afford to build your house, much less drill water wells and buy pivots."

I felt an internal groan building, but I managed to keep it muffled to a low rumble. I could only imagine how I would be appreciated at the next Animal Science meeting. Most of those lazy bastards already thought they were way overworked. When they realized that somehow, they got to share in another 12 or so hours of academic work while I got to go play like John Wayne my popularity would be at an all time low, if that were possible.

It didn't take Bohman long to handle the situation. He sent a letter to Bohmont indicating that he wished to resign his position as Department Chairman, immediately, because of an ever-expanding teaching and research load. I got wind of that decision about 4:30 one Friday afternoon, prior to having a cocktail with Pete, prior to my departure to the Gund. The more we thought about that the more we laughed, and the more we drank, sufficient to cause my departure to be delayed to early Saturday morning.

"You know what you should offer the Department?" Pete asked.

"My head on a platter?" I responded.

"No, seriously, you should offer to allow yourself to be considered as the Department Chair, and if selected, give up the Gund, except for research projects. Then Bohmont would have to hire a superintendent. Hello, I might apply for that job now that you got all the work done. Besides, it would give me more time to devote to my Salt Wells project!"

"That makes sense. Actually running the Gund will be a piece of cake from now on, your right I got the work done. You know, your right, even you could handle the job."

"Seriously, if you offered to take Bowman's job, and the Department turned you down, then you would never have to look back again," Pete concluded.

"You know, again seriously, you're right. The real work at the Gund is about done, whoever is out there, all you have to do now is keep the place together, and take credit for all the good programs. On the other hand, if the Department doesn't want me to be Chairman, then I'll move out there, take the credit myself, and they can kiss my ass from that point on. Sounds like a good program to me."

"Not to change the subject but what in the hell was that fire in front of Gina's that I read about in the paper the other day, sounded to me like your Basco heat got out of control before you got in the front door?" I asked.

"I don't go through the front door, you know that, but funny you should ask about that fire, as it might get kind of serious. Seems like old lady Banovich, the sheriff's wife took exception to Dave spending any time at Gina's. She tossed several Molotov cocktails through the front window, damn near burned the place down, in fact if one of the maids hadn't been damn handy with a fire extinguisher, it probably would have," Pete offered.

"So Big Dave the sheriff was beating your time with Gina, I thought you might be a little more protective than that," I threw at Pete while I was about to fall off the bar stool from laughter.

"Hope, I ain't going to put up with your funning, there wasn't much going on between Dave and Gina, at least as far as I know. He just patrols out there and makes sure everything is OK, maybe stops for a drink, I don't know."

"Come on Pete, that's what deputies are for, Banovich doesn't patrol, he runs the office, unless there is a big problem someplace. So, in my mind, if he's going to Gina's, then he's going for a little bit of that good stuff. Jeez, I didn't ever for one minute think a Basco would let a Bohunk get his girl, damn, sharing her with Banovich is just more than I can understand."

"You know what Hope, I am going to tell Banovitch just what you said. Now according to my recollection, you drive through Churchill County several times a week. I'll bet he just might like to talk to you so that you understand that his relationship with Gina is strictly plutonic."

That whole line of reasoning just sort of drifted away after another picon or two. However, at a later date I did remind Pete that Banovich might have a tendency to spend more time at Gina's, seeing how his wife would be spending a few months in jail.

Two weeks later a department meeting was scheduled to make recommendations on the new chairman. I had sent a letter to all Animal Staff, indicating that I was interested in the position, and that if selected, I would give up my assignment at the Gund, other than to continue to head up animal research at the facility.

Bohmont went crazy when he heard about it. "If you get selected, and I have to find a superintendent, Buddy, you'll pay plenty. I'll take his salary right out of Animal Science, and if I have my way, I'll take it out of your research projects."

"Relax, Dean. You know as well as I that I won't get a vote."

"Who else is running?"

"Nobody to my knowledge, guess none of them want to have to deal with you, a phenomenon that I can understand."

"Ok friend, I probably had that coming. But if nobody applies, and you don't get elected, wonder what happens then?"

"Don't worry, somebody will throw their hat in the ring. I hear Speth wants the job, but actually, I think it's his wife."

"Speth! He doesn't have a Ph.D. to begin with. Surely the job description requires that."

"Look again, no academic qualifications were listed, so he is eligible."

"Well, that sure wouldn't help the status of this College, much less the Animal Science Department, to have a non-Ph.D. head. I guess I'll deal with that if and when it happens."

Bohmont didn't have to wait long. The vote was taken at about two p.m. on a Friday afternoon. Bowman tallied the vote, and announced, "It's the overwhelming decision of this faculty that Charles Speth is to be your new Chairman." I never told Charlie, but even I voted for him. As I left for the Gund later that afternoon a thought wouldn't leave my mind. It was beyond me how Charlie would ever be able to pick up an additional twelve hours of academic teaching. He only taught one or two undergraduate courses.

Within six months we had moved to the Gund, living in a double wide, as we watched the house being built by Al Bruner slowly be surely taking place. The request for expanding a 160-acre water application to a full 640-acre right was approved by the State Engineer under special consideration, which meant nobody else got to try that stunt, until such time as the University proved it to be successful. The well was drilled by a company out of Winnemucca, Humboldt Drilling, and came in at around three thousand gallons per minute, more than twice what we needed. True to their word, R.M. Wade sold the required pivot, under bidding procedures, at 10% less than their cost. Wade's field representative, Bill Baxter, spent many hours at the Gund as the process unfolded. Baxter, and Wade, looked at this project as the most exciting project they had on a worldwide basis.

Other factors also just seemed to fall into place. The Gund Research and Demonstration Ranch started to become known as a center for all aspects of rangeland research. Dr. John Menke, University of California, Davis, and Dr. Jim Bartolome, University of California, Berkley, spent a year working with me to develop a rangeland course for their senior and graduate students. They would bring their combined classes to the Gund for a solid weeklong educational experience during their spring break in April. In turn, I was to teach part of the course, as well as attend a daylong session on their campuses to critique their students. For this I received the title of Visiting Professor, UCD.

It wasn't long before both Utah State University and Brigham Young University were inquiring about the same sort of program for their students. Finally, the range class from the University of Nevada started to actually use the ranch as a teaching tool.

And true to his word, Dr. Wehmeir from Stuttgart, Germany showed up with twenty graduate students for a weeklong field class. And Wehmeir indicated that the Commission for Foreign Studies was so pleased with the arrangement that he had received a grant for the next ten years to bring students to the Gund every other year.

My old friends, Hardesty and Elston of archeological fame also set up a school for archeological students interested in Great Basin lore. In cooperation with the University of Nevada, the State of Nevada established sufficient funds to initiate the Gund Research and Demonstration Ranch Historic and Prehistoric Archeology School to be held on an annual basis.

Prior to 1980, the University of Nevada had mandated that all colleges issue a ten year plan to coincide as near as possible with January 1. The Max C. Fleischmann College of Agriculture had their plan ready by late fall. It covered all aspects of the College, teaching, research and education. Under field stations it stated:

THE GUND RESEARCH AND DEMONSTRATION RANCH IS TO BECOME A MAJOR RANGE, RANGE LIVESTOCK, FORAGE CROP RESEARCH CENTER. THIS WILL REQUIRE ADDITIONAL CAPITAL IMPROVEMENTS AND STAFF.

In brief, it had become the top priority of the College of Agriculture.

In 1981, Bruner finished the house, and it was featured as the main attraction of the Ranch's annual field day, which was attended by several hundred people.

The more I became involved with the Gund, the less and less time I spent in Reno. That only bothered me to the extent that I didn't get to share picons with Pete very often at Louise anymore. However, Pete usually seemed to find a way around that problem, as one day, loud and clear over our new radio phone at the Ranch, he announced, "I am buying at Gina's. Now I know you will be going to Reno tomorrow afternoon for the College's annual conference, so the roadblock will be set up."

I hadn't seen Pete in nearly a year. Hadn't seen Gina in several, so what the hell. I always looked forward to hearing how Pete was doing with East Gate and Campbell Creek, which as I understood was fantastic. Besides, seeing Gina and her latest collection just sounded fun.

"Damn you Terry, you never come around here to give me a hug or size up my girls. You still have that free trick coming. Hell, who knows, interest being what it is these days, maybe its two free tricks now." I just couldn't shove away from her hug, those giant breasts and all.

"Give him hell, Gina. He is getting so old, hell he probably couldn't even get an erection, if all the girls paraded naked for him," Pete responded.

A course came from the other side of the bar, "Let's see, he looks plenty fit to me, Gina can we line up nude?"

I was about ready to leave, faster than I arrived, but things calmed down pretty fast. "How the hell have you been stud? Sure, do read lots about you in the papers."

"I been fine Pete, things have been great in Grass Valley. The grapevine tells me you got more cows than ever."

"Yeah, we're running 2,500 here now and still have about 500 up Buffalo way, but no more sheep, so Dad just barley gets involved anymore."

"I feel bad for him, but it sounds like you will be the cattle baron of all Nevada, that is if Salt Wells doesn't get the best of you."

"He can handle it, believe me." Gina responded as she was preparing her version of picons.

"Don't worry about me, Terry. I am a survivor. You're a survivor too, but I'll be damned if I know how you have survived this far. You probably don't have a friend left in Reno, but I guess you have neutralized that useless bunch. But that's not what I worry about anymore. Your involvement with the MX issue has probably really pissed some big boys off. That's what I worry about."

We talked long into the evening, often with Gina giving her opinion, and that included the fact that she was sure that the MX issue was much larger and far more dangerous than any of us realized. I wasn't really at liberty, at least in a Nevada whorehouse, to talk much about the MX, but Gina was right. If there was ever a brand to be fearful of, the concept of MX being burnt across the entire State of Nevada was enough to make anyone wonder where we were all headed.

MX AND THE SAGEBRUSH REBELLION
"A CONTRAST BEYOND BELIEF"

The history of the United States Air Force's involvement with the MX missile scheme is one of the most interesting, and at the same time, strangest periods in the military history of this country. Perhaps it was indicative of the paranoia associated with the "Cold War"; perhaps it was just indicative of the many problems associated with the Carter Administration. Either way, it just seemed to unfold gradually right in front of all Nevada. The first we ever heard of it was in a blaze across the January 28, 1978, Saturday morning edition of the Nevada State Journal. The headlines read, "Nevada Missile Site Studied, 14 million acre chunk hits 4 Counties". I can't rightly remember if I even took this seriously at the time, and I am reasonably sure most bonafide "Nevadans" didn't either.

President Carter had literally been out of control in regard to the military, east-west relations and about everything else that had any potential affect on the good old U.S. of A. He had torpedoed the B-1 bomber, read the riot act to the army on more than one occasion, and the salt treaty with the big bear in Russia was upside down at best. About the only part of the military, CIA, Secretary of State's Office or anything else that hadn't been reamed out for any apparent reason was the Department of Navy. And of course, most everybody assumed that was because Carter was himself an old submarine man.

It seemed somewhat impossible that the Air Force could pull off a project the magnitude of the proposed MX, without the full-scale support of the Department of Defense and President Carter. But the tea leaves would suggest that the Air Force indeed had that support, and strangely enough there never seemed to be any outcry from the Army, Navy, Marine Corps or anybody else. Perhaps they didn't believe it was for real either.

And there was good reason to question if indeed the MX would ever get past the dreaming stage to begin with. Throughout 1978 and into early 1979 the press was alive with MX stories, none of which seemed very consistent. The price of the project ranged from less than 20 billion to more than 80 billion. Sites ranged all over the west, in fact the governors of 10 states were put on notice that MX may come to their back door; including Colorado, Nebraska, Kansas, Oklahoma, Texas, New Mexico, Arizona, California, Utah and even Nevada. Fact is, no one really knew what the MX was actually even going to look like or how it would work. Confusion reigned, so why get excited?

Well, one good reason to get excited about the possibility of the MX actually occurring was because Nevada has always had a certain percentage of its elected officials that might be just a little bit hungry when it came to snapping up a fat carrot without ever considering the strings attached. In fact, the more MX stories that were in the press, the more it seemed that politicians from southern Nevada started to speak out in favor of wooing the Air Force to Nevada. Nevada's long standing senator, Howard Cannon didn't leave much to doubt when he came out full force for the MX, clearly stating that the economic upswing the project would create for Nevada would ultimately place Nevada among the Nation's job leaders. Considering his position as the Chairman of the Senate Armed Forces sub-committee, and his consistent ties to the aerospace industry through campaign contributions it seemed a pretty logical place for good old Howard to be.

However, former astronaut Brig. General Thomas Stafford in a special appearance in front of the Nevada Legislature fired the shot that really woke up Nevadans, both pro and con, on April 19, 1979.

Stafford promptly told the politicians that the only opposition MX faced was from a few that were simply misinformed. "The proposed $40 billion missile system will be deployed along Nevada's eastern border in sparsely settled valleys. The system will bring an estimated 25,000 persons and an estimated annual payroll of 400 million". Stafford went on to say that the likelihood of the MX coming to Nevada was at least 50-50, and those odds could be considerably increased with positive support from Nevada and the likes of the legislature. Stafford probably had Nevada sold at that point in time, but he seemed to want to drive home the point that no matter what, the MX really wouldn't cause Nevada any ecological damage. "The MX has been designed to create minimum impact on the environment. *Besides, much of the land in eastern Nevada where the MX will be located is for all practical purposes a wasteland. Probably its best and most productive use will be for national defense."* The Air Force probably never figured it out but labeling eastern Nevada as a "wasteland" put into effect many of the very forces that would ultimately bring down the MX concept.

It probably wasn't a timely decision on the part of the Air Force to label eastern Nevada as a wasteland. Seems like Nevadans had gotten pretty tired of federal domination of 86%, or more, of the State, in fact they had gotten so tired that they fired a missile of their own at the feds. It was called the Sagebrush Rebellion, a dream of state domination on the vast tracts of BLM land throughout Nevada; a dream conjured up by two Nevada politicians; Senator Norman Glaser and Assemblyman Dean Rhoads, both of Elko County. Glaser had brought forth SB 240 while Rhoads sponsored AB 413; both having similar language directing state agencies to inventory public lands before devising a mechanism to turn them over to private ownership. The State's case rested on two principles; the "equal footing doctrine" and the "trustee doctrine".

Equal footing asserted that states west of the Rocky Mountains had been denied the same treatment as their eastern counterparts where federal lands were turned over to state or private ownership during the nineteenth century. The trustee doctrine held that the federal government maintained the public lands in trust pending their disposal. But, because the feds had failed to divest themselves of these lands, it was guilty of breach of trust.

The Sagebrush Rebellion had created monumental interest, not only in Nevada, but throughout the west, as well as Washington D.C. Despite the problems that Nevada would have had in managing these vast tracts of land, to a man, woman and child, the "can do" attitude of Nevadans seemed quite capable of dealing with whatever the problems might be. The Assembly passed their version of the rebellion overwhelmingly, so everyone was watching the more conservative Senate when they voted on May 23, 1979. It was a slam-dunk, the Senate voted in the affirmative, 17-3. The prestigious Nevada State Journal said the decision to reclaim 49 million acres of federally owned land within Nevada's borders was about as close as a state could come to seceding from the union without actually doing so. The fact that the Air Force wanted perhaps as much as 20 million of these acres didn't seem to faze anybody. The little ugly state out west, born out of gambling, prostitution and other sinful endeavors was beginning to flex its muscles!

"Hope, what in the hell is going on with this MX, that's about all that I see in the papers anymore?" questioned my good friend Pete one springtime Friday afternoon as we sipped our occasional picons at Louie's.

"Not really sure I know, frankly I believe its just another bull shit deal of Carter's. He's so thoroughly pissed off the military so many times, maybe this is his olive branch to calm them down. I think people are going to get upset, I guess many are already, over that idiotic general calling eastern Nevada a wasteland. I'll bet before this is all over the Sierra Club and the cowboys will be best friends," I chuckled.

"Well, I am not too certain that will happen, but I suppose they might get together if anybody ever figures out if this is for real or not. My friends over in White Pine aren't even sure if it were to go, if it will hurt livestock production or not," Pete offered.

"Boy, I don't know about that. From what I have seen so far, if this racetrack concept is for real, I'll bet you it will be off limits for livestock, hey Manny another round and one for yourself," I concluded.

We both carried on at length about the MX, although in hindsight at that point in time neither of us had any idea about what we were talking about. Finally, we turned to something a little nearer and dearer to our hearts, the Sagebrush Rebellion. Pete asked out of a clear blue sky, "Do you trust Glaser and Rhoads?"

"I don't know, although one thing for sure that I do know, they got us way out on a limb. As much as I support the concept, one thing for sure, if we fail, I would imagine the feds will take an even dimmer view of rural Nevada. Maybe that's part of what is driving the MX, although at this time, it strikes me that the BLM is as confused on the subject as Nevada is. As to your question, can we trust Glaser and Rhoads; I think so, at least to a point. I believe Glaser firmly believes Nevada can do a far better job managing the federal lands than the feds have ever done, as to Rhoads, your guess is as good as mine. I do know that the talk in Elko is if we ever have a Republican president, Rhoads may have a shot at heading up Interior. Now that would be something, wouldn't it?"

"Yeah, I have heard that bull shit too, but I can't believe Ron Reagan would ever put a little-known Nevada Assemblyman in that position, if in fact he is our next president. Dean hasn't got balls enough to handle Reagan in my humble opinion," Pete responded.

"Sounds like you don't like Rhoads?" I questioned.

"Not particularly, he is a little bit too smooth for me, and I mean smooth in an artificial way if you know what I mean."

I guessed I did as I watched the constantly swirling motion on the top of my picon. "Well, I'm heading out to the Gund bright and early tomorrow. I suppose your heading to East Gate, with the usual pleasure stop at Gina's tonight?'

"Yup, eat your heart out, I took a new girl from Frisco out last week, tonight should be her first night on the line, so I kind of think I need to check that out, you know, make sure she knows all the positions and everything like that."

"You bastard, some day Nevada will become civilized enough to put people like you in jail," I mused.

"Well, when that day comes stud, you and I will be buried. And the truth of the matter is you like Nevada the way it is just as much as I do. Being a dedicated husband and father, you bypass some of our pleasures, but I can tell by the look on your face you wouldn't trade any part of this state for all of California."

"You know, you are probably right, I guess just knowing a person can go any direction they want to here, the freedom that represents to me, is worth it all – no, your right, I wouldn't trade it for anything, I think we both can say, we did it our way."

On Friday, July 14, 1979, Nevada Governor Robert List signed an emergency regulation coming out of the overwhelming legislative support for AB 413 that placed 49 million acres on Nevada land under state jurisdiction for 120 days. During that period the Division of State

Lands, and the State Land Registrar were to draw up final regulations and otherwise prepare for legal combat in the Rebellion with the feds.

Coincidently, just two days later, the Air Force unleashed the greatest fast-talking salesman that had ever worked for any part of this nation's defense from the days of General Washington to the present, Brigadier General Guy Hecker. The General gave a full-blown briefing for the multi billion-dollar shell game that the Air Force was proposing in front of 250 people for a White Pine Chamber of Commerce dinner. One has to understand that the giant Kennecott copper mine and smelter operation, that had been the economic backbone of White Pine County for over 80 years, was on the ropes and scheduled to be completely shut down within the year. So, to begin with the good town's folks were a bit apprehensive about their economic future, and Hecker had all that figured out before the first word was uttered. His casual estimate of the 22,000 jobs that would be coming to eastern Nevada was music to the Ely Chamber's ears.

One old time miner still seemed apprehensive when he asked; "Wouldn't Ely be the bulls eye for Russian missiles if all this happens?" The General seemed somewhat taken back that concern of this nature could conceivably be raised by a White Pine native. Carefully laying his cigar aside he met this challenge head on; "Hold on here, let's think this thing through carefully. First of all, without the MX, we'll all become bulls eye's. The coast of California is already a prime target for soviet missiles, along with the Fallon Naval Air Station and the Nevada Test Site. If we are hit west of here the wind will get us anyway, so what's the difference. Build the MX and Ely, Nevada will be the safest place in the world. Fact is, when I retire, I'd be happy to move here, move my whole family here. This will become a great place," he concluded as he took a long draw from his cigar, kind of like celebrating a victory lap, so to speak. And it didn't hurt anything that the General was speaking from a dais covered with Old Glory. When questioned about how much land might be involved and if folks would still have access, Hecker again rose to the occasion; "Not to worry, total land withdrawal will be a mere 25 square miles and you can still mine, hunt and look for rocks, and fact you can even shoot rabbits." The town's folks swooned, the County Commissioners seemed a little bit puzzled, and the cowboys and miners left scratching their heads.

Hecker's con job didn't quite fool everybody. About a week after his direct hit on Ely, the Reno Evening Gazette published a blistering editorial bashing President Carter, the Department of Defense, the Air Force and in particular Brigadier General Guy Hecker. The editorial pointed out that the missile system has been referred to as a "shell game". "We suspect that something of a similar nature is being played with the Nevada public. Somehow the prospects of rockhounds and rabbit hunters pursuing their hobbies within feet of our nation's prime atomic defense line stretches our imagination", concluded the editorial. And so it went, back and forth and back.

And as much press as the MX was receiving, the Sagebrush Rebellion was not to be outdone either. Solid western support for Nevada's efforts to rest control of the federal land from the government surfaced at a Western Conference of Attorneys General held in Fairbanks, Alaska in late July 1979. All ten western states pledged support for Nevada's efforts in the Rebellion. Enabling legislation was being planned in all of the western states. At first it seemed that the two entities, MX and the Rebellion, were ignoring each other.

But the Air Force's number one con artist, General Guy Hecker wasn't about to miss this opportunity. Seeing the apparent tidal wave of public support for state control of federal lands, the good General Hecker promptly told the executive secretaries of the Nevada Cattlemen's Association and the Nevada Mining Association, along with Governor List at a luncheon meting held in Reno, that, "we'd be happy with private ownership around the missile shelters." Apparently, the Air Force, or at least General Hecker, didn't much care who owned the land, it was pretty obvious that if the MX flew, there wasn't much an individual, or the State of Nevada could do about that to begin with. And it didn't hurt Hecker's campaign much to keep talking about shelters or silo's and only disturbing 25 square miles of land, when there were ominous hints that the MX would actually be housed on a racetrack concept that would disturb a thousand times more country.

Throughout the debate between the MX and the Rebellion, Nevada's junior senator, Paul Laxalt, had been strangely quiet. Laxalt, a second-generation Basque from the homeland was tied closely to Nevada and the land. His father, Dominique, a sheepherder from the old country, was a beloved figure. Paul's brother, Robert, was a world-famous author and professor at the University of Nevada. Laxalt had been one of Nevada's all time popular Governor's and was rapidly becoming known as a powerful senator. His close ties to former California Governor, Ron Regan, wasn't hurting his position at all. Laxalt was the kind of guy that could see through the smoking mirrors, and apparently during the summer of '79 he had seen enough. But finally, the dam broke in front of a bunch of journalists in Reno, when the Senator clearly stated, "Nevada is the first dumping ground for everything – I have great reservation." Laxalt went on to say, "We'd be the No. 1 target in the event of war. I find that a little heavy for my head."

Laxalt's position seemed to begin the real polarization of those for and against the MX, as well as those for and against the Rebellion. And it all fell pretty much along party lines; Republicans were against the MX and for the Rebellion, Democrats were for the MX and against the Rebellion. The one shining lone example was Nevada's single congressional representative, Jim Santini. Santini was a Democrat, albeit a conservative one, and Santini was dead set against, at least, the MX.

"You remember Wayne Hage", I asked Pete at our occasional monthly meeting at Louise?

"Yeah, sure, he didn't show up at the University until about a year or so after I graduated, but he and his wife, Jean, didn't they just buy that Pine Creek ranch over in Monitor?'

"Yes, they did, bought that place from the Arcularis family late last year, I have been there a few times, it a beautiful ranch", I concluded.

"So why the question about Hage?"

"Oh, nothing really, just was wondering if you knew him, your almost neighbors you know."

"Well yes, if you removed Reese River Valley and Smokey Valley, I guess you could rightly say we are neighbors, but leaving those two valleys in place, Wayne and I don't see each other very often. And I gather he doesn't like the Nevada Cattlemen's Association any better than I do, we don't even go to conventions very often!"

"Wayne called me the other night, he's pretty intense about this MX thing, in fact I would say he is very concerned that it may well put him right out of business."

"Well, Wayne may be just about right, in fact, I am beginning to get a bit worried about it also. Most of the maps that I have seen so far just about border on our spread, but what few meetings I have gone to seem to indicate that I haven't much to worry about. But it does look like Monitor Valley would be right smack dab in the middle of the whole thing", Pete concluded.

"Anyway, in our telephone conversation, he wanted me to go to a MX meeting in Ely next month. He seems to think that I should get involved, maybe prepare some white papers or something along the lines of how the proposed MX will impact the livestock industry. I don't know if I really want to do that, and likely Bohmont won't be too happy about that either. But I don't think that this issue is going to go away either, in fact I'll bet you a pecon that it's going to get nothing but bigger."

One thing about Bohmont, he was predictable. "MX meeting in Ely, hell no you can't go. If anybody representing the University goes to that thing it will be A.Z. Joy, it's an extension function, not a research or teaching function. Besides, I know you well enough that if you showed up, you would open that big mouth of yours and just about that quick the Air Force would write the University off their list of possible recipients of grants. It seems like I have to remind you about every week, you were hired to run the Gund Ranch, not be a roving ambassador for the University, much less the State."

And so began a journey for me that lasted well over three years, a journey taken entirely on my own, time wise and expense wise. A journey that would take me into the depths of the intrigue of the political-military-industrial relationships that so often runs this country without the average citizen even knowing they exist to be begin with. A journey that would forever change my career, my life, every fiber of my being.

I had lots of annual leave built up, so going to Ely, Nevada meant little more than failing to turn north off of Highway 50 at the Grass Valley turnoff, instead just continuing east for another 148 miles. The meeting was scheduled for Wednesday evening at the Bristlecone Motel and Restaurant. Whenever I stayed in Ely, I always liked the Jail House Motel, the name intrigued me, besides it was owned by a family that I had known for years. The Jail House was right downtown, besides, my favorite restaurant in Ely was in the historic Hotel Nevada, right across the street from the Jail House.

Earlier in the week I had called Wayne to let him know that I was going to be at the meeting, so we had agreed to meet for dinner.

Wayne Hage was a very unique individual. He came from old time ranching and mining stock in northern Nevada. He had never graduated from high school; in fact, he never really even went to high school. He choose early on to lead the buckaroo lifestyle, and he had led it well, working on most of the big northern Nevada ranches. He was into mining as well, or at least his father had been. Somehow, Wayne had inherited some old copper and gold claims up Mountain City way that he loved to talk about, but had never turned a profit. When Wayne turned 17 he somehow enlisted for a four-year stint in the Air Force. And after the four years, Wayne decided he wanted to go to college, which is where I first met him. I was astounded that this hayseed wanted to go to the University, yet he could not produce the slightest record of ever going to high school. Being on the admissions team for the College of Agriculture, it was my job to throw people like Wayne out. But Wayne had done his homework well, as I started to give my little spiel about not meeting admissions requirements, he politely showed me a small footnote in an obscure part of the catalogue that simply stated that any Nevada citizen over 21 years of age shall be entitled to attend the state university. Wayne's address was in Elko, and his birth certificate indicated that he was 21 and a few days.

When the first day of classes started that September, Wayne had already successfully challenged enough classes to make him academically a sophomore. Three short years later he graduated with nearly a straight A average. He married the former Jean Nichols from Sparks, also a graduate of the Ag College, and shortly after they bought a ranch in nearby Sierra Valley. After a year of ranching, Wayne worked part time at obtaining a Masters Degree in Agriculture Economics. It wasn't so many years later that they sold their Sierra Valley ranch holdings and purchased the Pine Creek ranch in central Nevada.

"So, tell me what you think about this MX scam", I inquired as we downed our rib steaks and baked potatoes.

"Well, first of all you're right, it's a scam. I firmly believe it was concocted by the Air Force officers at the mid level. It's clear that without a very major project of some kind the Air Force is overloaded with junior grade officers. That's been building ever since the Academy in Colorado Springs opened. Without some kind of project like MX, a whole lot of officers are going to either get downgraded, or just plain mustered out. I think that was the original driving force. But I think now it's grown far beyond what the original intent was. There's something sinister about the whole mess, it's a grab for land, for water, for power. I guarantee you if they are successful, ranching, mining, everything that goes on today in central and eastern Nevada, and in fact all rural Nevada will come to a halt, and likely in Utah as well. The Air Force will own rural Nevada and Utah and they will own all the water that goes with the land.

Now the question is, can that happen? I don't believe so, first of all the cost of this project has escalated beyond belief, nearly double what it was just six months ago. Congress can't go for that, simply because there just aren't that many dollars without bankrupting most other programs. On top of that I think the political mood of the country is changing. Carter won because he didn't have opposition, and we wanted a fresh face. He was that. But in the two years since he has been in office, he has laid claim to being the worst president this country has ever seen. Inflation, gas prices, Salt treaty, the list goes on and on. Plainly put he has pissed off enough of the electorate that he will never win a second term. If Regan wins the nomination, he will beat Carter hands down and the MX will be gone within 6 months, but that's all two years away. That's a dangerous two years."

"Well, I tend to agree with your analyses, but there are a whole lot of people in Nevada that are sure counting the hours until they think their

MX ship will be in. Sometimes even Governor List makes me nervous, but hopefully now that Laxalt has come out so strong, List will follow suit", I offered.

"I think List has just been walking a fine line waiting to see how the winds blow. I have talked with him, and I feel confident that deep down he is very much against the scam. I am pretty damn sure you are right about the Laxalt connection, once Paul came out strongly against the MX, List will pretty much have to eventually do the same thing."

"Where do you think people like us fit in, we are pretty small in the scheme of thing, you know. Hell, I had to take annual leave to even be here, and at that, Bohmont would probably want to fire me if he got wind of me being in Ely even on vacation time."

"Remember, Bohmont is just the Dean of a college, nothing more, nothing less. I don't think he understands Nevada, although I will admit, ever since your forced his hand on the Gund, he understands better. You understand Nevada, you understand the environment. You can put together the projections on what the impacts will be. Once the facts are clear, which I am hopeful they will be clearer after tonight, you can fire the papers out right and left. People like me can get them into the right hands in Congress, that will slow this locomotive down, buy us time. We have to put them on the defense so that we buy those two years. After that it will hopefully be in the hands of somebody other than President Carter."

"Well, Wayne, you make it sound simple, but remember, between teaching and the Gund, I work eight days a week, don't have a secretary, besides, now just about everyone at the University hates me."

"Good, at that rate they won't have the slightest idea of what you are up to, now let's go the this meeting and get ourselves educated."

Well, we got educated all right; however, not exactly the way that I had been educated thus far in my academic life. Up to that point, I hadn't really paid too much attention to who in the Air Force was pushing MX. Wayne had rattled off a number of names, including ranks, but I hadn't really been listening, except that a lot of majors and generals seemed to be involved. Well, they were all right there in little old Ely, Nevada; not only in front of God, but a bunch of cowboys, miners, townsfolk, councilmen, commissioners, and I suppose a prostitute or two, and what a show they put on.

General Guy Hecker led the charge; outlining what we already knew; nothing but a few missiles, a few atom bombs, just a few acres of wasteland involved; on and on. Actually, at first, it was kind of boring. Consequently, I spent a lot of time surveying the room. My interests were always along the lines on controversial issues as to who was on which side and why. However, in surveying the folks I couldn't help but notice one young officer in full dress. He indeed was a shining example of what I would guess most perceived the Air Force officer to be. He was blond, with flashing very blue eyes, stood about 6' 2" or so, and I guessed weighed about 210 or 220. Not knowing any better, I just sort of imagined that he played football at the Academy, probably either tight end or linebacker. He was, to put it mildly, an impressive looking guy.

After about 30 minutes of Hacker's pitch, he finally wound down by saying the Air Force had designated a new point man for their pitch, and it was his pleasure to introduce the new salesman. And with that he introduced Major Mike Hens haw, the very person I had just been studying. Yeah, and I was right, he was from Colorado Springs, played football for the Academy, and was a truly dedicated Air Force officer, at least so he said.

But amazingly enough, Hens haw, after a few introductory remarks, began to paint a different picture than what Hacker's line had been. We all had heard rumors that the final MX product was to be much larger than what had been alluded to thus far, but they were only rumors, and every time somebody like Hacker got called out on these "rumors", he would always successfully sidestep the obvious.

But Henshaw began to paint some different scenarios; including that the threat from the Russian bear was such, that maybe the MX would have to be expanded to the point that a whole new version might be necessary. He began to explain some "what if's"; including that it might be necessary to have the missiles on some kind of mobile launching platform, constantly moving throughout the Great Basin. This concept, he explained, would make a direct hit on any one launching site almost impossible. As his explanation continued, I couldn't help but notice the perplexed look an many locals, probably imagining thousands of war heads plummeting down on eastern Nevada, with the hope that one lucky hit would occur. Well, so much for General Hacker's previously stated philosophy that the Ely area would probably be the safest area in the U.S. during a nuclear holocaust.

Hens haw went on to say that if a mobile system was required, he envisioned miles of roads throughout the Basin, on which the mobile launching sites would be constantly traveling. Perhaps the mobile sites would be on a railroad, or perhaps they would be on giant trucks. He felt the Air Force was leaning towards independent vehicles, which would be harder to knock out.

A question came from the crowd, "Well, how many mobile vehicles with rockets?"

"Oh, perhaps hundreds, perhaps a thousand or so". was Henshaw's response.

"How many miles of roads?"

586

"I am not sure that we have determined that yet, but it could well be over a thousand miles or more."

Questions of this nature poured forth from the citizens, a citizenry that I might add was becoming a bit disgruntled. As this went on, I couldn't help but think about Hecker's more than controversial remark that the good folks would be able to rock hunt, even hunt for rabbits right up to the edge of the silos. Maybe you could still hunt in this scenario, but my thinking was that being flattened by a monster truck carrying an atom bomb equipped rocket was more likely than fetching a rabbit!

Finally, some old gentleman, that I judged to be a mining engineer, perhaps retired, asked what these monster vehicles loaded would weigh. Henshaw promptly responded by saying that information was classified, but obviously, they would be very, very heavy vehicles. And obviously, that would add a bit to the cost of MX, simply from the fact that these roadbeds would have to be built to specifications greatly in excess of present freeway construction.

But the old mining engineer wasn't satisfied, because Henshaw had previously said that maybe only one in ten of these mobile launching sites would actually have a rocket, the rest would be equipped with dummies, making it even harder for the big bad Bear to score a direct hit. "So, it only one in ten vehicles has the real thing, do you still have to build such superhighways?"

To me that seemed like a logical question. But Henshaw's answer, which I suppose in military concepts was logical enough, nevertheless, completely blew me away. In fact, I got to give Henshaw credit; his answer caused me to make the decision right then and there to fight the MX to the bitter end, regardless of the cost to me, mine and anything else ---

"Well, the answer to that is simple enough. The dummy vehicles must weigh the same as the real McCoy, because the Ruskies will have their folks out and about planting sensors under these roadways, in an attempt to determine if there is a difference in weight, which of course if there was a difference in weight, it would greatly improve their odds of obtaining a direct hit, so it is absolutely necessary that the dummy vehicles resemble the real deal in every aspect, including weight."

The evening wore on with charge and countercharge coming from all quarters. Henshaw took most of the questions head on, but occasionally his youth would get him in over his head, then the wily old General Hecker would invariably bail him out.

It didn't make much difference to me, however. I just couldn't get Henshaw's comments out of my mind. It was a comment made so casually, so matter of fact, that hardly anybody thought twice about it, except myself. I was stunned that a military representative, of considerable stature, could so casually imply that the Russians would know everything we were doing, because in fact they would be here observing, measuring or whatever. I thought of the test site and Dick Jensen's comments about always having to watch for Russians in Vegas wanting to access the test site. And yes, my old friend Tredwell even entered my mind.

It was just about midnight when everybody agreed that they had said everything that was worth saying. Fisticuffs were close but never actually occurred. Major Henshaw was pretty smooth in that regard, he seemed like he was everyone's friend. I hadn't talked to Wayne a bit throughout the meeting, and I really hadn't paid him any attention, so I wasn't privy as to what his thinking was. But as we began to head toward the exit, he asked, "You up to some late-night food or drink, maybe the Jail House is still open."

"Well, I am sure the bar is, maybe they will give us some pie or something."

The Jail House bar was just serving booze, but that was OK. The hour was such that most of the partygoers had probably either gone to bed or headed home, wherever that might be. At least Heacker and Henshaw weren't there. We both looked at a ditch, along with a cup full of peanuts and quietly contemplated what we had heard.

"Did you catch the significance of what Henshaw said about the vehicles all weighing the same", I inquired.

"Yeah, I did, and I turned and looked at you right then, and I would have laughed it hadn't been so serious. You looked like you had just swallowed a coyote, whole, and it was still pretty much alive."

We discussed the significance of that and all the other remarks that Henshaw had coughed up during his hour-long dissertation. Henshaw had impressed Wayne; "You know they really let the wolf out of the bag tonight. I had never seen this Henshaw guy before. He's polished, the all American boy for sure. The rest of those blowhards don't impress the folks, but Henshaw, I can see he is a different story. He will become your man in this debate, you can generate the facts, the science, and those are the only things that will possibly derail this guy. It will be tough, but you will have to be the one to do it, you have the academic standing, and that's what it will take. He's just too polished for the rest of us cowboys. You got to remember; he called it like it is tonight, no bullshit, just facts. And I guess we owe him a thanks for that, because now we sure know better where we stand."

It was late, well after midnight, and I had to be back at the Gund tomorrow before going to Reno. I agreed with Wayne's assessment, somebody had better start producing some white papers, papers with some hard solid facts before this monster got completely out of control.

It was close to two when I pulled the covers over my head, tried to ignore the 4 a.m. wake up call that seemed necessary, and continued to wonder how this mess ever came about to begin with.

The following week I made three trips back and forth between the Gund and Reno. Between equipment breaking down, grant proposals, trying to avoid Bohmont at all costs, I was busy. I was also making notes at every possible opportunity on how my first "white paper" would go. Sunday, July 22, I returned to the Gund, as we had actually moved to the Gund and were living in one of the vacated doublewides. The girls were all away in college at UNR so the move was not all that difficult. I had picked up a Sunday Gazette to read at my leisure that afternoon before starting haying on the second cutting of alfalfa. I ignored the front-page news, as it was all about Carter, and nothing could depress me more quickly than Jimmie Carter. The sports page featured some projections for the Nevada Wolf Pack's upcoming football season, a section I thoroughly enjoyed, as I was an avid Pack fan.

Directly I turned to the editorial page, and lo and behold there was an editorial titled "Sales Pitch for MX". Most of this was a rehash of the Ely meeting, so I just casually scanned the article. But then the editorial quoted Bob Hill, Governor List's Chief of his MX committee as saying joint planning and joint control would be necessary, as if the Air Force would ever allow "joint control" on such a project, much less joint planning, what in hell is this guy thinking?

Well it got worse fast, really fast. Two paragraphs later the editorial stated, "Apparently he (Hill) has the support of the Governor who, after giving the appearance of caution initially, has since come out foursquare in favor of having the system in Nevada". Well, so much for politics, so much for Laxalt having the power to influence List, in fact so much for rural Nevada!

One thing for sure, between the MX and the Rebellion, the one sure winner was the newspapers. One story or the other, often both made front-page headlines every day, and twice on Sunday. It was a journalistic holiday, as often as not the story in the Gazette would contradict the Journal's morning story, with the Journal contradicting the preceding day's Gazette's efforts. In fact, it got so bad that Dean Rhoads himself was forced to write a full-page editorial, which appeared in the Journal on August 13, 1979. Rhoads attacked an August 5th editorial titled "Whistling in the Wind" which also appeared in the Journal. That editorial suggested that the Rebellion was more or less a joke, and in the end would never fly. Rhoads, in his steady, but sometimes flamboyant style, took the editorial apart piece by piece. The only problem Rhoads had is that he boldly noted that the Rebellion was overwhelmingly supported by, "the Legislature, the Attorney General, and the Governor!" Well, Harry Ryan was Attorney General, a card carrying Democrat, and believe me, deep down in his heart, he hated the Sagebrush Rebellion and everything it stood for. Given the right opportunity he would scuttle such nonsense, even if it were supported by 10 western States, and 75% of voting Nevadans.

In this circus atmosphere I was pretty sure General Hecker wouldn't be letting too much grass grow under his feet. In fact, just 2 days after Rhoads blistering editorial, Hecker upped the anti for the support of the cowboys and miners by saying, "We'd be happy with private ownership around the missile shelters". The article, by a local Reno reporter was careful to not quote Major Henshaw however, because private ownership of land covered by the racetrack concept, he described just wouldn't seem too attractive, not even too a cowboy.

My desire to "lay low" couldn't go on forever. Fortunately, my name in regard to any aspect of the MX hadn't surfaced, but it had in relation to the Rebellion. Rhoads kept referring to work I had published in regard to wildlife and livestock grazing, as well as the economic impact of rangeland grazing for Nevada. It would only be a matter of time before my first "white paper" would surface, and if Bohmont read it out of a clear blue sky, I could readily imagine a coronary following shortly. So, I took the bull by the horns, marched directly into his office and laid it on the table.

"Hope, I am telling you point blank, you are a full professor with tenure, true enough. You are also a nutritionist by training, and currently, you are the superintendent of the Gund Research and Demonstration Ranch. But none of that qualifies you to be the official spokesperson for the anti MX crowd. I believe the majority of the Legislature is pro MX, the Governor is pro MX, and sure to hell Senator Cannon is pro MX. Even though you never stop to think about the consequences of your actions, you are coming out with these so called "white papers", which represent nothing more than your opinion could well jeopardize this College and the administration of this college. To put it in language that you can understand, if you persist with this idea of you writing anti MX papers, I will remove you from your position of Superintendent, your former position of Nutritionist has been filled by Speth, so you will come back to the Department without an office, without a laboratory and without any research funds. Do you understand me?"

Well, for a simple little comment saying that I would like to write a paper or two discussing some of the environmental ramifications of the proposed racetrack version of the MX, I got quite a response from the Dean and Director of the College of Agriculture! I just sat there across from Bohmont, with his monstrous desk in between, sort of like a buffer I was supposed to. I was sort of grasping for an appropriate response, but nothing intelligent seems to be occurring, at least from the standpoint of diffusing the situation. So, I went in the other direction.

"You know, I see last Friday, the Board of Regents spoke pretty highly of Acting President Crowley. I think he will become President of the University of Nevada. We have talked about that extensively, and you have always told me that would never happen, well guess what, it sure to hell looks like it well to me. I have told you repeatedly that it is my opinion that if good old Joe ever became President, he would have your ass; because of your past activities in firing Presidents. So, to get this conversation over with, I am going to write these papers, and I would advise you that if you wish to demote me, then you had better get with the program, because, if this happens, your position is in a whole lot more jeopardy than is mine. I am just exercising my academic freedom, and it will not interfere with my present assignment as Superintendent of the Gund Research and Demonstration Ranch."

In the hundreds of "discussions" Dean Bohmont and I had over the years since his arrival, most just ended in a better understanding of the problem once the yelling stopped. Sometimes, he would temporarily get the better of me, sometimes I would best him, but we always came together. This time it was vastly different. I had read the tealeaves correctly, and so had he. I was just blunt enough, crude enough if you will, to tell him point blank, that he was probably going to lose his Deanship under the leadership of Joe Crowley. I didn't have to tell him that as the dominoes fell, it would probably involve me sooner or later as well.

"You're right Professor, go write your papers. Maybe it will do some good and possibly bring some common sense to a situation that has become totally out of hand. If the MX is built like those idiots have been describing, there won't be much need for a College of Agriculture."

And so ended the only internal opposition that I had to begin my journey of challenging MX. It was over just that fast, I wasn't proud of what I had done to Bohmont, but I had already come to the conclusion that nothing was going to stop me from writing those papers. The MX was too real; the consequences of full implementation were too great. Whatever the cost of opposition was, it was incidental to the consequences of doing nothing.

Following the MX news for the remainder of 1979 was like following the antics of a three-ring circus. The cost of the project varied somewhere between 20 and 150 billion dollars, with little discussion of where the money would actually come from. I supposed that was something the taxpayers didn't want to hear, because ultimately, they would foot the bill, regardless.

The racetrack concept versus the stationary silo concept seemed to be gaining momentum. However, the racetrack concept varied between railroads or giant bomb carrying vehicles racing around on the tracks. The number of tracks varied greatly as well as to scope and location, no area was immune to the constantly changing concepts emerging from the Air Force. Congress wasn't short on ideas either. Reading between the lines, one couldn't be too sure about Congress, was it national defense, or the lure of billions that could be captured for contracts within specific congressional districts. By September, Laxalt and Santini had come out against the system, at least the system being implemented in Nevada. And Governor List began to see the picture a bit clearer, and he was beginning to question the sanity of everyone involved with the MX. Rumors of Russian spies began to appear everywhere; national television news to the Ely Times all reported that the FBI was trailing Russian infiltrators all over eastern Nevada. Everybody was beginning to be a self-proclaimed expert on the MX, based on secret discussions that they had had with another expert. Even General Hecker seemed to be getting confused, as he began referring to west Texas, where the racetracks would actually be deployed.

As the MX issue raged across the west, so did the Sagebrush Rebellion. Nearly 20 states had signed on to the Nevada effort. Strangely enough the two camps, MX and Rebellion paid absolutely no attention to each other, yet they were both focused on the same piece of western landscape. Hecker had covered his bases by saying he could work with private land ownership certainly as well as could work with the federal masters. On the other hand, Rhoads and Glaser never even acknowledged that the MX ever potentially might actually exist.

As support for the Rebellion grew throughout the west, so did opposition, at least from the environmental quarter. The environmental lobby, which was probably more concerned about raising money than saving the environment, had long since learned that the best avenue to promote their cause was through the federal government. Agencies like the BLM and the USFS were far easier to manipulate than States. They all realized that their mission would be essentially ruined if the lands in question, in fact, became private. That's not to say that private ownership cannot be equally committed to environmental concepts. Most livestock men had long since learned that a healthy landscape equated directly to better profits. But the environmentalists didn't like to paint that picture, instead they would find and publicize the worst possible environmental issues that related to owner or manager misuse; constantly pointing out that if the western ranges went from federal to state ownership, or worse yet private, then complete desertification of the entire west would undoubtedly occur shortly thereafter. Scientific fact, or even history seemed to have relatively little merit in the brouhaha that was developing around the Rebellion.

Rhoads and Glaser had no choice but to respond to the constant environmental bombardment if their political careers were to remain intact. To his credit Rhoads wrote many a good, soundly based, factual editorials, and they seemed to satisfy the citizenry. But there was a nagging question; did the citizens enjoy poking a stick in big brothers eye, or did they really understand what state ownership and management of the vast western rangelands really meant?

"I don't trust Rhoads, not even sure I trust Glaser," Pete voiced as we sipped one of our ever increasingly infrequent picons. "Rhoads is an opportunist, he knew he was going to get his hands on a ranch when he married his wife. He knew when he got into the legislature it would do nothing but help him. He takes advantage of every single federal program that will divvy up federal funds to any portion of his ranching efforts, I just don't trust him to do the right thing."

I didn't always agree with Pete, but I knew Pete got to know all the ranchers in Elko when he was a County Agent, and time and time again, his knowledge of that crowd had proven more right than wrong. "Well, I am not going to question Rhoads credibility, I don't know the man well enough. Of this, however, I am sure, and that is that Nevada now has only a handful of state lands to manage. If they suddenly find themselves owners of 50 or 60 million acres, some 2,000 livestock operations utilizing that forage resource, along with countless mines and other such endeavors, then somebody is going to have to step up to the plate. I just wish Rhoads and Glaser had paid a little attention to what we are trying to do at the Gund with this land transfer. I believe with minimal transfer of federal lands to private ownership this whole god damn mess would go away. If half of the 2,000 permittees in Nevada were able to get their hands on 5 to 10 thousand adjoining acres, it would only amount to 5 to 10 million acres reverting to non-federal ownership instead of 60 million acres. And maybe, just maybe, that is something Nevada could handle."

"Well stud, however this works out I just don't want to see Dean Rhoads profit from it more than anybody else. I know how the system works, and I can assure you Dean also knows the way."

With another pecon, talk drifted back to the MX, "You know what? Wayne Hage wants me to start writing environmental impact papers about MX possibilities. Been doing some research about possibilities, so I think I am going to get to learn about George Patton."

"What in the hell has General George S. Patton got to do with this god damn monster anyways."

"Don't you remember in range that Dr. Robertson said something to the effect that it was still very evident in the southern Nevada landscape where Patton practiced his tanks before the start of the war?" Pete remembered the lecture well in hindsight, "Yeah that always impressed me that you could still see the tank tracts," he continued.

"Patton organized a desert tank training center in Indio right after Pearl Harbor. He was placed in charge of both the first and second armored Divisions, so he had lots of tanks at his disposal, and from what I understand they trained in both southern California and Southern Nevada. If the tracks are still apparent in the desert after 40 years, I would guess it would be safe to say that the construction trail across Nevada and Utah from building these racetracks, whatever they might be, would be pretty obvious 40 years from now, say about 2019. So, I am planning on taking a weeks annual leave so Bohmont won't have a heart attack to go to Indio and find the locations of that tank activity. I think that's going to be the basis for my next paper.

"Well, its plain to see Dr. Hope that you are exercising your academic freedom. It's a good thing you called Bohmont's bluff, but I'll still bet he would like to tattoo your ass good and proper. His problem is he doesn't have anybody else to turn to, the rest of those idiots would never be able to find Indio, much less recognize a tank track, unless it ran over them. Manny lets have another pecon."

I just told Bohmont that I was taking a week off to go to Southern California to see my folks. I assured him that the Gund could take care of itself, hay was mostly up, and cattle would not come home for at least another 60 days. I had never been to Indio, went to college with kids from Indio, but that was about as close as it came. My old fireworks buddy from San Dimas days was from Indio.

Even though it was September, Indio was hot, 100 plus, and humid from the nearby Salton Sea. It didn't take long to determine that the Desert Tank Training site had been taken over by the California National Guard, and there wasn't too much information on what the General did, but this Division of the Guard was a motorized division, so they had tanks also. Desert training was no longer a major priority, but training still occurred, although relatively close to Indio. Finally, an old sergeant seemed to remember some World War II maps, and sure enough when we finally rolled them out and dusted them off, there it was, all of the intense training sites for the First and Second Armored Divisions under Patton's direction. It appeared most of the Nevada training had occurred in what is called Paiute Valley, between Searchlight and the California State line. The map showed several roads into the test areas, so it certainly seemed feasible to go and see what the damage, if any, looked like. And the good Sergeant volunteered to make a copy of the maps, seeing how they had long since been declassified.

Paiute is an extremely dry desert valley running on a north south transect from Searchlight to Needles in California, west of the Colorado River. The environment was the Mojave, the hot dry Mojave, and an environment that supported a very unique type of vegetation. A slow growing vegetation, one that reproduces only when the environment allows, which certainly isn't every year. Grasses and forbs are limited, except in wet cycles. Shrubs are more or less the dominant type of vegetation. I was pretty sure that if Patton's tanks had been practiced here, at least extensively, that the shrub population would pay a heavy price, even if this were nearly 40 years after the fact. I wasn't disappointed.

I wasn't very familiar with Mojave flora, but the obvious ones were there; creosote, yucca, hop sage, winter fat, and some sage species that I didn't clearly understand. There was an under story of forbs (dormant) and bits of grass, including Indian rice grass, giatta and even some cheat grass. I followed a road on the map the sergeant had provided me with in a general southwest direction leaving Searchlight. There wasn't much to indicate recent travel, on the other hand, who would want to go down this road to begin with. There were no obvious signs of water, no wildlife, except an occasional sparrow, parts of the Mojave can be pretty sterile.

After about 20 miles the vegetation started to change, less and less creosote and other shrubs, a more dominant under story of annuals, which appeared to be mostly dead weeds. After another five miles shrub vegetation was absent, weeds were abundant, berms from previous activity were everywhere, put bluntly, the desert was a mess, and it didn't appear that recovery was imminent.

A few pictures, some rudimentary range site measurements, a remnant from my range classes, and I had the foundation for a blockbuster "white paper".

When Wayne Hage saw what I had put together, he indicated he wanted 50 copies as he was planning on testifying in front of the House Subcommittee on National Parks, Forests and Public Lands, which was part of the House Committee on Natural Resources. "They are taking a look at this MX scam for the first time, so I want to be able to hit the Air Force as hard as I can. I'll just make it plain and simple, as bad as Patton tore up the desert, that will be a piece of cake compared to what Nevada and Utah will look like after they get through building these 32 racetracks or whatever number they finally come up with."

I was in Reno that day for our meeting, and as Wayne turned to head for Pine Creek he stepped back and asked, "Say, it looks like that damn Joe Crowley is going to become president, what's your take?"

"Pretty simple, he's got the votes, the Dems want him, the majority of the Board are card carrying Dems, its going to happen. Bohmont and I have talked a bit about that, but I will just about guarantee you, that within a year of him becoming president, Bohmont will be gone,

Crowley will be reorganizing the Ag College and that will be that," I responded.

"Well, I don't like the guy, two faced like most in academia, and I think you are right, agriculture is a bit below what Crowley would envision the University should be all about. Guess he thinks the land grant concept is a bit outdated. Well, I got to get on to Pine Creek, keep the papers coming."

And the papers kept coming. Copies routinely went to both Santini and Laxalt. However, they were the same old thing, always presented in a different form, but I never really had anything new to add. It was very obvious that the activity being presented by the Air Force in regard to MX construction would ultimately be hard on the Nevada environment, no matter how much care was taken. It was more difficult to get a handle on the economic impact on the livestock industry, as the Air Force was still hanging their hat on a relatively few acres of ultimate withdrawal. No hard figures were available, and they still clung to their concept that citizens would be able to rock hunt, rabbit hunt, or whatever, right along side of an atom bomb waiting for delivery to the mother bear. With all of that in place how could anyone with any authority say this monster is going to wipe out the livestock industry?

By mid September, I finally got my hands on some maps with enough clarity regarding location of racetracks to show that essentially all of the proposed tracks bisected existing livestock allotments. So I wrote a paper describing how disruptive it would be to the typical ranch to have their permit cut in half by a fenced racetrack. It wasn't long before Henshaw noted in a speech in Las Vegas that fencing would be too restrictive and too costly, so it was not being contemplated for the tracks. Further, he noted it wouldn't matter if train tracks were used or roadways to support the giant rocket carriers, in either case the machines would be moving too slowly to cause a problem with free grazing livestock. With front men like that how could the United States ever loose in this cold war?

And on top of everything else one Joe Crowley was inaugurated as the new president of the University of Nevada on October 5, 1979. That didn't bother me; my goal was set on beating the MX. Joe could go to hell as far as I was concerned; I would deal with that post MX.

Throughout the remainder of 1979, and well into the spring of 1980 the intrigue of MX did nothing but grow. Sides for and against became larger and more vocal daily. The Air Force would up the anti by suggesting the project cost were escalating, but that meant more money would be spent locally, and the locals loved that.

Arguments started over water requirements for the project. At first the listed water requirements were artificially low, but as the project expanded, the requirements for water expanded nearly logarithmically. At first, the Air Force said they would abide by Nevada water law, but then State Engineer, Bill Newman, noted that the MX water demand had escalated to over 30,000 acre feet of water, and with each new revision the demand seemed to grow further. Newman raised the probability that water volumes of that nature just might not be available, which shortly prompted General Hecker to question if it was necessary for the Air Force to abide by Nevada State water law at all. That statement alone sent a noticeable chill down the spine of all agriculture and environmentalists. Never did a day go by when more fuel wasn't dumped on the MX fire.

The papers kept coming, by February of 1980 I had pushed out number 4, much of the limited factual data just spit out in a new form, with as much environmental spin as I was capable of. Word came back indirectly from both Laxalt and Santini that my efforts were appreciated, but they needed more "meat". I couldn't have agreed more, but the Air Force was changing its options from silos to racetracks just about daily.

Further, racetracks were changing from railroads to superhighways just about that fast. My only option was to take all options, multiply them by 10, and summarize the impact.

Simultaneously, the politics of MX were changing. MX was Carter's baby from the beginning. And it appeared that former California Governor, Ronald Reagan, was likely to win the upcoming Republican primary, and if so, most political pundits felt that Regan would beat Carter to become the next President. A lot of people in Nevada were holding that as their hole card, the close working friendship between Reagan and Laxalt was well known, and based on Laxalt's total opposition to the MX it was assumed that would have some influence of Reagan as to the future of MX. Wayne Hage and I both totally agreed on that concept, the only problem was that even if Reagan won, inauguration was nearly 24 months away, 24 long months.

Money and politics seem to always go hand in hand. And there was no end to the amount of money being thrown around for MX, at least on paper. The number of Nevada firms to claim they already had valid MX construction contracts in hand was overwhelming. Nevada, and more particularly Clark County had been in an economic slump. Nothing could brighten the future, and win more votes, then a few hundred million dollars being casually thrown out for grabs during the cold winter of 1980.

And it didn't stop with Clark County. Years before the financial future of central Nevada had been forever dashed when old Highway 40 was chosen as the preferred Interstate Route across Nevada over old Highway 50. The towns of Fallon, Austin, Eureka and Ely were dealt a mortal blow by this decision, and had been winding down ever since. But MX possibilities tore the conservative hearts out of County Commissioners from Churchill, Lander, Eureka and White Pine Counties, they started counting the dollars before the first check ever showed up.

And old Tonopah, located on U.S. Highway 95 midway between Reno and Vegas wasn't going to be left out in the dark. Nevada Senator Howard Cannon, the prime supporter of MX, and head of the Senate Military Appropriations Committee decided that Tonopah would be the main base for the MX. Nobody paid too much attention to the fact that the Scott family out of Vegas owned most of Tonopah, and that Senator Cannon owned a half million dollars of Scott stock.

The greed for MX money was bubbling up through the sands of the Nevada desert everywhere you went. It was challenging for one's love of Nevada, but I had long since determined that I loved the Nevada environment far more than I loved the folks from the Silver State, albeit it was sometime damn difficult to separate the two.

One fine spring day in 1980, Jan reported that we got a very strange call over our new radio earth ground telephone. She had taken the call and relayed it best she could to me, but after listening to her version I was pretty sure that she had somehow mixed things up a bit. The jest part of the message was that I was supposed to return a call to a number that I determined was in Washington D.C. by its prefix, supposedly tonight about 6:00, which would make it 9:00 D.C. time. And, above all else, I was to make sure that the line was secure. Well, that left out our radiophone, as anyone with any radio knowledge could conveniently listen at any time. We had moved to the ranch permanently, but still maintained our Reno house, and I supposed that telephone was more secure than anything at the University. So, off to Reno I went that afternoon, still somewhat confused.

"Hello

"Yes, this Terry Hope returning a call to this number as I was advised to do today."

"The line is secure, according to my end it is at least."

"Well, to the best of my knowledge it is, its my home phone in Reno.'

"OK, don't offer any more information. I will not divulge my name, and as far as you and I are concerned this conversation never took place. I work for a congressman that greatly appreciates your white papers on MX. As you may or may not know, a Nevada Senator has a close working relationship with Ronald Reagan, and we feel it's a good gamble that Ronald Reagan will be the next President. We believe that Mr. Reagan will kill the MX, however, he has indicated that to defuse the political opposition to such a move he must have absolutely foolproof environmental facts. That will force him into aborting this mission. We have reviewed all of your papers and feel that with your credentials, as well as your practical knowledge, you are just about the only one that can provide the information Mr. Reagan will need when he becomes President. Do you understand."?

"Well yes, I guess I understand, but to pin down the Air Force to some fact that I can tear apart in such a manor as to provide Mr. Reagan what he needs is at best a very difficult assignment."

"We understand, that's why we are talking to you, we do not feel anyone else can came come up with that sort of information. I also must advise you again that this conversation has never occurred. If it surfaces in any fashion, we in D.C., or anywhere for that matter, we will distance ourselves from you immediately. I am sorry it has to be this way, but these are the most difficult of times."

"Again, I guess I understand, however, can I call you again at this number so I can think about this a bit more?"

"No, this number will terminate at the end of this conversation. I must caution you as to whatever you do, it must be kept an absolute secret for your welfare. You will provide the information Mr. Reagan will need, but it must be in some form that cannot be seen as coming from you, at least initially. Billions of dollars are at stake here, and there have already been numerous death threats, and we believe, based on some very strange events, some individuals have already paid the ultimate price."

"I see, and I guess once more I agree, but at this time I absolutely have no idea what trail I will take. I don't know where it will lead to, but I am sure as haphazard as this whole thing has been to this date, there must be some very vulnerable areas out there. I guess I don't have anything much else to say right now".

"Good, good luck, goodnight."

It took a long time to digest that conversation, and a hell of a lot longer to put it into effect. I was pretty sure the person I had talked to was one of Jim Santini's men in D.C., but what if it wasn't? Suppose it was a trap, a set up, done by someone else to make them look bad, after all they, Santini and Laxalt were the two most outspoken critics of MX. Well, no one knew I was in Reno, and of course the call could be traced to our phone. But what if it wasn't a trap, what if it was for real? And if it was, how in God's green acre was I going to be able to provide them the information, without having it provided directly to me to begin with, and what would that information be to begin with? My head was spinning, and I knew it wasn't time to act; I needed time to just think. I needed to be positive. It hadn't been more than 30 minutes since I hung up when it dawned on me that if I called back, I might just get some clarification.

"We're sorry, you have dialed a number which is not in use at this time. Please try again."

I guessed that was some type of clarification, regardless of whom I was talking to, they at least must have known how to do things.

I drove back to the Gund that evening, thinking all the way, what to do, where to go, on and on. I couldn't really tell anyone about the call, not even Jan. She was already paranoid about my anti MX involvement. Hearing the words that I heard tonight would drive her completely over the hill. So, I just dummied up, held to myself, and thought long and hard.

For the next week, I worked the Gund. We had already turned out, so I just rode all day, away from everybody, everything, trying to make sense out of the whole mess. I would ponder on how I always seemed to get myself into these predicaments, and this one was the best one of all; I am supposed to come up with some kind of significant information, significant enough to give the next President of the United States the justification he would need to kill the biggest military project in the history of the United States, and never allowing anybody to know it came from me! I was at a dead end with ideas, I was frustrated, and I began to realize that I was very lonely. I needed somebody that I could trust beyond all trust, somebody that could help me walk through this, somebody that could prop me up and give me the strength I desperately needed. There had only ever been one person in my life that could fill that void at this time, it was not my mother, it was not my dad, it was not my wife, and it sure to hell wasn't Dean Bohmont. That person was Peio Echegoyen. From our days as graduate students we have shared everything, every adventure, every problem, the highs, the lows, and his mom's death, just everything. We had drifted apart, not because of lost friendship, just the journeys through life, and the direction it takes us. Pete was a busy man these days, with both Buffalo and the Edwards/ Smith Creek ranches to manage, that I knew.

"Well, stud, by the nature of your voice over the phone I judge you have gotten yourself into some mess, a bit over your head," Pete said. He was right; out of frustration I had called him indicating that I just needed to talk. He didn't want to come to the Gund, he didn't have time to go to Reno, so he suggested a back room of Gina's establishment. "We won't be bothered, its really Gina's office, she will provide whatever we need, it's really pretty relaxing and we'll just sort out the problems whatever they may be. Remember, you took awful good care of me when we lost Mom, it's the least I can do".

So, I attempted to explain to Pete what the challenge was, without implicating either Santini or Laxalt. I just implied that to stop the MX, I had to come up with something that would be controversial enough to get the job done, and further to have this "thing" happen out of a clear blue sky, not implicating me or anybody else.

"Gina, my love, we will need picons, well made, and you remember those mountain oysters that I brought you the other day? I think some hor'dourves with the picons would be very helpful".

"Pete, if it were just you, I believe I would tell you to get packing. Even though we have been "friends" for over 20 years, I am not your servant. However, because Terry, the ultimate sexy gentleman, is here I might comply with your wish".

"That's good, he is trying to screw up his courage to take advantage of that free pass you gave him years ago, I assume its still good?" Pete responded.

"Well if I knew that was the case, I would get in the line up myself, if the girls find out he is ready, your peaceful afternoon is going to be disrupted," Gina responded with that totally sweet sexy soft drawl she could use so effectively.

"Ok, ok, I guess you guys have business, so I will make sure the picon jug is full, your nuts are being fried to your perfection, and we will stay out of your hair until you get ready to leave, but Terry, I am warning you, you will have to walk the gauntlet, something that has not been done very successfully by anyone. I think today, we are finally going to get our hands on your sexy body".

I just smiled and said nothing. However, all that would go through my mind was what in the hell all of this had to do with future President Reagan's needs to kill the MX.

So, after a picon and a few fried mountain oysters, admittedly done excellently by the cook, I tried to tell Pete what I was up against. In my stuttering careful approach, it took 15 to 20 minutes to get the short version out. Pete was patient, never said a word, just listened. When I finally stopped, Pete downed his picon, swallowed a couple of oysters, then opened up, "Those inconsiderate thoughtless bastards, they have placed you in an impossible position, to do an impossible task, with all the risk in the world, just to save their rotten fucking political asses."

I hadn't really thought this mess in quite that fashion, but basically Pete was right. I would risk everything; the only possible reward would be the knowledge that perhaps I may have contributed in some way to the destruction of the MX scam. Further, if it ever became known that I had pulled off such a stunt, I could just imagine a hit man from Martin Marietta or some other industrial giant ventilating me with the latest weapon. "You are right, they do take advantage, but I don't know that they really know how to scuttle MX without committing political suicide, its just that simple. If the MX survives, rural Nevada is finished as we know it," I concluded.

"You're right, I am not going to ask who or where this mission came from. I have no doubt that Laxalt is involved, but you can rest assured he will never know this meeting happened. Paul is a great guy, but he is a heartless bastard when it comes to things like this. I know, I am Basque," Pete finished.

We sat for a spell, contemplating a number of avenues that made absolutely no sense. Gina brought in more picons and oysters, laughing about how excited the girls were about the upcoming gauntlet. As I sipped the drink, a thought occurred to what was left of my brain. "You know what, they keep talking about their environmental impact statement, which is supposed to be thousands of pages long. They keep asking for 30 to 60 day delays. I don't think it is anywhere near done, there has been so many changes, so much uncertainty, that I'll bet the writers are going around in circles."

"So, who is writing this statement, surely not the Air Force, must be a contractor?" Pete questioned.

"It's an outfit located in Santa Barbara, called Henningson, Durham and Richardson, or more commonly known as HDR. I think the principles are mostly professors at the University there, and I suppose most of the work is being done by their graduate students," I answered.

"So, you're good at that sort of stuff, why not take a leave and go down there and help them?" asked the ever-practical Pete.

"My name is now on so many anti MX publications, newspaper clippings or whatever, I am sure they would just love to see me," I responded.

"Wait a minute, there is a new girl here, her name is Rhonda, I think I remember that she was pursuing her education at the University of Santa Barbara."

"Well, she might know something, ask Gina if we can talk to her."

"Hey, Gina Terry's made up his mind, he wants to talk to Rhonda."

Rhonda was a bubbly statuesque young lady with long blond hair, fully ready to comply with Pete's declaration. I explained that Pete didn't know what he was talking about, but we thought if she was from Santa Barbara, maybe she could help us.

"Yes, I am halfway through my junior year at Santa Barbara, majoring in Sociology. I ran out of money, and I needed some hands on work in sociology, don't know of a better place to accomplish both." She responded.

"Do you know anything about three professors named Henningson, Durham or Richardson?", I inquired.

"Santa Barbara is a big school, most of us barely know any real professors, and graduate students do most of the teaching. But I do remember one class on environmentalism, we had a guest lecturer, and I believe his name was Richardson, I believe Dr. Richardson," Rhonda replayed.

"Well, that's probably one of them," Pete volunteered.

"Are there lots of graduate students?" I inquired.

"Thousands, there seems like there are more graduate students than undergraduates at times, graduate students do almost all of the teaching, grading, that kind of stuff. I have been told that almost all of the laboratory work is done by graduate students. The only place there aren't graduate students is on the football and basketball teams."

I'll bet you a pecon Terry that graduate students are writing this EIS, what do you think?"

"I think you are right, and I am beginning to have some ideas, say, Rhonda, where do these graduate students hang out, local bars, clubs places like that?" I asked.

"Well, the University is not really in Santa Barbara, its in Goleta, which is around 9 miles north of Santa Barbara on the cost highway. There are dorms on campus, but mostly filled by underclassmen. Most everyone lives someplace around Santa Barbara, I am sure almost all graduate students live there, as they get paid pretty big salaries for graduate work. As to where they party, probably anywhere, everywhere. There are a lot of bars on State Street, I didn't have time to party much, but I would think that most grad students could be found on State Street, sooner or later."

We talked at length, or rather listened, to Rhonda's description of the University, Santa Barbara in general, and especially all the joints where grad students might hang us. I figured if the plan we were slowly formulating ever took place, I had better know something about Santa Barbara, and the lifestyle of the typical student.

"Rhonda, I have heard the front buzzer go off twice since you have been here, we're wasting your time, I think you have told us everything you know. Don't forget, Terry has to go through the gauntlet before we leave. Here is a couple of twenties to help pay for your time, good luck, and go back to school."

"Thanks, you guys are real gentlemen, sometimes we don't always get that in here, I'll remember this, hope I have helped you, love ya".

"You know stud, I got an idea. I'll bet you wouldn't have to hang around this State Street very long before you would meet a graduate student or two that are working on this EIS. It might be paying their way, and likely the Air Force has told them what to write. But I am under the impression from my days in Academia, that the basic environmental philosophy at Santa Barbara is fully left wing. I'll bet they hate the Air Force, at least after they cash their check."

"What are you saying, get to know some grad student working on the EIS, then convince them of the real picture? That could take months!"

"Na, not with your personality, most likely they are all girls, you could sweep them off their feet, an honest to God Nevada cowboy. I can see it now."

"Well, based on what you just said, sounds to me like the one to go should be you, not me."

"You know what, what I would do is have you go down there, size up the joint, get to know the folks, then when you get ready for the kill, call me in, I could handle this, especially if they were coed grad students."

"Well with your ego, it might just work, but no matter what, it will be a long shot, and I am not convinced it would really work even then. Besides, I believe it's a federal offense to try and covertly influence someone writing an EIS for the Government. I can imagine spending the next 10 years in the slammer, bet that would impress Joe Crowley."

We talked about possibilities for another pecan or two plus some more oysters. It was decided that I would attempt to find out as much about HDR as I could, along with the University and Santa Barbara in general. I had gotten to know Santa Barbara as a kid, and when I was going to San Luis Obispo, I drove through Santa Barbara every week or so, but that was about the extent of my knowledge. And, the University of California at Santa Barbara was part of the University of California System, but it had no land grant affiliations with the System in any way whatsoever, therefore, there wasn't a single person on the staff that I knew. Maybe that was just as well!

In the end, we agreed that I would go, incognito, attempt to make contact, if possible, then if I needed a "real" Nevada cowboy I would call Pete. Heaven helps us all. This reminded me of one of the old black and white slapstick comedies we all watched as kids.

Oh yeah, the gauntlet, will I beat it out the back door, left a hundred on Gina's desk with a note begging off one more time, but promised to come back.

"Well, Bohmont, I see Crowley is mumbling about starting an investigation about Ag College finances. I'll bet that doesn't bode well for you or me for that matter". Bohmont looked beat, looked exhausted, looked like he aged 5 to 10 since Crowley arrived.

"Well, he is going to raise hell and Molly isn't going to run for the Board again, so no matter who replaces her, we will have problems, I am sure. Hope, I know we haven't always gotten along, but you get the job done, and I respect that greatly. All I can promise is as this thing unfolds, I'll do my level best to protect you and the Gund, can't promise any more than that."

"Don't worry about that Dean, been here over 20 years, don't have a friend left on the staff, and frankly I am sick and tired of the whole mess. Say, speaking about all that, I would like to take up to two weeks off, everything is running perfect at the ranch, I would be back before haying starts, I just need some time away."

"I suppose you will be up to no good for the MX. I had enough problems not to worry about that. You got the two weeks, and I am sure you got a whole lot more time than that coming. All I ask is you keep your name out of the newspaper. Based on comments your old buddy Crowley has been making, I can only assume the Air Force has waved some big bills under his nose, I think he has bit hook line and sinker. I suspect if you get the credit for killing MX, he will gladly take the credit for killing you."

It was late May, the girls were now all in College, Jan went to spend time with her family, and I headed to Santa Barbara. Based on that phone call, which I still found disturbing, I had decided that this would be a trip that would be hard to follow me on. Cash only, no ID, no credit cards, in fact I was no longer Terry Hope, Ph.D. No, I was now Brock Mendenhill, rancher and cattle buyer from eastern Nevada, right clothes, right appearance, just rough stock. By the time I got to the coast, I even had myself believing all the b.s.

I figured that a rancher/buyer, especially one that was trying to locate some good purebred lines to start a ranch breeding herd would be fairly affluent, so I just walked into a reasonably attractive motel off of U.S. 101. I didn't know how the no credit card routine would work, and I hadn't even thought about the requirement for identification, which was more or less being required at all motels anymore, but a bluff never works if you don't try.

"Let's see, Mr. Mendenhill, you want this room for a week, and you want to pay in cash, right? At $75 a night for seven nights that will be $525, plus tax and Santa Barbara promotional fee, comes to $624.75. Well, we can accommodate that, but I will need to see your driver's license."

I really didn't want to show my drivers license, so I just casually said that I flew into town, took a taxi here, and was planning on meeting people here, so I had no need for a car. "Furthermore, I left my license home, so if its OK with you, here is an extra hundred to cover your needs."

I got a mighty funny look, some muttering about that this was highly irregular, however the c note slipped into the clerk's pocket pretty conveniently and so I was fully registered with a fictitious name, fictitious address, and no car or any other identifying characteristics. I was beginning to like my new identity. Brock Mendenhill, big time rancher and cattle buyer from eastern Nevada!

Rhonda, bless her sexy heart, had given me some advice on logical water holes; chief among them was the very original name, Joe's Bar and Grill. She remembered it somewhere on State Street. However, she seemed pretty adamant that the liberal environmental group would be there if anywhere.

So I headed out with my four wheel drive Ford pick-up, which seemed entirely proper for a cattle buyer from Nevada to find Joe's Bar, and any other liberal enticing water holes or eateries. It didn't take long to find Joe's, or at least what best fit Rhonda's description of Joe's, Joe's Bar and Grill, 508 State Street, pretty non descript from the outside, but who knows.

I ran State Street from Sterns Warf on the Pacific, to where State Street changes to Hollister. I drove several streets parallel to State, Anacapa and Chapala, then tried to cross streets, Cota, Ortega and Halaey. There were a lot of bars in Santa Barbara, as well as a lot of holes in the wall eateries. Any of these could be the local hide out for the do gooders; it would be like looking for a needle in a haystack. I slowly came to the conclusion that it may take a lot of booze before I found the gold mine, but for openers, thanks to Rhonda, I guessed I would try Joe's.

It was a Friday night, by design, as I figured after a hard week at the drawing board, EIS preparers would likely be looking for a bit of relaxation. It was about 6:30 or 7:00; the sun was setting over the blue Pacific as I entered Joe's. I had parked about a block away, paraded down Cota to State in my finest ranching attire, hopeful that these environmentalists didn't automatically hate anyone in a set of Tony

Lama's. It was crowded; no one gave me a second look, even though my attire stood out like a sore thumb. I did wear a cowboy hat, but it was a small brimmed one, not obnoxiously large, Levis, a semi western shirt, nothing too fancy, but obviously western, and obviously livestock orientated.

"What you want cowboy."

"Make it a Seagram's and seven, partner". I replied. Well at least the barkeep knew a cowboy when he saw one, which I judged to not be everyday. And Seagram's and seven was the best way I knew of to drink and not ultimately lose control.

I drank slowly, very slowly, listening to the bar chatter on all four sides, hoping to hear something that could open a door. There were probably 35 to 40 folks, mostly young, at least less than 25. It looked like girls outnumbered the men about two to one – good odds if you were looking for something new, and maybe even good odds for what I was looking for.

I noticed one young girl kept looking my way, however, she was also pretty occupied with two guys that looked the epitome of what the computer world were calling geeks. Well, I thought, I will just sit here in my cowboy finery; she will come over soon enough. Well, fortunately at least I was still on the first drink when she did.

"High, I hope you don't mind me asking, but you must be some kind of a cowboy?"

No, I laughed, "Not really, I am a rancher from eastern Nevada, and I am here looking at some purebred livestock, names Brock, Brock Mendenhill."

"Well Brock, glad to meet you, my name is Cindy, no last name or telephone number right now, just always wanted to talk to a real cowboy, and I'll bet you are one, even if you say you're not."

"Well, I can still ride a horse, and I can even rope a calf when all else fails," I laughed.

"Ok, so how in the world did you find Joe's?"

"Well, that's pretty simple, I arrived in Santa Barbara this afternoon, got to a motel down off the freeway, just had a bite to eat, and thought a night cap would be nice. Going to look at a bunch of purebred Angus cows and bulls tomorrow."

"Did, you eat here?"

"Nope, I ate at a restaurant by the motel," I lied.

"Joe's has really good food, as well as this great bar, you ought to try it tomorrow night if you are still here."

"Well, I probably will be, because I have made arrangements to view several sets of cattle, clear up to Santa Ynez. So what brings you to Joe's?"

"Oh, I come here almost every Friday night after work, just a great place to relax."

"So, what work do you do, say by the way, my glass is about empty, could I buy you a drink?"

"You sure can, I am drinking rose wine, they have an excellent white zinfandel here. As to work I am a graduate student at the College, one more semester to complete a master's degree in plant ecology".

"Get me another Seagram's and seven and this young lady a glass of your white zin, if you would sir."

"So, you are working in plant ecology, what type of plant work?"

"You would probably better understand what I am doing if I said rangeland ecology, but alas, that's not the case. I am working to study the relationship between wild oats and perennial grass vegetation and fire in the foothill areas of the California cost range."

I'll bet that's interesting, so what are you finding?'

I knew better than to ask the last question, as I had long since learned that no one is prouder of what they are doing to save the world, than a young lady working on masters degree in plant ecology under left wing leadership. And so after about 45 minutes, another round of white zin and another Seagram's and seven, I had the beginning understanding of the relationship between wild oats, an annual, and perennial bunchgrasses and fire. It wasn't much different than the relationship between cheat grass, perennial vegetation and fire in the Great Basin. Perennials lost, fire wins, and low and behold, the range all reverts to cheat grass. However, being more polite than normal, and desperate for some clue on who to talk to about MX, I played my cards a bit more carefully and marveled about Cindy's amazing grasp of scientific relationships, understanding of statistics, and most of all just plain common sense about the multitude of relationships in plant ecology.

It was getting close to nine, I really didn't want to gamble on many more Seagram's and seven, so I thought I would just bust right out there and see if she knew anything about MX. "You know what, we have a really serious problem in Nevada right now, the United States Air Force is proposing a giant project called MX. It will have mobile launching platforms all over Nevada and Utah, and I am totally afraid that the environmental impacts from this project will just about destroy rural Nevada and all of the absolutely beautiful desert and mountain landscapes we have. I know it will destroy wildlife, and probably ultimately put us ranchers out of business too."

"I have heard a lot about MX, in fact its one of the biggest projects our plant people are working on right now, the draft EIS. I have heard that the Air Force has spent millions here at the University. Several of our professors have formed a consulting group to do this type of work. They get the contract, pay the University a significant amount for using facilities, overhead, etc. hire all us grad students to write up this type of information, and that's how we get out degrees".

"You know, we can't find out anything that is going on in Nevada about this MX, and here you guys are writing all about the project and its impacts. That doesn't seem very fair to me."

"Well, its not, I really don't know much about MX, except a bunch of the plant students are working on it. I think they really hate what they are doing, because the Air Force has pretty much told them what to write, even dictated to them that their research results must support the conclusions that have already been told to them. But its what you have to do to get that degree," Cindy concluded.

"Golly sakes, I am wondering if it would be possible to talk to some of the people working on the MX. I would love to know what they are doing, what they think."

"I know two of the girls working on the project really well, they often come to Joe's but I don't see them tonight. I think they are both going to be here this weekend, I could see if they would like to meet you, say tomorrow night right here?'

"You bet, you say the food is great here, I could get done with my business tomorrow, probably be back here about 5, and I'll buy dinner, how does that sound?"

"I'll see what they are doing, I imagine they would love to get your perspective on not only MX, but the impacts as well. I am not even sure they have even been allowed to go to Nevada and see the real thing to begin with. I'll bet they would love to talk with you."

"OK Cindy, without the last name or telephone number. I'll meet you and your friends here tomorrow at 5. I may have a little dust on me, as I have got to look at about 500 head of cattle tomorrow, but other than that, I'll be here. If you guys don't show up, I will understand, and like I said, there are several other groups of cattle that I would like to study, so I'll be around for a few days."

So, Cindy and I parted for the night, she was not the cutest of young girls, but she was plenty intelligent, even if star struck. And I had to add, she was probably honest, which was more than could be said about me right now. False name, false occupation, a pack of lies just to get some information, and maybe slightly change history. Probably nothing that hadn't been done before, and probably nothing that wouldn't be done a thousand times over in the future, but why me, I guess my consciousness was really hurting as I tried to go to sleep. But I did have to recollect a bit – first bar stop, right out of the shot, meet someone that knows about MX, and a verbal commitment to maybe even meet some of the students actually writing the EIS. Who needs Pete, looks to me like I am doing right good by myself!

The next day, I really didn't care to see anything resembling cattle or anything else, so I ventured south on the 101 to Ventura, then east of 129 to my old hometown of Fillmore. Drove around a bit, not much change since high school graduation 32 years ago.

This relaxing drive did give me time to think about my situation, and that was that apparently a lot of people were relying on me to come up with something that would give Ron Reagan the tools he needed to scuttle MX, and survive politically, assuming he was elected to begin with. I was supposed to be caught trying to influence the preparation of an EIS would be some sort of Federal offense. However, I was even more sure that to have that meddling come about because of requests from officials in Congress would be totally politically incorrect to say the least. I had to laugh, I remember that phone call warning me about my own safety, I could only think that security for this adventure was being driven a whole lot more by political ramifications that my own personal well being!

I was back in Santa Barbara by 3, gathered my thoughts, and decided that I would be at Joe's by 4:45, sitting at the bar, drinking a seven up. I decided that the folks that I would be talking to tonight might not be avid supporters of the livestock industry, so I toned my attire to appear more as a businessman than a buckaroo. And right on schedule as advertised, Cindy walked in with two young ladies and another man. Introductions were in order, one young lady was named Margery Watros, and was introduced as an Environmental Scientist, fresh out of Stanford with a B.S., the other young lass was introduced as Mary Lambert, a geologist who had just graduated from New York State at Oneonta, also with a B.S. Mary was quick to point out that even though she was a geologist, she had a very strong background in plant ecology, and her work on the EIS was in that regard. Further, just because she was from New York didn't mean she didn't understand the West! The gentleman was named Steve Huckeba, and he held a B.A. in Fine Arts form the University of California, Riverside. Steve was an artist by training, but he was also one of the better computer geeks on staff, at least that's what he claimed.

My offer to buy a round was eagerly accepted by the three newcomers and Cindy, so began our social discussion. It was pretty obvious right off the bat, that these kids knew relatively little about eastern Nevada. For quite a while our roles were reversed, at least as I imagined, they were getting a lot more information from me than I was getting from them. Steve was pretty quiet, I kind of gathered he and Cindy were, at least friends, based on body language, placement of hands and other less conspicuous movements.

Margery and Mary were of a different nature, their quest for information on Nevada was overwhelming, and hopefully, I answered all of their questions reasonably accurately. After the third round of libations, the picture became somewhat clearer, at least to me. Mary was the first to unload, "We're supposed to be experts on the Great Basin, and I have learned more tonight just talking to you, Brock, then I ever learned in College. Of course, good old Fred, our project leader, a Lieutenant Colonel from Notre Dame, and a lawyer on top of that, pretty well tells how the Air Force sees the Great Basin."

Margery more or less cut her off at that point by saying, "What Mary is trying to say is that we all feel that we should spend some time on site instead of being spoon fed every scientific fact that they think we should now. The pay is good, but the Air Force could save a lot of money by just writing the damn thing themselves, because it's their baby, regardless of who the preparers actually are."

I let these comments ride, as it was pretty obvious with another round or two before we ate, the frustrations would probably really pour out. I was content to just listen, raise eyebrows pretty regularly and sympathize, sooner or later I was sure to find an area that I could jump on.

We did have one more round, but things were getting a bit sloppy, so I figured it might be time to eat, "Gosh I sure enjoy listening to all of this, it sure gives me a better idea of what MX will be like when it comes to Nevada, but I have had about all I can drink right now, so lets go get some dinner. I am more than willing to eat here, or wherever you guys want. Let's get one thing clear however, you are educating me, so as proper payment for that education, I'll buy, not going to have it any other way".

Everybody liked Joe's, and that was fine with me. I had requested, before everyone showed up, of the bar keep, that if we were to eat here could it be as private as possible. Joe's was a pretty quaint bar and restaurant, lots of hardwood, and pretty crowded. I didn't need noise and confusion! So, for an extra $20, we were ushered into a back room, just large enough to accommodate the 5 of us, the door was open, but most of the bar chatter stayed at the bar.

As we ordered, I couldn't help to note that the 4 students, three girls and one young man, all presumed to be left wing, cattle hating environmentalists, all ordered beef steaks of one kind or another. I brought everything back to normal by ordering a big dish of pasta!

Conversation was non-stop, mostly from Margery and Mary, Cindy and Steve mostly listened, but occasionally would verify a point the girls were making. It was plainly obvious that they didn't like the Air Force, that they didn't like being told what to do from an analytical point of view, and they sure as hell didn't like their Air Force contact, Fred, the Lieutenant Colonel from Notre Dame. Interestingly enough, I never did learn good old Fred's last name.

I definitely didn't want to push my luck, so I mostly listened, occasionally supporting comments that needed supporting to help open the doors wider. The girls had wanted wine with dinner, and they were on the second bottle of horribly inflated Zinfandel, which, fortunately, seemed to make the MX talk come more freely.

I was amazed as the evening wore on how advanced the MX concept was, at least in regard to the EIS. Reading all the newspaper articles about MX would lead one to believe that no one had really decided if it was going to be silo mounted missals, or a race track concept, and if the race track concept won out, would if be truck mounted vehicles, or a railroad concept. In fact, there had not even been a clear-cut description of how big, how wide, how many or any other description of what the track(s) would look like.

It became pretty obvious, that what the Air Force was releasing to the press, and what these kids were writing about in preparing the EIS were hardly the same thing. The EIS, as it was being described to me in bits and pieces, was set in concrete: hundreds of miles of roads, built far beyond the requirements of the interstate freeway system, built to support massive mobile rocket carriers, constantly on the move. As I listened, I couldn't help but to reflect on what Major Henshaw had told us in Ely, which seemed like a long time ago, although it was only three months, he had perfectly described the system that they were writing the EIS for. Because of time constraints, to get as much of this approved while Carter was still in office, it made absolutely no sense that the final system would be anything different than what the Major had described, totally contrary to all the garbage of vastly different systems that the Air Force, or folks in Congress were constantly throwing out. The only variable that hadn't changed in all of this nonsense, was that each rocket would have ten individual war heads, each packing a full-scale atom bomb, each designed to hit a specific Russian target. Just imagine, if at any one point in time ten mobile launchers were activated, out of the hundred that were running around, then 100 targets would evaporate instantaneously in Russia. And that scenario didn't take into account the submarine launch capability, the Minute Man silos, and the giant bombers always in the air. Mutual mass destruction, or self-destruction, I guess it didn't make much difference. It began to dawn on me why Mother Russia was complaining that the MX was not a defensive system as advertised!

Finally, I screwed up my courage and inquired about the actual so called track, "What are these tracks really going to be like, you said built better than the freeway, how wide will they be, how many miles?"

Mary had become the more talkative of the two, thanks to that second bottle of zin, so she promptly replied to my questions, "The tracks are big, several feet of hardened concrete, based on very compacted fill. Each track will be 100 feet wide, that's just the disturbed area as well as the concrete and the shoulders. We don't have a final figure, as they are still playing with some of the tracks in Utah. All roads, as well as tracks are considered to have a 100-foot-wide environmental impact. The final figure that I think is being used in the EIS is around 140,000 impacted acres. You can do the math yourself, 140,000 acres is about 7 billion square feet, so if a track is 100 feet wide, you would have to have about 11,000 miles of disturbance between tracks, primary roads, secondary roads, construction roads and so forth. We are not allowed to consider any more than a 100-foot wide path for any activity, regardless of what that activity might be. Gosh, suppose you are a Russian spy, we shouldn't be telling you all of this."

"Well, you can relax, not a spy, never been to Russia. I am just a Nevada businessman, mainly in livestock, and I am trying to figure out what this MX means to me and my future. I am pretty confident we will survive all of this nonsense, or I wouldn't be here in California trying to buy purebred stock."

That seemed to relax everyone, so the talk drifted on about the environment, their fears on what might really happen when all of this was put in place, on and on. Finally, Margery, who had been conspicuously quiet for the last few minutes, let her frustrations really show.

"We went over this track concept with Fred, and some high-ranking Air Force generals as to secondary impacts. This General, I think his name was Hecker or something like that got really upset with us, because we insisted that the secondary impact would be far greater. You know, I am sure you do, that each mobile launcher, and there will be at least 200 of them, will be stored under a shelter. These shelters are case hardened cement, sufficiently strong to essentially survive a direct hit. The catch is that there will be 4,600 of these shelters, designed so that the Russians will never know which shelter will be housing a rocket launcher. There will be enough cement between shelters and tracks to pave just about all Nevada. Yet, those bastards are insisting that the EIS conform to the 100 foot wide corridor, they are not going to allow us any secondary impact area whatsoever."

"You mean, all the construction equipment hauling cement, material will never venture out of that corridor," I asked, acting utterly amazed, which I guess I probably was.

Steve, who had little to offer up to this point chimed in, "We got into a really heated discussion over this very point. I am supposed to be accounting for secondary impacts, at least by drawing what they might look like, so I raised the question how contractors were going to turn some of the construction vehicles around, because they will actually be over 100' long. I have prepared many sketches to show just how far off the 100 foot wide track some of these vehicles will have to travel out through the sagebrush to simply turn around. Those turn around radiuses amount to hundreds of feet."

The frustrations continued to come forth. These kids were intelligent enough to clearly know the Air Force was forcing them to prepare a document that not only minimized impacts, in fact it was just plain old false. The more their frustrations came out, the madder they got.

I had placed the Patton photographs in my coat pocket in hopes our discussions would ultimately get around to such things as secondary impacts, because those photographs more clearly showed just how great secondary impacts can be.

"I am a great fan of General George C. Patton, and I guess you are aware of the fact that he practiced tank maneuvers in southeast California and southern Nevada. I happened to be in Searchlight the other day on business, so I ventured out into Paiute Valley to try and see what the impact of his activities might be. I have some pictures here if you would be interested."

Both Margery and Mary came forth in the affirmative at the same time. "We are aware of the Patton exercises, in fact we suggested that should be a model for long term impacts. We were told pretty bluntly that was not acceptable "science", and we were told that we wouldn't even be allowed to go see the site."

The pictures of the actual maneuver site clearly indicated that shrubs like creosote just never came back.

"Why haven't the shrubs ever returned," Cindy asked.

"If you look really close at those pictures you will see a heavy cover of annuals, all dormant. If you look at this picture of Paiute Valley about ten miles away from activity, you will see the near complete absence of annuals. You got to remember, the Mojave is pretty dry, less than 6 inches of annual precipitation, much of what they get is sporadic, and when it comes, the desert blooms, especially disturbed sites, which invariably plays home for the more invasive types of annuals. Once these guys get a foothold, they just simply out compete the perennials, like creosote for the water, so it's just about impossible for the original perennials to ever get reestablished."

"Damn the Air Force, this is the very kind of information that should be in this EIS", Mary grumbled.

I let them mull over the pictures from Paiute Valley awhile before showing the rest, "Let me show you some pictures taken about 2 miles up the valley from the last observable soil disturbance. You will see in these pictures the lack of new, or young shrubs, and again the heavy dominance of the ground cover. What has happened, after the establishment of the annuals at ground zero, they have gradually moved out into the surrounding area, again competing for all available moisture, out competing the shrubs. Establishment of shrub seed germination becomes nearly impossible in the presence of heavy annual cover, again simply because of moisture competition, so no new shrub seedlings survive. That's what you see in this picture, 40 years after the fact, and over two miles from any know disturbance by Patton's tanks, a slow and steady destruction of the native vegetation."

My pictures of Patton's playground were the hit of the evening. They were discussed, cussed and re-discussed for what seemed like hours. I didn't have much to offer, other than an occasional comment. I professed to understand little about plant ecology, just always coming back to the fact that I loved the Nevada landscape, and I just understood it from a common sense point of view. I tried to impart the concept that with their academic training, they were far better qualified to understand these complex relationships than I was.

It was past midnight, and the discussions were still going strong. I was pretty sure, by California law, Joe's would have to close by 2:00 a.m. so I was beginning to get a bit nervous about what the final conclusions might be.

Margery finally came to my rescue, thanking me profusely for sharing my common sense approach to the mess they were dealing with. "The MX EIS is set in concrete at this time. However, the MX document that most will see is a compilation of the 10, 15 or 20, I get mixed up how many, Environmental Technical Reports. The technical reports are still being prepared."

I asked, "You mean the final EIS is complete, but the technical reports are still being prepared?"

"You're right, completely opposite to the way it should be done. However, you got to remember, the Air Force basically wrote the final version. The technical reports are what we are preparing to make the final EIS be defensible."

"Marg", Mary inquired, "wouldn't it be possible for us to put in our report, native vegetation, and expanded area of possible conflict, say a half mile, or even more?"

"Maybe, we are under such a limited time frame, I am not even sure they are going to review the technical reports before they go out, especially ours. It's pretty dry reading, and they haven't paid much attention to it yet. We more or less have justified the 100-foot rule, but if you remember, there was that one sentence indicating that secondary impacts could exceed the 100-foot rule under the right set of circumstances. We might try to put in a section with a table or two, loosely written, that would allow a reader to come to their own conclusion. Carefully worded, it will either get rejected, or we may have to rewrite it, or it may sail right through. And, if we do this and get away with it, we may all get fired. Who knows"?

"Brock, will we be able to see you anymore this trip? Cindy inquired.

"Will, I have to look at a lot more cattle over the next few days, further north. I think I might move to Salinas tomorrow, so I won't be around Santa Barbara likely for a spell."

"We are supposed to go to some of the sites on a field trip in about 2 weeks, before June 15, as the schedule I am working under says our Native Vegetation Technical Report must be completed no later than July 15 of this year. Maybe we could spend some time with you, maybe you could introduce us to some of your friends to help us better understand what we are up against."

A sudden chill went through my entire body, I could just imagine somebody coming up to me when I was talking to these people and saying, "Terry Hope, how in the world have you been, anyway". Poor old Brock Mendenhill would have some pretty powerful explaining to do then. The webs we weave!

"Damn, I would love to, but your Air Force handlers might take a bit of an exception to that. However, unfortunately, I have to go to West Virginia in about a week on business, and I imagine I will be there most of June and July, then in August I will be in Florida to wrap up some business with a large overseas bank", I plainly lied.

"Well, that's probably best, we don't want to upset good old Fred, and just spending this evening with you has given us all the ammunition that we have needed to bring this whole mess back to reality. We simply cannot thank you enough," Mary concluded. And as we were all saying goodbye, hugging, shaking hands or whatever, I was already preparing Brock Mendenhill's obituary.

As I sat in the motel contemplating what had happened, I simply could not fathom that in two short days I may have set in motion events that ultimately could bring down the MX. What were the odds that I could have even met these people, what were the odds that I could have caught them at a time that they were so disgruntled with the Air Force that they would let every little dirty secret come out? I was good at statistics of probability, but not that good. This would have to be a jillion to one long shot if it worked, and I guessed I wouldn't know that until about August or September, when the long-awaited document finally surfaced. And to top it all off, I had to revel in the thought that the whole damn scam had been conceived in a Nevada whorehouse, with the help of a prostitute!

I hadn't been back at the Gund more than a week when Pete phoned on our new radiophone wanting to know how my trip to Santa Barbara went. "Never went, changed my plans" I lied.

"No shit, I thought you were really set on that, what changed your mind?"

"A bunch of things, just wanted to stay here and work on another paper."

"This doesn't make sense, guess you know best, at least as far as the MX goes. Talked to Hage the other day, he seems hell bent on staying in D.C. He seems to think he has those congressmen listening."

"Well he probably does, he is pretty good at that sort of thing, but he had also better spend some time at Pine Creek. This Sagebrush Rebellion is getting pretty serious, and I think both the BLM and the Forest Service are going to stop being nice about all this stuff, and put some pressure on permittees to behave."

"You may be right, Campbell Creek doesn't have any Forest, but my local friendly BLM range guy has been making noise about how we have been overusing certain pastures, and that we are not following our prescribed rest rotation program. So much B.S. because we have followed the rotation to the day, and my eyeballs tell me that we haven't overused anything, in fact we are only running about 60% of our allotted numbers. Doesn't make sense, in the meantime those damn nags have been increasing drastically. They had better propose a gather pretty soon. Or shortly I'll be feeding more government horses than I am feeding cows."

"Hey, this new-fangled radio phone is cutting out, barley hear you, lets get together, why don't you come out one of these days?"

"Good idea, I'll be moving some cows over by Umba in the Reese next week, that's only about 80 miles or so away from Grass Valley, I'll call if I get the opportunity.

I was pretty sure that I wasn't going to tell Pete, or anybody about Santa Barbara, just too risky. I was pretty sure those three girls and Steve would be immediately placed on the welfare rolls if any knowledge came out about our chance meeting. And I knew for sure I wasn't going to talk about it on our new radiophone. The Highway Department had fixed me up with this new apparatus, which was a thousand times better than the old earth ground line, had a receiver in the house and my pickup, both. The only problem, anybody with a frequency dial could readily pick up any conversation. And, the more I thought about my Santa Barbara adventure, the more I began to think that no one else, other than the five participants involved, ever needed to know it ever happened to begin with. Pete and the rest of the world would just have to wait!

MX controversy didn't wait because I was in Santa Barbara or anywhere else for that matter. It was a constant barrage of changing ideas, new concepts, the MX is going to be in New Mexico and Texas, because they want it, on and on, it just never even slowed down one bit. Finally, the Navy came out with their MX plan, mount it on boats, some with dummies, some with the real thing, let them float around the globe.

Governor List finally woke up to the fact that he had to choose sides on MX, no more fence riding. And he chooses right for that matter, he came out squarely against MX, once and for all. I always assumed there had been a little shove, or perhaps a rather big shove, from Senator

Laxalt, regardless, he finally came out firmly against MX, and that's all that really mattered.

And it only took about two weeks after that, that he and Utah's Governor Matheson came to the joint conclusion that everybody had better be ready to deal with the EIS when it came out, so they agreed to jointly put together an EIS review team. There were teams appointed to review every aspect of the EIS. However, most of the impacts were centered around what it would do to the two state's livestock industries, as well as their water resources.

Nevada's efforts were to be coordinated by a young lady by the name of Pamela Gene Cosby. Pam was a strikingly beautiful, a tall shapely blond. I didn't think she was a day over 28, if that. She was intelligent, but what she knew about MX was a mystery, as well as how she got the job in the first place, a position she had occupied for about 6 months.

She represented Governor List in all things MX. As such she was frequently across the table from Major Henshaw, a striking figure himself. I had seen them together at a number of meetings, he always wore his dress Air Force blues, she always wore attire that accentuated her long blond hair. It had been rumored for several months that they were having an affair, I certainly didn't know, nor did I particularly care. I was firmly convinced that the MX's future was definitely not dependent of either Major Henshaw's efforts or Miss Cosby's efforts for that matter.

One of the teams, perhaps the most important, was the Ranching MX EIS Review Team. A number of ranchers, and a few University personnel were rumored to make up the team, along with members from the Nevada Department of Agriculture and the United States Department of Agriculture. I really wasn't very interested in the review team, as I expected it to be dominated by University staff members, folks that couldn't make a decision if their life depended on it, at least without majority and minority reports. The list came out and from the bottom up there were no surprises, except at the top. Both Governors had agreed that there should be a joint chairmanship of this committee, none other than Wayne Hage and one Terry Hope, Ph.D.

Just about the next day Wayne and I agreed to meet, Eureka was most convenient for both of us travel wise. Wayne was adamant that he didn't want a bunch of, "useless academics and fence riding cowboys," screwing up his efforts in Congress up. I pretty much agreed.

"So far, your white papers have been tremendous help to me in D.C. They have to keep coming, and you don't need a committee to accomplish that," he added.

"Why don't I send out a letter to the committee, with a cc to Pam Cosby and the Governors, that each committee member will be provided a full copy of the EIS once it is available. We will expect your reviews to be completed individually within two weeks of that date, and we will call for meetings after that to coordinate all responses. In the meantime, Co-Chair Hage will continue to work with Congress, and I will continue to write white papers."

"Good, that will keep them off of our backs for the time being, can you get that sent out by tomorrow?"

"Yup", I answered.

And true to his word, a few days after Hage and I met in Eureka, Pete called and asked, "Can you meet me in Austin at the International for lunch today, I'll buy?"

"I'll be there at noon."

It was 50 miles by gravel road to Highway 50, 10 miles over Austin Summit to the front door of the historic International Restaurant and Bar. For safety's sake, the rooms upstairs had long since been closed off, as Austin, perched on the side of a steep canyon on the west side to the Toiyabes had the general appearance of slowly, but surely, sliding into Reese River Valley.

We both ordered a hamburger and beer. The place was just about deserted, two old timers at the bar, one bar keep, a waitress, and the inevitable Chinese cook, but he was good, at least at making hamburgers.

"Well. I don't believe your bullshit version of what happened in Santa Barbara for one second. I supposed you pulled your usual outmaneuvering crap, you maybe were successful, and I suppose you just don't want to talk about it."

"Yeah, you may be correct on all counts. Some people might be in jeopardy if I let my imagination go wild and tell you exactly just how successful I really was."

"OK, the MX is one problem, but I am really starting to get more concerned about this Sagebrush Rebellion that Rhoads and Glaser kicked off. I am not sure it knows where it is going or what it will do when it gets there."

"Well to tell you the truth, I just haven't gotten too excited about the Rebellion, the MX to me has just taken precedent. However, if there is a chance to get the land out of federal ownership, that would be a godsend, providing of course the State of Nevada had enough brains to manage this vast track of land, also assuming of course the Air Force doesn't get it first."

"Nevada has passed the law, I believe at least 10 other states have done so, it's getting close to the national level. Laxalt has let it be known that if Reagan becomes president, he would be more than willing to listen to the argument. All of that is good, but what happens if it all does happen? Does the Nevada State BLM Office and all five District offices automatically revert to the State. As near as I can figure, at the present time, the operation of the BLM within the Nevada is not cash flow positive, or anywhere near it. I don't see any aspect of Nevada government discussing what to actually do if we get the damn land to begin with, that's my concern," Pete concluded.

"You aren't telling me anything that I haven't thought about a thousand times already," I responded. "Furthermore, I have heard a lot of the Elko bunch say that they don't want to own the land, can't afford the taxes, and I know they will lean on Dean sooner or later, probably already have. If it just got turned over to the State, and the Nevada managed it like the BLM does, that would probably be OK, but like you say, somebody is going to have to come up with some bucks, or a whole bunch of BLM employees will get the boot when Nevada takes possession, which wouldn't be all bad by my book. However, I doubt that Congress is going to let that scenario happen either."

"I just wish we could get some people to listen to the concept we have been trying to push with that land transfer. And I am damn positive that with just half of the transfer land put into crested wheat and managed correctly, we have just about eliminated our dependence of the BLM allotment for at least the basic cow herd. But I would bet that half of the Nevada Cattlemen's Association doesn't support what we are trying to do."

"You are right on that. They don't like Bohmont, think he's too pushy, now that you have been reduced to nothing more or less than a ranch manager in their eyes, they think you are paid way too much, and most of them think that when you sell the calves, you are competing with their industry, and the University is subsidizing the whole process to begin with. Frankly, it is a no win situation for you, you should have stayed on Campus, no one complained about your salary then. But that's your problem, my concern is this rebellion, if we win, then what do we do, if we lose, won't there be vindictive actions taken by the Bureau against those that fostered this idea, teach us a lesson so to speak?"

"Well, maybe against Norm Glaser and his brother Art, but I'll bet you whatever, nothing is ever done against Dean. He is clever enough to have covered his butt throughout this process," I responded.

"Well, that even scares me more, because some of us, for example like me, are totally in favor of the Rebellion, but we are too involved in our work to do anything but just support it verbally. When the day of reckoning comes, you have got to remember, revolutionaries that lose often get hung by the neck, even if they were nothing more than bystanders. Buffalo was totally paid for, I lost my head, bought Campbell Creek, now I am in debt nearly a million dollars. A major change in my allotment use could readily cause me to go tits up faster than a New York second," Pete lamented.

"It's no different than anything else, you either take it head on, or get the hell out of the way. It's no different than where I am on the MX. I could well imagine if Reagan doesn't win, and we swallow the MX, I probably would have to be looking at some hole cards pretty quick. In your case, being a million in debt, you might want to go slow, because between you and me I don't think the land is ever going back to the State, even though I firmly believe that is the best thing that could ever happen to Nevada. But you got other options, you could always run Gina's joint!"

"You always throw that out, like I have said a thousand times, you're just jealous."

The International Bar didn't serve picons. In fact, they didn't serve much of anything but beer and whiskey. The hamburger was good, the beer was good, even the highball was good, all things being considered. But the setting was what counted, International was as old as Austin, the 1860's was when they struck gold, been here ever since. It had more or less burned down once or twice, but it had never lost its charm. It was a delightful place to just get plumb drunk, but, unfortunately, that wasn't our mission today. Pete was concerned about the Rebellion, and its impacts, regardless of what the outcome was. The MX was no different; fortunes were being gambled on both sides.

All the way back to the Gund I pondered over the whole mess, state ownership of the rangelands, or Air Force ownership of the rangelands. The MX price tag had escalated to over 50 billion dollars, with some projecting 70 billion. I don't know what the price tag would be for state ownership, but certainly the BLM spent millions in Nevada every year, and their budget never went down from one year to the next. You had to laugh, because I just never saw an acre of sagebrush bring a fifty-dollar bill or anything close, yet these were billion dollar stakes with deadly consequences. No wonder Pete was nervous, but on the other hand, maybe I should be too.

Nineteen hundred and eighty drug on for what seemed forever. The anti-MX forces became jubilant when Ronald Reagan received the Republican nomination for the presidency. Everyone felt he could beat Carter and were just as sure he would promptly kill the MX. The only problem with that was the fact that the Air Force was starting to let many very expensive contracts out to build parts of the MX. Wayne Hage felt it was a dead issue, but Wayne was unaware of the phone call that I had received, and my trip to Santa Barbara. I was pretty positive Reagan would kill the MX, but I was also equally sure that if he had a real environmental issue to use as his decision, it would make his life a whole lot easier.

Almost weekly, during the later half of 1980, the release of the pending EIS was supposed to occur the following week. Just as predictable, the following week a news release would indicate that "technical" problems had forced another delay.

During October, the folks at HDR revolted, claiming the EIS was nothing but a "whitewash" and avoided all real environmental conflicts. I was never able to determine if the revolutionaries were any of the folks that I had met, but I expected if they were, it might not help what I had attempted to accomplish. The revolution was followed shortly by a joint press release from the principles; Henningson, Durham and Richardson, indicating that their staff had worked tirelessly uncovering every single possible environmental conflict imaginable, had left "no stone unturned" to accomplish the critical EIS. They further went on to describe how they were a neutral third party and didn't reflect the views of the Air Force anymore than the views of the most vocal anti-MX groups. No mention was made of the fact that the Air Force had paid HDR an enormous sum of money, in the millions, to prepare the "neutral" report.

November rolled around, and Ronald Reagan won the Presidency with an overwhelming defeat of Jimmy Carter. Now only time would tell the fate of the MX.

Finally, on December 18, 1980, the official Environmental Impact Analysis report dealing with "Deployment Area Selection and Land Withdrawal/Acquisition", was released. This 1,800 page document was really just an introduction to the problems that MX would create. The meat of the subject was to be released momentarily in some 34 to 40 supplementary reports. The EIS indicated that some 139,515 acres of native vegetation would be removed due to MX activity in Utah and Nevada, which is about 218 square miles. Eighty percent of the disturbance would be in Nevada, and twenty percent would be in Utah. Hardly anything to get excited about, which was exactly what the information that had been continuously leaked out over the last two to three years led most people to believe. There was no indication that any figures to the contrary were forthcoming, but I wasn't too surprised. My friends in Santa Barbara had already forewarned me that the final version of the EIS was already set in concrete. If anything, contrary was going to show up it would be in the supplemental reports, which were promised to be delivered in January of 1981.

And in January 1981 Ronald Reagan became the 40th president of the United States, with little mention of the MX. What was of interest, however, was the appointment of one James Gaius Watt as Secretary of the Interior. Watt had worked for the Department of the Interior as deputy assistant secretary for water and power development. In 1976, Watt founded the Mountain States Legal Foundation, a law company that was devoted to individual liberty, the right to own and use property, limited and ethical government and economic freedom. Watt had strong feelings about the environmental movements that were surfacing across the nation. He had equally strong feelings about maximizing the use of federal lands for foresting, ranching and energy production. He was a natural for the Sagebrush Rebellion, between Reagan and Watt, how could the Rebellion be stopped?

In January of 1981, the Air Force was forced to extend the comment period on the controversial EIS by some 30 days, because the Technical Reports, all 33, had yet to be distributed. However, they promised copies would be available for all State review teams no later than January 31. The review date was set back from April 1 to May 1. It made me realize that if the reports were distributed by February 1, and our ranching review team had to have their report in the hands of the Air Force 89 days later it would be difficult, and likely something either Wayne Hage or I would likely have to do ourselves. Getting 15 to 20 Utah and Nevada ranchers to agree on anything, much less the MX EIS in 89 days would be a tall order indeed.

And about the last day of January, a UPS delivery truck showed up at the Gund with boxes of documents from the Air Force, my own copy of the EIS of 1800 pages, and 33 additional technical reports consisting of several thousand pages. It took the UPS driver and myself approximately 15 minutes to unload the many boxes.

I didn't much care to look at all the technical reports; I was only interested in one, ETR 14, Native Vegetation. And there on page 93 was all I could have ever hoped for! I will never forget the words,

"Indirectly impacted areas would be subject to vegetation degradation and invasion by toxic weeds. The proportion of the watershed which lies within 0.5 miles of disturbance provides a rough index to the frequency of vegetation clearing and the associated indirect impacts."

Those were almost exactly the words I had used at Joe's in Santa Barbara. Thank God for General Patton, he gave me all I needed, and thank God for Margery and Mary, they had done their work well, so well in fact, that on page 91, Table 2.4.2-1 had the amount, or percent, of each hydrologic subunit that would be impacted by off-site disturbance. General Patton had been gone for over 40 years, but I could somehow envision him giving me the "thumbs-up."

The math didn't take long, the off-site disturbance for Nevada and Utah amounted to slightly over five million acres, or almost 8,000 square miles, almost the size of White Pine County. By 8:00 a.m. the following morning I had my next "white paper" prepared analyzing the unbelievable environmental impacts the MX would really have on Nevada and Utah, near complete elimination of their multi-billion-dollar livestock industries; copies to Santini in the House, copies to Laxalt in the Senate, copies to Hage, copies to the Reno newspapers. Let the chips fall where they may!

I was good with math, good with environmental consequences, good at making an already bad situation much, much worse. Everything I wrote was based on the underlying theme that I had discovered these "true" facts in one of the thirty some environmental support documents. If all this devastating information was found in just one technical report, how many more such disturbing facts would be hidden in all the other technical reports?

It didn't take long for the other review teams to catch on to this concept, as well as the newspapers. The common theme for both Reno newspapers was, "what's next?"

It didn't take long for the Air Force to wake up to the fact that they had a big problem that was rapidly getting worse. Promptly on February 11, 1981, the Air Force's top brass, General Richard Ellis, commander in chief of the Strategic Air Command, strolled into the Legislative chambers to calm the fears. If Ellis would have been chomping on a cigar, he would have been the spitting image of his famous predecessor, Curtis Lamay. Ellis gave it his best shot, including, "It is now clear that the Soviets used the past two decades of Khrushchev's "peaceful co-existence" and Brezhnev's 'era of détente' to build a military structure that now surpasses our own." Ellis continued on pointing out that the only way to correct this "strategic imbalance" was to build the MX. It will be built, then he dropped the block buster, "it will be built, but if Nevadan's don't want it in Nevada, it will be built elsewhere."

Ellis's remarks, clearly theatrical in nature, were designed to get two points across; first, it will be built, and secondly, if you don't want it, it will be built where the economic benefits will be appreciated.

It took exactly 24 hours for the Clark County newspapers to go ballistic because of Ellis's remarks. They demanded for the immediate removal by recall of Washoe Republican Assemblyman Paul Prengaman, the most outspoken critic of the MX in the Nevada Legislature. Of course, this action was spurred on by the Democratically controlled Clark County Commission and Senator Howard Cannon, the sponsor of MX in Congress. The Clark County Commission had long since added up the economic impact that MX would bring to Las Vegas and Southern Nevada, of course helped by the good Senator. In the end, the only thing General Ellis accomplished was to add to the never-ending war of words between those that despised the MX, and those that were counting the dollars.

But Ellis and his buddies, namely Major Henshaw weren't quite through. The Air Force was getting more demanding concerning Nevada's limited water resources. The anti was upped by statements frequently being made that if Nevada didn't cooperate with water, federal authority over Nevada's waters would be requested. And believe me, nothing would send a chill down the average Nevadan's spine quicker than the thought of losing state control over water. I always felt these threats against Nevada were orchestrated by Henshaw. He had put all of his eggs for future advancement in the Air Force into one basket, the MX. Fortunately, however, Nevada historically had some pretty practical minded people in the Department of Conservation and Natural Resources. A lot of the time the cowboys were pretty upset with the Department, and especially the State Engineer, who for all practical purposes is, and had been for a long time, the water Czar of Nevada.

Water requirements for MX escalated on a daily basis, much like the projected costs. According to the Department, the Air Force had applied for 116 applications for ground water removal in 29 of Nevada's remote valleys. This all added up to a whopping 27.3 billion gallons of water required each year during the estimated 10-year construction phase, followed by a 4.2 billion gallon annual requirement during the 30 projected life of the development. Pete Morris, deputy director of Conservation and Natural Resources said those estimates are "conservative as hell."

Henshaw quickly responded to Morris's statement about being conservative, as that was what the Air Force needed, no more, no less. Morris, an old time Nevada sage responded by saying, "If you pardon the expression, you will have everything from whorehouses to car washes to everything else out there that the Air Force will have no control over." And Pete Morris was right, all of the Air Force's stated requirements for resources, such as land, water, and maybe even clean air was based specifically on what the Air Force needed, and never took into account the many rural villages that would be turned overnight into burgeoning cities.

And so, the point, counter point charges continued. My white papers only added fuel to the fire, constantly driving home how inadequate the 1,800 page EIS was when one finally read the fine print in the technical reports. A long-time friend, Julian Smith, the same Julian Smith that had turned the snapping sow loose at Poly Royal so many years before was now a lawyer working for the State Attorney Generals office, and coincidently chairman of Nevada's Multiple Use Advisory Board. Julian had contacted me asking if I would appear before the Board to give a discussion of MX.

"Your presence would pack the house, and our next meeting will be late February. You and Henshaw represent the two extremes on MX. I would love to see the two of you go at it, I think you could destroy Henshaw."

"I doubt that, because Henshaw is very capable, you can't shake him, no matter how hard you hit him with the real facts. He is totally dedicated to MX, his future is MX. Loose MX, and I'll bet you his Air Force career is over, no matter what. He either wins big. Or looses everything. However, I would love to rattle his cage a bit, I need some excitement, sitting around waiting for President Reagan to make his decision is rattling my composure a bit also."

And so, we met, February 27, 1981 in a packed house in the Assembly Chambers. To me, Henshaw was the epitome of the military warrior, totally programmed, and totally dedicated, much like a mechanical toy, wound tight. He could deflect any blow, no matter how bad it hurt; he was indestructible, short of outright killing.

We went at it for two straight hours, no quarter asked, no quarter given. Probably neither of us won, my comments were based on pretty indisputable facts, his comments were based on the overwhelming need for national defense. When it was over neither of us spoke to the other, we didn't even pause to shake hands, just went our separate ways. Most said I completely dominated the Major, but those were people that hated the MX, and their vision was questionable at best. I took no pride in dominating the Major, if in fact I did. The truth was that I felt rather sorry for him. For one of these days, President Reagan was going to say no to MX, and I suspected that Major Henshaw in his perfect blue uniform would become private citizen Henshaw, probably reduced to levis like most of the rest of us wore.

We got the ranching MX DEIS Review Team sufficiently organized during March to realistically prepare a team approach to responding to the EIS. It wasn't easy. Thirty cowboys will have 30 different opinions, probably none of them valid. We gathered everyone's comments, Hage said he was too busy to summarize, so I prepared the response; 65 pages with 323 individual responses, some one-liners to some being several pages long. We had a team meeting in Reno, well attended, one week before the May 1 deadline. Pam Cosby, fitted out in a form fitting white outfit, with a very short dress, chaired the meeting. The cowboys were mesmerized, so it went very well, except I was left holding the sack, with about a hundred or so corrections, requiring complete retyping. It was done and submitted to the State MX office on April 28. We had done our thing, even though I fully still believed that the President would axe the whole project shortly.

645

In July, the United States House of Representatives voted overwhelmingly to support the MX, by essentially a three to one margin. Of course, the House was Democratic, and the decision wasn't there's to make to begin with. The near complete absence of Reagan saying anything either for or against the MX was starting to get on people's nerves. A lot of "what if" games were being played out at all levels. Many suspected the overwhelming support shown by the House was putting Reagan between a rock and a hard place. Laxalt and Santini, however stood firmly against the project, Governor List still rode the fence to a certain extent. Political survival at all costs! Meanwhile, the projected cost of the MX, originally estimated to cost only 30 billion or so had escalated to 232 billion.

The first real hint of where the President stood on MX came out on the first of August, 1981. The Washington Post broke the story, saying Reagan was leaning towards using airplanes to keep the missals in air at all times rather than on the land-based shell game being proposed by the Air Force. Defense head, Casper Wineberger, seemed in total agreement. In fact, the article went so far as to say that Reagan was going to resurrect the B-1 bomber, scuttled by former President Carter. Needless to say, no one in the White House would verify the accuracy of the Post article.

Just when we thought the issue was near death, MX support struck again, big time. Members of the prestigious Defense Science Board recommended that the President go ahead with the land based shelter scheme as proposed by the Air Force. This recommendation, from what Pentagon insiders describe as the premier outside advisory group on technical defense matters would carry significant weight, especially in opposing Defense Secretary Wineberger's proposal to use airplanes. John Tower, a ranking Republican Senator from Texas came out in strong support for the land-based system proposed for Nevada and Utah. Secretary of State Alexander Haig Jr. also came out in strong support of the land-based system. Senator Tower, and Representative

Bill Dickinson, the ranking Republican on the House Armed Services Committee met with the President at his Santa Ynez Ranch to indicate strong support for the land-based scheme. Opposition against the concept of having B-1 bombers carry the MX in perpetual flight was growing daily, with most intelligent folks pointing out that it would be impossible to launch such a bulky missile from an airplane.

To add to the confusion, Reno Newspapers ran an extensive analysis of the MX issue in mid September, saying that the President would make his final decision on September 22, and it would include both the B-1 bomber version and 100 smaller MX missiles hidden in some 1,000 shelters located entirely in Lincoln and Clark Counties. Even the Air Force said this plan might be acceptable. I had to laugh; Clark County was totally supportive of the MX plan, as long as it wasn't in Clark County. The original EIS had very few structures, or miles of track near Vegas, but this plan put Vegas squarely in the bombsights of Mother Russia. I began to think that perhaps President Reagan wasn't above playing mind games in order to help make the final decision more acceptable. Well anyway, come September 22, 1981, President Reagan made no final MX decision, quiet contrary to what the Reno papers literally guaranteed.

The next shock wave came from Santana himself. The Nevada State Journal reported that an aid for Santana reported that the Defense Department would meet with 49 members of Congress, including Santana at a noon meeting in D.C., Friday, October 2, 1981, and discuss the President's final decision on MX basing among other items. I was at the Gund, and of course, any Reno Newspaper wouldn't get there until the following week. However, Patrick O'Driscoll, a reporter for the Journal called me Thursday evening to get my reaction, which basically was, "How many times to we have to go down this road before it over?"

It's funny how you remember monumental things that happen in your life, the Kennedy assignation, Pear Harbor, etc. I was disking a 160-acre field preparing it for a fall planting of crested wheat with our 140 hp Massey, which had a nice cab and a radio powerful enough to get KOH out of Reno. Based on what Pat had told me the night before, I was listening to KOH that morning as I made my half-mile runs pulling a 12' double offset disk slowly over the Nevada landscape. The 9:00 a.m. news had come and gone, and now we were into the morning music. It was about 9:20, I was just lumbering around a difficult turn, had raised the disk to facilitate the turn, when the music was disrupted by a voice saying we have a special news announcement from Washington D.C.

"The President has announced that he is scrapping the land based shuttle MX system in favor placing modified MX missiles in existing Minuteman and Titan silos, located mainly in the Dakota's, Montana and Wyoming". The President was further quoted as saying the ground-based system was too costly, was flawed from the beginning, but perhaps most important of all was the vast environmental impacts it would have had on rural Nevada and Utah. It would basically have killed agriculture in both states, a price too steep to pay."

I remembered shutting the tractor down, bending over the steering wheel, thanking God for having given me the strength to endure this nightmare. I especially asked Him to watch over those young ladies at HDR, they would need his protection. I asked him to watch over the President, Senator Laxalt, and especially Congressman Santini. I thanked Him over and over again. I remember thinking that you bastards beat me on the Test Site, but I won this one! Silly, the thoughts that creep into your brain at times like this.

It's funny how fast things can change, by mid October, the MX was nearly a forgotten thing. Committees were dissolved, my friend, Patrick

O'Driscoll prepared an editorial titled, "Nevada's Nevada Again". He went on to say, "And so, Nevada settles back into being Nevada again. But is it the same Nevada? The things so many people like about this hard-to-know state – its rugged, sere geography, its conservative but tolerant and open lifestyle, its sparsely settled hugeness – will remain that way a while longer, but not forever. The conflicts, disagreements and solutions about the use of their land – "Sagebrush Rebellion," wilderness, mining, Bureau of Land Management – are too pervasive to prevent change." Well said lad!

About a month after Reagan scuttled MX, I received two letters thanking me for my efforts in regard to MX. One from Senator Laxalt, carefully worded, the other from Congressman Santini. Buried within that letter was a "thank you" for the white papers, and a brief mention of "special efforts". I am sure neither ever knew about what old Brock Mendenhill did in Santa Barbara, because first of all, old Brock had long since vanished from this planet. I was pretty sure the original telephone call had somehow come out of the Santini camp. Whatever, it was never to be discussed. They asked me to do something, something that in hindsight was just about impossible, but it got done. President Reagan had reason to say that the environmental consequences were simply too great, he moved on rapidly after that, never looking back, and he never paid an ounce of political price for his decision. I liked to think I did one for the gipper, but in reality, it was for a whole lot more.

One would have thought that the Sagebrush Rebellion would have gained nothing but momentum after the MX died. Certainly, there was national support, more than 20 states had signed on. Rumors were coming back that Reagan was about ready to do something dramatic in regard to the Rebellion. Most Rebellion advocates thought that the President was going to use Nevada as a test to see if the Federal government could get out of land management. He was toying with the idea of turning the BLM land in Nevada over to state management. There was never a news release to that effect, but the rumor persisted from the highest sources, and it all pointed to Jim Watt, Reagan's appointment to the position of Secretary of Interior. Even though Watt had worked for the BLM in his early days, he was known as a critic of the Bureau as it existed in the early '80's. On numerous occasions he had indicated that it was his belief that western states could do a much better job of managing these lands than the Bureau could ever do. In his defense it was painfully obvious that the Bureau of Land Management had grown into a bloated, over manned, paper creating organization. Range Cons were supposed to be out on the land working with their ranching partners, but the truth of the matter was that their paperwork, much a result of the ever-encroaching environmental movements, was sufficient to basically keep them in the office full time.

So, in all likelihood there was much truth to the rumor that Nevada was going to get to manage the 50 to 60 million BLM acres. Surprisingly enough, the most vocal advocated of the Rebellion were not in Nevada, but in the surrounding western states. It seemed like once the MX died, the Nevada Cattlemen's Association became strongly quiet on the Rebellion subject. I couldn't understand that, but Pete, with his ever-present intelligence said, "You watch, once it appears like the land is going back to the state, and possibly back to the ranches, they are going to scatter like a bunch of chucker's. I have been telling you for years most of that the Elko County bunch would rather pay a grazing fee to the BLM than to have to pay taxes of their grazing land. Just cheaper for them, short sighted bastards."

Well, I never did figure out the exact reason, but Pete's comments made sense to me, as I had heard the same philosophy expressed more than once at livestock meetings. It was more than I could comprehend; there were so many advantages to state ownership. If the state owned the land, it would be far easier to accomplish what I had been preaching at the Gund, than federal ownership. After going through what I had to go through to get my hands of 8,000 acres of federal land, I doubted if any individual rancher could accomplish that.

650

I never did figure out exactly when it happened, probably about the middle of 1982. But I didn't hear this version until many years later. One of my former students, a great big kid from south of Burns Oregon had moved to Nevada to go to college. The U.S. Fish and Wildlife controls the water that goes into Harney Lake from upstate Oregon. Their ranch was on the edge of Harney. Well, one year the feds had a bit too much water, so they let her rip and ultimately the shoreline of Harney Lake ended up about a mile on the wrong side of their ranch. Needless to say, this young lad was a rather vocal critic of all things federal from that point on. Seems like shortly after he graduated, he got into a poker game over in Hotel Ely, located on Main Street. The stakes got pretty high, and ultimately the kid won, not much money, but he got a band of sheep out of the evening's entertainment. That youngster, Hank Vogler, ultimately went on to become the biggest sheep rancher in all Nevada. Sometime thereafter, around 1983, as near as I could ever figure, he had to go to a party in southern Idaho, Boise, I think. This was a high-powered party, several western congressmen in attendance, a senator or two, the Idaho Governor, and Jim Watt. About an hour after dark a telephone call came in for Jim, and he took it in a bedroom where it was quiet. The story as told to me was that after about 15 minutes Watt came out boiling mad, throwing things all over. Some kind folks restrained him before he blew a gasket, and he finally started yelling in decibels where he could be partially understood.

"The *&%$ bastards pulled the rug out from under us, myself and Reagan, that's the last chance." Will, it finally came out that the call was from somebody important in Nevada, and they said there was insufficient political support to accept the BLM land from the Feds. The caller said that from the Governor on down, there was no support, it was a done deal. I was told that Watt totally lost his temper threatening to kill somebody, anybody. List was still Governor in 1983, I knew that much, and he sure waffled on the MX, at least until there was no choice but to come out against it. He seemed like he had supported

651

the Rebellion, but that was in hindsight. However, the tea leaves also pretty clearly indicated that the next Nevada Governor would be big Bob Miller, a democrat from Vegas. Miller would never have supported the BLM land reverting to state ownership, much less private. Maybe it was payback time for axing the MX. I never really knew the real answer, in fact I never even learned who made that call, it was speculated that it was Dean Rhodes himself; he and Watt sure enough knew each other well enough. I knew Dean well over the years, never bothered to ask him if that story was true or not. It didn't really make much difference to me, as I had felt for a long time, just like Pete and a whole bunch of other folks that there was neither the desire, fortitude, or intelligence, if you well, in Nevada State government to really handle the rangelands. As bad as the BLM was somehow you had to figure Nevada politicians wouldn't have faired much better. I always thought that if the transfer had happened, that was one job I would go after hook line and sinker! But it wasn't to be, not even remotely close. At any rate, once Nevada pulled the rug, it hardly took six months before the Sagebrush Rebellion was almost totally forgotten, not only by Nevada, but all the rest of the Western States that had signed on. Some rebellions end peacefully, this was one such case. They didn't even hang the ringleaders, or for that matter, even slap their hands.

One day after the dust settled, I was sitting on the second story porch in the Gund house, just enjoying a late afternoon sunset. The landscape from the house gently sloped to the west, where it formed the playa of the ancient Pleistocene Lake Gilbert. That area was also more or less a meadow, formed from the many hot springs that dotted the area. It was a productive area, dominated by alkali tolerant vegetation, and some pretty good pasture grasses. It was also a productive area for jackrabbits, squirrels, voles, mice badgers, and a multitude of other long-standing members of the Grass Valley population. It was a classic area for coyote watching, something that every afternoon about sundown could be readily enjoyed, sometimes requiring binoculars, sometime being close enough to be plainly visible to the naked eye. Today was such a day.

I watched the antics of a young pup, not too well educated on the skills of survival yet, but with all the ambitions of youth. He had jumped, and then pounced on perhaps his third vole before being successful. Coyotes are unique in their meadow hunting style, sniffing, stalking, then at just the right second, coming forth with a gigantic leap, landing squarely on their next meal. This guy was learning, but he had a ways to go before the art was perfected. As I watched it became plainly obvious, the habitat of the human populations, playing home to vehicles, producing music and other sounds, seemed to not bother for a second this young pup. I had to laugh about the events of the last four or five years in the struggle for Nevada. Either the Air Force, through the MX was going to own her, lock stock and barrel, or the State, and likely ultimately the ranching community, would own her because of the Rebellion. The efforts spent by both entities, as represented by time and dollars, was unimaginable, but was surely in the billions, both efforts failed, Nevada remained the dominion of the coyote, and he probably would have remained in charge, regardless of what might have happened. I thought about that coyote I watched years ago on that day when Major Treadwell had in mind my elimination. We had set of enough atom bombs on the test site to kill probably 50% of the world's population, but that coyote was undaunted by the whole mess, including the confrontation that was taking place a few hundred yards away. This Gund Ranch coyote seemed to be sending the same message – you idiots do what ever you have to do, it shouldn't affect me too much one way or the other, I'll survive, reproduce, and we will still be here long after you give up trying to screw up my environment. Yeah, probably that damned coyote was the only real winner in the end, he was still there just doing his thing, while most folks involved with either the MX or the Rebellion had just about plumb wore themselves out. I had learned a lot from coyotes over the years, they didn't get too serious about anything but survival, and now my survival was facing me square on. I hoped I had learned my lessons well.

THE END OF CAMELOT, AND A WHOLE LOT MORE

Tony Lesperance pulling Hay out of the stack for the Winter Feeding of Cattle. Winter of 2018.

Bohmont had warned me on several occasions I was not making many friends because of my opposition to MX. "Company's like Martin Marietta, Boeing all have strong lobbyists working the Governor and the legislature right here in Nevada, and your name as a University Professor is linked to the anti MX group more than any one else. You got to remember, Joe Crowley is a Democrat, and MX is a Democratic fund-raising apparatus. Joe has already informed me in no uncertain terms that he feels you are stepping beyond the acceptable confines of academic freedom."

I had heard it a hundred times. Resources Concepts Inc., a Carson City consulting firm, working mostly with ranching problems, and long since been known as the rancher's friend in environmental issues with the federal land managers was rumored to be in line to help HGR with the next level of environmental analyses, a contract that could well be worth millions. RCI had already vented their anger with both Crowley and Bohmont. And I couldn't quite ever forget that late night call from Washington, clearly stating, "your life could be in danger."

In hindsight, I guessed a whole lot of things had started changing prior to MX, albeit subtle, but they were changes society would have to deal with, MX or no MX. In 1959, the year I went to work for the University, Nevada was the most rural state in the union. The population explosions of Las Vegas and Reno had only just begun, or weren't even on the horizon. Back in those days, the State Senate was made up of a single representative from each of Nevada's seventeen counties. At least half of those seventeen Senators had an agriculture background of some kind or another. Furthermore, because of the rural population base, the Assembly consisted of many rural members, again with ties to agriculture. The University's Board of Regents, consisting of nine members, had historically looked to it rural representative, for all situations involving the College of Agriculture, and normally the rural position was filled by someone that understood agriculture. So, in 1959 agriculture, rather it be at the University, or out in the field had as much political clout as any industry in Nevada, more than most, and in 1959, agriculture in Nevada meant range livestock production.

But it didn't take long for change to erode that rural power base. The United States Supreme Court, in its Reynolds vs. Sims 1964 decision mandated that one person is one vote in the apportionment of state legislatures. Chief Justice Warren wrote, "Legislators represent people, not trees or acres. Legislators are elected by voters, not farms or cities or economic interests." For Nevada, he might just as well said. "Legislators represent people, not cows."

Nevada had no choice but to make some mighty big changes shortly thereafter, even though the system had worked very well for 100 years. Nevada's seventeen Senators had represented individually one of Nevada's seventeen counties. After Reynolds vs. Sims, those seventeen senators each represented about 50,000 voters. Only two Nevada Counties had 50,000 or more population, Clark and Washoe. You had to throw quite a few rural counties together to come up with 50,000 voters.

So, in one Supreme Court decision, rural Nevada lost most of its power. Added to that problem, every ten years the legislature had to redistrict itself based on changing populations. So, by 1970, the majority of all elected legislators, either Assemblymen or Senators, came from Clark or Washoe, only a handful came from rural Nevada. Each subsequent 10 years, rural Nevada lost more clout. So, by 1982, when both the MX and the Sagebrush Rebellion perished, rural legislators were about as rare as a July snowstorm. It was often joked that when the rural legislators caucused, they only needed, at best, a single office.

The University of Nevada's Board of Regent was also impacted by Reynolds vs. Sims, but not to the extent that the legislature was. The Regents had for some time been elected from districts, and the districts represented the population reasonably well, but Reynolds vs. Sims made that representation more correct. Reynolds vs. Sims also required the Board to redistrict itself every ten years based on population change.

Dean Bohmont never let redistricting bother him too much. He was very capable in working the legislature, worked the Clark County representatives every bit as well as the rurals. The rural representative on the Board of Regents was Molly Magee, legendary Grass Valley rancher. Bohmont and Magee were close, very close. He saw to that relationship perhaps more than any other. Three previous University Presidents had felt the sting of being fired, pretty much to one extent or another as a result of that close relationship.

Molly Magee, who became Molly Knudtsen after divorcing her long-time husband Dick Magee and marrying her ranch foreman, Bill Knudtsen, became a regent in 1961, and remained a regent for the next 20 years, except for a two year period in the early seventies, when her health didn't allow her the time. Molly's Grass Valley Ranch was in the south part of Grass Valley, while the Gund Research and Demonstration Ranch existed in the more northerly parts of the Valley. Molly took a great deal of interest in the Gund, thanks to Belmont's constant efforts, and also thanks to my efforts. We frequently visited, kept her updated on all of the latest projects, rode with her, as no real fences separated the two range allotments. Additionally, I frequently helped Bill Knudtsen with his many mechanical projects.

Molly loved her ranch, she was an outstanding environmentalist, and was a recognized expert on central Nevada Indian lore and history. She was an avid student of the archeology work we were conducting at the Gund. But Molly's greatest love was her dedication to higher education and the work she accomplished through the Board of Regents.

Molly's association with the Grass Valley Ranch, and her purebred Hereford herd was something she worked at every single day. She loved her purebred herd, and rightly so, as it had won her many awards. But ranching life is also hard, and Molly, who did most everything from horseback, had paid a price. On several occasions she suffered injuries from horse wrecks, and these all took their toll. So, in early 1980, she made the decision not to run for another term on the Board. She told Bohmont before her own family had even heard the news. She had been protective of Bohmont, and all he had tried to accomplish, and I believe she was genuinely concerned that whoever the next rural regent might be, that person must be supportive of the College of Agriculture and its many programs.

But sometimes things don't go exactly as planned. Once the word got out that Molly wasn't going to run, long time Elko resident Dorothy Gallagher threw her hat into the ring. Mrs. Gallagher was well known in rural Nevada, and she was fairly well known by me because of her past activities.

"Dean, I'll be straight forward, Molly is not running, and Dorothy Gallagher is. You got problems."

"I know Mrs. Gallagher, and I think I can work with her as good as Molly."

"I don't think you know Mrs. Gallagher that well, or you might not have made that statement. Let me refresh your memory. Gallagher's dad was big in Nevada agriculture, as well as banking and grocery stores. He was a financial tycoon when there weren't very many tycoons in Nevada. She is a very ambitious woman, and always wanted to follow her father's footsteps". I continued, "I am sure you have heard of the Damele's of Eureka and Lander Counties; they got ranches everywhere. A few years back Tony Damele graduated from your college."

"Yes, I know the Damele's and I remember Tony."

"Well, it was twenty-five, maybe thirty years ago, the Damele's formed a corporation, bought the JD, and ran it like it should be, it was a classic old time ranching operation, believe me, hitting on all eight cylinders, a thing of beauty."

"I don't know the details but in the early 1960's, or possibly the late 50's they sold the JD, lock stock and barrel, to Dorothy, and I guess her husband, Tom. The reason I know all of this from way back then is because Mrs. Gallagher, and one of the Damele's, I have long since forgotten, came to my office for advice. The Galllagher's had not only bought the JD, but they also bought hay property in Diamond Valley. Their plan was to take the calves off of the JD, take them to their feedlot in Diamond, and take them to a finished weight. They called their property in Diamond Valley Liberty Land and Livestock. Well, anyways, after about two hours of listening to their plan they asked if I would work with them as a consultant. It was a nice offer, probably sincere, but I declined in an even a nicer manor."

"Why didn't you jump into this feet first, it sounds like a great opportunity?"

"Why, because first of all, Mrs. Gallagher didn't know all that much about Nevada ranching, and I don't think she had ever been around a feedlot operation. The Damele representative was just there to protect the family's interest, as they had financed most of this venture. And from what little I knew about the whole thing, no matter how hard the Damele's tried, things were going to be done Gallagher's way. I just didn't see how I could help them, besides, I was pretty sure that it is an Extension function, and last time I checked, I am not being paid to do Extension work."

"And there is more, your Extension beef guy, Bill Behrens, was asked out to evaluate the operation. He told me he filed a report that didn't go over very well. He found the crew running the feed mill were chopping bales of alfalfa with string and wire intact, mostly strings, but some wire. Well, that caused a hardware problem, and had lost quite a few steers. He also noted that no one was in charge of pharmaceuticals, and, if my memory is correct, they had mixed up red water and red nose shots, which caused some abortions, anyway, Bill's report goes on and on, ask him, he will tell you what he found."

"The Gallalgher's and their crew weren't there very long, I think less than ten years, when the Damele clan started getting nervous. Damele's were carrying the paper and they could see the ranch going down hill. Don't know which came first, chicken or the egg, but it all ended up with the Damele's getting their property back, slightly used. Tony Demale has told me their was a bankruptcy involved, but he was pretty young then, so I don't know what really happened, other than the Damele Corporation ended up owning at least the JD, don't know what happened to the farm land and feedlot in Diamond Valley. There were a lot of hard feelings, remember I ride with the Damele's when we gather so I have heard their version quite a bit, and I tend to believe the Damele version."

"Well, I still don't see how this is a problem for me or this college." Bohmont asked.

"Well, I can tell you why. I was in Elko the other day, talking to some old timers that I frequently work with; Bill Bellinger does a lot of our mechanical work. Anyways, Bills is about as old as Elko, not much gets by him. So, he tells me that he heard Mrs. Gallagher is going to run for the Board, and that will be bad news for the College because Mrs. Gallagher holds the College of Agriculture, Bill Behrens and Dean Dale W. Bohmont responsible for not still being in the ranching business."

"Well, that's ridiculous, but I appreciate the information. I will talk to Bill and get the straight story, then I probably better get to Elko and visit with Mrs. Gallagher, she is a republican, isn't she?"

"No, sorry, she is a Democrat, and pretty damned liberal from what I have heard. And if she is elected, I'll bet you a steak dinner right now that she and your brand new President, Crowley, will hit it off big time!"

Well, Mrs. Gallagher got elected sure enough, November 1980 and took office January 1981.

There are many versions of what happened next, I kind of always felt that Bohmont had gotten a lot of credit for the three previous presidents being retired early. And he had a lot of clout in the legislature, certainly at least with the College's budget, something that any University president would be leery of. But Bohmont was getting tired of the whole mess, and had informed the new President that he wished to retire on June 30, 1982. Anyways, suddenly out of a clear blue sky, Bohmon't resignation occurred as of June 30, 1981, at least according to Crowley. Unfortunately, the legislature was still in session; so, Crowley was called down to explain why he did this. In Crowley's own words, "I spent five to six hours that day in discussions. In the meantime, an appropriation affecting the University was being processed pending the conclusion of these negations, and we ended with an agreement that the Dean would serve through December 31, 1981." I knew some of the legislators involved in these "discussions" and their version was that if Crowley had been hired by the legislature, he would have been fired that day.

I never really knew all of the facts, Bohmont was not the kind of guy to talk much about these types of situations. And amazingly enough, he never ever really said anything negative about Crowley, at least in my presence.

I did many years later find another version of the differences between Regent Gallagher, Chairman Bob Cashell and Dean Bohmont. I remember an article, an interview of Gallagher that appeared in The Nevada Review. According to the article, Crowley was getting damn tired of every Dean, Department Head, and full professors hounding each and every legislator for their own project. Seems Cashell, Gallagher and Crowley decided that all budget requests henceforth would be considered internally on campus, and one budget only, for the whole University, would be sent to Carson. Well, either Bohmont didn't understand, or maybe he didn't get the memo, but he continued to work the legislature on behalf of the College. Crowley claimed that the College of Agriculture had an untold number of fiscal accounts, and all the money was mixed up, federal funds, state funds and grant funds. It was more than Crowley could stand, at least so he said, so he promptly removed Bohmont from his deanship.

I can attest to the statement about the funds being all mixed is blatantly false. Pete Test had every dollar in the College in the right category. Yes, there are federal dollars, there are state dollars, and there are all kinds of grants. Anybody that has ever been around a college of agriculture at a land grant university will attest to the fact that a complete understanding of the budget is most difficult at best. Crowley had dealt with this in a very interesting fashion however, called internal audits. Internal audits were conducted out of the Presidents Office, with little, if any, assistance from the Ag fiscal people like Test. Once the "internal audits" were complete, in record time, despite the complexity, they were released to the press. This technique took the offense completely from the administration of the College of Agriculture, causing them to have to respond to every negative charge about mismanagement that was being reported in the local papers. This unwarranted negative information, so willingly put forth by the press had placed the College of Agriculture, from the Dean down to field technicians in jeopardy. By December 31, 1981, Bohmont's official retirement date, I had lost all respect for Crowley and his merry band of henchmen, as had most of the faculty.

Even though Bohmont would remain Dean through 1981, Crowley did get his way to start a selection process early on. A selection team, consisting of the Department Chairmen and a very few other individuals was sending out invitations to apply for the job of Dean and Director by early March. Crowley was trying to create the impression that the selection of a new Dean would be basically accomplished by the Agriculture staff. He asked that three names be submitted and ranked. He maintained the right to privately interview each candidate, but implied he would mostly respect the rankings brought forth by the Chairs.

Each candidate was to give a presentation of one hour to the faculty, as well as tour facilities. All touring was basically on campus and did not include the Gund. I thought that was kind of strange, as the Gund now represented the most experiment station dollars, when our grants were considered. I thought it even stranger that the top three candidates for the position all declined the job offer when it was presented to them, in fact two withdrew from the search procedure shortly after being interviewed.

Larry Foster was a young animal range scientist from New Mexico State University down Las Cruces way. I had known Larry from my time at Oregon State and Squaw Butte where he had gone to work after obtaining his Ph.D. I hadn't talked to Larry in a number of years but was pleasantly surprised to hear from him during August.

After some pleasantries, he got right to the point of the conversation. One of the candidates had been the Chairman of the Soil Science Department at Las Cruces. I did not have the chance to meet this individual, but I had heard he was well liked by the faculty, and gave a bang up presentation. He was ranked one of the top two candidates.

Larry explained that the Soils man liked Reno very much, but had great apprehension after his interview with Crowley, and that's why he withdrew his name. After returning from Reno, he went straight to Larry, as he knew Larry and I were old friends.

That's when the conversation got very chilling, "Jim explained to me that the conversation with the President just blew him away. His assignment, if he accepted the position, was to greatly deemphasize the College's association with the agriculture industry in Nevada. The President indicated there was way too much outside support for an autonomous College, and that didn't help the image of the institution, especially during budget times with the legislature. He went on to say that there was a staff member that held the rank of full professor and was tenured that he insisted must go, and that would be one of the first jobs of the new Dean. Well, that tenured full professor was you. Jim knew quite a bit about your career, because he and I discussed Reno before he ever turned in his application. He told me that he wasn't taking any job with a requirement to ax people before he had the opportunity to see what they really were all about. He also wasn't about to ever do anything to any college of agriculture to destroy it support groups, rather it be here in New Mexico, Nevada, or any where else. In fact, he would work very hard to go the opposite direction. Jim said he was so stunned by that conversation, that after he got out of the Presidents Office he immediately called his secretary and had her prepare a letter for him to sign as soon as he returned, saying he was removing himself from any further consideration for Dean Bohmont's job."

"Well, about all I can do right now is say thank you, and please pass my remarks on to Jim. I greatly appreciate the fact that he saw fit to forewarn me. This may come as a surprise to you, but I more or less suspected that was the situation. A number of years ago, I was chairman of the Intercollegiate Athletic Board, and Joe Crowley came on that board shortly after he was hired. I guess I publicly said once that he was the weakest member of that board, and I suppose he didn't like it. But I don't think that is the reason. You know I was pretty active in beating down this MX thing, which I guess you know you almost got in New Mexico also, and I wouldn't be surprised if Aero Jet, Martin Marrietta, or the likes didn't lean on Joe pretty hard. Who knows, I am a full professor with tenure, so I'll damn well say what I please, and I am sure Joe Crowley doesn't like that one bit."

"In New Mexico we know all about you and MX, you were in the local papers everyday. Thank God, you got it killed, we sure didn't need that. Jim's thinking is that the MX probably isn't the reason, he thinks

Crowley is afraid of you because of your standing and reputation with the faculty. Crowley thinks you will fight whoever becomes Dean tooth and toenail if they try to downsize the College. He also knows that you are well liked in the legislature, those are all things that he has problems dealing with."

We probably talked for another 30 minutes. I asked repeatedly that my thanks be given to this Jim, strangely enough I never paid any attention to his name in the search procedure, and never ever met the man, just knew him as Jim, Dr. Jim.

Somehow real friends always seem to show up when they are needed the most. Amazingly enough, about an hour after my conservation with Foster, the radio phone rang, and it was Pete. "Need to see you, can we have lunch at the International tomorrow?"

"Yeah, its your turn to buy, I may need a bit more whiskey than usual, but I'll be there."

Yesterday's call from Larry was hitting me pretty hard. After 23 years, and accomplishing what I had accomplished, the new President, without any discussion with me in any form, wants me gone! What ever happened to academic freedom and tenure? These, and many more ugly thoughts about this Joe Crowley, drummed throw my brain as I negotiated the 50 miles of gravel road before hitting Highway 50, 10 miles from the International.

Acting nonchalant, I asked, "So what in the hell is your problem that caused both of us to drive 60 miles for a hamburger and a beer?"

"I am still upset about the Rebellion, shit you stopped the MX dead in its tracks, almost single handed. Yet you can't seem to do anything about the Rebellion, and it's dying before our very eyes."

"Its not dying, its dead, don't know the details, probably never well, but Jim Watt did a complete back flip, again don't know what or why, he seemed awful intent on seeing this thing through, so I have to conclude something or somebody got to him, maybe Reagan didn't think the battle was worth the price, but I doubt that, because he seems hell bent for leather to cut spending, and whittling on the BLM would create miracles in that regard."

"Well, you seem to be able to fix everything, so fix this, damn it" Pete shouted.

"Killing the MX was relatively easy, and I sure didn't do it by myself, maybe my efforts for whatever they were worth really had nothing to do with it. The MX was so top heavy with bullshit it was probably going to self destruct no matter what happened. The latest price tag I saw was abound 250 billion. I don't think anybody ever stopped to even ask where all that money was going to come from. Sure wasn't going to be agriculture in Nevada and Utah."

"The Rebellion is a little different story. Nothing I would like more to see than have Nevada in the drivers seat, managing the former federal lands. Incidentally, I would give my left nut to be the State Director of former federal lands, but I don't think that is ever going to happen. The time to put federal lands under state management came and went about 30 to 35 years ago, when Ike was President. Hell, the Government didn't even know how much land they owned west of the Mississippi, and environmental protection groups hadn't even been conceived. Try to do it now, and you will be under everyone's microscope. Nevada cowboys no longer have any political clout in Nevada, much less outside. Furthermore, I'll bet you a steak dinner at the Nugget, if the lands were going to revert to the State now, and most ranches would gain some sort of an advantage from that, that every cowboy from the other side of the Rockies would start claiming foul, unfair advantage or whatever. Pete, you know as well as I do that if you took a room full of cowboys from all over the west, got them a bit drunk, then threw some gold coins out on the floor you would start a major brawl. One cowboy could never stand the thought of another cowboy getting a leg up."

"Well, I know you are probably right, but what's left of this revolution sure needs somebody like you to save it."

"Thanks for the vote of confidence, I certainly appreciate your support, but I am tired, and this MX battle hasn't helped my marriage. On top of that I got a phone call from an old friend in New Mexico yesterday, I should tell you about it."

I told Pete about Larry, my work with him in Oregon, how he was successful in getting the job at Las Cruces. Then, slowly I went into the problems at Nevada in hiring an Ag dean, how everyone had turned the job offer down, and then, finally into the meat of the call.

After about ten minutes of listening, Pete finally let fly, "That God damned Crowley is going to destroy everything, you, the college, there won't be anything left when he is done."

"I think it totally depends on who they hire as the Dean. If it is somebody strong, things will be fine, if it somebody he can control, well then, we shall see."

"Yeah, but all the good ones have turned it down, how many were on the list anyway?"

"I have heard that they have about 10 on the list that completed resumes."

"OK, so we go to number 4, and he turns it down, what next?"

"Well, it will be a pretty good test of how far they want to push this thing, one thing that never sets well with the faculty is when a president becomes too involved in hiring specific college administrators."

"Let's have one more highball and then maybe we can get that Chinaman to cook hamburgers."

It was around August 15, President Crowley announced in a low-level news release that he had interviewed a candidate for the position of Dean, and that he had offered him the job and it was accepted. His name was Bernard Jones, which immediately rang a bell to me. I remembered a person named Jones that had been head of Animal Science at Fort Collins. So, in short order I was talking with some of my friends at Colorado State. Their enthusiasm for Dr. Jones was pretty well summed up by a statement that the Department seemed to be making in unison, the best thing that has happened at Colorado State in a long time is that Jones is going to Nevada!

MX had taken a lot of time, time which should have spent in developing programs at the Gund. So, I made the decision to get back to work, make the Gund hit on all eight cylinders. Get grants, improve the cooperative effort with the likes of Jim Young and the ARS staff, get more involved with the archeology program. We had to start planning for the 1982 field day, and both Berkely and Davis were sending their combined range students for a weeklong field trip in '82 also.

Shortly after Pete and I had our International lunch, I was back on campus. I searched out one of my old friends, Paul Tueller. Paul and I had gotten our MS degree at the same time, but he went straight on to Corvallis for his Ph.D. He was a range scientist and had risen to the point of being chairman of the Range Science Department. As such he was also on the Dean Search committee.

"Paul, how in the hell did you guys come up with this Jones guy from CSU, you know what they think of him there."

"Well, I'll tell you, we are kind of wondering ourselves. He was ranked number 10, dead last. In fact, we had made the decision that he wasn't even worth considering, his reputation was so lousy. We never did interview him. About all we know is about the same as you know, what you read in the newspaper. Even though the article says he was highly recommended by the search committee, nothing could be further from the truth. We are contemplating on filing a letter of protest with the faculty senate, but I think we should file a grievance with the Attorney General. Its terrible what Crowley has done."

We exchanged a few pleasantries, but it was painfully obvious that Crowley had hired a hit man, and that was the way things will be.

I only saw Bohmont once or twice during the remainder of 1981, he had turned most everything regarding field stations over to Ely and Test. It was sad to see him in his terminal days as Dean, he was a beaten man. I suggested that he should write a book about Nevada Agriculture and the College, "After all, Dean, when you entered the scene Nevada's College of Agriculture was pretty unknown. As you leave, we are unquestionably the third ranked land grant College of Agriculture west of the Rockies, that's no small accomplishment. You need to tell the story of how this was all accomplished."

"I have been thinking about doing just that, I know it's important to document what has been accomplished. Nothing I can do until I am out of here, Crowley would fight me tooth and nail to prevent such a book, and by all that I can gather, this college will be lucky to hold its own under this Jones guy."

Bohmont went on to say, "Pete is going to retire in six months, he feels he will owe Jones a couple of months to explain the budgets, allow him enough time to get a new fiscal officer, but Pete's mood is ugly these days, and I don't think he will likely last 6 months based on what we have heard to date. I think Ely is going to retire also. To tell you the truth, all of us are more worried about you than anybody."

"Me, you guys got to be out of your mind, don't worry about me. I have options, there are three jobs that are opening up in the west right now, and I would be a good candidate for any of those. But I am not sure that I want to go to another institution, getting kind of tired of academia, I think I would like to stay right where I am and see if this Jones guys got balls big enough to really do me in."

"Well, it certainly doesn't surprise me that you would like to take him on, but the odds would be that you could never win that fight. With Crowley behind him, he is going to have the Board behind him also, they went way out on a limb hiring Crowley, and they sure don't want to get mud in their face by admitting anything about Crowley, at least not now. Your friendship with John Marvel is probably the best thing going for you. If the Republicans hold the house, he will be head of Ways and Means, and that will carry a lot of weight. I talked to him just the other day, and he made it clear that Crowley and whoever the new Dean is that they had better not mess with your program."

I appreciated Bohmont's remarks, but I couldn't help but feel sorry for him, Pete and Ely as well. They had all gone out, way out, on a limb to make the Gund happen. That was not a popular decision with the rest of the Ag staff. A lot of individual programs didn't get the funding they had hoped for because of the Gund, and that obviously made a lot of professors upset, not only with me, but Bohmont, Test and Ely as well. But now the Gund was pretty secure financially, I had enough grants and cooperative projects that finances weren't the problem it once was, especially now that we had a viable cow herd that was actually producing a fair amount of income.

Shortly after January 1, 1982, I ventured back on campus to see and hear the new Dean. He had asked all the staff to come to a special introductory program that he wanted to have at Ascuaga's Nugget in Sparks. Dr. Ely had announced that he was resigning effective June 30, 1982, but still being on the staff, it was appropriate that he introduced Jones.

Jones was a tremendously big man, stood probably 6"1 or 2", tremendous girth, and I would guess his weight to be between 325 and 350. Actually, he looked like a fat slob. I had to laugh at myself as I was making the mental note that no matter what else I could outrun him! He briefly covered his background, which included many moves between institutions as he climbed the ladder of success. It sounded like he had never stayed at an institution for more than three years, always moving to a better job. I had obtained some background information from some of these institutions that he had graced, and it appeared that it never took too long for him to wear out his welcome, and as such he always got glowing support as he proposed to move to a new job, a trait not entirely uncommon among faculties of Universities.

After a few introductory remarks, he got right with the program, "President Crowley saw fit to hire me, he has laid out a plan which I like, and will see that it is carried out. Basically, this College has been spread too thin mainly because of the close association of faculty with the on ground industries of agriculture. That is the job for the Extension staff, not University professors. I am going to put professors back into the classroom and the laboratory. We are going to put the emphasis on research and publications. Every professor will be expected to produce annually two published articles in their appropriate journal, and these must be peer-reviewed articles, not just progress reports. The two publications will be expected for you to maintain your present status. Anything less than that will jeopardize your career, regardless of tenure or not. Future promotions will only occur for those of you that produce more than two publications annually."

By then there was absolutely stunned silence in the crowd, except that I could hardly contain myself from laughing out loud. There were a lot of professors sitting mighty low in their seats that hadn't produced two publications in the last five years. Regardless of my amusement on that, I couldn't help but feel some very deep concern. There was something sinister about this Jones guy; he had the appearance of totally lacking compassion, like a mechanical machine of sorts, just carrying out Crowley's orders, nothing more, nothing less.

He went on to say, "Dr. Crowley's wish is that this institution becomes a leader in basic research, research for the future, not anything akin to product testing or anything like that, that may give immediate help to the industry. It is his wish, and I firmly support that concept, that your research be aimed at solving the future of agriculture. We can look to the Extension Service to worry about today's agriculture problems."

By now the murmuring had grown to a high pitch, almost drowning out Jones. His face turned a dark black as he made his next proclamation, "I will be forming a research team, with one or two individuals from each Department to review the status of your present research projects. This will be an in-depth review of every staff member's research. Further, I am reserving the right to remove research dollars from those projects that do not meet the team's criteria. I will be announcing team members by this time next week."

He droned on about other details that his administration was going to change, but those were of little concern to me now. He had laid down the groundwork, basic research, laboratory research if you will. Although I had averaged far more that two publications a year, peer reviewed publications; they were certainly not basic research. I had plenty of grant money, and was not really dependent on any of the types of funds that Jones would have control of to begin with. The basic operation of the Gund was now being covered by income, so it seemed like I could survive this black terror. However, my friend Larry Foster's warnings were reverberating loud and clear through my head. For the time being my best bet was to do my job at the Gund, stay far away from campus, and perhaps think about some possible job opportunities.

Throughout early 1982 Jones had created so many administration problems that he just didn't have time to worry about me. Besides, I had to prepare for a field day to be held in June, teach a week long class on livestock ranching in the Great Basin to the combined range classes from Berkley and Davis in March, and Dr. Wehmeir was scheduled to bring his geography class from the University of Stuttgart in August. In addition to all that we had seven graduate students working on their Masters thesis's at the Gund throughout the spring and summer months.

It didn't take Jones long to catch everyone's attention for real. He may have been a fat slob, but his underhanded workings behind the scenes taught me a whole new meaning of college administration, and especially the use of internal audits.

Pete Test's replacement, David Charles, had kept me informed on what was really transpiring from a fiscal standpoint. Jones had gotten President Crowley to call for an internal audit of the College. As Charles described it, the internal audit was conducted by fiscal people out of Crowley's office who knew nothing about the fiscal requirements of a Land Grant University. Charles's only input was to provide fiscal information as requested. He further indicated that the internal audit was rewritten three times before it satisfied Jones that it was sufficiently critical for the College to accomplish his goals. The real test of Jones's ethics was the fact that the report was released to the press before any staff member had a chance to review it. It hadn't even been submitted to the Board of Regents for approval. Between May 20, 1982, a week after the report was sent to the newspapers, and August 21 there were 22 major front-page stories in the Reno newspapers about how bad things were at the College of Agriculture.

And it wasn't long before the newspapers hit the Gund Ranch. One article pointed out how the Gund Ranch spent $300,000 more in its first 5 years than the income it generated. No mention was made of the fact that the Gund was an experiment station, not an operating ranch, nor was any mention ever made of the fact that "ranch" had no livestock of its own at the start, and that the facilities (corrals, fences, etc.) were essentially non existence. But as in all such things, politically or otherwise, negative reporting leaves a mighty bad taste in most folk's mouth, especially, when little, if any, opportunity exists to set the record straight.

But I still had one shot left, my old cowboy buddy John Marvel. John had been in the Nevada Assembly for several years and had reached the point where he was definitely the "rural" legislator, and he was a long standing member of the Interim Finance Committee, which of course could well deal with the types of problems being reported about the College in the Reno press.

It was mid July when we met for lunch at Adel's in Carson. "This whole thing is a bunch of crap, orchestrated by Crowley, and it's all aimed at him getting much tighter control of the budget. The big loser will be rural Nevada and agriculture," John chimed in after I went over some of the facts.

"Would you be willing to submit to an investigation and hearing if I can convince the IFC to hold such a thing?"

"I sure would, I have nothing to hide. Pete Test is gone, he is so sick of this whole mess that I don't think you could get him to say a word. I am sure Bohmont would testify, and I am pretty sure David Charles would, although you may have to subpoena him."

674

"From what I have seen so far, the College is clean, but you know Crowley as well as I do. He has his man, this Jones, whom I have never met, so even if we have a hearing and you and the rest of the college gets a clean bill of health, you know as well as I do, that is just going to make Crowley hate you more than ever."

I couldn't disagree with that; I was beginning to see a side of Joe Crowley that was even uglier than I originally thought of him. And Jones? Well Jones was little more than a Chicago style hit man, probably wouldn't stop at anything.

The summer went off without a hitch, over 75 range students from Berkley and Davis for a week, Wehmeir brought 25 German grad students for a week. The field day during early July was attended by well over 100 people from all across Nevada, over 15 flew in by plane on our newly completed gravel runway. And we sponsored an eight-week field school in historic and prehistoric archeology in June under the direction of Don Hardesty and Bob Elston, Nevada's two prime archeologists.

Most of the pipe purchased in Oregon had been installed in 1982, so all of the meadows and fields were receiving more water than ever before, producing what certainly appeared to be a record hay harvest. And the movable pivot had been moved three times, irrigating over 390 acres of various crops. We didn't have enough economic data yet to say anything too strong about this project, but in another five years, the movable pivot might just rewrite Nevada's irrigated crop production potential.

Politically, everything was on a holding pattern between myself and Jones. Crowley and Jones were betting on the IFC coming out with a report that would substantiate the internal audit, I was betting the opposite. Jones hadn't bothered to come to our field day, but he had his henchmen, including the research review committee in attendance. The review committee was rapidly getting the nickname of the Death

Committee. They were obviously in Jones's camp, there wasn't a single one of them that had sufficient background to judge individual research efforts, but they were Jones's committee, bought and paid for. They had stood their distance at the field day, never asked a question, but were heard to say how isolated the facility was, how dusty the road was and other equally negative comments.

The IFC had reviewed the information provided by the University to their satisfaction, and established a hearing date of late October and early November. Pete, who was probably more frustrated by these proceedings than I was wanted to go to the hearing with me, and testify if he had the opportunity. I had picked Pete up at Campbell Creek the day before on my way to Carson. He was pretty well up to date when we hit town,

"Let's go to Adel's for dinner, all the big wigs will likely be there, maybe I can give them a piece of my mind!" he lamented.

Well, he was right. As we walked through the main door, I bumped squarely into Dorothy Gallagher, Pete was standing directly behind me. Dorothy apparently never noticed Pete, and I guessed if she did it wouldn't make any difference, as Dorothy wouldn't have know Peio Echegoyen from George Armstrong Custer. But Pete, bless his heart, had excellent hearing.

"You will be at the hearing tomorrow?" Gallagher asked.

"Yes, I will."

"Are you going to testify?"

"Certainly, if I am asked."

"Well, if you do, you had better testify correctly, you had better say the right things."

"Why Regent Gallagher, you certainly wouldn't expect me to say anything, but the truth would you?"

"You know exactly what I mean, your professional career depends on you saying the right things!"

About then the maître d' motioned Dorothy and her husband Tom to their table. Pete, who was still standing directly behind me said, "I heard every word that she said, and I would love to testify to that tomorrow if I get the chance."

"I doubt if you will get the chance, but I am pretty sure this thing will go well. John and several of his colleagues have pretty well seen through this whole bogus mess."

And John Marvel was right, the hearing lasted two days, I testified for about two hours, Pete never got the chance, but he did tell John what he had overheard. And it didn't take the IFC long to produce their findings. There were two major findings; first, the University's internal audit report did not disclose any illegal wrong doing, fraud or diversion of funds to illegal use, and secondly the internal audit was designed and written to unnecessarily discredit the former administration of the College and in particular, the Gund Research and Demonstration Ranch. The report recommended that the Board of Regents make "sufficient funds available in order for the Gund Ranch to continue operations as a demonstrational ranch facility".

The findings never received the press coverage that the original release of the internal audit got, but as far as I was concerned it was now a dead issue, I could again concentrate on making the Gund the number one experiment station in the Great Basin, or so I thought.

One reporter in particular had done most of the damage to the College by her negative and misleading reporting. Her name was Pamela Galloway Fay. I had never met this individual, and certainly had no inclination to do so. Her reporting, although clever, was extremely biased and very directed at making Crowley and Jones appear to be the good guys. However, one fine late winter day in 1983, the radio phone rang, and who should be on the other end, none other than Ms. Fay.

"Hello Dr. Hope, I would love to come out and interview you for a feature story. The Gund Ranch has been in the news a bit, and I think it would make a great story."

"Well, so far I don't think your reporting has been very fair, and frankly has been very misleading, so I don't see any reason why I should subject myself to any more of that nonsense."

"Oh, Dr. Hope, I was only reporting what has been told to me. I realize now, that some of that was very one-sided, as I had not really had access, or was even aware of the other side. I think a good feature story about the Gund, what you have accomplished, what your vision is about the future would be great."

"Well, all that is good, but quite frankly Ms. Fay, I simply don't trust you. Your reporting to date hasn't done very much to change my mind. You blew those original charges against the college all over the front page, and when the IFC gave us a clean bill of health, that only got a second page look, and then not much of a headline."

"Those decisions are the editors, not mine. I sent both articles in with the same request for front-page delivery. What happens after that is out of my hands."

"Well, I just don't see how any news about this facility would be good right now. We just work hard, keep our nose to the grindstone and try to keep out of any negative publicity."

"If I promised you the right to review anything I wrote, would you let me have the opportunity then?"

"I doubt it, but if you promised that I could make any appropriate changes before publication, I might consider it."

"Great, I will call you before we come out, I'll be bringing my photographer so that we can do a really good story."

"OK, but I'll negate this deal if anything comes out in the Journal in the meantime."

"It's a deal."

In hindsight, I must have been an idiot. Everything she had written was designed to make Jones look good. Why I even ever thought she would treat me fairly was beyond my comprehension. I suppose I was so anxious to see the Gund get some good publicity that I would agree to just about anything. Probably the stupidest thing I have ever done.

Well, Ms. Fay and some strange looking guy who was supposed to be a photographer showed up in early April. She seemed OK, kind a 1960 hippy version, but she seemed sincere. Most of the time was spent talking about what had transpired over the last ten years to make the ranch what it had become.

She asked a lot about how the operation was financed, so I gave her the latest breakdown, showing a very major part of the operation was financed by the various grants I had obtained. "What does it cost to maintain a cow on this ranch?" she asked.

"Remember this is not really a ranch anymore, all of that changed a few years back when we started doing major research. It is an experiment station now, but under those conditions, when everything is charged against the cowherd, including my salary, it makes the figure unrealistically high. You can figure that yourself, you have the most recent budget, and you have the number of producing cows, but that figure on a per cow basis is going to be way higher than the average Nevada ranch."

"OK, so if you took out all the research and demonstration costs, could you figure the actual operational cost of this ranch to see how it would compare with the average Nevada ranch?"

"That could be done easily enough, but I haven't looked at this thing in that light these few years. But even if I did that it, it still wouldn't be quite right, because our winter feeding costs would be artificially high."

"Why is that?"

"We do a lot of things here that a typical ranch just wouldn't do. For one thing, because of some of the research needs, we keep the cows on a higher plain of nutrition during winter months than would the typical ranch. This is a costly procedure, but necessary to get the research results we are trying to get."

"Well, I guess its fair to say that you don't know what your per cow cost are, or would be if you were just running this as a typical ranch?"

"I am not going to agree to that, as it is kind of putting me up for being the dumbest kid on the block the way your questioning is going. Probably the best ranches keep their per cow cost down in the 200 to 250 dollar range. Ours are a bit higher as I indicated, I think if I pulled out the so called other costs, reduced my salary to what a ranch manager would make, it still would be close to $400 per cow, which is not reasonable from a commercial standpoint. As I indicated, because of research problems, we have these cows on a winter plane of nutrition unnecessarily high from a commercial standpoint. I hope that answers your question."

"OK, you are probably correct, I am just beating a dead horse."

All in all, we spent about two hours talking, taking pictures around the headquarters, the new house, the cow herd, equipment and anything else she could think of. Then she and the strange looking photographer climbed into their van and headed to Reno. I hadn't asked how they would get the copy to me to read before publication, but she had the ranch address. I should have asked.

It was only about two weeks later, on a Sunday afternoon, when the phone rang, and a very irritated Wayne Marteney was on the other end.

I had known Wayne for 20 years at least. He was a giant of a man, had run the E.L. Cord Ranch in Fish Lake Valley under some difficult situations. Fish Lake joins Death Valley, and for some time he had to deal, successfully, with the likes of Charles Manson. More recently he had run the Maggie Creek Ranches in Elko County for the Searle Corporation. Wayne knew his business. He came out of Kansas, where he played football for the University. He had been voted "Cattleman of the Year" in both Kansas and Oklahoma, and just last year received the same honor in Nevada, to my knowledge the only individual to receive that honor in three states. Wayne was past president of the Nevada Cattlemen's Association, and on numerous occasions had voiced his opposition to what Crowley was trying to do with the University and the College. Today was no exception.

"I just read that god damn Reno Journal, your picture is on the front page and the article implies that you don't know what you are doing, wasted taxpayers money in building a house, don't even know what it costs to run a cow there. I have just had it with the whole damn bunch."

"Wait a minute, I haven't seen this article. The reporter, that Fay woman was out here and interviewed me but promised that I could see the article before it went to print. I guess that didn't happen!"

"Will I guess you are right. You wouldn't have approved of this even if you had been drunk for a week. That Fay woman is driving some of us cowboys crazy. Some think Jones is screwing her, or got some kind of a hold on her, she just reports what he tells her. Makes me sick."

"I am sorry, probably that article makes me look horrible, but more importantly, because the likes of you have supported everything I have done, it makes all of you look equally dumb."

"That's what's got me pissed, this has got to end. You know, I know that Bob Cashell is pretty good, he's now our Lieutenant Governor. Just got off the phone with him and I told him I want to bring you in with me so he can hear the whole story. He wants to see us Wednesday, so meet me at the Owl for breakfast Wednesday at 6:00 a.m., then we will drive in together."

"What about this Ryan guy," I asked, Harry Rryan, a long standing Democratic politician had just replaced List as Nevada's newest governor.

"We're not talking to any damned Democrats today, not on this issue. They got no love for the livestock industry to begin with, constantly on the side of the BLM and the environmentalist. They sure to hell couldn't help here. Besides Crowley is a card carrying Democratic, and it sure to hell would surprise me if that fat Jones was anything but," Marteney exploded.

No matter what, I knew better than to argue with Wayne Marteney, "OK, sounds good to me, bring me a copy of that paper so I can see what they are saying about me."

"Well do, see you Wednesday morning."

Six a.m. came, and Wayne was waiting at a table at the Owl. Battle Mountain was one of the oldest towns in Nevada, and its location on I-80 and the junction of the road to Austin gave it some importance. But as civilization progressed, major towns seemed to be getting further and further apart. Used to be a stop every 25 miles on the old trails that eventually became highways simply because 25 miles is about all a team wants to pull a stage coach. As the roads got better, stops began to be about 50 miles apart, and with better improvements, soon it was a hundred. It was about 220 miles between Elko and Winnemucca, and Battle Mountain was about in the middle. Elko and Winnemucca had won out, and Battle Mountain was sort of on the skids. It was the Lander County seat, which gave it some importance, and it was also home to the Battle Mountain District of the BLM, which gave it some government importance. The Owl, on old Main Street, which had been U.S. 40, seemed to persist no matter what. It was old Nevada at its finest, always a drunk or two passed out, the all night table, a couple of tired waitresses that were probably hookers in their younger days, but above all else, the OWL was the best breakfast stop on I-80, and also served the best chicken fried steak with mashed potatoes and gravy that had ever been created.

"When we see this Cashell, I am just going to point blank tell him he has to get rid of this Jones before he kills the whole College. The damn College is just too important to Nevada agriculture to allow this to happen. Hell, everybody I have talked to knows what you are up against, and to have that damned Journal print an article like that just can't be allowed to happen."

I didn't have much to do but listen, listen all the way to Carson. We had an 11:00 a.m. appointment with Cashell, and by the time we got there Marteney had raised his temper to a magnificent height!

I had never met Bob Cashell, he had been Chairman of the Board of Regents before being elected Lieutenant Governor. He wasn't at the recent hearing before the IFC, maybe he had already become Lieutenant Governor, I didn't know. He seemed to make the press a lot, had come to Reno sort of when I was a graduate student. He was a truck driver from Texas, got involved with a little casino and restaurant in Verdi, and soon ended up owning the whole thing and eventually built it into a major hotel gambling joint, the first one in Nevada when coming from California. He always struck me as a blow hard from Texas, but you had to give him credit, he was successful.

I had never been in the old state capitol building before, where the elected state officials from the Governor on down hung their hats. It was a beautiful old cut granite building, Cashell's office was on the second floor, everything was marble, I was sort of overwhelmed by the grandeur, but Marteney wasn't.

"Bob, this god damned Jones got to go, he is going to kill the College, and that is just too important to the industry."

"Wayne, you know I respect you and the rest of the cowboys, you have always supported me. I know this is a mess, its got way out of hand. I have already spoke to the Governor this morning, but you understand he is a Democrat, and he supports Crowley, politics, you understand."

"Yeah, I understand this bull shit, but I also understand this continued misinformation in the press is killing the industry. They have destroyed the former Dean, Bohmont, and he was one of the best friends agriculture ever had. Now the bastards have leveled their guns at

684

the Gund Ranch, and Terry. The industry has to have the Gund, it just about the only thing we have to counter the federal land management agencies."

"Tell you what, I'll give Dorothy Gallagher a call, she is the Rural Regent, and it's appropriate that I let her know how I feel on this subject. I am sure she supports the College, and what Terry is trying to accomplish at the Gund."

I had talked to Wayne about my concerns about Gallagher; I had to assume that he was totally aware of the many problems between Gallagher and Bohmont. By the time I had finished that conversation, the record was pretty straight. "Hell Bob, talking to Gallagher is like talking to the devil himself. She doesn't know the first thing about the industry, except how to go broke damn fast. As far as I can see, Gallagher is most of the problem, if it weren't for her, we wouldn't have Crowley, or Jones for that matter."

I didn't know if Wayne was reading Cashell like I was, but I was beginning to get the feeling we were getting lip service, and that in reality he wasn't, or perhaps couldn't, do anything about this mess. The dialogue continued about Nevada in general and how important agriculture was to the economy. Cashell never would come out and fully agree with Marteney about the mess at the College, but he did massage Wayne's ego by saying that he sure enough would look into the situation.

"Terry, you always have a field day about the middle of June, if my memory is correct, right?"

"Yes, Mr. Cashell, we do, and it's scheduled for June 18th this year."

"Tell you what, if I could make it out there this year would it be possible to put me on the agenda for, say, a 15-minute talk or so?"

"Sure, you bet. We normally get 100 to 125 ranchers and farmers from all over the State, lots fly in. I think they would love to hear from you. I haven't published the agenda yet, but I'll go ahead and put your name on it, say right before lunch for a 15-minute overview of the State, that sound OK?"

"You bet, I'll look forward to the opportunity, and especially seeing your operation."

After a few more useless pleasantries, we parted company, and Wayne and I started the long haul beck to Battle Mountain, although after a nice steak sandwich at Adel's.

We hadn't talked a whole bunch, long about Lovelock Wayne asked, "Say. What in the hell you so quiet about anyway, you should be feeling mighty proud, you just might have done in this Jones guy today."

"I don't think so Wayne, got a mighty bad feeling that we heard a copious quantity of bull shit today, nothing more, nothing less."

"Oh, come on, I think Bob's a good old boy, and I'll bet my bottom dollar if nothing else he will lean on Jonesy pretty heavy. For God's sake, he can't go against the Nevada Cattlemen's Association. No organization in the history of Nevada has elected more or voted out of office more politicians than the cattlemen."

"Wayne, this is 1983, not 1953," was my only reply.

"Well, you may be right, but I'll still bet my bottom dollar your situation gets a whole lot better really quick."

I didn't say anything to Wayne, he was too good of a supporter and too good of a friend, but I had already pretty much accepted the inevitable. I never was really sure what it was, my stand on the MX, or my arrogant attitude about Crowley, maybe one and the same, probably didn't really make any difference. I had already looked at three other positions, one at Oregon State, one at Montana State at Bozeman, and the Director's job at the USDA Sheep Experiment Station at Dubois, Idaho. I could probably have had any one of the three jobs, but I had grown to love Nevada, and just couldn't contemplate leaving this State. So unknown to anyone I had made an offer on a building in Elko, and was seriously thinking about going into some sort of agriculture supply business, along with consulting. The visit with Cashell just made me think more about going in a completely new direction.

The 1983 field day was going to be bigger and better than any of the previous ones, more good research results to report, more and better facilities, just more interest. Advance registration suggested that we might have as many as 150 people.

June 18th dawned bright and clear, a spectacular Nevada spring day. You could see a hundred miles, no wind, highs in the 80's, green grass everywhere, all streams running water, all five pipelines, fully installed delivering water to fields, meadows, agronomic plots – just about perfect.

The program started at 10:00 with research reports. John Marvel wanted to give a legislative update at 11:00, and by 11:30 I was beginning to wonder if Bob Cashell was going to show up at all, even if his name was featured in bold print on the program.

Not to worry at about 11:31, you could hear the thump, thump of a helicopter to the south, and by 11:35, it was setting down in the field adjacent to the High Place.

It's funny how a certain event can instantaneously make your whole life go through your mind, well watching Bob Cashell step out of that helicopter, along with Dean Jones was just such an event. It didn't take Bob more than 5 minutes to wind his way to the podium, their arrival pretty much messed up the program. A lot of folks couldn't wait to shake his hand. Jones followed right behind, and he got a lot of shakes too.

"Hello folks, let me tell you what a great pleasure it is to come to this field day and see so many interested folks from all over Nevada. Speaks mighty well for the University and the College. I want to put one thing right to rest before I give you my ideas on Nevada. There have been some wild rumors about me taking an active role in firing Dean Jones. I want to put that to rest right here, right now. I am not out to fire Dean Jones, quite the contrary, he has my full support, and I think he is doing a mighty fine job as Dean."

Cashell drowned on for the full 15 minutes about economic development, how important livestock and farming were to Nevada's economy, so forth and so on. I just leaned against the far side of the high place, just about as far away from the crowd as I could get.

It's funny, the thoughts that go through your head at a time like that. I kept thinking about our experimental irrigation project, where the State Engineer had given us permission to spread water over 640 acres, rather than the customary 160 acres, because of the movable pivot. All I could think of was that no one would ever profit from this work, because no one would be here to talk about its positive impacts. Why didn't Cashell talk about the transfer, and all that could potentially do for Nevada agriculture? Instead, he droned on and on about economic development in agriculture, something he knew absolutely nothing about.

It has been almost exactly 24 years since I took a temporary job with the University as a Junior Nutritionist. Now, as a full professor, with tenure, the author, or co-author of over 160 publications, I was listening to my obituary.

Both Wayne Marteney and John Marvel walked over to where I was standing, Wayne spoke first, "Well, I guess you were right, the prestige and power that went with the Nevada Cattlemen's Association has gone away. Its kind of a new day in Nevada, I day I wished I would never have lived to see."

Marvel was equally stunned, "That God Damned Texas wind bag, I'll settle the score with him somehow, but he has killed the College, and probably the Gund, and Lord only knows what will happen to you."

"Don't worry about me John, its time I changed my life anyway, I have thoroughly pissed off everyone at the College, the industry, and now I guess the State of Nevada. They don't understand, but regardless, my message to them would be, if Jones can do me in, then all the rest of you are in every bit as much trouble. And if they do in the College, the industry won't be far behind either. The difference is, I can make it on the outside, don't know about the rest."

Worrying about me wasn't what was on my mind at that point in time. No, it was far, far more. I realized, once and for all, as I listened to Cashell drone on in his Texas drawl, Nevada agriculture, at least the range livestock industry, just wasn't very important anymore. Perhaps in the scheme of things, nationwide, it was never very important. But to the thousands and thousands of families and their descendants that successfully settled this land, a land considered quite inhospitable by most, it was cruel beyond belief. Even though Cashell didn't represent the Governor, didn't represent the legislature, didn't even represent the Board of Regents anymore, what he did represent was the opinion of the uninformed, and the opinions of those that saw their economic future in the development of the urban metropolis, all at the expense of rural Nevada. When the Board of Regents hired Crowley, they had already made that decision. What Cashell was saying today, as he shook Bernard Jones's hand in front of all those cowboys, was essentially, *your world has come to an end!*

I don't remember much about the rest of the day, Jones and Cashell flew away about as quickly as they eat their lunch, which was at my personnel expense, a fact I doubt that they ever figured out. I listened to the thump thump as the copter flew to the south. I was thinking about how I was going to make my Elko business work.

There are some formalities about leaving an institution of higher education after 24 years. I hadn't offered anything resembling a resignation to anyone, I just wanted to see what they were going to do. I surely presented some sort of a problem. No matter how it was handled. So, I just sat back and waited to see what their plan was. It didn't take long.

Jones had been in office less than 18 months, and there had been a 100% plus change in all administrative positions under Jones. There had been two Experiment Station Directors for Ely's old job. Dave Charles, Pete Test's replacement, was already rumored to be on the way out. The Extension Directors position was in turmoil. Jones had hired a Korean by the name of Yun Kong to be his assistant.

Kong had a Ph.D. from some place, certainly knew nothing about Nevada agriculture, but was rumored to do all the Dean's dirty work. Right on schedule Yun called, and in his broken English more or less tried to tell me how I was going to be terminated.

"Director Hope, we are making some administrative changes that you need be aware of. We are changing field station superintend positions to classified. Since you professional we are transferring you to Reno July first."

"Really, that's interesting, so what will be my assignment when I am transferred."

"You will teach beginning cattle production, maybe beginning Feeds. You will develop your own research program, be expected to produce two publications this year."

"Will I have access to the Gund to do this research, and will I have a laboratory?"

"No, you will not have a laboratory, and all research at the Gund is being assigned to other researchers. You will develop own research."

There was more, "You should be aware that majority of Department chairs have given you poor evaluation. We could eliminate you the end of year."

"Really? I find that hard to believe, but anyway, what you are offering is a ridiculous offer. So to put things in the proper perspective, you can tell your fat friend that my answer is for both of you to shove that offer up your collective asses. My lawyer will be in touch to arrange the terms of my resignation. Goodbye!"

There was no future for me, and probably any other professor in the College that didn't totally support Jones, that was obvious. Ten years younger, and a little more "give a shit" attitude, I could probably have beaten Bernie at his own game, but I no longer had the desire.

So, after a great deal of explanation, I asked my old College buddy Julian Smith to represent me in negotiating a retirement from the University. Retirement, hell I was just 48 years old.

"So, exactly what would you take as a retirement package? I believe if you would fight this, I could probably get you a settlement of a half million or more, but it will be a fight."

"No, I don't think so, I am the youngest recipient of the full professor status in the history of the University. I would like to be the youngest recipient of the rank of emeritus also in their history. I just turned 48 two days ago; I have already signed a contract for 1983-1984. I expect to be paid for 1984-1985, until July 1, 1985, I will have just turned 50, so they pay me two years salary, I go do whatever I want, and I get the rank of emeritus, you do all that and I will go peacefully." I also added, "I will stay at the ranch until October 1, and, oh yeah, I don't trust those bastards, so I will insist on an actual cattle count inventory so that the cattle number agrees with my inventory. I am sure they would want to accuse me of stealing cattle.

"Well, I have already talked to their lawyer, I don't think they will argue too much, he actually confided that the way you were handled broke a whole lot of rules and he feels the University is very vulnerable."

"You don't know Jones, his ego is such that he will never agree to any of this," I answered.

The settlement meeting was set for July 3, 1983, to be held in the Chancellors private quarters, which was located in a seven-story office building in southwest Reno at 9:30 a.m. Those presents were to be the University Lawyer, Dean Jones, Yun Kong, Julian, myself and my wife Jan. We met Julian around 7:30 for breakfast and some last minute considerations.

"You still satisfied with this, I think I can get you more money if you are willing to forgo the emeritus status."

"No thanks, I kind of like the sound of being the youngest recipient of that rank in the history of the University."

"OK, that's what it will be then."

The Chancellors Office was pretty plush, beautiful solid oak table, adequate for 10 to 12 people, fancy chairs, fancy wallpaper, and beautiful pictures of the Reno campus. Jones had positioned himself in a far corner in one of the plush chairs, just big enough for his oversized carcass. Kelvin and the lawyer sat with their backs against the windows, we sat on the other side of the big oak table.

Julian started the proceedings, indicating I had agreed to retire from the University, based on the following stipulations, two years' pay, emeritus standing, etc.

As Julian drowned on with the demands, I could see the University lawyer was getting nervous, Jones was staring at the floor, and Kong wouldn't look at me, eyeball to eyeball. I had the feeling the other shoe was about to drop.

After Julian finished his presentation, the University mouthpiece indicated that before we go any further, Dr. Kong had a statement to present.

Kong stood up, cleared his throat, retrieved a single typewritten page from his briefcase, and began to read:

"It has been brought to attention that for many years Dr. Hope running experiment station he used extensive quantity of fuel for own personal. We estimate the value of this fuel to be excess of fifteen thousand dollars. Consequently, we are initiating legal procedures against Dr. Hope immediately."

I sat there in what was starting to be a world in very slow motion. Kong's statement seemed to go for an eternity, as I thought about the letter in my possession from Bohmont, way back in '73 giving me the right to use University fuel while at the Ranch in lieu of being provided a new pickup every few years.

The more I thought about what Kong was trying to say in his broken English, the more disgusted I got with the whole proceedings. As I looked around, everybody else was not moving, or if they were, it was like in slow motion. Kong had just about finished when I pushed my chair back and stood up, yet no one else hardly moved, except Jones, he started moving back in the corner very tightly. I had had it with Kong, making this totally unfair acquisition against me at this time was so unacceptable, that in my mind he could no longer partake in these proceedings, or life for that matter.

I slowly moved around the table, Kong was still talking, no one had really moved. The thought of twenty four years of my life having been devoted to this University, then to have to listen to a god damned Korean accuse me of stealing gas was more than I could handle. Yes, Kong had to leave, permanently.

By now I was nearly behind him, I grabbed the back of his coat with my right hand, coat, collar, and tie all in one bundle, and pulled as hard as I could. Kong started to gurgle, but it sounded like it was in slow motion. With my left hand, I flipped up the back of his coat, slid my hand in between his shirt and pants, gathered up the belt and top of his pants in my left hand, slowly wheeled him around from the table, to where he faced the window, still no one was moving, except that Julian was slowly starting to get up. I looked at Jones, and he had total fear on his face. I thought that was appropriate, because as soon as Kong went through the window, I was coming back for Jones.

By now I had Kong completely turned around, we were about six feet from the window, I took a couple of steps towards, stopped picked him up higher, he gurgled something awful by now. I stepped back a half step to perfect my aim, and I wanted to get a better run, I was concentrating of getting him through in a clean shot, making the hole as big as possible, because I was going to have to put that great big fat guy through the same hole next, the hole had to be large, very large.

I had started the motion towards the window, Kong was no longer gurgling, sort of just sounding like an old-fashioned steam engine running low on water. My aim was perfect, his feet were at least 6 inches off the ground, he was squirming, but not enough to slow me down.

Suddenly, just as I was making my final move, a tremendous thing hit me from my blind side, I was sent sprawling, but I didn't loosen my grip on Kong. Whatever hit me was knocking me over, but at least I had Kong for a cushion. We went down hard, whatever little air was still left in Kong cascaded out as I settled in on top of his skinny carcass.

Suddenly things returned to normal speed, Julian was sprawled along side of me, trying to get up. As he did, he announced in a very authoritative voice, "This meeting is over". And it was, Jones had already left the room, the lawyer was attempting to gather his paperwork, Koong had managed to sit in a chair, holding his neck and gasping for breath. Julian had a death grip on my left arm as he led me to the door, followed by my wife, now ghostly white.

We went straight to the ground floor, and outside as soon as possible. Julian was laughing, as he explained, "In all my life I have never seen anything like that. You moved so damn fast, that I honestly didn't think I could catch you. You probably had forgotten, but we were on the seventh floor, right up there, and even if you had succeeded in throwing him through the window, he would have landed on the Chancellors car, right here in front of you. Now, I could get you out of a whole lot of messes, but running the Chancellors car with Kong's body is beyond my pay grade."

There was one detail that I did want to clear up, and that was Kong's charge that the Department Chairs had given me a less than glowing evaluation. There was only one Chair that I cared about, and that was Charlie Speth, head of Animal Science. Charlie had been pretty damn sick, on and off, over the last 5 years. It was rumored that he had leukemia, which wouldn't be a surprise based on the time he spent on the east side of the Test Site. But to turn on me, that sure didn't seem reasonable.

I hadn't seen Charlie over the last year, he always came to our field days, but his health had caused him to miss a year ago and this year as well, this last missed field day I was kind of thankful for. "Charlie, how the hell you been anyway?" Actually, he looked a bit worse than death warmed over.

"Not well Terry, frankly, I am beginning to wonder if I am going to make it. I have been diagnosed with just about every ailment in the world, now they think maybe I get some rare form of leukemia."

"I am sorry as hell, I talked you into taking that job at Caliente. If this is a result of the Test Site, I don't think I could forgive myself."

"Who knows, I got sick about two years ago, it just keeps getting worse, I can't retire, too far in debt, I have used up all my sick leave and annual leave, so I just got to keep working."

"That's tough, I won't bother you, I guess you know I am resigning."

"Yes"

"There is just one question I need answered, Kong suggested that you gave me a bad evaluation, you haven't even talked to me in a year, so what is that all about?"

"You know I work for an absolute bastard, you surely know that. I have used up all my leave, starting just missing work. Jones said I would be terminated, unless I came up with something. I asked for an extended sick leave, he said he couldn't find a way for that to work. In a meeting with the Chairmen, he indicated that he wanted you gone, and he expected all of us to give you a bad recommendation. I told him I couldn't do that, and he responded by telling me he couldn't give me any more sick leave. It was obvious what I had to do."

I sat there looking at Charlie, and felt very, very sorry for him. I am sure he didn't want to write me up, but he had no strength left, not enough to fight this anyway, so he took the easy way out, probably thought I would never know to begin with.

I told Charlie I understood, didn't make a tinkers damn in the overall scheme of things to begin with. I just hoped he could get well and enjoy what was left of the rest of his life. I didn't waste much time leaving, I didn't ever really want to see Charlie again, or any of the rest for that matter. In fact, I didn't see Charlie ever again, except several years later, and then it was at his funeral. The whole thing disgusted me beyond belief, I just wanted away, far away.

Around July 15th, Julian called indicating that the University had agreed to all my demands, employed until June 30, 1985, Crowley would recommend me to the Board for Emeritus standing, could stay at the Gund until November 1, and the cattle count could be conducted by anybody I wished, and one representative from the fiscal department would be there representing the University.

"The lawyer even talked Kong out of filing an attempted murder charge against you, I guess you realize he could have done that, because I believe you had him convinced his life was over. Still the funniest damn thing I ever saw." Well, he was right, it probably was kind of funny in hindsight. I thought about reminding Julian about the snapping sow he released on the Poly Royal dance floor so many years ago, that was pretty damn funny too. Life did have its moments.

Some thirty days later we moved to a house in Spring Creek, Nevada, just south of Elko. I only ever went back to the Gund once, October 15th after the cattle had been brought in, to secure the final count so that nobody could accuse me of steeling cattle. Fact of the matter the final count indicated four more cows than my records showed. I should have sold them to Jones!

EPILOGUE

By the time my grandfather had gotten through telling me of his career at the University of Nevada, he was near the end. Throughout the University discussion, a lot of other things were mentioned, but without the detail that he placed on the University. There was no question that deep down he loved academia, and he loved the University of Nevada, but he hated with every ounce of energy that he had left, the events that transpired during those last three or four years of his University life. The impact of those years, coupled with his fight against the MX nearly consumed him, definitely consumed his marriage, all resulting in a period of his life that was obviously very difficult.

His move from the University to Elko occurred two years before I was born, so all of that period, the University, Elko and much thereafter occurred before I was either born, or certainly before I was old enough to even begin to understand his life.   In fact, I knew relatively little about his life until I sat down beside his hospital bed at the old Washoe Medical Center.   Some 45 days later, after his funeral, and after reviewing my hundreds and hundreds of pages of notes, I still felt like I still didn't really know him.   Much of what I had heard only seemed to deepen the mystery.   He loved Nevada, but he hated, even more, what had happened to Nevada. From my perspective, I couldn't really understand all of this. True enough, Nevada was dominated by Clark County politics, and to a lesser extent Washoe County. But the outback was still there, the ranches were still there, or at least I thought that to be the case. And the wildlife was still there, as an avid hunter of big horn sheep, I could attest to that. But when I put all of the notes together it began to dawn on me that he saw Nevada far differently than I. He knew it from the old timer's perspective, I saw it from a very modern viewpoint. I wondered what those differences were; I wondered how they came about. I slowly came to the conclusion that I could not really tell his story without knowing the real historical facts, not only of his lifetime, but also even perhaps before, long before he arrived in the Silver State.

Nevada's motto is "Battle Born". Knowing now what I had come to learn about Grampa, I guessed that title not only fit the State, but it fit him pretty well also.

"Battle Born" came about quite simply; Nevada could only have become a state if the facts were stretched a bit. It had to be separated from Utah, because Lincoln couldn't trust the Mormons to support the Union, and he even more desperately needed the immense wealth of the Comstock to fight the war, so Nevada became the 36th state of the Union, even though it had insufficient population to even qualify. Wealth always works miracles.

But battles in Nevada didn't exactly start with the Civil War. The Paiutes, Shoshone, Washoe and other Indian tribes were never given much credit as being warriors when compared to the plain's tribes, or even some of the eastern tribes for that matter. A review of the Indian wars in Thompson and West's 1881 History of Nevada might change one's opinion of that. The conflicts were bloody, were numerous, and cost hundreds and hundreds of lives, and they occurred from the onset of European mans entrance into the Great Basin until even in the early twentieth century.

Most Nevadan's, and certainly Grampa, have always considered themselves as residents of the Great Basin, although, the Basin proper only covers mostly the northern half of what is Nevada. For all practical purposes, the harshness of the surrounding areas might just as well be part of the Basin. The Great Salt Lake and the Salt Lake Desert, a nearly impassable obstacle, bound the Basin on the east. The Mojave Desert to the south isn't all that hospitable either. The west side is dominated by the Sierra Nevada, a totally impassable mountain range when covered by snow, which usually exists for at least six months each year. To the north, well that is an immense vastness of essentially nothing, called the Owyhee Desert.

The mighty Sierra set the stage for Nevada's first real battle with another state, and to a certain extent even the Federal Government. The early settlers of Honey Lake Valley, a hundred miles north of present-day Reno, thought they lived in the Nevada, Territory, as most everyone thought the eastern border of California, more or less lay on the spine of the Sierra, at least north of Lake Tahoe.

When Nevada became a territory in 1861, the Nevada Legislature promptly created a new county, which included Honey Lake and all the surrounding areas east of the Sierra and dubbed it Roop County. The good folks in California's Plumas County didn't take too kindly to the actions of Nevada, and promptly sent a small army of volunteers to Honey Lake Valley to correct the situation. The Honey Lake Militia fortified themselves in the old Roop trading posts and shots were fired. History indicates that no fatalities resulted, although several folks were, as Grampa would say, ventilated to one extent or another.

Calmer heads finally prevailed, eventually resulting in California Governor Stanford, and Nevada Governor Clemens agreeing to a jointly sponsored survey of the border north of Tahoe. Unfortunately for Nevada, the survey resulted in Honey Lake mostly being in California, so ended the Roop County war, and Roop County for that matter. It is interesting to note that Plums County referred to this misunderstanding,

701

via the local press, as the Sage-Brush Rebellion. It would not be the last such rebellion!

The western migration in the North American continent essentially started the day the first settlers arrived on the Atlantic coast. There was always land to the west. At first it was western Pennsylvania, western New York, the Carolinas, etc. Then it was how to get across the Alleghenies and homestead the Ohio and Mississippi Valleys. Lewis and Clark opened the northwest, and gold in California did the rest. Survivors of the Civil War always dreamed of heading west, because that's where the land was. There was always land to homestead, lay claim to. There was no shortage of that commodity, at least there didn't appear to be. That concept not only built the United States, but it was also as basic to the mind set as was the Constitution, perhaps even more so.

But, the final truth was, there was only so much land. Frederick Jackson Turner, a noted historian and professor at the University of Wisconsin, called attention to the fact that the western migration had indeed settled the west when he noted that the "frontier had ended". Along with Turner's words a movement started. History has never clearly defined exactly how, or even who started the movement, but start it did. It gradually became known as "The Conservative Movement". History certainly will never give Turner all the credit for the conservative movement. That came from a conglomeration essentially impossible to clearly identify, but included Teddy Roosevelt, eastern capitalists, foreign investments and politicians too numerous to name. Most involved in that movement long ago were quite different, philosophically, than those involved in the so-called environmental movement today.

Congressional passage of the Forest Reserve Act of 1891 was the beginning of federal attempts to stop what was beginning to be known as the great western land giveaway. It was also the beginning of a challenge to the very basis of the Constitution, although in 1891, very few, if any, considered it from that concept. The United States held title to a great tract of land throughout the west, land that had not been claimed yet by the homesteaders, most of it far too arid to grow meaningful crops without irrigation water, yet it did grow forage to one extent or another that could be harvested by livestock.

The high country grew timber, and those that supported the conservation theory claimed the vast timberlands were disappearing. The Forest Reserve Act of 1891 was passed and signed into law specifically to save that resource.

Suddenly, in Colorado, between 1891 and 1892, millions of acres of prime forestlands were carved out and placed into reserves by Congress and signed into law by President Benjamin Harrison. Rules greatly inhibited the Coloradoans' access to these lands they felt were theirs to begin with. For the next ten years all hell broke out in Colorado over the ownership and management of these so-called reserves. Finally, in 1907, the Colorado State Legislature called for a "Public Lands Convention" to be held in Denver to make some sort of sense out of the whole mess. For a week in June, federal officials sent to the Convention by then President Roosevelt faced the angry insurgents from all over the west. However, in the final hour, Gifford Pinchot confronted the assembly by saying clearly and emphatically that the government was right and that it would not back down. With that he walked out of the convention, and the revolution was over. And so, the United States Forest Service was born, right in the midst of the first real Sagebrush Rebellion. Additionally, although probably no one ever noticed, or mentioned it, but as Pinchot walked out of that great hall, public land became federal land forever afterwards.

Strangely enough, the Reserves created in Nevada, which eventually became know as the Humboldt – Toiyabe National Forest were created under exactly the opposite scenario, by request of the stock growers. Seems that hundreds of bands of migrant sheep had had been coming in ever increasing numbers out of California. This influx was becoming very detrimental to Nevada's high country, and had led to numerous encounters between locals and the California herders, several resulting in death and mayhem.

Nevada stock growers petitioned the Government to create reserves so that orderly grazing could be enforced and send the migrant California bands back home. Most of the Nevada forest reserves that would eventually build the Forest Service lands in Nevada were in place by 1910.

One would think that with the establishment of the forest reserves in Nevada that livestock grazing would return to its pastoral calm self, a state that perhaps never really ever existed in the first place.

And likely it didn't, for the underlying conflict itself; who will control Nevada, has been a matter of controversy since the beginning of time. Certainly, the Spanish didn't want it, simply dismissed it as the "northern mystery", the 49'ers certainly didn't want it, couldn't get through it fast enough. But don't get to feeling too sad for this unwanted land, because, early on, the intent of the powerful political and economic interests of the Northeastern States of the United States was made very clear: Nevada's tremendous mineral wealth and vast rangelands were to be controlled by them, and if not, certainly European interests were ready to strike.

All it took was the Comstock; the news of that lode went across the Nation like a tidal wave on the eve of the Civil War. Both north and south interests skirmished for the prize, but the North won out. Union activists organized a constitutional convention to gain statehood in 1863. That attempt failed, but the following year, 1864, success rained down on the Silver State. Lincoln desperately needed two more Senatorial votes to pass the 13th amendment with the required three-fourths majority, and the State of Nevada gave him just that. Joy reined on the Comstock, in Carson City, the small town on the Truckee called Reno and in innumerable mining camps and line camps throughout the region. But few truly understood the consequences of becoming a state under these unique circumstances.

As part of the enabling legislation that created the State of Nevada, Congress imposed conditions that the Supreme Court had already declared illegal. The Court had clearly indicated that new states must have "equal footing" with the original 13 states. However, in 1864 Congress, in their rush to get their hands on Nevada, not only forgot their history lessons, but also ignored the Supreme Court. And likely the Nevada legislature, that so strongly pushed for the legislation, never knew the history to begin with. The enabling act contained one provision that would haunt Nevada forever afterward; that provision stated that Nevada had to "forever disclaim all right and title to the unappropriated public lands lying within said territory and turn them over to the federal government." So, with a mere stroke of a legislative pen, 87% of Nevada remained federal territory in 1864 and essentially forever afterwards. So much for statehood!

For the early ranchers, federal property wasn't all that bad. Big time money moved into the State, Eastern money, European money. The Homestead Acts, passed in 1862 and 1864 were conceived as an attempt to mitigate some of these problems, and it worked on the plain's states and states east of the Mississippi, but not in Nevada. For the title to be transferred to the homesteaders by the government, it was necessary to start building structures within a short period of time and to have occupied the site for at least five years. Under Nevada's arid conditions and harsh winters, homesteaders just couldn't make it. However, with the practice of commutation, a settler could take title after the first year by paying $1.25 an acre. Waiting for that short period of time gave homesteaders the option of selling their acreage to large landholders and the eastern corporations, usually at a fair profit. Most every cowboy working for the large Nevada spreads was said to be a homesteader at least once, often many times. The big ranches just got bigger.

Massive ranching empires ruled the day, some having as many as 50,000 cows or more. The smart money realized that water was the key to survival in Nevada, and soon they filed, by homestead or other means, on the nearest 40-acre parcel for every water hole, spring or creek in Nevada. By the turn of the century a Nevada map showing private property looked like a dismembered octopus, tentacles stretching every which way, clearly indicating where every single water source in the State existed.

By the 1880's the Comstock was running out of precious metal, no other significant mineral finds had happened, and Nevada was drifting into a depression. Some even talked about returning to a territory, but you wouldn't have heard much of that talk in the livestock industry. The forage was still free for the taking, and the ranching industry grew accordingly. Nobody knew for sure, but there might have been over a million head of cattle, or more, in Nevada, and the Lord only knows how many sheep, some have put that number as high as a million head by 1885. Life was good, but hard lessons remained to be learned.

One very significant fact that was instrumental in the rapid growth of the Nevada livestock industry after the Civil War was a series of years where the winters were relatively mild, allowing stock to be out on valley bottom ranges throughout the winter, thus minimizing operating expenses as hardly any hay was produced or fed, according to existing County records. The 1870-1889 era, by all accounts available, were very moderate years. Additionally, having a transcontinental railroad running across Nevada, with numerous livestock shipping points throughout the line wasn't hurting livestock producers feelings either.

In the fall of 1889, something changed. It was first noticed by the cowboys around the booming cow town of Elko. Sometime in

September, the predominant winds from the west seemed to be replaced by a strange and very cold wind from the east, it was said to make cattle and horses very uneasy, some referred to it as the "devils wind". It likely made cowboys buy a bit more whiskey and some much warmer duds with their fall paychecks. Whatever, the wind blew for weeks on end, depending on which report you tend to believe, but eventually, the snow came with the wind. And it came in monumental amounts never before seen in Nevada, at least by white folk. The snows came first in the Northeast, eventually, all the way down the Humboldt to finally piling into the Sierra. From there, the storm seemed to bounce to the south. All the way to the Colorado River. But the hardest hit was the Humboldt River Basin, and from there north to Oregon and Idaho.

Weather records were not well kept in those days, reports varied, but no matter who or what you believe, the snow got pretty deep, Some say over ten feet in Elko, maybe five feet in Reno, but the depth was meaningless, because the wind simply piled the snow into drifts of monumental proportions. And it was far too cold for anything to melt, perhaps fifty below. Most trails and roads became impassable. Essentially every stage line gave up, horses couldn't handle it, broken legs, frozen animals, even frozen drivers. The transcontinental rail stayed open, barely. November turned into a winter that most thought would never end. Many people either just starved to death, or froze to death. No one could find their stock.

But no matter how bad a Nevada winter can be, spring will come, and it did. But as it did, it began to dawn on what was left of the livestock industry that once more, things would forever be different in Nevada. No one counted the dead carcasses, but there are estimates. Essentially every band of sheep, except for those few that managed to get far to the south, were lost, totally. Most county records, at least the few that exist, suggest that cattle loss was in excess of 80%, perhaps over 90% in Elko County. Stock horses, the work backbone of the industry, fared little better. For a less hardy group of people, the winter of 1889-

1890 would have been totally terminal. As it was the Nevada livestock industry was set back to the point that many of the giant spreads just went belly up, and those that did survive, survived by only the thinnest of threads.

The survivors of the winter of 1889-90 immediately came to the conclusion that harvested winter forage would henceforth be essential for their future survival. There was a run-on horse drawn mowing machines and rakes. There was a need for expertise in building large haystacks, a common occurrence in northern European countries. There was also a desperate need for irrigation water.

Most of the squabble over water had been over seeps, springs, creeks or other scattered sources of this valuable commodity that was so necessary for livestock to be able to harvest the vast areas of range forage. It suddenly occurred to anyone left in the industry, a whole lot more water was going to be required for crop production than was ever required to quench livestock thirst.

So, a new phase of Nevada agriculture began to grow; how to get stream and river water out of their channels and onto fields being prepared to grow harvestable forage. Obviously, those closest to the streams and rivers had the best chance. Those further away had a problem; they could help build ditches big enough to supply water to those ranches between themselves and the source, or they could take matters into their hands. As so often has been said in Nevada, "Whiskey is for drinking, water is for fighting".

The change from year around livestock grazing to winter-feeding was not overnight, simply because about 50% of the major livestock operations were wiped out by the winter of 1989-1890. The survivors often were poorly equipped financially to do much about changing their management. However, county records clearly indicate that significant amounts of hay were being harvested for winter-feeding by 1895 and did nothing but increase thereafter.

Chaos in general came out of the quest for irrigation water, especially on the tributaries to the Humboldt River, as well as the upper two thirds of the river itself. It was, so to speak, first come, first serve. It also had something to do with who had the most employees, who had the most guns, and who wanted the water the most. It is often noted that indeed it is an ill wind that blows no good whatsoever. For out of the chaos came the Nevada Irrigation Act of 1903. That act created the Office of the State Engineer and further stated:

All natural water courses and all natural lakes, and the waters thereof which were not held in private ownership, belong to the public and are subject to appropriation for a beneficial use. The right to the use of water so appropriated for irrigation would be appurtenant to the land to be irrigated, and beneficial use would be the basis, the measure, and the limit of the right.

Thus, Nevada water law began under what has become known as the Doctrine of Prior Appropriation. The 1913 Legislature improved Nevada water law by noting several very important facts, two of the most important were first, all Nevada water is covered by Nevada law, including any and all underground sources, and, secondly, establishment of vested water rights, which includes all rights that anyone can show proof of having been used historically by any operation. In short, Nevada flexed its muscle, albeit it small at that time, and told the whole world that it, the State of Nevada, owned the water, lock stock and barrel!

And so out of chaos, order began to evolve in the Nevada livestock industry. Ranchers were becoming recognizable entities, something greatly appreciated by the local county assessor. Ranches had deeded property, had buildings, corrals, irrigated fields, water rights, all things taxable. Grazing on the high country, where the good grass really was, was now controlled by the United States Forest Service. Essentially all ranches that existed near Forest Service lands, and could show use of such lands, were granted grazing rights, including a system of payment for the utilization of that forage basis.

However, there was still a problem in that no organization of the lower country, the valley bottoms, the foothills, and even the many mountain ranges not part of the Forest Reserve had occurred. It was not a problem the industry was particularly worried about, for the grazing was free, but it seemed to bother some folks, especially those that had no grazing rights, or were not in the livestock business to begin with, and it seemed to bother Congress. In Nevada there were sixty million acres out there being grazed by livestock, and that was federal property.

Nevada is arid; most of the north operates in the seven to nine inch annual precipitation zones, at least in the lower country. There is good evidence that, historically, most northern Nevada ranges supported a very good cover of perennial bunch grasses, interspersed with shrubs, including sagebrush and a host of other species. Bunch grass had survived historically for a very simple reason; there basically were few ungulates to consume it, essentially no grazing pressure. There is evidence that the various Indian tribes may well have periodically burned the landscape; however, fire would also certainly be a product of lightening strikes. Periodic fire would have done nothing but support such a diverse plant community. Regardless of what the factors were, most Nevada ranges prior to the arrival of European man were dominated by perennial species of bunch grass.

Pictures maintained by the Forest Service would suggest that by 1910, much of this bunch grass had simply been grazed on a yearlong basis to the point that it was gone. The resulting open space allowed sagebrush and other less desirable browse species to expand significantly.

But that open space also allowed exotic plants from far away places to also set up camp. Not many people know this, but the western ranges were devoid of annual weeds prior to the arrival of white man. But the misuse of this vast resource from 1870 to 1910 would forever change the western range ecology. First was cheat grass from China, followed by Halogeton from Manchuria, knapweeds from Russia, then species too numerous to name from all over the Old World. The end result was the Nevada range deteriorated, and everyone knew it, the stock growers, county officials (tax collector), state government, and even Congress knew it.

World War I caused the national focus to be pointed far from the western ranges, the roaring twenties focused on the booze wars, the good times and the rapidly growing national economy. Then came the depression and ultimately Franklin Roosevelt's New Deal.

During the administration of Herbert Hoover, numerous congressional hearings made it abundantly clear that ultimately some type of regulation of the western rangelands was needed. At that time, the vast portion of these lands were used for livestock grazing, and these hearings brought forth the concept that not only was management needed, but the scientific basis for wise range management was also desperately needed. These unreserved lands were under the direction of the Department of the Interior, but since the settling of the west, Interior had done little more than conduct mineral and water investigations. The use and value of these rangelands was poorly understood otherwise. The early scientific data, at least what there was, came mostly from scientists trained as plant ecologists from eastern Universities.

There was also a problem with terminology, a problem that would continue to add fuel to the fire of ownership and ultimate management of the western rangelands far, far into the future. These lands were always considered "public lands", and as such according to the Constitution, and innumerable subsequent court cases, were always meant to be dispersed of by the Government as the western migration continued. Nevada, and every western state, gave up their rights to one extent or another for most of these lands in the process of statehood. The actions of the Government were most egregious in Nevada, because, as noted, 87% of Nevada, including those lands eventually removed for Forest Reserves, reverted back to the Federal Government upon Nevada gaining statehood. Those lands became Federal Lands, not Public Lands, a fact poorly understood to this day.

Late in the Hoover administration, Congressman Don B. Colton of Utah, introduced a bill to create grazing districts, along the lines of what was assumed to be the grazing ranges of existing ranches; however, the bill failed to gain support in Congress. Edward E. Taylor, a Congressman from Colorado reintroduced the Colton bill in 1933, with it receiving support in both houses, and ultimately being signed into law by Roosevelt in 1934. Initially, this law established the Grazing Service in the Department of Interior to administer rangelands. However, the Grazing Service was merged with the General Land Office in 1946 to form what we know today as the Bureau of Land Management.

With the creation of the BLM, grazing districts were organized on essentially all BLM lands, the Battle Mountain District in Nevada being the last, was organized in 1955. Grazing allotments were assigned to each existing ranch, based on several factors, including tenure, their historic use patterns, livestock numbers, etc. Almost all of these grazing allotments were drawn along the original lines conceived by the State Engineer in those 1925 maps that my Grandfather often talked about. Ranchers were charged a fair market value of the forage they harvested off of the BLM lands. Market value was determined based on what is called an "Animal Unit Month, or the amount of forage required to sustain a cow and her calf for one month".

Range surveys were constantly being conducted by BLM employees during this period in an attempt to bring livestock usage in line with forage production. This was a difficult task, as most BLM employees, or range conservationists, were young, and often lacked practical experience. Additionally, an increasing number were from eastern liberal colleges, with nothing more than a degree in biology, thus poorly trained in the concepts of range forage production or livestock production.

During the 1950's and 1960's increasing tension was developing between the western livestock industry and the BLM. Across the board, permitted livestock use (numbers) were constantly being downgraded in an assumed attempt to bring forage harvest in line with production, at least as the BLM saw it. Livestock permittees were frequently seeing things almost the opposite. It must be remembered that throughout the rural west, state legislature were still dominated by rural interests, as the one man one vote principle had yet to be enacted. Consequently, considerable pressures were being put on each western state to do something about the heavy handedness of the federal government, as represented by the BLM.

Despite what efforts might have been put forth by the western states, the situation only grew worse, much worse. President Nixon signed into law the National Environmental Protection Act (NEPA) in early 1970. This law acknowledged that federal actions had potential environmental impacts, thus requiring that they (impacts) be analyzed before decisions were made. Strangely enough, NEPA contained language that protected the livestock industry utilizing the western ranges every bit as much as it seemed to protect the BLM. However, most ranchers failed to read the law that way, or even understand how to use NEPA to their advantage, consequently NEPA shortly became a dreaded word in the livestock vocabulary.

It didn't take Congress long to up the anti under both Presidents Nixon and Carter; passage of laws to protect air and water quality, endangered species, cultural resources, the list seemed to never end.

And President Nixon successfully created the Environmental Protection Agency in 1972.

During the seventies, Velma Johnson, a Reno secretary watched some folks out Dayton way gather up some wild horses, something that had been occurring for over a hundred years. But Velma didn't like what she saw, enlisted the aid of school kids across the nation, and suddenly old broken-down Nevada wild horses became a uniquely protected species, managed by the BLM under the auspices of the Free Roaming Wild Horse and Burro Act.

Then the final shoe dropped in 1976. The Bureau of Land Management, with the aid of eastern congressmen and conservation interests fought hard in three separate Congresses for the passage of an act to consolidate their land management interests, and it was accomplished in 1976 with the passage of the Federal Land Policy and Management Act or more commonly known as FLPMA.

FLPMA, also known as the BLM Organic Act, consolidated and articulated BLM's management responsibilities. But, with the help of Congress, and perhaps with the unwitting signature of then President Gerald Ford, FLPMA basically changed the intent of the founding fathers of this Nation, and essentially 200 years of American history, for FLPMA declared as policy that the remaining public domain lands would be retained in *Federal ownership.* Although to this day, the land management agencies including both the BLM and the USFS refer to these lands as "Public Lands", they are anything but. They are to be owned and managed for perpetuity by the Federal Government or their designated representatives such as the BLM or the USFS, it is the law of the land, at least until someone or some entity is clever enough to bring law suit against the Federal government to challenge the very basic legality of FLPMA, a task not easily accomplished.

It is difficult to understand how my Grandfather got title to the 7,800 acres or so of Federal Land for the University's Gund Research and Demonstration Ranch and successfully jumped through all of the hoops placed in his way by the likes of the BLM, and their use of FLPMA and all the acts prior to FLPMA. His concept of utilizing the transfer land to show the BLM how livestock use on remaining adjacent Federal lands could be reduced, and become more manageable was biologically very, very sound. However, politically, at least to the feds, it was unacceptable, especially as the ink had hardly dried on FLPMA. Once the Feds finally got wind of what he was really trying to do, one can be reasonably assured that they were never going to let it happen. If successful, it would have ultimately placed too much emphasis on the western livestock industry, and that was just plain unacceptable to the Feds. The Battle Mountain BLM director, Gene Nodine wasn't going to let the transfer happen to begin with, but he had placed all his marbles on the Federal Water Reserve, being the deciding factor. Once Grampa shot that down by chopping down that pinion tree, Nodine lost the battle.

The Antiquities Act was well in place when the University proposed the transfer. Clearing the land from an archeological or historical perspective would have been financially impossible on Grampa's budget, but finding the mastodon points was all he really needed. Having the archeological people on his side from that point on was the final accomplishment in saving the transfer, and it was the final blow against the BLM and their behind the scenes attempts to squash the transfer.

His dream of building the best research station in the Great Basin was alive and well. The agencies could do little to stop it at that point, other than to make the final steps in the transfer as miserable as possible, and that they did very well, although not successfully in the final analyses. Building the best experiment station in the Great Basin was his dream, it was his academic goal, it was indeed noble. I believe that Grampa knew that if he could indeed create this Great Basin Experiment Station, and show just how important Nevada agriculture really was, he could go a long way to protecting a very important and productive way of life. But I know he also greatly feared the constant urban growth throughout the west, and in particular in Nevada. He reckoned that unrestrained growth would ultimately make the politicians reset water priorities; the water would one day go to the great cities, totally at the detriment of agriculture, and perhaps more importantly, the environment. I believe his fear of that scenario drove him more than any other factor.

It was his fear of agriculture losing its water to urban growth that caused him to come up with the totally innovative irrigation scheme of using a movable pivot to effectively irrigate 640 acres, rather than the standard 160 acres. He was persuasive, no question about that. Getting the State Engineer to authorize such a deviation from the standard application probably couldn't have ever been accomplished by just anybody, regardless of the facts. I am sure his intent was to maximize every drop of irrigation water to the extent that it became so valuable, cities like Las Vegas and Reno would simply have to look to other alternatives.

Sometimes, I am not really sure my Grandfather really knew what hit him in the end. As indicated, along with NEPA and FLPMA, additional governmental acts happened faster than a Harold's Club slot machine paying off. Suddenly the environmental movement emerged, almost overnight. The environmentalist were, for the most part, young, educated and they knew how to use the law, three basic things the average western cowboy just didn't have at his disposal. In all actuality, both NEPA and FLPMA were very reasonably written; you just had to understand how to use them to your advantage. The average environmentalist would have wintered killed had they suddenly had to live the life of a cowboy, but the smart ones, often lawyers, never intended to be subjected to the rigors of the range they claimed they were trying to protect. But they did understand one thing very clearly, cleverly using these new federal laws in the courtroom was the quickest way to more riches and power than any of them had ever seen. And so, the war on the old west began in earnest.

The year 1981 was the modern-day peak year for cattle numbers grazing Nevada rangelands. Three short years later the University of Nevada had successfully pushed my Grandfather out the back door, forever ending every single thing he not only believed in, but that he had worked so hard to obtain. Ten years later Nevada livestock numbers had diminished by 25% and 20 years later the number of cattle roaming Nevada rangelands had been reduced to 50% of the 1981 numbers. Grampa had seen it coming at least to one extent, because early on he predicted the demise of the Nevada livestock industry, which incidentally, nearly got him fired from the University. He also predicted that the ecology of Nevada ranges would be forever altered, much to the worse, if livestock numbers were drastically reduced.

Within 10 years after the reduction in livestock numbers began, unused forage began to build up on Nevada ranges. And totally predictable, the fires came. Millions of acres burned, and within twenty years it was becoming difficult to find a Nevada range that hadn't been scarred by fire. And amazingly enough, as the perennial vegetation was destroyed by fire, it was rapidly replaced by annual grasses such as cheat grass, which unfortunately, burned even better. And if cheatgrass didn't dominate, then annual weeds, often labeled noxious, dominated.

As the ranges deteriorated, the ever-present environmentalists were there with all sorts of lawsuits, mostly against the BLM, which of course only resulted in further livestock reductions. Then came the rich and affluent class that liked to hunt wildlife. Nevada's mule deer population had always been the pride of wildlife management in Nevada. But there were those that wanted elk, always at the expense of deer, or antelope, or bighorn sheep, and not necessarily just the Desert Bighorn variety, and why not a few mountain goats also?

717

And don't forget the horses. The BLM management of the wild horse was a total disaster. They created what was later called Appropriate Management Levels, or AMP's for all allotments where horses were known to exist. And of course, the forage requirements for the AMP, or number of horses involved, came at the expense of livestock production. All of this might have worked, save for one small item. No one in the bureaucracy ever correctly estimated the potential for each band of free roaming horses to reproduce, or what the gathering of excess horses might cost, both financially as well as politically. For a while captured horses were successfully adopted out to folks all over the country, but that market was soon saturated. The final straw that broke the back of any reasonable horse management program fell, when Congress outlawed the slaughter of horses, either domestic or wild. It wasn't long before more captured mustangs resided in feeding facilities than actually foamed the western federal ranges.

And if all that wasn't enough to forever change range livestock production in Nevada, then came mining. GOLD! The word got out, tons of gold, microscopic gold that the cyanide process made it all possible. Pits so deep that one could hardly see the bottom of, pits so deep that the surrounding country had to be dewatered to keep the miners from being flooded out. Dewatering became the word of the land, dewatering required water rights, and the only place for the mines to get the water rights from was to buy out the big ranches. And that they did! By early in the 21st century almost all of the old historic ranches, ranches that Grampa loved, were now owned by the mining companies. Sure, they leased out the surface rights to folks that ran stock, but it was kind of like absentee ownership, the properties deteriorated, running less and less cattle.

And could the BLM possibly do anything about all of these problems, even if they wanted to, which has been debated ever more hotly in recent years. Most of the new BLM employees come from liberal arts types of colleges, where the closest thing to range management taught is

718

biology, conservation biology. And if that isn't enough to put the BLM behind the eight ball, then the constant multitude of environmental law suites aimed at the agency for their failure to manage the range lands correctly should just about put the ball in the corner pocket.

The growth of the metropolitan centers in the west has been phenomenal, and nowhere has it been more disproportional than in Nevada. In 30 short years Nevada went from the most rural state in the Union to the most urban. The sprawling cities of Las Vegas, and Reno to a lesser extent, in addition to tourism, recreation and industry, required water in ever increasing quantities. In an arid state like Nevada, where could that come from? In Vegas it was the Colorado River, while the Truckee kept folks' whiskey glasses full in Reno. But these watersheds can produce only so much. Out of panic over decreasing flows in the Colorado, the Southern Nevada Water Authority decided to take drastic action, action that would test the laws of Nevada to the extreme, as well as test the moral fibers of all Nevadans.

The Authority decided to buy most of the cattle ranches in White Pine and Lincoln Counties, petition the State Engineer to transfer the water from agriculture use to quasi-municipal usage. Never mind that the proposed pipeline, required to ship the water south, with, an inside height of seven feet, would cost maybe a billion dollars, Vegas needed water, and the price was, at most, incidental. After all, water had been transferred from one ground water basin to another in Nevada's history, so the precedence had long since been set. Smooth talking lawyers and "scientists" working for the Authority set about convincing the Nevada public that drying up thousands of acres of irrigated meadows and pastures in eastern Nevada wouldn't hurt the ecology of the area. They were successful to a point, the State Engineer granted them the right to transfer the water, but in far less quantities than the original proposal called for.

It hasn't exactly worked for Vegas yet, and it may not, considering all the regulations that SNWA seemed to forget about in their panic. However, mismanagement of the ranches they bought in White Pine has just about killed the livestock business there, driving another nail into what once was Nevada's number one industry. Most current pundits firmly believe that if, and when, the spigot is finally turned on for water transfers to Vegas, it will be the end or rural Nevada. Vegas isn't the only metropolitan area in Nevada considering stealing water from the north. The greater Reno area has no further options for growth. They have used just about all the water in western Nevada, so what to do? That's simple, do like Vegas did, buy the irrigated properties in Humboldt County, transfer the use from agriculture to quasi-municipal, and the problem is solved, with of course a billion or so for pipelines, pumping stations and a few other minor obstacles.

Grampa's old friend, Wayne Hage from the MX days, wrote a book, first published in 1989, titled "Storm Over Rangelands". Hage, although a range toughened rancher, was a true scholar of the constitution, the west and most of all property rights. And he successfully fought the tsunami that was gradually strangling the Nevada livestock industry, albeit at an unbelievable price.

Hage, and his wife the former Jean Nichols from Sparks, Nevada bought the sprawling Pine Creek Ranch in Monitor Valley, located in Nye County in 1978. Pine Creek had been successfully run for years by the Arcularius family, utilizing private property, and permits on both the Forest and BLM. The Ranch was said to run 2500 mother cows and a batch of yearlings. Pine Creek's Forest permit included Table Mountain, probably one of the most beautiful spots in all Nevada. The only problem with that was that the Nevada Department of Wildlife thought it would also be a beautiful place for elk, and so did the United States Forest Service. Table Mountain was also a beautiful place to summer a few hundred mother cows, cows that would always return a 600 pound calf or better. But there was an additional problem, and that was access to Table Mountain. As far as cattle and the cowboys were concerned, there was only one or two ways up and down, and these were steep rocky trails, with unforgiving drop-offs. Cows and Elk got along OK for a while, but then the wildlife folks arbitrarily changed the beginning hunt date to more or less overlap the customary livestock removal date. Cows, hunters and horses on the same trail system just didn't work, and suddenly, continued livestock use of Table Mountain become more trouble than it was worth.

And if that wasn't enough, Hage went to clean out some of historic ditches, which transversed federal lands to get water to the time-honored hay fields. Although his actions were totally legal, the feds tried their damndest to cite him for destroying federal property. Shortly after, he faced the possibility of prison for disrupting the ecology of Central Nevada, even though he was well within his legal rights. Hage's problems just didn't end, soon the Forest Service demanded his cattle be removed or be confiscated, and confiscated they were.

Hage had the customary two choices, sell out to the Forest Service, or fight the agency through the appeal process. The appeal process is designed to work on the agency's behalf, every time. Even the Judge is an agency employee. If you can successfully appeal your loss up through the levels of bureaucracy, usually four, successfully, then you are allowed to go to District Court. It doesn't look like hardly anybody has ever successfully accomplished that task!

Hage wasn't going to sell, and he wasn't going to fight the appeal process either. He devised a third option, go straight to the United States Federal Court of Claims, and sue for damages to his estate under the takings clause.

Hage's battle started shortly after he purchased the ranch in 1978. He won, but it cost him and his wife dearly. She died of a heart attack, and he died of cancer. Everyone familiar with the case clearly believed the many years of stress endured by the family ultimately resulted in their demise. Shortly after Hage passed away, his second wife, former Idaho Congresswoman, Helen Chenoweth was tragically killed on the ranch in an accident.

But Hage had children, and they were as committed to the battle as were the senior Hages. Wayne and Jean's son, affectionately known as "Little Wayne" not only runs Pine Creek but has become equally adapt at fighting the agency. He has received invaluable help from his sister, Ramona Morrison.

What has the Hage battle accomplished? First, the United States Forest Service currently owes millions to Hage, somewhere around 30 and still counting. The agency has appealed the decision, and it is likely the case, or any such cases will continue in the future. The Hage family have paid a price, a terrible price. In a way it kind of stands out like there is a warning to everyone else. If you fight the agency, this is kind of what you can expect.

However, Hage has shown that the livestock industry can successfully fight for their historic rights, and if they fight intelligently, they can win. However, not many folks have the determination of the Hage family. The legal issues eventually established by Hage, and his descendants, have done more for the reinstatement of the livestock industry throughout the west than essentially all other prior case history. Hopefully, these sacrifices will at least pave the way for more reasonable outcomes over range disputes, as well as preserve what is left of this once noble industry.

I never met Wayne Hage, he passed away many years before Grampa's demise. I did get to meet his children, Little Wayne and Ramona Morrison. I always thought that Wayne and Grampa were pretty close, and Wayne's kids verified that. Grampa did tell me that one of his proudest accomplishments after leaving the University was his help to Hage on establishing ownership on the Ranch's surface waters. Grampa not only measured all of the watershed on the ranch in relationship to their ability to produce water, but he successfully defended his work in Federal Court.

Grampa thought there were initially two factors that brought the world down on Hage. First, he wrote a book, titled "Storm Over Rangelands", which brought political and legal light to many of the West's problems. The book probably didn't set well with either the USFS or the BLM, and certainly it didn't set well with their legal arms, because it really did shed light on how the Constitution of the United States has been breached as the land management agencies gained control over the vast acreage of the western ranges. That's definitely not what our founding fathers envisioned. I don't doubt that Wayne's book brought about some of his problems.

But Grampa had another version, and it rang pretty true also. Deserved or otherwise, Wayne Hage and Terry Hope received the vast amount of the credit for doing in the MX. Wayne from his political work, and Grandpa from his environmental work. As Grampa always pointed out during his last days, within two years of winning the MX battle, Wayne was subjected to constant court battles for the rest of his days, and Grampa had been ushered out the back door of the University, despite being a very successful full professor with tenure. I kind of always wondered what they would have thought of him about his trip to Santa Barbara if that had become known, and the impact it had on the final MX decision. He always maintained that the Military/Industrial complex had as much to do with running the United States, as did any President or any Congress. Perhaps they were one and the same, certainly following the antics of Grampa's old advisory, Harry Ryan, would cause one to wonder.

Shortly before he passed away Grampa gave me two of his most prized possessions, letters from Paul Laxalt and Jim Santini thanking him for what he did in regard to the MX. Santini's letter was of extreme interest to me, because reading it carefully, and sort of reading between the lines, you can certainly sense that he was thanking Grampa for something more, far more. Grampa said I was the first person, outside of Pete, to ever hear of his Santa Barbara adventure. And I guess Pete never knew the truth for a long time. I came to the conclusion that perhaps Congressman Santini knew something special happened. Perhaps some history is just best left untold!

Grampa's life after he left the University is probably worth a book in itself. He was so turned off by academia, at least academia in Nevada; he just simply made a right-hand turn and never looked back. He established a business in Elko, just like he planned, got involved with mining from the reclamation standpoint, and made some money. But he never forgot the BLM or the USFS. If anyone had a fight with the agency, he was always available if needed. However, it's hard to imagine the feelings he surely had, as everything he believed in, everything he had worked so hard to create was literally taken away from him essentially overnight. It didn't help any, that so many in the industry tried to curry favor with the new administration of the College of Agriculture, or at least what was left of it. History clearly showed Bernard Jones became Dean for one purpose, and one purpose only, and that essentially was to destroy a college of agriculture. And history also showed that neither Bernard Jones, or Joe Crowley, for that matter showed much concern for the agriculture industries of Nevada, or what their actions might have caused to those industries.

Grampa's old friends, John Marvel, Wayne Marteney, Lloyd Sorenson, Stanley Ellison and their likes always stood behind Grampa over the years, but their time had come and gone as well. The newer generations sort of forgot the importance of science in the Great Basin, probably never realized that once upon a time there was a very strong College of Agriculture. Most just became so used to taking marching orders from the federal land management agencies that they just didn't know any difference to begin with.

Although he completely turned his back on the University, he did remain friends with a few of his old cronies. Dale Bohmont was instrumental in establishing a foundation to promote funds for scholarships for agriculture students. He had accomplished this before being fired, however he was very careful to make sure the funds were held in trust, off campus. When he got the axe Crowley apparently tried to grab the Foundation's funds for the University, but was unsuccessful. So, after retirement, Bohmont put his efforts into promoting the Foundation and it became pretty successful. However, students receiving scholarship help from the Foundation weren't required to go to Nevada, in fact most went elsewhere, due to the diminished role in agriculture that was occurring at Nevada. Grampa helped Bohmont in this regard over the years, in fact he became president of the Foundation for a nine-year span.

Grampa also remained close to Paul Tueller, his old research associate in the Ruby-Butte deer studies. They cooperated over the years in several consulting adventures, and remained close until their demise.

Jim Young and Al Bruner also remained close to Grampa. After leaving research, Young and his wife coauthored several books on western range situations. Grampa loved their books, and reviewed some of them for publication. Bruner was older than Grampa, but they always stayed close. I came to find out that Bruner had always wanted Grampa to write a book about their Gund Ranch adventures. Hopefully my efforts will fill the bill.

What happened to Grampa's old friend Pete, and his ever present girlfriend Gina? Well, this much I know from what Grampa told me, and my research. Harry Ryan fell in love with the Black Rock Desert, probably because of his old University of Nevada mentor, Dr. Robert Griffin. Seems like Harry suddenly decided that the Black Rock must be saved from advancing civilization, despite the fact that the Black

Rock plays home annually to sixty thousand plus free spirits for a week every year at the Burning Man Festival. What goes on in Black Rock City had best stay there, as I am not sure the God given beauty of the real Black Rock could quite handle those goings on. Anyway, Senator Ryan introduced legislation that ultimately created the Black Rock National Conservation Area, consisting of 1.2 million acres of federal lands receiving special designation. This included designating about 750,000 acres as wilderness. As the late nationally known author Tim Findley noted in an article in C.J. Hadley's award winning magazine "RANGE", "More government means less access. The feds are trying to close the Black Rock", and they essentially did for all, except Burning Man.

Pete had bought Campbell Creek, but Pete's dad stayed at Buffalo, finally pretty much by himself after the tragic death of Renee Echegoyan. The sheep had all gone, except for one small farm flock, but Marty still ran about two hundred cows, with the help of an old Basco friend. That was before Ryan's National Conservation Area showed up. Grazing restrictions were on the horizon and Marty clearly knew what that ultimately meant. With the final passage of NCA in Congress, Marty seemed to go into a deep depression, according to what Pete had told Grampa. Seems like one night Marty called Pete and was threatening to kill Ryan. Pete got scared, because he clearly knew Marty was totally capable of doing anything he might threaten, so early the next morning Pete arrived at Buffalo, only to find Marty dead of an apparent heart attack. Pete sold Buffalo shortly thereafter, and told Grampa he would never go back to Black Rock. He did once more, but it wasn't to Buffalo. And that's not quite the end of the story.

Seems like Ryan had other habits and wanted a secure place to enjoy those habits. Gina's Salt Wells had fallen on some difficult times, so she had some outstanding notes. Pete had tried to help her, but he had too many of his own problems to begin with, so other than consoling her he really couldn't do anything else. Seems like Harry bought up Gina's note, then politely told her he would appreciate a fairly regular supply of young girls, very young girls. Gina resisted, but Harry made it very clear that he held enough in the note that Gina would either comply or be put out of business. Gina told Pete of her predicament, and Pete, much like his father swore to kill Ryan.

Cooler heads prevailed, so Pete and Gina hatched a plan. They did get a young pretty hooker that supposedly could pass for 15 or so, then they invited Harry to enjoy the spoils. It was a slow night, and Harry preferred to never be seen at Salt Wells, so he always came in through the back. Harry didn't recognize Pete, certainly not from their college days, and Pete was acting as Bartender. A couple of special drinks and poor old Harry passed out before he ever got to taste the pleasures of youth.

He came two a few hours later into the vastness of the Black Rock sitting in Pete's pick-up along side of Pete. Pete calmly explained to Harry that his conduct was unacceptable, but he, Pete, was being very kind to Harry. "This time I will let you walk to Gerlach, which you can see on the horizon about 20 miles to the west, but next time you pull this stunt, or ever threaten Gina again, or for that matter ever grace Salt Wells again, I'll throw you out of my airplane at about 10,000 feet above this desert, and I will probably forget to provide you a parachute".

Grampa never said how Senator Ryan got to Gerlach, he probably never heard. And Grampa said that he didn't think Ryan ever bothered Gina again. Unfortunately, at least from Grampa's standpoint, Harry Ryan didn't really go away, at least not from Nevada. Despite the bitter opposition of nearly a majority of Nevada's voting citizens, Harry marched right on to the top of the United States Senate, and remained there for what seemed an eternity. He became an immensely powerful Senator. Grampa said he and Harry crossed paths many times over the years after he left the Gund. He didn't speak much about those encounters, other than to say Nevada always came out the loser.

Pete and Grampa stayed close over the years, they were undoubtedly each other's best friend. But Pete had a problem, an advanced case of prostrate cancer that was not responding to treatment very well. He apparently had had it for a number of years, and the treatment never beat it. Several years after the Black Rock incident Gina, who sold her joint many years before, called Grampa and said that he and Nancy had better come to see Pete, he was getting pretty sick. Grampa and Nancy had come to be even closer to Pete in their older years. Pete and Grampa were close, no two ways about it. They trusted each other without question. They had gone through so many adventures they could sit around the dinner table and keep everyone, including Nancy, in stitches for hours.

Grampa and Nancy went to Reno to see Pete based on Gina's call. He was at a little hospital east of Sparks, in the foothills. I don't know for sure, but I don't think Nancy had ever met Gina before. Anyways it was pretty obvious that Pete was not only sick, but he was close to the end. But he still had one more surprise – he was going to marry Gina. "Just wanted the two of you to witness the event, Nancy, you can be Gina's maid of honor, and Terry you be my best man. Now I am going to call in the preacher to make this final, should have done it 60 years ago when I met Gina in her beagle shop".

And so, they were married, and Pete passed away within a few months. Gina inherited Campbell Creek, and all of Pete's other assets. She wasn't a rancher for sure, and she was far too old to take on a new profession. According to Grampa, she put most of her money into some kind of a non-profit foundation to provide educational help for the children of former Nevada prostitutes. And, according to Grampa, it was pretty damn successful. By the time I came along, Gina had long since passed away. She had lived in San Francisco, and I could never really find any factual history of such an organization. But it made a good story, and Grampa seemed awfully pleased for both Pete and Gina.

You know, Grampa never said what, if anything, ever became of that free pass to Salt Wells.

The University? Well Bernie Jones stuck around long enough to completely destroy what once was ranked as the third best land grant College of Agriculture in the west. In fact, the American Association of University Professors claimed it was the most disastrous administrative fiasco in the annals of higher education in the history of the United States. Within five years after his arrival, Dr. Jones could lay claim to the fact that out of a staff of 100 scientists, some 75 were long gone, including several that became terminal because of the stress caused by the whole mess. After Jones' departure, there were halfhearted attempts to resurrect the College by various groups, but there simply was no political support. Eventually, most everything the University owned in the way of field stations got sold to support other activities, with the exception of one field station, the Gund Research and Demonstration Ranch. Research and demonstration had pretty much gone by the wayside, but the University just couldn't figure out how to sell something they never really owned to begin with. Most of the development Grampa had done was on the transfer lands, and thanks to Senator Laxalt's wisdom and foresight, the transfer land would all transfer back to the BLM if the University ever sold the property. The BLM didn't want it, and the University must have figured the bad publicity just wouldn't be worth the few dollars they would have gotten out of the original base property.

The Test Site, well that's another story. I think when Grampa finally figure out how devastating the early testing had been, not only on the soldiers forced to participate, but on all the ranches, communities and towns of southeastern Nevada and southern Utah, it was just about all that he could deal with. He talked about the Test Site three or four times during those last days, but it was always very emotional. He never forgave himself for not being more proactive in getting warnings out. I would always remind him that if he had talked to any extent about what he knew, for a long time after he had been there, that the Government would have silenced him one way or another. That fact never seemed to register; he just never forgave himself. Sometimes, when talking about the test site, he would mention Charlie Speth. I think he held himself responsible for Charlie's early death, because he talked him into taking that job in Caliente. Again, no amount of "what ifs" would change his feeling. As to Charlie writing that bad report about Grampa, he would say little more than, "its what he had to do."

In doing my research I realized just how devastating the MX controversy was to Nevada in those years long ago. Now 40 to 50 years after the fact it is difficult to find anybody that knows anything about the MX issues, or even exactly what the letters MX even stood for. When President Reagan pulled the switch, it must have been pulled pretty good. Within one year, it was rare to find any mention of the proposed project in any type of press. About the same could be said about the Sagebrush Rebellion. It died just about as fast. Although there have been periodic attempts ever since to turn federal land over to the states and possible private ownership, none have been successful. In fact, over the last 50 years, the BLM has actually expanded it holdings in the west, the Forest Service has even been more successful.

In order to better understand what the Gund Ranch was all about, one warm spring day, I drove to the Ranch. Likely, once past Fallon, old Highway 50 hadn't changed much over the years, with two exceptions. First, Salt Wells had burned to the ground years before. By the time I went by, there weren't even many charred remains still visible. And the Frenchman's was totally gone. I came to learn that the Naval Bombing Range had dropped some bombs relatively close in years past, so the Feds just bought the folks out, demolished the building and called it good. I doubt if anyone ever thought about the years and years of history there. Middlegate and Cold Springs appeared to me that they were likely in the same condition that Grampa had seen 50 years earlier or so, very old but still very functional. And Austin was still cleaning the side of the mountain. However, having moved the county seat of Lander County from Austin to Battle Mountain many years ago certainly had put the final nail in any potential plans for growth.

I took the Grass Valley Road slowly, trying to visualize what Grampa saw, at least on his first trip. The view of the Grass Valley Ranch, and Grass Valley itself was well worth a long stop and many photographs. However, it still looked like a long-lost land, possible just something far from the past. Other than the Grass Valley Ranch, I could see nothing else suggesting civilization. After 30 more miles of dust, I did come to the Gund. A quick stop produced one young person that claimed he was the Assistant Manager, however no one else was present. Based on Grampa's recollections, I judged there was a new barn and shop. And there was a new electricity line coming from the north, so some things must have happened over the years. The Assistant Manager told me that sometimes they had students out from the University, but no professors ever came out.

After leaving the Gund, I journeyed north to the old historic town of Cortez, Cortez Canyon, Crescent Valley, and eventually the historic railroad stops at Beowawee, then on back to Reno via I-80. It didn't appear that much had changed between Fallon and I-80, except for significant gold mining in Crescent Valley. There wasn't much at the Gund, couldn't see anything that resembled the High place that he loved to talk about, likely long since burned down and cleaned up, but it was overwhelmingly obvious that the dream that Grampa held so dearly about becoming the center of research excellence for the Great Basin, had vanished much like another Great Basin Desert dust devil.

After Grampa's death, and after the better part of two years doing research to make this book possible, I began to realize how different his world was from mine, at least certainly the early part of his life in Nevada. I am sure when he saw that map with all of the grazing allotments clearly marked throughout Nevada while doing the early research for his Masters Degree, he totally fell in love with Nevada.

It was livestock and ranches, wall to wall. Certainly, the wildlife was there as well, perhaps, even in better numbers and condition than today. There were streams with trout everywhere, a fact not so obvious today. The one ingredient missing from Grampa's youth was people; there just were so few people in Nevada then, that they really had no negative impact on his world.

But the people came, and the land management bureaucracy clearly recognized that their future was much brighter dealing with people rather than livestock and ranches. It is pretty easy in hindsight to clearly see that essentially all the acts, resolutions and environmental safeguards we now deal with resulted from people pressure. Have they helped? Before I embarked on this project, I was positive that all of the political involvement, from wild horses, through sage hen management, the endangered species act, the Antiquity act, and a million other such things were absolutely essential for preserving Nevada for all of us today. Now, I am not so sure, sometimes I think those old cowboys took pretty damn good care of the ecosystem themselves, even if they never even knew what the word "ecosystem" even meant. They probably did it a thousand times better than all the college-trained kids could ever do today.

The more I thought about all of this I began to realize the problems were very deep rooted, so deep rooted in fact, that they were the very life support system that supported the very growth of the bureaucracies, growth that has become so monstrously big over the last fifty years or so that they now can only add to the problems that they were originally created to solve. The Air Force had to have the MX to find employment homes for all of its new junior grade officers graduating from the Academy. They failed in that regard, and a lot of Air Force officers were forced to find other means of employment. Their failure unquestionably caught the attention of the other bureaucracies, positive growth was essential not only for job security, but the lucrative opportunities for early retirement, and the good life of retirement. The land management agencies strongly supported those concepts in management that would eventually require them to greatly expand their staffing in the attempt to manage these new concepts to begin with. The EPA? Will just about anybody can do the math there, the more regulations, the bigger budget and more employees will obviously be required. Even the University of Nevada; Joe Crowley realized early on that there was a lot more growth potential for the University in basic sciences, even liberal arts, than there ever would be for a college of agriculture, even if that College was nationally ranked. We blame our legislators, our congressmen for not reigning it all in, but didn't we put the Legislators, Representatives and Senators there in the first place? I guess that is progress, good bad or indifferent. However, it sure changed Grampa's world, probably to the point that today, we still haven't totally figured it out. Fortunately, Nevada will always be a beautiful state, its 108 distinct mountain ranges, each beautiful in their own right, will see to that, despite all the bureaucrats in the world.

Sometimes I find myself daydreaming about having lived in Grampa's time, or perhaps earlier. Working livestock from a camp wagon, being out a month or more, just chasing and doctoring cattle all day, maybe a bit of fishing before the evening chow, or perhaps knocking off a few sage hens for a special bar-b-que for the boys. That would have been a good life, a very rewarding life, but after all that's when it was Nevada, and that's not the way it is today, nor will it ever be again.

VITA

Dr. Lesperance holds the title of Professor of Animal and Range Science, Emeritus, University of Nevada, Reno. During his 25 year career at the University, he taught numerous undergraduate and graduate courses, published approximately 160 scientific publications and served on countless committees, not only at Nevada, but nationally as well. He directed over thirty successful graduate students. He developed and became Superintendent of the Gund Research and Demonstration Ranch located in Central Nevada. Lesperance has also served as Adjunct Professor, University of California, Davis, and Visiting Professor, Oregon State University, Corvallis, and was also a consultant to the Province of British Columbia regarding the Queen's Lands.

Since leaving the University, Lesperance and his wife, Nancy, have owned and operated a successful business in Elko, Nevada, dealing in agriculture and mining. He has served as a County Commissioner for Elko County, Nevada and served for three years as Director, Nevada Department of Agriculture.

The Lesperances own and operate a small ranch in Paradise Valley, Nevada. Both he and his wife, Nancy, will be celebrating their 79th birthdays during 2014.

Dr. Lesperance worked for the University of Nevada for 25 years. During that period, he taught numerous undergraduate and graduate classes. He published over 160 scientific and popular publications, served on countless committees both Nevada and nationally. He directed well over thirty successful graduate programs. In his later years he developed the Gund Research and Demonstration Ranch, located in central Nevada. He retired from the University in 1995 with the highest possible academic standing, being named Emeritus Professor of Animal and Range Science. During his academic career he also served as Adjunct Professor, University of California, Davis, and Visiting Professor, Oregon State University, Corvallis. Since leaving the University, Lesperance and his wife, Nancy, have owned and operated a successful business in Elko Nevada, dealing in agriculture and hard rock reclamation for the Nevada Mining industry. Lesperance also served as a County Commissioner for Elko County and assumed a three-year term Director of the Nevada Department of Agriculture. In 1997, the Lesperance's purchased a small ranch in Paradise Valley located in northern Humboldt County. He is considered an expert in the production of native grass, utilizing nothing but snow melt water and nitrogen from the occasional thunderstorm, as the above picture demonstrates.